THE PAPERS

of

JOHN C. CALHOUN

John C. Calhoun

This lithographic portrait, made in 1837 in Washington by Charles Fenderich, is now in the National Portrait Gallery, Smithsonian Institution. It was described by a contemporary newspaper as a "strikingly accurate" likeness.

THE PAPERS

of

JOHN C. CALHOUN

Volume XIII, 1835–1837

Edited by

CLYDE N. WILSON

Editorial Staff:

Shirley Bright Cook   Alexander Moore

Published by the UNIVERSITY OF SOUTH CAROLINA PRESS *for the*
SOUTH CAROLINA DEPARTMENT OF ARCHIVES AND HISTORY
and the SOUTH CAROLINIANA SOCIETY, *Columbia, 1980*

Copyright © 1980 by the
University of South Carolina

*Publication of this book was made possible
by a grant from the National Historical Publications
and Records Commission.*

*International Standard Book Number: 0–87249–392–X
Library of Congress Catalog Card Number: 59–10351*

Manufactured in the United States of America

CONTENTS

◫

PREFACE

0

This latest installment in the twenty-volume documentary record of the Carolina statesman that was begun a quarter of a century ago finds him in transition. The volume coincides with the last fifteen months of the Presidency of Andrew Jackson and the first nine months of that of Martin Van Buren. Calhoun is still the outsider, the Nullifier, but is on his way to that rapprochement with the Democratic party by which he managed to startle both friend and foe.

In the preparation of this volume a net has been cast far and wide. As a result, the volume is as complete as it reasonably can be made. All documents have been carefully compared in their various extant versions. A significant number of Congressional speeches and remarks have been found that were not reported at all or were reported differently in the familiar and readily-available sources for Congressional debates. In keeping with the practice of the series from its beginning, the more important and interesting documents have been included in full transcription. Some of the less important are included in careful summaries that are somewhat more than calendar entries. This procedure allows all the known documents for the period of the volume to be included.

Also in keeping with the plan of the series from the beginning, the concept of "papers" has been broadly construed. We have included letters to and from Calhoun, whether public or private; Calhoun's miscellaneous personal papers, such as accounts and deeds; the bills, resolutions, substantive motions, and petitions he presented to the Senate; his recorded remarks and speeches in Congress; and his few formal public speeches outside of Congress. In addition, a very few letters have been selected for inclusion from the rather extensive surviving correspondence of members of Calhoun's immediate family and from the correspondence of other persons that relates directly to him, especially when that correspondence is found preserved among his own papers.

In the ten years prior to 1836 Calhoun had been privileged to paint in broad strokes on a large canvas. His situation as Vice-President and as chief spokesman for a State in critical array against the federal government had allowed him to comment upon public issues from an elevated perspective. Senator Calhoun from 1836 to the mid-1840's was involved in the details of politics and legislation. His focus at this period, as reflected by his documents, is at times necessarily narrow.

The casual reader, therefore, is likely not to find this volume as interesting as some others in the series. It will require the more dedicated student of the intricacies of political events or the more subtle student of political thought to grasp the vision that underlay the day-to-day activities of the Senator. However difficult to discern, the vision is there. Whatever his immediate circumstances or necessities, Calhoun never entirely lost sight of the long view, which is one of the things that makes this imperfect record of his existential thought and expression of permanent interest. As he confessed somewhat apologetically to his more pragmatic and present-minded colleagues in the Senate, in a speech on January 5, 1837:

> It has, perhaps, been too much my habit to look more to the future and less to the present, than is wise; but such is the constitution of [my] mind, that, when I see before me the indications of causes calculated to effect important changes in our political condition, I am led irresistibly to trace them to their sources, and follow them out in their consequences.

The editor gratefully acknowledges the work of his predecessor, W. Edwin Hemphill, and the support of the sponsors of the Calhoun project. These sponsors are the South Carolina Department of Archives and History through its governing commission, chaired by Frederick M. Heath and John G. Sproat, its Director, Charles E. Lee, and its Assistant Director for Archives and Publications, Charles H. Lesser; the National Historical Publications and Records Commission; the University of South Carolina; and the South Caroliniana Society.

CLYDE N. WILSON

Columbia, S.C., July, 1979

INTRODUCTION

▯

During the years 1836 and 1837 Calhoun was largely occupied as a sectional tactician. "Sectional" means that the defense of that intangible but real social formation known as "the South" had become, for the first time, the central theme of his political thought and activity. "Tactician" is meant to convey that Calhoun had to adapt himself to the political game as it was played at that time. As a legislator and a tertium quid he found it unavoidable to calculate day-to-day the parliamentary and public effect of his words and actions. He had to formulate a program that was distinguishable from those of both the Democrats and the Whigs, but not so much so as to foreclose the possibility of constructive compromise with one or the other where it would further his ends.

The defense of the South had two aspects, in both of which Calhoun was a tactical innovator: the defense of its wealth and the defense of its honor. In at least one received view of republican liberty found among the political inheritances of nineteenth century Americans, property and honor were indispensable attainments of a citizen—or of a community of citizens. To put it another way, Calhoun's aim was to prevent the colonialization of the South. This was what his neighborhood newspaper meant when it referred to the South as a colony of the North and defined a colony as "a country governed, not with reference to its own interests, but to those of some other country."[1]

Southern Wealth

Defense of the South's wealth, in the Carolinian's view, was made necessary by the protective tariff that exploited the plantation States and by the ineluctable tendency of various Northern factions to view the government primarily as a source of plunder. The tariff had been adjusted downward as a result of the gallant gamble of South Carolina in 1832 and 1833. Taxes were coming down. They would reach a minimum in 1842 under the compromise that had ended the nulli-

[1] The Pendleton, S.C., *Messenger*, October 10, 1832, p. 1.

fication episode. Calhoun was not willing to disturb the gradual nature of that descent, in part because the honor of South Carolina was pledged to it, in part because he viewed proposals for faster reduction coming from the Jackson party as insincere and as likely to lead to a backlash from the tariff interests.

Meanwhile, in an expanding country, the Treasury was still full. Extravagance in appropriations could not easily be combatted under such conditions, and the Treasury surplus was a standing reproach to republicans. Such a surplus, according to republican teaching, promoted "consolidation," a political condition for which corruption, exploitation, and tyranny were synonyms. The dissipation of the surplus by distribution had been endorsed by both Henry Clay and Andrew Jackson. It was approved also by Calhoun. Agreeing upon the end, all three found defects in the manner of achieving the end proposed by the others, thus providing an interesting case study in the party legislative maneuvers of the time.

The question of the Treasury surplus inevitably ran into other questions. It pointed not only to the tariff, but to the other major source of federal revenue, the sale of public lands. And consideration of the public lands led inevitably into Indian policy, especially since 1836 saw the most serious frontier warfare since the War of 1812. Many people could not think of a federal Treasury surplus without thinking of internal improvements, a common American malady from which Calhoun had not always been immune. The Treasury surplus undoubtedly involved itself with questions of the handling of the government's deposits, unresolved since Jackson's demolition of the Bank of the United States. The handling of the government deposits, in turn, was inseparable from the vital question of control of currency and credit. This last was emphasized, if any emphasis was needed, by the banks' suspension of specie payment in the spring of 1837—the panic that Calhoun had been predicting since 1834.

Calhoun's approach to these issues, always distinctive, is fully documented herein. Though it was not self-evident at the time, in retrospect his course was transitional. During 1836 and 1837 his chief opponents were the Jacksonians; his major Senatorial combats were with Jacksonian spokesmen—James Buchanan of Pennsylvania, Silas Wright of New York, Robert J. Walker of Mississippi, Thomas H. Benton of Missouri, William R. King of Alabama, William C. Rives of Virginia. On numerous issues, like the efforts to expunge the 1834 censure of Jackson from the Senate records, the administration's Indian, foreign, and land policies, and the effort to rush through

Michigan Statehood for the Presidential election, Calhoun remained throughout this period a sharp thorn in Old Hickory's flesh. His stance toward Martin Van Buren, who donned the outsized toga of Old Hickory in March, 1837, had been unequivocally negative for seven years.

Nevertheless, as this volume ends, Calhoun's grappling with the issues had led him to support the "separation of the government and the banks." He had come to the verge of reunion with Van Buren and the Democratic party. In plain political terms "separation of the government and the banks" meant support for Van Buren's "Subtreasury" plan, devised to cope with the panic. And Calhoun, in keeping with his nature, could never be a temporizing or half-hearted advocate. If he jumped in, it was with both feet.[2] Thereby Calhoun earned the unending hostility of his late uneasy collaborators, the Whigs, whose heart's desire was a national bank. This apostasy, as it was viewed by many, meant that in the coming few years he would trade his lightweight Jacksonian opponents in the Senate for renewed mighty contests with Clay and Webster. It also created the most serious revolt at home that Calhoun ever faced, one put down with difficulty. But these are matters for the next volume of the series.

Calhoun's reunion with what was more and more often coming to be referred to as the Democratic party should not have surprised anyone. He had declared over and over in the Senate that his alliance with the Whigs was expedient. Doubtless, to many ordinary men who looked no farther than the last election, Calhoun appeared treacherous. How could one execrate Van Buren one day and embrace his major Presidential proposal the next! It was an easy assignment then and later to pin on Calhoun the label "opportunist." Sometimes the pinning was done by those who also found Calhoun to be "inflexible."[3] The explanation of his course is not so hard to come by or so damaging. Calhoun considered political parties as

---

[2] After Calhoun had entered into the effort to secure adoption of the Subtreasury, Daniel Webster reported to Nicholas Biddle: "Calhoun is moving heaven, earth & —— to obtain Southern votes for the measure. . . . His plausibility, & endless perseverance, have really effected a good deal." (Undated letter of *ca.* May or June, 1838, in the Nicholas Biddle Papers, Library of Congress.)

[3] Calhoun's alleged opportunism is one of the main themes of Thomas H. Benton's memoirs, *Thirty Years' View* . . . (2 vols. New York: D. Appleton and Company, 1854–1856). The view has been more recently elaborately overstated in Gerald M. Capers, *John C. Calhoun, Opportunist: a Reappraisal* (Gainesville: University of Florida Press, 1960).

instruments, not as ends, a distinction lost to the short-sighted who were gripped by the momentary enthusiasm and excitement of political strife and personalities.

As Calhoun's 1843 campaign biography put it: "The great ends in his system of life, whether public or private, he has ever held to be fixed by reason and general rules; but the time and mode of attaining them he regarded as questions of expediency, to be determined by the circumstances under which he is called to act."[4] Privately he wrote in 1837: "I felt in taking the course I did, that I assumed a very heavy responsibility, but I saw clearly as I do the light of heaven, that any other would be fatal to us. . . ."[5] The defense of the South, his chief aim, had little future with the Whigs, from whose ranks and general social ambience most of the attacks upon the South, both its wealth and honor, came.

Southern Honor

If the preservation of Southern wealth was a demanding chore, involving painful necessities, it was one for which there was considerable experience and precedent. Not so the defense of the good name of the South, the occasion for which was unexpected and unprecedented. Suddenly, antislavery was no longer limited to an occasional genteel Federalist or pacific Quaker, held as an opinion among other opinions. The Era of Reform had dawned. Abolitionism, along with other isms, radiated with camp meeting fervor out of the Burnt-Over District of New York, eastward into New England and westward into parts of the Old Northwest.

The suddenness and intensity of the phenomenon convinced many that it would be short-lived. Most Southerners and many Northerners, including certainly the greater part of the Jacksonians in both sections, were no more abolitionists than was Calhoun, but they were not willing to face, as Calhoun was, the fundamental and critical nature of the question that had been raised. The new abolitionist did not argue temperately with the slave owner about the political, economic, and social benefits of emancipation nor propose practical steps toward that goal. He could avow, quite rightly, that these actions were futile. The new abolitionist approached the planter class in the spirit of an exorcist about to deal with a demon.

[4] [Robert M.T. Hunter], *Life of John C. Calhoun, Presenting a Condensed History of Political Events from 1811 to 1843* (New York: Harper & Brothers, c. 1843), pp. 52–53.

[5] To John R. Mathewes, November 26, 1837, herein.

Abolition was obviously a threat to the economic and social orders of the South, both of which antedated the United States. But in the first instance, viewed from the perspective of Calhoun or any other sentient Southerner, it was an attack on the character, the honor, of the South. Do not expect, Calhoun told the Senate, "that the abolitionists will resort to arms, and commence a crusade to liberate our slaves by force." Rather,

> the war which the abolitionists wage against us is of a very different character, and far more effective. It is a war of religious and political fanaticism, mingled, on the part of the leaders, with ambition and the love of notoriety, and waged, not against our lives, but our character. The object is to humble and debase us in our own estimation, and that of the world in general. . . . We cannot remain here in an endless struggle in defence of our character, our property, and institutions.[6]

From the point of view of the traditional republican inheritance, honor, or virtue, was inseparable from the maintenance of liberty. He who could not maintain his own good name and order in his own household could hardly be expected to fulfill the strenuous demands of republican citizenship. What was true of a citizen was true of a community of citizens. "Of all questions, which have been agitated under our government," Calhoun went out of his way to tell a group of Georgians, "abolition is that in which we of the South have the deepest concern. It strikes directly and fatally, not only at our prosperity, but our existence, as a people."[7]

Calhoun knew that Northern society at large did not participate in or even countenance the tone and spirit of organized abolition. Most inhabitants of the free States were content to go about their business, and a not insignificant number had always looked to the planter class for ethical and disinterested leadership. Nevertheless, the challenge to Southern honor could not be treated as routine politics. As he told the Senate:

> However sound the great body of the non-slaveholding States are at present, in the course of a few years they will be succeeded by those who will have been taught to hate the people and institutions of nearly one half of this Union, with a hatred more deadly than one hostile nation ever entertained towards another. It is easy to see the end. By the necessary course of events, if left to themselves, we must become, finally, two people[s].[8]

[6] "Speech on Abolition Petitions," March 9, 1836, herein.
[7] To Augustin S. Clayton and others, August 5, 1836, herein.
[8] "Remarks on Receiving Abolition Petitions (Revised Report)," February 6, 1837, herein.

Calhoun looked ahead not a year but a generation. The wrath of abolition would not be turned aside by a soft answer or a cold shoulder. Whatever their opinions, politicians would hesitate to offend any determined group of voters at home, and if they did their opponents would not make the same mistake. The long-run alternatives for the South were surrender or fight. There was nothing in the heritage, temperament, or necessities of Southerners to suggest the possibility of the former alternative. If the only choice was fight, better now than later. Experience with other issues, like the tariff, had convinced Calhoun that in a government that operated to a considerable degree on a basis of accumulating precedents, all major questions had to be dealt with at threshold if they were truly to be dealt with at all.

This chain of reasoning led Calhoun to take the initiative on two fronts, one tactical, one ideological. Calhoun's opening of these new fronts could be, and was, characterized as either farseeing statesmanship or as unnecessary agitation of a matter better left alone. A majority of Southerners in 1836 were inclined to the latter view, but it is to be suspected that a quarter of a century later, most regretted that they had not answered Calhoun's alarum with more alacrity.

Tactically, there must be a hard line, no compromise, no temporizing with the spirit of the new abolition, wherever it appeared. The petitions for abolition in the District of Columbia that had almost literally buried the Congress were not to be set gently aside. The concerted deluge of abolition publications that inundated the Southern mails was not to be allowed quietly to subside. Both these offensives were to be met with total and unequivocal rejection, as were the abolition efforts of the British government whenever they encroached upon the jurisdiction of the American flag.

Ideologically, before Southerners could present the united front that was essential to the success of an embattled minority, they must free themselves of their own marginal but inhibiting equivocations about their society. Thus, on February 6, 1837, discussing the abolition petitions, Calhoun cast aside the polite evasions that had heretofore usually accompanied discussions of Southern slavery.

"Be it good or bad," he declared, slavery had "grown up with our society and institutions, and is so interwoven with them, that to destroy it would be to destroy us as a people."[9] Face the fact, he demanded, that the biracial society which had appeared in the New World through the workings of mysterious Providence presented problems of social organization never before encountered. Face also

[9] *Ibid.*

the fact that all societies had their laborers and their elites, whatever names they went by. The regime of the South, as he saw it, was an experiment in dealing with these facts. An experiment which had not yet run its course and the benefits or defects of which were not subject to final analysis. A different experiment was under way in the North and the rest of the Western world, an experiment in the relationship of capital and labor. Of the two experiments, "he would venture to predict" that the South's "would prove by far the most secure, and by far the most favorable to the preservation of liberty."[10]

Meanwhile, he rejected the insinuation that the South's honor was compromised by slavery. He appealed to all sides

> whether the South is not equal in virtue, intelligence, patriotism, courage, disinterestedness, and all the high qualities which adorn our nature. I ask whether we have not contributed our full share of talents and political wisdom in forming and sustaining this political fabric; and whether we have not constantly inclined most strongly to the side of liberty, and been the first to see and resist the encroachments of power. In one thing only are we inferior—the arts of gain.[11]

The fatal flaw of Calhoun's tactical and ideological offensives was that, in the long run, they aroused the fear and hostility of many Northern interests that were indifferent to slavery per se.

Patriarchical Politics

An implicit, unelaborated view of American society as a confederacy of patriarchs underlay Calhoun's response to abolition. Republican society operated through groups of gentlemen, local patriarchs who collectively made up the national will and who both led and represented their adherents and dependents. This is a paradigm which C. Vann Woodward has found to be descriptive of Southern society—a republicanized version of the seventeenth century Kentish gentry.[12] (Ironically, the historical connection was unrecognized by Calhoun himself, who in the same speech quoted above

---

[10] "Remarks on Receiving Abolition Petitions (First Report)," February 6, 1837, herein.

[11] "Remarks on Receiving Abolition Petitions (Revised Report)," February 6, 1837.

[12] See C. Vann Woodward, *American Counterpoint: Slavery and Racism in the North-South Dialogue* (Boston: Little, Brown & Co., 1971), pp. 134–138. This paradigm of Southern society is succinctly and cogently restated in Ludwell H. Johnson, *Division and Reunion: America, 1848–1877* (New York: John Wiley & Sons, c. 1978), pp. 73–74.

specifically rejected the monarchist doctrines of Sir Robert Filmer, the chief philosopher of the Kentish gentry.)[13]

A patriarchical society necessarily cohered in a considerable degree around the word of gentlemen. To Calhoun, and others, the Northern patriarchs had made an agreement in making the bargain of the Union that they would accept their confederated Southern brethren as they were—slavery and all. Having accepted slavery in the compact of 1787, the North could not turn against it without breaking the bond. Even assurance of sullen compliance with the letter of the Constitution was not enough, for the new spirit of abolition portended the inevitable breaking of the bargain. If such a spirit of hostility had existed previously, the bargain of the Union would never have been consummated. It was now, therefore, morally incumbent upon the Northern patriarchs to police themselves and their followers and maintain the agreement. Gentlemen did not renege on their solemnly pledged word merely due to convenience or a change of opinion.

That this view was not peculiar to Calhoun is indicated by language used by Andrew Jackson in reference to abolition publications in the mails. Jackson called upon the non-slaveholding States to exercise "their authority in suppressing, so far as in them lies, whatever is calculated to produce this evil." The federal Post Office, "which was designed to foster an amicable intercourse and correspondence between all the members of the confederacy," Jackson told Congress, should not be permitted to be "used as an instrument of an opposite character" by the abolitionists.[14] That the view of politics as bargain between communities of gentlemen was not brought forward expediently is supported by Calhoun's arguments on proposed tariff revisions. In opposing revision of the tariff downward faster than provided by the Compromise of 1833, he referred several times to the pledged honor of South Carolina. "Fair and honorable dealing," he said on one occasion, "has ever distinguished the Southern character; and I trust we have too much self-respect to complain, if the measure we now mete to others should hereafter be measured to ourselves."[15]

Fundamentally, what Calhoun and the South were seeking was an acknowledgment from the North, as a community, that they would

[13] "Remarks on Receiving Abolition Petitions (First Report)," February 6, 1837.

[14] *Senate Journal*, 24th Cong., 1st Sess., p. 31.

[15] "Speech on the Bill to Reduce the Duties on Certain Imports," February 23, 1837, herein.

bite the bullet and live up to the bargain, accepting the burdens as well as the benefits of Union.[16] But it was increasingly impossible, if it had ever been, for such an acknowledgment to come forth. Impossible because mainstream Jacksonian America, unlike antebellum South Carolina, was not an articulated community but an aggregate of competing individuals and interests who viewed the Constitution and government not as a static bargain but as an open-ended opportunity. Calhoun was doomed nostalgically to hanker to lock horns once more with the vanished Federalist gentlemen of old New England. However bitterly they might disagree with you, they could be counted upon to state their motives and intentions candidly and to do what they said they would do. They represented communities with a stable, articulated will, not a perpetual flux in which solemn understandings could be overturned by calculations of marginal advantage at the next election.

From this perspective, the activities of the abolitionists were not primarily in the realm of the rights of individuals. Individual rights related to the actions of a citizen within his community. The Constitution, at least in the question of slavery, pertained to relationships between communities. It was in that critical region where the relationship of the citizen with his sovereign community intersected with the relationships among sovereign communities that Calhoun, by the questions he posed, made his most significant contributions to political thought in this period. The traditional individual liberties like freedom of the press and of petition were rightly hallowed and essential. But, he asked, were they to be absolutized into negations of all other parts of the Constitution?

Few besides Calhoun saw immediately the potentially destructive paradox that absolutism as to individual rights posed for republican and constitutional government. The paradox had not been apparent prior to the age of romantic individualism. Did the right of petition, deemed sacred by the abolitionists as well as by many who disagreed with them, extend to the right to petition for unconstitutional or grossly improper objects? Did it extend to the right to use slanderous language in regard to other citizens or States? Did it extend to the right to bring a legislative body to its knees by the sheer volume and repetitiveness of the complaints and thereby thwart the will of the majority? Did the merely conventional and convenient right of

[16] A recent, brilliant, and intricately formulated statement coinciding with this point is found, with many other valuable insights on the sectional conflict, in J. Mills Thornton III, *Politics and Power in a Slave Society: Alabama, 1800–1860* (Baton Rouge and London: Louisiana State University Press, c. 1978).

the abolitionists to access to the Post Office for their publications override considerations of community survival? Where rights came into conflict, Calhoun urged, "the low must yield to the high; the convenient to the necessary; mere accommodation to safety and security."[17] There were questions yet to be answered before the survivability of American liberty had been fully tested.

The matter of the irregular course to Statehood of the Territory of Michigan also touched upon relations between sovereigns. Calhoun espied fundamental philosophical issues where others saw only questions of territorial land and elections. Congress at one and the same time had acted as if Michigan were a sovereign community for some purposes and a mere dependent territory for others, thereby obscuring the moment of immaculate conception when the inhabitants of a dependent region incorporated themselves into a sovereign people. Calhoun saw prophetically that the slavery question would come to center in the question of who governed the territories and thereby may be said to have anticipated the fundamental issues of the Dred Scott case of twenty years later and even of Reconstruction.[18]

A Balance of Power

The concept of American federal politics as primarily the governing of relations between patriarchical communities sheds some light on Calhoun's turning, in 1836, from plantation slavery as a necessary evil to plantation slavery as a positive good, a turn apt to seem incomprehensible and sinister to another and different era. The same conceptual framework can also perhaps lead us to a useful way of looking at the startling reunion with Van Buren in 1837 and at the overall role Calhoun played in the shaping of American destiny.

The most fashionable interpretation of Calhoun in recent decades has been as "the Marx of the Master Class."[19] By this view, Calhoun, a brutally realistic and prescient member of the "master class," had a clear (and proto-Marxist) conception of the incipient contradiction between capital and labor that was emerging in Northern society, a

---

[17] "Speech in Reply to Criticisms of the Bill to Prohibit the Circulation of Incendiary Publications through the Mail," April 12, 1836, herein.

[18] See Calhoun's speeches and remarks on Michigan, herein, dated January 26, April 2, and December 29, 1836, and January 2, 3, 4, and 5, 1837. He also may be said to have anticipated the Dorr Rebellion.

[19] This is argued cogently in the chapter with that title in Richard Hofstadter, *The American Political Tradition and the Men Who Made It* (New York: Alfred A. Knopf, 1948). It is also the theme of Richard N. Current, *John C. Calhoun* (New York: Washington Square Press, 1963).

phenomenon not yet grasped by most of his contemporaries. His perception led Calhoun, according to this interpretation, to hold out to the capital masters of the North, on the part of the slave masters of the South, a bargain of mutual support and alliance that would preserve each in its hegemony.

There is some evidence for this view, especially Calhoun's fatalistic (or candid) acquiescence in the inevitability of unequal rewards and privileges, which went against the American grain of that and later times. On the other hand, where Calhoun found followers in the North, it was more often among those who feared the growing power of capital than those who participated in it. And Calhoun felt ever free to chastise the business interests, whether freewheeling speculation or chartered privileges. For instance, his scorn for "stock-jobbers" and speculators was unstinting.[20] When it was proposed that Congress subsidize railroads through mail contracts, he remarked wryly:

> So long as it should be in the interest of these companies to fulfil their contracts, they would do so; but when it became their interest not to fulfil them, and they failed to comply with their engagements, there was no remedy but a suit for the return of the funds advanced.[21]

On one hand he deprecated the spirit that approved the casual abrogation of corporate charters. This he put upon grounds that stocks were a "sensitive" property whose fall threatened not only the owners but the whole community. But while protesting against such doctrines, he was "greatly alarmed with the thoughtless precipitancy (not to use a stronger phrase) with which the most extensive and dangerous [corporate] privileges have been granted of late. It can end in no good. . . . I have ever distrusted the banking system. . . ."[22] On balance, Calhoun cannot accurately be depicted as the ally of corporate wealth. In the emergent struggle of capital and labor Calhoun was not the ally of one side. He was an impartial observer.

An insight into Calhoun's strategy is given in a letter of 1836 to his intimate friend Samuel D. Ingham of Pennsylvania, explaining the grounds of his collaboration with Jackson's enemies. The South was the balance wheel of the Union, he said, the natural anchor of stability

[20] See his "Speech on the Bill to Regulate the Deposits of Public Money," May 28, 1836, and "Speech Against the Recommitment of the Public Land Bill to Committee," February 4, 1837, herein.

[21] Remarks on April 18, 1836, herein.

[22] "Second Speech on the Bill for the Admission of Michigan," January 5, 1837, herein.

that corrected the unsteady course of mass politics which otherwise would veer dangerously from extreme to extreme:

> We [the South] are the real conservative body, equally opposed to aristocracy and agra[ria]nism. So long as the tendency at the north was towards the former our natural union was with the democracy; but now that the democracy of the north tends to the agrarianism, our natural union is the other way.[23]

The South was not to be the ally of the capitalists, but rather the permanent balance wheel of the Union.

This strategy was appealed to again exactly nineteen months later when Calhoun undertook to explain to his friends in Edgefield District why he had used the occasion of the panic and Van Buren's Subtreasury proposal to rejoin the Democrats.[24] He had thought it his duty to counter the excesses of Jackson. But now Van Buren, who was no Jackson, was in office and in trouble. One must do more than relish throwing the rascal out. One must consider what manner of rascals were likely to take his place. The defeat of Van Buren by the Whigs would be the triumph of the party of the national bank, high expenditures, consolidation, and moralistic progressivism. These were not ends to be abetted by Southern support.

This joining with an old enemy against a rising one was classic balance-of-power strategy. It was also eminently compatible with American tradition. The South providing a rallying point for State rights for the Northern minority was a reprise of the campaigns of 1800 and 1828. The North, Calhoun said, "never had, and in the nature of things could not reform the Government: the South had never united for Reform without effecting it. . . ."[25]

To see Calhoun as the "Marx of the Master Class" is to see both Calhoun and his times through a glass distorted by theories of class conflict which, if they have any validity, are more appropriately applied to other societies than antebellum America. Opposition to the reform movements of the time, including abolition, did not make Calhoun a sinister opponent of democracy unless one assumes that the reform movements and democracy were identical. But the reform movements bore no necessary relation to majority rule or to the common man and could even be incompatible with them.

The goal of Calhoun's maneuvering was to prevent the colonialization of the South—a goal which for him and others was synonymous with preserving the American experiment in self-government. So,

[23] To Samuel D. Ingham, April 3, 1836, herein.
[24] To John Bauskett and others, November 3, 1837, herein.
[25] "Remarks at Charleston," March 17, 1837, herein.

in a particular way, Calhoun the sectional strategist was as much a national leader and patriot as he had ever been. A sectional strategy, in 1837 as in 1798, could be defended as the *sine qua non* of national health.

Nor was Calhoun's view primarily an economic one. The preservation of honor was at least as important to the survival of self-government as the preservation of property. Economic progress and profit were only incidents of the noble objective of republican liberty. Republican liberty, for Calhoun, was as much a challenge to strenuous duty as a call to bask in benefits. He repeatedly and even archaically deprecated the spirit of gain that marked his era. Invited to address his neighbors, Calhoun expressed gratification at the signs of a returning prosperity. But, he warned, "the love of gain" and "the eager pursuit of wealth" should not lead to neglect of higher objects: "virtue, patriotism[,] honor, and intelligence, and not wealth, are the only certain and durable foundation of national greatness."[26]

When he made his most sustained argument for the Subtreasury plan that would end the government's long-standing alliance with the private banking system, he put the argument primarily in moral terms. We should inquire, he told the Senate, whether the present system "is favorable to the permanency of our free republican institutions, to the industry and business of the country, and, above all, to our moral and intellectual development, the great object for which we were placed here by the Author of our being." Could that be favorable to liberty which concentrated power in a few hands, which created inequalities, which promoted instability, which allowed the cunning to profit at the expense of the industrious, and which turned "the whole community into stock-jobbers and speculators"?

> I object to the banking system, because it allots the honors and rewards of the community, in a very undue proportion, to a pursuit the least of all others favorable to the development of the higher mental qualities, intellectual or moral, [leading] to the decay of the learned professions, and the more noble pursuits of science, litera-ture, philosophy, and statesmanship, and the great and more useful

---

[26] "Speech at Pendleton," August 12, 1836, herein. Joseph A. Schumpeter has theorized that bourgeois, capitalist society, oriented toward goals of practical production, is unable to produce political leadership of the highest type, leadership sufficient to meet severe social crises. Capitalism needs a "protective strata" of "feudal" leadership whose motivation is not primarily economic in order to survive. It is instructive to apply this theory to Calhoun's vision of the role of the South in American politics. See Joseph A. Schumpeter, *Capitalism, Socialism, and Democracy*, 3rd edition (New York: Harper & Brothers, c. 1947), pp. 134–139.

pursuits of business and industry. . . . The rising generation cannot but feel its deadening influence.[27]

In fact, it is fair to say that almost all of Calhoun's major speeches have to do primarily with the moral consequences of public measures, which is surely a large part of his continuing appeal and importance.

To a young and trusted ally who in 1836 expressed despondency at the apparently irreversible downward course of civic virtue, Calhoun offered a few words of cheer. Since the end could not be known, it was a duty to struggle and hope for the best. "We have done much," he said, "and, if true to ourselves, can do much more to secure the country and to acquire honor & influence for the State. . . ."[28]

[27] "Speech on His Amendment to Separate the Government and the Banks," October 3, 1837, herein.
[28] To Francis W. Pickens, August 17, 1836, herein.

THE PAPERS

of

JOHN C. CALHOUN

▥

Volume XIII

DECEMBER 7, 1835–
JULY 4, 1836

(24th Congress, 1st Session)

▯

This seven-month session of Congress was as demanding as any in which Calhoun ever took part. He delivered five major speeches and made dozens of extended remarks. Scarcely a day passed when he was not on his feet in the Senate, and almost every item of the public business received his scrutiny. The major part of his attention, though, was devoted to two items of old business—the fiscal debacle and the depredations of Andrew Jackson's friends on good government—and to one item of new business—abolition.

Jackson in his message at the opening of Congress remarked upon the great recent increase in antislavery agitation. He urged Northern communities to discourage such activity, which he found repugnant to the Constitution, humanity, and religion; and he specifically called the attention of the legislators to a need to exclude "incendiary publications" from the mails. On December 21 Calhoun moved the appointment of a select committee to consider the President's recommendations. When he reported for the committee on February 4 Calhoun argued that suppressing "incendiary publications" was not the business of the federal government, which by the Constitution was expressly forbidden to interfere with freedom of the press. He introduced a bill directing postmasters to coöperate with the laws of the States on the subject, leaving to the States the definition of what was or was not incendiary.

Neither Calhoun's bill nor a Jacksonian substitute was passed at this session, though the Post Office by a combination of federal and local action had already stopped the flow of printed matter. During prolonged consideration of the question, Calhoun had the satisfaction of seeing the elusive Presidential nominee Martin Van Buren, as presiding officer of the Senate, forced to cast a tie-breaking vote in favor of his bill.

Meanwhile, abolition had been engaged on another front. Congress was almost literally buried under a deluge of evangelically inspired and worded petitions for the emancipation of slaves in the

3

District of Columbia. Custom called for a petition, when presented by a Senator, to be routinely received. In the case of abolition petitions there were three usual responses after reception. To table and forget, to refer to a committee for burial, or to refer to a committee for an unfavorable report.

On January 7, when Thomas Morris of Ohio presented two such petitions, Calhoun rose and invoked a standing but little used rule calling for the question to be taken as to whether the Senate would receive the petitions or not. He desired to discountenance abolition at the threshold. Rather than receive and deny the petitions, Congress should refuse to receive them at all as the only way to avoid encouraging a movement that otherwise would be relentlessly disruptive. He declared himself ready to demand the question on reception on every occasion.

Weeks of controversy and maneuver followed, during which Calhoun steadily called attention to the unprecedented and adamant nature of the new movement. Arguments that the best policy was to ignore the phenomenon did not move him at all. His tactics flowed from his principles, not his principles from his tactics. These arguments were based upon a false expectation, he said, that a low-key response would still the movement. Rather, concession would only lead to further demands. Those friendly Northerners who minimized the threat were doing the South no service. No matter that abolition was a minority movement. What would be the case after a generation of propaganda? What would happen when the same cunning political operators who had already brought so much corruption to the republic discovered that the antislavery men held a balance of power in some elections? Unless the movement was squelched right away, the South faced an endless war of attrition with only one possible outcome.

Finally, the Senate fell into an efficient way of dealing with a matter that otherwise would have consumed all its time: petitions were presented; the question was demanded on receiving them; a motion was adopted tabling the question of reception. This neat disposition of the whole matter satisfied the majority for the time. In the House of Representatives, where the Jackson stalwart and future President James K. Polk was Speaker, a different solution was adopted —the "gag rule" or automatic tabling of all such petitions. In the House ex-President John Quincy Adams insisted untiringly that the right of petition was at stake and that the liberties of Northern men were under attack by "the slave power." Calhoun had failed in his primary objective of promoting Southern solidarity on the question.

4

Calhoun's bill to restrict the President's power to remove office-holders without cause had passed the Senate during the previous session but had failed in the House. It was reintroduced in the current session, only to meet the same fate. In regard to dissipating the Treasury surplus which provided the base for Jacksonian corruption (in some way other than by expenditures) Calhoun was more successful. He greeted the new session by reintroducing his bill to regulate the "pet banks," which had passed the Senate last session, and his Constitutional amendment to authorize distribution of the Treasury surplus to the States for a limited time.

On February 17 he warned Senators that the Treasury surplus was at the center of impending disaster. He called their attention to "an inordinate increase of the banking system," which, unless corrected, "must produce an explosion," that is, the financial panic which indeed appeared the next year. On May 28 he made a major speech in favor of distribution. He declared himself the spokesman for the "great mass of the industrious and laboring portion of the community, whose hard earnings are extracted from them without their knowledge." He sensed, he said, a readiness in the administration forces to move in his direction. He would coöperate with them to the fullest extent. This overture received a friendly response. A select committee was appointed with Calhoun as a member, and on June 23 Jackson signed into law a bill for the gradual distribution of the Treasury surplus to the States.

Except for this happy interlude, however, Calhoun for most of the session kept up the biting attacks on Jackson and his friends that had characterized him during the previous three years. On January 18, for instance, he attacked Jackson's handling of relations with France, which he implied had been deliberately aimed at provoking war. War was being gotten up by the same political profiteers who had already plundered the Post Office, the public lands, the banking system, the customs, and the Indian administration, he said. Indian hostilities which had recently broken out in both Northwest and Southwest he put directly to the credit of the administration. Agents had been "sent out to make fortunes for themselves, and to oppress the Indians," he told the Senate on May 18.

Only rarely did Calhoun mention the pending Presidential election, but on February 17 in the Senate he was led to allude to the heir apparent, who happened to be occupying the chair. Andrew Jackson, despite his faults, had many admirable qualities, Calhoun said. His successor, however, was not "of the race of the lion or the tiger; he belonged to a lower order—the fox; and it would be in vain to

5

expect that he could command the respect or acquire the confidence of those who had so little admiration for the qualities by which he was distinguished."

It was the tendency of American republicans, like ancient ones, to emigrate to new lands and found colonies governed in the spirit of the mother country. In the far away Mexican province of Texas a one-star flag had been raised. Colonists, including men bearing the South Carolina names of Bowie, Bonham, and Travis, defended their liberties at a place called the Alamo during February and March. On April 21 a Texan army won a victory against long odds on San Jacinto creek. The army was commanded by Andrew Jackson's protegé Sam Houston. Its second in command was Thomas Jefferson Rusk, who had grown up in the shadow of Fort Hill. Reliable news took time to reach Washington, but on July 1 the Senate resolved to recognize the independent Republic of Texas. Many, including Calhoun, looked forward to receiving soon a new member into the Union. He closed out the session by serving on the joint committee assigned to commemorate the passing of James Madison.

▯

To E[lias] Brown, [former Representative from Md.,] 12/20. "The leading question of the session [of Congress] will grow out of the surplus revenue which is far greater than the administration are willing to admit. . . . The question is, whether the present and accruing surplus, should go back to the States as a fund for internal improvement, or shall remain in the hands of the Executive as a fund to corrupt and govern the country." PEx (from a manuscript in private possession) in Carl Brent Swisher, *Roger B. Taney* (New York: The Macmillan Company, c. 1935), p. 328.

To Dr. F[RANCIS] LIEBER, [South Carolina College, Columbia]

Senate Chamber [*ca.* December 21, 1835?]

My dear Sir, Judge [Willie P.] Mangum, the Senator from N[orth] Carolina, has at my request written to a friend at Raleigh to forward to you a copy of their new Constitution of the State, which I hope you may receive without delay.

I have received your remin[i]sce[nce]s of [Barthold Georg] Niebuhr, for which I am exceedingly obliged to you. I have not yet had leisure to read it, from which I anticipate much pleasure. I shall be very happy to receive your address.

The session will be ["an" *interlined*] important one—distinguished above most others for the number and importance of the questions that will be agitated.

I am much gratified to hear the College is getting on so well. With great respect I am &[c.] &[c.,] J.C. Calhoun.

ALS in CSmH, Francis Lieber Papers. NOTE: Lieber's *Reminiscences of an Intercourse with Mr. Niebuhr, the Historian, during a Residence with Him in Rome, in the Years 1822 and 1823* was published in Philadelphia by Carey, Lea & Blanchard in 1835. "Your address" mentioned by Calhoun was doubtless Lieber's *On History and Political Economy, as Necessary Branches of Education in Free States. An Inaugural Address, Delivered in South Carolina College . . . on Commencement Day, the 7th of December, 1835 . . .* (Columbia, S.C.: printed by A.S. Johnston, 1836).

MOTION AND REMARKS ON THAT PORTION OF THE PRESIDENT'S MESSAGE CONCERNING THE INCENDIARY PUBLICATIONS OF THE ABOLITIONISTS

[In the Senate, December 21, 1835]

[President Andrew Jackson devoted one portion of his annual message to Congress (dated 12/7) to deprecating the recent proliferation of antislavery agitation, which he characterized as "conduct so destructive of the harmony and peace of the country, and so repugnant to the principles of our national compact, and to the dictates of humanity and religion." Jackson relied upon the patriotism and good sense of the non-slaveholding States for promptness in exercising "their authority in suppressing, so far as in them lies, whatever

is calculated to produce this evil." However, he suggested that there was a need to prevent the Post Office Department "which was designed to foster an amicable intercourse and correspondence between all the members of the confederacy" from being "used as an instrument of an opposite character." He therefore called the attention of Congress to "the propriety of passing such a law as will prohibit, under severe penalties, the circulation in the Southern States, through the mail, of incendiary publications, designed to instigate the slaves to insurrection."]

Mr. Calhoun moved that so much of the President's message as relates to the transmission of incendiary publications by the United States mail be referred to a special committee.

Mr. C[alhoun] said that this was a subject of such importance as, in his opinion, to require the appointment of a special committee. It was one which involved questions of a complicated character, and such as did not properly come within the duties of the Committee on the Post Office and Post Roads, touching as they did on the constitutional powers of the Government. Another reason for the appointment of a special committee was to be found in the fact that, in the construction of the standing committees, there was only a single gentleman from that section of the country which was most deeply interested in the proper disposition of this very important subject. He did not anticipate any opposition to the motion, and hoped it would be at once adopted.

[William R. King of Ala. argued that the appointment of a special committee would tend to give to the subject "a greater degree of importance than was necessary."]

Mr. Calhoun replied that the Senator from Alabama had mistaken his object, which was not to produce any unnecessary excitement, but to adopt such a course as would secure a committee which would calmly and dispassionately go into an examination of the whole subject; which would investigate the character of those publications, to ascertain if they were incendiary or not, and, if so, on that ground to put a check in their transmission through the country. He could not but express his astonishment at the objection which had been taken to his motion, for he knew that the Senator from Alabama felt that deep interest in the subject which pervaded the feelings of every man in the Southern section of the country. He believed that the Post Office Committee would be fully occupied with the regular business which would be brought before them, and it was this consideration, and no party feeling, which had induced this motion. Whatever was to be done, whatever feeling to be expressed, it was earnestly to be desired that it should come from a committee, a majority of whom were of those who were most deeply interested in the matter; and he hoped this sentiment would be responded to by a general acquiescence on the part of the Senate.

[*Felix Grundy of Tenn. said that, as Chairman of the Committee on the Post Office and Post Roads, he neither wished for the labor of examining the subject in question nor desired to avoid any responsibility. William C. Preston of S.C. supported Calhoun's motion.*]

Mr. Calhoun stated that, if this subject had been within the ordinary duties of the Committee on the Post Office, he would not have objected to their taking charge of it; but every one must see that it involved considerations of a peculiar character, separate and distinct from the ordinary duties of that committee. He had no desire to bring into debate the important question of slavery, but merely the powers of the Government. The peculiar question of power now presented was a new one, and required to be examined with the utmost caution. In all free States, the most dangerous precedents had been founded on questions of this character. Great principles might be overlooked, and dangerous innovations adopted, from which the worst consequences would flow. He looked to the Constitution only. This was a great constitutional question, and he should deem himself a traitor to his section of the country if he could suffer any consideration as to the presidential election to be brought to bear upon it. It was a question of infinitely higher moment. His desire was to allay every excited feeling; to look calmly, not only at the main question, but at all the collateral. He looked only to the importance of the subject, as a new one, which was now to settle a great principle. He did not desire to assume any responsibility which the crisis did not demand, but he would not shrink from any necessary labor. The Southern people were deeply interested; they deemed that principles were involved in this subject which affected their rights, and on the right decision of which the peace and harmony of the nation depended. On these grounds he had desired a special committee.

From *Register of Debates*, 24th Cong., 1st Sess., cols. 26–33. Also printed in the Washington, D.C., *Daily National Intelligencer*, December 23, 1835, p. 2. Variant in the Washington, D.C., *Globe*, December 23, 1835, p. 2; *Congressional Globe*, 24th Cong., 1st Sess., pp. 36–37; the Charleston, S.C., *Southern Patriot*, December 28, 1835, p. 2. Another variant in the New York, N.Y., *Morning Courier and New-York Enquirer*, December 23, 1835, p. 2. NOTE: After further debate the Senate adopted Calhoun's motion by 23 aye votes. A select committee was then elected consisting of Calhoun, John P. King of Ga., Willie P. Mangum of N.C., John Davis of Mass., and Lewis F. Linn of Mo. The part of Jackson's annual message dealing with abolition publications is found in the *Senate Journal,* 24th Cong., 1st Sess., p. 31. The text of Calhoun's motion, as recorded in the same journal, p. 46, was: "*Resolved,* That so much of the last-mentioned message as relates to the attempts to circulate through the mails inflammatory appeals addressed to the passions of the slaves, calculated to stimulate them to insurrection, be referred to a select committee, to consist of five members, to consider and report thereon."

Petition of Frances Moore, presented by Calhoun to the Senate on 12/23. Frances Moore, as executrix of John Elias Moore, petitions to be remunerated by Congress for money lent by John Elias Moore's father to the State of S.C. during the Revolutionary War. (The petition was referred to the Committee on Revolutionary Claims, which reported unfavorably upon it on 2/8/1836.) PC in Senate Document No. 280, 24th Cong., 1st Sess. [In the next session of Congress, on 1/2/1837, Calhoun moved that this petition once more be referred to the Committee on Revolutionary Claims. This motion was adopted, but the committee was discharged from further consideration of the matter on 1/17. Endorsements on filing jacket of petition in DNA, RG 46 (Records of the U.S. Senate), 24A-G16.]

P[INKNEY] CALDWELL to "Col." John E[wing] Colhoun, Pendleton

Columbus [Ga.,] Decem[ber] 25[,] 1835
Dear Sir, I put off writing you from Lum[p]kin [County] for the purpos[e] of having a[n] Interview with G[eorge] W. Murr[a]y so as to be [*sic*] as I expected to of made a Satisfactory ar[r]angement about the ballance of a thousand dollars [due to Z.B. Hargraves] that you [along with John C. Calhoun] stand as one of the Indorsers after myself[.] I have the advice of the Messrs. Holts [Alfred B. and Hines Holt] and they say that none of the Indorsers are Lyable [*sic*]. I am determend [*sic*] that if the Indorsers should be made liable to *pay the debt, you* nor A.B. Holt shall neve[r] pay one Cent of that debt[.] If Murr[a]y dose sew [*sic*; sue,] fee a lawyer and I will pay all expence attendend [*sic*] on the Suit if you are *Sewed.* I payed off the debt of five hundred dollars that was gowing [*sic*] to G.K. Crissina [*sic*; Green K. Cessna]. I allso left with A.B. Holt the forty dolla[r]s for Esq[ui]r[e] Wilky and wrote to him whare [*sic*] the money was[.] I was not able to pay this dibt [*sic*] before I left as I expected[.] Do for God Sake Give yourself now [*sic*; no] unea[si]nenss [*sic*] about the

10

Murr[a]y debt[.]   I am now on my way to Texis [*sic*] but will Cor[r]ispond with the Messrs. Holts frequently and know what is gowing on till I return in June or July.   Respec[t]fully, P. Caldwell.

[P.S.]   I again say to you defend the Suit if you are sewed I will pay the debt and all Costs[.]   I secur[e]d myself in a great measure with McLaughlin.   I have Lands in Tixes [*sic*], and return to join the army to prevent my Lands from been [*sic*] confiscated so you m[a]y Judge the reason of my short stay in Georgia.   Respec[t]fully, P. Caldwell.

N.B.   I will write the Hon. J.C. Calhoun [*not found*] by the next Chan[c]e I have[.]   The stage is wateing [*sic*] on me.   P.C.

Do write to me [and] direct your letter to Nacogdoches Texis by way of [New] Orleans.

ALS in ScCleA.   NOTE: Caldwell had been involved with John C. Calhoun and John E. Colhoun in their gold mining operations in Ga.   He took part in the Texas War of Independence as a quartermaster in Samuel Houston's army and was killed by Indians near Victoria, Tex., in 1840.

To S[AMUEL] D. INGHAM, [New Hope, Pa.]

Washington, 27th Dec[embe]r 1835
My dear Sir, Shortly before I left home, I received yours of the 28th Oct[obe]r, which I would have answered immediately, but not having any thing worth communicating, I determined to postpone my reply till my arrival here.

I find the state of things ["here" *interlined*] very much as it was when we met last year; only something more slavish & base than even then.   The House is decidedly in a worse condition & the Senate certainly not improved, tho I hope we shall be able to maintain a majority in the body.   The tacticks of the Executive are visibly changed.   Having secured the affections of the lowest stratum of society, their present game is to enlist the highest & most fashionable, of which there is a striking proof in the ["change of the" *interlined*] social intercourse at the White house.   Levees are laid asside[?], after having been opened to all ranks & classes, and balls most brilliant & costly, consisting of *picked* parties, to use the language of the *Ton* [or "Town"].   To the power of the purse & the Sword, Fashion is to be added, and all are to be considered as vulgar, and to be excluded from the fashionable world who are not admitted ["to court favours" *canceled and* "within the perview of the court" *interlined*].   How uniform has been the progress to des[po]tism in all ages & countries! It begins with the canaille and ends ["with the" *interlined*] haut ton.

But to pass to graver subjects, if properly considered graver there can be. The war demonstration is considered as a mere trick. The best informed believe it to be a mere system of bull[y]ing & deception; bull[y]ing to get the greater credit on the payment of the debt, and deception to incite a war sperit [*sic*] in the country, in order to sustain the administration in asking nearly double, what any other has ever ventured to ask in time of peace. I say ask, for it is very doubtful, whether they really desire the appropriations, and whether the real object is not to cast the odium of their rejection on the Senate. Such I am strongly inclined to think is the object. The great increase of expenditures proposed should the appropriations be granted, will fall on the seaboard from Norfolk North; and whether granted, or not, are calculated greatly to strengthen the administration in that quarter. If granted, they will have all the patronage & influence belonging to the expenditure, and, if rejected, the odium must fall on the opposition, while the money, remaining in the Pet Banks, would be more potent ["to control publick opinion" *interlined*] under their control ["there" *interlined*], than, if expended. Such is the present disposition of the publick funds, that whether expended, or hoarded, ["they" *canceled*] in the banks they alike swell the influence & power of the Executive. Against this, I see no remedy, but in their distribution; and I shall accordingly renew my proposition for their distribution in the course of a few days, tho, I fear, with little prospect of success. I will, however, stand on higher ground, than at the last session. Then my estimate of the surplus was questioned; now no one will be so hardy, not even the Humbug [Thomas H. Benton] himself, to deny their moderation. So far from over, I am greatly under the actual receipts. The Sec[re]t[ar]y [of the Treasury, Levi Woodbury] himself is compelled to acknowledge a surplus of $19,-000,000 at the end of the year. It no doubt exceeds it by several millions, & will not be much, if any short, of $30,000,000 at the end of the first quarter; more than half the sum, I estimate for the whole 7 years. His report is the most bunggling [*sic*], and clumsy effort to conceal the truth, I have ever witnessed.

You will see by the ["mail" *canceled*] papers that I have had referred to a select Committee, so much of the President[']s Message as relates to the circulation of incendiary papers through the mail. The Subject is one, that involves the most important principles, to develope which fully will require a pretty full ["disc" *canceled*] explanation of the nature & structure of our Government. My present impression is, that the Govt. has not the right, and if it had, it could not be safely trusted with ["its" *canceled and* "the" *interlined*] exercise ["of the power" *interlined*] to determine, what discription [*sic*] of papers shall, or shall not be transmitted through the mail. It seems to me, that the power is the most odious & dangerous, that can be conceived.

I see that G[e]n[era]l [William Henry] Harrison has been nominated in your State. What are his prospects & what is the true state of things in Pennsyl[vani]a? Her influence will exercise a powerful control over the election. Should she be opposed ["to the administration" *interlined*] it would be a singular fact, and one not without its consolation & hope, that the three States, that elected G[e]n[era]l [Andrew] Jackson, Pennsyl[vani]a Carolina & Tennessee should be arrayed aga[in]st him at the close of ["the" *canceled and* "his" *interlined*] administration.

Anna Maria [Calhoun] is with me, & she joins her best regards to yourself & Mrs. [Deborah Kay Hall] Ingham. Mrs. [Floride Colhoun] Calhoun intended to accompany me, but the health of her mother [Floride Bonneau Colhoun] would not permit. Your friend, J.C. Calhoun.

ALS in ScU-SC, John C. Calhoun Papers. Note: In referring in his third paragraph above to "the war demonstration," Calhoun meant the strong language used by Jackson in his annual message to Congress in regard to recent action of the French legislature. The French had, during the recess of Congress, voted an appropriation to pay off U.S. claims for spoliations during the Napoleonic wars, conditional upon Jackson's apologizing for statements made in his annual message the previous year. Jackson emphatically rejected the condition.

Bill to amend the Tenure of Office Act of 1820, introduced in the Senate on 12/29. This bill was similar to the one for the same purpose that Calhoun had introduced in the previous session of Congress on 2/9/1835 [*The Papers of John C. Calhoun*, 12:448] except for minor changes in the language of the second and third sections. (Like its predecessor, this bill was passed by the Senate, on 2/5/1836, but failed in the House of Representatives.) Draft in DNA, RG 46 (Records of the U.S. Senate), 24A-B1; engrossed bill in DNA, RG 46, 24A-B11; incomplete PC in DLC, Congressional Bills, 24th Cong., 1st Sess., S-41.

Bill to regulate the deposits of the public money, introduced in the Senate on 12/29. This bill was nearly identical with one introduced by Calhoun on 2/9/1835 [*The Papers of John C. Calhoun*, 12:449–450] as it had been amended and passed by the Senate in the

23rd Cong., 2nd Sess. Here reintroduced in the 24th Cong., 1st Sess., it formed one of the major issues of the session. With amendments adopted by the Senate (including one introduced by Calhoun on 5/2 which provided for a distribution of the Treasury surplus to the States) and further amendments by the House of Representatives, the bill was expanded from nine to fifteen sections. As amended it passed the Senate on 6/17/1836 by a vote of 40 to 6, and passed the House on 6/21 by 155 to 38. It was signed into law by Andrew Jackson on 6/23. PC of the bill as introduced in DNA, RG 46 (Records of the U.S. Senate), 24A-B2; PC of the act adopted in Peters, *Statutes at Large of the U.S.A.*, 5:52–56.

"Motion by Mr. Calhoun to refer with instructions the report of the Sec[retar]y of the Treasury relative to a reduction or repeal of certain duties," submitted to the Senate on 12/29. "Resolved that the report of the Secretary of the Treasury [Levi Woodbury] of the 15th Inst[ant] relative to the duties that may be reduced, or repealed be referred to the Committee on manufactures, with instructions to report a bill providing for the reduction, or repeal of all duties, which in their opinion may be reduced or repealed consistently with a due regard to the manufacturing interest." ADU in DNA, RG 46 (Records of the U.S. Senate), 24A-B10; PC in *Senate Journal*, 24th Cong., 1st Sess., p. 66.

Remarks on His Motion to Reduce or Repeal Certain Tariff Duties

[In the Senate, December 29, 1835]
[Under consideration was the motion submitted today by Calhoun.]
Mr. Calhoun, on offering this resolution, adverted to the immense surplus which was daily accruing in the public treasury, to which we must look for an immense increase of power in the hands of the executive Government, and the overspreading of the country with corruption and subserviency. This was not a proper occasion to discuss the actual condition of the treasury; but, if it were, it would not be difficult to show that the actual surplus in the treasury was now from twenty-one to twenty-two millions, and that in the coming year it would be scarcely short of thirty millions. With this immense revenue at the disposal of the President, in banks under his control, and subject to be withdrawn at his discretion, it would be in vain, all our

efforts would be impotent, to oppose the executive will. On this point, therefore, the battle would have to be fought between power and liberty. All other measures which could be devised would fall short of correcting the danger to be apprehended from the march of power. But if all those who were opposed to the usurpations of the Government could be brought zealously to unite in arresting the funds arising out of the revenue, as far as they could, in their passage to the public treasury, and would snatch from the grasp of the Executive the funds which have already accumulated in his hands, there would be still ground for the hope that the course of power would be stayed. Every dollar we can prevent from coming into the treasury, or every dollar thrown back into the hands of the people, will tend to strengthen the cause of liberty, and unnerve the arm of power. He hoped that the Committee on Manufactures would take up the report with an earnest desire to repeal and reduce all those duties that can be reduced or repealed without injury to the manufacturing interest. In doing this they will then feel that they are not only aiding in the cause of reform, as far as it can be assisted by these means, but that they are also contributing to the prosperity of that particular interest of which they are the special guardians; since every reduction of duty, and every tax removed, while it cheapens the cost of production at home, and thus benefits our own manufacturer, will open the prospect of securing the foreign market. As there will be the two interests thus concurring to favor reduction, he hoped the Committee on Manufactures would consider the subject, and report, at as early a period as possible, all the reductions which can be made without injury to the manufacturing interest.

[*John Davis of Mass., Chairman of the Committee on Commerce, argued that the Senate should not press upon a committee "peremptory instruction, touching an interest of the first magnitude," without further time to examine the question. He requested Calhoun not to press a vote on the motion "at this moment."*]

Mr. Calhoun replied that there could be no difficulty on the subject. The Committee on Manufactures would have to examine and ascertain what duties might be reduced or repealed. The Secretary of the Treasury had recommended some, and given a list of others, and it was for the committee to investigate the subject. He would not wish to touch a single article that could injure the manufacturer.

[*After further discussion, Calhoun assented to allow his motion "to lie on the table until to-morrow."*]

From *Register of Debates*, 24th Cong., 1st Sess., cols. 53–54. Also printed in the Washington, D.C., *Daily National Intelligencer*, December 30, 1835, p. 3;

Niles' Weekly Register, vol. XLIX, no. 18 (January 2, 1836), p. 304; the Pendle-ton, S.C., *Messenger,* January 15, 1836, p. 2. Variant in the New York, N.Y., *Morning Courier and New-York Enquirer,* December 31, 1835, p. 2. Note: Secretary of the Treasury Levi Woodbury's report submitted to the Senate on 12/15 had been written in response to a motion made by Calhoun on 2/9/1835 and adopted on 2/12. The report can be found in Senate Document No. 14, 24th Cong., 1st Sess.

"Resolution proposing an amendment to the Constitution of the United States, providing for a distribution of the surplus revenues among the several States and Territories, until the year eighteen hundred and forty-three," introduced in the Senate on 12/29. This resolution was identical with that which Calhoun had introduced in the previous session of Congress on 2/9/1835. [See *The Papers of John C. Calhoun,* 12:451–452.] (This resolution passed its second reading. Further consideration was postponed several times, and it was finally tabled by the Senate on 3/4/1836. However, some features of this resolution were incorporated, by amendment during proceedings in 5/1836, into Calhoun's bill to regulate the public deposits.) Draft in DNA, RG 46 (Records of the U.S. Senate), 24A-B10; PC in DNA, RG 46, 24A-B6; PC in DLC, Congressional Bills, 24th Cong., 1st Sess., SR-3.

Further remarks on his motion to reduce or repeal certain tariff duties, 12/30. Expressing misgivings about Calhoun's motion of yesterday, Henry Clay suggested that it be amended to be a "subject of inquiry" rather than a "positive instruction." "Mr. Calhoun said that was already done. The resolution directed the committee first to inquire and then to report. If, continued Mr. C[alhoun], the land bill introduced by the Senator from Kentucky should pass, there would still remain a large surplus in the public treasury. The amount there already was twenty-one or twenty-two millions, and by the end of the first quarter of the coming year that amount will have swelled to thirty millions. If, as the Secretary of the Treasury [Levi Wood-bury] had stated, the expenditures can be reduced to thirteen mil-lions, there would be ample funds in the treasury, unless the reduc-tions of duty should go far beyond what he had imagined. He wished to impress upon the Senate the importance of two considera-tions: first, that there was an immense surplus in the public exche-quer, which might be employed for the degrading purposes of bribery and corruption; and, secondly, that, by a timely and liberal reduc-tion, all conflicting interests might be reconciled before the crisis which might be expected in 1842–'3. Every cent removed from the hands of Government is so much added to the wealth of the people. It cheapens production, and thus, by allowing a field for competition, it opens the foreign market at a shorter period." Later in the same discussion, Calhoun "said that if any doubt of the ability of the treasury to meet all demands upon it should arise during the progress of this bill, he would then move to lay it upon the table, or to refer it to the Committee on Finance." Clay then withdrew his objection, and the motion was agreed to by the Senate. From *Register of Debates*, 24th Cong., 1st Sess., cols. 54–55. Also printed in the Washington, D.C., *Daily National Intelligencer*, December 31, 1835, p. 3. Variant in the Washington, D.C., *Globe*, December 31, 1835, p. 2; *Congressional Globe*, 24th Cong., 1st Sess., p. 58; the Washington, D.C., *United States' Telegraph*, December 31, 1835, p. 2. Another variant in the New York, N.Y., *Morning Courier and New-York Enquirer*, January 1, 1836, p. 2.

To "Judge [John] McLean," [Associate Justice, U.S. Supreme Court,] 1836. "[Martin] Van Buren will have hard work to keep the [Democratic] party together." [The preceding words were quoted in an advertisement for sale of a letter of the above description by Burns and Son of New York City.] Abs in *American Antiquarian*, vol. IV, no. 1 (October, 1885), p. 301.

"Motion by Mr. Calhoun for amount of Revenue from all sources in 1835," submitted to the Senate on 1/5. "Resolved, that the Secretary of the Treasury be directed to Report to the Senate before the 3d Monday of the present instant [that is, before 1/18] the amount of Revenue from all sources, during the year ending on the 31st Dec[embe]r last, as far as returns have been Received, with an estimate of the amount to be received." (The motion was agreed to by the Senate with unanimous consent.) ADU in DNA, RG 46 (Records of the U.S. Senate), 24A-B10; PC in *Senate Journal*, 24th Cong., 1st Sess., p. 78. (In introducing this motion, Calhoun "said he desired to act early on this subject, as connected with the bills introduced by him, in relation to the surplus revenue. If the Secretary could not accomplish the object within the time specified, he would not hesitate to say so, when it could be enlarged." From the New York, N.Y., *Morning Courier and New-York Enquirer*, January 7, 1836, p. 2.)

From [James L. Edwards, Commissioner of Pensions,] War Department, "Jan. 6, 1835 [*sic*; 1836]." Although Maj. Hicks Chappell of S.C. performed valuable services in the Revolutionary War, he

did not serve in the Continental Army and is not eligible under an
1828 law for commutation of five years' full pay. He receives a pension of $400 per year under the 1832 pension law. FC in DNA, RG 15
(Records of the Veterans Administration), Letters Sent, 1831–1866.

From G O U V [E R N E U R] K E M B L E, [later a Representative from N.Y.]

Cold Spring, Putnam Co[unty], 6 Jan[uar]y 1835 [*sic*; 1836]
My dear sir, I understand from young [Hugh] Rose, the son of Mr.
James Rose of Charleston [S.C.] that it was through you that he received his appointment of Cadet at the military academy, and I am
therefore induced to write to you respecting him. The Boy is of
good parts and honorable feelings, but being untrained when he
entered at West Point, in any regular course of discipline or study,
fell so far behind in the first two months, that although he strove to
regain his standing in the last month, he was unable to effect it, and
would have been dismissed at the January examination, which by
a late rule of the [War] Department would have prohibited all chance
of his continuance at the institution; he has therefore, with the advice
of [Bvt. Lt.] Colo[nel René Edward] De Russy sent in his resignation, in the hope of procuring a reappointment for the next year—
the lad appears to feel his situation most sensibly, but acknowledges
that every justice has been done him, and that he has nobody to blame
but himself; he says that had he studied in the beginning of the
course as he did afterwards, he would have found no difficulty, and
might have taken a good standing in the class. Colo[nel] De Russy,
and the officers generally, speak in the highest terms both of his
head and heart, ["and fully confirm his statement," *interlined*] for
although behind hand in some of the studies, he is one of the best
soldiers and promised to be an excellent officer.

Laboring under the disadvantages of an only son, and residing
in a part of ["the" *canceled*] our country not famed for the early
discipline of its youth, it is not astonishing that a few months should
have elapsed before, with the best intentions, he could bring himself
into a regular course of study—unfortunately for him the studies of
the two first months, comprised the ground work of all his after
learning, and the time then lost, was not to be regained.

A letter which I have from Mr. [James] Rose expresses a great
desire that his son should continue at the institution, and the boy

himself would ["now" *interlined*] do any thing in his power to effect it—under these circumstances, and in the absence of his father, I have, with the concurrence of Colo[nel] De Russy, advised him to take lodgings in the neighbourhood, and promised that I would arrange with a professor of French and mathematics to give him private lessons, so that in case of his reappointment he should be thoroughly prepared, and if not, his studies would continue in progress; and I moreover promised to write to you as a friend of his father, stating all the circumstances, and asking your assistance to effect his restoration. I would however, have delayed troubling you until I could have heard from Mr. Rose but that the list of appointments is some times filled up early in February, and to wait for his answer might make it too late—besides, it were important that the application should be made at the same time that the Secretary of War is informed of the vacancy, lest it be otherwise filled. I trust you will excuse the liberty I have here taken, and will believe me always, Yours most truly, Gouv[erneur] Kemble.

ALS in DNA, RG 94 (Records of the Adjutant General's Office), Application Papers of Cadets, 1805–1866, 1835, 127 (M-688:100, frames 272–275).

REMARKS ON ADMITTING THE PUBLIC TO THE SENATE

[In the Senate, January 6, 1836]
[Under consideration was a motion by William C. Preston to repeal a recently adopted Senate regulation which restricted the access of the public to the Senate chamber and galleries. Preston and Alexander Porter of La. debated the expediency of the proposal in regard to the transaction of business in the Senate.]

Mr. Calhoun was disposed to put this question upon different grounds from what either of the gentlemen who had spoken upon it had. Our Government was a popular Government, and he was disposed to accommodate as much as possible the people that belonged to it. Those galleries were made for the accommodation of the public, and the public had a right to the use of them. The smaller gallery had been thrown open, but the more commodious one had been closed against aged persons and others, unless they had females under their charge. And shall we (said Mr. C[alhoun]) keep that gallery (turning to the circular gallery) continually shut against the people of this Union? He had higher objects in view than some of the gentlemen who advocated the passage of the resolution. He looked to the great struggle they were going to have in that body (the Senate) with one branch of the Government; and it was plainly to be seen, by the course pursued in relation to this resolution, who were the advocates of power, and by whom secrecy was desired. In a struggle between power and the people, between power and liberty, an audience was materially necessary. In the great struggle for liberty the galleries were thrown open. The reports were thrown coldly on the world, and could not be relied on. He would suggest that a certain number of tickets should be given out, in order to prevent the gallery from being crowded to excess. He would hold that the generous-minded ladies themselves would fully accord with his views. Mr. C[alhoun] concluded his remarks by demanding the yeas and nays.

[*John M. Clayton of Del. moved to substitute for Preston's proposal one that would allow spectators to be admitted to the circular gallery and allow each Senator to admit up to three persons "into the lobby of the Senate in front of the chair." Preston, Clayton, and Willie P. Mangum of N.C. engaged in a discussion.*]

Mr. Calhoun said he should vote for the resolution of his colleague, with the amendment of the Senator from Delaware, because he wished to take the question as to opening the galleries. If, hereafter, it should be found that the lobby could contain more than the amendment proposed to admit, without inconvenience, it might be further opened; but he was of opinion that the galleries ought to be opened. It was the nature of power to shut its doors, and hide its proceedings from the public eye; but those who resisted power had an interest in giving to their efforts the utmost publicity. He wished the whole people of the United States to have an opportunity of witnessing what passed in that chamber. As he desired to have the question essentially on the opening of the galleries, he should vote for the amendment.

[*Nathaniel P. Tallmadge of N.Y. proposed that Clayton's suggestion of allowing each Senator to admit a limited number of persons to the lobby be applied also to the circular gallery.*]

Mr. Calhoun said that the amendment to the amendment of the Senator from New York did not answer his purpose at all. He did not wish to be troubled with applications for admission there, nor did he wish to put the people to the trouble of asking for admission. They had a right to be there, to come there, and stay there, whenever the Senate was in session. It was impossible to look at that debate without seeing the nature of it, and from what quarter the opposition to the resolution came. Those who had got power were not willing that the truth should be heard boldly and openly. We, said he, who are on the opposite side, and who oppose power, ought to desire to give the utmost publicity to our proceedings. No, sir, said he, no modification of the amendment will answer my purpose; nothing which will exclude a single individual, will ever meet my consent.

[*James Buchanan of Pa. objected to Calhoun's "insinuation" that the question was one between a party supporting liberty and another supporting power. Calhoun replied that he had "affirmed" that, not insinuated it. Buchanan stated his willingness to open the chamber.*]

Mr. Calhoun remarked that he was much gratified at what had been said by the Senator from Pennsylvania, and hoped that every gentleman on the same side would concur with him. It was not for him or that gentleman to decide which of them were on the side of liberty in the contest between liberty and power—that must be left to time and to posterity for a fair decision. He was not called on then to show the many arbitrary acts of the present administration; but, on a proper occasion, he would be ready to go into the subject. He did hope that this session would show that the gentleman from Pennsylvania, and those with whom he acted, were not the advocates of power. He did hope that when that great measure, the expunging resolutions, came up, it would be seen that those gentlemen will be found on the side of liberty in its contest with power.

From *Register of Debates*, 24th Cong., 1st Sess., cols. 67–72. Also printed in the Washington, D.C., *Globe*, January 8, 1836, p. 2; *Congressional Globe*, 24th Cong., 1st Sess., pp. 71–72. Variant in the New York, N.Y., *Morning Courier and New-York Enquirer*, January 8, 1836, p. 2. NOTE: The first part of Clayton's amendment was adopted 35 to 7, the second part defeated 18 to 24. After further discussion Preston's motion, as amended, was adopted 31 to 11. The Alexandria, D.C., *Gazette*, as quoted by the Washington, D.C., *United States' Telegraph*, January 9, 1836, p. 2, introduced still another report of Calhoun's remarks on this occasion with the following account: "At the beginning of the present session, the Senate barred from the circular gallery everyone except privileged persons (Cabinet members, members of the House of Representatives, etc.) and ladies and their attendants. This left open to the general public only a small gallery above the presiding officer's head. It was usually overcrowded; some could gain no admittance; but the circular gallery was often more than half empty."

FIRST REMARKS ON RECEIVING
ABOLITION PETITIONS

[In the Senate, January 7, 1836]
Mr. [Thomas] Morris presented two petitions from Ohio, praying
for the abolition of slavery in the District of Columbia.

Mr. Calhoun demanded that the petitions should be read.

The Secretary having read the petitions,

Mr. Calhoun demanded the question on receiving them; which
was a preliminary question, which any member had a right to make.
He demanded it on behalf of the State which he represented; he demanded it, because the petitions were in themselves a foul slander
on nearly one-half of the States of the Union; he demanded it, because the question involved was one over which neither this nor the
House [of Representatives] had any power whatever; and that a stop
might be put to that agitation which prevailed in so large a section
of the country, and which, unless checked, would endanger the
existence of the Union. That the petitions just read contained a
gross, false, and malicious slander, on eleven States represented on
this floor, there was no man who in his heart could deny. This was,
in itself, not only good, but the highest cause why these petitions
should not be received. Had it not been the practice of the Senate
to reject petitions which reflected on any individual member of their
body; and should they who were the representatives of sovereign
States permit petitions to be brought there, wil[l]fully, maliciously,
almost wickedly, slandering so many sovereign States of this Union?
Were the States to be less protected than individual members on that
floor? He demanded the question on receiving the petitions, because
they asked for what was a violation of the Constitution. The question of emancipation exclusively belonged to the several States. Congress had no jurisdiction on the subject, no more in this District than
the State of South Carolina: it was a question for the individual
State to determine, and not to be touched by Congress. He himself
well understood, and the people of his State should understand, that
this was an emancipation movement. Those who have moved in it
regard this District as the weak point through which the first movement should be made upon the States. We (said Mr. C[alhoun])
of the South are bound to resist it. We will meet this question as
firmly as if it were the direct question of emancipation in the States.
It is a movement which ought to, which must be, arrested, *in limine*,
or the guards of the Constitution will give way and be destroyed.
He demanded the question on receiving the petitions, because of the

agitation which would result from discussing the subject. The danger to be apprehended was from the agitation of the question on that floor. He did not fear those incendiary publications which were circulated abroad, and which could easily be counteracted. But he dreaded the agitation which would rise out of the discussion in Congress on the subject. Every man knew that there existed a body of men in the Northern States who were ready to second any insurrectionary movement of the blacks; and that these men would be on the alert to turn these discussions to their advantage. He dreaded the discussion in another sense. It would have a tendency to break asunder this Union. What effect could be brought about by the interference of these petitioners? Could they expect to produce a change of mind in the Southern people? No; the effect would be directly the opposite. The more they were assailed on this point, the more closely would they cling to their institutions. And what would be the effect on the rising generation, but to inspire it with odium against those whose mistaken views and misdirected zeal menaced the peace and security of the Southern States? The effect must be to bring our institutions into odium. As a lover of the Union, he dreaded this discussion; and asked for some decided measure to arrest the course of the evil. There must, there shall be some decided step, or the Southern people never will submit. And how are we to treat the subject? By receiving these petitions one after another, and thus tampering, trifling, sporting with the feelings of the South? No, no, no! The abolitionists well understand the effect of such a course of proceeding. It will give importance to their movements, and accelerate the ends they propose. Nothing can, nothing will, stop these petitions but a prompt and stern rejection of them. We must turn them away from our doors, regardless of what may be done or said. If the issue must be, let it come, and let us meet it, as, I hope, we shall be prepared to do.

[*During the course of further discussion, Bedford Brown of N.C. remarked that a similar petition had several days earlier been received and laid on the table, a course which he favored. Calhoun explained "that himself and his colleague (William C. Preston) were absent from the Senate on the occasion alluded to." Discussion continued until Calhoun again took the floor.*]

Mr. Calhoun said that he could have no objection to the motion to postpone, as he was desirous that every Senator should have ample time to deliberate before he was called on to record his vote; but as the opinion of some of the Senators might be more or less influenced by the course which he might think proper to pursue in relation to the question, he deemed it proper to declare that no consideration could induce him to withdraw the demand which he had made for the question [to be taken] on the reception of the petition. He had made it on full deliberation, and it was impossible that he could be induced to change his opinion. He desired the question to be put to the vote; and were there no other reason, there is one, to him imperious, why he should not forego this desire—the insolent, the false, and calumnious language which the petitions held towards the slaveholding States and every slaveholder in the Union. This body (said Mr. C[alhoun]) presented to him a portentous, an amazing spectacle. Here are assembled the representatives of twenty-four confederate States, to deliberate on their common interest and prosperity, seriously discussing the question, whether they shall or shall not receive petitions which basely calumniate the institutions of eleven of those States, which denounce their citizens as pirates, kidnappers, and dealers in human flesh! That a single individual from the States thus slandered should avow a determination to vote to receive so base a libel on the State he represents, as well as the entire South, was to him truly wonderful; and yet more wonderful, if possible, were the arguments he advanced in support of his intention. But more of this in its proper place.

Why, said Mr. C[alhoun], should there be any hesitation to reject these petitions in any quarter? Is it from a feeling of delicacy to the petitioners? If such be the feelings of regard on the part of the Senators from the non-slaveholding States towards these mischievous agitators, what ought to be our feelings, to behold the entire South, by whose confidence we have been selected and placed here to guard their interest and honor, basely vilified in the face of the world? Is the hesitation because there are feelings diffused throughout the non-slaveholding States in relation to the subject of these petitions, so strong and so general, that, for political reasons, it is not thought desirable to disturb them? Are the two great parties who divide those States afraid to come into conflict with those opinions? If so, it is a decided reason why we of the South should insist on taking the question. It is important to our constituents that the fact should be known. He, said Mr. C[alhoun], wished to be perfectly explicit on a point where our interest is so deeply concerned. He, with others, felt, as ought to be felt, for the open, manly, and decided course of a large portion of our Northern brethren during the last summer, against the criminal conduct of the fanatics; but he feared it has not checked the disease. He feared the true reason why there should be the least hesitation in rejecting these vile and libellous attacks on nearly half of the members of this Union was, that both parties are afraid to incur the displeasure of a party so strong as the incendiaries. He could not doubt but all who heard him reprobated the language of these petitions; and with such feelings he could not discover any other reason that was even plausible, but the one he apprehended. There were other reasons which induced him to fear the motive to which he referred was the true one. He had received, a few days since, a printed copy of a protest, signed by Arthur Tappan and several of his associates, remonstrating against the language used in the President's message against the fanatics, in which it is stated, boastingly, that, so far from being repressed by the proceedings against them to the North during the last summer, the number of their societies had increased from (if my memory be accurate) 250 to 350. In addition to this, he regarded the fact to which the Senator from Virginia (Mr. [Benjamin W.] Leigh) referred as proof but too strong that the fanatical spirit at the North was strong and increasing. He had not seen Dr. [William Ellery] Channing's book;* but that a divine of his eminence, and one of the most eloquent and polished writers of the country, should publish such a book at this time, was a matter for serious reflection to those he represented, as well as all who had similar interests. If he might judge of the whole from some of its extracts, it might be well compared with the incendiary publications of [William Lloyd] Garrison himself. It is a sad omen of the times, that he should lend the aid of his talents and character to criminal designs, the direct tendency of which is to work asunder the Union and subvert the Constitution. But, said Mr. C[alhoun], though the false and slanderous language of these petitions are to him imperious reasons for their rejection, there were others of a character not less decisive. The parties, as he stated when he was first up, call on Congress to abolish slavery in this District. He again repeated that Congress had no such power, no more than it has to abolish slavery in the States.

The fifth amendment of the Constitution offers an insuperable barrier, which provides, among other things, that "no person shall be deprived of life, liberty, or property, without due process of law; nor shall private property be taken for public uses without just compensation." Are not slaves property? and if so, how can Congress any more take away the property of a master in his slave, in this District, than it could his life and liberty? They stand on the same

---

*Editor's note: Calhoun refers here to Channing's *Slavery*, first published by James Munroe and Company at Boston in 1835 and issued in revised second and third editions in 1836.

ground. The one, in the eye of the Constitution, is as sacred as the other. He would pass over the latter part of the sentence cited, on which his colleague had touched, and conclusively show that the proviso which it contained also opposed impassable barriers to emancipation by Congress in this District.

He, said Mr. C[alhoun], felt the profoundest gratitude and respect to those watchful and jealous patriots who, at the time of the adoption of the Constitution, would not agree to its ratification without proposing these amended articles, which were subsequently agreed to, and which contain those great limitations on power, of the importance of which he daily became more sensible. But it is said that Congress has, by the Constitution, the exclusive right of legislation in this District. Grant it; and what then? Does the Constitution mean that it has absolute power of legislation here? Certainly not. There are many important limitations on its powers in the District as well as in the States. Congress cannot, in the District, abridge the liberty of the press; it cannot establish a religion by law; it cannot abolish jury trial. In granting exclusive right of legislation, the Constitution only intended to exclude all other legislative authority within the District, and not to create an absolute and despotic power in Congress over the lives and property of its citizens. Nor was the opinion less erroneous that Congress has the same unlimited power here that the States had within their respective limits. The two powers are wholly different. The latter was original, inherent, and sovereign; while the former was a derivative and delegated trust-power, given by the States for special purposes, and subject to be altered and rescinded at their pleasure.

But it is said that it would be a violation of the Constitution not to receive these petitions. He denied that there was any provision in that instrument that made it their duty to receive them. He had again and again read the Constitution, and could find none such, nor any thing like it. It is true that there is a provision that "Congress should pass no law to abridge the right of the people peaceably to assemble and to petition the Government for a redress of grievances." Is a refusal to receive these slanderous petitions a passage of a law for the purpose forbidden in the Constitution? Is there any man of sense, who has for a moment reflected on the subject, who can have the assurance to say so? How, then, can the refusal to receive be construed into a violation of the Constitution?

He, said Mr. C[alhoun], could not but be struck with one remarkable fact. When the question is as to the right of these fanatics to attack the character and property of the slaveholding States, there

26

are Senators on this floor who give a latitude to the Constitution wider than the words can possibly mean; but when the object is to defend the rights and property of these States, they give the most rigid and narrow construction to the instrument.

But, (said Mr. C[alhoun]) the Senator from North Carolina [Bedford Brown] objects to a refusal to receive these slanderous and abusive petitions, for fear it should cause excitement and agitation. To avoid this, he recommends that they should be received and laid on the table, there to slumber quietly. He (said Mr. C[alhoun]) well knew that there were two modes to prevent agitation, which, according to the difference of temperament and character, were resorted to: the one to receive and quietly pocket the insult, and the other by repelling it promptly and decisively. Now, he would ask the Senator whether, if one should petition him, and pronounce him in his petition to be a robber, kidnapper, pirate, with all the other abusive terms used in these petitions, to which of the two modes would he resort? Would he quietly take the petition and put it in his pocket, (lay it on the table,) or would he knock the scoundrel down? I am sure I need not wait an answer. Will, then, he, representing a sovereign State, whose confidence has placed him here to guard her honor and interest, agree to receive a paper, and place it, by his vote, on the permanent records of the Senate, which he would indignantly repel, if offered to himself personally? Is he prepared to show himself less jealous of the honor of his State than his own? As vigilant as we may be to guard our honor and interest, let us be still more watchful in guarding the honor and interest of those we represent. To meet these studied attacks, which come here in the shape of petitions, in that spirit, is the mode, and only safe and effectual mode, to put down agitation—the only mode to preserve our peace and security at home, and the union and institutions of the country generally. Show these fanatics, by a decided refusal, by shutting the door in their face, that they have nothing to hope by agitation, and they will soon cease to agitate.

An objection of a different character is made (said Mr. C[alhoun]) by the Senator from Virginia near me, (Mr. [John] Tyler). He objects that, to refuse to receive the petitions is not strong enough; is not, to use his expression, up to the occasion; and thinks that the proper course is to refer them to the Committee for the District of Columbia, which, he assures us, would be united in denying to Congress any constitutional power to touch the question of emancipation in this District. He also expressed his conviction that the Senate would unanimously sustain the committee, with, perhaps, the exception of [Thomas Morris] the Senator who presented these petitions. He was (said Mr. C[alhoun]) at a loss to see how the course he had adopted fell short of the occasion. What was the occasion? Petitions basely slandering the States, which he and all the other Senators from the same section represented, were presented by the Senator from Ohio. This was the occasion. By the parliamentary rules, the question is, shall they be received? Shall we who represent the States, thus openly and in our own presence insulted, pocket the insult? or shall we indignantly repel it? Did he fall short of the occasion in demanding the question on the reception, and in calling on the Senate to join him in repelling the indignity?

But (said Mr. C[alhoun]) I am rejoiced to learn from the Senator that he is in favor of stronger measures; in favor of a direct declaration by the Senate, denying the right to touch the question of emancipation in the District; doubly rejoiced that the Committee for the District was unanimous on this important point; and trebly so to hear from the Senator that there were just grounds to expect almost perfect unanimity in the Senate itself. I trust he is not mistaken, and I am happy to inform him that there is not the slightest incompatibility between the course he (Mr. C[alhoun]) had pursued, and the one the Senator recommends. A reference of these petitions is not necessary to give jurisdiction to the Committee for the District, in order to bring out their opinion and that of the Senate on the highly important point on which the Senator anticipated so much unanimity. A resolution may be moved expressly denying the power of Congress, and referred to the committee; and, if no other should move it, he (Mr. C[alhoun]) would, if acceptable to the Senator from Virginia. So far from the two courses being incompatible, they were, in his opinion, in perfect harmony, and, together, formed the true course. Let the Senate, by a unanimous rejection of these vile slanders on the slaveholding States, show a just indignation at the insult offered them; and let it be followed by the passage of a resolution, with like unanimity, denying the power of Congress to touch the subject of emancipation in this District; and much, very much, would be done to put down agitation, to restore confidence to the South, and preserve harmony to the Union.

The question of postponement till Monday [1/11] was then determined in the affirmative.

From *Register of Debates*, 24th Cong., 1st Sess., cols. 72–99. Also printed in the Washington, D.C., *Daily National Intelligencer*, January 11, 1836, pp. 1–3; the Washington, D.C., *United States' Telegraph*, January 12, 1836, p. 2, and January 14, 1836, p. 2. Variant in the Washington, D.C., *Globe*, January 11,

1836, pp. 2–3; *Congressional Globe,* 24th Cong., 1st Sess., pp. 75–81. Another variant in the New York, N.Y., *Morning Courier and New-York Enquirer,* January 9, 1836, p. 2.

From H[ENRY] H. TOWNES

Calhoun[']s Mills, S.C., Jan[uar]y 7th 1836

Dear Sir, Mr. W[illia]m Smith applied for a pension under the late act of Congress, & it was refused because he could not prove his service by a *living witness.* He regards this as a hard case, & particularly requests that you will call for his papers at the Pension Office, & determine whether it is worth his while to petition Congress &c. The reason why he applies to you in stead [*sic*] of his immediate representative [Francis W. Pickens] is that you once did him a great service[,] he says[,] after other persons had failed, in procuring the bounty land of his son who died in the service of the U.S. during the last war.

The old man is in very necessitous circumstances, & no doubt is entertained in this neighborhood, where he has lived, I believe for 30 or 40 years, but that he is a revolutionary soldier. You will see among his papers a certificate of this fact signed by highly respectable gentlemen well known to you. I am unacquainted with the rules of the Pension Office, but suppose such a ["letter"(?) *canceled and* "note" *interlined*] as you will find on the opposite page will be necessary. The old man must get his pension soon if it is ever to benefit him, as he is not likely to live till spring. Very sincerely Yours, H.H. Townes.

ALS with En in DNA, RG 15 (Records of the Veterans Administration), Revolutionary War Pension and Bounty-Land Warrant Application Files, 1800–1900, R–9875½. NOTE: An enclosed certificate was dated 1/7/1836, signed by Townes as Smith's agent, and addressed to J[ames] L. Edwards, Commissioner of the Pension Office. It said: "You are requested by Mr. Wm. Smith to hand over all of his papers to the Hon. John C. Calhoun." Dr. Henry H. Townes had married in 2/1827 Calhoun's niece, Lucretia Ann Calhoun.

"Foederatus" to "His Grace the Duke of Pendleton," [published at Greenville, S.C., 1/9]. The author of this public letter considers Calhoun as "a subject for moral speculation" and accuses him of being an immoral "villain who aims at the dissolution of the Federal Union." Calhoun's association during the nullification crisis with [Robert J. Turnbull], a man considered by "Foederatus" to be a traitor to the U.S., is cited as a proof of disunionism. That the qualities of cowardice and cunning are deeply ingrained in Calhoun's nature is widely known, according to "Foederatus." Calhoun is advised to "commence not the work of patching up your character, for that would be labor lost, but that of repentance. You have nothing to fear from the people of the United States in the way of temporal punishment, for they despise you too much to injure you—but even I, my Lord, would be sorry to see you defy the avenging justice of Heaven." PC in the Greenville, S.C., *Mountaineer,* January 9, 1836, p. 2; PC in the Washington, D.C., *Globe,* January 28, 1836, p. 2.

To [Lewis] Cass, [Secretary of War,] 1/11. If Cass can comply with the contents of the enclosed letter [from Gouverneur Kemble to Calhoun, dated 1/6 and concerning Hugh Rose,] he will much oblige Calhoun. (Papers filed with the foregoing indicate that Rose was reappointed to the U.S. Military Academy for 1836, as requested.) ALS with En in DNA, RG 94 (Records of the Adjutant General's Office), Application Papers of Cadets, 1805–1866, 1835, 127 (M-688:100, frames 259–261 and 272–275).

Further remarks on the reception of abolition petitions, 1/11. James Buchanan presented a petition from certain members of the Society of Friends in Pa. asking that slavery in the District of Columbia be abolished. He moved "that the memorial be read, and that the prayer of the memorialists be rejected." "Mr. Calhoun thought the debate which commenced on Thursday [1/7] ought to be resumed and continued. He saw no reason why this memorial should take priority over the one presented from Ohio; why we should break away from that petition to receive this, merely because the language in which it was couched was respectful; that is, as respectful as could be expected. For, however temperate it might seem, the same principle was imbodied in it; and the innuendoes conveyed were as far from being acceptable as the bare-faced insolence of the other. He hoped the debate would go on on the first petition; that the question would be met manfully; and that, at the same time, we should not encroach upon the hour which ought to be devoted to other business." From *Register of Debates,* 24th Cong., 1st Sess., col. 100. Also printed in the Washington, D.C., *Daily National Intelligencer,* January 12, 1836, p. 2. Variant in the Washington, D.C., *Globe,* January 12, 1836, p. 2; *Congressional Globe,* 24th Cong., 1st Sess., p. 83. Another variant in the New York, N.Y., *Morning Courier and New-York Enquirer,* January 14, 1836, p. 2.

Remarks on executive patronage, 1/11. "The bill introduced by Mr. Calhoun, to repeal the second section of an Act limiting the term of certain officers therein named, and for other purposes, was now taken up and considered." Calhoun "briefly advocated the Bill; argued that the power of removal was a legislative and not an Executive power, inasmuch as Congress were authorized by the Constitution to pass laws to carry all constitutional powers into effect; he stated that the removals by the present Executive [Andrew Jackson] had been at least ten or twenty to one greater than all made by all our former Executives; he described the enormous extent of Executive power over the public and the various officers of Government by means of removal, patronage, and the use of the surplus revenue; and declared that the President must be a bungler who could not by these means control the public will." After further discussion the bill was ordered to a third reading by a vote of 24 to 18. From the Washington, D.C., *United States' Telegraph*, January 12, 1836, p. 3.

Remarks on the bill for the relief of the sufferers by fire in New York City, 1/12. Calhoun "expressed his ardent desire to extend relief so far as it could constitutionally be done. He objected, however, to several features of the Bill, as inadmissible on principle, and unequal in their results. He was in favor of granting every possible indulgence in the way of delay; and he would even remit the duties on the merchandise destroyed. He was also in favor of making loans to the sufferers; the money would be better employed than in the Executive banks." From the Washington, D.C., *United States' Telegraph*, January 13, 1836, p. 3. Variant in the New York, N.Y., *Morning Courier and New-York Enquirer*, January 14, 1836, p. 2.

Further Remarks on the Bill to Relieve the Sufferers by Fire at New York City

[In the Senate, January 13, 1836]

Mr. Calhoun moved to strike out from the bill the second section. He was opposed to all that did not provide for the actual sufferers. He was opposed to becoming the general ensurers for all losses, whether of an agricultural, manufacturing, or commercial community.

[*An extended debate followed in which a dozen Senators took
part and during which Thomas Ewing of Ohio offered an amendment which he said would overcome the objection that the bill violated the Constitutional provision against laws preferring one port
over another.*]

Mr. Calhoun said he had listened with great attention to those
gentlemen who had taken part in this debate, but his objections to
the second section still remained unchanged. It was admitted on
all hands that this second section contained a novel principle, and
that no precedent for it was to be found on our statute books. Here
indulgence was extended to those who had not suffered by the fire,
and the argument in support of it was that it was not a regulation as
to revenue, but that we were as creditors dealing with our debtors.
But might not this apply as well when the commercial community
of a city had suffered by any other calamity, by the breakage of
banks, or by shipwrecks? You may at no time (said Mr. C[alhoun])
say that this particular city has suffered and we must extend relief
to it. Let it be recollected that it was not for the misfortunes of
small towns that so much sympathy was excited; but that the calamities of large cities create an excitement which is apt to cause the
Constitution to be overlooked, and a dangerous precedent established by giving a preference to that city over the other ports of the
Union. You must (said Mr. C[alhoun]) extend relief only to those
who have suffered, or you will establish, a dangerous precedent.
He felt deeply for the losses sustained by this great city, and he
would with the greatest pleasure vote for the bill if its objectionable
features were removed; but principle with him was stronger than
feeling, and he was compelled to oppose it. He was not sent there
to exercise his sympathies, but for a higher purpose. He would
much prefer leaving this money in the hands of the merchants to
placing it in the monopolizing banks, which made such great profits
by the use of it; for he believed the merchants would make a better
use of it. He would vote for the amendment of the gentleman from
Ohio, but even if that prevailed he must vote against the bill, unless
his objections to the second section were removed.

From *Register of Debates*, 24th Cong., 1st Sess., cols. 115–129. Also printed in
the Washington, D.C., *Globe*, January 15, 1836, p. 2; *Congressional Globe*, 24th
Cong., 1st Sess., pp. 96–100. Variant in the New York, N.Y., *Morning Courier
and New-York Enquirer*, January 15, 1836, p. 2. NOTE: The bill under discussion provided no direct relief. It would extend consideration in the payment of
tariff duties to those who had lost merchandise in the fire. The first section of
the act extended such consideration to actual sufferers in the fire. The second

section extended it in a general way to others whose bonds fell due before the fire of 12/16/1835. The bill as passed can be found in *Register of Debates,* 24th Cong., 1st Sess., Appendix, pp. i–ii.

Speech on the President's Message on Relations with France

[In the Senate, January 18, 1836]

[*The Senate received a message from President Andrew Jackson describing communications between the United States and the French government over the payments to be made under the treaty of 1831, reporting hostile naval preparations being made by France, and recommending the closing of American ports to French vessels and "adequate preparations on our part." Henry Clay moved to refer the President's message to the Committee on Foreign Relations. James Buchanan rose to express his "entire approbation" of the "general tone and spirit" of the President's message.*]

When Mr. Buchanan had concluded,

Mr. Calhoun rose and said,

I rise (said Mr. C[alhoun]) with feelings entirely different from those of the Senator from Pennsylvania. He said he never listened to any message with greater satisfaction than the present. That which has excited such agreeable sensations in his breast, I have heard with the most profound regret. Never did I listen to a document with more melancholy feelings, with a single exception, the war message [of 1/16/1833 on nullification] from the same quarter a few years since, against one of the sovereign members of this confederacy.

I arrived here (said Mr. C[alhoun]) at the beginning of the session, with a strong conviction that there would be no war. I saw, indeed, many unfavorable and hostile indications; but I thought the cause of difference between the two nations was too trivial to terminate so disastrously. I could not believe that two great and enlightened nations blessed with constitutional Governments, and between whom so many endearing recollections existed to bind together in mutual sympathy and kindness, would, at this advanced stage of civilization, plunge into war for a cause so frivolous. With this impression, notwithstanding all I saw and heard, I still believed peace would be preserved; but the message, and the speech of the Senator from Pennsylvania, have dispelled the delusion. I will not undertake to pronounce with certainty that war is intended, but I will say that, if the recommendations of the President be adopted, it will be almost inevitable.

I fear (said Mr. C[alhoun]) that the condition in which the country is now placed has been the result of a deliberate and systematic policy. I am bound to speak my sentiments freely. It is due to my constituents and the country to act with perfect candor and truth on a question in which their interest is so deeply involved. I will not assert that the Executive has deliberately aimed at war from the commencement; but I will say that, from the beginning of the controversy to the present moment, the course which the President has pursued is precisely the one calculated to terminate in a conflict between the two nations. It has been in his power, at every period, to give the controversy a direction by which the peace of the country might be preserved, without the least sacrifice of reputation or honor; but he has preferred the opposite. I feel (said Mr. C[alhoun]) how painful it is to make these declarations; how unpleasant it is to occupy a position which might, by any possibility, be construed in opposition to our country's cause; but, in my conception, the honor and the interests of the country can only be maintained by pursuing the course that truth and justice may dictate. Acting under this impression, I do not hesitate to assert, after a careful examination of the documents connected with this unhappy controversy, that, if war must come, we are the authors—we are the responsible party. Standing, as I fear we do, on the eve of a conflict, it would to me have been a source of pride and pleasure to make an opposite declaration; but that sacred regard to truth and justice, which, I trust, will ever be my guide under the most difficult circumstances, would not permit.

I cannot (said Mr. C[alhoun]) but call back to my recollection the position which I occupied twenty-four years since, as a member of the other House. We were then, as I fear we are now, on the eve of a war with a great and powerful nation. My voice then was raised for war, because I then believed that justice, honor, and necessity, demanded it. It is now raised for peace, because I am under the most solemn conviction that, by going to war, we would sacrifice justice, honor, and interest. The same motive which then impelled to war now impels to peace.

I have not (said Mr. C[alhoun]) made this assertion lightly. It is the result of mature and deliberate reflection. It is not my intention to enter into a minute examination of that unhappy train of events which has brought the country to its present situation; but

I will briefly touch on a few prominent points, beginning with that most unfortunate negotiation, which seems destined to terminate so disastrously for the country.

From the accession of the present King, his ministry avowed itself favorable to the settlement of our claims. It could scarcely be otherwise. The King had just been raised to the throne, under a revolution originating in popular impulses, which could not but dispose him favorably towards us. Lafayette at the time possessed much power and influence, and had greatly contributed to elevate Louis Philippe to his present station. His feelings were known to be decidedly favorable to us. But with all this favorable inclination, the ministry were fearful of concluding a treaty. They dreaded the Chambers; they knew how odious all treaties of indemnity were to the entire French nation, and how difficult it would be to bring the Chambers to agree to make an appropriation to carry a treaty of indemnity into effect, even with our country. With these impressions, they frankly stated to Mr. [William C.] Rives, our minister, that the difficulty was not with them, but with the Chambers; that if a treaty were made, it could not be carried into effect without a vote of appropriation from the Chambers; and it was very doubtful whether such a vote could be obtained. These declarations were not made once or twice; they were repeated again and again, throughout every stage of the negotiation, and never more emphatically than in the very last, just before the conclusion of the treaty.

The President of the Council, M. Perrier [*sic*; Casimir Pierre Périer], in a conversation with Mr. Rives, at that late period, stated that there would be no difficulty in arranging the question, were it not that he feared opposition on the part of the Chambers, which might place the relations between the two countries in a more dangerous state, by refusing to make the appropriation. How prophetic! as if he had foreseen what has since come to pass. I do not profess to give his words; I did not anticipate the discussion, and have not come prepared with documents; but what I state is substantially what he said. With this apprehension, he asked our minister to wait the short period of two months, for the meeting of the Chambers, that they might be consulted before the conclusion of the treaty, in order to avoid the possibility of the embarrassment which has since occurred, and which has so dangerously embroiled the relations of the two countries. Mr. Rives objected, and the treaty was concluded.*

*Editor's note: At this point most of the published versions of Calhoun's remarks included a long footnote headed "Extract of a part of the correspondence

Now, I submit (said Mr. C[alhoun]) to every man of integrity and honor, whether we, in accepting the treaty after these repeated declarations, did not accept it subject to the condition which they implied; that is, whether, in point of fact, the stipulation of the French Executive ought not to be fairly construed, with these declarations made at the formation of the treaty, to amount simply to an engagement to use his best endeavors to obtain the assent of the Chambers to the appropriation. Such would certainly be the understanding, in a similar case, between honorable and conscientious individuals; and such, I apprehend, will be the opinion hereafter, when passions shall have subsided, of every impartial inquirer after truth.

The question (said Mr. C[alhoun]) is now presented, has the French Executive complied with his promise? Has he honorably, faithfully, and earnestly, endeavored to obtain the assent of the Chambers? To these questions I shall not reply. I leave the answer to our Executive and to our ministers. They have explicitly and honorably acquitted the French Executive on this important point.

But (said Mr. C[alhoun]) let us turn to the conduct of our own Executive in relation to this important part of the controversy. If the implied obligation on the part of the French Executive was such as I suppose, there was a corresponding one on the part of ours, to interpose no obstacle in obtaining the assent of the Chamber. How stands the fact? Mr. Rives, in communicating to our Executive the result of the negotiation, boasted of his skill, and the advantage which he had acquired over the French negotiators. I pass him by. It was, perhaps, natural for him to boast. What does the Executive do? With a full knowledge of all the facts, forewarned of the difficulty which the French ministry would have to encounter in the Chambers, he publishes to the world this boastful communication, which produced a sensation in France, such as might have been expected, which increased in the same proportion the difficulty of obtaining the assent of the Chambers to the appropriation. The next step increased the difficulty. Knowing, as he did, that the appropriations depended upon the Chamber, the then Secretary of the Treasury [Louis McLane], without waiting for its action, drew a bill for the payment of the first instalment before the appropriation was

---

between Mr. [William C.] Rives and the French minister during the negotiations [of 1830–1831], taken from the report of the Committee on Foreign Relations during the last session." The footnote was intended to support Calhoun's contentions in the preceding two paragraphs and to exhibit the frankness and reasonableness of the French in the discussions.

made, and before, of course, it could possibly be paid. A protest necessarily followed, accompanied with much irritation on both sides.

With these obstacles, created by our own acts, the treaty was submitted to the Chambers. Every effort was made to obtain the appropriation. The minister displayed uncommon zeal and ability in defence of the treaty but in vain, under these multiplied difficulties. The bill was rejected by a majority of eight votes; a number so small, in so large a body, that it may be fairly presumed, without any violence, that, had not Mr. Rives's letter been published, and the draft drawn before the appropriation was made, the majority would have been on the other side, and all the unhappy train of consequences which have since followed would have been prevented. So earnest were the French ministry in their efforts to carry the bill, that their defeat dissolved the administration.

With these facts before us, who can doubt where the responsibility rests? We had thrown the impediments in the way—we who had been so urgent to obtain the treaty, and we who were to profit by its execution. It matters not, in the view in which I am considering the question, to what motives the acts of our Executive may be attributed; whether to design or thoughtlessness, it cannot shift the responsibility.

Let us now (said Mr. C[alhoun]) proceed to the next stage of this most unfortunate affair.

I pass over the intervening period; I come to the opening of the next session of Congress. In what manner does the President, in his message at the opening of the session, notice the failure of the French Chambers to make the appropriation? Knowing, as he must, how much the acts to which I have referred had contributed to the defeat of the bill, and that his administration was responsible for those acts, it was natural to expect that he would have noticed the fate of the bill in the calmest and most gentle manner; that he would have done full justice to the zeal and fidelity of the French Executive in its endeavors to obtain its passage, and would have thrown himself with confidence on the justice and the honor of the French nation for the fulfilment of the treaty. In a word, that he would have done all in his power to strengthen the executive Government in France in their future efforts to obtain the appropriation, and carefully avoid every thing that might interpose additional obstacles. Instead of taking this calm and considerate course, so well calculated to secure the fulfilment of the treaty, and so befitting the dignity and justice of our Government, he sends a message to Congress, couched in the strongest terms, and recommending that he should be invested with authority to issue letters of marque and reprisal in the event of the appropriation not being made—a measure, if not tantamount to war, leading to it by almost a necessary consequence. The message was received in France with the deep feeling of irritation which might have been expected; and under this feeling, with all the impediments which it was calculated to create, the bill to carry the treaty into effect had the second time to make its appearance in the Chambers. They were surmounted. The bill passed; but not without a condition—a condition [that Andrew Jackson apologize] which causes the present difficulty.

I deeply regret (said Mr. C[alhoun]) the condition. In my opinion the honor of France did not require it; and the only vindication that can be offered for the ministry in accepting it, is the necessity of the case—that it was indispensable to its passage. But surely, in the midst of the difficulties which it has caused, we ought not to forget that the acts of our own Executive were the cause of its insertion.

This (said Mr. C[alhoun]) brings us to the present stage of this unhappy controversy. I shall not offer an opinion on the message and documents which have just been read, till I have had time to read them at leisure, and more fully comprehend their character and bearing. The Senator from Pennsylvania has probably had the advantage of me in knowing their contents. (Here Mr. Buchanan signified his dissent.) I will not (said Mr. C[alhoun]) make the remarks that I intended, but I am not satisfied with much that I have heard in the reading of the message and the documents. I am, in particular, very far from being satisfied with the reasons assigned by the Secretary of State [John Forsyth] why he did not accept the copy of the letter from the Duke de Broglie to the French Chargé d'Affaires here, which the latter offered to put in his possession. I regret exceedingly that we have not that document. It might have shed much light on the present state of this unhappy controversy. Much mystery hangs over the subject.

There is another point (said Mr. C[alhoun]) which requires explanation. There is certainly some hope that the message at the opening of the session may be favorably received in France. The President has in it expressly adopted the explanation offered by Mr. [Edward] Livingston, which affords some hope, at least, that it may prove to be satisfactory to the French Government. Why, then, send this message at this time? Why recommend preparations and non-intercourse, till we have heard how the message has been received in France? Suppose its reception should be favorable, in the absence of a representative of our Government at the French court, nothing could be done till the message which we have just received shall have passed the Atlantic, and reached Paris. How unfortunate would be the consequence! What new entanglements and difficulties would be caused in the relations of the two countries! Why all this? Who can explain? Will any friend of the administration rise in his place and tell us what is intended?

I might ask (said Mr. C[alhoun]) for like explanation, why our Chargé was recalled from Paris at the time he was. Why not wait until the annual message was received? Whom have we there to represent us on its reception, to explain any difficulty which might remain to be explained? All these things may have a satisfactory explanation. I cannot, however, perceive it. There may be some deep mystery in the whole affair, which those only who are initiated can understand.

I fear (said Mr. C[alhoun]) that with the message which we have this day received, the last hope of preserving the peace of the country has vanished. This compels me to look forward. The first thing that strikes me, in casting my eyes to the future, is the utter impossibility that war, should there unfortunately be one, can have an honorable termination. We shall go into war to exact the payment of five millions of dollars. The first cannon discharged on our part would be a receipt in full for the whole amount. To expect to obtain payment by a treaty of peace would be worse than idle. If our honor would be involved in such a termination of the contest, the honor of France would be equally involved in the opposite. The struggle then would be, who should hold out longest in this unprofitable, and, were it not for the seriousness of the occasion, ridiculous contest. To determine this point, we must inquire which can inflict on the other the greater injury, and to which the war must be most expensive. To both a ready answer may be given. The capacity of France to inflict injury upon us is ten times greater than ours to inflict injuries on her; while the cost of the war, in proportion to her means, would be in nearly the same proportion less than ours to our means. She has relatively a small commerce to be destroyed, while we have the largest in the world, in proportion to our capital and population. She may threaten and harass our coast, while her own is safe from assault. Looking over the whole ground, I do not, said Mr. C[alhoun], hesitate to pronounce that a war with France will be among the greatest calamities, greater than a war with England herself. The power of the latter to annoy us may be greater than that of the former; but so is ours, in turn, greater to annoy England than France. There is another view connected with this point, deserving the most serious consideration, particularly by the commercial and navigating portion of the Union. Nothing can be more destructive to our commerce and navigation than for England to be neutral, while we are belligerent [*sic*] in a contest with such a country as France. The whole of our commercial marine, with our entire shipping, would pass almost instantly into the hands of England. With the exception of our public armed vessels, there would be scarcely a flag of ours afloat on the ocean. We grew rich by being neutral while England was belligerent. It was that which so suddenly built up the mighty fabric of our prosperity and greatness. Reverse the position, let England be neutral while we are belligerent, and the sources of our wealth and prosperity would be speedily exhausted.

In a just and necessary war, said Mr. C[alhoun], all these consequences ought to be fearlessly met. Though a friend to peace, when a proper occasion occurs, I would be among the last to dread the consequences of war. I think the wealth and blood of a country are well poured out in maintaining a just, honorable, and necessary war; but in such a war as that with which the country is now threatened—a mere war of etiquette—a war turning on a question so trivial as whether an explanation shall or shall not be given—no, whether it has, or has not been given, (for that is the real point on which the controversy turns,) to put in jeopardy the lives and property of our citizens, and the liberty and institutions of our country, is worse than folly—is madness. I say the liberty and institutions of the country. I hold them to be in imminent danger. Such has been the grasp of executive power, that we have not been able to resist its usurpations, even in a period of peace; and how much less shall we be able, with the vast increase of power and patronage which a war must confer on that department? In a sound condition of the country, with our institutions in their full vigor, and every department confined to its proper sphere, we would have nothing to fear from a war with France, or any other Power; but our system is deeply diseased, and we may fear the worst in being involved in a war at such a juncture.

I have, said Mr. C[alhoun], in conclusion, no objection to the message and documents going to the Committee on Foreign Relations. I have great confidence in the committee, and have no doubt that they will discharge their duty to the Senate and to the country with prudence and wisdom, at the present trying juncture. But let me suggest a caution against the hasty adoption of the recommendations of the message. To adopt them, would be to change for the worse the position which we now occupy in this unfortunate controversy, and lead, I fear, directly to war. We are told that a French fleet has been sent to the West Indies, which has been considered as a menace, with the intention of frightening us into hasty measures. The French Government itself has said, in its official journal, that it acts on the defensive, and that there is no legitimate cause of war between the two countries. We would not be justified, with these declarations, connected with the circumstances of the case, were we to regard the sending the fleet as a menace. We must not forget that we, in this controversy, are, as my colleague [William C. Preston] said the other day in debate, the plaintiffs, and France the defendant. If there must be war, it must come from us, not France. She has neither motive nor cause to make war. As we, then, must declare the war, it is not strange that France, after what has passed, should prepare for the worst; and such preparation ought fairly to be considered, not as a menace, but as a precautionary measure, resulting from our own acts. But should we in turn commence arming, it must be followed on the part of France with increased preparation, and again on ours with a corresponding increase, till, at length, the pride and passions of both parties would be so wrought up as to burst out to open violence.

I have, said Mr. C[alhoun], thus freely expressed my opinion upon this important subject, feeling a deep conviction that neither justice, honor, nor necessity impel to arms; and that a war with France, at all times, and more especially at the present, would be among the greatest calamities that could befall the country.

From *Register of Debates*, 24th Cong., 1st Sess., cols. 169–177. Also printed in the Washington, D.C., *Daily National Intelligencer*, January 20, 1836, pp. 2–3; the Washington, D.C., *United States' Telegraph*, January 20, 1836, p. 3; the Charleston, S.C., *Mercury*, January 28, 1836, p. 2; the Pendleton, S.C., *Messenger*, February 12, 1836, pp. 1–2; *Speech of Mr. Calhoun, of South Carolina, in Senate, January 18, 1836, on the Motion to Refer the Messages [sic] of the President of the United States, concerning the Relations of the United States with France, to the Committee on Foreign Relations* [Washington?: 1836]; Crallé, ed., *Works*, 3:14–27 (mistakenly dated 2/14/1837). Variant in the Washington, D.C., *Globe*, January 20, 1836, p. 3; *Congressional Globe*, 24th Cong., 1st Sess., pp. 114–115. Another variant in the New York, N.Y., *Morning Courier and New-York Enquirer*, January 20, 1836, p. 2. NOTE: In a document dated 1/19 various Senators, including Calhoun, John Tyler, John J. Crittenden, Thomas Ewing, and John Davis, signed themselves as subscribers for a pamphlet publication of Calhoun's speech on this occasion. (DS advertised for sale in 1963 by Kingston Galleries, Somerville, Mass., and in 1966 by Hobart House, Haddam, Conn.)

REMARKS ON THE RECEPTION OF THE
OHIO ABOLITION PETITION

[In the Senate, January 19, 1836]
The Senate proceeded to the consideration of the question on the petition, from sundry citizens of Ohio, to abolish slavery in the District of Columbia; the question being, "Shall the petition be received?"

[*Benjamin W. Leigh of Va. spoke in favor of Calhoun's motion of 1/7 against the reception of the petition.*]

Mr. Calhoun then called for the reading of the petition, and it was accordingly read.

Mr. C[alhoun] then observed that he did not rise to say one word on the subject of these petitions, which he considered had been sufficiently elucidated by the very able argument just heard, of his friend from Virginia. He did not know when he [had] heard an argument more forcible, more full, more modest, and more comprehensible. He rose to make some remarks on the particular petition then before the Senate, which had been selected from the others, to induce a part of the Southern delegation to consent to receiving it. It was certainly, he admitted, less objectionable in its language than the petition coming from the ladies of the same State. This memorial, however, contained language highly reprehensible. It spoke of "dealing in human flesh." Will our friends of the South, said Mr. C[alhoun], agree that they keep shambles, and deal in human flesh? And this petition was selected from the others, and pushed forward, in order to obtain the votes of gentlemen from the South. There was another phrase in the petition to which he objected. It speaks of us, said Mr. C[alhoun], as pirates. Strange language! Piracy and butchery? We must not permit those we represent to be thus insulted on that floor. He stood prepared, whenever petitions like this were presented, to call for their reading, and to demand that they be not received. His object was to prevent a dangerous agitation, which threatened to burst asunder the bond of this Union. The only question was, how was agitation to be avoided. He held that receiving these petitions encouraged agitation, the most effectual mode to destroy the peace and harmony of the Union.

[*Silas Wright of N.Y. spoke at length in support of the Senate's receiving abolition petitions and then tabling them without discussion and by unanimous vote.*]

Mr. Calhoun could not concur with the gentleman from New

York that so much delicacy was to be shown to the very small part of his own State he referred to, that these petitions were not to be rejected, lest the refusal to receive them might be considered as a violation of the right of the citizen to petition Congress. But, (said Mr. C[alhoun],) does the gentleman look at our side of the question? If his constituents (continued Mr. C[alhoun]) are to be treated with so much respect, that their petitions are to be received, what is to be considered as due to our constituents? The Senator considered the petition before the Senate as moderate in its language—he did not say otherwise—language (said Mr. C[alhoun]) which treats us as butchers and pirates. The Senator said that they must receive this petition, and reject it, lest it might be considered as violating the right of petition. To receive it, and immediately reject it. This looked something like juggling. Was the petition of sufficient consequence to be received, and at the same time of so little consequence as to be immediately rejected? Was it intended merely that this petition was to be put on the files of the Senate as a record to show the opinion entertained of the people of the South by these abolitionists? The Senator told them that this abolition spirit had subsided at the North. He told them that this convention of Utica, which he spoke of as an exception to the general in his State, was compelled to disperse. Well, within a few days a newspaper, published at Utica, had been handed to him, called Oneida Standard and Democrat. He supposed the gentleman was acquainted with its character; it was headed "For President, Martin Van Buren, of New York; for Vice-President, Richard M. Johnson, of Kentucky." This paper contained a most violent attack on the Southern States and their institutions.

(Mr. Wright explained. He only wished to state that it was the office where this paper was published which had been forcibly entered, and the types thrown into the street, as he had before related; that it was for that offence against this paper, when the grand jury of the county refused to find bills of indictment; that neither himself nor his friends could be responsible for the names which such a paper might choose to place at its head; but that of this one fact he could assure the Senator, of his own knowledge, that no other paper in the whole State was more universally or distinctly understood to be hostile to the political party to which he belonged than this paper, and he did not doubt that its columns would establish his position.)

Mr. Calhoun continued. He had always supposed that there was something inexplicable in the politics of New York, and the explanation of the gentleman confirmed the opinion. But to return to the petitions. The gentleman said that unanimity of opinion in the Senate was very desirable. He said so too. Let the gentleman and his friends join us, (said Mr. C[alhoun],) and in that way we can obtain unanimity of opinion. If, as the gentleman said, the petition was to be immediately rejected, why receive it at all? Would the gentleman say that a refusal to receive the petition would press in the slightest degree on the constitutional right of the people peaceably to assemble and petition for a redress of grievances? If the gentleman had made up his mind to reject the petition, he could have no insuperable objection to refuse to receive it. He repeated, that so long as these petitions could be received in the Senate, so long would agitation on the subject continue. The question must be met on constitutional grounds, or not at all.

[*Robert H. Goldsborough of Md. spoke in favor of not receiving the petition in question, but also advocated not using that decision as a rule for guidance "upon the whole subject."*]

Mr. Calhoun would only remark that these petitions might be rejected on various grounds. First, on the unconstitutionality of their object; second, for containing improper and disrespectful language; third, for the impropriety and unreasonableness of their prayers, and for the inexpediency of granting their requests.

[*Thomas Morris of Ohio, who had presented the petitions that had aroused the present discussion, stated that he wished to avoid agitation and excitement. In order to "disembarrass this question of the right of petition of the difficulties as to the language of the petitions," Morris asked leave to withdraw the petitions so that the question of reception could be decided on one of more moderate language that had been presented by James Buchanan of Pa. (on 1/11). Calhoun objected to the petition under consideration being withdrawn at that stage of proceedings, but was overruled by the chair. The Senate then accepted Buchanan's motion that a petition from the Caln Quarterly Meeting of Friends in Pa. be substituted for the Ohio petition. Calhoun called for the reading of the former petition, and it was read.*]

Mr. Calhoun said that the language even of this petition was very strange. It held up the buying and selling of slaves in the Southern States to be as flagrant a wrong as the slave trade itself on the coast of Africa; declaring "that it was as inconsistent in principle, as inhuman in practice, as the foreign slave trade." The foreign slave trade, Mr. C[alhoun] said, consisted in seizing on the Africans by violence, and selling them into slavery. Now, he was not willing to admit the parallel between slavery in the Southern States and this foreign slave trade. We ourselves, said he, have denounced this African slave trade, and made it piracy; though he did not himself believe that the offence could be properly designated as piracy, and ever should regret that this term had been applied to it in our laws. With regard to the petition, if he had no other objection to it than that of its using this language, he would not on that account receive it.

[*William R. King spoke in favor of the Senate receiving the petition in question and then stamping it with disapprobation, thus vindicating both the right of petition and the rights of the States.*]

Mr. Calhoun had heard, with much regret, the argument of his friend from Alabama, (Mr. King). He understood the gentleman to put this question of receiving the petition on constitutional grounds. He asked the Senator if he was aware of the extent to which this doctrine would carry him. Was he prepared to receive petitions to abolish slavery in the navy yards and arsenals of the United States, in the Southern section of the Union? Was he prepared to receive petitions couched in abusive and indecorous language?

(Here Mr. King said, No!)

The Senator answered no. Then I ask him, said Mr. C[alhoun], to show the distinction between such petitions as he had described and the one before the Senate. If the right to have petitions received was constitutional, then there could be no qualification of that right. The Senator from Alabama, by saying no, surrendered the ground he had taken. Then, by what possibility, he asked him, was he prepared to receive petitions to abolish slavery in this District? If he was prepared to receive such petitions, what was to prevent him from receiving petitions to abolish slavery in every arsenal and navy yard in every State in the Union[?]

He confessed he was astonished at the gentleman's arguments. The right of petition was cautiously guarded in the Constitution; "Congress shall make no law prohibiting the right of the people peaceably to assemble and petition for a redress of grievances." By these plain terms it was expressly limited; and yet, when gentlemen came to the petitions of these fanatics, for abolishing slavery in this District, they were disposed to enlarge the construction. I know, said Mr. C[alhoun], that the Senator from Alabama represents constituents more deeply interested in this question than mine. The Southwestern States were more deeply interested than the South Atlantic States, as the former had a growing slave population, continually augmenting by purchases from Maryland, Virginia, North and South Carolina, and Georgia; and he was, therefore, the more astonished at his argument.

Not to receive these petitions was considered wonderfully disrespectful to these petitioners; but to receive and reject them immediately was considered entirely respectful. What did gentlemen mean? He could not, for the life of him, make out why gentlemen were so anxious to receive these petitions, when they were determined to reject them.

[*After further discussion the Senate adjourned without taking the question.*]

From *Register of Debates*, 24th Cong., 1st Sess., cols. 185–210. Also printed in the Washington, D.C., *Globe*, January 21, 1836, p. 2; *Congressional Globe*, 24th Cong., 1st Sess., pp. 119–122. Variant in the Washington, D.C., *Daily National Intelligencer*, January 25, 1836, pp. 1–3; the Washington, D.C., *United States' Telegraph*, January 25, 1836, pp. 2–3. Another variant in the New York, N.Y., *Morning Courier and New-York Enquirer*, January 21, 1836, p. 2.

To [James L.] Edwards, Pension Office, 1/20. Calhoun enquires on what grounds the claim enclosed [of William Smith of Abbeville District, S.C., for a Revolutionary War pension] was rejected? "If it be a case of any doubt I will thank you to send me the papers; but if not it will not be necessary." ALS in DNA, RG 15 (Records of the Veterans Administration), Revolutionary War Pension and Bounty-Land Warrant Application Files, 1800–1900, R-9875½.

From J[AMES] L. EDWARDS

War Department, Pension Office, January 22d 1836
Sir, I received this morning your note of the 20th instant. The claim of William Smith has not been admitted, because it was considered of so doubtful a character as to require some proof of his service other than his own declaration, so long ago as in the year 1818. No such proof has yet been exhibited. Since that period he has applied for the benefits of the act of 7 June 1832. The papers which were first transmitted to this Department in 1818, [were] returned to him, and have not since been in this Office. I enclose herewith the papers in support of his claim under the act of 1832; and I will be obliged to you if you will be so kind as to acknowledge the receipt of them. I have the honor to be, very respectfully, Your Ob[edien]t Serv[an]t, J.L. Edwards.

LS in DNA, RG 46 (Records of the U.S. Senate), 24A-D12; CC in DNA, RG 15 (Records of the Veterans Administration), Revolutionary War Pension and Bounty-Land Warrant Application Files, 1800–1900, R-9875½.

To Duff Green

Washington, 24th Jan[uar]y 1836

My dear Sir, I was much gratified with the contents of your letter and hope you may realise your anticipations.

I send you a copy of my speech on the French question. It was made on the Spur of the occasion. I was compelled to acquiesce in Mr. [James] Buchanan's indorsement for the Senate, or signify my dissent. I did not hesitate, as bold as the move was. I stood alone. The Senate I fear is subdued. I never saw so little sperit in the body. There has, however, sprung up a fine sperit in the House [of Representatives] among the young men from the South and West. I have long looked to them to reform the country, and now, that all the leaders of the Nat[ional] Republican party have withdrawn from the House, the lead in the opposition has fallen into proper hands, the young and the daring from the only section, that can overthrow an administration. Among this band [Henry A.] Wise [of Va.] has taken a noble stand. He has made the most effective speech ever delivered against the Administration. It was full of disclosures shameful to the party, and told with great boldness and point. I look on the movement in the House as the commencement of a new era. Your presence is greatly needed. The Telegraph in your absence is far from being effective. The period has arrived, when bold and decided movements must be made. On your return, arrangements must be made for effective operations through the press here. Can you not associate [Richard K.] Crallé with you, and take charge between you of both the Telegraph and the [Washington?] Sun? They would present a powerful point from which to act. As the nationals go down, we must come into action. The final and successful resistance must be with us. Our principles only can overthrow power.

I see [John Hampden] Pleasants [editor of the Richmond *Whig*] has printed, what I said on the French question, without a single remark. What does it mean? Is he afraid to speak out on the question? If so, it would show a fearful state of things in Virginia.

I fear, that Mr. [Benjamin W.] Leigh and Mr. [John] Tyler [Senators from Va.], may act differently under their instructions, should instructions come [from their legislature], which could not but be disasterous [*sic*] to our cause in the State. I think Mr. Leigh has taken his ground firmly not to obey, at least at once. It is highly desirable that the two Senators should act together, and it seems to me a mutual ground may be found. In voting for Mr. [Henry]

Clay's resolution [to censure Andrew Jackson in 1834], they voted under instructions, or what amounted to it, and if they should be instructed to expunge, it would [be] instruction against instruction, and would constitute, it seems to me, a fair occasion to make the appeal to the people, at the approaching election. Let their resignation abide that event, on an able communication to the Gov[erno]r [Littleton W. Tazewell] on receiving the instructions. I know you cannot act in relation to it, but you might suggest these views to some of our friends. I think it is the only safe course and the one that would meet with the approbation of our friends here.

PC in Jameson, ed., *Correspondence*, pp. 356–357. NOTE: Green's whereabouts at the time this letter was addressed to him has not been determined. He was perhaps travelling in connection with some of his many business ventures.

To [LITTLETON W.] TAZEWELL, Governor [of Va.]

Washington, 24th Jan[uar]y 1836

My dear Sir, It is long since, I have either received a letter from you or written one to you. We have been moving along, in such a beaten and almost hopeless track of baseness & corruption, that I have had but little spirit to write to my friends. But the disease is now coming to a head, and the terrible reaction of all the vice, folly, & corruption of this the most vicious, mad, and corrupt administration, that ever disgraced the ["country" *canceled and* "government" *interlined*], is about to recoil on the country with fearful disasters.

I now hold it certain, that Gen[era]l [Andrew] Jackson is bent on a French war. He said to a lady a few days since, as I understand, that nothing could induce him to take a third term, but a war with France, and ["the" *canceled and* "his" *interlined*] desire to retain power is the only satisfactory explanation, that can be offered, for the course he has pursued. In the mean time, there is no real war spirit in Congress. No party is in favour of it, and none more opposed to it, than [Martin] Van Buren & his friends. They see clearly it must be fatal to them; but they dare not openly ["to" *canceled*] oppose the will of their master. But they will covertly do all they can, by delay & otherwise, to defeat the war, taking special care not to be discovered by Jackson. To hide their design, they will be most clamorous for ["appro" *canceled*] preperations [*sic*], and the most forward to denounce all, who shall oppose them. In this, they will have two objects, one to conceal their moves, and the other to plunder the treasury, under the name of preperation. While Jackson's aim is France & reelection, theirs ["are" *canceled*] is to defeat him & to seize on the immense surplus of about $30,000,000 now in the Treasury. ["Wh" *canceled*.] In the mean time, the opposition, I fear, will go freely into the measures, that may be proposed for arming & preparing; some from timidity, others from a false conception of the real danger, and others to seize the occasion to drop into the arms of the administration. Those who will have the courage to resist will be very few.

It must be obvious, that all this will ultimately create a war feeling in the country; which added ["to" *interlined*] that large & powerful party, which from a variety of reasons, must ever exist in a country like ours, in favour of war, will prepare the way for the moment, for which Jackson is waiting; when a war Message will compel all those, who are playing the disgraceful game, which I have described, will be compelled [*sic*] to vote for war—a war I fear much more ["intended to" *canceled*] against the institutions of the country, than against France. The spoil party is in the natural course of events succeeded by the military party. It is more natural & more manly to plunder by force, than fraud; and I fear that there are thousands of the young & desperate, whose morals have been cor[r]upted by the examples of the last few years, who will be found ["to be" *canceled*] ready to second Jackson, or any other Chieftain, ["who" *canceled and* "that" *interlined*] may ["be ready" *canceled and* "attempt" interlined*] to set up dominion of the Sword. I fear the Senate can oppose no effectual resistance to the dangers I apprehend. Certainly none, if your Senators be instructed [by the legislature] out of their place, of which I suppose there is great probability. The question is constantly asked will they obey and what ought to be done? A question in which not only Virginia, but the whole Union has a deep interest.

The impression here is, that they are disposed to pursue different directions; Mr. [John] Tyler to obey & Mr. [Benjamin W.] Leigh not, which I fear is the fact. Nothing it appears to me could be more disasterous [*sic*; "than seperation" *interlined*], and under this impression I have ventured to touch the subject. There is but one opinion here among all our friends, that to divide would ["be" *interlined*] the worse [*sic*] possible course in any view that can be taken both for the State & the country at large. It ["must" *canceled and* "would" *interlined*] end in a conflict between the friends of the two gentlemen, with all the disasters that must follow. And this I fear will happen, unless prevented at Richmond, by bringing your weight

& influence with that ["of" *interlined*] our friends generally in your quarter into action.

From what I learn, neither will yield to the views of the other, which makes it necessary to find a mid[d]le ground, if one can be found. It appears to our friends here, that there is such a ground.

If we understand the case correctly, in voting for Mr. [Henry] Clay's resolutions [to censure Andrew Jackson], your Senators voted in fact under instructions. Should they be instructed to vote for expunging these resolutions, it would be a case of instructions against instructions, and would ["be" *interlined*] a proper one to wait the action of another Legislature. The suggestion then is, that instead of obeying, ["that" *canceled*] the two Senators should come out in a communication to the Governor, through whom they would, I suppose, be received, with a full statement of the case and to take their ground, that they will abide the result of the Spring elections. It does seem to me, that, if ever a case ["jus" *canceled*] could justify so bold a course, it is the present, and that it would be in their power on a full view of all the circumstance[s] and exposition of the facts to take ground, on which they & their friends could firmly stand. It is a clear case of the abuse of instruction, and on taking the ground indicated, the stand would be to maintain the right of instruction against the abuse. But I know that the propriety of the course must depend on the peculiar feelings & temper of your people, of which none can judge, but a Virginian; and you must consider, what I have said merely as suggestions for your consideration. I have ventured to make them from the deep interest I feel, that the course ["that" *canceled and* "which" *interlined*] may be adopted at this critical juncture by your Senators may be in ["union" *canceled and* "concert" *interlined*], and be such as may ["best" *canceled*] preserve harmony & support our common interest. They have been made without consultation with either, & without their consent or knowledge.

From all I can learn, the abolition party are making rapid advances in the Northern States. I had a letter from a friend ["a few days since" *interlined*] in the interior of New York, on whom I can rely, who says that they are car[ry]ing every thing before them in that quarter, and will in a few years carry all the elections. With sincere respect Yours truely [*sic*], J.C. Calhoun.

[P.S.] I have enclosed [this letter] with a document and got a friend to direct & frank [it] that it might reach you more certainly.

ALS in DLC, John C. Calhoun Papers. NOTE: The Virginia General Assembly had instructed that State's Senators by resolution to vote for the 1834 censure of Jackson. As Calhoun predicted above the General Assembly reversed its position and in 2/1836 instructed the Senators to support Thomas H. Benton's expunging resolution. Tazewell resigned as Governor rather than transmit the latter instructions. Tyler resigned from the Senate rather than obey them. Leigh refused either to obey or resign, but resigned later the same year for other reasons. These actions occurred even though Benton's resolution never came to a vote in the Senate during this session of Congress.

Remarks on "the memorial from the Legislature of Michigan, on the subject of her admission into the Union," 1/26. A prolonged debate about receiving this memorial had been carried on by nine other Senators when Calhoun took the floor. "Mr. Calhoun regarded the political existence of Michigan as a State, as a nonentity. The gentleman from Massachusetts (Mr. [John] Davis) had said that we were not bound to recognise a petitioner as a manufacturer, because he called himself one in the petition. That case did not apply to a corporate body, and especially to a political body. The petition must or must not be received. The position it assumed was strongly illustrative of the position some gentlemen had assumed on this floor. To receive this petition would amount to a recognition of Michigan as a State, and he could therefore not agree to receive it." After further debate the petition was referred to the select committee on the admission of Michigan that had been appointed on 1/22. From *Register of Debates*, 24th Cong., 1st Sess., cols. 286–290. Also printed in the Washington, D.C., *Globe*, January 28, 1836, p. 2; *Congressional Globe*, 24th Cong., 1st Sess., pp. 139–141. Variant in the Washington, D.C., *Daily National Intelligencer*, January 27, 1836, p. 3.

Remarks on the reception of an abolition petition, 1/28. Benjamin Swift of Vt. presented a petition praying that slavery in the District of Columbia be abolished. Calhoun "desired to know if the language of the petition was respectful to those who had sent them there. He therefore wished to hear the petition read." After the reading Calhoun "demanded the preliminary question on receiving the petition. The Senator from Vermont, he said, objected to the calling these petitioners incendiaries, and yet (said Mr. C[alhoun]) he does not object to the language used by them towards those who sent us here." Swift said that Senators could judge of the language used in the petition for themselves and asserted that the motives of the signers were pure. Calhoun "cared not what their motives were; he cared not whether they acted from ignorance or design; he only judged of the effect. Those persons who presented this petition knew of the existence of the Southern institutions, and yet they spoke of them as unjust, wicked, and diabolical. Whatever might be the design of these men, the course they were pursuing was calculated to destroy this Union and subvert its institutions. He did not mean to enter into any argument with the gentleman from Vermont, but he demanded the preliminary question, and on it he asked for the yeas and nays." A few other remarks followed, including some unreported ones by Calhoun, before his motion was laid on the table. From *Register of Debates*, 24th Cong., 1st Sess., cols. 302–303. Also printed in the Washington, D.C., *Globe*, January 30, 1836, p. 2; *Congressional Globe*, 24th Cong., 1st Sess., p. 147; the Washington, D.C., *Daily National Intelligencer*, February 5, 1836, pp. 2–3. Variant in the New York, N.Y., *Morning Courier and New-York Enquirer*, January 30, 1836, p. 2; the Richmond, Va., *Enquirer*, February 2, 1836, p. 2.

Remarks on the reception of an abolition petition, 2/2. Samuel L. Southard of N.J. offered a petition asking for the abolition of slavery in the District of Columbia. Calhoun "objected to the reception of the petition and demanded the question thereon." He "said some decision should be given by the Senate, and he urged that it should be made speedily." The Senate, however, adopted a motion by Alfred Cuthbert of Ga. to table Calhoun's demand for the preliminary question. From the New York, N.Y., *Morning Courier and New-York Enquirer*, February 4, 1836, p. 2.

From "C. of C.," [published at Richmond, Va., 2/4]. This pseudonymous open letter responds to Calhoun's speech [of 1/18] on U.S. relations with France. The writer seems to have three purposes: to affirm that war is not as likely as Calhoun thinks because there is no sufficient cause for it and no desire for it on the part of France or Congress; to explain steps by which the President [Andrew Jackson] can resolve the present difficulties; and to insist that, whatever happens, the $5,000,000 owed to American merchants by the French as a result of an acknowledged thirty-year-old injury ought to be paid either by France or the U.S. government, preferably with $10,000,000 interest. PC in the Richmond, Va., *Whig and Public Advertiser*, February 4, 1836, p. 1; PC in the Washington, D.C., *United States' Telegraph*, February 8, 1836, p. 2.

REPORT FROM THE SELECT COMMITTEE ON
THE CIRCULATION OF INCENDIARY
PUBLICATIONS

In Senate of the U.S., Feb[ruar]y 4, 1836
Mr. Calhoun made the foll[owin]g report with S[enate] bill No. 122.

The Select Committee, to whom was referred, that portion of the President's Message, which relates to the attempts to circulate through the mail inflammatory appeals to excite the slaves to insurrection, submit the following Report;

The Committee fully concur with the President [Andrew Jackson], as to the character and tendency of the papers, which have been attempted to be circulated in the South, through the mail, and participate with him in the indignant regret, which he expresses at conduct so destructive of the peace and harmony of the country, and so repugnant to the Constitution, and the dictates of humanity and religion. They also concur in the hope that, if the strong tone of disapprobation which these unconstitutional and wicked attempts have called forth, does not arrest them, the non-slave-holding States will be prompt to exercise their power to suppress them, as far as their authority extends. But, while they agree with the President as to the evil and its highly dangerous tendency, and the necessity of arresting it, they have not been able to assent to the measure of redress which he recommends; that Congress should pass a law prohibiting under severe penalty the transmission of incendiary publications, through the mail, intended to instigate the slaves to insurrection.

After the most careful and deliberate investigation, they have been constrained to adopt the conclusion that Congress has not the power to pass such a law; that it would be a violation of one of the most sacred provisions of the Constitution, and subversive of reserved powers essential to the preservation of the domestic institutions of the slave-holding States, and, with them, their peace and security. Concurring, as they do, with the President, in the magnitude of the evil and the necessity of its suppression, it would have been the cause of deep regret to the Committee, if they thought the difference of opinion, as to the right of Congress, would deprive the slave holding States of any portion of the protection, which the measure recommended by the President was intended to afford them. On the contrary, they believe all the protection intended may be afforded, according to the views they take of the power of Congress, without infringing on any provision of the Constitution, on one side, or the reserved rights of the States on the other.

The Committee, with these preliminary remarks, will now proceed to establish the positions, which they have assumed, beginning with the first—that the passage of a law would be a violation of an express provision of the Constitution.

In the discussion of this point, the Committee do not deem it necessary to enquire, whether the right to pass such a law can be derived from the power to establish Post-offices and Post roads, or from the trust "of preserving the relation created by the Constitution between the States," as supposed by the President. However ingenious, or plausible the arguments may be, by which it may be attempted to derive the right from these, or any other sources, they must fall short of their object. The jealous spirit of liberty, which characterized our ancestors at the period, when the Constitution was adopted, for ever closed the door, by which the right might be implied from any of the granted powers, or any other source, if there be any other. ["They" *canceled and* "The Committee" *interlined*] refer to the amended Article of the Constitution which, among other things, provides, that Congress shall pass no law, which shall abridge the liberty of the press—a provision, which interposes, as will be hereafter shown, an insuperable objection to the measure recommended by the President. That the true meaning of this provision may be fully comprehended, as bearing on the point under consideration, it will be necessary to recur briefly to the history of the adoption of the Constitution.

It is well known, that great opposition was made to the adoption of the Constitution. It was acknowledged, on all sides, at the time, that the old Confederation, from its weakness, had failed, and that something must be done to save the country from anarchy and convulsion; yet, so high was the spirit of liberty—so jealous were our ancestors of that day of power, that the utmost efforts were necessary, under all the then existing pressure, to obtain the assent of the States to the ratification of the Constitution. Among the many objections to its adoption, none were more successfully urged, than the absence in the instrument of those general provisions, which experience had shown to be necessary, to guard the outworks of liberty; such as the freedom of the press and of speech, the rights of conscience, of trial by Jury, and others of like character. It was the belief of those jealous and watchful guardians of liberty, who viewed the adoption of the Constitution with so much apprehension, that all these sacred barriers, without some positive provision to protect them, would, by the power of construction, be undermined and prostrated. So strong was this apprehension, that it was impossible to obtain a ratification of the instrument in many of the States, without accompanying it with the recommendation to incorporate in the Constitution various articles, as amendments, intended to remove this defect, and guard against the danger apprehended, by placing these important rights beyond the possible encroachment of Congress. One of the most important of these is that, which stands at the head of the list of amended articles, and which, among other things, as has been stated, prohibits the passage of any law abridging the freedom of the press, and which left that important barrier against power under the exclusive authority and control of the States.

That it was the object of this provision to place the freedom of the press beyond the possible interference of Congress is a doctrine not now advanced for the first time. It is the ground taken and so ably sustained by Mr. [James] Madison in his celebrated report to the Virginia Legislature in 1799, against the Alien and Sedition Law, and which conclusively settled the principle, that Congress has no right, in any form, or in any manner, to interfere with the freedom of the press. [*Footnote*: The article is in the following words: "Congress shall make no law respecting an establishment of religion, or prohibiting the free exercise thereof; or abridging the freedom of speech, or of the press; or the right of the people peaceably to assemble and to petition the Government for a redress of grievances."] The establishment of this principle not only overthrew the sedition act, but was the leading cause of the great political revolution which, in 1801, brought the Republican party, with Mr. [Thomas] Jefferson at its head, into power.

With these remarks, the Committee will turn to the Sedition Act, in order to show the identity in principle between it and the act, which the Message recommends to be passed, as far as it relates to the freedom of the press. Among the other provisions, it inflicted punishment on all persons, who should publish any false, scandalous, or malicious writing against the Government, with intent to defame the same, or bring it into contempt or disrepute. Assuming this provision to be unconstitutional, as abridging the freedom of the press, which no one now doubts, it will not be difficult to show that if, instead of inflicting punishment for publishing, the act had inflicted punishment for circulating through the mail, for the same offence, it would have been equally unconstitutional. The one would have abridged the freedom of the press as effectually as the other.

The object of publishing is circulation, and to prohibit circulation is, in effect, to prohibit publication. They both have a common object, the communication of sentiments and opinions to the public, and the prohibition of one may as effectually suppress such communication, as the prohibition of the other, and, of course, would as effectually interfere with the freedom of the press, and be equally unconstitutional.

But to understand more fully the extent of the control, which the right of prohibiting circulation through the mail would give to the Government over the press, it must be borne in mind, that the power of Congress over the Post Office and the mail is an exclusive power. It must also be remembered, that Congress, in the exercise of this power, may declare any road, or navigable water, to be a post road, and that by the Act of 1825 it is provided "that no stage, or other vehicle, which regularly performs trips on a post road, or on a road parallel to it, shall carry letters." The same provision extends to packets, boats, or other vessels on navigable waters. Like provision may be extended to newspapers and pamphlets, ["newspapers" *canceled*] which, if it be admitted, that Congress has the right to discriminate in reference to their character, what papers shall, or what shall not be transmitted by the mail, would subject the freedom of the press, on all subjects, political, moral, and religious, completely to its will and pleasure. It would, in fact, in some respects, more effectually control the freedom of the press, than any sedition law, however severe its penalties. The mandate of the Government alone would be sufficient to close the door against circulation through the mail, and thus, at its sole will and pleasure, ["might" *interlined*] intercept all communication between the press and the people; while it would require the intervention of Courts and Juries to enforce the provisions of a sedition law, which experience has shown, are not always passive and willing instruments in the hands of Government, where the freedom of the press is concerned.

From these remarks it must be apparent, that to prohibit publication on one side, and circulation through the mail, on the other, of any paper ["in reference to" *canceled and* "on account of" *interlined*] its religious, moral, or political character, rests on the same principle, and that each is equally an abridgement of the freedom of the press, and a violation of the Constitution. It would indeed have been but a poor triumph for the cause of liberty, in the great contest of [17]99 had the Sedition Law been put down on principles, that would have left Congress free to suppress the circulation through the mail of the very publications, which that odious act was intended to prohibit. The authors of that memorable achievement would have had but slender claims on the gratitude of posterity, if their victory over the encroachment of power had been ["left" *interlined*] so imperfect.

It will, after what has been said, require but few remarks to show, that the same principle, which applied to the Sedition Law, would apply equally to a law punishing, by Congress, such incendiary publications as are referred to in the Message, and, of course, to the passage of a law prohibiting their transmission through the mail. The principle on which the Sedition Act was condemned, as unconstitutional, was a general one, and not limited in its application, to that act. It withdraws from Congress all right of interference with the press, in any form, or shape whatever; and the Sedition Law was put down, as unconstitutional, not because it prohibited publications against the Government, but because it interfered, at all, with the press. The prohibition of any publication on the ground of its being immoral, irreligious, or intended to excite rebellion, or insurrection, would have been equally unconstitutional; and from parity of reason, the suppression of their circulation, through the mail, would be no less so.

But as conclusive as these reasons are, against the right, there are others not less so, derived from the powers reserved to the States, which the Committee will next proceed to consider.

The Message, as has been stated, recommends, that Congress should pass a law to punish the transmission, through the mail, of incendiary publications, intended to instigate the slaves to insurrection. It, of course, assumes for Congress a right to determine, what papers are incendiary and intended to excite insurrection. The question then is, has Congress such a right? A question of vital importance to the slave holding States, as will appear in the course of the discussion.

After examining ["it" *canceled and* "this question" *interlined*] with due deliberation in all its bearings, the Committee are of ["the" *canceled*] opinion, not only that Congress has not the right, but to admit it would be fatal to those States. Nothing is more clear, than ["that" *interlined*] the admission of the right on the part of Congress to determine what papers are incendiary, and as such to prohibit their circulation through the mail, necessarily involves the right to determine, what are not ["incendiary," *interlined*] and to enforce their circulation. Nor is it less certain, that to admit such a right would be virtually to clothe Congress with the power to abolish slavery, by giving it the means of breaking down all the barriers which the slave holding States have ["created" *canceled and* "erected" *interlined*] for the protection of their lives and property. It would give Congress, ["without regard to the prohibitory laws of the States," *interlined*] the authority to open the gates to the flood of incendiary publications, which are ready to break into those States, and to punish all, who dare resist, as criminals. Fortunately Congress has no such right. The internal peace and security of the States are under the protection of the States themselves, to the entire exclusion of all authority and control on the part of Congress. It belongs to them, and not to Congress, to determine what is, or is not, calculated to disturb their peace and security, and of course, in the case under consideration, it belongs to the Slave holding States to determine, what is incendiary and intended to incite to insurrection, and to adopt such defensive measures, as may be necessary for their security, with unlimited means of carrying them into effect, except such as may be expressly ["prohibited" *canceled and* "inhibited" *interlined*] to the States by the Constitution. To establish the truth of this position, so essential to the safety of those States, it would seem sufficient to appeal to their constant exercise of this right, at all times, without restriction, or question, both before and since the adoption of the Constitution. But on a point of so much importance, which may involve the safety, if not the existence itself, of an entire section of the Union, it will be proper to trace it to its origin, in order to place it on a more immoveable foundation.

That the States, which form our federal union are sovereign and independent communities, bound together by a constitutional compact, and possessed of all the powers belonging to distinct and separate States, excepting such as are delegated to be exercised by the General Government, is assumed as unquestionable ["fact" *canceled*]. The compact itself expressly provides, that all powers, not delegated, are reserved to the States and the people. ["Then" *canceled and* "To ascertain, then," *interlined*] whether the power in question is delegated or reserved, it is only necessary to ascertain, whether it ["is to be found" *interlined*] among the enumerated powers, or not. If it be not among them, it belongs, of course, to the ["reserved" *canceled and* "reserved powers" *interlined*]. On turning to the Constitution, it will be seen, that while the power of defending the country against external danger is found among the enumerated, the instrument is wholly silent as to the power of defending the internal peace and security of the States, and, of course, reserves to the States this important power, as it stood before the adoption of the Constitution, with no other limitation, as has been stated, except such as are expressly prescribed by the instrument itself. From what has been stated, it may be inferred, that the right of a State to defend itself against internal dangers is a part of the great, primary and inherent right of self-defence, which, by the laws of nature, belongs to all communities; and so jealous were the States of this essential right, without which their independence could not be preserved, that it is expressly provided by the Constitution, [*Footnote*: See 4th Article(,) 4th Section, of the Constitution.] that the general Government ["should" *canceled and* "shall" *interlined*] not assist a State, even in case of domestic violence, except on the application of the authorities of the State itself; thus excluding, by a necessary consequence, its interference in all other cases.

Having now shown that it belongs to the Slave holding States, whose institutions are in danger, and not to Congress, as is supposed by the Message, to determine what papers are incendiary and intended to excite insurrection among the slaves, it remains to inquire, in the next place, what are the corresponding duties of the general Government, and the other States, from within whose limits and jurisdiction their institutions are attacked—a subject ["immediately" *canceled and* "intimately" *interlined*] connected with that with which the Committee are immediately charged, and which, at the present juncture, ought to be fully understood by all the parties. The Committee will begin with the first.

It may not be entirely useless to premise, that rights and duties are reciprocal; the existence of a right always implying the corresponding duty. If, consequently, the right to protect her internal peace and security belongs to a State, the general Government is bound to respect the measures adopted by her for that purpose, and to co-operate in their execution, as far as its delegated powers may admit, or the measure may require. Thus, in the present case, the slave-holding States having the unquestionable right to pass all such laws as may be necessary to maintain the existing relation between master and slave, in those States, their right, of course, to prohibit the circulation of any publication, or any intercourse, calculated to disturb or destroy that relation is incontrovertible. In the execution of the measures, which may be adopted by the States for this purpose, the powers of Congress over the mail, and of regulating commerce with foreign nations and between the States, may require co-operation on the part of the general Government; and it is bound, in conformity with the principle established, to respect the laws of the State in their exercise, and so to modify ["by" *canceled*] its acts, as not only not to violate those of the States, but, as far as practicable, to co-operate in their execution. The practice of the Government has been in conformity to these views.

By the act of the 28th of February, 1803, entitled "An act to prevent the importation of certain persons into certain States," where by the laws of those States their importation is prohibited, Masters or captains of ships, or vessels, are forbidden, under severe penalty, "to import or bring, or cause to be imported, or brought, any negro or mulatto, or person of colour, not being a native, or citizen, or registered seaman, of the United States, or seamen, natives of countries beyond the Cape of Good Hope, into any port or place which shall be situated in any State which, by Law, has prohibited, or shall prohibit, the admission or importation of such negro, mulatto, or other person of colour." This provision speaks for itself, and requires no illustration. It is a case in point, and fully embraces the principle laid down. To the same effect is the Act of the 25th of February, 1799, respecting quarantine and health laws, which, as belonging to the internal police of the States, stand on the same ground. The Act, among other things, "directs the Collectors and all other Revenue officers, the masters and crews of the Revenue Cutters, and the military officers in command on the station, to co-operate faithfully in the execution of the Quarantine and other restrictions, which the health laws of the State may establish."

The principles embraced by these acts, in relation to the commercial intercourse of the country, are equally applicable to the intercourse by mail. There may indeed be more difficulty in co-operating with the States in the latter, than in the former, but that cannot possibly affect the principle. Regarding it ["then" *interlined*] as established, both by reason and precedents, the Committee, in conformity ["to it," *canceled and* "with it," *interlined*] have prepared a Bill, and directed their Chairman to report the same to the Senate, prohibiting under the penalty of ["fine and" *interlined*] dismission from office, any Deputy Postmaster, in any State, Territory, or District, from knowingly receiving and putting into the mail, any letter, packet, pamphlet, ["or" *canceled*] paper, or pictorial representation, directed to any Post office or person in a State, Territory or District, by the laws of which the circulation of the same is forbidden; and also prohibiting, under a like penalty, any Deputy Postmaster in said State, Territory or District, from knowingly delivering the same, except to such persons as may be authorized to receive them by the Civil authority of said State, Territory, or District.

It remains next to inquire into the duty of the ["United" *canceled*] States, from within whose limits and jurisdiction the ["the" *can-*

celed] internal peace and security of the slave holding States are endangered.

In order to comprehend more fully the nature and extent of their duty, it will be necessary to make a few remarks on the relations, which exist between the States of our federal Union, with the rights and obligations reciprocally resulting from such relations.

It has already been stated, that the States, which compose our federal Union are sovereign and independent communities, united by a constitutional compact. Among its members the laws of nations are in full force and obligation, except as altered, or modified by the compact; and, of course, the States possess, with that exception, all the rights, and are subject to all the duties, which separate and distinct communities possess, or to which they are subject. Among these are comprehended the obligation, which all States are under, to prevent their citizens from disturbing the peace, or endangering the security of other States; and in case of being disturbed, or endangered, the right of the latter to demand of the former to adopt such measures as will prevent their recurrence; and, if refused, or neglected, to resort to such measures as its protection may require. This right remains, of course, in force among the States of this Union, with such limitations as are imposed expressly by the Constitution. Within their limits, the rights of the Slave holding States are as full to demand of the States, within whose limits and jurisdiction their peace is assailed, to adopt the measures necessary to prevent the same, and, if refused, or neglected, to resort to means to protect themselves, as if they were separate and independent communities.

Those States, on the other hand, are not only under all the obligations, which independent communities would be, to adopt such measures, but also ["under" *interlined*] the obligation, which the Constitution super-adds, rendered more sacred, if possible, by the fact, that while the Union imposes restrictions on the right of the slave holding States to defend themselves, it affords the medium through which their peace and security are assailed. It is not the intention of the Committee to enquire what those restrictions are, and what are the means which, under the Constitution, are left to the slave holding States to protect themselves. The period has not yet come, and, they trust never will, when it may be necessary to decide those questions; but come it must, unless the States, whose duty it is to suppress the danger, shall see in time its magnitude, and the obligations which they are under to adopt speedy and effectual measures to arrest its further progress. That the full force of this obligation may be understood by all parties, the Committee propose, in conclusion, to touch briefly on the movements of the abolitionists, with the view of ["slavery and" *canceled and* "showing" *interlined*] the dangerous consequences to which they must lead, if not arrested.

Their professed object is the emancipation of slaves in the Southern States, which they propose to accomplish through the agency of organized Societies, spread throughout the non-slave holding States, and a powerful press, directed mainly to excite, in the other States, hatred and abhorrence against the institutions and ["usages" *canceled and* "citizens" *interlined*] of the slave holding States, by addresses, lectures and pictorial representations, abounding in false and exaggerated statements.

If the magnitude of the mischief affords, in any degree, the measure by which to judge of the criminality of a project, few have ever been devised to be compared with the present, whether the end be regarded, or the means by which it is proposed to be accomplished. The blindness of fanaticism is proverbial. With more zeal than understanding, it constantly misconceives the nature of the object at which it aims, and towards which it rushes with headlong violence, regardless of the means, by which it is to be effected. Never was its character more fully exemplified, than in the present instance. Setting out with the abstract principle, that slavery is an evil, the fanatical zealots come at once to the conclusion, that it is their duty to abolish it, regardless of all the disasters, which must follow. Never was conclusion more false, or dangerous. ["Assuming it to be an evil," *canceled and* "Admitting their assumption," *interlined*] there are innumerable things, which, regarded in the abstract, are evils, but which it would be madness to attempt to abolish. Thus regarded government itself is an evil, with most of its institutions intended to protect life and property, comprehending the civil as well as the criminal and military code, ["and" *canceled and* "which" *interlined*] are tolerated only because to abolish ["them evil" *canceled and* "them" *interlined*], would be to increase, instead of diminishing ["it" *canceled and* "the evil" *interlined*]. The reason is equally applicable to the case under consideration, to illustrate which, a few remarks on slavery, as it actually ["exists in the" *interlined*] Southern States, will be necessary.

He who regards slavery in those States simply under the relation of master and slave, as important as that relation is, viewed merely as a question of property to the slave holding section of the Union, has a very imperfect conception of the institution, and the impossibility of abolishing it, without disasters unexampled in the history of the world. To understand its nature and importance fully, it must be borne in mind, that slavery, as it exists in the Southern States, (including under the Southern all the slave holding States) involves not only the relation of master and slave, but also the social and political relations of two races, of nearly equal numbers, from different quarters of the Globe, and the most opposite of all others in every particular, that distinguishes one race of men from another. Emancipation would destroy these relations—would divest the masters of their property, and subvert the relation, social and political, that has existed between the races from almost the ["first" *interlined*] settlement of the Southern States.

It is not the intention of the Committee to dwell on the pecuniary aspect of this vital subject; the vast amount of property involved, equal ["at least" *interlined*] to ["at least" *canceled*], $950,000,000; the ruin of families and individuals, the impoverishment and prostration of an entire section of the Union, and the fatal blow, that would be given to the productions of the great agricultural staples, on which the commerce, the navigation, the manufactures and the Revenue of the country, almost entirely depend. As great as these disasters would be, they are nothing compared to what must follow the subversion of the existing relation between the two races, to which the Committee will confine their remarks.

Under ["its protection" *canceled and* "this relation" *interlined*], the two races have long lived in peace and prosperity, and if not disturbed would long continue so to live. While the European race has rapidly increased in wealth and numbers, and at the same time has maintained an equality, at least, morally and intellectually, with their brethren of the non-slave holding States, ["while" *canceled*] the African race has multiplied with not less rapidity, ["with" *canceled and* "accompanied by" *interlined*] great improvement, physically and intellectually, and the enjoyment of a degree of comfort, with which the laboring class in few countries can compare, and confessedly, greatly superior, to what the free people of the same race possess in the non slave holding States. It may indeed be safely asserted, that there is no example in history in which a savage people, such as their ancestors were, when brought into the country, have ever advanced, in the same period, so rapidly in numbers and improvement.

To destroy the existing relations would be to destroy this prosperity, and to place the two races in a state of conflict, which must end in the expulsion, or extirpation of one or the other. No other can be substituted, compatible with their peace, or security. The difficulty is in the diversity of the races. So strongly drawn is the line between the two, in consequence of ["it," *interlined*] and so strengthened by the force of habit and education, that it is impossible for them to exist together in the same community, where their numbers are so nearly equal, as in the slave holding States, under any other relation, than which now exists. Social and political equality between them is impossible. No power on earth can overcome the difficulty. The causes resisting ["it" *canceled*], lie too deep in the principles of our nature to be surmounted. But, without such equality, to change the present condition of the African race, were it possible, would be but to change the form of slavery. It would make them the slaves of ["a" *canceled and* "the" *interlined*] community instead of the slaves of individuals, with less responsibility and interest in their welfare on the part of the community, than is felt by their present masters; while it would destroy the security and independence of the European race, if the african should be permitted to continue, in their changed condition, within the limits of those States. They would look to the other States for support and protection, and would become, virtually, their allies and dependents; and would thus place in the hands of those States the most effectual instrument to destroy the influence and control the destiny of the rest of the Union.

It is against this relation between the two races, that the blind and criminal zeal of the abolitionists is directed—a relation that now preserves in quiet and security more than 6,500,000 human beings, and which cannot be destroyed, without destroying the peace and prosperity of nearly half the States of the Union, and involving their entire population in a deadly conflict, that ["would" *canceled and* "must" *interlined*] terminate either in the expulsion, or extirpation of those, who are the object of the misguided and false humanity of those who claim to be their friends.

He must be blind indeed, who does not perceive, that the subversion of a relation, which must be followed with such disastrous consequences, can only be effected by convulsions, that would devastate the country, burst asunder the bonds of the Union, and engulph, in a sea of blood, the institutions of the country. It is madness to suppose, that the slave holding States would quietly submit to be sacrificed. Every consideration: interest, duty, and humanity, the love of country, the sense of wrong, hatred of oppressors, and ["traitorous" *canceled and* "treacherous" *interlined*] and faithless confederates, and finally, despair—would impel them to the most daring and desperate resistance in defence of property, ["family," *interlined*] country, ["family" *canceled*] liberty, and existence.

But wicked and cruel, as is the end aimed at, it is ["fully" *interlined*] equalled by the criminality of the means, by which it is proposed to be accomplished. These, as has been stated, consist in organized Societies and a powerful press, directed mainly with a view to excite the bitterest animosity and hatred of the people of the non-slave-holding States, against the citizens and institutions of the slave holding States. It is easy to see, to what disastrous results such means must tend. Passing over the more obvious effects, their tendency to excite to insurrection and servile war, with all its horrors, and the necessity, which such tendency must impose on the slave-holding States to resort to the most rigid discipline and severe police, to the great injury of the present condition of the slaves, there remains another[,] threatening incalculable mischief to the country.

The inevitable tendency of the means, ["to" *interlined*] which the abolitionists have resorted ["to" *canceled*], to effect their object, must, if persisted in, end in completely alienating the two great sections of the Union. The incessant action of hundreds of societies, and a vast printing establishment, throwing out, daily, thousands of artful and inflam[m]atory publications, must make, in time, a deep impression on the section of the Union, where they freely circulate, and are mainly designed to have effect. The well informed and thoughtful may hold them in contempt, but the young, the inexperienced, the ignorant and thoughtless, will receive the poison. In process of time, when the number of proselytes is sufficiently multiplied, the artful and profligate, who are ever on the watch to seize on any means, however wicked and dangerous, will unite with the fanatics and make their movements the basis of a powerful political party, that will seek advancement by diffusing, as widely as possible, hatred against the slave holding States. But, as hatred begets hatred, and animosity animosity, these feelings would become reciprocal, till every vestige of attachment would cease to exist between the two sections, when the Union and the Constitution, the offspring of mutual affection and confidence, would forever perish.

Such is the danger, to which the movements of the abolitionists expose the country. If the force of the obligation is in proportion to the magnitude of the danger, stronger cannot be imposed, than is at present, on the States within whose limits the danger originates, to arrest its further progress—a duty they owe, not only to the States, whose institutions are assailed, but to the Union and Constitution, as has been shown, and, it may be added, to themselves. The sober and considerate portions of citizens of non-slave holding States, who have a deep stake in the existing institutions of the country, would have little forecast not to see, that the assaults, which are now directed against the institutions of the Southern States, may be very easily directed against those, which uphold their own property and security. A very slight modification of the arguments used against the institutions, which ["maintain" *canceled and* "sustain" *interlined*] the property and security of the South, would make them equally effectual against the institutions of the North, ["particularly" *canceled and* "including" *interlined*; "the" *interlined and canceled*] Banking, in which so vast an amount of its property and capital ["are" *canceled and* "is" *interlined*] invested. It would be well for those interested to reflect, whether there now exists, or ever has existed, a wealthy and civilized community, in which one portion, did not live on the labor of another; and whether the form, in which slavery exists, in the South, is not but one modification of this universal condition; and finally, whether any other ["under all the circumstances of the case" *interlined*] is more defensible, or stand [*sic*] on stronger ground of necessity. It is time to look these questions in the face. Let those who are interested remember, that labor is the only ["ground" *canceled and* "resource" *interlined*] of wealth, and how small a portion of it, in all old and civilized countries, even the best governed, is left to those by whose labor wealth is created. Let them also reflect, how little volition, or agency the operatives in any country have in the question of its distribution—as little, with a few exceptions, as the African of the slave holding States has in the distribution of the proceeds of his labor. Nor is it the less oppressive, that in the one case it is effected by the stern and powerful will of the government, and in the other, by the more feeble and flexible will of a master. If one be an evil so is the other. ["In both cases he who makes is not permitted to consume." *canceled.*] The only difference is the amount and mode of the exaction and distribution, and the agency by which they are effected.

CC in DNA, RG 46 (Records of the U.S. Senate), 24A-D18; PC in Senate Document No. 118, 24th Cong., 1st Sess.; PC in the Washington, D.C., *United States' Telegraph,* February 9, 1836, pp. 2–3; PC in the Washington, D.C., *Daily National Intelligencer,* February 10, 1836, p. 2; PC in the Charleston, S.C., *Courier,* February 11, 1836; PC in *Niles' Weekly Register,* vol. XLIX, no. 24 (February 13, 1836), pp. 408–411; PC in *Register of Debates,* 24th Cong.,

1st Sess., Appendix, pp. 72–76; PC in *Speeches of John C. Calhoun*, pp. 189–197; PC in Crallé, ed., *Works*, 5:190–208. NOTE: The manuscript clerk's copy of the report that is transcribed above is apparently the copy from which the official Senate document was set in type. After Calhoun's report and the bill which accompanied it had been presented to the Senate, Willie P. Mangum of N.C. moved that 5,000 extra copies be printed. Calhoun said "he hoped his friend from North Carolina would modify his motion, so as to include the printing of the bill with the report. It would be seen, by comparing both together, that there was no *non sequitur* in the bill, coming as it did after this report." After discussion by William R. King of Ala. and John Davis of Mass., Calhoun "said that a majority of the committee did not concur in the report, though there were two members of it, himself and the gentleman from North Carolina [Mangum], who concurred throughout; three other gentlemen concurred with the greater part of the report, though they dissented from some parts of it, and two gentlemen concurred also with some parts of it. As to the bill, two of the committee would have preferred a different one, though they had rather have that than none at all; another gentleman [Davis] was opposed to it altogether. The bill, however, was a natural consequence of the report, and the two did not disagree with each other." Mangum's motion was amended as requested and then adopted. (See *Register of Debates*, 24th Cong., 1st Sess., cols. 383–385, or *Congressional Globe*, 24th Cong., 1st Sess., p. 165.) Among the replies elicited by this report was "Cincinnatus," *Freedom's Defence: or a Candid Examination of Mr. Calhoun's Report on the Freedom of the Press, Made to the Senate of the United States, Feb. 4, 1836* (Worcester, Mass.: printed by Dorr, Howland & Co., 1836).

BILL FROM THE SELECT COMMITTEE ON THE CIRCULATION OF INCENDIARY PUBLICATIONS

In the Senate, February 4, 1836

Mr. Calhoun from the select committee to whom was referred so much of the President's message as relates to the circulation of incendiary publications, reported the following bill; which was read, and passed to a second reading.

A Bill Prohibiting deputy postmasters from receiving or transmitting through the mail to any State, Territory, or District, certain papers therein mentioned, the circulation of which, by the laws of said State, Territory, or District, may be prohibited, and for other purposes.

Be it enacted by the Senate and House of Representatives of the United States of America in Congress assembled, That it shall not be lawful for any deputy postmaster, in any State, Territory, or District, knowingly to receive and put into the mail any pamphlet, newspaper, handbill, or other paper, printed or written, or pictorial representation, touching the subject of slavery, addressed to any person or post office in any State, Territory, or District, where, by the laws of the said State, Territory, or District, their circulation is prohibited. Nor shall it be lawful for any deputy postmaster, in said State, Territory, or District, knowingly to deliver to any person any such pamphlet, newspaper, handbill, or other paper, printed or written, or pictorial representation, to any person whatever, except to such person or persons as are duly authorized, by the proper authority of such State, Territory, or District, to receive the same.

Sec. 2. *And be it further enacted by the authority aforesaid,* That it shall be the duty of the Postmaster General to dismiss from office any deputy postmaster offending in the premises, and such deputy postmaster shall, on conviction thereof in any court having competent jurisdiction, be fined in any sum not less than [*blank space*; "one hundred" *inserted*] dollars, and not more than [*blank space*; "one thousand" *inserted*] dollars, according to the aggravation of the offence, at the discretion of the court.

Sec. 3. *And be it further enacted by the authority aforesaid,* That it shall be the duty of deputy postmasters, mail carriers, and other officers and agents of the Post Office Department, to co-operate, as far as may be, to prevent the circulation of any pamphlet, newspaper, handbill, or other paper, printed or written, or pictorial representation, as aforesaid, in any State, Territory, or District, where, by the laws of said State, Territory, or District, the same are prohibited, and that nothing in the acts of Congress to establish and regulate the Post Office Department, shall be construed to protect any deputy postmaster, mail carrier, or other officer or agent of said Department, convicted of knowingly circulating in any State, Territory, or District, as aforesaid, any such pamphlet, newspaper, handbill, or other paper, printed or written, or pictorial representation, forbidden by the laws of such State, Territory, or District.

Sec. 4. *And be it further enacted,* That it shall be the duty of the Postmaster General to furnish to the deputy postmasters, and the agents and officers of the Department, copies of the laws of the several States, Territories, and Districts, prohibiting the publication or circulation of any pamphlet, newspaper, handbill, or other paper, printed or written, or pictorial representation, within the limits of said States, Territories, or Districts, for their government in the premises; and make such regulations and give such instructions in carrying this act into effect as may not be contrary to law.

Sec. 5. *And be it further enacted by the authority aforesaid,*

That the deputy postmasters of the offices where the pamphlets, newspapers, handbills, or other papers, printed or written, or pictorial representations aforesaid may be deposited, shall, under the instructions of the Postmaster General, from time to time give notice of the same, so that they may be withdrawn by the person depositing them; and if not withdrawn in the space of one month thereafter, shall be burnt or otherwise destroyed.

PC in DNA, RG 46 (Records of the U.S. Senate), 24A-B2; draft in DNA, RG 46, 24A-B1; engrossed bill in DNA, RG 46, 24A-B11; PC in DLC, Congressional Bills, 24th Cong., 1st Sess., S-122; PC in *Register of Debates*, 24th Cong., 1st Sess., Appendix, pp. 76–77; PC in Senate Document No. 118, 24th Cong., 1st Sess., pp. 11–12; PC in the Washington, D.C., *Daily National Intelligencer*, February 5, 1836, p. 3; PC in *Niles' Weekly Register*, vol. XLIX, no. 23 (February 6, 1836), p. 391; PC in the Washington, D.C., *United States' Telegraph*, February 9, 1836, p. 3. NOTE: The first source cited above also includes PC's of two proposed amendments. One offered by John M. Niles of Conn. would have substituted the words "the design or tendency of which is to excite insurrection among slaves" for "touching the subject of slavery" in the first section. Felix Grundy of Tenn. offered changes which would have permitted any deputy postmaster who was guilty under the act to be "forthwith removed from office" without the requirement of trial and conviction. This bill underwent prolonged consideration in the Senate and, after being amended, was defeated on its third reading on 6/8 by a vote of 18 to 25.

Remarks on the Treasury surplus and the prospects of a French war, 2/5. Under discussion was a bill to appropriate one million dollars to continue construction of the Cumberland Road through Ind. and Ill. "Mr. Calhoun moved to lay the bill upon the table, upon the ground that to vote such large appropriations for such a purpose was inconsistent with the apprehensions of a French war which the friends of the Administration had urged upon the Senate. He stated that the money in the Treasury was the means of sustaining the war; and that if Senators were indeed apprehensive of a rupture with France they would not make such long drafts upon it for such purposes. He hoped that the proposition to lay the bill on the table would be considered a test question. That if those who spoke so much of the necessity of preparing for war were found voting away the 'sinews,' without which it could not be maintained, it would be conclusive proof that there was in reality no serious expectation of war, and that all that had fallen from the friends of the Administration upon that subject, was intended to humbug the people." From the Washington, D.C., *United States' Telegraph*, February 9, 1836, p. 3. Variant in the New York, N.Y., *Morning Courier and New-York Enquirer*, February 8, 1836, p. 2.

To "Maj[o]r" C[HRISTOPHER] VANDEVENTER, [near Buffalo, N.Y.?]

Washington, 7th Feb: 1836

My dear Sir, A great pressure of business has prevented me from answering your letters at an earlier date. I am exceedingly gratified to learn that your health is better, and do hope that a kind Providence may long spare you for the benefit of your ["families" *altered to* "family"] & friends. My own health remains good, fully as much so as when we last parted.

You give a fearful picture of the progress of the Fanaticks, which is confirmed from every quarter we hear in the North. I fear a direct issue between them & us cannot long be delayed—an issue, which, if it does not rent [*sic*] our political fabrick assunder [*sic*], will shake it to the centre.

I made a few days since a report on the part of the President's Message, which relates to incendiary publications, in which I have discussed some very important points. The report, I think, was well received on all sides. I will send you a copy as soon as it is printed, which I hope will be tomorrow.

The prospect of peace has brightened. The mediation is said to be accepted, of which, however, there is no official information. I trust it is true, and that it will save us from the disasters & folly of a French war.

The times are daily becoming worse. This year is more corrupt & sycophantick than the last, and I fear the next will be more so than this. God only knows what is to become of the ["times" *canceled*] country. Without a timely & thor[o]ugh reform all will be lost, for which our fathers fought & bled.

Anna [Maria Calhoun], who is with me, joins her kind regards to yourself, Mrs. [Sally Birckhead] V[andeventer] & family.

Wishing you an improvement of health, and long continuance of life, I remain your friend, J.C. Calhoun.

ALS in DLC, Christopher Vandeventer Papers; PC in Jameson, ed., *Correspondence*, pp. 357–358.

To [Lewis Cass, Secretary of War, *ca.* 2/9]. Calhoun requests Cass to review the case represented by the enclosed papers [concerning the pension claim of William Smith of Abbeville District, S.C.]. "I have no doubt it is an honest claim. I know the petitioner, and all the persons named, to be entitled to full credit." ALS in

DNA, RG 15 (Records of the Veterans Administration), Revolutionary War Pension and Bounty-Land Warrant Application Files, 1800–1900, R-9875½.

Remarks on the bill "for the relief of the several corporate cities of the District of Columbia," 2/11. Nine Senators had engaged in a discussion of the merits and details of the bill to provide relief to Washington, Georgetown, and Alexandria (for debts due individuals in Holland in connection with the Chesapeake and Ohio Canal). "Mr. Calhoun did not understand the only question on this bill to be whether the Government should pay the debt now due; but it was to pay to the corporations all they had paid; to refund every expenditure. The only justification rests on the ground of an improvident contract. On what principle was the Government to pay back to the corporations what they had paid? He had heard this debate with infinite pain. It appeared to him as if he was living in the last stage of a corrupt age. He wished to know if his constituents were to be taxed to pay this money. There was no constitutional power to give the money. As far as he could, he would afford relief, but it must be only as far as the necessity of the case requires, and that under all possible indemnities. He was willing to go as far as the million and a half, and would take a mortgage on the property, with the right to receive dividends, and to make sale. He wished to recommit the bill, with instructions to report it in that form." Later in the debate, Calhoun "insisted that all which was necessary to be done to place Georgetown and Alexandria on a footing of equality with Washington was to give to these two cities as much interest as had been given to Washington, and not to pay all the debt and the interest of the Washington part of the loan twice over." From *Register of Debates*, 24th Cong., 1st Sess., cols. 466–470. Also printed in the Washington, D.C., *Daily National Intelligencer*, February 15, 1836, p. 2. Variant in the Washington, D.C., *United States' Telegraph*, February 12, 1836, p. 3. Another variant in the New York, N.Y., *Morning Courier and New-York Enquirer*, February 13, 1836, p. 2.

REMARKS IN DEBATE ON THE RECEPTION OF ABOLITION PETITIONS

[In the Senate, February 12, 1836]

The Pennsylvania memorial, praying for the abolition of slavery in the District of Columbia, was called up, as the first on the list of general orders.

[*There followed a discussion in which several Senators sought postponement of the matter on the grounds that the time was almost at hand that had been scheduled for the consideration of private bills. Calhoun defended the right of Gabriel Moore of Ala., who was entitled to the floor, to speak. Moore addressed the Senate in support of Calhoun's motion not to receive the petition. Then John P. King of Ga. spoke against the motion.*]

Mr. Calhoun said that the discussion was to him entirely unexpected; and as it had interfered with the arrangement, allotting this day to private business, he felt bound to explain the motive which governed him in resisting the motion to postpone the question, in order to afford the Senator from Alabama (Mr. Moore) an opportunity to deliver his remarks. It is known that that Senator had, several weeks since, risen to discuss this subject, so important to his constituents, but the Senate adjourned before he had finished his remarks. After so long a lapse, he felt it to be due to that Senator that he should now have an opportunity of concluding what he then intended to say. As he was known to be generally brief in his remarks, I did suppose that he would not have occupied the Senate beyond the usual time of taking up the orders; and much less did I suppose that other Senators, who were not in a similar situation, would succeed him in the discussion. Had I anticipated such a result, I would certainly have acquiesced in the postponement of the question, in order to take up the business to which the day was allotted; and in order that I may occupy as little time as possible, I will not undertake to follow the Senator from Georgia in the course of his argument. I propose to touch upon a few points only, in the hope that, after I have concluded my remarks, the question may be disposed of for the present.

I have heard (said Mr. C[alhoun]) with deep mortification and regret the speech of the Senator from Georgia; not that I suppose that his arguments can have much impression in the South, but because of their tendency to divide and distract the Southern delegation on this, to us, all-momentous question. We are here but a handful in the midst of an overwhelming majority. It is the duty of every member from the South, on this great and vital question, where union is so important to those whom we represent, to avoid every thing calculated to divide or distract our ranks. I, (said Mr. C[alhoun],) the Senate will bear witness, have, in all that I have said on this subject, been careful to respect the feelings of Southern members who have differed from me in the policy to be pursued. Having thus acted, on my part, I must express my surprise at the harsh expressions, to say the least, in which the Senator from Georgia has indulged.

(Mr. King here asked that the expressions might be specified.)

Mr. C[alhoun] replied that he understood the Senator to designate the demand of the question on the receiving of the petition as a mere pretext.

(Mr. King disclaimed having done so.)

Mr. Calhoun said that he certainly understood the Senator from Georgia as having used the expression, but was gratified that he had disclaimed it; but he could not be mistaken in saying that the Senator had represented the course which I, and other Senators who think with me, have pursued in reference to this subject, as aiding and playing into the hands of A[rthur] Tappan & Co., and calculated to produce agitation. I would ask (said Mr. C[alhoun]) upon what possible authority such assertion can be made? What has been my course? Has it not been purely defensive? I am averse to Congress touching the subject of abolition, and from the beginning of the session have prescribed to myself, as a rule not to be departed from, a resistance of all attempts to bring the subject within the sphere of the action of this body. Acting on this principle, I felt myself bound (said Mr. C[alhoun]) to demand the question on receiving the various petitions which have been presented, in order to shut the doors of the Senate against the admission of the wicked and fanatical agitators. Had I not a right, (said Mr. C[alhoun],) secured by the parliamentary rules of this body, to demand this question, and was I not bound to exercise it on this occasion? When the incendiaries present themselves here, in violation of the Constitution, with petitions in the highest degree calumnious of the people of the South, holding them up as despots, dealers in human flesh, and pirates, was it for me, representing one of the Southern States, to be silent on such an occasion, and to endorse such slanders on my constituents, by receiving them? I certainly do not so estimate my duty. I consider it the proper occasion to exercise the right, which belongs to me as a Senator, to demand the question on the reception; for doing this I have been accused as an agitator. This is the utmost extent of my offending. But (said Mr. C[alhoun]) let us inquire, if there has been agitation, who are the agitators, and who is responsible for discussion? Is it I and those who have acted with me; who have acted on the defensive; who have demanded a question which every Senator has the acknowledged right of demanding on every petition, or those who have resisted that demand? And on what ground has this demand been resisted? Can any be more extraordinary than that to refuse to receive is a violation of the Constitution? What are the words of that instrument? That "Congress shall pass no law prohibiting the people from peaceably assembling and praying for a redress of grievances." Has any such law been passed? Have these agitators been prohibited from praying for a redress of grievances? Does any one pretend that such is the fact? How, then, can it be asserted that, to refuse to receive these slanderous petitions, praying the enactment of unconstitutional laws, is a violation of the Constitution?

I (said Mr. C[alhoun]) am gratified that the Senator from Georgia concedes the point that Congress has no power to abolish slavery in the District [of Columbia]—a concession which atones for much which he has said. To yield the right here, is to yield the right to Congress to abolish slavery in the States. I would proclaim (said Mr. C[alhoun]) to the whole South that, if the right be surrendered to abolish slavery in the District, their most effectual guard is surrendered. But I will ask the Senator from Georgia, if Congress has no right to abolish slavery in this District more than to do so in the States, upon what principle can he vote upon the reception of this petition which, he concedes, prays the Senate to pass a law in violation of the Constitution? Let us change the question, to test the principle on which the Senator acts. He admits the constitutional power of Congress over the subject, whether in this District or in the States, to be the same. I ask him, then, (said Mr. C[alhoun], addressing Mr. King,) is he prepared, as a Senator from Georgia, to vote to receive a petition for the abolition of slavery in that State —a petition, too, for his principles go to that extent, couched in the most abusive and slanderous language against the State and its institutions?

(Mr. King replied, yes.)

All, then, (said Mr. C[alhoun],) that I can say is, that the Senator and myself are so organized as to have feelings directly dissimilar. Rather than receive such a petition against South Carolina, against those whom I represent, I would have my head dissevered from my body.

I feel (said Mr. C[alhoun]) that I have transgressed upon the time of the Senate; I must postpone much that I have to say to a more suitable occasion; but so deeply am I impressed with the magnitude of the subject, that it was impossible that I could say less than I have said. No question of equal magnitude has been agitated since the formation of the Government, and, in my opinion, the only way to arrest their progress is to meet them at the threshold with a stern refusal to permit them to enter these doors. If I stand alone, I shall continue to occupy this ground, regardless of the unfounded charges of agitation. I hold this question too deep and too serious to be mixed up with the presidential or any other question of the day. I accuse no one of so mixing it, or of seeking to agitate it for party purposes; but I must say that, if there be agitators, those only are such who resist the course which I feel it my duty to pursue, and which I believe to be the only one compatible with the interests and security of the slaveholding States.

[*Here Isaac Hill of N.H. spoke at length in reply to Calhoun. He presented evidence of opposition to abolitionism in New England, attributing the antislavery movement to a "certain description of the clergy" who had sympathized with Great Britain during the War of 1812. He was once called to order by Calhoun for a reference to the "deep disgrace" which S.C. had brought upon herself in 1832, but was allowed by the chair to proceed. Hill continued, deprecating the recent report of the Select Committee on Incendiary Publications and maintaining that "the democracy of the North are strenuously contending for the rights of the South."*]

Mr. Calhoun said the Senator from New Hampshire could not expect him to reply to him. That Senator had availed himself of the position he occupied on that floor to indulge very freely in assailing the motives of others. He was persuaded that no Senator who had any respect for himself would stoop to notice any thing of this character which had fallen from him. For himself, he would as soon condescend to notice the mendacious and filthy columns of the [Washington, D.C.,] Globe, as to notice the general remarks of the Senator from New Hampshire. That Senator had, however, stated what purported to be a fact, that the abolition excitement in New Hampshire was entirely extinct. But here was a statement of facts in relation to what that gentleman said of the abolition question in New Hampshire. It was found in a publication coming from one of the incendiary publications [*sic*; societies] in that State, and he would lay it before the Senate, in order that it might judge for itself. He would not institute a comparison between the relative degree of veracity in the statement contained in this paper and the one made by the Senator from New Hampshire. He would lay the paper before the Senate, in order that it might judge of the truth as to the abolition spirit in New Hampshire. It was a paper that had been sent to him through the mail, but he did not know from what quarter it came.

(Here Mr. C[alhoun] handed to the Secretary a newspaper containing an article impugning a statement made by Mr. [Franklin] Pierce, of New Hampshire, in the House of Representatives, as to the number of abolitionists in his State, with severe strictures on the state of slavery in the South; said article stating that a great number of petitions in favor of the abolition of slavery in the District of Columbia would be forwarded to Congress from New Hampshire.)

The paper having been read, Mr. Hill inquired the title of it.

(The Secretary answered, "The Herald of Freedom," published at Concord, New Hampshire.)

[*Hill maintained that though the paper was printed in Concord, "those who were engaged in it were ashamed to circulate it in its own neighborhood." He then deplored the reading of a paper attacking a member of the House of Representatives and spoke of "the contempt and disgust" felt for Calhoun in N.H. Then Henry Hubbard of N.H., who was in the chair, apologized to the Senate for the reading of the newspaper article, which he said he would not have allowed had he known its import.*]

Mr. Calhoun said he was entitled to the floor, and objected to being interrupted by the Chair.

(Mr. Hubbard replied, he had said all he wished to say. The Senator was entitled to the floor, and could proceed if he wished.)

Mr. Calhoun continued. He knew nothing of the paper just presented. He had seen it for the first time that morning, and had presented it to the Senate for no other purpose than to show from another quarter the state of the abolition spirit in New Hampshire. He knew the gentleman (Mr. [Franklin] Pierce) who was assailed in that paper, and was ready to bear testimony to his worth and high standing. He meant no disrespect to him. He had presented the paper because it was important that the real state of things should be known. It was due from gentleman [*sic*] of the North to those of the South, to give correct information. He did not call those friends of the South who would disguise the state of things at the North. He believed as yet that the real number of abolitionists was small; but he also believed that the number of those who contemplated ultimate abolition was very great; and that those ardent addresses in favor of liberty, so constantly made at the North, must have a deep effect on the young and rising generation. The spirit of abolition was not to be trifled with. It had had its bad effect on one of the most powerful Governments of Europe, and ended disastrously to its colonial possessions. It was commencing in the same manner here, and must be met at once with the most decided resistance. He repeated that he had the greatest respect for the member from New Hampshire mentioned in the paper just read; and he took pleasure bearing testimony to his high standing and moral worth. He had only presented the paper to show the state of things in New Hampshire, and that the Senate might judge whether the abolition spirit was subsiding there.

[*James Buchanan and Thomas H. Benton spoke briefly, and the Senate adjourned.*]

From *Register of Debates,* 24th Cong., 1st Sess., cols. 471–497. Variant in the Washington, D.C., *Globe,* February 17, 1836, p. 2, and February 18, 1836, p. 2; *Congressional Globe,* 24th Cong., 1st Sess., Appendix, pp. 89–93. Another variant in the New York, N.Y., *Morning Courier and New-York Enquirer,* February 15, 1836, p. 2.

Remarks on the reception of abolition petitions, 2/15. John M. Niles of Conn. accused Calhoun of agitating this subject. Calhoun "rose to explain. He said he had not urged on a debate—he had done nothing to cause a debate—he had only made the question that the petition be not received; and, if a debate had ensued, he was not responsible for it, but those who had opposed his motion." Later in Niles's speech Calhoun queried whether Niles "doubted the sincerity of his declaration, when he asserted that he was opposed to agitating the question." From *Register of Debates,* 24th Cong., 1st Sess., cols. 513–514. Also printed in *Congressional Globe,* 24th Cong., 1st Sess., Appendix, p. 118. Variant in the Washington, D.C., *United States' Telegraph,* February 16, 1836, p. 3.

Remarks in Reply to Silas Wright on Admitting the Public to the Senate

[In the Senate, February 16, 1836]
[*Under consideration was James Buchanan's proposal to restrict admission to the Senate lobby to ladies, three to be admitted by each Senator. Silas Wright of N.Y. criticized remarks made by Calhoun when the subject was last under discussion (on 1/6), remarks to the effect that the issue under consideration involved a conflict between those in power and the people.*]

Mr. Calhoun rose to correct the misapprehension of Mr. Wright. It was not that he had considered the decision of the question as to whether the galleries should be open to the public at large, as deciding a contest between the Executive and the people. He had said that there was a great contest now going on between power and the people. The Executive, he said, had taken upon himself to nominate his successor through the medium of a convention got up by office holders; that he had seized upon the whole treasury of the country, now amounting to more than thirty millions of dollars, to use it as he and his friends chose; that by means of it and by his proscriptive policy, forcing all the officers of the government to become either active partizans in favor of the Executive and his views, or to become neutral in order to retain office. By these means he expected, and was striving to nominate his successor. He has, said Mr. Calhoun, the treasury of the country at his disposal. He has the offices and the honors, and he has the Post Office, with all its patronage and power of corruption. And these, said he, are used without stint, or regard to law or decency. Letters are broken up; yes, said he, my own letters and those of my family have been broken open in their passage through the post office.

With all these overwhelming means of corrupting, of deceiving, and of deluding the people, possessed by the Executive, let us be permitted to have this Hall in which the people can freely hear what transpires on this floor. If, said he, the whole people of the United States could have been here and listened to the debates of the last four years, we should not now hear the gentleman from New York referring to the people as approving the course of the Administration. No! There would have been on their part one unanimous voice of disapprobation.

Mr. Calhoun acknowledged the talent, ability, and adroitness of the Senator from New York. It was, he believed, from those qualities in that gentleman, and from his stern adherence to party discipline, that the State of New York exhibited the aspect she now did in her fiscal and political relations. Who controls the Safety Fund Banks? Look at the decrease of the stock of the Chartered Companies. How is that Stock divided? Who gets the profit of them?

This contest, said Mr. Calhoun, between power on one side, the Executive encroaching on the other powers of the Government, and the people, is one that has existed in every free Government. It goes on increasing and increasing, always getting what it can, and never giving up any: and it must be met on the threshhold [*sic*] and resisted from the commencement, or the Executive soon usurps all amidst the corruption it produces.

From the Washington, D.C., *United States' Telegraph*, February 17, 1836, p. 3. Variant in the New York, N.Y., *Morning Courier and New-York Enquirer*, February 18, 1836, p. 2.

REMARKS ON THE TREASURY SURPLUS

[In the Senate, February 17, 1836]

[Under consideration was a resolution introduced by Thomas H. Benton "for appropriating the surplus revenue to objects of permanent national defence." Silas Wright had spoken at length in support of the resolution.]

Mr. Calhoun said that he regarded the declaration of the Senator from New York, who had just taken his seat, (Mr. Wright,) that the danger of a war with France is past, as an annunciation, almost official, that the peace of the country is to be preserved. He was gratified with the information. He rejoiced that the country had been saved from the calamities of a French war—a war, had it occurred, the termination of which no one could conjecture, and which would have proved disgraceful and ruinous to us. We might now look forward to the speedy restoration of amicable relations between the two countries, unless, indeed, the late unseasonable message of the President [Andrew Jackson], and the ill-timed and imprudent speeches of his friends, delivered since on this floor, should prevent it. Should they be received in France before the difference between the two countries is finally adjusted, it would be impossible to tell the consequence; particularly the speech of the Senator from Pennsylvania, (Mr. [James] Buchanan,) who is supposed to represent the Executive on the floor of the Senate on all questions connected with our foreign relations. That Senator directly impeached the sincerity and integrity of Louis Philippe, contrary to the admission of the President himself, and this even after the mediation had been accepted. The Senate would recollect that, after the message was read, he (Mr. C[alhoun]) expressed his deep regret that the President had not waited to learn how his annual message had been received by the French Government before he sent in the message in question, the direct tendency of which was to involve the country in war. He then expressed his fears that the message just received would arrive in France before the favorable impression that the first was calculated to make could be acted on, as unfortunately our representative at the French court had been withdrawn; but, thanks to the wise and magnanimous conduct of the British Government, there was reason to hope, notwithstanding all these adverse causes, that this unwise and frivolous quarrel would terminate without destroying the friendly relations between the two countries.

He would next (Mr. C[alhoun] said) make a few remarks on the fiscal statement presented by the Senator from New York, (Mr. Wright). He furnished a statement from the Treasury, showing that the unexpended balance on the 1st of January last was upwards of $26,000,000. From this he properly deducted the unavailable funds, equal to about $1,000,000, and leaving a balance in the treasury of something more than $25,000,000. The Senator attempted a farther reduction by substracting [sic], as the Secretary of the Treasury has been in the habit of doing for some years, the outstanding and unsatisfied appropriations, amounting to $7,000,000 or $8,000,000; but very little reflection will show that no reduction ought to be made on that account. These appropriations, in point of fact, constituted a running account of nearly the same amount from year to year, and which the accruing revenue would be more than sufficient to meet, without touching the existing surplus, long before they would be demanded. If, indeed, we were about to terminate our political partnership, and to distribute the balance, after closing our accounts, it might be proper to take the outstanding appropriations into the estimate; but as such was not the case, it was calculated to deceive to make the deduction. The true amount, then, of surplus revenue in the treasury on the 1st of January last may, on the showing of the Secretary [Levi Woodbury] himself, be fairly estimated at $25,000,000 at least, without comprehending the Government share of the United States Bank stock. How forcibly does this statement bring up the incidents of the last session? What a striking illustration of the ultimate triumph of truth! Who does not remember the vociferous charges of extravagance which were, a year ago, made against his (Mr. C[alhoun]'s) estimates? Since then, time has come round, the year has terminated, and we have now the result of the Treasury itself; and, instead of being extravagant, his estimate has fallen far short of the truth. He anticipated that such would be the fact. He wished to be on the safe side, and made, at the time, ample allowances for possible contingencies.

After furnishing the Senate with the statement from the Treasury, the Senator from New York undertook to explain the error which the Secretary is now compelled to admit in his estimate of the receipts of the last quarter of the last year. But what explanation can be offered? What apology made for errors so gross? In his annual report, the Secretary estimates the receipts of the quarter at less than $5,000,000, and it is now admitted to be $11,000,000, making a difference of more than $6,000,000. Was it ever heard of before, that an officer at the head of the fiscal department of any Government ever made so gross an error—an error of more than $6,000,000 in the estimate of the income of a single quarter, and that estimate made within twenty days of the termination of the quarter? The actual returns of the receipts of the quarter to the Treasury must, at the time, have exceeded the Secretary's estimate of the income of the whole quarter. This is the way in which our affairs are now managed. I aver I have looked into scarcely a single fiscal report from the Treasury for some years, without discovering errors calculated to destroy all confidence in the head of that Department.

The Senator from New York has spoken of the defenceless state of the country. This song has been sung from the beginning to the end of this discussion; and yet, not a man of the party had undertaken to review the state of our preparation, and to designate what fortifications were completed, and what remained to be erected, and what was the state of our supplies of arms and munitions, and what remained to complete them. He (Mr. C[alhoun]) would not undertake to say particularly what was the state of our preparations. Some years had elapsed since he had bestowed particular attention on the subject; but if the appropriations which have been made for the defences of the country have been properly expended, as they no doubt had under the excellent arrangement of the military branch of the War Department, the country was infinitely in a better state of defence than at the commencement of the late war with Great Britain, which terminated with so much credit to our arms. Gentlemen spoke of the state of our fortifications with as much confidence as if they possessed the skill of a [Simon] Bernard or a

[William] McRee, and yet he would venture to assert that neither the
Senator from New Hampshire, (Mr. [Henry] Hubbard,) who spoke
so long and so emphatically on the subject, nor any of those who
followed him on the same side, could enumerate what fortifications
were completed, where they were situated, what were their dimensions, or what were to be constructed in order to complete our
defences. He would tell those gentlemen that, so far from being
defenceless, as far as fortifications are concerned, the country was,
with some exceptions, in a state of admirable defence. In making
this declaration he wished not, however, to be understood as desiring to stop where we were. He wished the system to progress till
every portion of the country was in a suitable state of defence. But
in thus advocating a system of fortifications, he did not think we
ought to rely on them principally for defence. Our reliance ought
to be on the navy, which, in his opinion, ought to be augmented to
the extent of our capacity to man and officer.

Mr. C[alhoun] said the discussion on the subject of the fortifications recalled the recollection of former years. It was with pride
that he heard the high eulogy of the system which he had for so
many years defended, against the attacks of the party to which the
Senator from New York belonged, and which now, if we may judge
from professions, were its warmest advocates. For seven long years
he (Mr. C[alhoun]) had maintained the system of fortifications,
which he had perfected and matured, against the incessant attacks
of the party. He would now ask his former opponents, what would
have become of the system, and what would have been the present
condition of the defences of the country, if he had yielded to those
attacks—if he had shrunk from an honest and fearless discharge of
his duty[?] He felt a proud satisfaction in what he now beheld.
He saw those who formerly so strenuously opposed and denounced
him coming forward and approbating the very measures which formerly he sustained against their attacks, but who have not the magnanimity to do him justice. If, in their former attacks on him while
fearlessly performing his duty, they excited his indignation, their
conduct now made them the object of his pity. But what I see
strengthens my confidence in the cause of truth—nerves me in the
performance of my duty. I perceive, more clearly than ever, that,
in the dispensations of Providence, justice must in the end prevail.
We shall (said Mr. C[alhoun]) have, before long, other illustrations
of this consoling truth. Before many years shall have elapsed, many
who have opposed his course of late will be the foremost to approve
it. He saw the brewing of a storm. That most lawless and uncon-

stitutional act, the removal of the deposites, has given a fatal blow to the currency of the country. It was now producing its legitimate consequences—an inordinate increase of the banking system. The causes in operation must produce an explosion, the like of which has scarcely ever been witnessed in any country. To this catastrophe the surplus revenue, deposited where it is, is destined to contribute its full share. It is, in fact, in its present state, banking capital in its worst possible form, whether we regard its effects on the currency of the country, or its political institutions. The time has gone by when nations could safely accumulate a surplus revenue. The currency of the world no longer consisted of gold and silver. Bank notes and bank credit now constitute far the greater part of the currency of commercial and civilized countries. It is almost exclusively our currency, and it is difficult to imagine greater folly than for a Government to hoard up its revenue when collected in such a currency. The consequences must, in the end, prove fatal, unless the greatest discretion and foresight are exercised. Every dollar in bank notes drawn from circulation by being deposited in the treasury, but makes room for the issue of another note of equal amount in its place. But that is not all. The note deposited in bank becomes banking capital, and, as such, the means of making still farther issues; and thus, between the notes in deposite and those in circulation, the currency of the country must receive an unnatural and dangerous enlargement. While the funds are accumulating in banks, and in the absence of any political or commercial disaster, no immediate shock can take place; but let it be reversed, let the funds be suddenly withdrawn, or disaster befall the country, and widespread ruin must be the consequence. The time is coming when all he said would be realized, and when those who have been most forward to advocate the measures which have given rise to the present dangerous condition of the currency will, when it is too late, condemn it as bitterly as they have ardently approved it.

Mr. C[alhoun] said that the Senator from New York had spoken much of the President's popularity, and the power and talents of the opposition, which it had successfully resisted. It was not for him to offer any opinion on the degree of talents possessed by the opposition, as he constituted a portion of a portion of it; but he would say that, whatever might be its talents, the opposition was essentially weak; so much so, that any man possessing a moderate degree of intellect and firmness, with the patronage possessed by the President, and occupying the position which he has, might easily maintain himself against all the opposition which he has encountered.

The attacks of the opposition were made from so many different points, and carried on with such different views, and on such different principles, that nothing could be more feeble, however talented the members who composed it. With whatever vigor their assaults might be made at the commencement, at the very moment victory seemed near, the opposition were resolved into their separate and opposing elements. He said that the friends of the administration smiled at this confession. He would give them something at which they would not. The opposition was not only weak in the particular to which he had adverted, but the position occupied by the President, though not such as an honest and patriotic man would choose, was exceedingly strong. To be understood, he must revert to the circumstances under which the present incumbent was first elected President.

We all remember the two great hostile and sectional parties into which the country was divided for so many years, on the subject of the tariff. With the election of Mr. [John Quincy] Adams, the majority in favor of the tariff became fixed. In order to prevent his re-election, the South was reduced to the necessity of making a choice of evils, and to offer, as their candidate, a man whose opinions were undefined on the great question in controversy between the two sections. General Jackson was accordingly selected as a judicious tariff man, and although we of the South had our fears in relation to him, we were compelled to adopt him, rather than to submit to Mr. Adams's re-election. We hoped that, receiving our support, and being identified with us in interests, he (General Jackson) would use his influence, if elected, gradually to correct the excesses and abuses of the system, and to bring the revenue to the standard which the wants of the Government required. Under this impression, he received our support, and was elected. But he deceived us. We soon saw that, instead of fulfilling the conditions under which he was elected, he was intent on using the position which he occupied as the means of personal influence and aggrandizement. Without identifying himself either with the tariff or anti-tariff interest, he assumed a middle position between the contending parties, now leaning towards the one, and again to the opposite party, as circumstances required; and at the same time using the immense patronage which the system placed in his hands, as a means of recruiting from the ranks of both parties all who preferred themselves to their country; and thus creating a party, for the first time in our country, purely personal—a party held together, not by principle, or by a system of public policy, but by the hopes of personal gain and advancement. It was thus the principles of the spoils party, which had originated in the State of New York, gained the ascendant in the Union, with its rigid and despotic system of discipline, by which all who held or expected office were compelled to rely on partisan service for success or security; a party whose base and low-minded system is rapidly contaminating the whole community. Thus, standing on middle ground, and surrounded by a numerous host of devoted personal partisans, it was impossible for the opposition, acting upon conflicting principles, to make any effective resistance to General Jackson. The North preferred him to a nullifier, and the South to a consolidationist. In the mean time, it was impossible to unite the South against the administration, however unconstitutional and outrageous its acts. The circumstance that we had elected General Jackson gave him great advantage in effecting his scheme of keeping the South. Without it the tenth part of the sins of the administration would long since have united the South in opposition.

When the South was divided (continued Mr. C[alhoun]) the opposition must ever be feeble. It was an historical fact, that all effective opposition to the administration of this Government has come from the South. The North has never been able to turn out an administration. He intended no disparagement to that great section. He spoke of the fact simply, without pretending to go into the cause; while, on the other hand, the South has never failed to overthrow an administration to which it was opposed. But two administrations had come in against its choice, both of which were speedily and decisively overthrown. General Jackson would soon be out of power, and the administration that may succeed him could not keep the South divided. He would tell the coming administration to beware. If there be any who expected that the President's nominee could successfully play the game which he has, he would be wo[e]-fully mistaken. With all his objections to the President, he (Mr. C[alhoun]) would not deny him many high qualities: he had courage and firmness, was bold, warlike, audacious; though not true to his word, or faithful to his pledges. He had, besides, done the state some service. He terminated the late war gloriously at New Orleans, which has been remembered greatly to his advantage. His nominee [Martin Van Buren] had none of these recommendations; he is not, as remarked by his (Mr. C[alhoun]'s) friend from North Carolina, [Willie P. Mangum,] of the race of the lion or the tiger; he belonged to a lower order—the fox; and it would be in vain to expect that he could command the respect or acquire the confidence of those who had so little admiration for the qualities by which he was distinguished. By the dexterous use of patronage, for which he and his party were so distinguished, an individual here and there, who preferred himself to the country, might be enlisted; but the great mass, all that were independent and sound in the South, would be finally opposed to him and his system.

Mr. C[alhoun], in conclusion, observed that he did not intend to take any part in the present debate, but the remarks of the Senator from New York excited a train of reflection in his mind that would not permit him to remain silent.

From *Register of Debates*, 24th Cong., 1st Sess., cols. 551–556. Also printed in the Washington, D.C., *Daily National Intelligencer*, March 3, 1836, p. 2; the Washington, D.C., *United States' Telegraph*, March 5, 1836, p. 2, and March 7, 1836, p. 2; the Charleston, S.C., *Mercury*, February 27, 1836, p. 2. Variant in the Washington, D.C., *Globe*, February 25, 1836, p. 2; *Congressional Globe*, 24th Cong., 1st Sess., Appendix, pp. 112–114. Another variant in the New York, N.Y., *Morning Courier and New-York Enquirer*, February 19, 1836, p. 2. NOTE: Later in the debate Calhoun twice made brief remarks in exchange with Garrett D. Wall of N.J. who said that Calhoun's speech had been "unsuitable to the decorum" of the Senate. (*Register of Debates*, 24th Cong., 1st Sess., col. 557.)

[Nathaniel] B[everly] Tucker, Williamsburg, Va., to James H. Hammond, [Representative from S.C.,] 2/17. Writing of the nullification crisis, Tucker says that he had told Calhoun at the time that "had S.C. met the force bill by secession, there might have been a sharp struggle, but a short one; and the whole South would soon have joined her." ALS in DLC, James Henry Hammond Papers.

Amendment to Thomas H. Benton's resolutions, 2/18. Under consideration were two resolutions. The first called for applying the surplus revenue to permanent objects of national defense; the second called upon the President for proposals and estimates for various such objects. "Mr. Calhoun moved to lay the whole subject on the table. The change (he said) in the state of our relations with France rendered the resolutions unnecessary, and the appropriations for national defense would more appropriately be made in the general appropriation bills." This motion was defeated 15 to 23. From *Congressional Globe*, 24th Cong., 1st Sess., pp. 192–193. Later in the same debate Calhoun "moved to amend the resolutions by inserting, at the end of the first resolution, a new series of resolutions [*not found*]." Calhoun's resolutions, he said, were offered "principally with a view, to declare whether, there was any surplus revenue at present in the Treasury, and upon which they were to legislate."

Subsequently Calhoun withdrew this amendment. Benton's resolutions, after being amended to delete all reference to "surplus" revenue, were adopted. From *Register of Debates*, 24th Cong., 1st Sess., cols. 571–577, and the New York, N.Y., *Morning Courier and New-York Enquirer*, February 20, 1836, p. 2. Variant in the Washington, D.C., *Daily National Intelligencer*, February 19, 1836, p. 3; the Washington, D.C., *United States' Telegraph*, February 19, 1836, p. 3.

From LEW[IS] CASS, [Secretary of War]

War Department, February 19[t]h, 1836

Sir, I have examined the papers in the case of William Smith about which you have expressed a solicitude, and I have also conversed with the Commissioner of Pensions [James L. Edwards] on the subject. Although there are strong circumstances in favor of Mr. Smith's representations, yet it appears to me, on full consideration, that I cannot allow the claim. Any additional statements which would remove, or explain, the difficulty suggested by the Commissioner of Pensions, would incline the balance in favor of Mr. Smith. Very respectfully Y[ou]r mo[st] Ob[edien]t Serv[ant,] Lew[is] Cass.

LS in DNA, RG 46 (Records of the U.S. Senate), 24A-D12.

From AMOS KENDALL, [Postmaster General]

[Washington, February] 19th [1836]

My attention has just been called to the enclosed report taken from the United States Tellegraph [*sic*] of the 17th Ins[tan]t of remarks made by you in the Senate on a previous occasion. I feel it my duty to request to be informed, whether so much of your remarks as relates to the Post Office Department be therein correctly reported. Amos Kendall.

FC in DNA, RG 28 (Records of the Post Office Department), Letters Sent by the Postmaster General, 1789–1836, A:468. NOTE: Kendall undoubtedly enclosed the Washington, D.C., *Telegraph* of 2/17 reporting Calhoun's remarks on 2/16 during the debate over the regulations for admitting the public to the Senate galleries. Compare those remarks and the editorial note accompanying them above. No reply from Calhoun to Kendall has been found, and it is entirely possible that none was written. It is also possible that if such a reply existed it was lost when the Post Office Department quarters burned in 1836.

Remarks on the reception of a petition to abolish slavery in the District of Columbia, 2/19. After a motion had been made to reconsider the Pa. petition that had been previously tabled, Calhoun "observed that it never was his wish to bring on the debate on this subject. His whole object had been, from the beginning, defensive —to resist. He had not any agency in bringing on the debate in the first instance; for he had restricted himself simply to demanding the question, without argument. While up, he would remind the Chair of the parliamentary rule, which had hitherto been lost sight of. He held it to be the duty of the Chair, when any doubt existed as to a petition's being unanimously received, to present to the House the question, 'shall the petition be received?' without waiting for a member to demand it. This was the correct parliamentary rule, as laid down by Mr. [Thomas] Jefferson in his Manual [of parliamentary practices]; and the Chair, by adhering to it, would relieve him from the necessity of demanding the preliminary question when such petitions were presented." William R. King of Ala. differed with Calhoun's interpretation of the rule. Calhoun said that he "had made no question of order. He had merely suggested his construction of what the parliamentary rule was. It was the duty of the Chair not to put any question of receiving a petition until a regular motion was made. There was either a rule to receive or not to receive. If there was no such rule, he had no right to insist. He considered it put down as one of the rules applicable to this country. He wished it to be settled that when a petition is to be received hereafter, the question should be made by the Chair as to receiving it. Mr. C[alhoun] here read from Jefferson's Manual the rule in substance that, when petitions are presented, the preliminary question is, whether they shall be received." From *Register of Debates*, 24th Cong., 1st Sess., cols. 578–579. Also printed in the Washington, D.C., *Globe*, February 22, 1836, p. 3; *Congressional Globe*, 24th Cong., 1st Sess., pp. 197–198. Variant in the Washington, D.C., *United States' Telegraph*, February 20, 1836, p. 3. Another variant in the New York, N.Y., *Morning Courier and New-York Enquirer*, February 22, 1836, p. 2.

[To Lewis Cass, Secretary of War,] 2/22. An entry in a register of letters received indicates that Calhoun's letter of this date concerning the Cadet application of Benjamin Berry was received on 2/23. The letter was referred to the Engineer Dept. Entry in DNA, RG 107 (Records of the Office of the Secretary of War), Registers of Letters Received, 1800–1870, 38:C-298 (M-22:38).

Anna [Maria Calhoun], Washington, to J[ames] Ed[ward] Colhoun, Terrysville, S.C., 2/26. Anna sends regards to her uncle from old acquaintances in Washington. She writes nothing of politics except to note the general disapprobation "all the Southerners" and "indeed many of the Northerners also" feel at the course of Henry L. Pinckney [Representative from S.C.] "on the subject of abolition." "Pa [John C. Calhoun] is quite well and desires to be remembered to you." ALS in ScU-SC, John C. Calhoun Papers.

"Foederatus" to "His Grace the Duke of Pendleton," [published at Greenville, S.C., *ca.* 2/27]. In this pseudonymous public letter to Calhoun, the author bitterly attacks Calhoun's speech [of 1/18 concerning Andrew Jackson's message] on U.S. relations with France. He contends that Calhoun's speech avoided the main point of the discussion, "that the French, from the month of February, 1832, had accepted, and were receiving all the advantages which the Treaty afforded them." From that time, France was "bound to execute" the conditions of the treaty, in his opinion. The fact that Calhoun did not discuss this point is ascribed to his hope of "involving the whole subject in confusion, and embarrassing your own government." "Foederatus" insists upon the probability of a clandestine understanding between Calhoun and the French government. Calhoun's support of the War of 1812 is cited as evidence of his long involvement in French intrigues. "Foederatus" closes by commending Calhoun's consistency in attempting to force a dissolution of the Union. From the failure of these efforts, "despair may yet drive you to the commission of some act, which may require the interposition of the Law, and terminate your career in a manner worthy of your life." PC in the Greenville, S.C., *Mountaineer,* February 27?, 1836, p. 4.

"Memorial of James Nicholson [of Charleston, S.C.], Attorney of Elias Carter of England," presented to the Senate by Calhoun on 3/1. According to the memorial and supporting documents, Carter has invented and holds a British patent for "an improved apparatus for regulating the supply of Gas to the burners and for the stopping of the same." Congress is petitioned to "Authorize and direct the issuing of Letters Patent" for the invention in the U.S. (Endorsements indicate that the memorial was referred to the Committee on the Judiciary and that the committee was discharged from further consideration of it on 7/4.) DS with Ens in DNA, RG 46 (Records of the U.S. Senate), 24A-G7.

[To Lewis Cass, Secretary of War, 3/3.] Calhoun apparently requests that Capt. Benjamin Huger of the Ordnance Corps be assigned to serve with the Topographical Engineers who will make a survey in connection with the proposed railroad between Charleston and Cincinnati. Jacket with endorsements (letter missing) in DNA, RG 156 (Records of the Office of the Chief of Ordnance), Letters Received, 1812–1894, 259.

Motion about a mail route in S.C. and Ga., submitted to the Senate on 3/7. "Resolved that the Committee on Post offices & post roads be instructed to enquire into the expediency of establishing a line of two horse coaches to carry the mail from Pendleton So[uth] Carolina, ["to" *canceled*] by Clarkesville [Ga.] to Dahlonega Georgia." (This motion was adopted by the Senate by unanimous consent with the words "mail route" substituted for "line of two horse coaches to carry the mail." A related document [*not found*] which Calhoun submitted at the same time was referred to the same committee.) ADU in DNA, RG 46 (Records of the U.S. Senate), 24A-B10; variant PC in *Senate Journal,* 24th Cong., 1st Sess., p. 204.

"Memorial of the City Council & Chamber of Commerce of Charleston, South Carolina, for the establishment of a Navy Yard at that place," presented to the Senate by Calhoun on 3/9. This memorial, dated 2/29, calls the attention of the Senate to previous memorials presented to Congress on the subject and to a report made by the Committee on Naval Affairs of the House of Representatives on 6/24/1834 on the advantages of the proposal. The document is signed by Edward W. North, Intendant; William Roach, Clerk of Council; David Alexander, President of the Chamber of Commerce; and R[oger] Heriot, Secretary of the Chamber of Commerce. (The petition was referred to the Committee on Naval Affairs which reported favorably on 5/6. On 5/24 the Senate concurred in the Committee report and referred the subject to the Executive.) DS in DNA, RG 46 (Records of the U.S. Senate), 24A-G11.

SPEECH ON ABOLITION PETITIONS

[In the Senate, March 9, 1836]
The Senate proceeded to consider the petition of the Society of Friends in Philadelphia, on the subject of the abolition of slavery in the District of Columbia. The question being on the motion "that the petition be not received,"

Mr. Calhoun rose and said: If we may judge from what has been said, the mind of the Senate is fully made up on the subject of these petitions. With the exception of the two Senators from Vermont [Samuel Prentiss and Benjamin Swift], all who have spoken have avowed their conviction, not only that they contain nothing requiring the action of the Senate, but that the petitions are highly mischievous, as tending to agitate and distract the country, and to endanger the Union itself. With these concessions, I may fairly ask, why should these petitions be received? Why receive, when we have made up our mind not to act? Why idly waste our time and lower our dignity in the useless ceremony of receiving to reject, as is proposed, should the petitions be received? Why finally receive what all acknowledge to be highly dangerous and mischievous? But one reason has been or can be assigned—that not to receive would be a violation of the right of petition, and, of course, that we are bound to receive, however objectionable and dangerous the petitions may be. If such be the fact, there is an end to the question. As great as would be the advantage to the abolitionists, if we are bound to receive, if it would be a violation of the right of petition not to receive, we must acquiesce. On the other hand, if it shall be shown, not only that we are not bound to receive, but that to receive, on the ground on which it has been placed, would sacrifice the constitutional rights of this body, would yield to the abolitionists all they could hope at this time, and would surrender all the outworks by which the slave-holding States can defend their rights and property here, then a unanimous rejection of these petitions ought of right to follow.

The decision, then, of the question now before the Senate is reduced to the single point—are we bound to receive these petitions? Or, to vary the form of the question, would it be a violation of the right of petition not to receive them?

When the ground was first taken that it would be a violation, I could scarcely persuade myself that those who took it were in earnest, so contrary was it to all my conceptions of the rights of this body and the provisions of the Constitution; but, finding it so earnestly maintained, I have since carefully investigated the subject, and the result has been a confirmation of my first impression, and a conviction that the claim of right is without shadow of foundation. The question, I must say, has not been fairly met. Those opposed to the side which we support have discussed the question as if we denied the right of petition, when they could not but know that the true issue is not as to the existence of the right, which is acknowledged by all, but its extent and limits, which not one of our opponents has so much as attempted to ascertain. What they have declined doing, I undertake to perform.

There must be some point, all will agree, where the right of petition ends, and that of this body begins. Where is that point? I have examined this question carefully, and I assert boldly, without the least fear of refutation, that, stretched to the utmost, the right cannot be extended beyond the presentation of a petition, at which point the rights of this body commence. When a petition is presented, it is before the Senate. It must then be acted on. Some disposition must be made of it before the Senate can proceed to the consideration of any other subject. This no one will deny. With the action of the Senate its rights commence—rights secured by an express provision of the Constitution, which vests each house with the right of regulating its own proceedings, that is, to determine by fixed rules, the order and form of its action. To extend the right of petition beyond presentation is clearly to extend it beyond that point where the action of the Senate commences, and, as such, is a manifest violation of its constitutional rights. Here, then, we have the limits between the right of petition and the right of the Senate to regulate its proceedings clearly fixed, and so perfectly defined as not to admit of mistake, and, I would add, of controversy, had it not been questioned in this discussion.

If what I have asserted required confirmation, ample might be found in our rules, which embody the deliberate sense of the Senate on this point, from the commencement of the Government to this day. Among them the Senate has prescribed that of its proceedings on the presentation of petitions. It is contained in the 24th Rule, which I ask the Secretary to read, with Mr. [Thomas] Jefferson's remarks [in his manual of parliamentary practices of the Senate] in reference to it:

> [*The Secretary of the Senate read:*] Before any petition or memorial addressed to the Senate shall be received, and read at the table, whether the same shall be introduced by the President or

a member, a brief statement of the contents of the petition or memorial shall verbally be made by the introducer.—Rule 24.

[*Then the Secretary read*] Mr. Jefferson's remarks: Regularly a motion for receiving it must be made and seconded, and a question put whether it shall be received; but a cry from the House of "receive," or even a silence, dispenses with the formality of the question.

Here we have a confirmation of all I have asserted. It clearly proves that when the petition is presented the action of the Senate commences. The first act is to receive the petition. Received by whom? Not the Secretary, but the Senate. And how can it be received by the Senate but on a motion to receive, and a vote of a majority of the body? And Mr. Jefferson accordingly tells us that regularly such a motion must be made and seconded. On this question, then, the right of the Senate begins; and its right is as perfect and full to receive or reject as it is to adopt or reject any other question, in any subsequent stage of its proceedings. When I add that this rule was adopted as far back as the 19th of April, 1789, at the first session of the Senate, and that it has been retained, without alteration, in all the subsequent changes and modifications of the rules, we have the strongest evidence of the deliberate sense of this body in reference to the point under consideration.

I feel that I might here terminate the discussion. I have shown, conclusively, that the right of petition cannot possibly be extended beyond presentation. At that point it is met by the rights of the Senate; and it follows, as a necessary consequence, that so far from being bound to receive these petitions, so far would a rejection be from violating the right of petition, were it [*sic*; we are] left perfectly free to reject or to receive at pleasure; to deprive us of which would violate the rights of this body secured by the Constitution.

But on a question of such magnitude, I feel it to be a duty to remove every difficulty; and, that not a shadow of a doubt may remain, I shall next proceed to reply to the objections our opponents have made to the grounds I have taken. At the head of these, it has been urged, again and again, that petitioners have a right to be heard, and that not to receive petitions is to refuse a hearing. It is to be regretted that, throughout this discussion, those opposed to us have dealt in such vague generalities, and ventured assertions with so little attention to facts. Why have they not informed us, in the present instance, what is meant by the right to be heard, and how that right is violated by a refusal to receive? Had they thought proper to give us this information, it would at least have greatly facilitated my reply; but, as it is, I am constrained to inquire into the different senses in which the assertion may be taken, and then to show that in not one of them is the right of petition in the slightest degree infringed by a refusal to receive.

What, then, is meant by the assertion that these petitioners have a right to be heard? Is it meant that they have a right to appear in the Senate chamber in person to present their petition, and to be heard in its defence? If this be the meaning, the dullest apprehension must see that the question of receiving has not the slightest bearing on such right. If they have the right to be heard personally at our bar, it is not the 24th rule of our proceedings, but the 19th, which violates that right. That rule expressly provides that a motion to admit any person whatever within the doors of the Senate to present a petition, shall be out of order, and of course excludes the petitioners from being heard in person. But it may be meant that petitioners have a right to have their petitions presented to the Senate, and read in their hearing. If this be the meaning, the right has been enjoyed in the present instance to the fullest extent. The petition was presented by the Senator from Pennsylvania (Mr. [James] Buchanan) in the usual mode, by giving a statement of its contents, and on my call was read by the Secretary at his table.

But one more sense can be attached to the assertion. It may be meant that the petitioners have a right to have their petitions discussed by the Senate. If this be intended, I will venture to say that there never was an assertion more directly in the teeth of facts than that which has been so frequently made in the course of this discussion—that to refuse to receive the petition is to refuse a hearing to the petitioners. Has not this question been before us for months? Has not the petition been discussed day after day, fully and freely, in all its bearings? And how, with these facts before us, with the debates still ringing in our ears, any Senator can rise in his place and gravely pronounce that to refuse to receive this petition is to refuse a hearing to the petitioners—to refuse discussion, in the broadest sense—is past my comprehension. Our opponents, as if in their eagerness to circumscribe the rights of the Senate, and to enlarge those of the abolitionists, (for such must be the effect of their course,) have closed their senses against facts passing before their eyes, and have entirely overlooked the nature of the question now before the Senate, and which they have been so long discussing.

The question on receiving the petition not only admits discussion, but admits it in the most ample manner; more so, in fact, than any other, except the final question on the rejection of the prayer of the petition, or some tantamount question. Whatever may go to show that the petition is or is not deserving the action of this body, may be freely urged for or against it, as has been done on the present occasion. In this respect there is a striking difference between it and many of the subsequent questions which may be raised after reception, and particularly the one made by the Senator from Tennessee, (Mr. [Felix] Grundy,) who now is so strenuous an advocate in favor of the right of the petitioners to be heard. He spoke with great apparent complacency of his course, as it respects another of these petitions. And what was that course? He who is now so eager for discussion, to give a hearing, moved to lay the petition on the table—a motion which cuts off all discussion.

But, it may be asked, if the question on receiving petitions admits of so wide a scope for discussion, why not receive this petition, and discuss it at some subsequent stage? Why not receive it in order to reject its prayer, as proposed by the Senator from Pennsylvania, (Mr. Buchanan,) instead of rejecting the petition itself on the question of receiving, as we propose? What is the difference between the two?

I do not intend, at this stage, to compare, or rather to contrast, the two courses, for they admit of no comparison. My object, at present, is to establish, beyond the possibility of doubt, that we are not bound to receive these petitions; and, when that is accomplished, I will then show the disastrous consequences which must follow the reception of the petition, be the after disposition what it may. In the mean time, it is sufficient to remark that it is only on the question of receiving that opposition can be made to the petition itself. On all others, the opposition is to its prayer. On the decision, then, of the question of receiving, depends the important question of jurisdiction. To receive is to take jurisdiction, to give an implied pledge to investigate and decide on the prayer, and to give the petition a place in our archives, and become responsible for its safe keeping; and who votes for receiving of this petition, on the ground on which its reception is placed, votes that Congress is bound to take jurisdiction of the question of abolishing slavery both here and in the States—gives an implied pledge to take the subject under consideration, and orders the petition to be placed among the public records for safe keeping.

But to proceed, in reply to the objections of our opponents. It is next urged that precedents are against the side we support. I meet this objection with a direct denial. From the beginning of the Government to the commencement of this session, there is not a single precedent that justifies the receiving of these petitions, on the ground on which their reception is urged. The real state of the case is, that we are not following but making precedents. For the first time has the principle been assumed, that we are bound to receive petitions; that we have no discretion, but must take jurisdiction over them, however absurd, frivolous, mischievous, or foreign from the purpose for which the Government was created. Receive these petitions, and you will create a precedent which will hereafter establish this monstrous principle. As yet there are none. The case [from the 1st Congress] relied on by the Senator from Tennessee (Mr. Grundy) is in no respect analogous. No question, in that case, was made on the reception of the petition. The petition slipped in without taking a vote, as is daily done, where the attention of the Senate is not particularly called to the subject. The question on which the discussion took place was on the reference [to committee], and not on the reception, as in this case; but what is decisive against the precedent, and which I regret the Senator (Mr. Grundy) did not state, so that it might accompany his remarks, is the fact that the petition was not for abolishing slavery. The subject was the African slave trade; and the petition simply prayed that Congress would inquire whether they might not adopt some measure of interdiction prior to 1808, when, by the Constitution, they would be authorized to suppress that trade. I ask the Secretary to read the prayer of the petition:

> But we find it indispensably incumbent on us, as a religious body, assuredly believing that both the true temporal interests of nations, and eternal well-being of individuals, depend on doing justly, loving mercy, and walking humbly before God, the creator, preserver, and benefactor of men, thus to attempt to excite your attention to the affecting subject (slave trade), earnestly desiring that the infinite Father of Spirits may so enrich [y]our minds with his love and truth, and so influence your understanding by that pure wisdom which is full of mercy and good fruits, as that a sincere and an impartial inquiry may take place, whether it be not an essential part of the duty of your exalted station to exert upright endeavors, to the full extent of your power, to remove every obstruction to public righteousness, which the influence or artifice of particular persons, governed by the narrow, mistaken views of self-interest, has occasioned; and whether, notwithstanding such seeming impediments, it be not really within your power to exercise justice and mercy, which, if adhered to, we cannot doubt must produce the abolition of the slave trade.

Now, I ask the Senator where is the analogy between this and the present petition, the reception of which he so strenuously urges? He is a lawyer of long experience and of distinguished reputation; and I put the question to him, on what possible principle can a case so perfectly dissimilar justify the vote he intends to give on the present occasion? On what possible ground can the vote of Mr. [James] Madison to refer that petition, on which he has so much relied, justify him in receiving this? Does he not perceive, in his own example, the danger of forming precedents? If he may call to his aid the authority of Mr. Madison, in a case so dissimilar, to justify the reception of this petition, and thereby extend the jurisdiction of Congress over the question of emancipation, to what purpose hereafter may not the example of his course on the present occasion be perverted?

It is not my design to censure Mr. Madison's course, but I cannot refrain from expressing my regret that his name is not found associated, on that occasion [in the House of Representatives in the 1st Congress], with the sagacious and firm representatives from the South —[William Loughton] Smith, [Thomas Tudor] Tucker, and Barber [sic; Aedanus Burke], of South Carolina, James Jackson, of Georgia, and many others who, at that early period, foresaw the danger, and met it, as it ought ever to be met by those who regard the peace and security of the slaveholding States. Had he added the weight of his talents and authority to theirs, a more healthy tone of sentiment than that which now unfortunately exists would this day have been the consequence.

Another case has been cited, to justify the vote for reception. I refer to the petition from the Quakers, in 1805, which the Senator from Pennsylvania (Mr. Buchanan) relies on to sustain him in receiving the present petition. What I have said in reply to the precedent cited by the Senator from Tennessee applies equally to this. Like that, the petition prayed legislation, not on abolition of slavery, but the African slave trade, over which subject Congress then in a few years would have full jurisdiction by the Constitution, and might well have their attention called to it in advance. But, though their objects were the same, the manner in which the petitions were met was very dissimilar. Instead of being permitted to be received silently, like the former, this petition was met at the threshold. The question of receiving was made, as on the present occasion, and its rejection sustained by a strong southern vote, as the [Senate] journals will show. The Secretary will read the journal:

Mr. [George] Logan presented a petition, signed Thomas Morris, clerk, on behalf of the meeting of the representatives of the people called Quakers, in Pennsylvania, New Jersey, &c., stating that the petitioners, from a sense of religious duty, had again come forward to plead the cause of their oppressed and degraded fellow-men of the African race. On the question, "Shall this petition be received?" it passed in the affirmative: yeas, 19, nays, 9.

Among those, to receive the petition there were but four from the slaveholding States, and this on a single petition praying for legislation on a subject over which Congress in so short a time would have full authority. What an example to us on the present occasion. Can any man doubt, from the vote, if the southern Senators on that occasion had been placed in our present situation, that, had it been their lot, as it is ours, to meet the torrent of petitions which is now poured in on Congress, not from peaceable Quakers, but ferocious incendiaries; not to suppress the African slave trade, but to abolish slavery, they would, with united voice, have rejected the petitions with scorn and indignation? Can any one who knew him doubt that one of the Senators from the South, (the gallant Sumpter [*sic*; Thomas Sumter],) who on that occasion voted for receiving the petition, would have been among the first to vindicate the interests of those whom he represented, had the question at that day been what it is on the present occasion? [*Here Buchanan asked Calhoun's permission to read the names of the Southern Senators who voted with Sumter to receive the petition. When that had been done, Calhoun resumed:*] We are next told that, instead of looking to the Constitution, in order to ascertain what are the limits to the right of petition, we must push that instrument aside, and go back to magna charta and the declaration of rights for its origin and limitation. We live in strange times. It seems there are Christians now more orthodox than the Bible, and politicians whose standard is higher than the Constitution; but I object not to tracing the right to these ancient and venerated sources; I hold in high estimation the institutions of our English ancestors. They grew up gradually through many generations, by the incessant and untiring efforts of an intelligent and brave people struggling for centuries against the power of the Crown. To them we are indebted for nearly all that has been gained for liberty in modern times, excepting what we have added. But may I not ask how it has happened that our opponents, in going back to these sacred instruments, have not thought proper to cite their provisions, or to show in what manner our refusal to receive these petitions can violate the right of petition as secured by them? I feel under no obligation to supply the omission—to cite what they have omitted to cite, or to prove, from the instruments themselves, that to be no violation of them which they have not proved to be a violation. It is unnecessary. The practice of Parliament is sufficient for my purpose. It proves conclusively that it is no violation of the right, as secured by those instruments, to refuse to receive petitions. To establish what this practice is, I ask the Secretary to read from [John] Hatsel[l] [*Precedents of Proceedings in the House of Commons*], a work of the highest authority, the several paragraphs which are marked with a pencil, commencing at page 760, under the head of Petitions on Matter of Supply:

> On the 9th of April, 1694, a petition was tendered to the House, relating to the bill for granting to their Majesties several duties upon the tonnage of ships; and the question being put, that the petition be received, it passed in the negative.
>
> On the 28th of April, 1698, a petition was offered to the House against the bill for laying a duty upon inland pit coal; and the question being put, that the petition be received, it passed in the negative. See, also, the 29th and 30th of June, 1698, petitions relating to the duties upon Scotch linens, and upon whale fins imported.— Vide 20th of April, 1698.
>
> On the 5th of January, 1703, a petition of the maltsters of Nottingham being offered, against the bill for continuing the duties on malt; and the question being put, that the petition be brought up, it passed in the negative.
>
> On the 21st December, 1706, *Resolved*, That this House will receive no petition for any sum of money relating to public service, but what is recommended from the Crown. Upon the 11th of June, 1713, this is declared to be a standing order of the House.
>
> On the 29th of March, 1707, *Resolved*, That the House will not proceed on any petition, motion, or bill, for granting any money, or for releasing or compounding any money owing to the Crown, but in a Committee of the Whole House; and this is declared to be a standing order. See, also, the 29th of November, 1710.
>
> On the 23rd of April, 1713, *Resolved*, That the House will receive no petition for compounding debts to the Crown, upon any branch of the revenue, without a certificate from the proper officer annexed, stating the debt, what prosecutions have been made for the recovery thereof, and what the petitioner and his security are able to pay.
>
> On the 25th of March, 1715, this is declared to be a standing order. See the 2d of March, 1735, and the 9th of January, 1752, the proceedings upon petitions of this sort.
>
> On the 8th of March, 1732, a petition being offered against a bill depending for securing the trade of the sugar colonies, it was refused to be brought up. A motion was then made that a committee be appointed to search precedents in relation to the receiving or not receiving petitions against the imposing of duties; and the question being put, it passed in the negative.

Nothing can be more conclusive. Not only are petitions rejected, but resolutions are passed, refusing to receive entire classes of petitions, and that, too, on the subject of imposing taxes—a subject, above all others, in relation to which we would suppose the right ought to be held most sacred, and this within a few years after the declaration of rights. With these facts before us, what are we to think of the assertion of the Senator from Tennessee, (Mr. Grundy,) who pronounced in his place, in the boldest and most unqualified manner, that there was no deliberative body which did not act on the principle that it was bound to receive petitions? That a member of his long experience and caution should venture to make an assertion so unfounded, is one among the many proofs of the carelessness, both as to facts and argument, with which this important subject has been examined and discussed on that side.

But it is not necessary to cross the Atlantic, or to go back to remote periods, to find precedents for the rejection of petitions. This body, on a memorable occasion, and after full deliberation, a short time since, rejected a petition; and among those who voted for the rejection will be found the names (of course I exclude my own) of the most able and experienced members of the Senate. I refer to the case [in the last Congress] of resolutions in the nature of a remonstrance from the citizens of York, Pennsylvania, approving the act of the President [Andrew Jackson] in removing the deposites. I ask the Secretary to read the journals on the occasion:

> The Vice-President communicated a preamble and a series of resolutions adopted at a meeting of the citizens of York county, Pennsylvania, approving the act of the Executive removing the public money from the Bank of the United States, and opposed to the renewal of the charter of said bank; which having been read, Mr. [Henry] Clay objected to the reception. And on the question, Shall they be received? it was determined in the negative: Yeas, 20, nays, 24.
>
> On motion of Mr. [William C.] Preston, the yeas and nays being desired by one-fifth of the Senators present, those who voted in the affirmative are,
>
> Messrs. [Thomas H.] Benton, [Bedford] Brown, [John] Forsyth, [Felix] Grundy, [William] Hendricks, [Isaac] Hill, [Elias K.] Kane, [William R.] King of Alabama, [John P.] King of Georgia, [Lewis F.] Linn, [Samuel] McKean, [Willie P.] Mangum, [Thomas] Morris, [John M.] Robinson, [Ether] Shepley, [Nathaniel P.] Tallmadge, [John] Tipton, [Hugh L.] White, [William] Wilkins, [Silas] Wright.
>
> Those who voted in the negative are,
>
> Messrs. [George M.] Bibb, [John] Black, Calhoun, Clay, [John M.] Clayton, [Thomas] Ewing, [Theodore] Frelinghuysen, [Joseph] Kent, [Benjamin W.] Leigh, [Gabriel] Moore, [Arnold] Naudain, [George] Poindexter, [Alexander] Porter, [Samuel] Prentiss, Preston, [Asher] Robbins, [Nathaniel] Silsbee, [Nathan] Smith, [Samuel L.] Southard, [Peleg] Sprague, [Benjamin] Swift, [Gideon] Tomlinson, [George A.] Waggaman, [Daniel] Webster.

In citing this case, it is not my intention to call in question the consistency of any member on this floor; it would be unworthy of the occasion. I doubt not the vote then given was given from a full conviction of its correctness, as it will doubtless be in the present case, on whatever side it may be found. My object is to show that the principle for which I contend, so far from being opposed, is sustained by precedents, here and elsewhere, ancient and modern.

In following, as I have, those opposed to me, to magna charta and the declaration of rights, for the origin and the limits of the right of petition, I am not disposed, with them, to set aside the Constitution. I assent to the position they assume, that the right of petition existed before the Constitution, and that it is not derived from it; but while I look beyond that instrument for the right, I hold the Constitution, on a question as to its extent and limits, to be the highest authority. The first amended article of the Constitution, which provides that Congress shall pass no law to prevent the people from peaceably assembling and petitioning for a redress of grievances, was clearly intended to prescribe the limits within which the right might be exercised. It is not pretended that to refuse to receive petitions trenches, in the slightest degree, on those limits. To suppose that the framers of the Constitution—no, not the framers, but those jealous patriots who were not satisfied with that instrument as it came from the hands of its framers, and who proposed this very provision to guard what they considered a sacred right—performed their task so bunglingly as to omit any essential guard, would be to do great injustice to the memory of those stern and sagacious men; and yet this is what the Senator from Tennessee (Mr. Grundy) has ventured to assert. He said that no provision was added to guard against the rejection of petitions, because the obligation to receive was considered so clear that it was deemed unnecessary; when he ought to have known that, according to the standing practice at that time, Parliament was in the constant habit, as has been shown, of refusing to receive petitions; a practice which could not have been unknown to the authors of the amendment; and from which it may be fairly inferred that, in omitting to provide that petitions should be received, it was not intended to comprehend their reception in the right of petition.

I have now, I trust, established, beyond all controversy, that we are not bound to receive these petitions, and that, if we should reject them, we would not, in the slightest degree, infringe the rights of petition. It is now time to look to the rights of this body, and to see whether, if we should receive them, when it is acknowledged that the

101

only reason for receiving is that we are bound to do so, we would not establish a principle which would trench deeply on the rights of the Senate. I have already shown that where the action of the Senate commences, there also its right to determine how and when it shall act also commences. I have also shown that the action of the Senate necessarily begins on the presentation of a petition; that the petition is then before the body; that the Senate cannot proceed to other business without making some disposition of it; and that, by the twenty-fourth rule, the first action after presentation is on a question to receive the petition. To extend the right of petition to the question of receiving, is to expunge this rule; to abolish this unquestionable constitutional right of the Senate, and that for the benefit, in this case, of the abolitionists. Their gain would be at the loss of this body. I have not expressed myself too strongly. Give the right of petition the extent contended for; decide that we are bound, under the Constitution, to receive these incendiary petitions, and the very motion before the Senate would be out of order. If the Constitution makes it our duty to receive, we would have no discretion left to reject, as the motion presupposes. Our rules of proceeding must be in accord with the Constitution. Thus, in the case of received [*sic;* revenue] bills, which, by the Constitution, must originate in the other House, it would be out of order to introduce them here, and it has accordingly been so decided. For like reason, if we are bound to receive petitions, the present motion would be out of order; and, if such be your opinion, it is your duty, as the presiding officer, to call me to order, and to arrest all further discussion on the question of reception. Let us now turn our eyes for a moment to the nature of the right, which, I fear, we are about to abandon, with the view to ascertain what must be the consequence if we should surrender it.

Of all the rights belonging to a deliberative body, I know of none more universal, or more indispensable to a proper performance of its functions, than the right to determine at its discretion what it shall receive, over what it shall extend its jurisdiction, and to what it shall direct its deliberation and action. It is the first and universal law of all such bodies, and extends not only to petitions, but to reports, to bills and resolutions, varied only in the two latter in the form of the question. It may be compared to the function in the animal economy, with which all living creatures are endowed, of selecting, through the instinct of taste, what to receive or reject, on which the preservation of their existence depends. Deprive them of this function, and the poisonous as well as the wholesome would be indifferently received into their system. So with deliberative bodies; deprive them of the essential and primary right to determine at their pleasure what to receive or reject, and they would become the passive receptacles, indifferently, of all that is frivolous, absurd, unconstitutional, immoral, and impious, as well as what may properly demand their deliberation and action. Establish this monstrous, this impious principle (as it would prove to be in practice,) and what must be the consequence? To what would we commit ourselves? If a petition should be presented praying the abolition of the Constitution, (which we are all bound by our oaths to protect,) according to this abominable doctrine it must be received. So, if it was prayed, the abolition of the decalogue, or of the Bible itself. I go farther. If the abolition societies should be converted into a body of atheists, and should ask the passage of a law denying the existence of the Almighty Being above us, the creator of all, according to this blasphemous doctrine we would be bound to receive the petition, to take jurisdiction of it. I ask the Senators from Tennessee and Pennsylvania, (Mr. Grundy and Mr. Buchanan,) would they vote to receive such a petition? I wait not an answer. They would instantly reject it with loathing. What, then, becomes of the unlimited, unqualified, and universal obligation to receive petitions, which they so strenuously maintained, and to which they are prepared to sacrifice the constitutional rights of this body[?]

I shall now descend from these hypothetical cases to the particular question before the Senate. What, then, must be the consequences of receiving this petition, on the principle that we are bound to receive it and all similar petitions whenever presented? I have considered this question calmly, in all its bearings, and do not hesitate to pronounce that to receive would be to yield to the abolitionists all that the most sanguine could for the present hope, and to abandon all the outworks upon which we of the South rely for our defence against their attacks here.

No one can believe that the fanatics, who have flooded this and the other House with their petitions, entertain the slightest hope that Congress would pass a law at this time to abolish slavery in this District. Infatuated as they are, they must see that public opinion at the North is not yet prepared for so decisive a step, and that seriously to attempt it now would be fatal to their cause. What, then, do they hope? What but that Congress should take jurisdiction of the subject of abolishing slavery; should throw open to the abolitionists the halls of legislation, and enable them to establish a permanent position within their walls, from which hereafter to carry on their operations against the institutions of the slaveholding States[?] If we receive this petition, all these advantages will be realized to them to the fullest extent. Permanent jurisdiction would be assumed over the subject of slavery, not only in this District, but in the States themselves, whenever the abolitionists might choose to ask Congress, by sending their petitions here, for the abolition of slavery in the States. We would be bound to receive such petitions, and, by receiving, would be fairly pledged to deliberate and decide on them. Having succeeded in this point, a most favorable position would be gained. The centre of operations would be transferred from Nassau Hall to the halls of Congress. To this common centre the incendiary publications of the abolitionists would flow, in the form of petitions, to be received and preserved among the public records. Here the subject of abolition would be agitated session after session, and from hence the assaults on the property and institutions of the people of the slaveholding States would be disseminated, in the guise of speeches, over the whole Union.

Such would be the advantages yielded to the abolitionists. In proportion to their gain would be our loss. What would be yielded to them would be taken from us. Our true position, that which is indispensable to our defence here, is, that Congress has no legitimate jurisdiction over the subject of slavery, either here or elsewhere. The reception of this petition surrenders this commanding position; yields the question of jurisdiction, so important to the cause of abolition and so injurious to us; compels us to sit in silence to witness the assaults on our character and institutions, or to engage in an endless contest in their defence. Such a contest is beyond mortal endurance. We must, in the end, be humbled, degraded, broken down, and worn out.

The Senators from the slaveholding States, who most unfortunately have committed themselves to vote for receiving these incendiary petitions, tell us that whenever the attempt shall be made to abolish slavery, they will join with us to repel it. I doubt not the sincerity of their declaration. We all have a common interest, and they cannot betray ours without betraying, at the same time, their own. But I announce to them that they are now called on to redeem their pledge. The attempt is now making. The work is going on daily and hourly. The war is waged, not only in the most dangerous manner, but in the only manner it can be waged. Do they expect that the abolitionists will resort to arms, and commence a crusade to liberate our slaves by force? Is this what they mean when they speak of the attempt to abolish slavery? If so, let me tell our friends of the South who differ from us, that the war which the abolitionists wage against us is of a very different character, and far more effective. It is a war of religious and political fanaticism, mingled, on the part of the leaders, with ambition and the love of notoriety, and waged, not against our lives, but our character. The object is to humble and debase us in our own estimation, and that of the world in general; to blast our reputation, while they overthrow our domestic institutions. This is the mode in which they are attempting abolition, with such ample means and untiring industry; and now is the time for all who are opposed to them to meet the attack. How can it be successfully met? This is the important question. There is but one way: we must meet the enemy on the frontier, on the question of receiving; we must secure that important pass—it is our Thermopylae. The power of resistance, by universal law of nature, is on the exterior. Break through the shell, penetrate the crust, and there is no resistance within. In the present contest, the question on receiving constitutes our frontier. It is the first, the exterior question, that covers and protects all the others. Let it be penetrated by receiving this petition, and not a point of resistance can be found within, as far as this Government is concerned. If we cannot maintain ourselves there, we cannot on any interior position. Of all the questions that can be raised, there is not one on which we can rally on ground more tenable for ourselves, or more untenable for our opponents, not excepting the ultimate question of abolition in the States. For our right to reject this petition is a truth as clear and unquestionable as that Congress has no right to abolish slavery in the States.

Such is the importance of taking our stand immoveably on the question now before us. Such are the advantages that we of the South would sacrifice, and the abolitionists would gain, were we to surrender that important position by receiving this petition. What motives have we for making so great a sacrifice? What advantages can we hope to gain that would justify us?

We are told of the great advantages of a strong majority. I acknowledge it in a good cause, and on sound principles. I feel in the present instance how much our cause would be strengthened by a strong and decided majority for the rejection of these incendiary petitions. If any thing we could do here could arrest the progress of the abolitionists, it would be such a rejection. But as advantageous as would be a strong majority on sound principles, it is in the same degree dangerous, when on the opposite—when it rests on improper concessions, and the surrender of principles, which would be the case at present. Such a majority must in this instance be purchased by concessions to the abolitionists, and a surrender, on our part, that would demolish all our outworks, give up all our strong

105

positions, and open all the passes to the free admission of our enemies. It is only on this condition that we can hope to obtain such
a majority—a majority which must be gathered together from all
sides, and entertaining every variety of opinion. To rally such a
majority, the Senator from Pennsylvania [Buchanan] has fallen on
the device to receive this petition, and immediately reject it, without
consideration or reflection. To my mind the movement looks like
a trick—a mere piece of artifice to juggle and deceive. I intend no
disrespect to the Senator. I doubt not his intention is good, and
believe his feelings are with us; but I must say that the course he
has intimated is, in my opinion, the worst possible for the slaveholding States. It surrenders all to the abolitionists, and gives nothing in turn that would be of the least advantage to us. Let the
majority for the course he indicates be ever so strong, can the Senator
hope that it will make any impression on the abolitionists? Can he
even hope to maintain his position of rejecting their petitions without consideration, against them? Does he not see that, in assuming
jurisdiction by receiving their petitions, he gives an implied pledge
to inquire, to deliberate, and decide on them? Experience will teach
him that we must either refuse to receive, or go through. I entirely
concur with the Senator from Vermont (Mr. Prentiss) on that point.
There is no middle ground that is tenable, and, least of all, that
proposed to be occupied by the Senator from Pennsylvania and those
who act with him. In the mean time, the course he proposes is calculated to lull the people of the slaveholding States into a false security, under the delusive impression which it is calculated to make,
that there is more universal strength here against the abolitionists
than really does exist.

But we are told that the right of petition is popular in the North,
and that to make an issue, however true, which might bring it in
question, would weaken our friends, and strengthen the abolitionists. I have no doubt of the kind feelings of our brethren from the
North, on this floor; but I clearly see that, while we have their feelings in our favor, their constituents, right or wrong, will have their
votes, however we may be affected. But I assure our friends that
we would not do any thing, willingly, which would weaken them
at home; and, if we could be assured that, by yielding to their wishes
the right of receiving petitions, they would be able to arrest, permanently, the progress of the abolitionists, we then might be induced
to yield; but nothing short of the certainty of permanent security
can induce us to yield an inch. If to maintain our rights must increase the abolitionists, be it so. I would at no period make the

least sacrifice of principle for any temporary advantage, and much less at the present. If there must be an issue, now is our time. We never can be more united or better prepared for the struggle; and I, for one, would much rather meet the danger now, than to turn it over to those who are to come after us.

But putting these views aside, it does seem to me, taking a general view of the subject, that the course intimated by the Senator from Pennsylvania is radically wrong, and must end in disappointment. The attempt to unite all, must, as it usually does, terminate in division and distraction. It will divide the South on the question of receiving, and the North on that of rejection, with a mutual weakening of both. I already see indications of division among northern gentlemen on this floor, even in this stage of the question. A division among them would give a great impulse to the cause of abolition.

Whatever position the parties may take, in the event of such division, one or the other would be considered more or less favorable to the abolition cause, which could not fail to run it into the political struggles of the two great parties of the North. With these views, I hold that the only possible hope of arresting the progress of the abolitionists in that quarter is to keep the two great parties there united against them, which would be impossible if they divide here. The course intimated by the Senator from Pennsylvania will effect a division here, and instead of uniting the North, and thereby arresting the progress of the abolitionists, as he anticipates, will end in division and distraction, and in giving thereby a more powerful impulse to their cause. I must say, before I close my remarks in this connexion, that the members from the North, it seems to me, are not duly sensible of the deep interest which they have in this question, not only as affecting the Union, but as it relates immediately and directly to their particular section. As great as may be our interest, theirs is not less. If the tide continues to roll on its turbid waves of folly and fanaticism, it must in the end prostrate in the North all the institutions that uphold their peace and prosperity, and ultimately overwhelm all that is eminent, morally and intellectually.

I have now concluded what I intended to say on the question immediately before the Senate. If I have spoken earnestly, it is because I feel the subject to be one of the deepest interest. We are about to take the first step; that must control all our subsequent movements. If it should be such as I fear it will, if we receive this petition, and establish the principle that we are obliged to receive all such petitions, if we shall determine to take permanent jurisdiction over the subject of abolition, whenever and in whatever manner the abolitionists may ask, either here or in the States, I fear that the consequence will be ultimately disastrous. Such a course would destroy the confidence of the people of the slaveholding States in this Government. We love and cherish the Union; we remember with the kindest feelings our common origin, with pride our common achievements, and fondly anticipate the common greatness and glory that seem to await us; but origin, achievements, and anticipation of coming greatness are to us as nothing, compared to this question. It is to us a vital question. It involves not only our liberty, but, what is greater, (if to freemen any thing can be,) existence itself. The relation which now exists between the two races in the slaveholding States has existed for two centuries. It has grown with our growth and strengthened with our strength. It has entered into and modified all our institutions, civil and political. None other can be substituted. We will not, cannot, permit it to be destroyed. If we were base enough to do so, we would be traitors to our section, to ourselves, our families, and to posterity. It is our anxious desire to protect and preserve this relation by the joint action of the Government and the confederated States of the Union; but if instead of closing the door, if, instead of denying all jurisdiction and all interference in this question, the doors of Congress are to be thrown open, and if we are to be exposed here, in the heart of the Union, to endless attacks on our rights, our character, and our institutions; if the other States are to stand and look on, without attempting to suppress these attacks, originating within their borders; and, finally, if this is to be our fixed and permanent condition, as members of this confederacy, we will then be compelled to turn our eyes on ourselves. Come what will, should it cost every drop of blood, and every cent of property, we must defend ourselves; and, if compelled, we would stand justified by all laws, human and divine.

If I feel alarm, it is not for ourselves, but the Union and the institutions of the country, to which I have ever been devotedly attached, however calumniated and slandered. Few have made greater sacrifices to maintain them, and none is more anxious to perpetuate them to the latest generation; but they can and ought to be perpetuated only on the condition that they fulfil the great objects for which they were created—the liberty and protection of these States.

As for ourselves, I feel no apprehension. I know to the fullest extent the magnitude of the danger that surrounds us. I am not disposed to under-estimate it. My colleague [that is, Senator Preston of S.C.] has painted it truly. But, as great as is the danger, we have nothing to fear if true to ourselves. We have many and great resources; a numerous, intelligent, and brave population; great and valuable staples; ample fiscal means; unity of feeling and interest, and an entire exemption from those dangers originating in a conflict between labor and capital, which at this time threatens so much danger to constitutional Governments. To these may be added, that we would act under an imperious necessity. There would be to us but one alternative—to triumph or perish as a people. We would stand alone, compelled to defend life, character, and institutions. A necessity so stern and imperious would develop to the full all the great qualities of our nature, mental and moral, requisite for defence—intelligence, fortitude, courage, and patriotism; and these, with our ample means, and our admirable materials for the construction of durable free States, would ensure security, liberty, and renown.

With these impressions, I ask neither sympathy nor compassion for the slaveholding States. We can take care of ourselves. It is not we, but the Union, which is in danger. It is that which demands our care—demands that the agitation of this question shall cease here—that you shall refuse to receive these petitions, and decline all jurisdiction over the subject of abolition, in every form and shape. It is only on these terms that the Union can be safe. We cannot remain here in an endless struggle in defence of our character, our property, and institutions.

I shall now, in conclusion, make a few remarks as to the course I shall feel myself compelled to pursue, should the Senate, by receiving this petition, determine to entertain jurisdiction over the question of abolition. Thinking as I do, I can perform no act that would countenance so dangerous an assumption; and as a participation in the subsequent proceedings on this petition, should it unfortunately be received, might be so construed, in that event I shall feel myself constrained to decline such participation, and to leave the responsibility wholly on those who may assume it.

From *Register of Debates*, 24th Cong., 1st Sess., cols. 765–778. Also printed in the Washington, D.C., *Daily National Intelligencer*, March 24, 1836, pp. 2–3; the Washington, D.C., *United States' Telegraph*, March 26, 1836, pp. 2–3; the Washington, D.C., *Globe*, April 8, 1836, pp. 1–2; the Edgefield, S.C., *Advertiser*, April 21, 1836, pp. 1–2; the Charleston, S.C., *Mercury*, April 29, 1836, p. 2, September 7, 1836, p. 2, and September 8, 1836, p. 2; *Congressional Globe*, 24th Cong., 1st Sess., Appendix, pp. 223–226; *Speech of the Hon. J.C. Calhoun, of South Carolina, on the Abolition Petitions. Delivered on Wednesday, March 9, 1836* (Washington: printed by Duff Green, [1836?]); *Speeches of John C. Cal-*

houn, pp. 197–210; Crallé, ed., *Works,* 2:465–490. Variant in the Washington, D.C., *Globe,* March 11, 1836, p. 2; *Congressional Globe,* 24th Cong., 1st Sess., pp. 238–239. Another variant in the New York, N.Y., *Morning Courier and New-York Enquirer,* March 11, 1836, p. 2. NOTE: Later the same day the Senate voted 36 to 10 to receive the petition.

From [Lewis Cass, Secretary of War,] 3/10. In reply to Calhoun's letter of 3/3, Cass states that on consultation with Col. [George] Bomford, he finds the services of Capt. [Benjamin] Huger of the Ord[nance] Corps are of such a nature that he cannot consistently with the public interest be assigned to duty on the railroad survey in S.C. CC in DNA, RG 156 (Records of the Office of the Chief of Ordnance), Letters Received, 1812–1894, 259.

FINAL REMARKS ON RECEIVING ABOLITION PETITIONS

[In the Senate, March 11, 1836]
[Under consideration was the memorial from the Caln Quarterly Meeting of Friends (petitioning Congress to abolish slavery in the District of Columbia) which had been received by the Senate on 3/9. Samuel McKean of Pa. moved that "it is inexpedient at this time to legislate on the subject of slavery in the District of Columbia." His motion was rejected 2 to 37. The question was then on James Buchanan's motion "that the prayer of the petition be rejected."]

Mr. Calhoun rose and said that, as the question was about to be put, he felt himself constrained to make a few remarks explanatory of the course he intended to pursue. He could not vote in favor of the motion now before the Senate. If the question of the rejection of this petition had been presented without connexion with the one which had been previously raised and discussed, the objection which he felt against the motion would not have existed; but it was impossible for him, after what had passed, to regard the present motion separately from the motion to receive. They in fact constituted but one question. It was avowed by the mover, while the question on receiving was pending, that he voted for the reception with the view of immediately moving the rejection. Regarding them, then, as constituting a single question, it was impossible for him, with the opinions he entertained, to give his support to the present motion.

The Senate has, by voting to receive this petition, on the ground on which the reception was placed, assumed the principle that we are bound to receive petitions to abolish slavery, whether in this District or the States; that is, to take jurisdiction of the question of abolishing slavery whenever and in whatever manner the abolitionists may think proper to present the question. He considered this decision pregnant with consequences of the most disastrous character. When and how they were to occur it was not for him to predict; but he could not be mistaken in the fact that there must follow a long train of evils. What, he would ask, must hereafter be the condition on this floor of the Senators from the slave-holding States? No one can expect that what has been done will arrest the progress of the abolitionists. Its effects must be the opposite, and instead of diminishing must greatly increase the number of the petitions. Under the decision of the Senate, we of the South are doomed to sit here and receive in silence, however outrageous or abusive in their language towards us and those whom we represent, the petitions of the incendiaries who are making war on our institutions. Nay, more, we are bound, without the power of resistance, to see the Senate, at the request of these incendiaries, whenever they think proper to petition, extend its jurisdiction on the subject of slavery over the States as well as this District. Thus deprived of all power of effectual resistance, can any thing be considered more hopeless and degrading than our situation; to sit here, year after year, session after session, hearing ourselves and our constituents vilified by thousands of incendiary publications in the form of petitions, of which the Senate, by its decision, is bound to take jurisdiction, and against which we must rise like culprits to defend ourselves, or permit them to go uncontradicted and unresisted? We must ultimately be not only degraded in our own estimation and that of the world, but be exhausted and worn out in such a contest.

Whatever may be the feelings of others, he for one, if he stood alone, would not give his countenance to so dangerous an assumption of jurisdiction in any manner or form whatever. To vote for the motion now pending would, in his opinion, give such countenance; and, if he had no other reason, would prevent him from giving it his support.

But he had other reasons. In his view of the subject, the vote to receive gave a fatal stab to the rights of the people of the slaveholding States, as far as it could be given here; and the present motion was vainly intended to pour a healing balm into the wound. So far from doing good, it can but do mischief. It can have no influence whatever in stopping the mischief at the North, while it is calculated to throw the South off its guard. Thus viewed, he was compelled to say that the very worst possible direction has been given to the subject, as far as we were concerned, and that in voting for the present motion we would increase rather than diminish the mischief. What the votes of Senators from other quarters would not be able to effect standing alone, to create a false security among those we represent, might be effected with the aid of ours.

Entertaining these views, it was impossible for him to vote for the motion. But could he vote against it? No. It would put him in a false position, which he did not choose to assume. With these alternatives there was but one course left for him to pursue, consistently with his sense of duty—to abstain from all participation in the further progress of this question.

From *Register of Debates*, 24th Cong., 1st Sess., cols. 804–805. Also printed in the Washington, D.C., *Daily National Intelligencer*, March 14, 1836, p. 2; the Washington, D.C., *United States' Telegraph*, March 16, 1836, p. 2; the Charleston, S.C., *Mercury*, May 4, 1836, p. 2. Variant in the Washington, D.C., *Globe*, March 14, 1836, p. 3; *Congressional Globe*, 24th Cong., 1st Sess., p. 247. Another variant in the New York, N.Y., *Morning Courier and New-York Enquirer*, March 14, 1836, p. 2. NOTE: After further debate the Senate adopted Buchanan's motion to reject the prayer of the petitioners by 34 to 6. A text of the petition is printed in *Register of Debates*, 24th Cong., 1st Sess., col. 803.

Remarks on the distribution of the surplus, 3/14. Thomas Ewing of Ohio moved that the Senate proceed to consider the "bill to distribute the proceeds of the public lands amongst the several States." Calhoun supported the motion. He "believed it by far the most important bill which they could have up this session; he should regard the taking up of any other bill in preference to it, as a decision whether, it was their intention to distribute the surplus revenue, or not. He might be peculiar in his views, but his opinion was, that if Congress separated without passing a bill for that object—when they next met, they would have little, possibly, to dispose of. The present large sales of public lands that were made was [sic] perfectly easy to account for. The whole circulation of the country was diseased, and would continue worse and worse, until the result would be, that the General Government would have paper, rags, for their lands! With the U.S. Bank stock they now had 36 or 40 millions of dollars—they would have in the Treasury on the 1st January fifty millions, unless heavy appropriations were made; and were they to sit there and see that vast fund further increasing? He put to the Senators from the West, if they or those of the South, were willing to abandon their proportion of the public revenue? Or would they rather let it lie in Deposit banks, to the general injury of the country?" Ewing's motion was defeated 20 to 26. From the New York, N.Y., *Morning Courier and New-York Enquirer*, March 16, 1836, p. 2. Variant in the Augusta, Ga., *State Rights' Sentinel*, March 25, 1836, p. 2.

[Nathaniel] B[everly] Tucker, Williamsburg, Va., to James H. Hammond, 3/15. Tucker tells Hammond that he had expressed his opinions on secession to Calhoun in a letter "last summer" and assumes that if Calhoun received the letter, he would have disapproved of Tucker's opinions. Tucker is curious to discover whether Calhoun did receive the letter. "For I would have him pass his judgment on the same subject five years hence." ALS in DLC, James Henry Hammond Papers.

Remarks on the preemption law, 3/16. Robert J. Walker of Miss. introduced two bills providing for extension of time for proving preemption rights granted under an act of 1834 and moved to refer them to the Committee on Private Land Claims. "Mr. Calhoun moved to refer them to the Committee on the Public Lands; and advocated this motion by contending that they involved the policy of the Government in regard to the pre-emption law, to the further extension of which, he believed, a large majority of the Senate was opposed." From *Register of Debates*, 24th Cong., 1st Sess., col. 838. Also printed in *Congressional Globe*, 24th Cong., 1st Sess., p. 259.

[To Lewis Cass, Secretary of War,] 3/17. An entry in a register of letters received indicates that Calhoun's letter of this date enclosing a "letter from Gen[era]l [Robert Y.] Hayne respecting a survey in So[uth] Ca[rolina] &c." was received by the War Dept. on 3/18. The letter was referred to the Topographical Bureau. A Clerk's EU reads: "ans[were]d unofficially Mar[ch] 17, [18]36." Entry in DNA, RG 107 (Records of the Office of the Secretary of War), Registers of Letters Received, 1800–1870, 39:C-346 (M-22:39).

From L[ewis] C[ass, Secretary of War], "Unofficial," 3/17. As promised to Calhoun, Cass has requested Col. [John J.] Abert "to make his final arrangements without delay to send a party of Engineers" to S.C. Capt. [William George] Williams will wait upon Calhoun at the Senate "and let you know when he can leave here. You may rely upon it that no unnecessary delay shall take place."

FC in DNA, RG 107 (Records of the Office of the Secretary of War), Confidential and Unofficial Letters Sent, 1814–1847, 2:40 (M-7:2).

FURTHER REMARKS ON THE TREASURY SURPLUS

[In the Senate, March 17, 1836]
[*A report had been received from the Secretary of the Treasury containing financial statements of banks that had been designated by President Andrew Jackson as depositaries of public funds. Daniel Webster moved the printing of 3,000 extra copies of the report.*]

Mr. Calhoun said that, until he saw this document, he had no conception of the great and imminent danger which awaited us. No man now, however, could deny or shut his eyes as to the cause of it. Its commencement took date some three or four years back; and its results had been distinctly foreseen, by himself at least. The disease is on us, and there is a fearful responsibility somewhere as to its cause. This is the point. Something must be done, and done speedily. Delay till this session has passed, and a wound will be inflicted on our currency and our country, from which neither will recover. All who have any of this worthless capital in their possession will be rushing to invest it in the public lands. And shall we stand calmly by, and permit this fraud? Shall this Senate enlist on the side of speculators and swindlers? Sir, a worse state of things is, we are on the eve of a frightful political catastrophe—a catastrophe which will terminate in nothing but the government of the strongest. He understood these military schemes; they were leading, by a rapid and fiery process, to absolute despotism. The Government was no longer elective; it had become hereditary. The demoralizing influence of gold has been already exercised: the age of steel is coming; and with steel will the conflict close. Vain will be the efforts of patriotism, of virtue, of eloquence, to withstand the advances of arbitrary power. The great and durable interests of society will be destroyed, and executive power will rise over them, strong in the ruin of every counteracting authority; strongest in the possession of consolidated power.

Some honest and equitable manner of getting rid of this surplus revenue must be devised. He put it to the gentleman from New York, (Mr. [Silas] Wright,) whether fifteen millions of money, belonging to the whole country, ought to remain at the disposal of his particular constituents? Will he, as a friend of his country, permit this robbery? He was confident that the Senate would not adjourn without applying some remedy. Let all party feeling be put aside. Let Senators consider themselves as citizens of the confederated States, sent here to legislate for the whole Union. He felt under great obligation to the Senator from Massachusetts [Webster] for the motion he had made. He trusted it would prevail. Let the document be printed, and, take my word for it, (said Mr. C[alhoun],) it will be considered as a phenomenon in the eyes of all Europe. The disease which is spreading over the whole body politic demands, and should receive, our notice. Let us break up this stagnant pool, and throw back upon the people the treasure which is legally and equitably theirs.

[*Here Wright replied to Calhoun.*]

Mr. Calhoun said that the Senator from New York had displayed his usual tact and ingenuity in the remarks which he had just made. He (Mr. C[alhoun]) had stated the existing evil as it stands. He had said that there was fifteen millions of the people's money in the deposite banks of New York, and that these funds were used without interest. He did not question the Senator's patriotism; he only appealed to it. The gentleman, however, had given to his remarks a totally different turn. As to transfer drafts, he would rather the money should remain where it was, than give to the Secretary of the Treasury the power of issuing them.

The gentleman wishes to know why a remedy was not offered before. Did not he (Mr. C[alhoun]) offer one? Did he not introduce a bill which would have met and obviated these evils; and was it not lost in the other House? As to any comparison of his political life with that of the Senator from New York, he was perfectly willing to go into it at any moment when the gentleman saw fit. He should not shrink from any comparison which should involve forecast, patriotism, and a manly meeting of responsibility. The majority in this body had changed, and in some measure he rejoiced at it; for the Executive and those who supported him had now the whole responsibility.

[*Wright spoke again at this point.*]

Mr. Calhoun said that the Executive had a fixed majority in the other House; we poor Senators, who were called a factious majority, had done all that was possible to avert these evils. Why were we not seconded by the friends of the administration in the other branch of Congress? The Senator could answer that question if he chose.

There were three measures introduced in this body which would have had the desired effect: one to take away from the Executive the power, by means of the public treasure, of disciplining and regulating the ranks of his party; another, to regulate the deposites of the public money; the third, a proposition so to amend the Constitution as to permit the distribution of the surplus revenue equitably among the whole people. All his reasoning on this last subject was pronounced wild and visionary. There was no prospect of pushing it through at the last session; and he had thought it better to let it sleep over until the amount of the surplus was ascertained.

The Senator from New York wishes us to turn our eyes upon the past. He (Mr. C[alhoun]) wished to consider the future; and it was for this purpose he had endeavored to awaken the attention of the gentleman. The subject was indeed full of interesting considerations. It was the greatest and most momentous question that had ever occupied the attention of the nation.

From *Register of Debates*, 24th Cong., 1st Sess., cols. 842–844. Also printed in the Washington, D.C., *Daily National Intelligencer*, March 19, 1836, p. 3; the Washington, D.C., *United States' Telegraph*, March 22, 1836, p. 2. Variant in the Washington, D.C., *Globe*, March 19, 1836, p. 3; *Congressional Globe*, 24th Cong., 1st Sess., p. 262; the Pendleton, S.C., *Messenger*, April 1, 1836, p. 2. Another variant in the New York, N.Y., *Morning Courier and New-York Enquirer*, March 19, 1836, p. 2.

To J[ames] L. Edwards, Pension Office, [*ca.* 3/20]. "I will thank you to transmit to me the papers in the case of William Smith of South Carolina for a pension." ALS in DNA, RG 15 (Records of the Veterans Administration), Revolutionary War Pension and Bounty-Land Warrant Application Files, 1800–1900, R-9875½.

To Thomas J. Johnson

Washington, 20th March 1836

Dear Sir, It at all times affords me much pleasure to render any aid to youths seeking information, and improvement; and I really regret my incompetency to advise your young friend on a general course of reading on law & jurisprudence. I remained only two years at the bar, and have not read a law book in 25 years, so that I am far in the rear of the profession as it now stands. But I would say to your friend: study attentively all the best elementary treatises; be assiduous in his attendance in court, and attentive to the ro[u]tine of office. He will of course make himself master of the particular laws of the State where he intends to practise. But no previous preperation [*sic*] can supercede the necessity of the minutest & closest attention to the cases he may undertake after he is admitted to practise, both as to the facts and law. On this point the success of a lawyer mainly depends. The study of particular cases is better calculated, than any thing else to give full & accurate legal knowledge. As to history, he will of course study all the ancient classicks; to be followed by [Edward] Gibbon's decline & fall of the Roman Empire. To which the history of England & that ["of" *interlined*] our own country ought to succeed. Both ought, not only to be read, but studied. Add to these some good general History, and a foundation will be laid, which may be built on, from time to time, by reading at leisure the histories of the more celebrated States of modern times. With respect I am & & J.C. Calhoun.

ALS in DLC, Breckinridge Long Papers; typescript in DLC, Carnegie Institution of Washington Transcript Collection.

To [Lewis] Cass, Secretary of War, [3/21]. Calhoun encloses a letter [*not found*; from J.C.S. Dustan, requesting information as to the employment of his father as Keeper of the Arsenal at Fort Richmond, N.Y., during the War of 1812]. Calhoun does not remember the papers referred to [by Dustan]. However, if received in the War Department, "they can no doubt be traced, and I will thank you to cause the information to be given, which is requested." ALS in DNA, RG 77 (Records of the Office of the Chief of Engineers), Letters Received, 1826–1866, C-1509.

[To Lewis Cass, Secretary of War, *ca.* 3/21.] An entry in a register of letters received indicates that the War Dept. received a letter on this date from Calhoun "relative to a small error in the instructions to Capt. [William George] Williams in reference to the survey in South Carolina." The letter was referred to the Topographical Bureau. Entry in DNA, RG 107 (Records of the Office of the Secretary of War), Registers of Letters Received, 1800–1870, 39:C-358 (M-22:39).

Petition of Samuel Warner, [brought by Calhoun to the Senate *ca.* 3/21]. Endorsements indicate that the petition of Samuel Warner of Mass., requesting a pension by reason of having been a seaman in the service of the U.S., was presented by Calhoun. According to the journal, however, the petition was presented by Nehemiah R. Knight of R.I. (It was referred to the Committee on Naval Affairs, which reported a bill for Warner's relief which passed the Senate on 5/11.) Endorsements on jacket (petition missing) in DNA, RG 46 (Records of the U.S. Senate), 24A-G12; Abs in *Senate Journal,* 24th Cong., 1st Sess., p. 232.

To [Lewis Cass, *ca.* 3/24]. Calhoun asks whether there is not some mistake in an enclosed document [*not found*]. "If my memory serves me Mr. [Hugh] Rose was appointed [as a Cadet at the U.S. Military Academy] last year, and was reinstated last winter after having ["been" *interlined*] dismissed." ALS in DNA, RG 77 (Records of the Office of the Chief of Engineers), Letters Received, 1826–1866, C-1510.

From [James L. Edwards], Pension Office, 3/24. "In compliance with your request [of *ca.* 3/20] I have the honor to enclose herewith the papers in the case of William Smith. Be pleased to acknowledge the receipt of them." CC in DNA, RG 15 (Records of the Veterans Administration), Revolutionary War Pension and Bounty-Land Warrant Application Files, 1800–1900, R-9875½.

Motion on the safekeeping of public records, submitted to the Senate on 3/24. "Resolved, that the Committee on the Judiciary be instructed to enquire into the expediency of providing proper measures for the safekeeping of the Journal[s] of the two Houses, and other publick records; and of protecting them by proper legal enac[t]-ments from being mutilated, obliterated, enrased [*sic*], defaced, expunged, disfigured, altered, or otherwise destroyed; or injured." ADU in DNA, RG 46 (Records of the U.S. Senate), 24A-B10; PC in *Senate Journal,* 24th Cong., 1st Sess., p. 242.

REMARKS ON HIS MOTION ON THE SAFEKEEPING OF PUBLIC RECORDS

[In the Senate, March 25, 1836]
[Under consideration was Calhoun's motion, submitted yesterday, to instruct the Committee on the Judiciary to enquire into means for the protection of the public records. Calhoun's motion obviously had reference to the continued efforts of the friends of Andrew Jack-

son to expunge from the Senate journal that body's censure resolution of 3/28/1834.]

Mr. Calhoun rose, and said that there is no evil without some accompanying good. The truth of the remark is illustrated by the measure which has occasioned the introduction of this resolution. As unconstitutional and as odious as is the attempt to expunge a portion of the journals of the proceedings of this body, it has had the good effect of rousing attention, for the first time, to the unprotected condition of the journals of the two Houses, and the other public records. I have caused diligent search to be made, and the result is, that, with the exception of the 18th section of the act of 1790, to punish certain crimes against the United States, which provides for punishing in certain cases the falsifying for fraudulent purposes the records of the courts, there is no law whatever to protect the public records. As strange as it is, it is no less true, that they may be mutilated, obliterated, falsified, expunged, or destroyed by those in whose possession they are, or any person who may have access to them, without subjecting the person perpetrating the crime to the slightest punishment. Our Secretary, who is in charge of our journals, if so disposed, might destroy them before our eyes, without exposing himself to any legal penalty. All who hear me, whatever may be their opinions on particular points, must agree that such a state of things ought not to continue. Setting aside the obligation imposed by the Constitution on us in reference to our journals, the great importance of the public records would of itself make it our duty to preserve and protect them with the utmost care. They contain the only authentic account of the proceedings of the legislative and judicial departments of the Government, and from them must be drawn mainly the materials for the true political history of the country, to say nothing of the important interests, both public and private, involved in their being preserved free from all alterations or changes, or suspicion of being altered or changed.

But, as sacred as is the duty of adopting the requisite measures for their protection, regarded in the light presented, it becomes far more so, when to that is added the obligation imposed by the Constitution on this and the other House to keep a journal of their proceedings. Yes, we are under the obligation of an oath to *keep* our journals—a word of the most comprehensive meaning, and, at the same time, free from all ambiguity, as applied in this instance. It implies that our proceedings shall be fully and accurately recorded, and, when so recorded, that the journal containing them shall be carefully protected and preserved. Without recording, it would be impossible to preserve, while the injunction to record would be vain and absurd, without the obligation to preserve. The very object of recording is to preserve, for the use of the present and all future generations, a true and faithful account of the acts of this body. Such is the extent of the obligation imposed on the Senate by the Constitution, in providing that it shall keep a journal of its proceedings; and in taking the oath to support the Constitution, we have all solemnly sworn faithfully to perform this duty, with the others imposed by that instrument. To discharge this obligation, we are bound not only to abstain from destroying, altering, or in any respect injuring the journals ourselves, but to adopt all proper measures to guard them against destruction, alteration, or injury by others.

The impression that they are our journals, and that we may do with them as we please, is the result of a gross misconception. They, indeed, contain an account of our proceedings, but they belong not to us. They are the property of the public. They belong to the people of these confederated States; and we have no more right to injure, alter, or destroy them, than the stranger that walks the streets; no more than we have to alter or destroy the journal of the other House, or the records of the courts of justice. We are, it is true, the representatives and the agents of those to whom our journals rightfully belong; and, as such, are their keepers, placed under the sacred obligation of an oath to perform our duty in that capacity, but which, so far from giving us any right to destroy or injure them, would but add to the enormity of the crime; just as it would be more criminal in a guardian to defraud or destroy his ward than any other person.

In making these remarks, I am aware that no law can restrain us from doing what we may think proper in our official characters as Senators; and that, while acting in that character, we are not amenable to any court. It follows, of course, that whatever act may be passed by Congress to protect the journals of the two Houses, cannot prevent either House from passing resolutions, with a view to mutilate, obliterate, expunge, alter, disfigure, or otherwise destroy or injure their journals, or subject the members to punishment for passing such resolutions; but still a law, making it penal to destroy or injure them, will not be without great and salutary effect in protecting the journals, even against the two Houses. We may order the expunging or destroying of the journal either in whole or in part, but we cannot perform the act. That must be the work of an agent. Some one must be ordered to do it; either the Secretary, or some one else. Though the order may not make us amenable to the laws, it cannot exempt the Secretary, or whoever may be ordered to perform the odious and unconstitutional act, from responsibility. In a court of justice, on an indictment for the violation of law, it would be so much waste paper when opposed to an act of Congress, and an express provision of the Constitution. Our Secretary, as well as all our other officers, from you (addressing the Vice-President [Martin Van Buren]) to the lowest clerk, are all under oath to support the Constitution. Each, when he comes to act, must judge for himself, and act on his own individual responsibility. If the members of this body should misconstrue or disregard the injunctions of the Constitution to keep the journal, that would not justify the Secretary [Walter Lowrie, a former Senator from Pa.,] should he be ordered to expunge or destroy the journal. What he ought to do in such an event is a case of conscience; that he must decide for himself; and I do trust that, if the members of this body should be so regardless of the solemn obligation imposed by their oath, as to give such an order, neither our present nor any future Secretary would be found wanting in the requisite firmness and virtue to resist an order so clearly unconstitutional. But such may not always be the case, and, in such event, the beneficial effects of proper penal enactments to protect the journals from being expunged or destroyed would be experienced. He who might not be restrained by the sanctity of an oath, may be by the terror of punishment; and a Senate, impelled, by party spirit and party discipline, to order the performance of an act in subversion of the Constitution, might find itself arrested by the refusal of its selected agent, under the terrors of the laws, to perpetrate the criminal act. Thus, a law to preserve and protect the journals of the two Houses, and other public records, by inflicting condign punishment on all who may destroy or injure them, may be found in practice to be an efficient protection against the danger to which they may be exposed in high and violent party times from the Houses themselves.

It is too late to suppose that party violence and discipline could not possibly drive the Houses to an act so palpably in violation of the Constitution, and the high duty they are under to preserve the public record as the precious and sacred depository of the acts of the legislative and judicial departments of the Government. After what has already passed here, as well as in several of the State Legislatures, the danger can no longer be considered imaginary. As monstrous as it may seem, it can no longer be doubted that those who by the Constitution are made the keepers of the journals, their protectors and guardians, may so far forget their duty as to be the first to aim at their destruction. Admonished by what has occurred, and looking forward to what may hereafter follow from the present attempt, every one, be his party what it may, who is desirous to see some restraint imposed on the violence and madness of party, ought to aid to throw around the journals and other public records every guard that may contribute to protect them against the destruction to which the rage of party war may hereafter expose them.

I have great confidence in the Committee on the Judiciary, and have no doubt, should the resolution be adopted, they will give the subject a thorough investigation; and should their opinion concur with mine, they will, I doubt not, be able to devise the proper measures to effect the important object intended to be accomplished.

From *Register of Debates*, 24th Cong., 1st Sess., cols. 970–977. Also printed in the Washington, D.C., *Daily National Intelligencer*, March 29, 1836, p. 2; the Washington, D.C., *United States' Telegraph*, March 30, 1836, p. 2; the Charleston, S.C., *Mercury*, May 3, 1836, p. 2. Variant in the Washington, D.C., *Globe*, March 28, 1836, p. 3; *Congressional Globe*, 24th Cong., 1st Sess., pp. 289–290; Crallé, ed., *Works*, 2:490–495 (misdated 3/26). Other variants in the Washington, D.C., *United States' Telegraph*, March 28, 1836, p. 2, and the New York, N.Y., *Morning Courier and New-York Enquirer*, March 28, 1836, p. 2. NOTE: Later the same day Calhoun's motion was tabled by a vote of 19 to 15. Some of the reports of Calhoun's above remarks present them as having been made at three different points in the debate rather than all at once. In the variant first cited, Calhoun was reported, in part, as saying in reply to John M. Niles of Conn., "that it has been long since established, that the common law forms no part of the laws of the Union." In a reply to Ether Shepley of Me. Calhoun was reported in the same source as acknowledging that a pending expunging motion submitted by Thomas H. Benton was the occasion of his offering his motion. However, his object was a general one, and the deficiency in the laws he had alluded to should be supplied on general principles, Calhoun said.

From [Lewis Cass,] War Department, 3/28. "The letter of Mr. [J.C.S.] Dustan, encl[osed] in y[ou]rs of the 21st ins[tant,] is herewith returned, with report of the Ch[ief] Eng[inee]r [Charles Gratiot] & the Col. of Ordnance [George Bomford]." The examination of the files of the War Department and its bureaus has been unsuccessful. CC in DNA, RG 77 (Records of the Office of the Chief of Engineers), Letters Received, 1826–1866, C-1509.

Motion submitted to the Senate on 3/28. "Resolved that the Committee on pensions be instructed to enquire into the propriety of placing the name of William Smith of [South] Carolina on the pension list." (This motion was agreed to on 3/28 by unanimous consent.) ADU in DNA, RG 46 (Records of the U.S. Senate), 24A-B10; CC in DNA, RG 46, 24A-D12; PC in *Senate Journal*, 24th Cong., 1st Sess., p. 247.

To David Porter, [U.S.] Chargé d'Affaires, Constantinople, 3/28. Calhoun introduces Dr. [John] Breckinridge of Baltimore, who will visit Constantinople during his tour to Jerusalem. "Mr. Breckinridge is a Presbyterian divine of the first standing and respectability in our country. He is a son of the Hon. Mr. [John] Breckinridge formerly a Senator from Kentucky, and afterwards attorney General of the U[nited] States." ALS in DLC, Breckinridge Family Papers, 71: 12728–12729.

To Henry Wheaton, [U.S.] Chargé d'Affaires, Berlin, 3/28. Calhoun introduces Dr. [John] Breckinridge, a Presbyterian minister from Baltimore, who will visit Europe "with the intention of making an extensive tour by way of the Rhine and the Danube to Constantinople." ALS in DLC, Breckinridge Family Papers, 71:12730–12731.

To JOHN G. MILLER, [Columbus, Ohio]

Washington, March 29, 1836
Dear Sir: I have been honored by your note inviting me, in the name of the Committee of Arrangements, to attend a public dinner to be given at Columbus on the 13th of April, by the State Rights Association of the city of Columbus and county of Franklin, in memory of the birth day of Thomas Jefferson.

You were correct in supposing that it might not be compatible with my public engagements to attend; but I cannot permit the occasion to pass without the expression of my cordial approbation of the object of your celebration.

When the General Government was formed, it is not at all surprising, that the wise and patriotic should have differed in opinion, as to what would be its tendency. This difference gave rise to the two great, and, let me add, honest and patriotic parties, which for so long a period divided the country; the one apprehending that the General Government would prove to be too strong for the States, and that the system would end in consolidation; while the other believed, that the tendency would be in the opposite direction. These opposing views, on this fundamental question, influenced and directed all the views and movements of the two contending parties, and caused all the conflicts between them, which for so many years agitated the country. But time has at length decided the controversy. The States have, in less than half a century, virtually sunk into mere corporations; and, with their decay, faction, corruption, and subserviency, have rapidly overspread the land, and prepared the way, as was from the beginning predicted by those who dreaded consolidation, for the utter subversion of our institutions, and the erection on their ruins of lawless and despotic power. Already great progress has been made towards this fatal termination. Already has a great and powerful party, held together by the "spoils of victory," obtained the ascendancy—a party which knows no law but the will of the Executive [Andrew Jackson], and no principle but obedience to that will. Already has the present Chief Magistrate, at the head of the party, nominated through a mock Convention his successor [Martin Van Buren], and entered personally into the canvass, with all the power and influence, which the vast patronage of the Government and the almost unlimited control over the public treasury, with its millions of surplus, give him.

Against a danger so pressing and fearful, there is but one certain and efficient protection; and that is to be found in the rights and sovereignty of the States. It is only through them, that the encroachments of the Executive can be successfully resisted, and the threatened catastrophe averted. Opposition, on any other principle, is vain and hopeless. It has ever proved so, and ever will continue so to do, as long as our system may last.

In conclusion, I take the liberty of offering the following sentiment [as a toast for your celebration]:

The Rights and Sovereignty of the States; our history has proved, that with them no opposition to Executive encroachments has ever failed of success, and that without them none has ever been successful.

With great respect I am &c. &c., J.C. Calhoun.

PC in the Washington, D.C., *United States' Telegraph,* May 6, 1836, p. 2; PC (reprinted from the Columbus, O., *Spirit of Seventy-Six*) in the Columbus, O., *Ohio State Journal, and Columbus Gazette,* June 11, 1836. NOTE: As reported in the issue of the *Ohio State Journal* cited above, the Jefferson's Birthday dinner of which Miller was chairman passed resolutions endorsing Calhoun for President. Miller was described by the *Journal* as the editor of the *Spirit of Seventy-Six,* "a thorough going Nullification print." The Washington, D.C., *United States' Telegraph* of May 6, 1836, p. 2, gave an account of the dinner to which Calhoun declined an invitation above. Several toasts to him were made at the dinner including one which went: "John C. Calhoun. He wears the mantle of Jefferson—lofty in intellect, pure in patriotism, in honesty stern, in virtue severe; we hail him *even now* as the hope of our country."

Remarks on a bill to reduce the price of public lands for actual settlers, 3/28. Robert J. Walker of Miss. introduced "a bill to reduce and graduate the price of the public lands to actual settlers alone, &c.," and moved that the bill be referred to a select committee of five. "Mr. Calhoun rose and opposed the provisions of the bill, particularly the clause reducing the price of the public lands and granting pre-emption to settlers, and closed by moving a reference of this bill to the Committee on the Public Lands." (After further debate among eight Senators, in which Calhoun made unreported remarks, Calhoun's motion was lost 19 to 25.) From *Register of Debates*, 24th Cong., 1st Sess., col. 1032. Variant in the Richmond, Va., *Enquirer*, April 5, 1836, p. 2.

To A A R O N V A I L, [U.S.] Chargé d'Affaires [in London]

Washington, April 1836

Dear Sir, I take the liberty of making you acquainted with the Rev[eren]d Mr. [Richard] Fuller of South Carolina, who visits Europe for the restoration of his health.

Mr. Fuller is distinguished for his piety and abilities, as well as his amiable and gentlemanly deportment. He proposes to try the effect of the climate of France & Italy on his constitution.

Knowing your disposition to bestow any attention in your power on our citizens, who visit Europe, I feel confident I need not say more than I have to recommend him to your particular regard. With great respect I am & & J.C. Calhoun.

ALS in NHi, Vail Collection, 2:19.

Remarks on "the bill to establish the northern boundary line of Ohio, and to provide for the admission of the State of Michigan," 4/1. "Mr. Calhoun (half past seven) said he would make one more effort to obtain time to look into the amendments, many of which were new, and required to be examined. He moved that the Senate now adjourn; which was negatived: Yeas 12, nays 24." (The bill was then ordered to be read a third time and engrossed by a vote of 23 to 8.) From *Register of Debates*, 24th Cong., 1st Sess., col. 1048. Variant in the New York, N.Y., *Morning Courier and New-York Enquirer*, April 4, 1836, p. 2.

Speech on the Bill to Provide for the Admission of Michigan

[In the Senate, April 2, 1836]
[*Under consideration, on third reading, was a bill to establish the northern boundary of Ohio and to make arrangements for the admission of Mich. Territory as a State. A motion by Alexander Porter of La. was being debated. It would, if adopted, recommit the bill for the purpose of amending it in respect to the right of suffrage and in order to secure more effectually the rights of the U.S. to the public lands in the new State. William C. Preston of S.C. had spoken in favor of the recommitment but in opposition to the principle of interfering with the right of the proposed State to prescribe the qualifications of its voters. Calhoun said:*]

I regret that my colleague [Preston] has thought proper to raise the question, whether a State has a right to make an alien a citizen of the State. The question is one of great magnitude—presented for the first time—and claiming a more full and deliberate consideration, than can be bestowed on it now. It is not necessarily involved in the present question. The point now at issue is, not whether a State or territory has a right to make an alien a citizen; but whether Congress has a right to prescribe the qualifications of the voters for members of the convention to form a constitution, preparatory to the admission of a territory into the Union. I presume, that even my colleague will not deny that Congress has the right. The Constitution confers on Congress the power to govern the territories; and, of course, to prescribe the qualifications of voters within them—without any restriction—unless, indeed, such as the ordinance and the Constitution may enforce—a power that expires only when a territory becomes a State. The practice of the Government has been in conformity with these views; and there is not an instance of the admission of a territory into the Union, in which Congress has not prescribed the qualifications of the voters for members of the convention to form a constitution for the government of the State, on its admission. The power which Congress has thus invariably exercised, we claim to exercise on the present occasion—by prescribing who shall be the voters to form the constitution for the government of Michigan, when admitted into the Union. Michigan is not yet a State. Her constitution is not yet formed. It is, at best, but in an incipient state—which can only be consummated by complying with the conditions which we may prescribe for her admission. A convention is to be called, under this bill, to agree to these conditions. On motion of the Senator from New-

York (Mr. [Silas] Wright) a provision was introduced into the bill, giving the right to the people of the territory at large—without limitation, or restriction, as to age, sex, color, or citizenship—to vote for the members of the convention. The Senator from Kentucky (Mr. [Henry] Clay), while the amendment of the Senator from New-York was pending, moved to amend the amendment by striking out people, and inserting free white male citizens of twenty-one years of age— thus restricting the voters to the free white citizens of the United States, in conformity with what has been usual on such occasions.

Believing that Congress had the unquestionable right to prescribe the qualifications of voters, as proposed by the Senator from Kentucky, and that the exercise of such right does not involve, in any degree, the question whether a State has a right to confer on an alien the rights of citizenship, I must repeat the expression of my regret, that my colleague has felt it to be his duty to raise a question so novel and important, when we have so little leisure for bestowing on it the attention which it deserves. But, since he considers its decision as necessarily involved in the question before us, I feel it to be my duty to state the reasons why I cannot concur with him in opinion.

I do not deem it necessary to follow my colleague and the Senator from Kentucky, in their attempt to define or describe a citizen. Nothing is more difficult than the definition, or even description, of so complex an idea; and hence, all arguments resting on one definition in such cases, almost necessarily lead to uncertainty and doubt. But though we may not be able to say, with precision, what a citizen is, we may say, with the utmost certainty, what he is *not*. *He is not an alien.* Alien and citizen are correlative terms, and stand in contradistinction to each other. They, of course, cannot coexist. They are, in fact, so opposite in their nature, that we conceive of the one but in contradistinction to the other. Thus far, all must be agreed. My next step is not less certain.

The Constitution confers on Congress the authority to pass uniform laws of naturalization. This will not be questioned; nor will it be, that the effect of *naturalization is to remove alienage*. I am not certain that the word is a legitimate one.

(Mr. Preston said, in a low tone, it was.)

My colleague says it is. His authority is high on such questions; and with it, I feel myself at liberty to use the word. To remove alienage, is simply to put the foreigner in the condition of a native born. To this extent the act of naturalization goes, and no further.

The next position I assume is no less certain: that, when Congress

127

has exercised its authority by passing a uniform law of naturalization (as it has), it excludes the right of exercising a similar authority on the part of the State. To suppose that the States could pass naturalization acts of their own, after Congress had passed an uniform law of naturalization, would be to make the provision of the Constitution nugatory. I do not deem it necessary to dwell on this point, as I understood my colleague as acquiescing in its correctness.

I am now prepared to decide the question which my colleague has raised. I have shown that a citizen is not an alien, and that alienage is an insuperable barrier, till removed, to citizenship; and that it can only be removed by complying with the act of Congress. It follows, of course, that a State cannot, of its own authority, make an alien a citizen without such compliance. To suppose it can, involves, in my opinion, a confusion of ideas, which must lead to innumerable absurdities and contradictions. I propose to notice but a few. In fact, the discussion has come on so unexpectedly, and has been urged on so precipitately, through the force of party discipline, that little leisure has been afforded to trace to their consequences the many novel and dangerous principles involved in the bill. I, in particular, have not had due time for reflection, which I exceedingly regret. Attendance on the sick bed of a friend drew off my attention till yesterday; when, for the first time, I turned my thoughts on its provisions. The numerous objections which it presented, and the many and important amendments which were moved to correct them, in rapid succession, until a late hour of the night, allowed but little time for reflection. Seeing [last night, Friday,] that the majority had predetermined to pass the bill, with all its faults, I retired, when I found my presence could no longer be of any service, and remained ignorant that the Senate had rescinded the order to adjourn over till Monday, until a short time before its meeting this [Saturday] morning: so that I came here wholly unprepared to discuss this and the other important questions involved in the bill. Under such circumstances, it must not be supposed that, in pointing out the few instances of what appear to me the absurdities and contradictions necessarily resulting from the principle against which I contend, there are not many others, equally striking. I but suggest those which first occurred to me.

Whatever difference of opinion there may be as to what other rights appertain to a citizen, all must at least agree, that he has the right to petition, and also to claim the protection of his Government. These belong to him as a member of the body politic—and the possession of them, is what separates citizens of the lowest condition from aliens and slaves. To suppose, that a State can make an alien a citizen of the State—or, to present the question more specifically, can confer on him the right of voting, would involve the absurdity of giving him a direct and immediate control over the action of the General Government, from which he has no right to claim the protection, and to which he has no right to present a petition. That the full force of the absurdity may be felt, it must be borne in mind, that every department of the General Government is either directly or indirectly under the control of the voters in the several States. The Constitution wisely provides, that the voters for the most numerous branch of the legislatures in the several States, shall vote for the members of the House of Representatives, and, as the members of this body are chosen by the legislatures of the States, and the Presidential electors either by the legislatures, or voters in the several States, it follows, as I have stated, that the action of the General Government is either directly or indirectly under the control of the voters in the several States. Now, admit, that a State may confer the right of voting on all aliens, and it will follow as a necessary consequence, that we might have among our constituents, persons who have not the right to claim the protection of the Government, or to present a petition to it. I would ask my colleague, if he would willingly bear the relation of representative to those, who could not claim his aid, as Senator, to protect them from oppression, or to present a petition through him to the Senate, praying for a redress of grievance?—and yet such might be his condition on the principle for which he contends.

But a still greater difficulty remains. Suppose a war should be declared between the United States and the country to which the alien belongs—suppose, for instance, that South Carolina should confer the right of voting on alien subjects of Great Britain residing within her limits, and that war should be declared between the two countries; what, in such event, would be the condition of that portion of our voters? They, as alien enemies, would be liable to be seized under the laws of Congress, and to have their goods confiscated and themselves imprisoned, or sent out of the country. The principle that leads to such consequences cannot be true; and I venture nothing in asserting, that Carolina, at least, will never give it her sanction, or consent to act on it. She never will assent to incorporate, as members of her body politic, those who might be placed in so degraded a condition and so completely under the control of the General Government.

But let us pass from these (as it appears to me conclusive) views, and inquire what were the objects of the Constitution in conferring on Congress the authority of passing uniform laws of naturalization—from which, if I mistake not, arguments not less conclusive may be drawn, in support of the position for which I contend.

In conferring this power the framers of the Constitution must have had two objects in view: one to prevent competition between the States in holding out inducements for the emigration of foreigners, and the other to prevent their improper influence over the General Government, through such States as might naturalize foreigners, and could confer on them the right of exercising the elective franchise, before they could be sufficiently informed of the nature of our institutions, or were interested in their preservation. Both of these objects would be defeated, if the States may confer on aliens the right of voting and the other privileges belonging to citizens. On that supposition, it would be almost impossible to conceive what good could be obtained, or evil prevented by conferring the power on Congress. The power would be perfectly nugatory. A State might hold out every improper inducement to emigration, as freely as if the power did not exist; and might confer on the alien all the political privileges belonging to a native born citizen—not only to the great injury of the Government of the State, but to an improper control over the Government of the Union. To illustrate what I have said, suppose the dominant party in New-York, finding political power about to depart from them, should, to maintain their ascendency, extend the right of suffrage to the thousands of aliens of every language and from every portion of the world, that annually pour into her great emporium—how deeply might the destiny of the whole Union be affected by such a measure. It might, in fact, place the control over the General Government in the hands of those who know nothing of our institutions and are indifferent as to the interests of the country. New-York gives about one-sixth of the electoral votes in the choice of President and Vice-President; and it is well known that her political institutions keep the State nearly equally divided into two great political parties. The addition of a few thousand votes either way might turn the scale, and the electors might, in fact, owe their election, on the supposition, to the votes of unnaturalized foreigners. The Presidential election might depend on the electoral vote of the State, and a President be chosen in reality by them; that is, they might give us a king—for, under the usurpations of the present Chief Magistrate, the President is in fact a king. I ask my colleague if we ought willingly to yield our assent to a principle that would lead to such results—and if there be any danger on the side for which I contend, comparable to those which I have stated? I know how sincere he is in the truth of the position for which he contends, and that his opinion was founded anterior to this discussion. We have rarely differed in our views on the questions which have come before the Senate; and I deeply regret, as I am sure he does, that we should differ on this highly important subject.

My colleague cites, in support of his position, the example of Vermont, North Carolina, and, if I recollect rightly, Rhode Island—under whose constitutions aliens, it seems, may vote. It is a sufficient answer to say, that their constitutions were adopted before the existence of the General Government, and that the provisions which permitted aliens to vote constituted a portion of their constitutions when they came into the Union. North Carolina has since amended hers, and limited the right of voting to citizens. If Vermont and Rhode Island have not done the same, it must be attributed to that *vis inertia* which indisposes most States to alter their constitutions, or to accidental omission. But we have the authority of the Senator from North Carolina (Mr. [Willie P.] Mangum), and also the Senator from Vermont (Mr. [Samuel] Prentiss), that under the decision of the courts of the respective States, their constitutions have been so construed, since they entered the Union, as to confine the right of voting and holding lands to citizens of the States, so as to conform to the principle for which I contend. To cite a case in point, my colleague ought to show that, under the constitution of any State, formed since the adoption of the Constitution of the Union, the right of voting has been conferred on an alien. There is not, I believe, an example of the kind—from which I infer the deep and universal conviction which has pervaded the public mind, that a State has no authority to confer such right; and thus the very example cited by my colleague, serves but to strengthen instead of refuting the position which I seek to maintain.

My colleague also cites the example of Louisiana, which was admitted into the Union without requiring the inhabitants, at the time, to conform to the act of naturalization. I must think the instance is not in point. That was a case of the incorporation of a foreign community, which had been acquired by treaty, as a member of our confederacy. At the time of the acquisition, they were subjects of France, and owed their allegiance to that government. The treaty transferred their allegiance to the United States; and the difficulty of incorporating Louisiana into the Union, arose, not under the act of naturalization, but the right of acquiring foreign possession by purchase, and the right of incorporating such possessions into the

Union. These were felt, at the time, to be questions of great difficulty. Mr. [Thomas] Jefferson himself, under whose administration
the purchase was made, doubted the right, and suggested the necessity of an alteration of the Constitution to meet the case; and if the
example of the admission is now to be used to establish the principle
that a State may confer citizenship on an alien, we may all live to
regret that the Constitution was not amended according to the suggestion. My colleague insists that, to deny the right for which he
contends, would be to confer on Congress the right of prescribing
who should or should not be entitled to vote in the State, and exercise
the other privileges belonging to citizens; and portrayed in strong
language the danger to the rights of the States from such authority.
If his views are correct in this respect, the danger would, indeed, be
imminent; but I cannot concur in their correctness. Under the view
which I have taken, the authority of Congress is limited to the simple
point of passing uniform laws of naturalization, or, as I have shown,
simply to remove alienage. To this extent it may clearly go, under
the Constitution; and it is no less clear that it cannot go an inch
beyond, without palpably transcending its powers, and violating the
Constitution. Every other privilege except those which necessarily
flow from the removal of alienage, must be conferred by the constitution and the authority of the State. My remarks are, of course, confined to the States; for, within the territories, the authority of Congress is as complete, in this respect, as that of the States within their
respective limits, with the exception of such limitations as the ordinance to which I have referred may impose.

But, to pass to the question immediately before us. This, as I
have stated, does not involve the question whether a State can make
an alien a citizen; but whether Congress has a right to prescribe the
qualifications to be possessed by those who shall vote for members
of a convention to form a constitution for Michigan. Reason and
precedent concur, that Congress has the right. It has, as I have
stated, been exercised in every similar case. If the right does not
exist in Congress, it exists nowhere. A territory, until it becomes a
State, is a dependent community, and possesses no political rights
but what are derived from the community on which it depends. Who
shall or shall not exercise political power? and what shall be the
qualifications possessed by them? and how they shall be appointed?
are all questions to be determined by the paramount community;
and in the case under consideration, to be determined by Congress,
which has the right, under the Constitution, to prescribe all necessary
rules for the government of the territories, not inconsistent with the

provisions of the Constitution. This very bill, in fact, admits the right. It prescribes that the people of Michigan shall vote for the convention to form her constitution, on becoming a State. If it belongs to the territory of Michigan (she is not yet a State) to determine who shall vote for the members of the convention, this attempt on our part to designate who shall be the voters, would be an unconstitutional interference with her right, and ought to be objected to, as such, by those opposed to our views. But if, on the other hand, the view I take be correct, that the right belongs to Congress, and not to the territory, the loose, vague, and indefinite manner in which the voters are described in the bill, affords a decisive reason for its recommitment. I ask, who are the people of Michigan? Taken in the ordinary sense, it means every body, of every age, of every sex, of every complexion, white, black, or red, aliens as well as citizens. Regarded in this light, to pass this bill, would sanction the principle that Congress may authorize an alien to vote, or confer that high privilege on the runaway slaves from Kentucky, Virginia, or elsewhere; and thus elevate them to the condition of citizens, enjoying under the Constitution all the rights and privileges in the States of the Union which appertain to citizenship. But my colleague says that this must be acquiesced in, if such should be the case, as it results from the principles of the Constitution. I know we are bound to submit to whatever are the provisions of that instrument; but surely my colleague will agree with me, that the danger of such a precedent would be great; that the principles on which it is justified ought to be clear and free from all doubt; and I trust I have, at least, shown that such is not the fact in this case.

But, we are told, that the people of Michigan means, in this case, the qualified voters. Why, then, was it not so expressed? Why was vague and general language used, when more certain and precise terms might have been employed? But, I would ask, who are the qualified voters? Are they those authorized to vote under the existing laws established for the government of the territory? or are they those who, under the instrument called the constitution, are authorized to vote? Why leave so essential a point in so uncertain a condition, when we have the power to remove the uncertainty? If it be meant by the people of Michigan, the qualified voters under her incipient constitution (as stated by the Senator from New-York), then are we sanctioning the right of aliens to vote. Michigan has attempted to confer this right on that portion of her inhabitants. She has no authority to confer such right under the Constitution. I have exclusively shown that a State does not possess it—much less a Territory, which possesses no power except such as is conferred by Congress. Congress has conferred no such power on Michigan—nor, indeed, could confer it—as it has no authority, under the Constitution, over the subject, except to pass uniform laws of naturalization.

But this is only one of the many objections to the bill before us; and I regret to say, that the friends of the measure have not even attempted to explain the many, and, to my mind, decided objections which have been urged against it. Among others, it leaves open the question of the public lands—to be settled hereafter between Congress and the State, contrary to all past precedents, and at the imminent danger, ultimately, of our rights to the lands within her limits. This is the more remarkable, as an opposite course, I understand, has been adopted in the bill for the admission of Arkansas.

What has caused the distinction? Why has one measure been meted out to the one, and another to the other?

Here let me express my regret that this Bill for the admission of Michigan has been furthered so far ahead of that for the admission of Arkansas. They ought to have progressed together, and both been sent to the House of Representatives at the same time. We all remember the difficulty of admitting Missouri, and ought to be admonished by the example, to use all possible precaution that a similar difficulty may not occur in the instance of Arkansas.

But, I again ask, why not at once settle the question of the public lands in Michigan, as has invariably been done on the admission of other territories? What must be the effect of leaving it open, but to throw the State into the hands of the dominant party, at this critical moment, when the Presidential election is pending? It is a misfortune that the power and influence of the Executive over the new States are so great. Through the medium of the public lands they are ramified in every direction, accompanied by that corruption and subserviency, which are their never failing companions. It is our duty to check, instead of increasing this evil; but, instead of this, we seem to seek every opportunity of increasing its impulse. In the present case, we have placed Michigan in a position calculated to give almost unlimited control to executive influence, as the final arrangement in respect to the public lands (a question of such deep importance to her) must mainly depend on that branch of the Government. Not satisfied with this, we have divested ourselves of the right to determine whether Michigan shall comply with the condition which we are about to prescribe for her admission, and to confer it on the President, with the corresponding diminution of our influence and the increase of his over the State. In our eagerness to divest the

Senate of its power, we propose to go still further. In direct violation of an express provision of the Constitution, which confers on this body the right to judge of the qualifications of its members, this bill provides for the creation of two Senators by law, the first instance of the kind ever attempted since the commencement of the Government.

Such are the leading objections to the bill. There are others of no inconsiderable magnitude. I have never read one, containing more objectionable provisions, submitted to the consideration of Congress. And yet it has been urged with as much precipitancy through the body, as if its provisions were in accordance with those which are usual on such occasions. A trained and despotic majority have resisted every attempt at amendment, and every effort to gain time to reflect on the extraordinary and dangerous provisions which it contains. If there were any reason for this urgency, I would be the last to complain; but none has been assigned, or can be imagined. We all agree that Michigan should be admitted, and are anxious for the admission. I, individually, feel solicitous that the bill should be so modified that I can reconcile it to my conscience and views of expediency to vote for it. For this purpose, I only ask that it shall be put in the usual form; and that the numerous precedents which we have, shall not be departed from. But the majority, as if anxious to force a division, seem obstinately bent on refusing compliance to so reasonable a request.

From Crallé, ed., *Works*, 2:496–509. Variant in the Augusta, Ga., *State Rights' Sentinel*, April 15, 1836, p. 2, and in the Charleston, S.C., *Mercury*, April 20, 1836, p. 2 (both reprinted from the Baltimore, Md., *Chronicle* of unstated date). Another variant in the New York, N.Y., *Morning Courier and New-York Enquirer*, April 4, 1836, p. 2. NOTE: No text similar to the one presented above and existing earlier than Crallé's edition of Calhoun's *Works* has been found. It is not possible to determine where Crallé derived the text, which he gave the title in his table of contents of "Speech on the Power of the States in respect to Aliens." Since no contemporary text has been found, it is possible that the above text was a written elaboration, after the fact, of impromptu remarks made on this day. The Baltimore *Chronicle* report for this date said: "Mr. Calhoun supported the motion [to recommit] in a short speech distinguished by his usual force and thought, and that indignant and somewhat vehement eloquence with which he is accustomed to assail the corruption and unprincipled management of the [Jacksonian] party. He reminded the Senate of the strong objections that had already been dwelt upon by him and others, to the admission of Michigan under present circumstances. She had come into the halls of Congress without knocking at the portal. Her constitution gave to aliens and even to runaway slaves the elective franchise. The last point he urged with extraordinary power and made a powerful appeal to the Southern Senators to unite in stamping on this provision, their decided and indignant reprobation." The issue taken up in this speech in some respects anticipates the Dred Scott case of two decades later. On the same day as the above speech Calhoun "moved to amend the bill by general consent, by inserting a clause providing that the assent of Michigan to this bill shall be given by a convention elected by the free white male citizens of the United States over the age of twenty-one years residing in the said Territory; but the amendment requiring the unanimous consent of the Senate" was defeated by the objection of Silas Wright of N.Y. Porter's motion to recommit failed by a vote of 19 to 24. (*Congressional Globe*, 24th Cong., 1st Sess., p. 313.)

REMARKS ON THE BILL TO PROVIDE FOR THE ADMISSION OF ARKANSAS

[In the Senate, April 2, 1836]
[The Senate, which had just approved the bill making preliminary arrangements for the admission of Mich., took up, on the motion of James Buchanan, the bill for the admission of Ark., which action prompted the following remarks by Calhoun.]

Mr. Calhoun protested against the indecent haste with which, after a most fatiguing and anxious sitting, the measure was pressed, at so late an hour. He denounced in strong terms the iron despotism of the majority. He concluded, by intimating that if he should be forced to vote to-night, he would do so on the faith of his friend from Kentucky, Mr. [John J.] Crittenden, since he had not been allowed time to examine the provisions of the bill. As for the gentlemen of the [Democratic] majority, he regarded them as the very worst authority on this subject that the country could boast of.

[At this point Samuel L. Southard and Thomas Ewing spoke to the same effect.]

Mr. Calhoun [then] put some searching questions to Mr. Buchanan, and boldly declared that the majority could have no motive for their present conduct, but to make two new States available at the coming election for President. It is a part of the "spoils" system of management.

From the Augusta, Ga., *State Rights' Sentinel*, April 15, 1836, p. 2, and the Charleston, S.C., *Mercury*, April 20, 1836, p. 2 (both quoting the Baltimore, Md., *Chronicle* of unstated date). Variant in the Washington, D.C., *United States' Telegraph*, April 5, 1836, p. 3. NOTE: The *Telegraph* reported Calhoun as saying: "Put it off until Monday—force it not through now, amid a darkness and gloom befitting deeds of similar character. Take not advantage of the absence of Senators; wield not the majority to such abominable purposes. We wish to see this bill through, but for the sake of decency put it off until Monday. The Senate weary with sessions of unusual length; members jaded and worn out; the night wasting away; postpone its consideration. . . . I understand it all.

I see the irregular way in which this whole matter has been got up and carried through. I see in it the destruction of our institutions. I can see no other motive in hastening these Territories into States, than to gain them as allies in the contest for President that is approaching." On 3/14 Calhoun had been appointed one of the five members of a select committee on the constitution and government of Arkansas.

To S[AMUEL] D. INGHAM, [New Hope, Pa.?]

Washington, 3d April 1836
My dear Sir, I have read with interest & pleasure your letters from Harrisburgh. That there should ["be" *interlined*] any symptoms of returning health in a State so deeply diseased, as Pennsylvania opens a ray of hope, that the body politick may yet be restored to health. Were it not for the surplus revenue, I would have no small confidence in the ultimate restoration of the Constitution; but as it is, I fear, that before it can be disposed of, the publick mind will have become too much debauched ever to be restored. The surplus now, including our stock in the U[nited] States bank, cannot be much short of $40,000,000; fully half the amount of the debt of the Revolution; and all of which, I fear, is destined to become the means of rewarding partisan services.

There is, I think, no prospect of the passage of Mr. [Henry] Clay's land bill. The whole weight of the administration is concentrated against it; and not a few of the opposition have insuperable constitutional objections, and among others myself. But were it to pass, it could not become a law, as it would certainly be arrested by the veto. As to my proposition to amend the Constitution, I fear the prospect is not less desperate; and even could it pass Congress, it would be too slow for the disease, so rapid has been its progress. I see but one alternative left, to advance the money to the States to be returned whenever the government shall require it, without interest; or in other words, (for such would be the effect) to make the States instead of the State banks the depository of the publick funds. There is I believe, but one difficulty in the way of the measure; the preference, which Mr. Clay and his immediate friends have for his land bill, from the natural feelings of parentage. Were this out of the way, I feel confident, the measure, I have suggested would succeed. I have conversed with him on the subject, and tho' he avows a disposition to support any measure calculated to meet the evil, I can see & feel the resistance of his influence.

137

We are at last in a minority in the Senate. The majority are disposed to exercise their power imperiously; but I doubt, whether they will not find a loss, instead of gain, in their ascendency. They have now the sole responsibility.

Looking to the future, I can see no hope of a complete restoration of our system, till the men of wealth and talents in the North, shall become convinced, that their true interest is to rally on the South & on Southern doctrines. We are the real conservative body, equally opposed to aristocracy and agra[ria]nism. So long as the tendency ["to" *canceled*] at the north was towards the former our natural union was with the ["former" *canceled and* "democracy" *interlined*]; but now that the democracy of the north tends to the ["agrarians side" *canceled and* "agrarianism" *interlined*], our natural union is the other way. The misfortune is that the old Federal party is like the Bourbons. Time stands still with them. But, I think, I see many indications, that among the young men of the party, in fact I wou[l]d say among the young men generally there is the commencement of a sounder state of things. The remark appears to me to be applicable to every part of the country.

I sent you some time since a copy of my remarks [on 3/9] on the question of receiving abolition petition[s]. I hope you have received it, and accord in the views I have taken. I will at all times be happy to hear from you.

Make my kind respects to Mrs. [Deborah Kay Hall] Ingham & the family & believe me to be truely yours & J.C. Calhoun.

ALS in ScU-SC, John C. Calhoun Papers. NOTE: On 12/29/1835 Clay had introduced a bill to provide for distribution among the States of the proceeds of sales of public lands for the period 1833–1837. A similar bill had passed Congress in 1833 and had been the subject of a pocket veto by Jackson.

Remarks on his bill to prevent the circulation of incendiary publications by mail, 4/6. "Mr. Calhoun said the bill assumed as a principle that the right of legislating upon the subject of slavery was confined to the slaveholding States; that Government could not interfere in the matter, but must act in conformity with such State legislation. All it asked of the General Government was, that they should abstain from violating the laws of a State by means of their agents. The bill went no further, and he trusted the Senate would consent to its passage." Calhoun then moved to fill up the first blank in the 2d section with "$100," and the second blank in the same section with "$1,000" (as the minimum and maximum fines to be imposed on deputy postmasters for violations of the law). John Davis of Mass.

expressed a wish that the bill be laid on the table until he was prepared to speak on it, after which the bill was tabled until 4/7. From the Washington, D.C., *Daily National Intelligencer*, April 7, 1836, p. 3. Variant in the Washington, D.C., *Globe*, April 8, 1836, p. 2; *Congressional Globe*, 24th Cong., 1st Sess., p. 325. Another variant in the New York, N.Y., *Morning Courier and New-York Enquirer*, April 8, 1836, p. 2. (Another variant version of Calhoun's remarks, in the Washington, D.C., *United States' Telegraph*, April 7, 1836, p. 3, reads thus: "Mr. Calhoun said the main principle on which the Bill was based, is that the General Government has no power or right whatever to interfere with slavery in the States. He briefly explained the objects of the Bill in its several provisions, and summed them up by saying that its whole design is to require those belonging to the Post Office Department, to obey the laws, on the subject, of the respective States where they reside.")

REMARKS ON THE STATE OF THE CURRENCY

[In the Senate, April 6, 1836]
[Under consideration was the bill making appropriations for payments of Revolutionary and other pensions for 1836. Several amendments had been offered which, with various qualifications, would require payments by the government to be made in specie or in notes convertible to specie at the place where they were paid out.]

Mr. Calhoun doubted whether much if any good could come out of this proposition. He could see nothing in it that could cure the wretched state of the currency. It would be better to draw the fifteen millions of Government money out of these deposite banks, and distribute it where it could be usefully employed. They were using this money without paying any thing for the use of it, and drawing from the Government something like two and a half millions of dollars profit. The administration was responsible for that thoughtless, mischievious [*sic*], and imprudent act, of withdrawing the deposites from the United States Bank, and placing them in these pet banks; notwithstanding they were told that, instead of stopping the evils of banking, these Hydras would spring up like mushrooms. It was amazing to see the majority sitting quietly by, without proposing a remedy to this evil, which was making beggars of thousands, and enriching speculators. These pet banks had an agent by the name of [Reuben M.] Whitney, (Mr. C[alhoun] did not know him,) who had a control over the pecuniary affairs of the country which no other man ever had. He could raise or depress stocks at pleasure. There was an awful responsibility resting on the supporters of the administration. The gulf into which they were rushing was before their eyes. The dreadful explosion was coming. The injury to the manufacturers would be immense. But, he thanked God, it would not be so great to those of the South. If the growing crop should be cut off, no one could tell the state of things it would bring about. Money that had been won by blood was put into public lands, and drawn out to be put into pet banks. Withdraw them (the deposites) from the banks, said he, and if you cannot return them to the people in any other way, loan them without interest. The money of the United States deposited in these irresponsible banks was an annual tax of something like two millions of dollars. He approved of the spirit in which this resolution [*sic*] was offered, but it would not meet the crisis. Let the Senate follow up this resolution with measures that would make this money cease to be banking capital. The Senate would do him justice for predicting, in 1834, that the state of things then would shake the country to its very centre. He could not let the matter pass without warning the Senate and the country of the dangers that threatened the country.

[*Thomas H. Benton here endorsed Calhoun's bill to regulate the public deposits, which was due for consideration soon, and said he would propose various provisions to strengthen the regulation of the deposit banks and to prevent their notes from becoming currency. He was in favor of a specie circulation, but it must be brought about gradually.*]

Mr. Calhoun rose to express his approbation of the measures the Senator from Missouri proposed to introduce, and said he would co-operate in any measures that would prevent the greatest of all calamities to any country, a ruined currency, a state of things which gave the sagacious and cunning man the advantage over the honest laborer.

[*John M. Niles of Conn. then spoke at length, criticizing Calhoun for exaggerated alarm over the evils of the large treasury surplus which was in the deposit banks.*]

Mr. Calhoun, in reply to Mr. Niles, said the gentleman had misunderstood him. His argument was, that the removal of the deposites, and the breaking down of the Bank of the United States, had given rise to innumerable State banks; and not that the surplus would not have accumulated in the Bank of the United States; and that the idea of limiting bank capital by removing the deposites had turned out to be wholly fallacious. But it was the security of the public money to which he had alluded; for he would venture to assert that, if an ensurance was opened, they could not get the public money ensured in the deposite banks, against loss, for a premium of twenty per cent. In the Bank of the United States the public money would have been safe; and, what was more, they would, as stockholders, be drawing an interest of $400,000 for this money, which the deposite banks used without interest. There would have arisen another advantage from leaving the public money in that bank. Had it remained there, there would have been no objection, as now, to the distribution of it among the States, because the Government was in a state of hostility to the bank. President [Andrew] Jackson had twice recommended this measure, and it was surprising to see the facility with which his friends changed their opinions to please him. When he first recommended the distribution, they highly applauded it; the recommendation was eagerly hailed by New York; Pennsylvania followed suit, and the whole party sung hosannas to it; now they were all opposed to it. He saw a great difference in having the public money where it was safe, from having it where it was not safe. Banking capital had increased more than one hundred millions, and he held the administration responsible for it, as well as for all the evils with which they were threatened. He had predicted this state of things again and again, as a consequence of the measures of the administration, but he had not been listened to, and they had proposed no measure to remedy or prevent the evils acknowledged to exist. They came into power in 1830—they saw the public debt was about to be paid—they saw the tariff throwing millions into the treasury which it ought not to have collected; and they recommended no measures to meet these emergencies. Instead of being employed in attending to these objects, they were employed in turning out one Cabinet and putting in another, and regulating social intercourse, declaring who they should visit, and who they should not visit. He held the administration responsible for the existing state of things in regard to the currency, and for converting the public lands, the property of the people, into useless paper.

From *Register of Debates*, 24th Cong., 1st Sess., cols. 1096–1099. Also printed in the Washington, D.C., *Globe*, April 8, 1836, p. 2; *Congressional Globe*, 24th Cong., 1st Sess., pp. 326–327. NOTE: Later in the same day's proceedings, Silas Wright of N.Y. expressed a hope that Calhoun's bill for the regulation of the public deposits would come up for consideration soon, and he presented an amendment (actually a substitute) he would offer to it. Calhoun "expressed his gratification that the gentleman from New York and the Senator from Missouri [Benton] had taken this bill under their protection. They had the power to carry it through, and he was glad that they had it in their charge." (*Register of Debates*, 24th Cong., 1st Sess., col. 1101.)

Remarks on his bill to prohibit the transmission of incendiary publications through the mail, 4/7. John Davis of Mass. delivered a speech opposing the bill as unconstitutional. "Mr. Calhoun said that the Senator from Massachusetts had certainly raised a very important point; and he could not do justice to his argument and to himself, without previously arranging the various points of it. The Senator, however, was mistaken in his view of the subject. It was because the subject particularly belonged to the States, and it was the duty of the general Government to aid and co-operate with them in carrying their laws into effect, that the bill was framed. He ventured to assert that not only did this duty result from the relations between the States and the federal Government, but that it was an indispensable duty. The principle was not a new one; it had been applied more than once; but it was an old principle applied to a new case. He threw out these hints to prevent any erroneous impressions resulting from the remarks of the gentleman from Massachusetts." From *Register of Debates*, 24th Cong., 1st Sess., col. 1108. Also printed in the Washington, D.C., *Globe*, April 9, 1836, p. 2; *Congressional Globe*, 24th Cong., 1st Sess., p. 332. Variant in the Washington, D.C., *United States' Telegraph*, April 8, 1836, p. 3.

Remarks on the Bill to Authorize Mail Contracts with Railroads

[In the Senate, April 7, 1836]
[*Felix Grundy, from the Committee on the Post Office and Post Roads, made a report "on the subject of the bill to authorize contracts with the railroad companies." Thomas Ewing of Ohio moved that 5,000 extra copies of the report be printed so that the public could become informed of the "important matter" which it contained.*]

Mr. Calhoun said that the report was an important one, but he could not but apprehend that it might be difficult to carry out the views which it contained. He feared that the Postmaster General

[Amos Kendall] would derive, as the agent of the Government to contract with these companies, too great an addition to his power, and in this respect the bill could not be too carefully guarded. He had not had sufficient time to turn in his mind the many difficulties which seemed to stand in the way of this plan. Whenever the bill should come before the Senate, he would co-operate heartily in guarding against too much power being given to the Department. He doubted the propriety of printing so large a number. It was often the case that these *ex parte* reports held out flattering prospects, which were doomed to be clouded, and to lead to expectations which were never realized. He hoped there would be a postponement of the question to print the extra number.

[*Grundy assured Calhoun that the bill would confer no new powers on the Postmaster General.*]

Mr. Calhoun said he should be happy to concur in all the provisions of the bill which appeared to him to be practicable; but even in the modified form in which the bill was now presented by the Senator from Tennessee, he saw much difficulty. We are about to make a new movement. We had frequently seen plans which were equally plausible in their appearance, but which finally turned out to be mere fallacies. He was desirous that the motion to print the extra number should be postponed until there had been a little more time allowed for examination into the report.

From *Register of Debates*, 24th Cong., 1st Sess., cols. 1101–1102. Also printed in the Washington, D.C., *Daily National Intelligencer*, April 8, 1836, p. 3. Variant in the Washington, D.C., *Globe*, April 9, 1836, p. 2; *Congressional Globe*, 24th Cong., 1st Sess., p. 331.

Remarks on the bill to grant to the State of Mo. certain lands for the purpose of internal improvement, 4/8. Calhoun "inquired whether the principles contained in this bill were not contained in the bill of the same nature introduced by the Senator from Mississippi [Robert J. Walker]." Walker "replied that the equalising principle was." Calhoun "said that the bill introduced by the Senator from Mississippi had been referred to a select committee, and they ought at least to wait for the report of that committee, before they proceeded further with this bill. He would move, therefore, to lay it on the table." This motion was carried by a vote of 26 to 8. From *Register of Debates*, 24th Cong., 1st Sess., col. 1123. Also printed in the Washington, D.C., *Globe*, April 11, 1836, p. 2; *Congressional Globe*, 24th Cong., 1st Sess., p. 339.

REMARKS ON THE MAINE RESOLUTIONS
ABOUT ABOLITION PUBLICATIONS

[In the Senate, April 8, 1836]

[John Ruggles of Me. presented resolutions passed by the Legislature of Me. in response to resolutions from N.C., S.C., Ga., and Ala. "calling upon the non-slaveholding States to suppress, by law, abolition publications." The Me. resolutions declared that the federal government was one of limited powers and had no authority over slavery in the States, and they deplored interference by the people of one State in the affairs of another. The resolutions further declared that it was "inexpedient to legislate on the subject of abolition publications, because there is no abolition publication printed within the State, and because all discussion on this subject has been arrested by the decided expression of public disapprobation." Ruggles remarked that the resolutions provided an example which he wished to call to the attention of "certain honorable Senators": they passed through the Legislature almost unanimously "without one word of agitating and exciting debate."]

Mr. Calhoun expressed his gratification at the tenor of the resolutions, which he said gave the correct view of the subject in discussion, going back to the good old republican principles. He was also gratified to understand from her Senator that the reasons which induced Maine not to legislate on the subject, were, that no abolition papers were printed in that State, and no discussion of the kind was carried on there. He would now ask the Senator whether there was not an abolition society in Maine, and whether it did not issue addresses that were extensively circulated. He put these questions because he was anxious to give correct information to the South on the subject.

[Ruggles replied that the resolutions justified "the belief that there were now no proceedings relating to abolition in that State, which it was necessary to suppress by law."]

Mr. Calhoun observed, he had put the question because, shortly after his arrival here, he saw a publication, drawn up with great ability, said to be issued by a society calling itself the Maine Abolition Society, having numerous signatures appended to it. Now, he held the existence of such a society to be as dangerous to the South as an abolition newspaper; and he thought if the State could suppress the one, it could suppress the other. He hoped that in time public sentiment would be such at the North as to put down all such societies; but he confessed he was incredulous as to the result. The

Senator from Maine went so far as to cite the example of the legislature of Maine, as worthy to be followed by certain Senators on that floor; meaning, he supp[o]sed, himself for one. He thanked the Senator for his advice, and was, perhaps, so weak-minded as to require it; but he who offered this advice ought to have himself followed the example recommended by him to others. He would tell the Senator, that so long as his constituents sent here denunciations against the people he represented, terming them pirates, murderers, and villains, he should take the liberty to treat such denunciations with the scorn they deserved. He held it to be a solemn truth, that as long as they were compelled to discuss the subject of abolition on petitions received there, the abolitionists had gained all they wanted; and so long as they were permitted to come there he would take the liberty to speak of them in the terms they deserved.

[*Bedford Brown of N.C. praised the resolutions as showing the weakness of abolition sentiment in Me. and remarked that it was impracticable "to expect a State to eradicate every folly or infatuation from the minds of all its citizens." He further remarked that, while the language of the petitions "was bad enough," he did not believe any had used the words "pirates, robbers, and murderers" for the people of the South. Calhoun thereupon asked Thomas Morris of Ohio for the petitions that he had presented and then withdrawn earlier in the session. Morris gave Calhoun some petitions but said he could not consent for them to be used "at that time."*]

Mr. Calhoun said he was utterly astonished at the remarks of the gentleman from North Carolina. These charges were made when the Ohio petitions were presented and read, and in the gentleman's presence. Memory was frail, but he could hardly be mistaken as to the offensive epithets used in the Ohio memorials. Certainly, said he, all remembered that we were charged with dealing in human flesh, an allegation as strong as any he had quoted. The Senator from North Carolina could not rejoice more strongly than himself to see this spirit of abolition arrested, but he feared that it was too strong to be easily subdued.

The feelings, as indicated in these resolutions of the Legislature of Maine, were certainly to be highly commended, and he had taken occasion to express the satisfaction with which he received them. He had thought it, however, right for the people of the South to know that there was an abolition society in Maine, which put forth very able and extensive publications.

[*After further discussion Calhoun again took the floor.*]

Mr. Calhoun was very happy that the Senator from North Carolina [Brown] had at last made up his mind to reject petitions that were such as he would deem offensive in their language; and he hoped that he and all other southern Senators would in time see the propriety of rejecting all abolition petitions, no matter in what language they were couched, for, from the very nature of the subject they treated, they must be offensive to the South.

[*Brown said that the expressions used by Calhoun had not appeared in any petition or Calhoun would have read them to the Senate; instead they had been drawn by inference from the petitions in question. He further asserted that both Senators from S.C. had voted to receive similar petitions in the previous session of Congress.*]

Mr. Calhoun said the Senator from North Carolina certainly did not hear his remarks. The Senator from Ohio (Mr. Morris) had put the petitions in his hands, and suggested to him not to use them. He would now refer to some of the expressions found in one of these petitions; among them was the phrase, "traffic in human flesh," a phrase borrowed from the shambles, from the butchers, holding up to all the world, that the gentleman and his constituents treated human beings as they treated beeves. That was the first. The petition went on to say, that (dealing in slaves) "had been solemnly declared piracy by the laws of our own, and all Christian nations"; assimilating the acts of himself and those whom he represented, with the acts of those who seize Africans on the coast of Africa, and sell them for slaves. If he could lay his hands on the other petitions, he could point out the epithets he had quoted; but those he had given were, he thought, sufficiently offensive to justify a southern representative in voting to reject them. But he would read a little further. "It (slavery) was sinful because it violated the laws of God and man"; "because it (slavery) corrupted the public morals." This was some of the language of the petitions which had been withdrawn to make way for the Quaker petitions which were first tried in order to obtain the sanction of the southern representatives to that most dangerous of all principles, that they were bound to receive petitions, no matter in what language they were drawn. The Senator from North Carolina had mistaken him in supposing he had found nothing in these petitions that was as offensive as he had termed them. The Senator from Ohio, on putting them in his hands, had requested him not to use them at that time.

[*Brown remarked that "he would vote to reject petitions that violated the rules of the Senate, by the use of language indecorous towards individual members of the body or to the body itself." Willie P. Mangum of N.C. chided Brown for being more ready to reject*] *insults to himself than to his constituents and for dividing the South by crying "'all's well,' while the storm was rushing over their heads."*]

Mr. Calhoun rose to say, the Senator from North Carolina (Mr. Brown) was utterly mistaken when he said that he (Mr. C[alhoun]) voted to receive a petition on this subject. No vote of his would be found on the journal. He might have suffered petitions to pass at former sessions, when there was but a few of them presented. He confessed he had neglected this matter too long. The gentleman from North Carolina (Mr. Brown) said he (Mr. C[alhoun]) had not made good his word. He (Mr. C[alhoun]) thought the expressions in the petition to which he had referred were as strong as the terms used by him. It seemed, however, that the Senator cared for nothing but the precise words. He had shown that these petitions likened his constituents to pirates, and spoke of them as dealers in human flesh. This, he thought, was sufficiently strong to make good his position.

From *Register of Debates*, 24th Cong., 1st Sess., cols. 1109–1116. Also printed in the Washington, D.C., *Globe*, April 11, 1836, p. 2; *Congressional Globe*, 24th Cong., 1st Sess., pp. 335–338. Variant in the Washington, D.C., *United States' Telegraph*, April 9, 1836, p. 2, and April 11, 1836, p. 3. Another variant in the New York, N.Y., *Morning Courier and New-York Enquirer*, April 10, 1836, p. 2.

Speech in Reply to Criticisms of the Bill to Prohibit the Circulation of Incendiary Publications through the Mail

[In the Senate, April 12, 1836]

The Senate having resumed consideration of the bill to prohibit the circulation through the mails of incendiary publications,

Mr. Calhoun addressed the Senate:

I am aware (said Mr. C[alhoun]) how offensive it is to speak of one's self; but as the Senator from Georgia on my right (Mr. [John P.] King) has thought proper [in his speech yesterday] to impute to me improper motives, I feel myself compelled, in self-defence, to state the reasons which have governed my course in reference to the subject now under consideration. The Senator is greatley [*sic*] mistaken in supposing that I was governed by hostility to General [Andrew] Jackson. So far is that from being the fact, that I came here at the commencement of the session with fixed and settled principles on the subject now under discussion, and which, in pursuing the course that the Senator condemns, I have but attempted to carry into effect.

As soon as the subject of abolition began to agitate the South last summer, in consequence of the transmission of incendiary publications through the mail, I saw at once that it would force itself on the notice of Congress at the present session; and that it involved questions of great delicacy and difficulty. I immediately turned my attention, in consequence, to the subject, and after due reflection arrived at the conclusion that Congress could exercise no direct power over it, and that, if it acted at all, the only mode in which it could act, consistently with the Constitution and the rights and safety of the slaveholding States, would be in the manner proposed by this bill. I also saw that there was no inconsiderable danger in the excited state of the feelings of the South; that the power, however dangerous and unconstitutional, might be thoughtlessly yielded to Congress, knowing full well how apt the weak and timid are, in a state of excitement and alarm, to seek temporary protection in any quarter, regardless of after consequences, and how ready the artful and designing ever are to seize on such occasions to extend and perpetuate their power.

With these impressions I arrived here at the beginning of the session. The President's message was not calculated to remove my apprehensions. He assumed for Congress direct power over the subject, and that on the broadest, most unqualified, and dangerous principles. Knowing the influence of his name, by reason of his great patronage and the rigid discipline of his party, with a large portion of the country, who have scarcely any other standard of constitution, politics, and morals, I saw the full extent of the danger of having these dangerous principles reduced to practice, and I determined at once to use every effort to prevent it. The Senator from Georgia will, of course, understand that I do not include him in this subservient portion of his party. So far from it, I have always considered him as one of the most independent. It has been our fortune to concur in opinion in relation to most of the important measures which have been agitated since he became a member of this body, two years ago, at the commencement of the session during which the deposite question was agitated. On that important question, if I mistake not, the Senator and myself concurred in opinion, at least as to its inexpediency, and the dangerous consequences to which it would probably lead. If my memory serves me, we also agreed in opinion on the connected subject of the currency, which was then incidentally discussed. We agreed, too, on the question of raising the value of gold to its present standard, and in opposition to the bill for the distribution of the proceeds of the public lands, introduced by the Senator from Kentucky, (Mr. [Henry] Clay). In recurring to the events of that interesting session, I can remember but one important subject on which we disagreed, and that was the President's protest. Passing to the next, I find the same concurrence of opinion on most of the important subjects of the session. We agreed on the question of executive patronage, on the propriety of amending the Constitution for a temporary distribution of the surplus revenue, on the subject of regulating the deposites, and in support of the bill for restricting the power of the Executive in making removals from office. We also agreed in the propriety of establishing branch mints in the South and West—a subject not a little contested at the time.

Even at the present session we have not been so unfortunate as to disagree entirely. We have, it is true, on the question of receiving abolition petitions, which I regret, as I must consider their reception, on the principle on which they were received, as a surrender of the whole ground to the abolitionists, as far as this Government is concerned. It is also true that we disagreed in part in reference to the present subject. The Senator has divided, in relation to it, between myself and General Jackson. He has given his speech in support of his message, and announced his intention of giving his vote in favor of my bill. I certainly have no right to complain of this division. I had rather have his vote than his speech. The one will stand for ever on the records of the Senate (unless expunged) in favor of the bill, and the important principles on which it rests, while the other is destined, at no distant day, to oblivion.

I now put to the Senator from Georgia two short questions. In the numerous and important instances in which we have agreed, I must have been either right or wrong. If right, how could he be so uncharitable as to attribute my course to the low and unworthy motive of inveterate hostility to General Jackson? But if wrong, in what condition does his charge against me place himself, who has concurred with me in all these measures? (Here Mr. King disclaimed the imputation of improper motives to Mr. C[alhoun].) I am glad to hear the gentleman's disclaimer, (said Mr. C[alhoun],) but I certainly understood him as asserting that such was my hostility to General Jackson, that his support of a measure was sufficient to insure my opposition; and this he undertook to illustrate by an anecdote, borrowed from [Daniel?] O'Connell and the pig, which

149

I must tell the Senator was much better suited to the Irish mob to which it was originally addressed, than to the dignity of the Senate, where he has repeated it.

But to return from this long digression. I saw, as I have remarked, that there was reason to apprehend that the principles embraced in the message might be reduced to practice; principles which I believed to be dangerous to the South, and subversive of the liberty of the press. The report fully states what those principles are, but it may not be useless to refer to them briefly on the present occasion.

The message assumed for Congress the right of determining what publications are incendiary, and calculated to excite the slaves to insurrection, and to prohibit the transmission of such publications through the mail; and, of course, it also assumes the right of deciding what are not incendiary, and of enforcing the transmission of such through the mail. But the Senator from Georgia denies this inference, and treats it as a monstrous absurdity. I had (said Mr. C[alhoun]) considered it so nearly intuitive, that I had not supposed it necessary in the report to add any thing in illustration of its truth; but as it has been contested by the Senator, I will add in illustration a single remark.

The Senator will not deny that the right of determining what papers are incendiary, and of preventing their circulation, implies that Congress has jurisdiction over the subject; that is, of discriminating as to what papers ought or ought not to be transmitted by the mail. Nor will he deny that Congress has a right, when acting within its acknowledged jurisdiction, to enforce the execution of its acts; and yet the admission of these unquestionable truths admits the consequence asserted by the report, and so sneered at by the Senator. But, lest he should controvert so plain a deduction, to cut the matter short, I shall propound a plain question to him. He believes that Congress has the right to say what papers are incendiary, and to prohibit their circulation. Now, I ask him if he does not also believe it has the right to enforce the circulation of such as it may determine not to be incendiary, even against the law of Georgia that might prohibit their circulation? If the Senator should answer in the affirmative, I then would prove by his admission the truth of the inference for which I contend, and which he has pronounced to be so absurd; but if he should answer in the negative, and deny that Congress can enforce the circulation against the law of the State, I must tell him he would place himself in the neighborhood of nullification. He would in fact go beyond. The denial would assume the right of nullifying what the Senator himself must, with his views, consider a constitutional act, when nullification only assumes the right of a State to nullify an unconstitutional act.

But the principle of the message goes still farther. It assumes for Congress jurisdiction over the liberty of the press. The framers of the Constitution (or rather those jealous patriots who refused to consent to its adoption without amendments to guard against the abuse of power) have, by the first amended article, provided that Congress shall pass no law abridging the liberty of the press, with the view of placing the press beyond the control of congressional legislation. But this cautious foresight would prove in vain, if we should concede to Congress the power which the President assumes of discriminating in reference to character, what publications shall not be transmitted by the mail. It would place in the hands of the general Government an instrument more potent to control the freedom of the press than the sedition law itself, as is fully established in the report.

Thus regarding the message, the question which presented itself on its first perusal was, how to prevent powers so dangerous and unconstitutional from being carried into practice. To permit the portion of the message relating to the subject under consideration to take its regular course, and be referred to the Committee on the Post Office and Post Roads, would, I saw, be the most certain way to defeat what I had in view. I could not doubt, from the composition of the committee, that the report would coincide with the message, and that it would be drawn up with all that tact, ingenuity, and address, for which the chairman of the committee [Felix Grundy] and the head of the Post Office Department [Amos Kendall] are not a little distinguished. With this impression, I could not but apprehend that the authority of the President, backed by such a report, would go far to rivet in the public mind the dangerous principles which it was my design to defeat, and which could only be effected by referring the portion of the message in question to a select committee, by which the subject might be thoroughly investigated, and the result presented in a report. With this view I moved the committee, and the bill and report, which the Senator has attacked so violently, are the result.

These are the reasons which governed me in the course I took, and not the base and unworthy motive of hostility to General Jackson. I appeal with confidence to my life to prove that neither hostility nor attachment to any man or any party can influence me in the discharge of my public duties; but were I capable of being influenced by such motives, I must tell the Senator from Georgia that I have too little regard for the opinion of General Jackson, and, were it not for his high station, I would add, his character too, to permit his course to influence me in the slightest degree, either for or against any measure.

Having now assigned the motives which governed me, it is with satisfaction I add that I have a fair prospect of success. So entirely are the principles of the message abandoned, that not a friend of the President has ventured, and I hazard nothing in saying will venture, to assert them practically, whatever they may venture to do in argument. They well know now that, since the subject has been investigated, a bill to carry into effect the recommendation of the message would receive no support, even from the ranks of the administration, devoted as they are to their chieftain.

The Senator from Georgia made other objections to the report besides those which I have thus incidentally noticed, to which I do not deem it necessary to reply. I am content with his vote, and cheerfully leave the report and his speech to abide their fate, with a brief notice of a single objection.

The Senator charges me with what he considers a strange and unaccountable contradiction. He says that the freedom of the press, and the right of petition, are both secured by the same article of the Constitution, and both stand on the same principle; and yet I, who decidedly opposed the receiving of abolition petitions, now as decidedly support the liberty of the press. To make out the contradiction, he assumes that the Constitution places the right of petitioners to have their petitions received, and the liberty of the press, on the same ground. I do not deem it necessary to show that in this he is entirely mistaken, and that my course on both occasions is perfectly consistent. I take the Senator at his word, and put to him a question for his decision. If, in opposing the receiving of the abolition petitions, and advocating the freedom of the press, I have involved myself in a palpable contradiction, how can he escape a similar charge, when his course was the reverse of mine on both occasions? Does he not see that, if mine be contradictory, as he supposes, his, too, must necessarily be so? But the Senator forgets his own argument, of which I must remind him, in order to relieve him from the awkward dilemma in which he has placed himself in his eagerness to fix on me the charge of contradiction. He seems not to recollect that, in his speech on receiving the abolition petitions, he was compelled to abandon the Constitution, and to place the right, not on that instrument, as he would now have us believe, but expressly on the ground that the right existed anterior to the Constitution, and that we must look for its limits, not to the Constitution, but to the *magna charta* and the declaration of rights.

Having now concluded what I intended to say in reply to the Senator from Georgia, I now turn to the objections [in his speech on 4/7] of the Senator from Massachusetts (Mr. [John] Davis,) which were directed, not against the report, but the bill itself. The Senator confined his objections to the principles of the bill, which he pronounces dangerous and unconstitutional. It is my wish to meet his objections fully, fairly, and directly. For this purpose, it will be necessary to have an accurate and clear conception of the principles of the bill, as it is impossible without it to estimate correctly the force either of the objections or the reply. I am thus constrained to restate what the principles are, at the hazard of being considered somewhat tedious.

The first and leading principle is, that the subject of slavery is under the sole and exclusive control of the States where the institution exists. It belongs to them to determine what may endanger its existence, and when and how it may be defended. In the exercise of this right, they may prohibit the introduction or circulation of any paper or publication which may, in their opinion, disturb or endanger the institution. Thus far all are agreed. To this extent no one has questioned the right of the States; not even the Senator from Massachusetts, in his numerous objections to the bill.

The next and remaining principle of the bill is intimately connected with the preceding; and, in fact, springs directly from it. It assumes that it is the duty of the general Government, in the exercise of its delegated rights, to respect the laws which the slaveholding States may pass in protection of its institutions; or, to express it differently, it is its duty to pass such laws as may be necessary to make it obligatory on its officers and agents to abstain from violating the laws of the States, and to co-operate, as far as it may consistently be done, in their execution. It is against this principle that the objections of the Senator from Massachusetts have been directed, and to which I now proceed to reply.

His first objection is, that the principle is new; by which I understand him to mean that it never has heretofore been acted on by the Government. The objection presents two questions: is it true, in point of fact; and, if so, what weight or force properly belongs to it? If I am not greatly mistaken, it will be found wanting in both particulars; and that, so far from being new, it has been frequently acted on; and that, if it were new, the fact would have little or no force.

If our Government had been in operation for centuries, and had been exposed to the various changes and trials to which political institutions, in a long-protracted existence, are exposed in the vicissitudes of events, the objection, under such circumstances, that a principle had never been acted upon, if not decisive, would be exceedingly strong; but when made in reference to our Government, which has been in operation for less than half a century, and which is so complex and novel in its structure, it is very feeble. We all know that new principles are daily developing themselves under our system, with the changing condition of the country, and doubtless will long continue so to do, in the new and trying scenes through which we are destined to pass. It may, I admit, be good reason, even with us, for caution—for thorough and careful investigation, if a principle proposed to be acted upon be new; for I have long since been taught by experience that whatever is untried is to be received with caution in politics, however plausible. But to go further, in this early stage of our political existence, would be to deprive ourselves of means that might be indispensable to meet future dangers and difficulties.

But I take higher grounds in reply to the objection. I deny its truth in point of fact, and assert that the principle is not new. The report refers to two instances in which it has been acted on, and to which for the present I shall confine myself: one in reference to the quarantine laws of the States, and the other more directly connected with the subject of this bill. I propose to make a few remarks in reference to both, beginning with the former, with the view of showing that the principle, in both cases, is strictly analogous, or, rather, identical with the present.

The health of the State, like that of the subject of slavery, belongs exclusively to the State. It is reserved, and not delegated; and, of course, each State has a right to judge for itself what may endanger the health of its citizens, what measures are necessary to prevent it, and when and how such measures are to be carried into effect. Among the causes which may endanger the health of a State is the introduction of infectious or contagious diseases, through the medium of commerce. The vessel returning with a rich cargo, in exchange for the products of a State, may also come freighted with the seeds of disease and death. To guard against this danger, the States, at a very early period, adopted quarantine or health laws. These laws, it is obvious, must necessarily interfere with the power of Congress to regulate commerce—a power as expressly given as that to regulate the mail, and, as far as the present question is concerned, every way analogous; and, acting accordingly, on the principles of this bill, Congress, as far back as the year 1796, passed an act making it the duty of its civil and military officers to abstain from the violation of the health laws of the States, and to co-operate in their execution. This act was modified and repealed by that of 1799, which has since remained unchanged on the statute book.

But the other precedent referred to in the report is still more direct and important. That case, like the present, involved the right of the slaveholding States to adopt such measures as they may think proper, to prevent their domestic institutions from being disturbed or endangered. They may be endangered, not only by introducing and circulating inflammatory publications, calculated to excite insurrection, but also by the introduction of free people of color from abroad, who may come as emissaries, or with opinions and sentiments hostile to the peace and security of those States. The right of a State to pass laws to prevent danger from publications is not more clear than the right to pass those which may be necessary to guard against this danger. The act of 1803, to which the report refers as a precedent, recognises this right to the fullest extent. It was intended to sustain the laws of the States against the introduction of free people of color from the West India Islands. The Senator from Massachusetts, in his remarks upon this precedent, supposes the law to have been passed under the power given to Congress by the Constitution to suppress the slave trade. I have turned to the journals in order to ascertain the facts, and find that the Senator is entirely mistaken. The law was passed on a memorial of the citizens of Wilmington, North Carolina, and originated in the following facts:

After the successful rebellion of the slaves of St. Domingo, and the expulsion of the French power, the Government of the other French West India islands, in order to guard against the danger from the example of St. Domingo, adopted rigid measures to expel and send out their free blacks. In 1803, a brig, having [on board] five persons of that description who were driven from Guadaloupe, arrived at Wilmington. The alarm which this caused gave birth to the memorial, and the memorial to the act.

I learn from the journals that the subject was fully investigated and discussed in both Houses, and that it passed by a very large majority. The first section of the bill prevents the introduction of any negro, mulatto, or mustee, into any State by the laws of which they are prevented from being introduced, except persons of the description from beyond the Cape of Good Hope, or registered seamen, or natives of the United States. The second section prohibits the entry of vessels having such persons on board, and subjects the vessels to seizure and forfeiture for landing or attempting to land them, contrary to the laws of the States; and the third and last section makes it the duty of the officers of the general Government to co-operate with the States in the execution of their laws against their introduction. I consider this precedent to be one of vast importance to the slaveholding States. It not only recognises the right of those States to pass such laws as they may deem necessary to protect themselves against the slave population, and the duty of the general Government to respect those laws, but also the very important right, that the States have the authority to exclude the introduction of such persons as may be dangerous to their institutions —a principle of great extent and importance, and applicable to other States as well as slaveholding, and to other persons as well as blacks, and which may hereafter occupy a prominent place in the history of our legislation.

Having now, I trust, fully and successfully replied to the first objection of the Senator from Massachusetts, by showing that it is not true, in fact, and, if it were, that it would have little or no force, I shall now proceed to reply to the second objection, which assumes that the principles for which I contend would, if admitted, transfer the power over the mail from the general Government to the States.

If the objection be well founded, it must prove fatal to the bill. The power over the mail is, beyond all doubt, a delegated power; and whatever would divest the Government of this power, and transfer it to the States, would certainly be a violation of the Constitution. But would the principle, if acted on, transfer the power? If admitted to its full extent, its only effect would be to make it the duty of Congress, in the exercise of its power over the mail, to abstain from violating the laws of the State in protection of their slave property, and to co-operate, where it could with propriety, in their execution. Its utmost effect would then be a modification, and not a transfer or destruction of the power; and surely the Senator will not contend, that to modify a right amounts either to its transfer or annihilation. He cannot forget that all rights are subject to modification, and all, from the highest to the lowest, are held under one universal condition—that their possessors should so use them as not to injure others. Nor can he contend that the power of the general Government over the mail is without modification or limitation. He himself admits that it is subject to a very important modification, when he concedes that the Government cannot discriminate in reference to the character of the publications to be transmitted by the mail, without violating the first amended article of the Constitution, which prohibits Congress from passing laws abridging the liberty of the press. Other modifications of the right might be shown to exist, not less clear, nor of much less importance. It might be easily shown, for instance, that the power over the mail is limited to the transmission of intelligence, and that Congress cannot, consistently with the nature and the object of the power, extend it to the ordinary objects of transportation, without a manifest violation of the Constitution, and the assumption of a principle which would give the Government control over the general transportation of the country, both by land and water. But, if it be subject to these modifications, without either annihilating or transferring the power, why should the modification for which I contend, and which I shall show hereafter to rest upon unquestionable principles, have such effect? That it would not, in fact, might be shown, if other proof were necessary, by a reference to the practical operation of the principle in the two instances already referred to. In both, the principle which I contend for in relation to the mail has long been in operation in reference to commerce, without the transfer of the power of Congress to regulate commerce to the States, which the Senator contends would be its effect if applied to the mail. So far otherwise, so little has it affected the power of Congress to regulate the commerce of the country, that few persons, comparatively, are aware that the principle has been recognised and acted on by the general Government.

I come next (said Mr. Calhoun) to what the Senator seemed to rely upon as his main objection. He stated that the principles asserted in the report were contradicted by the bill, and that the latter undertakes to do indirectly what the former asserts that the general Government cannot do at all.

Admit (said Mr. C[alhoun]) the objection to be true in fact, and what does it prove, but that the author of the report is a bad logician, and there is error somewhere, but without proving that it is in the bill, and that it ought therefore to be rejected, as the Senator contends? If there be error, it may be in the report instead of the bill; and till the Senator can fix it on the latter, he cannot avail himself of the objection. But does the contradiction which he alleges exist? Let us turn to the principles asserted in the report, and compare them with those of the bill, in order to determine this point.

What, then, are the principles which the report maintains? It asserts that Congress has no right to determine what papers are incendiary, and calculated to excite insurrection, and as such to prohibit their circulation; but, on the contrary, that it belongs to the States to determine on the character and tendency of such publications, and to adopt such measures as they may think proper to prevent their introduction or circulation. Does the bill deny any of these principles? Does it not assume them all? Is it not drawn up on the supposition that the general Government have none of the powers denied by the report, and that the States possess all for which it contends? How, then, can it be said that the bill contradicts the report? But the difficulty, it seems, is, that the general Government would do through the States, under the provisions of the bill, what the report denies that it can do directly; and this, according to the Senator from Georgia, is so manifest and palpable a contradiction, that he can find no explanation for my conduct but an inveterate hostility to General Jackson, which he is pleased to attribute to me.

I have, I trust, successfully repelled already the imputation, and it now remains to show that the gross and palpable errors, which the Senator perceives, exist only in his own imagination; and that, instead of the cause he supposes, it originates, on his part, in a dangerous and fundamental misconception of the nature of our political system—particularly of the relation between the States and general Government. Were the States the agents of the general Government, as the objection clearly presupposes, then what he says would be true, and the Government, in recognising the laws of the States, would adopt the acts of its agents. But the fact is far otherwise. The general Government and the Governments of the States are distinct and independent departments in our complex political system. The States, in passing laws in protection of their domestic institutions, act in a sphere as independent as the general Government passing laws in regulation of the mail; and the latter, in abstaining from violating the laws of the States, as provided for in the bill, so far from making the States its agents, but recognises the right of the States, and performs on its part a corresponding duty. Rights and duties are in their nature reciprocal. The existence of one presupposes that of the other, and the performance of the duty, so far from denying the right, distinctly recognises its existence. The Senator, for example, next to me, (Mr. [Hugh L.] White,) has the unquestionable right to the occupation of his chair; and I am of course in duty bound to abstain from violating that right; but would it not be absurd to say that, in performing that duty, by abstaining from violating his right, I assume the right of occupation? Again: suppose the very quiet and peaceable Senator from Maine (Mr. [Ether] Shepley,) who is his next neighbor on the other side, should undertake to oust the Senator from Tennessee, would it not be strange doctrine to contend that, if I were to co-operate with the Senator from Tennessee in maintaining possession of his chair, it would be an assumption on my part of a right to the chair? And yet this is the identical principle which the Senator from Georgia assumed, in charging a manifest and palpable contradiction between the bill and the report.

But to proceed with the objections of the Senator from Massachusetts. He asserts, and asserts truly, that rights and duties are reciprocal; and that if it be the duty of the general Government to respect the laws of the States, it is in like manner the duty of the States to respect those of the general Government. The practice of both has been in conformity to the principle. I have already cited instances of the general Government respecting the laws of the States, and many might be shown of the States respecting those of the general Government.

But the Senator from Massachusetts affirms that the laws of the general Government regulating the mail, and those of the Governments of the States prohibiting the introduction and circulation of incendiary publications, may come into conflict, and that in such event the latter must yield to the former; and he rests this assertion on the ground that the power of the general Government is expressly delegated by the Constitution. I regard the arguments wholly inconclusive. Why should the mere fact that a power is expressly delegated give it paramount control over the reserved powers? What possible superiority can the mere fact of delegation give, unless, indeed, it be supposed to render the right more clear, and, of course, less questionable? Now, I deny that it has in this instance any such superiority. Though the power of the general Government over the mail is delegated, it is not more clear and unquestionable than the rights of the States over the subject of slavery—a right which neither has been nor can be denied. In fact, I might take higher grounds, if higher grounds were possible, by showing that the rights of the States are as expressly reserved as those of the general Government are delegated; for, in order to place the reserved rights beyond controversy, the tenth amended article of the Constitution expressly provides that all powers not delegated to the United States by the Constitution, nor prohibited by it to the States, are reserved to the States, respectively, or to the people; and as the subject of slavery is acknowledged by all not to be delegated, it may be fairly considered as expressly reserved under this provision of the Constitution.

But while I deny his conclusion, I agree with the Senator that the laws of the States and general Government may come into conflict, and that, if they do, one or the other must yield. The question is, which ought to yield? The question is one of great importance. It involves the whole merit of the controversy, and I must entreat the Senate to give me an attentive hearing while I state my views in relation to it.

In order to determine satisfactorily which ought to yield, it becomes necessary to have a clear and full understanding of the point of difficulty; and for this purpose, it is necessary to make a few preliminary remarks.

Properly considered, the reserved and delegated powers can never come into conflict. The fact that a power is delegated, is conclusive that it is not reserved; and that it is not delegated, that it is reserved, unless, indeed, it be prohibited to the States. There is but a single exception: the case of powers of such nature that they be exercised concurringly by the State and general Governments—such as the power of laying taxes, which, though delegated, may also be exercised by the States. In illustration of the truth of the position I have laid down, I might refer to the case now under consideration. Regarded in the abstract, there is not the slightest conflict between the power delegated by the Constitution to the general Government to establish post offices and post roads, and that reserved to the States over the subject of slavery. How, then, can there be conflict? It occurs not between the powers themselves, but the laws respectively passed to carry them into effect. The laws of the State, prohibiting the introduction or circulation of incendiary publications, may come into conflict with the laws of the general Government in relation to the mail; and the question to be determined is, which, in the event, ought to give way?

I will not pretend to enter into a full and systematic investigation of this highly important question, which involves, as I have said, the merits of the whole controversy. I do not deem it necessary. I propose to lay down a single principle, which I hold to be not only unquestionable, but decisive of the question, as far as the present controversy is concerned. My position is, that, in deciding which ought to yield, regard must be had to the nature and magnitude of the powers to which the laws respecting it relate. The low must yield to the high; the convenient to the necessary; mere accommodation to safety and security. This is the universal principle which governs in all analogous cases, both in our social and political relations. Wherever the means of enjoying or securing rights come into conflict, (rights themselves never can,) this universal and fundamental principle is the one which, by the consent of mankind, governs in all such cases. Apply it to the case under consideration, and need I ask which ought to yield? Will any rational being say that the laws of the States of this Union, which are necessary to their peace, security, and very existence, ought to yield to the laws of the general Government regulating the Post Office, which at best is a mere accommodation and convenience, and this when this Government was formed *by the States* mainly with a view to secure more perfectly their peace and safety? But one answer can be given. All must feel that it would be improper for the laws of eleven States in such case to yield to those of the general Government, and, of course, that the latter ought to yield to the former. When I say *ought*, I do not mean on the principle of concession. I take higher grounds. I mean under the obligation of the Constitution itself. That instrument does not leave this important question to be decided by mere inference. It contains an express provision which is decisive of the question. I refer to the provision which invests Congress with the power of passing laws to carry into effect the granted powers, and which expressly restricts its power to laws necessary and proper to carry into effect the delegated powers. We here have the limitation on the power of passing laws. They must be necessary and proper. I pass the term *necessary* with the single remark, that whatever may be its true and accurate meaning, it clearly indicates that this important power was sparingly granted by the framers of the Constitution. I come to the term *proper*; and I boldly assert, if it has any meaning at all, if it can be said of any law whatever that it is not proper, and that, as such, Congress has no constitutional right to pass it, surely it may be said of that which would abrogate, in fact, the laws of nearly half of the States of the Union, and which are conceded to be necessary for their peace and safety. If it be proper for Congress to pass such a law, what law could possibly be improper? We have heard much of late of States' rights. All parties profess to respect them, as essential to the preservation of our liberty. I do not except the members of the old federal[ist] party—that honest, high-minded, patriotic party, though mistaken as to the principles and tendency of the Government. But what, let me ask, would be the value of the States' rights, if the laws of Congress in such cases ought not to yield to the States? If they must be considered paramount, whenever they come into conflict with those of the States, without regard to their safety, what possible value can be attached to the rights of the States, and how perfectly unmeaning their reserved powers? Surrender the principle, and there is not one of the reserved powers which may not be annulled by Congress under the pretext of passing laws to carry into effect the delegated powers.

The Senator from Massachusetts next objects that if the principles of the bill be admitted, they may be extended to morals and religion. I do not feel bound to admit or deny the truth of this assertion; but if the Senator will show me a case in which a State has passed laws, under its unquestionable reserved powers, in protection of its morality or religion, I would hold it to be the duty of the general Government to respect the laws of the States in conformity to the principles which I maintained.

His next objection is, that the bill is a manifest violation of the liberty of the press. He has not thought proper to specify wherein the violation consists. Does he mean to say that the laws of the States prohibiting the introduction and circulation of papers calculated to excite insurrection are in violation of the liberty of the press? Does he mean that the slaveholding States have no right to pass such laws? I cannot suppose such to be his meaning; for I understood him throughout his remarks to admit the right of the States—a right which they have always exercised, without restriction or limitation, before and since the adoption of the Constitution, without ever having been questioned. But if this be not his meaning, he must mean that this bill, in making it the duty of the officers and agents of the Government to respect the laws of the States, violates the liberty of the press, and thus involves the old misconception, that the States are the agents of this Government, which pervades the whole argument of the Senator, and to which I have already replied.

The Senator next objects that the bill makes it penal on deputy postmasters to receive the papers and publications which it embraces. I must say that my friend from Massachusetts (for such

I consider him, though we differ in politics) has not expressed himself with his usual accuracy on the present occasion. If he will turn to the provisions of the bill, he will find that the penalty attaches only in cases of knowingly receiving and delivering out the papers and publications in question. All the consequences which the Senator drew from the view which he took of the bill of course fall, and thus relieve me from the necessity of showing that the deputy postmasters will not be compelled to resort to the espionage into letters and packages in order to exonerate themselves from the penalty of the bill, which he supposed.

The last objection of the Senator is, that under the provision of the bill every thing touching on the subject of slavery will be prohibited from passing through the mail. I again must repeat that the Senator has not expressed himself with sufficient accuracy. The provisions of the bill are limited to the transmission of such papers in reference to slavery as are prohibited by the laws of the slaveholding States; that is, by eleven States of the Union, leaving the circulation through the mail without restriction or qualification as to all other papers, and wholly so as to the remaining thirteen States. But the Senator seems to think that even this restriction, as limited as it is, would be a very great inconvenience. It may, indeed, prove so to the lawless abolitionists, who, without regard to the obligations of the Constitution, are attempting to scatter their firebrands throughout the Union. But is their convenience the only thing to be taken into the estimate? Are the peace, security, and safety of the slaveholding States nothing? Or are these to be sacrificed for the accommodation of the abolitionists?

I have now replied, directly, fully, and, I trust, successfully, to the objections to the bill; and shall close what I intended to say by a few general and brief remarks.

We have arrived at a new and important point in reference to the abolition question. It is no longer in the hands of quiet and peaceful, but I cannot add harmless, Quakers. It is now under the control of ferocious zealots, blinded by fanaticism, and in the pursuit of their object, regardless of the obligations of religion or morality. They are organized throughout every section of the nonslaveholding States; they have the disposition of almost unlimited funds, and are in possession of a powerful press, which, for the first time, is enlisted in the cause of abolition, and turned against the domestic institutions and the peace and security of the South. To guard against the danger in this new and more menacing form, the slaveholding States will be compelled to revise their laws against the introduction and circulation of publications calculated to disturb their peace and to endanger their security, and to render them far more full and efficient than they have heretofore been. In this new state of things, the probable conflict between the laws which those States may think proper to adopt, and those of the general Government regulating the mail, becomes far more important than at any former state of the controversy; and Congress is now called upon to say what part it will take in reference to this deeply interesting subject. We of the slaveholding States ask nothing of the Government, but that it should abstain from violating laws passed within our acknowledged constitutional competency and conceded to be essential to our peace and security. I am anxious to see how this question will be decided. I am desirous that my constituents should know what they have to expect, either from this Government or from the non-slaveholding States. Much that I have said and done during the session has been with the view of affording them correct information on this point, in order that they might know to what extent they might rely upon others, and how far they must depend on themselves.

Thus far (I say it with regret) our just hopes have not been realized. The Legislatures of the South, backed by the voice of their constituents expressed through innumerable meetings, have called upon the non-slaveholding States to repress the movements made within the jurisdiction of those States against their peace and security. Not a step has been taken; not a law has been passed, or even proposed; and I venture to assert that none will be; not but what there is a favorable disposition towards us in the North, but I clearly see the state of political parties there presents insuperable impediments to any legislation on the subject. I rest my opinion on the fact that the non-slaveholding States, from the elements of their population, are, and will continue to be, divided and distracted by parties of nearly equal strength; and that each will always be ready to seize on every movement of the other which may give them the superiority, without much regard to consequences, as affecting their own States, and much less, remote and distant sections.

Nor have we been less disappointed as to the proceedings of Congress. Believing that the general Government has no right or authority over the subject of slavery, we had just grounds to hope Congress would refuse all jurisdiction in reference to it, in whatever form it might be presented. The very opposite course has been pursued. Abolition petitions have not only been received in both Houses, but received on the most obnoxious and dangerous of all grounds—that we are bound to receive them; that is, to take jurisdiction of the question of slavery whenever the abolitionists may think proper to petition for its abolition, either here [in the District of Columbia] or in the States.

Thus far, then, we of the slaveholding States have been grievously disappointed. One question still remains to be decided that is presented by this bill. To refuse to pass this bill would be virtually to co-operate with the abolitionists—would be to make the officers and agents of the Post Office Department in effect their agents and abettors in the circulation of their incendiary publications, in violation of the laws of the States. It is your unquestionable duty, as I have demonstrably proved, to abstain from their violation; and by refusing or neglecting to discharge that duty, you would clearly enlist, in the existing controversy, on the side of the abolitionists against the Southern States. Should such be your decision, by refusing to pass this bill, I shall say to the people of the South, look to yourselves—you have nothing to hope from others. But I must tell the Senate, be your decision what it may, the South will never abandon the principles of this bill. If you refuse co-operation with our laws, and conflict should ensue between your and our law, the southern States will never yield to the superiority of yours. We have a remedy in our hands, which, in such event, we shall not fail to apply. We have high authority for asserting, that, in such cases, "State interposition is the rightful remedy"—a doctrine first announced by [Thomas] Jefferson—adopted by the patriotic and republican State of Kentucky by a solemn resolution, in 1798, and finally carried out into successful practice on a recent occasion, ever to be remembered, by the gallant State which I, in part, have the honor to represent. In this well-tested and efficient remedy, sustained by the principles developed in the report and asserted in this bill, the slaveholding States have an ample protection. Let it be fixed, let it be riveted in every southern mind, that the laws of the slaveholding States for the protection of their domestic institutions are paramount to the laws of the general Government in regulation of commerce and the mail, and that the latter must yield to the former in the event of conflict; and that, if the Government should refuse to yield, the States have a right to interpose, and we are safe. With these principles, nothing but concert would be wanting to bid defiance to the movements of the abolitionists, whether at home or abroad, and to place our domestic institutions, and, with them, our security and peace, under our own protection, and beyond the reach of danger.

From *Register of Debates*, 24th Cong., 1st Sess., cols. 1136–1148. Also printed in the Washington, D.C., *United States' Telegraph*, April 25, 1836, p. 2; the Washington, D.C., *Daily National Intelligencer*, May 28, 1836, p. 2; *Speech of the Hon. J.C. Calhoun, of South Carolina, on the Bill to Prohibit Deputy Post Masters from Receiving and Transmitting through the Mail to Any State, Territory, or District, Certain Papers therein Mentioned, the Circulation of Which Is Prohibited by the Laws of Said State, Territory, or District. Delivered in the Senate, April 12, 1836* (Washington: no publisher, 1836); *Speeches of John C. Calhoun*, pp. 210–222. Slightly variant version in Crallé, ed., *Works*, 2:509–533. Variant in the Washington, D.C., *Globe*, April 14, 1836, p. 3; the Charleston, S.C., *Mercury* (reprinted from the New York *Commercial Advertiser* of unstated date), April 30, 1836, p. 2; *Congressional Globe*, 24th Cong., 1st Sess., pp. 347–348.

Further Remarks on the Bill to Prohibit the Circulation of Incendiary Publications through the Mail

[In the Senate, April 13, 1836]

[*Four Senators spoke on the bill, including Felix Grundy of Tenn. who asked Calhoun's consent to postpone consideration of the bill for a few days "so that gentlemen might turn their attention particularly to it, and, if it did not suit them, to offer them such a bill as they could support."*]

Mr. Calhoun said that, in bringing this subject before the Senate, he had done his duty. He had brought it before them with the aid of the special committee appointed for that purpose, and it depended on them whether it should pass. All he asked was, that there should be a final vote on this subject; and this was due to those he represented, that they might distinctly know whether there was a power in this Government to arrest the evil that all acknowledged to exist; and if there be such a power, whether there was a disposition to exercise it for the remedy of that evil. The attacks of these incendiaries was [sic] through the mails, using the press as an auxiliary. This was an acknowledged evil, and the question was, had they the power to arrest it? If we have no power (said Mr. C[alhoun],) let us say so at once; but if we have the power, let us understand the extent of it, and why this power is not exercised. Let this

166

(said he) be told to our constituents. Let it be told to them, if the mere convenience or inconvenience of the mails is considered of more importance than their existence. He had done his duty, and the responsibility now rested on the majority. He could not but be surprised at the course of the friends of the Executive [Andrew Jackson]. He had heard Senators denounce this measure, recommended by the Executive, as unconstitutional, as tyrannical, or an abuse of power, who never before dared whisper a word against the Administration. What was he to understand from this? Was it because the present Executive was going out of power, that his influence was declining? Was he to understand from this, that it was now for the first time discovered that the man who never erred had committed the most monstrous errors, recommending an abridgement of the liberty of the press and a tyrannical espionage over the post office? The very thing they denounced as proposed to be done by Congress, was now informally done by one branch of this Administration. They all knew that many of the postmasters at the North, and all of the postmasters at the South, had refused to receive these incendiary publications for transmission through the mails; yet this bill, giving the authority of law to that which was now done without authority, was denounced by Administration members as a most tyrannical abuse of power, while they did not raise a whisper against those officers of the Administration who now exercise this power.

He must express his surprise, that gentlemen who now denounced this measure, which was to legalize what had been done without authority, had sat there silent during the whole session, knowing that what they deemed such an unconstitutional abuse of power was carried on. Why did they not introduce a resolution to inquire into these abuses? Why did they not denounce them at first, instead of waiting until the action of Congress was proposed? There was a strange disease in the public mind. They permitted the Executive to do without censure what they refused to permit Congress to do. If the Executive trampled on the laws and Constitution, not a word was said; but when Congress came to legalize what the Executive had done, and to do what he had recommended, then the liberty of the press was assaulted and the Constitution violated. Mr. C[alhoun] here referred to the President's protest, and to the removal of the deposits, citing them as abuses of power, and spoke of the deposit banks as being a greater evil than the Bank of the United States.

[*Grundy said that administration supporters were free to vote as they pleased on issues and indicated that he also wished for a "final action" during the present session on the subject of abolition publications.*]

Mr. Calhoun said the Senator from Tennessee (Mr. Grundy) was much mistaken in supposing he reflected any censure upon him as an Administration man. The President himself had given his recommendation, going much further in this matter than he had. The gentleman was correct in saying that, in the general range of party discipline, they reserved the right to act for themselves; but he saw in this House men who, by raising their finger, could make this a party question. It was his opinion that they made nothing a party question that was not connected with the spoils. The same party had been brought to bear on the expunging resolution, the deposit question, the surplus funds, and which had kept those funds where they now were, in the hands of speculators, who were to be brought to bear on the people. That power was brought to bear on the spoils; and although the Senator from Connecticut (Mr. [John M.] Niles) had dissented in this case, he would have found it a little hazardous to have went against the executive recommendation in regard to the removal of the deposits, or the recharter of the United States Bank. The Senator from Tennessee (Mr. Grundy) had put Tuesday as the day to postpone the bill to. That Senator and himself agreed in the general. They had had conversations respecting the bill, and his remarks were not intended to apply to him; but he feared that the bill, having grown out of the subject of the executive message, might take a part of the Administration from its support.

[*Grundy said that "it was hard that the Senator from South Carolina and himself could not get along when they agreed."*]

Mr. Calhoun said that his remarks had no application to the Senator from Tennessee, whom he knew, from frequent conversations with him, was in favor of the principles of the bill.

[*Grundy continued, followed by Alfred Cuthbert of Ga. who regretted that "southern rights might be injuriously affected" by Calhoun's repeated references to the party motives of administration Senators.*]

Mr. Calhoun touched those topics because he knew there was a potent power in this Government, and when he heard the opposition coming from the quarter it did this morning, he confessed he thought it withdrawn from this bill. He differed from the Senator from Georgia (Mr. Cuthbert) in adverting to the responsibility of the majority in regard to this matter. It was salutary to bring public attention to it. He was sorry to see the Senator from Tennessee (Mr. Grundy) employ his wit in so grave and solemn a question. He must say his wit was good and his reasons feeble. He alluded to the power invested in the Government by its patronage, and the immense amount of money at its disposal, and its control of the press. All he asked was that the Executive should keep the people in a state of harmony. He objected to the power exercised, because he had seen its abuse when applied to the removal of the public deposits, and its distribution of the spoils. The Executive had expressed himself boldly in regard to suppressing these publications, and he would say, manly; and he would do him the justice to say he believed him sincere, although mistaken in this matter. He (Mr. C[alhoun]) had not abandoned his interest in this bill; he had put it into the hands of a stronger party. He was happy to hear the general remarks of the Senator from Georgia (Mr. Cuthbert). He wanted the country should have their eyes upon it. One point he could not abandon, and that was to have a final vote on the bill, and that he was determined to have. If the Senator from Tennessee would call it up in a reasonable time, he would consent to its postponement.

From *Congressional Globe*, 24th Cong., 1st Sess., pp. 351–353. Also printed in the Washington, D.C., *Globe*, April 15, 1836, p. 2; *Register of Debates*, 24th Cong., 1st Sess., cols. 1155–1162. Variant in the Washington, D.C., *United States' Telegraph*, April 14, 1836, p. 3; the Charleston, S.C., *Mercury*, April 21, 1836, p. 2. Another variant in the New York, N.Y., *Morning Courier and New-York Enquirer*, April 15, 1836, p. 2. NOTE: Some reported versions of the above debate, apparently erroneously, reversed the order of Calhoun's remarks.

"Motion by Mr. Calhoun for information from the Treasury Dept. rel[ative] to Deposite Banks and receipts into the Treasury," submitted to the Senate on 4/13. "Resolved, That the Secretary of the Treasury [Levi Woodbury] be directed to report to the Senate, with as little delay as may be practicable, the amount of money in the Treasury on the 1st of this month, when ["it was" *canceled*] deposited, and the amount of the liabilities of the several Banks of deposite, respectively, with their means of meeting the same; and also the receipts of the Treasury for the quarter ending the 31st of March last, arranged under the heads of customs, public lands, and incidental receipts." (This motion was adopted on 4/13 by unanimous consent.) CC in DNA, RG 46 (Records of the U.S. Senate), 24A-B10; PC in *Senate Journal*, 24th Cong., 1st Sess., p. 286.

REMARKS ON THE REMOVAL OF
DAVID MELVILL FROM OFFICE

[In the Senate, April 15, 1836]
Mr. Calhoun said that a petition had been sent to him, with a request that he would present it to the Senate, by a Mr. David Melville [*sic*], late an officer of the customs at Newport, Rhode Island, complaining of his removal from office. Mr. C[alhoun] said that he had no acquaintance with this individual, and why he had been selected to present the petition he was at a loss to know. He had therefore inquired into his character, and had understood that he was a highly respectable and worthy man. He had examined his petition, and he must say that Mr. Melville had made out a very strong case. He was weigher and gauger, and had been uniform and consistent in his politics as a Jeffersonian democrat. He had taken a decided part in the late war, having been principally instrumental in raising a volunteer corps which had been highly serviceable. Yet, notwithstanding all this, the purity of his character, the correctness of his deportment in his official duties, and non-interference with elections, he had been dismissed from office—and on what grounds? Because he would take no part in elections, and having a small freehold, he had disposed of it, and could no longer vote. These facts were all stated in plain and perspicuous language. Mr. C[alhoun] said he knew that this might be considered a small affair; but this, he thought, was very far from diminishing its importance. It laid bare the manner in which those who administered this Government abused their trusts. Nothing was too high and nothing was too low for them. It laid bare the manner in which the conditions under which they came into office have been fulfilled. He confessed that sad impressions were made on his mind by the perusal of this petition. He could not but remember the great struggle which brought the President [Andrew Jackson] into power. He could not but remember that one of the principal objects they had in view was that the power and patronage of the Government should not be brought to bear on the freedom of elections. He never could forget the scene which took place when the President was inaugurated, and when he declared openly, in the presence of thousands of our citizens assembled on that occasion, the principles on which he would administer the Government. It was a short and noble address, and was received with shouts of approbation by congregated thousands; and particularly that part of the address was applauded, which declared that he would reform those abuses by which the power and patron-

age of the Government had been brought to bear on the freedom of elections. How that promise had been carried out, let the case of this humble individual answer.

Mr. C[alhoun] referred to the reasons given for the removal of Mr. Melville, as stated in the petition, and to his correspondence with the Secretary of the Treasury [Levi Woodbury] on the subject. On writing to the Secretary, he received an answer, by which he only found out that the collector had exercised the legal authority vested in him. Not satisfied with that, he wrote for a copy of the report of the collector on the subject, and was answered, that the report, being confidential, could not be communicated. Sir, (said Mr. C[alhoun],) under what Government could such an act of injustice and oppression be perpetrated? Many of the friends of the administration there would hardly believe it possible such things had occurred. The individual made application to the collector for the reasons of his dismissal, and the collector told him, in a friendly, verbal reply, that no fault had been found with his official conduct, but that his case was one on which he could give no written answer. Mr. C[alhoun] moved that the petition and papers be referred to the Committee on Commerce. He thought no remedy could be applied; but he wished the committee to take the matter into their consideration. He wished particularly to see the report made by the collector to the Secretary of the Treasury, on the dismissal of Mr. Melville. He had often heard it stated on that floor, that this administration was supported by the votes of freemen; but if the facts stated in this petition be true, it was easily seen how they controlled the fifty or sixty thousand officeholders who supported them.

[*An extended discussion of this petition took place. Then Robert H. Goldsborough of Md. moved to lay it on the table.*]

Mr. Calhoun said, if the petition should be referred, the committee would have all the facts before them. If the Secretary did not know of this underwork, the case presented a state of things which, to his mind, made it little better. Did he understand the Senator from New Hampshire [Henry Hubbard] to hold that, because a man had lost his freehold, he should be turned out of office? Was there any Senator here who would subscribe to such a doctrine? Where a man had conducted himself properly, and was well qualified to discharge the duties of his office, that he should be turned out of it for no other reason than because he had lost his freehold qualification to vote? The Senator from Tennessee [Felix Grundy] thought this representation of the memorialist not correct. The facts set out seemed to him [that is, Calhoun] to be a plain, unvarnished narration of his wrongs; and it seemed Mr. Melville was reluctantly turned out, as he was acknowledged to be a good officer. It might appear to some Senators that it was so small a case that no one would think it worth while to notice it. He did not think so. The principles involved in it gave it great importance. The Senator from Connecticut (Mr. [John M.] Niles) had said that he (Mr. C[alhoun]) had given an opinion that public offices should be perpetual. If the Senator had stated so in a newspaper at Hartford, he would not have noticed it; but stating it, as he did, in his place, he felt bound to say not one word of it was true.

[*Hubbard said that Calhoun's remarks indicated his belief that the Secretary of the Treasury was at fault.*]

Mr. Calhoun made no accusation against the Secretary. He had said that it was the duty of the Secretary to look into all the facts of the case; and if the collector had turned out Mr. Melville only because he had no freehold, and could take no part in elections, to apply the proper remedy. This the Senator from New Hampshire could not deny.

(Mr. Hubbard said, certainly not.)

Mr. Calhoun continued. But the gentleman said that the collector had power to remove the officer, without giving any reasons for it. Against this doctrine he protested. All these high offices were held as trusts for the benefit of the people, and not as the property of the individual or his party. The officer having appointments to make was bound to appoint men capable and worthy, and to sustain them if they did their duty faithfully, and he had no right to turn them out to put in men who would serve the party. If the office was the property of the collector, and not held as a trust, he admitted that he would have a right to turn out and put in whom he pleased. He said nothing against the Secretary, but he thought, from his correspondence with Mr. Melville, he had a knowledge of all the facts, and it was his duty to inquire further into them, and if the collector had done wrong, to apply the remedy. This was all he had said, for it might turn out that the collector gave good reasons for the removal.

[*Discussion continued, at the end of which the petition and related papers were referred to the Committee on Commerce.*]

From *Register of Debates*, 24th Cong., 1st Sess., cols. 1177–1187. Also printed in the Washington, D.C., *Globe*, April 18, 1836, p. 3; *Congressional Globe*, 24th Cong., 1st Sess., pp. 361–364. Variant in the Charleston, S.C., *Mercury*, April 25, 1836, p. 2. Another variant in the New York, N.Y., *Morning Courier and*

New-York Enquirer, April 18, 1836, p. 2. NOTE: Melvill's petition, dated 3/21/1836, states that he had been a Weigher and Gauger in the Newport Customs House from 1824 to March, 1835, and had ably served two Collectors before being removed by a third, William Littlefield. He relates in great circumstantial detail political party influences and considerations which, he maintains, led to the dismissal of himself and other workers in the Customs House. He encloses documents indicating his patriotism during the War of 1812. DS with Ens in DNA, RG 46 (Records of the U.S. Senate), 24A-G2. On 5/6 Calhoun submitted to the Senate additional documents supporting Melvill's petition, which were also referred to the Committee on Commerce. On the last day of the session the Committee reported sympathetically on Melvill's petition but recommended no specific course of action. The report and related papers are printed in Senate Document No. 430, 24th Cong., 1st Sess.

[To Lewis Cass, Secretary of War, *ca.* 4/16.] An entry in a register of letters received indicates that the War Dept. received a letter on this date from Calhoun, enclosing a "letter from Cha[rle]s C. Mayson [of Jackson, Miss.?] inquiring respecting the claim of heirs of Col. Ja[me]s Mayson to bounty land." The letter was referred to the Bounty Land Office. Entry in DNA, RG 107 (Records of the Office of the Secretary of War), Registers of Letters Received, 1800–1870, 39:C-403 (M-22:39).

Remarks on Francis Lieber's memorial, 4/18. "Mr. Calhoun presented a memorial of Professor Lieber [of South Carolina College], on the subject of a statistical work on the United States, in preparation by him, and praying for the aid of Congress. Mr. Calhoun spoke of the work in terms of high approbation, and moved the printing." Daniel Webster stated that he had read the memorial and found it an "able and comprehensive plan or outline" which ought to be given extensive publicity whether or not Congress was inclined to patronize it. On Webster's suggestion, "Mr. Calhoun modified his motion so as to make it for printing double the usual number, and in this form it was agreed to." (Lieber's memorial, dated 4/6 and addressed to the Senate, can be found in Senate Document No. 314, 24th Cong., 1st Sess.) From *Register of Debates,* 24th Cong., 1st Sess., col. 1198. Also printed in the Washington, D.C., *Globe,* April 20, 1836, p. 2; *Congressional Globe,* 24th Cong., 1st Sess., p. 370.

Remarks on "the bill to authorize contracts for the transportation of the United States mail and property on railroads," 4/18. "Mr. Calhoun admitted that, if something was not done, the transmission of intelligence would be transferred from the general Government to the railroad corporations. He thought, with the gentleman from Pennsylvania [James Buchanan], there were great objections to this bill. He saw very clearly, if they commenced this system, that there was great danger of its utimately ending in a system of internal improvements. There was no knowing the extent to which these contracts would be carried; and there was also a great difficulty in fixing what would be an adequate compensation. He would mention another difficulty that could not well be guarded against. So long as it should be the interest of these companies to fulfil their contracts, they would do so; but when it became their interest not to fulfil them, and they failed to comply with their engagements, there was no remedy but a suit for the return of the funds advanced." From *Register of Debates,* 24th Cong., 1st Sess., col. 1205. Also printed in the Washington, D.C., *Globe,* April 20, 1836, p. 2; *Congressional Globe,* 24th Cong., 1st Sess., pp. 372–373.

To V[irgil] Maxcy, Soli[cito]r of the Treasury, 4/21/[1836?; or possibly 1832 or 1834]. "When you can make it convenient to call I would be glad to see you in reference to Mr. Walsh's note, which you enclosed [to] me." ALS in DLC, Galloway-Maxcy-Markoe Papers, 60:20608.

From P[eter] H[agner, Third] Auditor [of the Treasury], 4/22. In reply to Calhoun's note of 4/21 [*not found*] enclosing a letter to himself from B. Chisholm, which Hagner returns, he states that no payment has been made to Thomas P. Green in behalf of the legatees of Maj. John Brent for the latter's Revolutionary services. So that Chisholm may understand the matter better, a copy of Hagner's letter of 2/11/1834 to R[ichard] M. Johnson is enclosed to Calhoun. FC in DNA, RG 217 (Records of the General Accounting Office), Third Auditor: Congressional Letterbooks, 3:418.

Remarks on a private relief bill, 4/22. "Mr. Calhoun, after some remarks against the bill, said he did not see why the Senate should be so very particular about these small matters, when their attention was so little directed to the millions of money in the deposite banks, independent of the seven millions of stock in the Bank of the United States, and the money arising from the Chickasaw purchase. He wished the hundredth part of the zeal was directed to these large items, while the country was on the brink of ruin, that there was to small matters. He hoped the money of the Government would be taken out of the hands of these public plunderers, and that Congress would not adjourn till it made an equitable disposition of it." From *Register of Debates*, 24th Cong., 1st Sess., col. 1253. Also printed in the Washington, D.C., *Globe*, April 25, 1836, p. 2; *Congressional Globe*, 24th Cong., 1st Sess., p. 384. Variant in the New York, N.Y., *Morning Courier and New-York Enquirer*, April 25, 1836, p. 2.

REMARKS ON REQUIRING SPECIE IN PAYMENT FOR PUBLIC LANDS

[In the Senate, April 23, 1836]
[*Under consideration was a motion introduced by Thomas H. Benton to instruct the Committee on the Public Lands to report a bill requiring that nothing but gold and silver be received in payment for the public lands.*]

Mr. Calhoun observed that he should be very much governed in the vote he should give on this occasion by the opinions of gentlemen coming from the new States, where the public lands were. He saw a great many advantages that would result from the measure, and particularly in the check it would give to that spirit of speculation by which bank rags were given in exchange for the valuable public domain. If the gentlemen coming from the West were of opinion that the measure would not affect the settlement and prosperity of the new States, he would cheerfully give it his support.

[*Several other Senators spoke.*]

Mr. Calhoun agreed with the Senator from North Carolina [Willie P. Mangum] as to the appointment of a select committee, and hoped that it would be appointed by the Chair, selecting a majority from the new States.

In reply to the Senator from Connecticut [John M. Niles], he would observe that, during the time of the pecuniary pressure, he said nothing, because he believed that it would be temporary. He never did doubt that the removal of the deposites would produce the greatest distress, and the most disastrous consequences; but he always did believe that there would be an excess in the Treasury. We make great mistakes in supposing that certain events do not follow their causes, because they do not come at once. In the ordinary course of Providence, causes and their consequences are frequently remote; but this was no reason for neglecting the caution, that the one necessarily followed the other.

The great distress that pervaded the country, the changes of property, and the derangement of the currency—all these were seen and predicted; and the present majority were justly chargeable with them. He never had any thing to do with the Bank of the United States, though he opposed the removal of the deposites, as leading to a ruinous derangement of the currency by the unlimited use of State bank paper. Since that measure, one hundred millions had been added to the currency by these banks, which would not have been the case had there been a Bank of the United States to control them. As to the superabundance of the Treasury, he had always foreseen it. Ever since the fatal tariff of 1828, he foresaw the evil, and his subsequent course, which had brought on him so much opprobrium, (he alluded to the proceedings of South Carolina in opposition to the tariff,) was dictated by the knowledge that this tariff would produce an overwhelming accumulation of money in the Treasury, which ought never to be there. There was a deep responsibility on those who had caused these evils. But let us, said he, not look to the past, but to the future. Let us apply what remedies are in our power; and, above all, let us endeavor to prevent this noble domain, the public lands, from passing out of our hands into those of speculators, in exchange for worthless bank rags. His only desire was that the measure under consideration should be approved of by the Western gentlemen, and, if it was so, he should give it his hearty support.

From *Register of Debates,* 24th Cong., 1st Sess., cols. 1271–1274. Also printed in the Washington, D.C., *Daily National Intelligencer,* May 2, 1836, p. 4; the Washington, D.C., *Globe,* April 26, 1836, p. 2; *Congressional Globe,* 24th Cong., 1st Sess., pp. 392–393.

To Maj. C[HRISTOPHER] VANDEVENTER, [Erie County, N.Y.?]

Senate Chamber, 24th April 1836
My dear Sir, I am exceedingly happy to learn from your last, that you have made so favourable a disposition of your farm, as to leave you perfectly at ease as to property, and to select such situation, for your future residence, as your health & comfort may require. It will afford me great pleasure to give you all the information in my power, with my best advice in making your selection. Taking your general suggestions as my guide, I would think your selection will be con-

fined to Charlotte[s]Ville[,] Virginia, the seat of the University, Raleigh[,] N. Carolina, Chappell [*sic*] Hill, [or] Hillsborough [N.C.], Athens[,] Georgia & my own immediate neighbourhood. They are all healthy, but in that respect I should think Charlot[t]esVille, and my neighbourhood ["has(?)" *changed to* "have"] the advantage. Mine is very healthy. As it regards education, CharlottesVille, and Chappell Hill would probably rank first, tho' I understand the University of Georgia, is flourishing, and that the ["advantage" *altered to* "advantages"] of Education ["is" *changed to* "are"] good in Raleigh. My neighbourhood [at Pendleton] is ["good" *canceled*] not good in that particular. I have to employ a private teacher. As it regards religion, in [being] near[?] a pious society, and a flourishing church, I would suppose that Raleigh has the advantage. It is the residence of the Episcopal Bishop and I understand the community is a regular & moral one. We have a good church, well attended in the summer but as our society is much reduced in the winter, ["the" *interlined*] church service is suspended during that season. As it regards society, Chappell Hill is probably the most defective; and Raleigh as a perman[en]t one the best. Ours is good in the summer, & fall, but much less so in winter & spring, when it is much dispersed. I would think the society at the other places very respectable. Living is cheap in all of them. I have not added Columbia [S.C.] to the list, as I would be doubtful as to health.

If you should think the advantages held out, by our neighbourhood would suit you, I would [be] delighted to have you for a neighbour; but if the absence of society for a large part of the year, with the suspension of church service, and the want of schools, would not make it desirable, I would think that Raleigh in the maine [*sic*], holds out the greatest advantages, taking all things into consideration. Its health is good, its advantages of education highly respectable of itself, and it is but 28 miles from the university, its situation quite a pretty one, being cheap, the population orderly, and it will soon be connected by railroad with Baltimore through the whole line, except the link of steam boat navigation from this [city] to Baltimore.

I would be very happy to add any farther information, if you should desire additional, or to see and converse with you, if you could make it convenient to come on before the adjournment.

Anna [Maria Calhoun] joins her affectionate regards to yourself & family. I sincerely hope, that your health may continue to improve, till your [*sic*] are completely restored. I do not doubt, that a Southern climate would be of service to you, and looking to your particular case; I would suppose healthy situations remote from the mountains, like Raleigh, Athens, Hillsbo[ro]ugh, & Chappell Hill, ought to be preferred ["as the climate is more mild" *interlined*]. Your Physicians, however, is [*sic*] the best judge of what may best suit you. Sincerely & truly yours & & J.C. Calhoun.

ALS in MiU-C, Christopher Vandeventer Papers.

DAVID ALEXANDER to John C. Calhoun and W[illiam] C. Preston, Senators from S.C.

Charleston, 26th Ap[ri]l 1836

Gentlemen, By desire of the Chamber of Commerce, I have the Honor to inclose you their Memorial on the Bill (now before the House of representatives), *"to fix the number & Compensation of Officers of the Customs."* Should your Views on the subject Coincide with those of the Memorialists when the Bill Comes before the Senate, the Memorialists flatter themselves with Obtaining your powerful aid in removing the Objections which have been pointed out. With Great Respect, I have the Honor to be, Gentlemen, Your mo[st] Ob[e]d[ien]t Serv[an]t, David Alexander, President Charleston Chamber [of] Com[mer]ce.

ALS with En in DNA, RG 46 (Records of the U.S. Senate), 24A-H3. Note: Enclosed with this letter is a memorial of 4/25/1836 signed by David Alexander and R[oger] Heriot, President and Secretary, respectively, of the Charleston Chamber of Commerce, protesting against a bill proposing a reduction in the number and salaries of Customs officers at Charleston. The memorial was presented to the Senate and laid on the table on 6/17.

CH[ARLE]S EDMONDSTON to John C. Calhoun and W[illia]m C. Preston

[Charleston, *ca.* April 26, 1836]

Gentlemen, In compliance with the wishes of the great majority of the merchants of this City I now do myself the pleasure of transmitting to you the accompanying memorial on the subject of a Bill now before Congress, regulating the duties and compensations of Customhouse officers[,] requesting that you will bring it before the Senate of the United States in that form most likely to attain the objects of the memorialists. I am Gentlemen With esteem & the most profound respect Your Obed[ien]t Servant, Ch[arle]s Edmondston.

ALS with En in DNA, RG 46 (Records of the U.S. Senate), 24A-H3. NOTE: The enclosure is a printed memorial signed by over one hundred merchants of Charleston protesting against the proposed reduction in the number and salaries of Custom House officers there. The memorial was presented to the Senate by Calhoun on 6/17 and was "read & laid on the table."

Remarks on James Buchanan's motion to direct the Committee on Finance "to inquire into the expediency of contracting with Luigi Persico for two groups of statues to complete the ornaments of the east front of the Capitol," 4/28. "Mr. Calhoun said that, when this resolution was first introduced, his attention was called to it, and he really did think that they ought to reserve objects of this description for native artists; one of whom [Hiram Powers?] was, at that time, in Europe, at the head of his profession. At the solicitation of the mover, he would not make any opposition to the resolution now. Let it go (said Mr. C[alhoun]) to the committee, and let them report on it, and should the report be unfavorable, he would then have an opportunity of expressing his views further on the subject. Mr. Persico was a gentleman of talents, and would no doubt do justice to the subject; but the Government had but little patronage of the kind, and he thought they owed it to native artists to reserve it for them." After further debate on the subject, Calhoun said that he "was of opinion that they should reserve such matters for native artists, many of whom were highly distinguished. The very fact being known that they had such works in reservation for native talent, would have a powerful influence in stimulating their exertions to attain excellence in their professions." From *Register of Debates*, 24th Cong., 1st Sess., cols. 1314 and 1318. Also printed in the Washington, D.C., *Globe*, April 30, 1836, p. 2; *Congressional Globe*, 24th Cong., 1st Sess., pp. 406–407.

REMARKS ON THE SMITHSON LEGACY

[In the Senate, April 30, 1836]
[Under consideration was a bill "authorizing the President of the United States to appoint an agent or agents to prosecute and receive from the British court of chancery the legacy bequeathed to the

179

United States by the late James Smithson of London, for the purpose of establishing at Washington city an institution for the increase of knowledge among men, to be called the Smithsonian University." A complex discussion occurred which revealed a variety of opinions as to the exact terms of the legacy and as to the propriety and constitutionality of any action to be taken by the Congress in response to it. John M. Clayton of Del. stated that Calhoun had been wrong on an earlier occasion in characterizing the bequest as a "donation to the United States." Rather, the Congress was merely the trustee for carrying out a charitable bequest in the District of Columbia, an action for which there was precedent.]

Mr. Calhoun said, if his memory served him, there was opposition made to the passage of those acts.

Mr. Clayton said he believed there was some objection made to the policy, but not to the power, of making the donation. It was to be located in the city of Washington, and persons in this city would be more benefited by it than any others.

Mr. Calhoun was of opinion that this donation was made expressly to the United States. By reading the terms in which the bequest was made, it was impossible to conceive otherwise. The bequest was "to the United States of America, for the purpose of establishing, *at the city of Washington,* an institution for the increase of knowledge among men." Now, take out the words "the city of Washington," and the donation was clearly to the United States. The words "the city of Washington," were only used to designate the place where the university was to be established, and not by any stretch of the meaning of language to be considered as making the donation to the city. He understood the Senators, on all hands, to agree that it was not in the power of Congress to establish a national university, and they all agreed that they could establish a university in the District of Columbia. Now, on this principle, they could not receive the bequest; for the District of Columbia was not even named in it; the city of Washington being only designated as the place where the university was to be established, and the bequest being expressly made to the United States. He thought that acting under this legacy would be as much the establishment of a national university, as if they appropriated money for the purpose; and he would indeed much rather appropriate the money, for he thought it was beneath the dignity of the United States to receive presents of this kind from any one. He could never pass through the rotundo [*sic*] of the Capitol without having his feelings outraged by seeing that statue of Mr. [Thomas] Jefferson, which had been placed there contrary to their consent.

[*Debate continued. John Davis of Mass. argued that institutions other than universities could be involved in the diffusion of knowledge. He would agree with Calhoun if he thought a bequest to the government was involved. However, since he considered it only a question of incorporating an institution in the District of Columbia, he would vote for the bill.*]

Mr. Calhoun asked the Senator from Massachusetts (Mr. Davis) what construction he would put upon the bill, if the words "at Washington" had been left out of it.

[*Davis reiterated his position. Debate continued until the question was taken on engrossing the bill for a third reading, which passed 31 to 7.*]

From *Register of Debates*, 24th Cong., 1st Sess., cols. 1374–1377. Also printed in the Washington, D.C., *Globe*, May 2, 1836, p. 3; *Congressional Globe*, 24th Cong., 1st Sess., p. 413.

AMENDMENT TO THE BILL TO REGULATE THE DEPOSITS OF PUBLIC MONEY

In Senate of the U[nited] States
["April" *canceled*] May 2d. 1836

Amendment Proposed by Mr. Calhoun to the "Bill [introduced by him on 12/29/1835] to regulate the Deposites of the public money," viz:

Add the following as new sections—

Sec[tion] 10 And be it further enacted, That the unexpended balance remaining in the Treasury on the thirty-first of December of each year, after deducting therefrom the sum of [*blank space*] dollars, shall be divided and deposited with the several States of the Union, in the manner and on the conditions hereinafter provided for.

Sec[tion] 11 And be it further enacted, That it shall be the duty of the Secretary of the Treasury to divide the said balance, after making the deduction aforesaid, into as many parts as there are States of the Union at the time, and to allot to each a part, which shall bear to the entire sum to be divided, the same proportion, that the Representation of the State in both Houses of Congress bears to the aggregate Representation of all the States in both Houses;

and shall forthwith notify to the chief executive officer of each State the sum allotted to the State, and that the same will be transferred and deposited in the Treasury of the State on the warrant of the officer of the State who may be duly qualified to receive the same: Provided, always, There shall be an existing law of the State at the time, authorizing the receiving of the sum that may be allotted to it under this act, and which shall pledge the State to return the same without interest in such instalments and at such times, ["giving at least (*blank space*) months notice," *canceled*] as Congress shall by law provide. [*Inserted*: "Provided also that (*blank space*) months notice shall be given and that the instalments shall be in proportion to the amount deposited with the several States respectively."]

Sec[tion] 12 And be it further enacted, That immediately after the termination of the present session, it shall be the duty of the Secretary of the Treasury to make an estimate of the probable receipts and expenditures for the residue of the year, ending the thirty-first of December next, and that after adding the probable receipts to the sum in the Treasury at the close of the session, and deducting therefrom the probable expenditures, and from the balance the sum of [*blank space*] dollars, he shall divide the residue and allot the shares to the several States, in the manner provided for in the second section [of the amendment], and notify the chief executive magistrate of each State of the sum allotted to the State, and that the same will be transferred and deposited in the Treasury of the State on the warrant of an officer duly qualified to receive the same, so soon as the State shall pass an act in conformity to the condition contained in the second section of this act.

Sec[tion] 13 And be it further enacted, That the 10, 11 and 12th sections of this act shall continue in force till the 30th of June, eighteen hundred and forty-two, and no longer.

Draft in DNA, RG 46 (Records of the U.S. Senate), 24A-B1; PC's in DNA, RG 46, 24A-B2; PC's in the Washington, D.C., *United States' Telegraph*, May 12, 1836, p. 2, and June 29, 1836, p. 2. NOTE: On 5/25 Calhoun received the approval of the Senate to incorporate these amendments into the bill which he had introduced on 12/29/1835. On that day the blanks in the 10th and 12th sections were filled with the sum of "$3,000,000," and the blank in the 11th section with "six months." For the further history of this bill, see below the note to the "Speech on the Bill to Regulate the Deposits of Public Money" of 5/28/1836.

To Lt. Gen. Baron [SIMON] BERNARD, Paris

Senate Chamber, 4th May 1836

My dear Sir, I take much pleasure in making you acquainted with my friend, the Hon: Mr. [James H.] Hammond, member of Congress from South Carolina.

Mr. Hammond took his seat in Congress for the first time, at the begin[n]ing of the present session, and altho' he has been prevented by indisposition, during a large portion of the time, from taking an active part, few members have at any time in so short a period acquired equal reputation for soundness of judgement and power of speaking.

He visits Europe, with his family, under the advice of his physicians, with the view to the restoration of his health, and intends to spend a portion of his time in Paris. That his residence there might me [*sic*; be] more agreeable, I have taken the liberty of giving him this letter in order to afford him the pleasure of forming the acquaintance of yourself and your agreeable family.

Your attention to my friend will place me under lasting obligations. With great respect I am & & J.C. Calhoun.

ALS in DLC, James Henry Hammond Papers, vol. 6. NOTE: Calhoun addressed the above letter as follows: "Lieut. G[e]n[era]l Baron Bernard[,] Aid de Campt. due Roi[,] Paris." It is possible that this letter was actually written on 6/4 and was misdated by Calhoun as of 5/4. Compare below the related letters of 6/4 to Henry Wheaton and G.W. Lafayette.

From JOHN ALEX[AND]ER KEITH and A[BRAM?] MYERS, "Comm[itt]ee of Council"

Geo[rge] Town [S.C.,] 5th May 1836

Dear Sir, We transmit to you, by direction of the Town Council of Georgetown, a memorial to be presented to the U.S. Senate, praying for a survey of the Bar and Harbor of Georgetown, and the adjacent coast. The Council trust that your views, as to the utility and practicability of the scheme, will authorize your active co operation in the accomplishment of an object which is anxiously desired by the people of this neighborhood generally. Sea faring men have expressed the opinion that the scheme is entirely practicable.

We are instructed to request that you will confer with your colleagues on the subject. We are, with very high respect, Y[ou]r

Mo[st] Ob[edient] Ser[van]ts, Jno: Alex[and]er Keith, A. Myers, Comm[itt]ee of Council.

[P.S.] Since the memorial has been printed, we believe, on the authority of sea faring men, well acquainted with the Bar, that the same work which would improve the Northern would also encrease the depth of water in the Southern entrance.

[Enclosure]

To the Hon. the ["Speaker" *canceled and* "President" *interlined*] and Members of the ["H. of Representatives" *canceled and* "Senate" *interlined*] of the United States.

The Town Council of Georgetown in the State of South Carolina in Council assembled—Respectfully represent to your Honorable body that the entrance into the harbor of this place does not at present, at high water, admit vessels drawing more than nine feet except under extraordinary circumstances. They believe for many reasons that the northern Bar which, although less circuitous than the southern, has hitherto been rarely used in consequence of its greater shallowness, is susceptible of great improvement. Among these reasons are, the nature of the soil of the neighboring shore, the relative position of certain shoals with the extreme southern point of North Island, known on some of the maps as Lafayette, and the manifest change which has, within the last few years, taken place in the direction of the current, the effect of which change has been a considerable increase in the depth of water.

In consideration of the great advantage to the interests of this section of country, in which the Pee Dee Districts are included, that would necessarily result from the contemplated improvement, the consequent benefit accruing to the Treasury of the United States, and its entire practicability, your memorialists trust that your Honorable Body will direct a survey to be ["immediately" *inserted*] made of the Bar and Harbor of Georgetown and of the adjacent coast with a view to ascertaining whether the said Bar may not be improved in such a manner as to admit vessels of greater burthen than can at present enter. Such survey your memorialists confidently believe will fully sustain the views which they have presented.

And your petitioners will ever pray, [*signed*] John Harrelson[,] Intendant, In behalf of the Council. Attest[:] James Smith[,] Cl[er]k & Treas[ure]r.

LS with printed En in DNA, RG 46 (Records of the U.S. Senate), 24A-G2. NOTE: Calhoun presented this petition to the Senate on 5/12. It was referred to the Committee on Commerce, which never reported on it specifically. However, on 7/4, the last day of the session, the Senate adopted a resolution from that committee directing the President of the U.S. to collect, arrange, and transmit all available information relative to surveys of harbors and rivers.

Remarks on the payment of $20,000 to Matthew St. Clair Clarke and Peter Force for continuation of their documentary history of the American Revolution, 5/5. "Mr. Calhoun hoped the Senate would agree to strike out the section [of the general appropriation bill providing for the payment], and allow the publishers liberal compensation for what they had done, and stop its further progress. They [the government?] had made a most improvident contract. And, besides, he had strong constitutional doubts as to the power of Congress to contract for such a work; and if they had, there were few, in his opinion, who were qualified to perform a work of so sacred a character." From *Register of Debates*, 24th Cong., 1st Sess., cols. 1408–1409. Also printed in the Washington, D.C., *Globe*, May 7, 1836, p. 3; *Congressional Globe*, 24th Cong., 1st Sess., pp. 421–422.

"Additional documents in the case of David Melville [*sic*]," presented to the Senate by Calhoun on 5/6. The documents include an affidavit by Melvill testifying to the correctness of the facts stated in his memorial (presented to the Senate on 4/15) concerning his removal as Weigher and Gauger at the Newport, R.I., Customs House; a memorial signed by 15 persons who affirm their faith in Melvill's integrity and veracity; and affidavits by Caleb C. Mumford and Alexander Barker, both of whom were removed from the Newport Customs House at the same time as Melvill, stating that they also had been removed for political reasons. The papers were referred to the Committee on Commerce, which reported on 7/4. DS's in DNA, RG 46 (Records of the U.S. Senate), 24A-D2; PC's (along with the Committee report) in Senate Document No. 430, 24th Cong., 1st Sess.

To [Stephen] Pleasonton, Fifth Auditor [of the Treasury, *ca.* 5/9]. Calhoun requests certified copies of documents referred to in an enclosed letter [from James Nicholson; *not found*]; he also requests that the En be returned. ALS in DNA, RG 26 (Records of the U.S. Coast Guard), Bureau of Lighthouses: Miscellaneous Letters Received from Individuals, C:1836.

From S[tephen] Pleasonton, Fifth Auditor and Acting Commissioner of the Revenue, 5/10. "I had the honor to receive your note enclosing a letter from James Nicholson, and asking to be furnished with copies of the documents referred to in said letter, that were placed in this Office[,] on the application to Congress for Light-houses and Lightboats to be placed on or near the Capes of Florida and the Bahama Banks." In reply Pleasonton encloses a copy of a letter of 4/8/1824 from Secretary of the Navy [Samuel L. Southard] and a copy of Lt. James Ramage's report on the subject. He also returns Nicholson's letter. FC in DNA, RG 26 (Records of the U.S. Coast Guard), Bureau of Lighthouses: Lighthouse Letters, Fifth Auditor's Office, 11:275.

REMARKS ON THE FORTIFICATIONS BILL

[In the Senate, May 12, 1836]
[*Under consideration was the "bill making appropriations for the purchase of sites, the collection of materials, and for the construction of fortifications."*]

Mr. Calhoun was not disposed to depart from the usual course of legislation in this case. Bills for fortifications usually originated in the House of Representatives, and the Senate could add to or reduce the amount of appropriations contained in them, as they thought proper. They had before them two propositions: to complete old, and to erect new fortifications. He thought they ought, as far as possible, to complete the old fortifications before new ones were taken up. By pursuing the course indicated, which was that of waiting for the action of the other House, it would prevent confusion, caused by the Senate sending their fortification bill to the House of Representatives, and the House of Representatives sending theirs to the Senate; while both branches would be acting on the same subject in distinct bills.

[*Calhoun then moved to lay the bill on the table, a motion which was lost by a vote of 17 to 22. An extended debate ensued, near the end of which Calhoun again spoke.*]

Mr. Calhoun observed, that the Senator from Maine [Ether Shepley] put these large appropriations on the ground that the Secretary would make the contracts to run through the whole time. Now he had had some little experience in these matters, and well knew the disadvantages attending the making [of] long contracts. If they were made when prices were high, the profit consequent on the fall of prices enured to the contractor; and if they were made when prices were low, the contractor was sure to violate his contract, when he found himself losing by the fall of prices; so that in either case the Government must be a great loser. One great objection that he had to the large appropriations in this bill was, that they were calculated to empty the public purse and fill the pockets of the contractors.

The Senator from Connecticut [John M. Niles] said that labor is now falling. Well, what would be the result? Why, the fall in the price of labor would put thousands into the pockets of individuals, for no earthly benefit to the public. There never was a time better fitted to make fortunes for contractors than the present. He understood this thing very well. He would not attribute motives to any gentleman; but it had been almost openly avowed on that floor, that the design was to retain the public money where it is, and prevent it from going back to the people, to whom it rightfully belonged. There were powerful combinations interested in this matter. Millions were deposited in these deposite banks, who paid no interest on it, and were, therefore, deeply interested in retaining this money; a vast number of individuals who were indebted to them, were equally interested in the same object; and this powerful combination would make every effort to prevent the withdrawal of this money. If this bill was a question of fortifications, there would be no difficulty; it would be passed at once, but these were not the real objects in view. The question now was not for fortifications, for they were not even dreamed of; but how to prevent this immense amount of public money from being withdrawn from the deposite banks. With respect to these appropriations, the passing them at this time, and in the absence of surveys and sufficient information, would be a departure from the long settled practice of the Government, for which no sufficient reason could be given. Their custom had been, to wait for the action of the other House, and to pass such fortification bills as came from that body. There was a fortification bill now in progress there, and there was no danger of its not being sent to the Senate in time to be acted on. It was not expected to expend this money this year, for the Secretary would have too much discretion to make contracts at this time.

There never was a time when there was so little use in expending money on new fortifications as the present. There were only two nations in the world against whose attacks they would be wanted, and these were France and Great Britain. Our difficulties with France were, thanks to Providence, happily settled; and with Great Britain there was not the slightest expectation of our coming in conflict. Her magnanimous interference to settle our foolish and wicked quarrel with France, plainly showed her friendly intentions towards this country, and her strong desire to maintain her friendly relations with us. Our danger (said Mr. C[alhoun]) lies not on the seacoast; it lies in another way—in the southwest [that is, toward Texas]. Let me tell you, (said Mr. C[alhoun],) that every dollar of our surplus may be wanted, and that soon. They knew not even what the next mail might bring them. Wait then (said Mr. C[alhoun]) a few days, and watch the progress of events; let this bill lie, and rest until the Senate has time to consider and reflect upon it. They were proceeding with too much precipitation on idle schemes to prevent the surplus money from going back to the people, from whom it was derived. He was anxious to have the bill to provide for the safety of the public money taken up and considered; it being, in his opinion, a more important matter than any that could be brought before them; and he had hoped that the Senator from New York (Mr. [Silas] Wright) would have called it up before this. He now gave notice that he would himself call up that bill on Saturday next [5/14], if the Senator from New York did not call it up before that day.

From *Register of Debates*, 24th Cong., 1st Sess., cols. 1431–1432, 1446–1447. Also printed in the Washington, D.C., *Globe*, May 14, 1836, p. 3; *Congressional Globe*, 24th Cong., 1st Sess., pp. 449–451. Variant in the New York, N.Y., *Morning Courier and New-York Enquirer*, May 14, 1836, p. 2.

To D[avid] Daggett, [Kent Professor of Law, Yale College,] New Haven, 5/13. Calhoun introduces and requests Daggett's kind attentions to "Mr. Martin of South Carolina," who is "a son of an old acquaintance of mine, and visits New Haven with the intention, of joining the law school over which you preside." [Martin cannot be identified with certainty, but the graduates of Yale Law School included Benjamin Y. Martin, 1836, and August W. Martin, 1840, both of Augusta, Ga.] ALS in CtY, Sterling Library, David Daggett Papers.

Further remarks on the bill for the relief of the city corporations of the District of Columbia, 5/14. The bill under discussion had been returned from the House of Representatives with amendments. "Mr. Calhoun said the chairman of the Committee for the District of Columbia (Mr. [William R.] King of Alabama) had avowed this appropriation to be a donation. He (Mr. C[alhoun]) doubted the propriety and also the constitutionality of making it. He would much rather support the bill as sent from the Senate. He believed, when the [Chesapeake and Ohio] canal was extended to the mineral regions, the stock would rise above par. He would much rather the bill would be sent back to the House of Representatives as it had originally passed the Senate. He doubted the right of Congress to vote away the money of the people, without making provision to have it returned to their Treasury again." From *Register of Debates*, 24th Cong., 1st Sess., cols. 1450–1451. Also printed in the Washington, D.C., *Globe*, May 16, 1836, p. 2; *Congressional Globe*, 24th Cong., 1st Sess., p. 458.

REMARKS ON THE INDIAN APPROPRIATIONS

[In the Senate, May 18, 1836]

[Under discussion was "the bill making appropriations for the current expenses of the Indian department, for Indian annuities, and other similar objects, for the year 1836." Daniel Webster, as Chairman of the Committee on Finance, said that recent information had induced the committee to offer several amendments to the bill previously reported. He "submitted several communications from the War Department, showing that a considerable addition would be required to the appropriations for removing Indians." Several amendments were offered and agreed to by the Senate. Then Hugh L. White of Tenn. moved to provide an appropriation of $40,000 to remove "the Indians of Wisconsin to the neutral ground on the borders of Missouri."]

Mr. Calhoun hoped that some gentleman who understood the subject would explain the uses for which this appropriation was intended, and the prospect there was of its being applied so as to accomplish the object in view. For his part, he feared that it would, like other appropriations of the kind, be productive only of the greatest frauds. He had long anticipated things of this kind. He had long believed that this Indian department was one of the branches of the Government under which the greatest frauds would be perpetrated—that, and the public lands, and the banking system. He only regretted that the speculators in Indian lands were not the persons to suffer, instead of the frontier inhabitants. It made his heart bleed to think of the sufferings of the innocent frontier settlers. All these evils, he said, had been the result of mismanagement. The persons appointed had been generally incapable or unfaithful. The Government ought to have appointed men of intelligence, of firmness, and of honor, who would have faithfully fulfilled their obligations to the United States and to the Indians. Instead of that, men were sent out to make fortunes for themselves, and to oppress the Indians. He believed that the two Indian wars they had had were the result of mismanagement, and that the one that was announced that morning [by Senator William R. King of Ala. reporting Creek hostilities] might be traced to the same cause. All this resulted from want of capacity or honesty in the agents sent out by the Government. Did he not see, on one hand, large fortunes built up, and, on the other, the most degrading subserviency to those in power?

The prominent cause of these Indian disturbances had been the reservations, which he had invariably opposed from the first, predicting that they would be followed by speculations, the grossest frauds, and by the greatest injustice to the Indians themselves. He recollected that when the first Indian treaty, containing reservations, was brought in the Senate, it was strenuously opposed by a distinguished Senator from New York, (Rufus King,) who demonstrated the evils that these reservations would lead to. That treaty was confirmed; and since that time the system had been kept up, always accompanied by the same abuses. There was no remedy for this state of things, but in the appointment of honest, capable men, who would consult the interest of the Government and the welfare of the Indians, rather than their own selfish purposes. Let gentlemen think of the course of this administration, and the consequences of its mismanagement of public affairs. First, there was a French war threatened; then a Seminole war; next the probability of a war with Mexico; and now a Creek war. All this was the consequence of converting this Government into a political electioneering machine, instead of properly administering the high trusts that had been confided by the people. He hoped that some gentleman who understood this matter would explain the necessity of the appropriation.

[*White explained that the appropriation was necessary to deal with Indians who had removed but had returned. Lewis F. Linn of Mo. said that it was too late to inquire whether these Indians "had been cheated, which had been admitted from the beginning." Calhoun was mistaken, however, about the Black Hawk war, he said. "In that case, the Indians were bought off by salt and corn, and came back again expecting to be bought off again, and, being disappointed in not being bought off, commenced hostilities."*]

Mr. Calhoun regretted much that the Senator from Indiana, (Mr. [John] Tipton,) who knew more about the origin of Black Hawk's war than any body else, was not in his place. That gentleman rose in his place [several years ago], and declared that that war broke out in consequence of the mismanagement of the officers of the Government. Let the Senator from Missouri [Linn] recollect that this acknowledgment came from one of the warmest friends of the administration.

He acknowledged, with the Senator from Missouri, that the Indians had been treated wrong[ly] from beginning to end; which, unfortunately, would ever be the case, when savage and civilized man came in conflict; but this was no reason why they should suffer their agents to practise frauds both against the Indians and the Government. They ought to have honest, intelligent, and active men to manage their Indian affairs, or there never would be an end to these abuses. There were no people on earth so easy to deal with as our half-civilized Indians. It only required ordinary justice, a mild but firm course of conduct, with a strict adherence to truth in all transactions with them; and it was the easiest thing in the world to keep them quiet. The Senator spoke of the cordons of Indians around the frontier; but let him look to the heavy annuities paid them, which made it their interest to keep at peace. With proper management, they were the best allies we could have to keep off the wild Indians at a distance. He saw, he said, very plainly, the progress of events. These Indian disturbances were to furnish the pretext for a large increase of the standing army. This was the consequence of carrying out the principles of the spoils party, enriching men with large jobs and contracts, and the system to be kept up by a large military force. He repeated that there never was a time when it was so easy to keep the Indians at peace. Their frontier posts were greatly extended, and the Indians were driven back into the prairies; and, though they were formidable in the woods, being the best light troops in the world, they were entirely helpless in the open plain. If they would appoint honest, faithful, intelligent men, to transact their business with the Indians, instead of broken down politicians, men sent out to be rewarded for party services, these Indian disturbances would soon cease; but unless that was done, it was apparent that there would be continual disturbances, creating causes for wars, to be followed by a large increase of the standing army. He should not oppose the appropriation after the explanation of the Senator from Tennessee, but he feared that it would be used to give jobs to reward some political partisans.

From *Register of Debates*, 24th Cong., 1st Sess., cols. 1458–1462. Also printed in the Washington, D.C., *Globe*, May 20, 1836, p. 2; *Congressional Globe*, 24th Cong., 1st Sess., pp. 468–469. Variant in the New York, N.Y., *Morning Courier and New-York Enquirer,* May 20, 1836, p. 2. NOTE: The term "reservations" used by Calhoun above refers specifically to parcels of land retained or reserved by Indians, such as the Creeks in Ala., within a territory most of which was ceded.

REMARKS ON THE REPORT OF THE CONFERENCE COMMITTEE ON THE VOLUNTEER BILL

[In the Senate, May 20, 1836]

[On 5/18 William R. King of Ala. announced to the Senate the news of Creek Indian hostilities in the Southwest and urged that that body immediately take up a pending bill from the House of Representatives "authorizing the President to accept the services of volunteers." The Senate incorporated several amendments and passed the bill on the same day. On 5/19 word was received that the House had concurred in all the Senate amendments except one. The Senate resolved to insist upon this amendment, "without which," according to King, "the corps to be raised would not be an efficient one." Calhoun remarked that he understood "that the effect of this disagreement of the House was to change the character of this volunteer force from regular soldiers to volunteer militia." He thought the intention of the House "was sufficiently expressed that this should be a volunteer militia, and not a regular force." Calhoun moved that the Senate ask for a conference committee. The motion was adopted and the Chair, Martin Van Buren, with unanimous consent, appointed King, Calhoun, and James Buchanan to serve. The committee reported on 5/20.]

Mr. Calhoun, from the committee of conference appointed on the part of the Senate, to confer with a committee of the House on the disagreeing votes of the two Houses as to the Senate's amendment to the bill authorizing the President to accept the services of ten thousand volunteers for the defence of the western frontiers, reported that the committees of the two Houses had had a meeting, but that they had not been able to effect the objects for which they were appointed, having sat the whole day without coming to any agreement whatever.

[William R. King complained that the committee had discussed the entire bill rather than the amendment under dispute.]

Mr. Calhoun replied that the committee did confine themselves to the subject of disagreement, until finding that there was no possibility of coming to an agreement on that point, they entered into a more enlarged discussion, for the purpose of ascertaining whether the bill could not be so framed as to meet the concurrence of both Houses. His understanding was, that when a committee of conference came to a proposition that could not be agreed on, the whole subject was open to them.

[*King said that "the proposition last made was, that they should extend the term of service of the militia force of the United States for a year, instead of its being a volunteer militia force."*]

Mr. Calhoun said it was true that that proposition was made, but another one was also made, and that was that the President [Andrew Jackson] should receive these volunteers from the States by battalions, regiments, and brigades, officered by the States. The committee of the other House was unanimous in the opinion that it was unconstitutional for the President to officer this force, unless it was made a part of the regular army, and that then he must appoint the officers in the same way that other officers of the regular army are appointed. He must say this bill had been passed under the pressure of very extraordinary circumstances, and that, consequently, that consideration was not given to it in this particular that its importance deserved. It had been called up by the Senator from Alabama, under the apprehension of a Creek war, and its immediate passage was insisted on. They were told that there were precedents to sanction it; but, on examination, he found that there was not one. The precedent referred to, was the volunteer bill of 1812, which was passed the very day preceding the adjournment of Congress. By it, authority was given to the President to commission these volunteers; but on what condition? Why, on the condition of enrolment. The bill provided, that, after these companies should be organized, and their services accepted, they should enrol themselves as part of the army; and then, and not till then, the President was to commission them. Now, he would ask gentlemen to consider the difference between this bill, which had been cited as a precedent, and the one before them. By the present bill, they were to have a dormant military force in the country, mixed up with the militia; and this dormant force was to be officered by the President, to mingle with our citizens, entirely contrary to the provisions of the Constitution. They ought to be cautious how they established precedents. They all remembered the circumstances under which this volunteer bill of 1812 was passed. Unfortunately, some of the New England States held up their militia, and Congress wanted to get that military force without going to the Executives of those States for them. They authorized the President to accept the services of this militia in companies; and what was the next step? It was first to enrol and then commission them. And what was the next step now? We get, said Mr. C[alhoun], a military force mixed up with the citizens of the United States, not organized as part of the standing army, but officered by the President; thus having, at the same time, two militia forces, one officered by the States and the other by the President. Again: the power of appointment of the subordinate officers was virtually taken from the President, and given to the men. He wished to know the necessity for this departure from the Constitution. The gentleman from Alabama said that the mode of appointment, provided by the bill, would render the force more effective. Why should it be so? Why would a force officered by the President be more effective than one officered by the States? He did not think that the description of force contemplated by the bill could be raised. The difficulty would be in getting the men to enrol themselves; for officers who were in the late war said that the same thing had been ineffectually tried then. There were but two ways of getting men for a military force; the one was by volunteers raised on the spur of the occasion; and the other was by enlisting men for the regular army from the dregs of society. Now, the men could not be raised under the provisions of this bill, and the result would be, that there would be a multitude of officers appointed by the President, and no men to be commanded by them.

[*Later a message was received from the House of Representatives "stating that that body insisted on its disagreement to the amendment of the Senate." Calhoun moved that the Senate insist on its amendment and that it ask for another conference committee. King supported this motion, hoping that "one more effort might be made, so that we might have a force in the field sufficient to meet the emergency."*]

Mr. Calhoun said there had not been, nor should there be, any thing wanting on his part to give a safe, prompt, and efficient force for the protection of the frontiers. If the gentleman from Alabama believed that, for the sake of having an efficient force, these volunteers should be officered by the President, he had wholly overlooked the Constitution. He entertained the deliberate opinion, that this bill was wholly unconstitutional, and was not supported by a single precedent. In reply to the Senator from Alabama, he asked, if it was not under the pressure of extraordinary circumstances, that this bill was called up and hurried through?

[*James Buchanan spoke at length on his disagreement with Calhoun on the matter and asked to be excused from the conference committee if it was again appointed. He said that he had proposed in the conference committee an amendment to the Senate amendment which he still favored as the best solution. That amendment would provide "that none of the officers should be appointed by the President, until the volunteers were actually mustered into the service of the United States." Until so mustered the volunteer companies would be considered "as mere voluntary associations."*]

Mr. Calhoun would have been glad if the Senator from Pennsylvania had stated the whole of his objections to this bill. He did object to the President's appointment of the officers in the recess; because he believed there was no necessity for giving him such power. The volunteer bill of 1812, referred to as a precedent, was passed on the last day of the session, and there was therefore no time to have the appointments submitted to the revision of the Senate. But here there was no such exigency; if this force was to be at all valuable in the Creek war, they would certainly sit there long enough to provide for its constitutional organization. The Senator from Pennsylvania had omitted another of his objections. This bill conferred on the companies the power of appointing the officers, from the rank of captain, down; and there was not the slightest authority for this in the Constitution. Remember (said Mr. C[alhoun]) that this bill provides for an army of the United States: it can only be defended on that ground; and the bill conferred on the companies the power of appointing their own officers, while the Constitution provided that they should be appointed by the President, by and with the advice and consent of the Senate. The proposition was to treat all the officers, from captain, down, as inferior officers, and this, too, in the regular army; and to have them appointed by the President, without the previous consent of the Senate. They well knew how an ambitious man would proceed, when he wanted to seduce the army to aid his views. He would not go first to the general officers; it would be the subordinates that he would first practise on; Cromwell like, he would take the corporals to his bed. The proposition was, in creating this regular army, to confer on the President the power of appointing the officers of every grade.

A member of the committee of the other House, [Eleazar W. Ripley of La.,] who was a distinguished officer in the late war, told them that it would be impossible to raise the force contemplated by the bill, as it now stood; that the experience of the late war had fully shown that but an inconsiderable force could be raised in this way. This gentleman was most decidedly in favor of a volunteer force in the constitutional way. He said further, that, if officered by the States, a trained force of twenty thousand men could be got in a very short time, without the least difficulty. Mr. C[alhoun] believed that if the bill passed in its present form, there would be a multitude of officers, without men to be commanded; and that if it passed in the form recommended by the Senator from Pennsylvania, there would be neither men nor officers; and this Creek war would have to be ended without this volunteer force. He hoped that it would soon pass off; indeed, he had just been informed that it was not likely to prove as serious as had at first been apprehended. He believed that a volunteer militia force would be as efficient as the force proposed by the Senator from Alabama. Why should not a volunteer militia force, the officers having commissions in their pockets signed by Governor [Clement Comer] Clay of Alabama, Governor [Charles] Lynch of Mississippi, or Governor [Newton] Cannon of Tennessee, be as efficient as if their commissions were signed by Andrew Jackson? With respect to himself, he was not ambitious of serving in this committee of conference, neither had he any objections to doing so. He held himself at the disposal of the Senate, and was content to serve, or not to serve, as it pleased.

[*Discussion continued among four Senators, during which Buchanan defended the compromise amendment he had proposed in the conference committee.*]

Mr. Calhoun stated his impressions in reference to that amendment; and, as he understood it, the members of the committee who voted for the amendment, voted for it as preferable to the bill of the Senate. The question was put distinctly, whether they would prefer their own bill of the Senate, or the bill as amended by the Senator from Pennsylvania? and they decided in favor of their own bill. The cases cited as precedents for this bill were not analogous; and by the act of July, 1812, the distinction was still broader, which was "upon the express condition of enrolling"; which, by changing the phraseology of a single word, it would read, "on the express condition of enlisting." The question was discussed in committee as to what was the condition of these men before being called into service, after their service was tendered. They were citizens; and, he would ask, could they be tried by a court-martial? The question was, simply, whether the President could enrol a number of men as an army, and leave them in the midst of the citizens? He could not bring his mind to the conclusion to consent that the officers should be appointed without the consent of the Senate. The act of

196

the 3d of July was passed under peculiar emergencies at the very close of the session, and he could not consent to recognise it as a general precedent.

[After further debate the Senate decided to insist on its own amendment and appointed as members of the committee Calhoun, King, and Robert C. Nicholas of La.]

From *Register of Debates*, 24th Cong., 1st Sess., cols. 1503–1512. Also printed in the Washington, D.C., *Globe*, May 24, 1836, pp. 2–3; *Congressional Globe*, 24th Cong., 1st Sess., pp. 477–480. Variant in the New York, N.Y., *Morning Courier and New-York Enquirer*, May 23, 1836, p. 2. NOTE: The proceedings of 5/19 concerning the first appointment of the conference committee can be found in *Register of Debates*, 24th Cong., 1st Sess., cols. 1463–1464.

Report from the second conference committee on the Volunteer Bill, 5/21. Calhoun "reported that they had had a meeting with the committee of the House of Representatives, and that they had jointly agreed to recommend an amendment to their respective Houses, in substance as follows: The President is authorized to accept the service of volunteers, the number not exceeding ten thousand, in companies, regiments, brigades, and divisions; the officers to be commissioned in the manner prescribed by the laws of the several States from which these volunteers may offer themselves. Where regiments, brigades, or divisions volunteer, they shall be commanded by the same officers by whom they shall be commanded at the time of volunteering; and that, for volunteers offering their services in single companies, the President shall organize them into battalions, regiments, brigades, and divisions, and apportion the battalion and field officers among the States from which said companies shall come." (Both the Senate and the House concurred in this report before the end of the day.) From *Register of Debates*, 24th Cong., 1st Sess., col. 1523. Also printed in the Washington, D.C., *Globe*, May 24, 1836, p. 3; *Congressional Globe*, 24th Cong., 1st Sess., p. 482.

REMARKS ON THE INDEPENDENCE OF TEXAS

[In the Senate, May 23, 1836]
[Several Senators presented resolutions adopted by public meetings in their States urging the recognition of the Republic of Texas by the United States. Robert J. Walker of Miss. moved the reference

of all such memorials to the Committee on Foreign Relations. An extended discussion ensued in which ten Senators took part.]

Mr. Calhoun was of opinion that it would add more strength to the cause of Texas to wait for a few days, until they received official confirmation of the victory and capture of Santa Anna, in order to obtain a more unanimous vote in favor of the recognition of Texas. He had been of but one opinion from the beginning, that, so far from Mexico being able to reduce Texas, there was great danger of Mexico herself being conquered by the Texans. The result of one battle had placed the ruler of Mexico in the power of the Texans; and they were now able, either to dictate what terms they pleased to him, or to make terms with the opposition in Mexico.

This extraordinary meeting had given a handful of brave men a most powerful control over the destinies of Mexico; he trusted they would use their victory with moderation. He had made up his mind not only to recognise the independence of Texas, but for her admission into this Union; and if the Texans managed their affairs prudently, they would soon be called upon to decide that question. No man could suppose for a moment that that country could ever come again under the dominion of Mexico; and he was of opinion that it was not for our interests that there should be an independent community between us and Mexico. There were powerful reasons why Texas should be a part of this Union. The southern States, owning a slave population, were deeply interested in preventing that country from having the power to annoy them; and the navigating and manufacturing interests of the North and East were equally interested in making it a part of this Union. He thought they would soon be called on to decide these questions; and when they did act on it, he was for acting on both together—for recognising the independence of Texas, and for admitting her into the Union.

Though he felt the deepest solicitude on this subject, he was for acting calmly, deliberately, and cautiously, but at the same time with decision and firmness. They should not violate their neutrality; but when they were once satisfied that Texas had established a Government, they should do as they had done in all other similar cases—recognise her as an independent nation; and if her people, who were once citizens of this republic, wished to come back to us, he would receive them with open arms.

If events should go on as they had done, he could not but hope that before the close of the present session of Congress, they would not only acknowledge the independence of Texas, but admit her into the Union. He hoped there would be no unnecessary delay, for in such cases delays were dangerous; but that they would act with unanimity, and act promptly.

[*After several other Senators spoke, Calhoun made some unreported remarks. Then William C. Rives of Va. spoke in favor of referring the matter to the Committee on Foreign Relations and remarked that "it was strange that Senators, who stated that their opinions were made up," should oppose referring the matter to the committee for a report.*]

Mr. Calhoun explained. He stated that he was not prepared now to take either course that he had suggested. But he said that the questions, both of the recognition of Texas, and her incorporation into the Union, would soon be brought before them. He stated that the Texans, having the power, could make good terms with Santa Anna, or with the opposing party in Mexico; and that if they acted with prudence, Congress would soon be called upon to decide whether they should be incorporated into the Union. The gentleman from Virginia, he presumed, would not oppose this. He was not so prudent as to wait for the opinion of the committee. He had the fullest confidence in the committee, but having made up his mind long ago, he did not rely on the opinions of any one. It was not that he considered action to be now premature, but because he desired to see a greater unanimity of opinion, that he wished this matter delayed.

[*Rives replied that he considered it prudent to await the formal report of the committee before forming an opinion; he believed that Calhoun "had stated his feelings as a Southern man."*]

Mr. Calhoun explained. He stated that all parts of the Union, the manufacturing, navigating, and commercial interests, were all equally interested in the independence of Texas.

[*After further discussion the memorials on Texas were referred to the Committee on Foreign Relations.*]

From *Register of Debates,* 24th Cong., 1st Sess., cols. 1531–1537. Also printed in the Washington, D.C., *Globe,* May 25, 1836, p. 3; *Congressional Globe,* 24th Cong., 1st Sess., pp. 487–489. Variant in the Washington, D.C., *United States' Telegraph,* May 25, 1836, p. 3; the Charleston, S.C., *Mercury,* May 30, 1836, p. 2; the Augusta, Ga., *State Rights' Sentinel,* June 3, 1836, p. 2. Another variant in the New York, N.Y., *Morning Courier and New-York Enquirer,* May 25, 1836, p. 2. NOTE: The *Telegraph* reported Calhoun's remarks on this occasion as follows: "Mr. Calhoun said that he considered the subject as one involving the most momentous consequences. He had from the first entertained but one opinion as to the result of the contest carried on in Texas. He had never for a moment doubted that the Texians would succeed. In his opinion the danger always had been, not that Mexico would subdue Texas, but that Mexico would fall under the power of the Texians. The late events had, however, precipitated the result, and had given to a handful of brave men in Texas a most tremendous power. They have in their hands the very Government of Mexico itself; for Santa An[n]a may be considered as the Government. They can thus negotiate with the greatest effect with both of the parties which decide that country. We shall, said Mr. Calhoun, in time, be called upon to decide questions of the most momentous interest connected with the state of affairs now existing, and soon to exist in Texas. We shall have to decide whether we shall have in Texas an independent State, or whether that country shall be admitted to our Union as one of our States. He confidently expected that before the close of the session events would have made such progress, that the Senate might and would be called on to decide the great and momentous questions involved in the subject. He would wish, therefore, that the motion be laid on the table for a few days. He wished to get as much unanimity as possible in the Senate, and as some members thought it premature, he would prefer a short delay. He made the motion, therefore, hoping that it might be voted by a strong vote." Thomas H. Benton in his memoirs quoted the first part of Calhoun's remarks above, preceded by the observation that "Mr. Calhoun went beyond all other speakers, and advocated not only immediate recognition of the independence of Texas, but her simultaneous admission into the Union; was in favor of acting on both questions together, and at the present session; and saw an interest in the slaveholding States in preventing Texas from having the power to annoy them." Benton intentionally or unintentionally confused the debates of 5/23 and 7/1 in his history of the Texas question. Nor does his assertion that Calhoun "went beyond all other speakers" accurately reflect the reported remarks of Calhoun or of others on either date. See [Thomas H. Benton,] *Thirty Years' View; or a History of the Working of the American Government . . . from 1820 to 1850 . . .* (2 vols. New York: D. Appleton and Co., c. 1854–1856), 1:667.

Remarks on an increased appropriation for fortifications at Portsmouth, N.H., 5/24. Henry Hubbard of N.H. offered an amendment, passed 17 to 16, doubling the appropriation provided for Portsmouth in the fortifications bill. "Mr. Calhoun said this question involved so important a principle, that, without plans or estimates, he was not willing to trust it even to the discretion of the Secretary of War, and must, therefore, oppose it." After remarks by Hubbard and Thomas H. Benton, Calhoun "said that in detailed estimates the quantity of materials of each kind was minutely put down, and, when the cost of construction greatly exceeded the estimates, they knew who was to blame. But, he asked, upon whom did the responsibility rest in the case of conjectural estimates? They did not do their duty in regard to the trust reposed in them by acting in this general way, and there was something more at the bottom of this than mere fortifications." Later Calhoun "asked why the Senate should act before the surveys and estimates were made, when the Secretary of War himself would think it unwise to proceed without them? They were in no danger of a war at this time with any European Power; and why the necessity of acting at this time with such precipitation?" Benton remarked on the unreliability of estimates, alluding to a certain fort in Va. "where the cost exceeded the detailed estimate as two to one." Calhoun "said if Congress should make a call on the engineer in the case of a detailed estimate, he could explain where the fault was, and who was to blame. He stated the reason of the excess of cost in the case of Fort Calhoun, which was owing to its being built on a sand-bar." (A motion to strike the appropriation was defeated 10 to 25.) From *Register of Debates*, 24th Cong., 1st Sess., cols. 1550–1551. Also printed in the Washington, D.C., *Globe*, May 30, 1836, p. 2. Variant in the New York, N.Y., *Morning Courier and New-York Enquirer*, May 26, 1836, p. 2.

To S[AMUEL L.] GOUVERNEUR, [New York City]

Washington, 25th May 1836

My dear Sir, Tho' I am not much of a sportsman, I would have been delighted to attend your approaching races had circumstances permitted me to visit New York at this time. But it is quite impossible for me to leave my place in the Senate at this time. The deposit bill, of which I have special charge, is now before the Senate, and will not be disposed of till it will [be] too late for your noble sport. From the renown of the competitors, an arduous struggle is anticipated, which I would delight to witness; tho' my sympathy would be such, between friendship on one side, and local attachment on the other, that whatever result fate may decree, would be mingled with a due proportion of pain & pleasure. Anna [Maria Calhoun] joins me in thankful acknowledgement for the hospitable invitation of yourself and Mrs. [Maria Hester Monroe] Gouverneur, which, had it been in our power to visit your city, we would have accepted with much pleasure. Yours truely, J.C. Calhoun.

ALS in NN, Gouverneur Papers; PC in New York Public Library *Bulletin*, vol. III, no. 8 (August, 1899), pp. 332–333. NOTE: The event which Calhoun above declined to attend was a North/South challenge race sponsored by the New York Jockey Club on 5/31. "John Bascomb" owned by John Crowell of Ala. defeated "Post Boy" owned by Robert Tillotson of N.Y.

Remarks on the bill making appropriations for fortifications, 5/26. "Mr. Calhoun observed that this system of fortifications was likely to be run down by extravagant appropriations. It added something like two millions to the usual appropriation bill, and, considering the present prices, at least a million beyond what the appropriations ought to be. As the bill now stood, he felt himself compelled to vote against it." From *Register of Debates,* 24th Cong., 1st Sess., col. 1579. Also printed in the Washington, D.C., *Globe,* May 28, 1836, p. 2; *Congressional Globe,* 24th Cong., 1st Sess., p. 501; the Washington, D.C., *Daily National Intelligencer,* June 22, 1836, p. 1.

Remarks on the bill to regulate the deposits of public money, 5/27. During discussion of this bill, Silas Wright modified his substitute bill [offered on 4/6] by leaving blank the "amount of surplus to be retained for the floating demands upon Government." Calhoun "said as *he* had [on 5/25] filled up the blank, in the amendment proposed by him, to divide the surplus among the States of the Union, over *three* millions; he would modify it, so as also to leave the sum to be retained in blank; which was, by consent, agreed to." Wright then spoke "at length in favor of his project," after which Calhoun commented "on the necessity of proceeding, day after day, until this measure was disposed of; he desired time to reply to the observations of the Senator from N.Y., and moved an adjournment; which motion prevailed." From the New York, N.Y., *Morning Courier and New-York Enquirer,* May 31, 1836, p. 2.

Speech on the Bill to Regulate the Deposits of Public Money

[In the Senate, May 28, 1836]
The Senate then proceeded to the consideration of the bill to regulate the deposites of the public money [which had been introduced by Calhoun on 12/29/1835].

After some words from Mr. [Silas] Wright [of N.Y.], in explanation [of the substitute bill he had introduced on 4/6],

Mr. Calhoun said: This bill, which the Senator from New York proposes to strike out, in order to substitute his amendment, is no stranger to this body. It was reported at the last session by the select committee on Executive patronage, and passed the Senate, after a full and deliberate investigation, by a mixed vote of all parties, of twenty to twelve. As strong as is this presumptive evidence in its favor, I would, notwithstanding, readily surrender the bill, and adopt the amendment of the Senator from New York, if I did not sincerely believe that it was liable to strong and decisive objections. I seek no lead on this important subject; my sole aim is to aid in applying a remedy to what I honestly believe to be a deep and dangerous disease of the body politic; and I stand prepared to co-operate with any one, be he of what party he may, who may propose a remedy, provided it shall promise to be safe and efficient. I, in particular, am desirous of co-operating with the Senator from New York, not only because I desire the aid of his distinguished talents, but, still more, of his decisive influence with the powerful party of which he is so distinguished a member, and which now, for good or evil, holds the destiny of the country in its hands. It was in this spirit that I examined the amendment proposed by the Senator; and, I regret to say, after a full investigation, I cannot acquiesce in it, as I feel a deep conviction that it will be neither safe nor efficient. So far from being substantially the same as the bill, as stated by the Senator, I cannot but regard it as essentially different, both as to objects and means. The objects of the bill are, first, to secure the public interest, as far as it is connected with the deposites; and, next, to protect the banks in which they are made against the influence and control of the Executive branch of this Government, with a view both to theirs and the public interest. Compared with the bill, in respect to both, the proposed amendment will be found to favor the banks against the people, and the Executive against the banks. I do not desire the Senate to form their opinion on my authority. I wish them to examine for themselves; and, in order to aid them in the examination, I shall now proceed to state, and briefly illustrate, the several points of difference between the bill and the proposed amendment, taking them in the order in which they stand in the bill.

The first section of the bill provides that the banks shall pay at the rate of two per cent. per annum on the deposites for the use of the public money. This provision is entirely omitted in the amendment, which proposes to give to the banks the use of the money without interest. That the banks ought to pay something for the use of the public money, all must agree, whatever diversity of opinion there may be as to the amount. According to the last return of the Treasury Department, there was, on the 1st of this month, $45,000,000 of public money in the thirty-six depository banks, which they are at liberty to use as their own, for discount or business, till drawn out for disbursements; an event that may not happen for years. In a word, this vast amount is so much additional banking capital, giving the same, or nearly the same, profit to those institutions as their permanent chartered capital, without rendering any other service to the public than paying away from time to time the portion that might be required for the service of the Government. Assuming that the banks realize a profit of six per cent. on these deposites (it cannot be estimated at less,) it would give, on the present amount, nearly three millions of dollars per annum, and, on the probable average public deposites of the year, upwards of two millions of dollars; which enormous profit is derived from the public by comparatively few individuals, without any return or charge, except the inconsiderable service of paying out the drafts of the Treasury when presented. But it is due to the Senator to acknowledge that his amendment is predicated on the supposition that some disposition must be made of the surplus revenue, which would leave in the banks a sum not greater than would be requisite to meet the current expenditure—a supposition which necessarily must affect, very materially affect, the decision of the question of the amount of compensation the banks ought to make to the public for the use of its funds; but, let the disposition be what it may, the omission in the amendment of any compensation whatever is, in my opinion, wholly indefensible.

The next point of difference relates to transfer warrants. The bill prohibits the use of transfer warrants, except with a view to disbursement; while the amendment leaves them without regulation, under the sole control of the Treasury Department. To understand the importance of this difference, it must be borne in mind that the transfer warrants are the lever by which the whole banking operations of the country may be controlled, through the deposites. By them, the public money may be transferred from one bank to another, or from one State or section of the country to another State or section; and thus one bank may be elevated, and another depressed; and a redundant currency created in one State or section, and a deficient in another; and, through such redundancy or deficiency, all the moneyed engagements and business transactions of the whole community may be made dependent on the will of one man. With the present enormous surplus, it is difficult to assign limits to the extent of this power. The Secretary, or the irresponsible agent unknown to the laws, who, rumor says, has the direction of this immense power, (we are permitted to have no certain information,) may raise and depress stocks and property of all descriptions, at his pleasure, by withdrawing from one place and transferring to another, to the unlimited gain of those who are in the secret, and the certain ruin of those who are not. Such a field of speculation has never before been opened in any country; a field so great, that the Rothschilds themselves might be tempted to enter it, with their immense funds. Nor is the control which it would give over the politics of the country much less unlimited. To the same extent that it may be used to affect the interests and the fortunes of individuals, to the like extent it may be employed as an instrument of political influence and control. I do not intend to assert that it has or will be so employed: it is not essential at present to inquire how it has or will be used. It is sufficient for my purpose to show, as I trust I have satisfactorily, that it may be so employed. To guard against the abuse of so dangerous a power, the provision was inserted in the bill to prohibit the use of transfer warrants, except, as stated, for the purpose of disbursement; the omission of which provision in the amendment is a fatal objection to it, of itself, were there no other. But it is far from standing alone: the next point of difference will be found to be not less striking and fatal.

The professed object of both the bill and the amendment is to place the safe keeping of the public moneys under the regulation and control of law, instead of being left, as it now is, at the discretion of the Executive. However strange it may seem, the fact is nevertheless so, that the amendment entirely fails to effect the object which it is its professed object to accomplish. In order that it may be distinctly seen that what I state is the case, it will be necessary to view the provisions of the bill and the amendment in reference to the deposite separately, as they relate to the banks in which the public funds are now deposited, and those which may hereafter be selected to receive them.

The bill commences with the former, which it adopts as banks of deposite, and prescribes the regulations and conditions on the observance of which they shall continue such; while, at the same time, it places them beyond the control and influence of the executive department, by placing them under the protection of law so long as they continue faithfully to perform their duty as fiscal agents of the Government. It next authorizes the Secretary of the Treasury to select, under certain circumstances, additional banks of deposite, as the exigency of the public service may require, on which it imposes like regulations and conditions, and places in like manner under the protection of law. In all this the amendment pursues a very different course. It begins with authorizing the Secretary to select the banks of deposite, and limits the regulations and conditions it imposes on such banks; leaving, by an express provision, the present banks wholly under the control of the Treasury or the executive department, as they now are, without prescribing any time for the selection of other banks of deposite, or making it the duty of the Secretary so to do. The consequence is obvious. The Secretary may continue the present banks as long as he pleases; and so long as he may choose to continue them, the provisions of the amendment, so far as relates to the deposites, will be a dead letter; and the banks, of course, instead of being under the control of the law, will be contrary, as I have said, to the professed object both of the bill and amendment—subject exclusively to his will.

The Senator has attempted to explain this difference, but I must say very unsatisfactorily. He said that the bill prohibited the selection of other banks; and, as he deemed others to be necessary at certain important points, in consequence of the present enormous surplus, he inserted the provision authorizing the selection of other banks. The Senator has not stated the provisions of the bill accurately; so far from not authorizing, it expressly authorizes, the selection of other banks where there are now none; but I presume he intended to limit his remarks to places where there are no existing banks of deposite. Thus limited, the fact is as he states; but it by no means explains the extraordinary omission (for such I must consider it) of not extending the regulations to the existing banks, as well as to those hereafter to be selected. If the public service requires additional banks at New York and other important points, in consequence of the vast sums deposited there (as I readily agree it does,) if no disposition is to be made of the surplus, it is certainly a very good reason for enlarging the provisions of the bill, by authorizing the Secretary to select other banks at those points; but it is impossible for me to comprehend how it proves that the regulations which the amendment proposes to impose should be exclusively limited to such newly-selected banks. Nor do I see why the Senator has not observed the same rule in this case, as that which he adopted in reference to the compensation the banks ought to pay for the use of the public money. He omitted to provide for any compensation, on the ground that his amendment proposed to dispose of all the surplus money, leaving in the possession of the banks a sum barely sufficient to meet the current expenditure, for the use of which he did not consider it right to charge a compensation. On the same principle, it was unnecessary to provide for the selection of additional banks where there are now banks of deposite, as they would be ample if the surplus were disposed of. In this I understood the Senator himself to concur.

But it is not only in the important point of extending the regulations to existing banks of deposite, that the bill and the amendment differ. There is a striking difference between them in reference to the authority of Congress over the banks of deposite embraced both in the bill and the amendment. The latter, following the provision in the charter of the late Bank of the United States, authorizes the Secretary to withdraw the public deposites, and to discontinue the use of any one of the banks, whenever, in his opinion, such bank shall have violated the conditions on which it has been employed, or the public funds are not safe in its vaults, with the simple restriction, that he shall report the fact to Congress. We know from experience how slight is the check which this restriction imposes. It not only requires the concurrence of both Houses of Congress to overrule the act of the Secretary, where his power may be improperly exercised, but the act of Congress itself, intended to control such exercise of power, may be overruled by the veto of the President, at whose will the Secretary holds his place; so as to leave the control of the banks virtually under the control of the executive department of the Government. To obviate this, the bill vests the Secretary with the power simply of withdrawing the deposites and suspending the use of the bank as a place of deposite, and provides that, if Congress shall not confirm the removal, the deposite shall be returned to the bank after the termination of the next session of Congress.

The next point of difference is of far less importance, and is only mentioned as tending to illustrate the different character of the bill and the amendment. The former provides that the banks of deposite shall perform the duties of commissioners of loans, without compensation, in like manner as was the duty of the late Bank of the United States and its branches, under its charter. Among these duties is that of paying the pensioners—a very heavy branch of disbursement, and attended with considerable expense, and which will be saved to the Government under the bill, but will be lost if the amendment should prevail.

Another difference remains to be pointed out, relating to the security of the deposites. With so large an amount of public money in their vaults, it is important that the banks should always be provided with ample means to meet their engagements. With this view, the bill provides that the specie in the vaults of the several banks, and the aggregate of the balance in their favor with other specie-paying banks, shall be equal to one fifth of the entire amount of their notes and bills in circulation, and their public and private deposites—a sum, as is believed, sufficient to keep them in a sound and solvent condition. The amendment, on the contrary, provides that the banks shall keep in their own vaults, or the vaults of other banks, specie equal to one fourth of its notes and bills in circulation, and the balance of its accounts with other banks payable on demand.

I regret that the Senator has thought proper to change the phraseology, and to use terms less clear and explicit than those in the bill. I am not certain that I comprehend the exact meaning of the provision in the amendment. What is meant by specie in the vaults of other banks? In a general sense, all deposites are considered as specie; but I cannot suppose that to be the meaning in this instance, as it would render the provision in a great measure inoperative. I presume the amendment means special deposites in gold and silver in other banks, placed there for safe keeping, or to be drawn on, and not to be used by the bank in which it is deposited. Taking this to be the meaning, what is there to prevent the same sum from being twice counted in estimating the means of the several banks of deposite? Take two of them, one having $100,000 in specie in its vaults, and the other the same amount in the vaults of the other bank, which, in addition, has besides another $100,000 of its own: what is there to prevent the latter from returning, under the amendment, $200,000 of specie in its vaults, while the former would return $100,000 in its own vaults, and another in the vaults of the other bank, making, in the aggregate, between them, $400,000, when, in reality, the amount in both would be but $300,000?

But this is not the only difference between the bill and the amendment, in this particular, deserving of notice. The object of the provision is to compel the banks of deposite to have, at all times, ample means to meet their liabilities, so that the Government should have sufficient assurance that the public moneys in their vaults would be forthcoming when demanded. With this view, the bill provides that the available means of the bank shall never be less than one fifth of its aggregate liabilities, including bills, notes, and deposites, public and private; while the amendment entirely omits the private deposites, and includes only the balance of its deposites with other banks. This omission is the more remarkable, inasmuch as the greater portion of the liabilities of the deposite banks must, with the present large surplus, result from their deposites, as every one who is familiar with banking operations will readily perceive.

I have now presented to the Senate the several points of difference which I deem material between the bill and the amendment, with such remarks as may enable them to form their own opinion, in reference to the difference, so that they may decide how far the assertion is true, with which I set out, that, wherever they differ, the amendment favors the banks against the interests of the public, and the Executive against the banks.

The Senator, acting on the supposition that there would be a permanent surplus, beyond the expenditure of the Government, which neither justice nor regard to the public interest would permit to remain in the banks, has extended the provisions of his amendment, with great propriety, so as to comprehend a plan to withdraw the surplus from the banks. His plan is to vest the commissioners of the sinking fund with authority to estimate, at the beginning of every quarter, the probable receipts and expenditures of the quarter; and if, in their opinion, the receipts, with the money in the Treasury, should exceed the estimated expenditure by a certain sum, say $5,000,000, the excess should be vested in State stocks [that is, bonds]; and if it should fall short of that sum, a sufficient amount of the stocks should be sold to make up the deficit. We have thus presented for consideration the important subject of the surplus revenue, and with it the question so anxiously and universally asked, What shall be done with the surplus? Shall it be expended by the Government, or remain where it is, or be disposed of as proposed by the Senator? Or, if not, what other disposition shall be made of it? Questions, the investigation of which necessarily embraces the entire circle of our policy, and on the decision of which the future destiny of the country may depend.

But before we enter on the discussion of this important question, it will be proper to ascertain what will be the probable available means of the year, in order that some conception may be formed of the probable surplus which may remain, by comparing it with the appropriations that may be authorized.

According to the late report of the Secretary of the Treasury, there was deposited in the several banks little upwards of $33,000,000 at the termination of the first quarter of the year, not including the sum of about $3,000,000 deposited by the disbursing agents of the Government. The same report stated the receipts of the quarter at about $11,000,000, of which lands and customs yielded nearly an equal amount. Assuming for the three remaining quarters an equal amount, it would give for the entire receipts of the year $44,000,000. I agree with the Senator, that this sum is too large. The customs will probably average an amount throughout the year corresponding with the receipts of the first quarter; but there probably will be a considerable falling off in the receipts from the public lands. Assuming $7,000,000 as the probable amount, which I presume will be ample, the receipts of the year, subtracting that sum from $44,000,000, will be $37,000,000; and subtracting from that $11,000,000, the receipts of the first quarter would leave $26,000,000 as the probable receipts of the last three quarters. Add to this sum $33,000,000, the amount in the Treasury on the last day of the first quarter, and it gives $59,000,000. To this add the amount of stock in the United States Bank, which at the market price is worth at least $7,000,000, and we have $66,000,000, which I consider as the least amount at which the probable available means of the year can be fairly estimated. It will probably very considerably exceed this amount. The range may be put down at between $66,000,000 and $73,000,000, which may be considered as the two extremes, between which the means of the year may vibrate. But in order to be safe, I have assumed the least of the two.

The first question which I propose to consider is, shall this sum be expended by the Government in the course of the year? A sum nearly equal to the entire debt of the war of the Revolution, by which the liberty and independence of these States were established; more than five times greater than the expenditure of the Government at the commencement of the present administration, deducting the payments on account of the public debt, and more than four times greater than the average annual expenditure of the present administration, making the same deduction, extravagant as its expenditure has been. The very magnitude of the sum decides the question against expenditure. It may be wasted, thrown away, but it cannot be expended. There are not objects on which to expend it; for proof of which I appeal to the appropriations already made and contemplated. We have passed the navy appropriations, which, as liberal as they are admitted to be on all sides, are raised only about $2,000,000, compared with the appropriations of the last year. The appropriations for fortifications, supposing the bills now pending should pass, will amount to about $3,500,000, and would exceed the ordinary appropriations, assuming them at $1,000,000, which I hold to be ample, by $2,500,000. Add a million for ordnance, seven or eight for Indian treaties, and four for Indian wars, and supposing the companies of the regular army to be filled as recommended by the War Department, the aggregate amount, including the ordinary expenditures, would be between thirty and thirty-five millions, and would leave a balance of at least $30,000,000 in the Treasury at the end of the year.

But suppose objects could be devised on which to expend the whole of the available means of the year, it would still be impossible to make the expenditure, without immense waste and confusion. To expend so large an amount regularly and methodically, would require a vast increase of able and experienced disbursing officers, and a great enlargement of the organization of the Government in all the branches connected with disbursements. To effect such an enlargement, and to give suitable organization, placed under the control of skillful and efficient officers, must necessarily be a work of time; but, without it, so sudden and great an increase of expenditure would necessarily be followed by inextricable confusion and heavy losses.

But suppose this difficulty overcome, and suitable objects could be devised, would it be advisable to make the expenditure? Would it be wise to draw so vast an amount of productive labor, to be employed in unproductive objects, in building fortifications, dead walls, and in lining the interior frontier with a large military force, neither of which would add a cent to the productive power of the country?

The ordinary expenditure of the Government, under the present administration, may be estimated say at $18,000,000—a sum exceeding, by five or six millions, what, in my opinion, is sufficient for a just and efficient administration of the Government. Taking eighteen from sixty-six, would leave forty-eight millions as the surplus, if the affairs of the Government had been so administered as to avoid the heavy expenditures of the year, which, I firmly believe, with early and prudent counsel, might have been effected. The expenditure of this sum, estimating labor at $20 a month, would require 200,000 operatives, equal to one third of the whole number of laborers employed in producing the great staple of our country, which is spreading wealth and prosperity over the land, and controlling, in a great measure, the commerce and manufactures of the world. But take what will be the actual surplus, and estimate that at half the sum which, with prudence and economy, it might have been, and it would require the subtraction of 100,000 operatives from their present useful employment, to be employed in the unproductive service of the Government. Would it, I again repeat, be wise to draw off this immense mass of productive labor, in order to employ it in building fortifications, and swelling the military establishment of the country? Would it add to the strength of the

Union, or give increased security to its liberty, or accelerate its prosperity?—the great objects for which the Government was constituted.

To ascertain how the strength of any country may be best developed, its peculiar state and condition must be taken into consideration. Looking to ours with this view, who can doubt that, next to our free institutions, the main source of our growing greatness and power is to be found in our great and astonishing increase of numbers, wealth, and facility of intercourse? If we desire to see our country powerful, we ought to avoid any measure opposed to their development, and, in particular, ought to make the smallest possible draught, consistent with our peace and security, on the productive powers of the country. Let these have the freest possible play. Leave the resources of individuals under their own direction to be employed in advancing theirs and their country's wealth and prosperity, with the extraction of the least amount required for the expenditure of the Government; and draw off not a single laborer from their present productive pursuits to the unproductive employment of the Government, excepting such as the public service may render indispensable. Who can doubt that such a policy would add infinitely more to the power and strength of the country than the extravagant scheme of spending millions on fortifications and the increase of the military establishment?

Let us next examine how the liberty of the country may be affected by the scheme of disposing of the surplus by disbursements. And here I would ask, is the liberty of the country at present in a secure and stable condition; and if not, by what is it endangered? And will an increase of disbursements augment or diminish the danger?

Whatever may be the diversity of opinion on other points, there is not an intelligent individual of any party, who regards his reputation, that will venture to deny that the liberty of the country is at this time more insecure and unstable than it ever has been. We all know that there is in every portion of the Union, and with every party, a deep feeling that our political institutions are undergoing a great and hazardous change. Nor is the feeling much less strong, that the vast increase of the patronage and influence of the Government is the cause of the great and fearful change which is so extensively affecting the character of our people and institutions. The effect of increasing the expenditures at this time, so as to absorb the surplus, would be to double the number of those who live, or expect to live, by the Government, and in the same degree augment its patronage and influence, and accelerate that downward course which, if not arrested, must speedily terminate in the overthrow of our free institutions.

These views I hold to be decisive against the wild attempt to absorb the immense means of the Government by the expenditures of the year. In fact, with the exception of a few individuals, all seem to regard the scheme either as impracticable or unsafe; but there are others who, while they condemn the attempt of disposing of the surplus by immediate expenditures, believe it can be safely and expediently expended, in a period of four or five years, on what they choose to call the defences of the country.

In order to determine how far this opinion is correct, it will be necessary first to ascertain what will be the available means of the next four or five years; by comparing which with what ought to be the expenditure, we may determine whether the plan would, or would not, be expedient. In making the calculation, I will take the term of five years, including the present, and which of course will comprehend 1840; after the termination of which, the duties above twenty per cent. are to go off, by the provisions of the compromise act [of 1833], in eighteen months, when the revenue is to be reduced to the economical and just wants of the Government.

The available means of the present year, as I have already shown, will equal at least $66,000,000. That of the next succeeding four years (including 1840) may be assumed to be twenty-one millions annually. The reason for this assumption may be seen in the report of the select committee at the last session, which I have reviewed, and in the correctness of which I feel increased confidence. The amount may fall short of, but will certainly not exceed, the estimate in the report, unless some unforeseen event should occur. Assuming, then, $21,000,000 as the average receipts of the next four years, it will give an aggregate of $84,000,000, which, added to the available means of this year, will give $150,000,000 as the sum that will be at the disposal of the Government for the period assumed. Divide this sum by five, the number of years, and it will give $30,000,000 as the average annual available means of the period.

The next question for consideration is, will it be expedient to raise the disbursement during the period to an average expenditure of $30,000,000 annually? The first and strong objection to the scheme is, that it would leave in the deposite banks a heavy surplus during the greater part of the time, beginning with a surplus of upwards of thirty millions at the commencement of next year, and decreasing at the rate of eight or nine millions a year, till the termination of the period. But, passing this objection by, I meet the question directly. It would be highly inexpedient and dangerous to attempt to keep up the disbursements at so high a rate. I ask, on what shall this money be expended? Shall it be expended by an increase of the military establishment? by an enlargement of the appropriations for fortifications, ordnance, and the navy, far beyond what is proposed for the present year? Have those who advocate the scheme reflected to what extent this enlargement must be carried, to absorb so great a sum? Even this year, with the extraordinary expenditure upon Indian treaties and Indian wars, and with profuse expenditure in every other branch of service, the aggregate amount of appropriations will not greatly exceed $30,000,000, and that of disbursements will not probably equal that sum. To what extent, then, must the appropriations for the army, the navy, the fortifications, and the like, be carried, in order to absorb that sum, especially with a declining expenditure in several branches of the service, particularly in the pensions, which, during the period, will fall off more than a million of dollars? But, in order to take a full view of the folly and danger of the scheme, it will be necessary to extend our view beyond 1842, in order to form some opinion of what will be the income of the Government when the tariff shall be so reduced, under the compromise act, that no duty shall exceed twenty per cent. ad valorem. I know that any estimate made at this time cannot be considered much more than conjectural; but still, it would be imprudent to adopt a system of expenditure now, without taking into consideration the probable state of the revenue a few years hence.

After bestowing due reflection on the subject, I am of the impression that the income from the imposts after the period in question will not exceed $10,000,000. It will probably fall below, rather than rise above, that sum. I assume as the basis of this estimate, that our consumption of foreign articles will not then exceed $150,000,000. We all know that the capacity of the country to consume depends upon the value of its domestic exports, and the profits of its commerce and navigation. Of its domestic exports it would not be safe to assume any considerable increase in any article except cotton. To what extent the production and consumption of this great staple, which puts in motion so vast an amount of the industry and commerce of the world, may be increased between now and 1842, is difficult to conjecture; but I deem it unsafe to suppose that it can be so increased as to extend the capacity of the country to consume beyond the limits I have assigned. Assuming, then, the amount which I have, and dividing the imports into free and dutiable articles, the latter, according to the existing proportion between the two descriptions, would amount in value to something less than $70,000,000. According to the compromise act, no duty, after the period in question, can exceed twenty per cent., and the rates would range from that down to five or six per cent. Taking fifteen per cent. as the average, which would be probably full high, and allowing for the expenses of collection, the nett [sic] income would be something less than $10,000,000.

The income from public lands is still more conjectural than that from customs. There are so many and such various causes in operation affecting this source of the public income, that it is exceedingly difficult to form even a conjectural estimate as to its amount beyond the current year. But, in the midst of this uncertainty, one fact may be safely assumed, that the purchases during the last year, and thus far [during] this, greatly exceed the steady progressive demand for public lands, from increased population, and the consequent emigration to the new States and Territories. Much of the purchases have been unquestionably made upon speculation, with a view to resales, and must, of course, come into market hereafter in competition with the lands of the Government, and to that extent must reduce the income from their sales. Estimating even the demand for public lands from what it was previous to the recent large sales, and taking into estimate the increased population and wealth of the country, I do not consider it safe to assume more than $5,000,000 annually from this branch of the revenue, which, added to the customs, would give for the annual receipts between fourteen and fifteen millions of dollars after 1842.

I now ask whether it would be prudent to raise the public expenditures to the sum of $30,000,000 annually, during the intermediate period, with the prospect that they must be suddenly reduced to half of that amount? Who does not see the fierce conflict which must follow between those who may be interested in keeping up the expenditures, and those who have an equal interest against an increase of the duties as the means of keeping them up? I appeal to the Senators from the South, whose constituents have so deep an interest in low duties, to resist a course so impolitic, unwise, and extravagant, and which, if adopted, might again renew the tariff, so recently thrown off by such hazardous and strenuous efforts, with all its oppression and disaster. Let us remember what occurred in the fatal session of 1828. With a folly unparalleled, Congress then raised the duties to a rate so enormous as to average one half the value of the imposts [sic], when on the eve of discharging the debt, and when, of course, there would be no objects on which the immense income from such extravagant duties could be justly and constitutionally expended. It is amazing that there was such blindness then as not to see what has since followed—the sudden discharge of the debt and an overflowing Treasury, without the means of absorbing the surplus; the violent conflict resulting from such a state of things; and the vast increase of the power and patronage of the Government, with all its corrupting consequences. We are now about, I fear, to commit an error of a different character: to raise the expenditure far beyond all example in time of peace, and with a decreasing revenue, which must, with equal certainty, bring on another conflict not much less dangerous, in which the struggle will not be to find objects to absorb an overflowing Treasury, but to devise means to continue an expenditure far beyond the just and legitimate wants of the country. It is easy to foresee that, if we are thus blindly to go on in the management of our affairs, without regard to the future, the frequent and violent concussions which must follow from such folly cannot but end in a catastrophe that will ingulf our political institutions.

With such decided objections to the dangerous and extravagant scheme of absorbing the surplus by disbursements, I proceed to the next question, Shall the public money remain where it now is? Shall the present extraordinary state of things, without example or parallel, continue, of a Government calling itself free, exacting from the people millions beyond what it can expend, and placing that vast sum in the custody of a few monopolizing corporations selected at the sole will of the Executive, and continued during his pleasure, to be used as their own from the time it is collected till it is disbursed? To this question there must burst from the lips of every man who loves his country and its institutions, and who is the enemy of monopoly, injustice, and oppression, an indignant *no*. And here let me express the pleasure I feel, that the Senator from New York, in moving his amendment, however objectionable his scheme, has placed himself in opposition to the continuance of the present unheard-of and dangerous state of things; and I add, as a simple act of justice, that the tone and temper of his remarks in support of his amendment were characterized by a courtesy and liberality which I, on my part, shall endeavor to imitate. But I fear, notwithstanding this favorable indication in so influential a quarter, the very magnitude of the evil (too great to be concealed) will but serve to perpetuate it. So great and various are the interests enlisted in its favor, that I greatly fear all the efforts of the wise and patriotic to arrest it will prove unavailing. At the head of these stand the depository banks themselves, with their numerous stockholders and officers; with their $40,000,000 of capital, and an equal amount of public deposites, associated into one great combination extending over the whole Union, under the influence and control of the Treasury Department. The whole weight of this mighty combination, so deeply interested in the continuance of the present state of things, is opposed to any change. To this powerful combination must be added the numerous and influential body who are dependant on banks to meet their engagements, and who, whatever may be their political opinions, must be alarmed at any change which may limit their discounts and accommodation. Then come the stock-jobbers, a growing and formidable class, who live by raising and depressing stocks, and who behold in the present state of things the most favorable opportunity of carrying on their dangerous and corrupting pursuits. With the control which the Secretary of the Treasury has over the banks of deposite, through transfer warrants, with the power of withdrawing the deposites at pleasure, he may, whenever he chooses, raise and depress the stock of any bank; and, if disposed to use this tremendous power for corrupt purposes, may make the fortunes of the initiated, and overwhelm in sudden ruin those not in the secret. To the stock-jobbers must be added speculators of every hue and form; and, in particular, the speculators in public lands, who, by the use of the public funds, are rapidly divesting the people of the noble patrimony left by our ancestors in the public domain, by giving in exchange what may in the end prove to be broken credit and worthless rags. To these we must add the artful and crafty politicians who wield this mighty combination of interests for political purposes. I am anxious to avoid mingling party politics in this discussion; and that I may not even seem to do so, I shall not attempt to exhibit, in all its details, the fearful, and, I was about to add, the overwhelming power which the present state of things places in the hands of those who have control of the Government, and which, if it be not wielded to overthrow our institutions and destroy all responsibility, must be attributed to their want of inclination, and not to their want of means.

Such is the power and influence interested to continue the public money where it is now deposited. To these there are opposed the honest, virtuous, and patriotic, of every party, who behold in the continuance of the present state of things almost certain convulsion and overthrow of our liberty. There would be found on the same side the great mass of the industrious and laboring portion of the community, whose hard earnings are extracted from them without their knowledge, were it not that what is improperly taken from them is successfully used as the means of deceiving and controlling them. If such were not the case—if those who work could see how those who profit are enriched at their expense—the present state of things would not be endured for a moment; but, as it is, I fear that from misconception, and consequent want of union and co-operation, things may continue as they are, till it will be too late to apply a remedy. I trust, however, that such will not be the fact; that the people will be roused from their false security, and that Congress will refuse to adjourn till an efficient remedy is applied. In this hope I recur to the inquiry, what shall that remedy be? Shall we adopt the measure recommended by the Senator from New York, which, as has been stated, proposes to authorize the commissioners of the sinking fund to ascertain the probable income of each quarter, and, if there should be a probable excess above $5,000,000, to vest the surplus in the purchase of State stocks; but, if there should be a deficiency, to sell so much of the stock previously purchased as would make up the difference.

I regret that the Senator has not furnished a statement of facts sufficiently full to enable us to form an opinion of what will be the practical operation of his scheme. He has omitted, for instance, to state what is the aggregate amount of stocks issued by the several States—a fact indispensable in order to ascertain how the price of the stocks would be affected by the application of the surplus to their purchase. All who are in the least familiar with subjects of this kind, must know that the price of stock rises proportionably with the amount of the sum applied to their purchase. I have already shown that the probable surplus at the end of this year, notwithstanding the extravagance of the appropriations, will be between thirty and thirty-five millions; and before we can decide understandingly whether this great sum can with propriety be applied as the Senator proposes, we should know whether the amount of State stocks be sufficient to absorb it, without raising their price extravagantly high.

The Senator should also have informed us, not only as to the amount of the stock, but how it is distributed among the States, in order to enable us to determine whether his scheme would operate equally between them. In the absence of correct information on both of these points, we are compelled to use such as we may possess, however defective and uncertain, in order to make up our mind on his amendment.

We all know, then, that while several of the States have no stocks, and many a very inconsiderable amount, three of the large States (Pennsylvania, Ohio, and New York) have a very large amount, not less in the aggregate, if I am correctly informed, than thirty-five or forty millions. What amount is held by the rest of the States is uncertain; but I suppose that it may be safely assumed that, taking the whole, it is less than that held by those States. With these facts, it cannot be doubted that the application of the surplus, as proposed to be applied by the Senator, would be exceedingly unequal among the States, and that the advantage of the application would mainly accrue to these three States. To meet these objections, the Senator, while he does not deny that the application of the surplus will greatly raise the price of stocks, insists that the States issuing them will not derive any benefit from the advance, and consequently have no interest in the question of the application of the surplus to their purchase.

If by States he means the Government of the States, the view of the Senator may be correct. They may, as he says, have but little interest in the market value of their stocks, as they must be redeemed by the same amount, whether that be high or low. But if we take a more enlarged view, and comprehend the people of the State, as well as the Government, the argument entirely fails. The Senator will not deny that the holders have a deep interest in the application of so large a sum as the present surplus in the purchase of their stocks. He will not deny that such application must greatly advance the price; and, of course, in determining whether the States having stocks will be benefited by applying the surplus as he proposes, we must first ascertain who are the holders. Where do they reside? Are they foreigners residing abroad? If so, would it be wise to apply the public money so as to advance the interest of foreigners, to whom the States are under no obligation, but honestly to pay them the debts which they have contracted? But if not held by foreigners, are they held by citizens of such States? If such be the fact, will the Senator deny that those States will be deeply interested in the application of the surplus as proposed in his amendment, when the effects of such application must be, as is conceded on all sides, greatly to enhance the price of the stocks, and consequently to increase the wealth of their citizens? Let us suppose that, instead of purchasing the stocks of the States in which his constituents are interested, the Senator's amendment had proposed to apply the present enormous surplus to the purchase of cotton or slaves, in which the constituents of the southern Senators are inter-

219

ested: would any one doubt that the cotton-growing or slave-holding States would have a deep interest in the question? It will not be denied that, if so applied, their price would be greatly advanced, and the wealth of their citizens proportionably increased. Precisely the same effect would result from the application to the purchase of stocks, with like benefits to the citizens of the States which have issued large amounts of stock. The principle is the same in both cases.

But there is another view of the subject which demands most serious consideration. Assuming, what will not be questioned, that the application of the surplus, as proposed by the amendment, will be very unequal among the States, some having little or none, and others a large amount of stocks, the result would necessarily be to create, in effect, the relation of debtor and creditor between the States. The States, whose stocks might be purchased by the commissioners, would become the debtors of the Government; and as the Government would, in fact, be but the agent between them and the other States, the latter would, in reality, be their creditors. This relation between them could not fail to be productive of important political consequences, which would influence all the operations of the Government. It would, in particular, have a powerful bearing upon the Presidential election; the debtor and creditor States each striving to give such a result to the elections as might be favorable to their respective interests; the one to exact, and the other to exempt themselves from the payment of the debt. Supposing the three great States to which I have referred, whose united influence would have so decided a control, to be the principal debtor States (as would, in all probability, be the fact) it is easy to see that the result would be, finally, the release of the debt, and consequently a correspondent loss to the creditor, and gain to the debtor States.

But there is another view of the subject still more deserving, if possible, of attention, than either of those which have been presented. It is impossible not to see, after what has been said, that the power proposed to be conferred by the amendment of the Senator, of applying the surplus in buying and selling the stocks of the States, is one of great extent, and calculated to have powerful influence, not only on a large body of the most wealthy and influential citizens of the States which have issued stocks, but on the States themselves. The next question is, in whom is the exercise of this power to be vested? Where shall we find individuals sufficiently detached from the politics of the day, and whose virtue, patriotism, disinterestedness, and firmness, can raise them so far above political and sinister motives, as to exercise powers so high and influential, exclusively for the public good, without any view to personal or political aggrandizement? Who has the amendment selected as standing aloof from politics, and possessing these high qualifications? Who are the present commissioners of the sinking fund, to whom this high and responsible trust is to be confided? At the head stands the Vice President of the United States [Martin Van Buren], with whom the Chief Justice of the United States [Roger B. Taney], the Secretary of State [John Forsyth], the Secretary of the Treasury [Levi Woodbury], and the Attorney General [Benjamin F. Butler], are associated; all party men, deeply interested in the maintenance of power in the present hands, and having the strongest motives to apply the vast power which the amendment would confer upon them, should it become a law, to party purposes. I do not say it would be so applied; but I must ask, would it be prudent, would it be wise, would it be seemly, to vest such great and dangerous powers in those who have so strong a motive to abuse them, and who, if they should have elevation and virtue enough to resist the temptation, would still be suspected of having used the power for sinister and corrupt purposes? I am persuaded that, in drawing the amendment, the Senator from New York has, without due reflection on the impropriety of vesting the power where he proposes, inadvertently inserted the provision which he has; and that, on review, he will concur with me, that, should his amendment be adopted, the power ought to be vested in others, less exposed to temptation, and consequently less exposed to suspicion.

I have now stated the leading objections to the several modes of disposing of the surplus revenue, which I propose to consider; and the question again recurs, What shall be done with the surplus? The Senate is not uninformed of my opinion on this important subject. Foreseeing that there would be a large surplus, and the mischievous consequences that must follow, I moved, during the last session, for a select committee, which, among other measures, reported a resolution so to amend the Constitution as to authorize a temporary distribution of the surplus among the States; but so many doubted whether there would be a surplus at the time, that it rendered all prospect of carrying the resolution hopeless. My opinion still remains unchanged, that the measure then proposed was the best; but so rapid has been the accumulation of the surplus, even beyond my calculation, and so pressing the danger, that what would have been then an efficient remedy, would now be too tardy to meet the danger; and, of course, another remedy must be devised more speedy in its action.

After bestowing on the subject the most deliberate attention, I have come to the conclusion that there is no other so safe, so efficient, and so free from objections, as the one I have proposed—of depositing the surplus that may remain at the termination of the year in the treasuries of the several States, in the manner provided for in the amendment. But the Senator from New York objects to the measure, that it would, in effect, amount to a distribution, on the ground, as he conceives, that the States would never refund. He does not doubt but that they would, if called on to refund by the Government; but he says that Congress will in fact never make the call. He rests this conclusion on the supposition that there would be a majority of the States opposed to it. He admits, in case the revenue should become deficient, that the southern or staple States would prefer to refund their quota, rather than to raise the imposts to meet the deficit; but he insists that the contrary would be the case with the manufacturing States, which would prefer to increase the imposts to refunding their quota, on the ground that the increase of the duties would promote the interests of manufactures. I cannot agree with the Senator that those States would assume a position so utterly untenable as to refuse to refund a deposite which their faith would be plighted to return, and rest the refusal on the ground of preferring to lay a tax, because it would be a bounty to them, and would consequently throw the whole burden of the tax on the other States. But, be this as it may, I can tell the Senator that, if they should take a course so unjust and monstrous, he may be assured that the other States would most unquestionably resist the increase of the imposts; so that the Government would have to take its choice, either to go without the money, or call on the States to refund the deposites. But I so far agree with the Senator as to believe that Congress would be very reluctant to make the call; that it would not make it till, from the wants of the Treasury, it should become absolutely necessary; and that, in order to avoid such necessity, it would resort to a just and proper economy in the public expenditures as the preferable alternative. I see in this, however, much good instead of evil. The Government has long since departed from habits of economy, and has fallen into a profusion, a waste, and an extravagance in its disbursements, rarely equalled by any free state, and which threatens the most disastrous consequences.

But I am happy to think that the ground on which the objection of the Senator stands may be removed, without materially impairing the provisions of the bill. It will require but the addition of a few words to remove it, by giving to the deposites all the advantages, without the objections which he proposes by his plan. It will be easy to provide that the States shall authorize the proper officers to give negotiable certificates of deposite, which shall not bear interest till demanded, when they shall bear the usual rates till paid. Such certificates would be, in fact, State stocks, every way similar to that in which the Senator proposes to vest the surplus, but with this striking superiority: that, instead of being partial, and limited to a few States, they would be fairly and justly apportioned among the several States. They would have another striking advantage over his. They would create among all the members of the confederacy reciprocally the relation of debtor and creditor, in proportion to their relative weight in the Union; which, in effect, would leave them in their present relation, and would of course avoid the danger that would result from his plan, which, as has been shown, would necessarily make a part of the States debtors to the rest, with all the danger resulting from such relation.

The next objection of the Senator is to the ratio of distribution, proposed in the bill, among the States, which he pronounces to be unequal, if not unconstitutional. He insists that the true principle would be to distribute the surplus among the States in proportion to the representation in the House of Representatives, without including the Senators, as is proposed in the bill; for which he relies on the fact, that, by the Constitution, representation and taxation are to be apportioned in the same manner among the States.

The Senate will see that the effect of adopting the ratio supported by the Senator would be to favor the large States, while that in the bill will be more favorable to the small.

The State I in part represent occupies a neutral position between the two. She cannot be considered either a large or a small State, forming, as she does, one twenty-fourth part of the Union, and of course it is the same to her whichever ratio may be adopted. But I prefer the one contained in my amendment, on the ground that it represents the relative weight of the States in the Government. It is the weight assigned to them in the choice of the President and Vice President in the electoral college, and, of course, in the administration of the laws. It is also that assigned to them in the making of the laws by the action of the two Houses, and corresponds very nearly to their weight in the judicial department of the Government; the judges being nominated by the President and confirmed by the Senate. In addition, I was influenced in selecting the ratio by the belief that it was a wise and magnanimous course, in case of doubt, to favor the weaker members of the confederacy. The larger can always take care of themselves, and, to avoid jealousy and improper feelings, ought to act liberally towards the weaker members of the confederacy. To which may be added, that I am of the impression that, even on the principle assumed by the Senator, that the distribution of the surplus ought to be apportioned on the ratio with direct taxation, (which may be well doubted,) the ratio which I support would conform in practice more nearly to the principle than that which he supports. It is a fact not generally known, that representation in the other House, and direct taxes, should they be laid, would be very far from being equal, although the Constitution provides that they should be. The inequality would result from the mode of apportioning the Representatives. Instead of apportioning them among the States, as near as may be, as directed by the Constitution, an artificial mode of distribution has been adopted, which in its effects gives to the large States a greater number, and to the small a less, than that to which they are entitled. I would refer those who may desire to understand how this inequality is effected, to the discussion in this body on the apportionment bill, under the last census. So great is this inequality, that, were a direct tax to be laid, New York, for instance, would have at least three members more than her apportionment of the tax would require. The ratio which I have proposed would, I admit, produce as great an inequality in favor of some of the small States, particularly the old, whose population is nearly stationary; but, among the new and growing members of the confederacy, which constitute the greater portion of the small States, it would not give them a larger share of the deposites than what they would be entitled to on the principle of direct taxes. But the objection of the Senator to the ratio of distribution, like his objection to the condition on which the bill proposes to make it, is a matter of small comparative consequence. I am prepared, in the spirit of concession, to adopt either, as one or the other may be more acceptable to the Senate.

It now remains to compare the disposition of the surplus proposed in the bill with the others I have discussed; and, unless I am greatly deceived, it possesses great advantages over them. Compared with the scheme of expending the surplus, its advantage is, that it would avoid the extravagance and waste which must result from suddenly more than quadrupling the expenditures, without a corresponding organization in the disbursing department of the Government to enforce economy and responsibility. It would also avoid the diversion of so large a portion of the industry of the country from its present useful direction to unproductive objects, with heavy loss to the wealth and prosperity of the country, as has been shown; while it would, at the same time, avoid the increase of the patronage and influence of the Government, with all their corruption and danger to the liberty and institutions of the country. But its advantages would not be limited simply to avoiding the evil of extravagant and useless disbursements. It would confer positive benefits, by enabling the States to discharge their debts, and complete a system of internal improvements by railroads and canals, which would not only greatly strengthen the bonds of the confederacy, but increase its power, by augmenting infinitely our resources and prosperity.

I do not deem it necessary to compare the disposition of the surplus which is proposed in the bill with the dangerous, and, I must say, wicked scheme of leaving the public funds where they are, in the banks of deposite, to be loaned out by those institutions to speculators and partisans, without authority or control of law.

Compared with the plan proposed by the Senator from New York, it is sufficient, to prove its superiority, to say that, while it avoids all the objections to which his is liable, it at the same time possesses all the advantages, with others peculiar to itself. Among these, one of the most prominent is, that it provides the only efficient remedy for the deep-seated disease which now afflicts the body politic, and which threatens to terminate so fatally, unless it be speedily and effectually arrested.

All who have reflected on the nature of our complex system of government, and the dangers to which it is exposed, have seen that it is susceptible, from its structure, to two dangers of opposite character: one threatening consolidation, and the other anarchy and dissolution. From the beginning of the Government we find a difference of opinion among the wise and patriotic, as to which the Government was most exposed; one party believing that the danger was that the Government would absorb the reserved powers of the States, and terminate in consolidation; while the other were equally confident that the States would absorb the powers of the Government, and the system end in anarchy and dissolution. It was this diversity of opinion which gave birth to the two great, honest, and patriotic parties which so long divided the community, and to the many political conflicts which so long agitated the country. Time has decided the controversy. We are no longer left to doubt that

the danger is on the side of this Government, and that, if not arrested, the system must terminate in an entire absorption of the
powers of the States.

Looking back, with the light which experience has furnished,
we now clearly see that both of the parties took a false view of the
operation of the system. It was admitted by both that there would
be a conflict for power between the Government and the States,
arising from a disposition on the part of those who, for the time
being, exercised the powers of the Government, and the States, to
enlarge their respective powers at the expense of each other, and
which would induce each to watch the other with incessant vig-
ilance. Had such proved to be the fact, I readily concede that the
result would have been the opposite to what has occurred, and the
Republican, and not the Federal party, would have been mistaken
as to the tendency of the system. But so far from this jealousy,
experience has shown that in the operation of the system a majority
of the States have acted in concert with the Government at all times,
except upon the eve of a political revolution, when one party was
about to go out, to make room for the other to come in; and we now
clearly see that this has not been the result of accident, but that the
habitual operation must necessarily be so. The misconception resulted from overlooking the fact, that the Government is but an
agent of the States, and that the dominant majority of the Union,
which elect and control a majority of the State Legislatures, would
also elect those who would control this Government, whether that
majority rested on sectional interests, on patronage and influence,
or whatever basis it might; and that they would use the power both
of the general and State Governments jointly, for aggrandizement
and the perpetuation of their power. Regarded in this light, it is
not at all surprising that the tendency of the system is such as it
has proved itself to be, and which any intelligent observer now sees
must necessarily terminate in a central, absolute, irresponsible, and
despotic power. It is this fatal tendency that the measure proposed
in the bill is calculated to counteract, and which I believe would
prove effective if now applied. It would place the States in the relation in which it was universally believed they would stand to this
Government at the time of its formation, and make them those
jealous and vigilant guardians of its actions on all measures touching the disbursements and expenditure of the Government, and
which it was confidently believed they would be, which would arrest the fatal tendency to the concentration of the entire power of
the system in this Government, if any power on earth can.

But it is objected that the remedy would be too powerful, and would produce an opposite and equally dangerous tendency. I coincide [sic] that such would be the danger, if permanently applied; and under that impression, and believing that the present excess of revenue would not continue longer, I have limited the measure to the duration of the compromise act. Thus limited, it will act sufficiently long, I trust, to eradicate the present disease, without superinducing one of an opposite character.

But the plan proposed is supported by its justice, as well as these high considerations of political expediency. The surplus money in the Treasury is not ours. It properly belongs to those who made it, and from whom it has been unjustly taken. I hold it an unquestionable principle, that the Government has no right to take a cent from the people beyond what is necessary to meet its legitimate and constitutional wants. To take more intentionally, would be robbery; and if the Government has not incurred the guilt in the present case, its exemption can only be found in its folly—the folly of not seeing and guarding against a vast excess of revenue, which the most ordinary understanding ought to have foreseen and prevented. If it were in our power—if we could ascertain from whom the vast amount now in the Treasury was improperly taken, justice would demand that it should be returned to its lawful owners. But as that is impossible, the measure next best, as approaching nearest to restitution, is that which is proposed—to deposit it in the treasuries of the several States, which will place it under the disposition of the immediate representatives of the people, to be used by them as they may think fit, till the wants of the Government may require its return.

But it is objected that such a disposition would be a bribe to the people. A bribe to the people! to return it to those to whom it justly belongs, and from whose pockets it should never have been taken. A bribe! to place it in the charge of those who are the immediate representatives of those from whom we derive our authority, and who may employ it so much more usefully than we can. But what is to be done? If not returned to the people, it must go somehow [sic; somewhere?]; and is there no danger of bribing those to whom it may go? If we disburse it, is there no danger of bribing the thousands of agents, contractors, and jobbers, through whose hands it must pass, and in whose pockets, and those of their associates, so large a part would be deposited? If, to avoid this, we leave it where it is—in the banks—is there no danger of bribing the banks in whose custody it is, with their various dependants, and the numerous

swarms of speculators which hover about them in hopes of participating in the spoil? Is there no danger of bribing the political
managers, who, through the deposites, have the control of these
banks, and, by them, of their dependants and the hungry and vo-
racious hosts of speculators who have overspread and are devouring
the land? Yes, literally devouring the land. Finally, if it should
be vested as proposed by the Senator from New York, is there no
danger of bribing the holders of State stocks, and, through them,
the States which have issued them? Are the agents, the jobbers,
and contractors; are the directors and stockholders of the banks;
are the speculators and stock-jobbers; are the political managers
and holders of State securities, the only honest portion of the community? Are they alone incapable of being bribed? And are the
people the least honest, and most liable to be bribed? Is this the
creed of those now in power? of those who profess to be the friends
of the people, and to place implicit confidence in their virtue and
patriotism?

I have now (said Mr. C[alhoun]) stated what, in my opinion,
ought to be done with the surplus. Another question still remains—
not what shall, but what will, be done with the surplus? With a few
remarks on this question, I shall conclude what I intended to say.

There was a time, in the better days of the republic, when to
show what ought to be done, was to ensure the adoption of the
measure. Those days have passed away, I fear, forever. A power
has risen up in the Government greater than the people themselves,
consisting of many and various and powerful interests, combined
into one mass, and held together by the cohesive power of the vast
surplus in the banks. This mighty combination will be opposed to
any change; and it is to be feared that such is its influence that no
measure to which it is opposed can become a law, however expedient and necessary, and that the public money will remain in their
possession, to be disposed of, not as the public interest, but as theirs
may dictate. The time, indeed, seems fast approaching, when no
law can pass, nor any honor be conferred, from the Chief Magistrate
to the tide-waiter, without the assent of this powerful and interested
combination, which is steadily becoming the Government itself, to
the utter subversion of the authority of the people. Nay, I fear we
are in the midst of it, and I look with anxiety to the fate of this
measure as the test whether we are or not.

If nothing should be done; if the money, which justly belongs to
the people, be left where it is, with the many and overwhelming objections to it, the fact will prove that a great and radical change has

been effected; that the Government is subverted; that the authority of the people is suppressed by a union of the banks and Executive—a union a hundred times more dangerous than that of church and state, against which the Constitution has so jealously guarded. It would be the announcement of a state of things, from which, it is to be feared, there can be no recovery—a state of boundless corruption, and the lowest and basest subserviency. It seems to be the order of Providence that, with the exception of these, a people may recover from any other evil. Piracy, robbery, and violence, of any description, may, as history proves, be followed by virtue, patriotism, and national greatness; but where is the example to be found, of a degenerate, corrupt, and subservient people, who have ever recovered their virtue and patriotism? Their doom has ever been the lowest state of wretchedness and misery; scorned, trodden down, and obliterated forever from the list of nations. May Heaven grant that such may never be our doom!

From *Register of Debates*, 24th Cong., 1st Sess., cols. 1616–1635. Also printed in the Washington, D.C., *Daily National Intelligencer*, June 21, 1836, pp. 2–3; the Washington, D.C., *United States' Telegraph*, June 22, 1836, pp. 1–3; the Charleston, S.C., *Mercury*, July 13, 1836, p. 2, and July 14, 1836, pp. 2–3; the Washington, D.C., *Globe*, August 30, 1836, p. 2, and September 2, 1836, p. 2; *Congressional Globe*, 24th Cong., 1st Sess., Appendix, pp. 644–650; *Remarks of the Hon. John C. Calhoun, of South Carolina, on the Bill to Regulate the Deposites of Public Money. In Senate, June [sic] 1836* (Washington: printed by Duff Green, 1836); *Speeches of John C. Calhoun*, pp. 226–243; Crallé, ed., *Works*, 2:534–569. Variant in the Charleston, S.C., *Mercury*, June 6, 1836, p. 3. Another variant in the New York, N.Y., *Morning Courier and New-York Enquirer*, May 31, 1836, p. 2. NOTE: On 5/2 Calhoun had submitted an amendment to his own bill which provided for a distribution of surplus revenue to the States under certain conditions. The Senate had allowed him to incorporate this amendment into the bill on 5/25. On 5/31 Calhoun moved that the bill be referred to a select committee of nine to be chosen by ballot. The motion was adopted and a committee was elected consisting of Wright, Calhoun, Daniel Webster, William R. King, James Buchanan, Ether Shepley, Benjamin W. Leigh, William Hendricks, and Thomas Ewing. Calhoun's bill, with amendments by the Senate and House of Representatives, was eventually passed and was signed by President Jackson on 6/23.

REMARKS ON PRINTING THE MESSAGE FROM SAMUEL GWIN

[In the Senate, June 1, 1836]
[President Andrew Jackson communicated to the Senate a message received by the Treasury Department from Samuel Gwin, a Land

Office Register in Miss. In the message Gwin responded to "charges affecting his official conduct and character, which were set forth in the evidence taken under the authority of the Senate, by the Committee on Public Lands," pursuant to a Senate resolution of 3/3/1835. Thomas H. Benton moved that Gwin's "defence might be printed, and sent abroad in the same manner as the accusations against him had been."]

Mr. Calhoun said that he knew nothing at all relative to the charges made against Mr. Gwin; but it appeared to him that the regular course would be to refer the whole subject to the Committee on Public Lands. If Mr. Gwin had satisfactorily refuted the charges made against him, or had not succeeded in doing so, the fact would appear by the report of the committee. The best way of doing justice to all parties would be to subject the whole matter to the investigation of a committee.

[*Several Senators spoke in opposition to Calhoun's motion, including Thomas Ewing, Chairman of the Committee on Public Lands.*]

Mr. Calhoun very much regretted that the chairman of the Committee on Public Lands should object to the reference of this paper. His object was that full justice should be done to Mr. Gwin, to Mr. [George] Poindexter [former Senator from Miss. and former Chairman of the Committee on Public Lands], and to the Senate. He would not agree that the Senate had not the right to inquire into the conduct of public officers when serious frauds had been charged against them, as he had heard alleged on that floor. Serious frauds had been alleged against Mr. Gwin, and among other charges was one that he had amassed a large fortune in a very short time. This, alone, was very suspicious, and an investigation was ordered. The session [of 1834–1835] was a short one, and the committee reported that they could not get through with the examination before its close, the [then] chairman [Poindexter] proposing, by a resolution, that he should be authorized to go on with the examinations in the recess. This was agreed to. He did not now propose to inquire whether these examinations were conducted properly or not. One thing was now assumed here, and that was, the innocence of Mr. Gwin, and the guilt of Mr. Poindexter. Now, something was due to the absent; and an investigation by a committee was necessary before coming to the conclusion that Mr. Poindexter was culpable. Now, as these papers had taken an accusatory course against Mr. Poindexter, he would ask, was that gentleman called on for his evidence? Was he notified that he was to take Mr. Gwin's place, and that depositions were to be taken to implicate him? Was this an *ex parte* examination? If it was so improper on the part of the Senate to clothe Mr. Poindexter with these extraordinary powers, he would ask were they prepared to sanction the same thing done by the Executive, who had given to Mr. Gwin, or somebody else, the power to examine into the conduct of Mr. Poindexter?

Now they were called on to vote in the dark for the printing of these papers, of which they knew nothing, for the purpose of implicating Mr. Poindexter and the Senate itself. He took it for granted that the inquiry into alleged frauds, relative to the public lands, was a proper one; and if Mr. Poindexter abused the power with which he was intrusted, it was not the fault of the Senate; and the fact whether this was so or not, could be best ascertained by the examination of a committee. They had been told that there was nothing for the action of a committee. Now he thought otherwise. The character of an officer of the Government had been implicated; he had been charged with an abuse of office, and his defence was before them. Now, if Mr. Gwin was innocent, he ought to be called so. When he voted for the inquiry, his object was to do justice to Mr. Gwin and to the public; and in voting now for the reference, he had the same object in view. Justice, both towards Mr. Gwin, and one who had formerly been a member of that body, required the reference. If they condemned Mr. Poindexter, it ought to be with their eyes open. They all knew what an arduous task a Senator in high party times had to perform, and how liable the strict execution of his duty was to subject him to censure. No member of that body would be willing that his conduct should be censured after he left here without an examination; and he called upon gentlemen by what was due to themselves, as well as to justice, to vote for the reference.

[*Other Senators spoke.*]

Mr. Calhoun agreed partly with his friend from North Carolina [Willie P. Mangum], but was clearly of opinion that the printing ought to be after the report of the committee. Not a single Senator had read the whole of this evidence; not a Senator knew whether it exculpated the officer implicated, or whether it implicated the conduct of the [former] chairman; and in the dark they were asked to print the testimony. Now, he thought that to do justice to all parties, to Mr. Gwin himself, as well as others, the proper course was to refer it to a committee. If the object in sending this document here was to implicate a former member of that body, who had, in the discharge of arduous duties, been implicated, every principle of honor and justice required that they should be referred and examined before sending them abroad to the world. As to the dangerous doctrine, that this body is not to look into malfeasances in office, it had been avowed here for the first time. Never had it been avowed in the British Parliament, from which we took our practice, nor had it been advanced in any of the State Legislatures. Such a doctrine would surrender entirely the Legislative power of the Senate.

Mr. C[alhoun] continued his remarks to some considerable length; after which [*nine other Senators spoke.*]

From *Register of Debates*, 24th Cong., 1st Sess., cols. 1658–1668. Also printed in the Washington, D.C., *Globe*, June 3, 1836, p. 3; *Congressional Globe*, 24th Cong., 1st Sess., pp. 516–519. Variant in the New York, N.Y., *Morning Courier and New-York Enquirer*, June 4, 1836, p. 2. NOTE: The next day the matter of Gwin was tabled on Calhoun's motion and not taken up again during the session.

Amendment to the bill to prohibit the circulation of incendiary publications, submitted to the Senate on 6/2. Under consideration in Committee of the Whole was a proposal by Felix Grundy to strike out all of the bill after the enacting clause and insert a substitute. Calhoun moved "to amend the proposed amendment, by striking out, sec[tion] 3, line 5, after 'shall,' the words 'under the instructions of the Postmaster General, from time to time, give notice of the same, so that they may be withdrawn by the person who deposited them originally to be mailed; and if the same shall not be withdrawn in one month thereafter, shall be burnt, or otherwise destroyed:' and, in lieu thereof, inserting '*deliver them to such person or persons as may be duly authorized by such State, Territory, or District, to receive the same; but if there be no such person or persons, or in case there be such, if no application be made, during the space of three months, by them, for the delivery of such pamphlets, newspapers, hand-bills, or other printed papers or pictorial representations, they shall be burnt, or otherwise destroyed, under such regulations as the Postmaster General shall prescribe.*' " Calhoun's amendment failed by a vote of 15 to 15, the division being strictly sectional. Grundy's substitute was adopted. (A text of Grundy's bill, which differed only in minor respects from Calhoun's, can be found in *Register of Debates*, 24th Cong., 1st Sess., col. 1721. Later the same day a vote was taken on the motion to engross the bill, as amended, for its third reading. The vote was 18 to 18, with Vice-President Martin Van Buren giving his casting vote in favor of the motion.) PC in *Senate Journal*, 24th Cong., 1st Sess., pp. 398–399.

To Prof. [BENJAMIN] SILLIMAN, [Yale College], New Haven, Conn.

Senate Chamber, 2d June 1836

My dear Sir, I take pleasure to introduce you to Mr. [John S. or Thomas L.?] Preston, the brother of my Colleague [in the Senate from S.C., William C. Preston], who is desireous [*sic*] of forming your acquaintance.

I feel confident, that it requires no solicitation on my part to ensure your particular attention to Mr. Preston. With the highest esteem I am & & J.C. Calhoun.

ALS in CtY, Sterling Library, Silliman Family Papers. NOTE: This visit to Silliman, a chemist, was perhaps related to the salt works owned by the Preston family in Washington County, Va.

To Monsieur G[EORGE] W[ASHINGTON DE] LAFAYETTE, Paris

Senate Chamber, 4th June 1836

My dear Sir, I take much pleasure in making you acquainted with my friend, the Hon: Mr. [James H.] Hammond, member of Congress from South Carolina.

Mr. Hammond, during the short period he has been in Congress, tho' much indisposed a large portion of the time, has greatly distinguished himself, by his abilities and eloquence. He visits Europe, with his family, under the advice of his physicians, with the view to the restoration of his health.

None of our intelligent citizens can visit France, without des[ir]-ing to form the acquaintance of one, who besides the esteem with which he is personally regarded among us, stands so nearly connected with him, whose name must be ever dear to Americans. To afford my friend this pleasure, I have taken the liberty of giving him this letter. Your attention to him will place me under lasting obligations. With great resp[ec]t I am & & J.C. Calhoun.

ALS in DLC, James Henry Hammond Papers, vol. 6.

To HENRY WHEATON, [U.S.] Chargé d'Affaires, Berlin

Senate Chamber, 4th June 1836

My dear Sir, I take much pleasure in introducing to you, my friend, the Hon: Mr. [James H.] Hammond, member of Congress from South Carolina.

Mr. Hammond commenced his Congressional career at the begin[n]ing of the present session, and tho he has been indisposed a large portion of the time, he has greatly distinguished himself by his abilities and eloquence.

He visits Europe, with his family, under the advice of his physicians, with the view to the restoration of his health.

He will visit Berlin in his tour, where, I feel assured, you will take pleasure in making his stay agreeable to him. Your attention will place me under lasting obligations. With great respect I am & & J.C. Calhoun.

ALS in DLC, James Henry Hammond Papers, vol. 6.

FURTHER REMARKS ON THE BILL TO PROHIBIT DEPUTY POSTMASTERS FROM TRANSMITTING INCENDIARY PUBLICATIONS

[In the Senate, June 8, 1836]

[The question was on the passage of the bill as amended. Daniel Webster and John Davis of Mass. spoke against the bill. Henry Clay considered the bill unnecessary. James Buchanan and Felix Grundy supported the bill, taking pains to distinguish their positions from Calhoun's.]

Mr. Calhoun could not concur with the views taken by the Senators from Massachusetts [Webster] and Kentucky [Clay], that this bill would comprehend in its provisions all publications touching the subject of slavery. In order to bring any publication within the provisions of the bill, two qualifications were necessary. The first was, that it must relate to the subject of slavery; and the next was, that it must be prohibited by the laws of the State to which it is transmitted. He thought that this was the view that would be taken of it by the courts. The object of this bill was to make it the duty of the postmasters in the States to conform to the laws of such States, and not to deliver out papers in violation of their laws. The simple question was, had this Government the power to say to its officers, you shall not violate the laws of the States in which you reside? Could it go further, and make it their duty to co-operate with the States in carrying their laws into effect? This was the simple question. Now could any man doubt that Congress possessed the power to pass both measures, so that their officers might not come into conflict with the State laws? Indeed, he looked upon measures of this kind to prevent conflicts between the General and State Governments, which were likely to ensue, as essentially necessary; for it was evident that when such conflicts took place, the State must have the ascendancy. Mr. C[alhoun] then briefly recapitulated the principles on which this bill was founded, and contended that it was in aid of laws passed by the States as far as Congress had the power constitutionally to go, and assumed no power to prohibit or interfere with the publication or circulation of any paper whatever; it only declared that the officers of the Government should not make their official stations a shield for violating the State laws. Was there any one there who would say, that the States had not the power to pass laws prohibiting and making penal, the circulation of papers, calculated to incite insurrection among their slaves? It being admitted that they could, could not Congress order its officers to abstain from the violation of these laws? We do not (said Mr. C[alhoun]) pass a law to abridge the freedom of the press, or to prohibit the publication and circulation of any paper whatever—this has been done by the States already. The inhibition of the Constitution was on Congress, and not on the States, who possessed full power to pass any laws they thought proper. They knew that there were several precedents to sanction this bill. Congress had passed laws to abstain from the violation of the health laws of the States. Could any one say that the Constitution gave to Congress the power to pass quarantine laws? He had not adverted to the message of the President [Andrew Jackson] on this subject, because he believed that the President acted from the best motives, and that that part of the message was drawn up without sufficient reflection. He denied, however, that this message was in conformity with the Constitution. It would be directly abridging the liberty of the press for Congress to pass such laws as the President recommended. One part of the message he would refer to, which was in these words:

"I would, therefore, call the special attention of Congress to the subject, and respectfully suggest the propriety of passing such a law as will prohibit, under severe penalties, the circulation in the southern States, through the mail, of incendiary publications, intended to instigate the slaves to insurrection."

This was clearly unconstitutional; for it not only recommended the prohibition of publications and circulation of incendiary papers, (abridging the freedom of the press,) but it recommended also the infliction of severe penalties, which powers were expressly prohibited by the Constitution. On no other principle could this ever be defended, than that it was simply abstaining from a violation of the laws of the States.

The Senator from Kentucky contended that this bill was useless; and he (Mr. C[alhoun]) agreed that it was so in one sense, and that was, with or without this bill, the southern States would execute their own laws against the circulation of such papers. It was a case of life and death with them; and did any body suppose that they would permit so many magazines in their bosom to blow them to destruction, as these post offices must be, if these incendiary publications continued to be circulated through them? While the southern States contained so many postmasters opposed to their institutions, as it was in his own State, where almost every postmaster was opposed to it, it was absolutely necessary for them to take effectual measures for their own security. It was the assertion of the principle, that the States had a right to protect themselves, which made the bill valuable in his eyes; it prevented the conflict which would be likely to take place between the General and State Governments, unless some measure of the kind should be adopted. The States had a right to go to the extent of this bill; and they would be wanting to themselves and to posterity if they omitted to do it. It was on the doctrine of State rights and State intervention that he supported this bill, and on no other grounds.

The Senator from Massachusetts objected to the returning of these papers whose delivery was prohibited. He regretted this as much as the Senator did; but his objection was, that it did not go far enough: he thought that these papers should be delivered to the prosecuting officers of the States, to enable them to ferret out the designs of the incendiaries.

From *Register of Debates,* 24th Cong., 1st Sess., cols. 1729–1731. Also printed in the Washington, D.C., *Globe,* June 20, 1836, p. 2; *Congressional Globe,* 24th Cong., 1st Sess., Appendix, pp. 456–458. NOTE: The bill failed on this day by a not strictly sectional vote of 19 to 25. Calhoun's remarks on this occasion seem to have been crudely reported and the above account of them to lack coherence.

John E[wing] Colhoun to [THOMAS J. RUSK in Texas]

Pendleton, June 9, 1836

D[ea]r Sir, I beg leave to introduce to your acquaintance Mr. Bernard [*sic*; Barnard] E. Bee of Charleston, and latterly a resident of this neighbourhood. He goes to Texas with the view of making a permanent settlement. From your situation, and knowledge of the country, you may have it in your power to render him important services in aid of his views. You will find him intelligent and efficient, & a useful member of your new govt.

Permit me to congratulate you on the unparalle[le]d success which has crowned your efforts in obtaining possession of the country[;] the advantages commercially and politically will be immense.

Should you see Pinckney [*sic*; Pinkney] Caldwell do say to him that I wrote some time since as he requested, and that I should be very glad to hear from him. I am D[ea]r Sir very respectfully yours, John E. Colhoun.

ALS in TxU, Thomas Jefferson Rusk Papers. NOTE: Rusk was a native of Pendleton whose education Calhoun had reportedly forwarded and who had succeeded Samuel Houston as commander of the Texas Republic Army. Bee was subsequently Secretary of State of the Republic.

Remarks on the bill to regulate the public deposits, 6/9. "Mr. Calhoun denied that this was intended as a distribution bill—it was in good faith a deposite bill, and nothing more. Gentlemen on all sides, he said, admitted that there would be a very large surplus at the end of the year, and that it would continue to increase for two or three years to come. Now, he put it to gentlemen, could they consider this vast sum safe as it was? Was there not a necessity for depositing it somewhere? and where could that be so safely done as in the treasuries of the States? If the Government was only economically administered, the money would probably never be called for; but if there should be war, or if the revenue of 1842 should fall short, the States would pay it without the slightest difficulty, rather than have a direct tax, as the events of the last war proved. Mr. C[alhoun] replied to the objections of Mr. [Robert J.] Walker, as to the inequality of the distribution, by saying that it was proposed in the only way that it could be made; that is, on the principle on which the direct taxes would have to be levied; so that if Mississippi lost now, she would have a corresponding gain when a direct tax came." From *Register of Debates*, 24th Cong., 1st Sess., col. 1745.

Also printed in the Washington, D.C., *Globe*, June 11, 1836, pp. 2–3; *Congressional Globe*, 24th Cong., 1st Sess., pp. 541–542.

Remarks on "the bill to increase the present military establishment of the United States," 6/10. Thomas H. Benton spoke for the bill at length. Robert C. Nicholas of La. "moved to recommit the bill, with instructions to report an organization precisely similar to that which was adopted for the peace establishment in 1815." Subsequently, "Mr. Calhoun called for a division of the question, so as to take the question first on the recommitment generally, and afterwards on the instructions. He had thought that there ought to be an increase of the army by filling up the companies; but he was opposed to a new organization of the army. There was nothing in the character of our foreign relations to shake the belief that it would depend on our own prudence only to remain at peace with all nations. It was only in reference to our Indian relations that any additional force was necessary. He would be willing to give as much increase as would place us in a situation of defence, but not a man more than was necessary for that purpose." After some debate the Senate agreed to recommit the bill. During debate on the instructions, Calhoun "took a view of the present force of the country, and indicated in what manner the regiments we now have might be stationed, in order to effect an efficient defence of our frontier. He was disposed to fill up the companies, so as to render the regiments more competent." Nicholas's motion as to instructions was defeated 18 to 25. From *Register of Debates*, 24th Cong., 1st Sess., cols. 1755–1756. Also printed in the Washington, D.C., *Daily National Intelligencer*, June 11, 1836, p. 3. Variant in *Congressional Globe*, 24th Cong., 1st Sess., pp. 543–544.

Remarks in debate on the bill to regulate the public deposits, 6/13. "Mr. Calhoun was in hopes that some Senator, coming from that portion of the Union where the specie condition [for deposit banks] would operate oppressively, would move to strike it out. After hearing the debate, he was satisfied it would operate oppressively in some States, while in others the banks would not be affected by it. Mr. C[alhoun] then moved to strike out the second clause of the section." After debate, Calhoun's motion was agreed to. Thomas H. Benton moved an amendment giving to the President the power "to direct transfers to be made . . . to the branch mints of the United States, either for supplying metal for coining or for safe-keeping." "Mr. Calhoun was opposed to the amendment, as it might be the means of oppressing some individual bank, by transferring all the specie in its vaults for the purpose of coining." Later, in reference to the same amendment, Calhoun "supposed the object was to obtain a large circulation of the coin of the United States. That could only be done by repealing the laws making foreign coin a tender, and next by suppressing the circulation of bank notes from ten dollars down, which Congress could not do. He was opposed to the amendment, and should vote against it." The part of the amendment allowing transfers for coinage passed by a vote of 22 to 17; the provision providing for the transfers for the purpose of safekeeping was lost. Benton offered an amendment exempting from distribution to the States "the amount received from the sales of public lands, and subject to distribution under the bill for appropriating the proceeds of the sales of the public lands." "Mr. Calhoun said, that in order to effect the object of the Senator from Missouri, and remove any ambiguity that might exist, he would move to amend the amendment, by adding the words 'provided said bill shall become a law.' He had no doubt that, if both bills passed, the land bill, making a special appropriation, would have the preference. But if this amendment passed, his addition to it would be necessary." After remarks by other Senators, Calhoun said that he "did not see the slightest difficulty between this bill and the other, with or without the amendment. The one was specific, and the other was general; and if both passed, all sound lawyers would say that the first would take the precedence. It was under these impressions that in drawing this bill he did not think it necessary to take any notice of the land bill; but as the Senator from Missouri (Mr. Benton) had thought it necessary to offer an amendment to remove an apparent incongruity, he had no objections to it, provided his proviso was also added, to render it perfectly clear." After some further discussion, Calhoun's proviso to Benton's amendment was adopted; shortly thereafter the amendment itself was rejected. Calhoun then "moved to fill the blank in the thirteenth section [for the sum to be retained in the Treasury before making the distribution of the surplus to the States] with two millions." No vote was taken on this motion before the Senate adjourned. From *Register of Debates,* 24th Cong., 1st Sess., cols. 1763–1769. Also printed in the Washington, D.C., *Globe,* June 15, 1836, pp. 2–3; *Congressional Globe,* 24th Cong., 1st Sess., pp. 548–549.

Remarks on the bill to regulate the public deposits, 6/14. Silas Wright moved an amendment to provide "that the outstanding appropriations shall be deducted prior to making the distribution of the surplus to the States. Mr. Calhoun opposed the amendment as unnecessary, and as contrary to the objects of the bill. Considering the very heavy and unusual appropriations of this year, he estimated the amount of the outstanding balances at eight or nine millions; and he submitted to Senators whether it was wise and consistent with the objects of the bill to leave so large a sum where it now was. Was it for the convenience of the deposite banks? He could not suppose that gentlemen had that object in view. He thought that the appropriations of this year were so large that the balances to be carried over would be sufficient for the whole of the appropriations for the next year." After further discussion Calhoun "moved to fill the blank in the third section, for the sum to be retained in the Treasury, with five millions." This motion was carried by a vote of 22 to 18. From *Register of Debates*, 24th Cong., 1st Sess., cols. 1775–1778. Also printed in the Washington, D.C., *Globe*, June 16, 1836, p. 2; *Congressional Globe*, 24th Cong., 1st Sess., pp. 552–553. Variant in the New York, N.Y., *Morning Courier and New-York Enquirer*, June 17, 1836, p. 2.

Remarks on Silas Wright's motion to recommit the bill to regulate the public deposits, 6/16. The question was on Wright's "motion to recommit the original bill, with the substitutes reported by the select committee, and the amendments adopted by the Senate, to the Committee on Finance, with instructions to divide them into two separate bills," one relating to the regulation of the deposit banks, the other to the distribution of the surplus. "Mr. Calhoun had no desire to embarrass this motion by any indirection or technicality; but he was exceedingly desirous that the parliamentary rule should be observed within a reasonable degree. The first question was on striking out the original bill, introduced by himself, and inserting the substitute; and in that state of the question, the gentleman from New York [Wright] moved to refer it, with the substitute and amendments, to the Committee on Finance, with instructions. He [Calhoun] held that they could not refer amendments under any parliamentary rule, and that, in recommitting the bill, all the amendments not concurred in in the House fell to the ground. Now, these instructions referred to the amendments made to the bill in Committee of the Whole; and therefore they referred to a matter which, under the parliamentary rule, could not go before the Committee on Finance. He contended that when a bill was referred to a committee, all that it could do was to recommend amendments to it. (Mr. C[alhoun] here read the rule relating to the subject.) The only parliamentary way in which the gentleman could get at his object would be to move to strike out the thirteenth section, and bring it in as another bill." The Chair decided that Wright's motion was in order, although the motion was subsequently defeated. Robert J. Walker offered an amendment proposing that the distribution of the surplus revenue among the States should be based on the number of each State's Representatives and Senators in Congress. "Mr. Calhoun had been in favor of the plan of distribution proposed by the Senator from Mississippi, but had yielded his wishes in the committee, on the ground that it could not be carried through. It was in vain to contend against the opposition of six of the large States; and under these impressions he was constrained, though reluctantly, to vote against the amendment." Walker's amendment was adopted by a vote of 23 to 22. From *Register of Debates*, 24th Cong., 1st Sess., cols. 1781–1783. Also printed in the Washington, D.C., *Globe*, June 18, 1836, p. 3; *Congressional Globe*, 24th Cong., 1st Sess., pp. 558–560. Variant in the New York, N.Y., *Morning Courier and New-York Enquirer*, June 18, 1836, p. 2.

Remarks on the bill to regulate the public deposits, 6/17. Silas Wright spoke at length, giving the history of his and Calhoun's relations with the bill, outlining what he considered to be the prospective expenditures of the government, and affirming his opposition to the distribution features of the bill. "Mr. Calhoun said the Senator had made use of the best of all possible arguments for preserving the surplus. No Senator had estimated the whole surplus at the end of the year, including the $7,000,000 in the United States Bank, and exclusive of the year's expenditures, at less than $66,000,000. The Senator from New York had earnestly endeavored to prove that the expenditures of this year of this administration would amount to this $66,000,000. Mr. C[alhoun] made a solemn appeal to Senators, whether they were prepared to rise so soon from an annual Government expenditure of $12,000,000, then deemed prodigal, to the enormous sum of $66,000,000, and that in a time of profound peace. There could possibly be no stronger argument in favor of taking care of the surplus. Mr. C[alhoun] made a comparison between the State stock and State deposite projects, and drew the obvious deductions in favor of the latter, expressing his satisfaction at the great unanimity of the Senate on the subject, and his belief that but for the opposition from the Senator from New York, the vote would have been unanimous." Lengthy debate followed Calhoun's remarks. Just before a vote was taken on the bill, he "expressed a hope that the harmony of the debate would not be disturbed. He thought there was no mischief in the measure, and it was a mere measure of precaution." The bill passed 40 to 6. From *Register of Debates,* 24th Cong., 1st Sess., cols. 1800 and 1845. Variant in the New York, N.Y., *Morning Courier and New-York Enquirer,* June 20, 1836, p. 2.

To ALEX[ANDER] W. JONES and Others, Norfolk

Washington, 18th June, 1836
Gentlemen: I have been honored by your note of the 8th inst[ant], inviting me in the name of the Norfolk Junior Volunteers, to partake of a dinner to be given to their Captain, James F. Hunter, on the 4th of July. My official duties here forbid an acceptance; but in declining, I avail myself of the opportunity to express the pleasure I feel at the growing disposition which I see among our youths to bestow increased attention on the militia, which has been so shamefully permitted to fall into a state of almost perfect decay. It is the only safe description of force on land, against external or internal danger; and I have regarded it as one of the bad symptoms of the times, that it has been of late so much neglected.

Permit me to offer the following sentiment:

Our youths; may they ever remember that those who have not spirit and courage enough to defend themselves, must basely seek protection under the sword of a master.

PC in the Norfolk and Portsmouth, Va., *Herald and General Advertiser,* July 8, 1836, p. 2. NOTE: According to the *Herald,* the committee addressed by Calhoun consisted of "Lieut. Alex. W. Jones, Sergt. W. Pearce, Corpl. G.W. Camp, Pioneer W.H. Smith, and Private S.S. Stubbs." Calhoun and William C. Preston of S.C. seem to have been the only non-Virginians invited to this dinner. In regard to the interest in military affairs above indicated, it is noteworthy that the news of the summer of 1836 was dominated by reports of hostilities in Tex. and Fla.

To James H. Hammond,
[former Representative from S.C.]

Washington, 19th June 1836

My dear Sir, Since you left us, as short as is the period, a very great change has taken place in the aspect, if not the condition, of parties. I had for weeks perceived, that something was going on; but was not aware of the extent of the change till the bill for the regulation of the deposites was brought up. You will remember, that I reported the bill at the last session from the Select Committee on Executive ["patronage" *interlined*]. It then passed the Senate and was sent to the other House, where it remained till the end of the session without being taken up. I introduced it on leave in the early part of this session, and while I was waiting for a favourable opportunity to take it up, the opposition in the Senate sunk [*sic*] into a minority. Seeing after this, that there was no opportunity of passing it without the aid of the administration party, I seized on the first suitable occasion to announce my intention of ["pass" *canceled*] abandoning the bill, and throwing the deposit question, wholly on the responsibility of the administration and their party. The result of ["which" *canceled*] that announcement was the offer of Mr. [Silas] Wright, a few days after, of a substitute by way of amendement [*sic*] for ["the" *interlined*] bill, and which in addition to the provisions to regulate the banks of deposites, contained provisions to dispose of the surplus revenue by vesting it in State securities. I seized on this movement, and offered an amendment to my bill, providing that the surplus should be deposited in the Treasury of the several States rateably on condition of returning it without interest whenever required.

I soon saw, that Mr. Wright became shy of the subject, and was indisposed to call up the bill in conformity to his promise. After much delay, I determined to call it up myself. In his opening speech, I clearly saw, that his intention was to get clear of the subject altogether, tho' he professed ["a" *interlined*] strong desire, that something should be done. I determined to act on his professions, and not his real intention, and accordingly joined him in a tone of great moderation in the expression of an equally strong desire that something should be done, and a determination on my part to sacrifice any thing, except principle, to effect so desirable an object.

The result, after some remarks from Mr. [Daniel] Webster & others, ["of" *canceled and* "was" *interlined*] the appointment of a special Committee of 9, on my motion, from all the parties in the

Senate, of which Mr. Wright was chairman. The Committee with great unanimity reported an amendment, as a substitute for the bill, on the principle and with most of the leading details of the original bill, and my amendment[,] but with important modifications in ["others" *canceled and* "some particulars" *interlined*]. Mr. Wright's desire to defeat the bill and amendment now became very appeant [*sic*; apparent]; but after every expedient he could devise for that purpose, the bill was ordered to a third reading on thursday last [6/16], by a vote of 40 to 6, the latter consisting of Mr. Wright, Mr. [Thomas H.] Benton, Mr. [Felix] Grundy, Mr. [Alfred] Cuthbert [Senator from Ga.], and the two Mississippi ["Senators" *interlined*; John Black and Robert J. Walker] for special reasons arising out of some difficulty in their State Constitution. The next day after this remarkable vote, the real state of things in the Senate disclosed itself on the question of the passage of the bill. It was furiously opposed by Benton and artfully, but earnessly [*sic*] by Wright. This brought out [William C.] Rives and [Nathaniel P.] Tallmadge, Wright's Colleague [from N.Y.], in ["a" *interlined*] warm and eloquent defence of it, on the old doctrines of the Republican party, of economy, retrenchment, and decidedly attacking the extravagance of the appropriations passed & contemplated, as well as Mr. Benton[']s gold Humbug. The bill, after the debate closed, passed 38, to 6, Mr. [Arnold] Naudain of Delaware having resigned, and Mr. [Thomas] Mor[r]is [of Ohio] being accidentally absent.

Yesterday a motion was made in the House to take up the bill, and tho' it was the day for private bills and had of course to encounter some opposition from that cause, the vote stood 130 ["to" *canceled and* "for" *interlined*] taking up and 70 against. It will be taken up on monday [6/20], and there can be no doubt, I think, of its passage.

The effect has been a complete disorganization of ["party" *altered to* "parties"] for the present. The President [Andrew Jackson] is furious, and threatens to veto the bill, should it pass, but I have no fears of that. The Globe took a decided stand against it, and Mr. [Martin] Van Buren is understood to be warmly opposed; but all in vain. The schism may not be permanent, but I am inclined to think it lies pretty deep, and will not be easy to heal. There is unquestionably a good deal of rivalry and jealousy between the interests of Rives & Benton, which tend strongly to distract the ["party" *altered to* "parties"], and to which a good deal of what has occurred may be attributed.

But there is another and more powerful cause of distraction, which begins to disclose itself; I refer to the growing conflict between the more honest portion of the party, and the real plunder & humbug portion, who are willing to go all length. Things have arrived at the point, at which it is difficult for these two portions to go on together much longer.

Looking over the whole ground, I am inclined to think, that we are at the commencement of events which must lead to important and salutary changes, if we act with moderation and prudence. It is said Gen[era]l Jackson threatens to veto the bill should it pass. I cannot think ["so" canceled and "he will" interlined], and, if he should, I think, it will only accelerate the overthrow of those in power. The result would not be so speedy, but would be no less certain, should the bill become a law.

At this interesting stage of our affairs, I cannot but regret your absence from the councils of the Union. It is the more to be regretted at this time, not only on account of the importance and delicacy of the juncture, but because we are so weak in the House. [Francis W.] Picken[s]'s health is still delicate, which prevents his constant attendance, and [Waddy] Thompson leaves this [city] with his family for Carolina this evening, on account of ["the" canceled] unfavourable intelligence in relation to the health of Mrs. Thompson's mother [Behethaland Foote Moore (Mrs. William) Butler].

Should you see [James] Hamilton [Jr.] before you sail do not forget to say to him, that I am extremely anxious to see him on many accounts, and that he must expedite his visit here as much as possible.

I hope your health has improved, and that you met your family in health, and entirely recovered from the effects of their rough passage.

I would be glad to hear from you before you sail, and as often as you can make it convenient while abroad. Make Anna's [Anna Maria Calhoun's] and my kind respects to Mrs. [Catherine E. Fitzsimons] H[ammond] and believe me to be yours truely & sincerely, J.C. Calhoun.

ALS in DLC, James Henry Hammond Papers, vol. 6; PC in Jameson, ed., *Correspondence*, pp. 358–361. NOTE: Hammond had resigned his seat in the House on 2/26 because of ill health and was to spend about two years in Europe.

[John C. Calhoun "& others, Members of Congress," to Lewis Cass, Secretary of War, 6/20.] An entry in a register of letters indicates that a letter of this date was received which recommended "Benjamin H. Johnson" for a commission in a new regiment of dragoons. Entry in DNA, RG 107 (Records of the Office of the Secretary of War), Registers of Letters Received, 1800–1870, 40:C-540 (M-22:40).

Remarks on the bill to increase the military peace establishment, 6/20. Calhoun "moved to strike out the 7th and 8th sections of the bill, providing for an increase of the medical staff, and for the appointment of three additional paymasters, on the ground that bills for this purpose had already passed the Senate, and been sent to the other House." Thomas H. Benton indicated his intention to "insert a proviso that these sections should not take effect" if those bills should become law. Calhoun then withdrew his motion. From *Register of Debates*, 24th Cong., 1st Sess., col. 1853. Also printed in the Washington, D.C., *Globe*, June 23, 1836, p. 2; *Congressional Globe*, 24th Cong., 1st Sess., p. 568. (The Washington, D.C., *Daily National Intelligencer*, June 21, 1836, p. 3, reported that on this occasion Calhoun requested "an estimate of the increased expense of the military establishment," and that on his motion "the 15th and 16th sections[,] relating to changes in the Quartermaster's department, were stricken out" of the bill by the Senate.)

L[ewis] C[ass, Secretary of War], to John C. Calhoun "& Others," 6/21. "Gentlemen, In answer to your letter of yesterday in favor of Mr. [Benjamin H.] Johnston [*sic*], I have the honor to inform you that, the selections for officers of the new Regiments of Dragoons were all made some time since. But should any vacancies occur in the Corps, Mr. Johnston[']s claims shall receive respectful consideration." FC in DNA, RG 107 (Records of the Office of the Secretary of War), Letters Sent by the Secretary of War Relating to Military Affairs, 1800–1861, 16:117 (M-6:16).

To [SAMUEL D. INGHAM, New Hope, Pa.]

Washington, 21st June 1836

My dear Sir, I am highly gratified to learn, that your health is so far restored; and hope by your next to hear of its entire restoration.

You know how fully I agree with you, that we have long been marching in the direct road to despotism; and that too by the operation of causes, which have seldom failed to terminate short of that point. With us, events have taken, what may be considered their natural order.

The first false step was to convert that, in practise, which was designed for a confederative into a national Government; or to express it differently, ["to convert" *interlined*] the Government itself, instead of the people of the States, into the supreme power. The effect was to give the dominant interest of the Union the supreme and unlimited control. From this the American system draws its origin; out of that rose the excessive fiscal action of the system; and from that the spoil party, and the spoil party, if events ["take" *canceled and* "continue" *interlined*] their natural course, ends necessarily in military despotism. We are near this point, of which we have had many indications this session; but, I think, we will stop short; because I beleive [*sic*], we are in a fair way of arresting ["effec-(t)ually" *interlined*] the cause. The first step towards it, was the act of our State. Nullification has completely arrested the American system; and is gradually healing the sectional difference to which it was both parent and offspring. It has had a double effect. It is drying up that fiscal deludge [*sic*], out of which the spoil party arose, while it is gradually restoring the federative character of our system, and, thereby, eradicating the original cause of all our political disorders. Our present difficulty is to get clear of a temporary excess of revenue, resulting from the American system. It is a symptom, that remains after the ["dis" *canceled*] cause of the disease is removed; but a symptom hard to get clear of, and which might prove fatal in its consequence. I think, a remedy will be applied. The bill to deposite the surplus in the ["State Treasuries" *altered to* "Treasury of the States"] at the end of the year has passed the Senate, 40 to 6, and is now before the House with every prospect of passing that body by a large majority. The leaders of the spoil party are in a state of consternation. [Andrew] Jackson is in a perfect rage; and threatens his veto, which, however, I think, will hardly be applied, and, if applied, will so weaken and distract the party, as to endanger its overthrow. Should the measure pass, and be repeated by a renewal of the act for a few years, the progress to despotism will be effectually arrested, and the system will be thoroughly reformed. The party at present is completely seperated [*sic*]; the portion, who prefer the country to party interests, [is separated] from that, which rely so[le]ly on plunder and humbug[g]ery to retain power.

In regard to Texas, I almost entirely concur in your views. The fate of Mexico is sealed. The tide of our population moving towards the West and South West will not stop till it reaches the pasifick [*sic*] and the Ist[h]mus [of Panama or California?]. It is desirable, that its progress shall be gradual; to drive before, and not overrun. The Mexicans will not present a ["restance" *canceled and* "resistance" *interlined*] stronger, than what the indian tribes have. I hold the inco[r]poration of Texas into the Union, as indispensible [*sic*]. A seperate government there would endanger every thing.

Looking over the whole ground, I have hopes ["for" *canceled and* "of" *interlined*] the country. We will take a new lease for our liberty, with a vast increase of expe[rie]nce[?] & wisdom. Whether [Martin] Van Buren is elected or not, reform must come—a thorough & radical reform. The only doubt is, whether ["the" *interlined*] taint of the last few years ["have" *canceled and* "has" *interlined*] not reached the body of the people, in many of the States.

ALU (signature and closing clipped) in ScU-SC, John C. Calhoun Papers.

Remarks on a House amendment to the deposit bill, 6/22. A message was received that the House of Representatives agreed to the bill, with one amendment to the distribution portion allowing the Secretary of the Treasury to call for repayment from the States under certain conditions when money "shall be wanted . . . to meet the appropriations made by law." Calhoun moved "that the Senate concur in the amendment." During discussion of his motion Calhoun "said the principle of the bill had not been changed, and he hoped the Senate would come to a vote. No Secretary of the Treasury will ever call for this money." Later, in response to a suggestion to amend the House amendment, "Mr. Calhoun said that few, if any, of the [State] Legislatures would be in session before the 1st of January, when the bill will take effect." The amendment was accepted. From *Register of Debates*, 24th Cong., 1st Sess., cols. 1858–1859. Also printed in the Washington, D.C., *Daily National Intelligencer*, June 24, 1836, p. 2. Variant in the New York, N.Y., *Morning Courier and New-York Enquirer*, June 24, 1836, p. 2.

Remarks on "the bill to change the mode of conducting the sales of the public lands," 6/23. When this bill came up for consideration, Robert J. Walker moved for its indefinite postponement. "Mr. Calhoun said that this motion was intended to defeat the bill; but, as it was a measure of considerable importance, he hoped it would not be thrown aside without some discussion. He would be glad to hear the arguments for and against it before he gave his vote." (After debate Walker's motion was carried 25 to 15 with Calhoun voting in the majority.) From *Register of Debates*, 24th Cong., 1st Sess., col. 1867. Also printed in the Washington, D.C., *Globe*, June 25, 1836, p. 2; *Congressional Globe*, 24th Cong., 1st Sess., pp. 578–579.

Motion to amend the bill for the relief of Charles J. Catlett, submitted to the Senate on 6/24. "The bill [reported by the Committee on Finance] was amended, on motion of Mr. Calhoun, so as to refer the bill to the officers of the Treasury, to report on the principle." [Catlett, a merchant of Alexandria, D.C., had petitioned Congress for compensation for flour and tobacco burned by the British at his warehouse during the War of 1812.] From *Register of Debates*, 24th Cong., 1st Sess., col. 1872.

To L[EWIS] S. CORYELL, [New Hope, Pa.?]

Washington, 27th June 1836

Dear Sir, I shall be very happy to see and examine Mr. Reading's invention, and to afford him any aid in my power to bring his improvement into useful operation. As far as I have been able to obtain information, nothing promises so much profit as the successful extraction of oil from cotton seed, to which I understand his invention relates. The material is most abundant and abounds in oil, of an excellent quality as it is said by those, who have attended to the subject. A friend informs me, that an establishment in Mississippi for the extraction of the oil has proved exceedingly profitable. Should Mr. Reading's invention facilitate the existing process by making it cheaper, or better he ought by all means to go South. I hope he will come on to Washington before I leave the city.

I am rejoiced to learn that Mr. [Samuel D.] Ingham is recovered, and that Mrs. [Deborah Kay Hall] Ingham is well. I wrote to him a few days since and addressed to N[ew] Hope. I hope my letter has been received.

I trust that your anticipation as to the result of your [Pa.] election may be realized. It is indeed a sad atlernative [*sic*] to be reduced to a ["chance"(?) *canceled and* "choice" *interlined*] of evils; but I trust that better times are coming. There is certainly a great change going on here, as the passage of the deposite bill indicates. That measure will of itself go far to reform the gover[n]ment, and to give an ascendancy to the old Republican doctrines of '98. With great respect I am & & J.C. Calhoun.

ALS in PHi, Coryell Papers. NOTE: The choice of evils referred to by Calhoun may have been the Presidential contest between Martin Van Buren and William Henry Harrison in Pa. Or possibly he referred to the split between the Van Buren and George M. Dallas factions of the Democratic party in that State which came into the open at about this time.

Remarks on the bill to establish armories, arsenals, a foundry, and arms depots in the South and West, 6/27. Calhoun "thought that it was too late in the session to act on a bill of such importance, involving such heavy appropriations; and he would therefore move that it be indefinitely postponed." Calhoun's motion was rejected by 12 to 22. From *Register of Debates*, 24th Cong., 1st Sess., cols. 1882–1884. Also printed in *Congressional Globe*, 24th Cong., 1st Sess., pp. 588–589.

To A[RMISTEAD] BURT, [Abbeville, S.C.]

Washington, 28th June 1836
My dear Sir, I have received from Mr. [William G.] Overton [our attorney in Va.] what he estimates to be due to my brothers, and will bring it out with me. I expect to leave here Friday, or Saturday next [7/1 or 7/2] and probably may take Abbeville on my way. I take the Salisbury [N.C.] route.

I am gratified to learn, that my constituents so generally approve of my course. I am of the impression, that much has been effected during the session. We stand stronger than we [*one word or partial word canceled*] ever did on the slave question. The South is more united, and the nature of the question is better understood both north & South than it has ever been. But we must not relax. The abolitionists are numerous, Zealous & active. They have a powerful press and abundant friends. But it ["is" *interlined*] not only on the slave question, that we have gained. The bill regulating the deposites and disposing of the surplus, which has become a law, will do much to restore the ascendancy of the States, and effect a deep political reform. It is the most decisive measure that has ever been adopted to regu[l]ate the government. It is the consummation of the action of our State. No measure has for a long time been received with such universal joy.

Make mine and Anna's [Anna Maria Calhoun's] best & kindest

respects to Martha [Calhoun Burt], and believe me to be yours Truly & sincerely, J.C. Calhoun.

ALS in NcD, John C. Calhoun Papers; PC in Jameson, ed., *Correspondence*, pp. 361–362.

Remarks on the fortifications bill, 6/29. "Mr. Calhoun moved to recommit the bill to the Committee on Finance, with instructions to reduce the amount of appropriations, on the ground that it was impossible to expend so large a sum as that appropriated during the remainder of the year, economically or profitably. The old rate of expenditure for fortifications, he said, had never exceeded $800,000 in a year; and now it was proposed to appropriate, in time of profound peace, when there was not the slightest prospect of a war, in this bill, and the one that had been sent from the Senate to the House, at least four and a half millions of dollars. He wished to know, and he earnestly desired gentlemen to answer him, why it was sought to make this vast and unusual appropriation at this time. Was it intended that it should remain locked up in the Treasury, or remain in the hands of the disbursing agents? It was perfectly clear, he said, that this money would not be required, and ought not to be appropriated; and he therefore moved to recommit the bill, with instructions to reduce the appropriations one half." John M. Clayton of Del. said he would "submit an amendment, providing that it [the money appropriated] shall not be drawn from the Treasury until it is wanted for the expenditures authorized by the bill." Calhoun "withdrew his motion to recommit, in order to give way to the above amendment by" Clayton. Later in the proceedings Calhoun "moved to recommit the bill to the Committee on Finance, with instructions to reduce the appropriations to an amount not exceeding one million six hundred thousand dollars." After further debate the Senate agreed to recommit the bill, without instructions. From *Register of Debates*, 24th Cong., 1st Sess., cols. 1902–1906. Also printed in the Washington, D.C., *Globe*, July 2, 1836, p. 3; *Congressional Globe*, 24th Cong., 1st Sess., pp. 594–595. Variant in the New York, N.Y., *Morning Courier and New-York Enquirer*, July 1, 1836, p. 2.

Further remarks on the bill to establish new arsenals and armories in certain States, 6/30. Calhoun argued, "with great force, that public armories ought now to be gradually reduced, rather than augmented, the U.S. having already 800,000 stand of small arms, fully equal to the number possessed by the British empire in 1817; and yet augmenting by means of the public armories now in operation at the rate of 37,000 stand per annum. He characterized the aug-

251

mentation of armories under such circumstances as an almost un-exampled instance of madness." (The bill was passed by a vote of 24 to 15.) From the Washington, D.C., *United States' Telegraph,* July 1, 1836, p. 3.

Further remarks on the fortifications bill, 6/30. "Mr. Calhoun adverted to the necessity for some point at which the accumulation of arms must stop, and when there would be a tremendous reaction, when the losses in consequence of risk, ensurance, impediment, &c., would be infinitely greater than the value of the arms." From *Register of Debates,* 24th Cong., 1st Sess., cols. 1910–1911. Also printed in the Washington, D.C., *Daily National Intelligencer,* July 1, 1836, p. 3.

To J[OSIAH] W. WARE, [Clarke County, Va.]

Washington, 30st June 1836

Dear Sir, So incessantly has my time been employed that it has been utterly out of my power to avail myself of your kind & hospitable offer to spend some time with you on a visit.

Had circumstances permitted, I would have been much delighted to visit your section of the State, not only to extend my acquaintance in that quarter; but also to obserrve [*sic*] your mode of cultivation, which I think would suit well our mountain region, in which I reside.

I hope that on some future occasion, I may have leisure to do, what my engagements have prevented me from doing at present.

I enclose copies of my several speeches during the session and report[s] on the abolition and deposite questions. With great re-sp[ec]t I am & & J.C. Calhoun.

ALS in OFH, J.W. Ware Papers. NOTE: Josiah William Ware (1802–1883) was a prominent planter, sheep raiser, and stock breeder of the lower Shenandoah Valley and later a Colonel in the Confederate States Army. He was a cousin of Lucy Webb who in 1852 married Rutherford B. Hayes.

Amendment to a motion in the Senate, 7/1. A motion offered by Daniel Webster [to require various reports from the Secretary of the Treasury] was amended by Calhoun "so as to require the Secretary of the Treasury to report at the next session the amount of credit allowed to the several disbursing agents of the Government." From the Washington, D.C., *United States' Telegraph,* July 2, 1836, p. 3.

From J[AMES] K. PAULDING

New York [City], 1st July 1836

Dear Sir, I perceive that Mr. [William C.] Preston is nominated as Chairman of the Senate Committee, for carrying into effect the joint Resolution of Congress in relation to the four Pictures for the Rotunda, and as I have not the honour of being acquainted with him, take the liberty of addressing you in behalf of an artist of my acquaintance.

Mr. John G. Chapman, is a native of Virginia, but now resident here, where I have had ["ample" *canceled*] opportunities of judging of his talents as a Historical Painter. From the knowledge thus acquired, and the specimens he has already produced, I do not hesitate to assure Mr. Preston, that should Mr. Chapman be selected to paint one of these pictures he will do ample justice to the choice.

With the advantage of a residence of some years in Italy, which were zealously and industriously devoted to a study of his art, he combines a fertility of invention, a facility of design, and a skill in colouring, superior to any artist with whom I have ever been acquainted. To these high requisites he unites an intimate and extensive knowledge of all the principles of his art, an ardent desire to distinguish himself, and what I consider indispensible [*sic*] to the success of an undertaking of this kind, an ardent feeling of Patriotism. Be assured that if I were not confident, that Mr. Chapman, will do honour to any preference in this instance, I would not have troubled you on the subject, for no personal consideration, or feeling of private regard could induce me to recommend any man, whose incapacity might degrade the reputation of my Country, in any way whatever.

Many applications will probably be made in behalf of persons utterly disqualified for the fulfilment of the just expectations of the Public. These paintings belong to the highest department of the art. It is not sufficient that an artist can paint a Landscape from nature, or a likeness from the original. The conception & grouping a number of figures, and combining them in one action, so as to produce one great effect, is one of the highest efforts of inventive genius, and requires a combination of powers rarely bestowed, or acquired. Without them no man, can fulfill the expectations of the Country, or justify the selection of the Committee. I pledge myself on my own personal knowledge that Mr. Chapman, combines in a ["high" *canceled and* "great" *interlined*] degree the requisite qualifications for producing a national Picture of a high order.

My desire that these Paintings may do credit to the state of the arts in this Country, not less than to do justice to an artist of great merit, must be my apology for troubling you with this Letter. I am Dear Sir, Your Sincere friend & Serv[an]t, J.K. Paulding.

ALS in ViU, Barrett Library, Paulding Collection.

Remarks on the independence of Texas, 7/1. The Senate was considering a resolution reported from the Committee on Foreign Relations, favoring the recognition of the independence of Texas when satisfactory information was received that a civil government was in operation capable of performing the duties of an independent power. "Mr. Calhoun congratulated the Senate on the tone of the discussion; stated that he had hoped we should be ready to recognise Texas before now; but under existing circumstances, he thought we should only go at present so far as the report and resolution contemplate." From *Register of Debates*, 24th Cong., 1st Sess., col. 1916. Also printed in the Washington, D.C., *Daily National Intelligencer*, July 2, 1836, p. 3; the New York, N.Y., *Morning Courier and New-York Enquirer*, July 4, 1836, p. 2.

Remarks on a pension bill, 7/2. Calhoun and John P. King "moved to amend the bill by confining its benefits to the widows and orphans of those who have died or may die of wounds actually received in service, or who have been killed or may be killed in action." (This amendment was adopted.) From *Register of Debates*, 24th Cong., 1st Sess., col. 1929. Also printed in *Congressional Globe*, 24th Cong., 1st Sess., p. 608.

Remarks on the bill to "provide for the better protection of the western frontier," 7/2. Calhoun "said a few words in opposition to the bill, and proposed laying it on the table, that the subject might be taken up next winter, when they would be in possession of the estimates and surveys for the military road contemplated." (The bill was approved.) From *Register of Debates*, 24th Cong., 1st Sess., col. 1930. Also printed in the Washington, D.C., *Globe*, July 6, 1836, p. 2; *Congressional Globe*, 24th Cong., 1st Sess., p. 608.

To [JAMES H.] HAMMOND

Senate Chamber, 4th July 1836
My dear Sir, We are within a few minutes of the adjournment sine die, and I expect to take my departure home in the course of the day. I have but a few minutes to devote to drop[p]ing you a line to acknowledge your last.

The deposite bill has already begun its salutary work. It has limited the appropriations by many millions; but they are still great, about $35,000,000. The surplus to be deposited with the States will be about an equal sum. We adjourn under very favourable auspices. Party discipline is broke[n] and I trust before you return [from Europe], the great work of reform will have made great progress. By that time I trust that your health will be completely reinstated, so that we may have your aid in accomplishing the great work. The deposite act consum[m]ates our Carolina movements and, I feel increased confidence, it will effect all that its friends contemplated.

You must write me often & fully. Let me have your impression on all you see & hear.

With ardent wishes for the complete restoration of yours & Mrs. [Catherine E. Fitzsimons] Hammond[']s health & your safe return I remain your friend, J.C. Calhoun.

ALS in DLC, James Henry Hammond Papers, vol. 6; PC in Jameson, ed., *Correspondence*, p. 362.

Remarks about the suspension of a joint Congressional rule, 7/4. The Senate received from the House of Representatives a message that the House had suspended the rule providing that no bills be sent to the President for his signature on the last day of the session, insofar as it related to certain enumerated bills. "Mr. Calhoun said they all knew that this rule was adopted after many years of experience, and that, on the last day of the session, the Executive had no opportunity to examine a number of bills. He felt obliged to the Senator from North Carolina [Willie P. Mangum] for making his objection, as he thought it highly important that the rule should not be relaxed." (After an amendment was made, the House message was concurred in.) From *Register of Debates*, 24th Cong., 1st Sess., col. 1937. Also printed in the Washington, D.C., *Daily National Intelligencer*, July 6, 1836, p. 3; the Washington, D.C., *Globe*, July 6, 1836, p. 2; *Congressional Globe*, 24th Cong., 1st Sess., p. 615. Variant in the Richmond, Va., *Enquirer*, July 8, 1836, p. 2.

JULY 5–DECEMBER 4
1836

◫

Taking the Piedmont route homeward from Washington, Calhoun was at Pendleton before July 17, arriving simultaneously with news of Jackson's "Specie Circular," issued as soon as Congress adjourned. In early August Calhoun travelled to Athens to participate in the commencement of the University of Georgia, which was presided over by his brother-in-law, Moses Waddel. In Athens he helped to settle bloodlessly a pending student duel. However, he told a student group, including Howell Cobb, Jr., future President of the Confederate Provisional Congress, that, though he hoped not, they might be called upon someday to defend with their muskets the way of life he defended with his talents. For the time being, Southern military ardor could be expressed by raising volunteers for the Seminole campaign going on in the wilderness of Florida Territory and for the threatened new Texas Republic westward of the Sabine River.

Addressing Athens citizens who tendered him an honorary dinner, Calhoun was mutedly optimistic. He saw signs of an abatement of the corruption and consolidation that had marked government action in recent years and of a returning prosperity in the South. And he mentioned a favorite idea, the great potential benefits of a railroad to connect the South Atlantic States and the Mississippi Valley. These themes were repeated when he spoke to Pendleton neighbors on August 12.

Not content to be an armchair advocate, Calhoun set out in September on an extended exploring expedition deep in the Appalachians. He hoped to find the best pass over the mountains for the proposed railroad, a company for which had been organized at Knoxville in July. He was accompanied by the engineer James Gadsden and his neighbor William Sloan and returned to publicize what he believed was the best railroad passage through the mountains. However, his high hopes for the project soon dwindled as it bogged down in localistic competitions.

In November, while voters in the States were selecting Presidential Electors, Calhoun paid a visit to his gold mine in Georgia to make arrangements for the next season's work. Much rode on the profitability of that venture. Because of hail, unusual cold, and his long absence, his cotton crop was "the worst I have ever had." Calhoun seldom mentioned the election in his surviving correspondence, though with his usual failure in short-term prophecy, he predicted that Van Buren would lose.

Van Buren won, defeating a diverse field of opponents. His majority varied according to whether or not Michigan was a State, an ambiguity that Calhoun had pointed out in the last Congress. Daniel Webster carried only Massachusetts. The stalwart Jackson States of Georgia and Tennessee rejected Van Buren to vote for Hugh L. White, even though Jackson had personally campaigned against White. The antique General William Henry Harrison showed surprising though insufficient strength as a candidate in the Middle States and Northwest. South Carolina, as in the previous election, refused to countenance any of the candidates and bestowed her electoral votes on friends—Senator Willie P. Mangum of North Carolina for President and Senator John Tyler of Virginia for Vice-President.

In the election for the Vice-Presidential office that Calhoun had once held the Electoral College returned no majority. Virginia had swallowed Van Buren but not his unsavory running mate Richard M. Johnson. There was no winner, and the Senate would be required to pick a Vice-President from the front runners when it assembled.

Another interesting though minor aspect of the campaign was Calhoun's appearance as the hero of a futuristic romance. The Virginian Nathaniel Beverly Tucker, half-brother of John Randolph and already a convinced secessionist, wrote pseudonymously and Duff Green published incognito The Partisan Leader; a Tale of the Future. This half-novel, half-campaign document portrayed events that were to transpire during Van Buren's fourth term on the "Presidential throne," when a successful Southern confederacy would be established under the leadership of a brilliant and dynamic "Mr. B——." Few readers could miss a resemblance between "Mr. B——" and a well-known Senator from South Carolina.

⊞

From J[OHN] E[WING] BONNEAU

Charleston, 11th July 1836

D[ea]r Sir, I received 49 Bales of your Cotton from Pendleton—18 Bales of which were prime, & sold at $\frac{20}{100}$ [per pound], & the remainder[,] 31 Bales were inferior, & sold @ $\frac{16}{100}$.

Enclosed is the sale & a statement of your account Current to this day, leaving a balance to your Credit, of $505.$\frac{76}{100}$.

The 2 Boxes mentioned in your letter of 20th Ult[imo] to be sent to my Care from New York [City] by [J.] Ed[ward] Boisseau, ["one" *interlined*] for James Ed[ward] Colhoun & the other for his sister [Floride Colhoun Calhoun] have not yet arrived. As soon as they do, they shall be forwarded with as little delay as possible. Respectfully Y[ou]r's &c &c, J.E. Bonneau.

ALS with Ens in ScU-SC, John C. Calhoun Papers. NOTE: The enclosed report of the sale of Calhoun's cotton indicates net proceeds of $2,192.19. The enclosed "account Current" begins with a debit of $1,875.59 which Calhoun had owed [to Mathewes & Bonneau] on 6/25/1835. Subsequent obligations for purchases and payments made in his behalf are itemized. Credited against his obligations were the above-mentioned net proceeds from the sale of his cotton and a payment of $2,093.11 "By Cash rec[eive]d from Planters and Mechanics Bank for a Certificate of Deposit in the Bank Metropolis at Hamburg," [S.C.]. The net balance due to Calhoun from the firm stood, therefore, at $505.76.

From E[LIAS] D. EARLE and Others

Rowland's Hotel [Greenville, S.C.], July 12 [1836]

Dear Sir: The citizens of Greenville, a portion of your constituents, having heard of your arrival, and highly appreciating your eminent public services, beg leave to tender to you, on to-morrow, and request your acceptance of a dinner, as a slight testimony of the feelings with which they regard the successful and faithful discharge of the high trusts confided to you. With sentiments of the highest esteem, we have the honor to be, very respectfully, your obedient servants, E.D. Earle, G[eorge] F. Townes, J[ohn?] H. Joyce, F[ountain] F. Beattie, W. Robinson, and R[ichard] Thruston.

PC in the Greenville, S.C., *Mountaineer*, July 16, 1836, p. 3.

To E[LIAS] D. EARLE and Others

Greenville [S.C.], 12th July, 1836

Gentlemen: I have been honored with your note of this inst[ant], inviting me, in the name of the citizens of Greenville, to a dinner to be given to-morrow, as a mark of their approbation of my public conduct.

I regret exceedingly, that it is not in my power to accept the invitation. My long absence from home, and great desire to see my family, I trust, will be a sufficient apology for declining the acceptance.

For the flattering terms you have used in speaking of my public conduct, you will please accept my sincere acknowledgements. Whatever services I may have rendered the country, must be attributed to the virtue and intelligence of those, whom it is my honor to represent, and whose approbation and support are only to be won and preserved by a faithful discharge of duty. With such constituents, the path of duty loses its ruggedness, and becomes one of comparative ease and pleasure. With great respect, I am, &c. &c. J.C. Calhoun.

PC in the Greenville, S.C., *Mountaineer*, July 16, 1836, p. 3.

To F[RANCIS] W. PICKENS, [Representative from S.C.], Edgefield, S.C.

Fort Hill, 17th July 1836

My dear Sir, The last mail brought your letter with the check, which is as convenient to me as would be the money itself; the advance of the money was not the slightest inconvenience to me. I have destroyed your due bill.

I arrived on Wednessday [*sic*] last [7/13] and found all well except Margaret [Green Calhoun], who was a good deal indisposed, but is now pretty well again. I regret to learn, that your father's [Andrew Pickens's] sperits [*sic*] are so much depressed. Say to him, that his friends in this quarter would be glad to see him, and that he would probably find gentle exercise and change of scene among the most efficient restoratives. Floride [Colhoun Calhoun] and myself would be glad to see him & Mrs. [Mary Harrison] Pickens, and would be happy, that they should spend with us as much of the summer as they could conveniently. Your father's constitution is naturally so good and he has taken such care of it, that I cannot but ["think" *interlined*] that its present derangement is the result of one of those transitions to which our system is liable in our passage through life. I hope your health has improved since your return.

Anna [Maria Calhoun] did not return with me. In conformity to the arrangement before you left us, she joined Col. & Mrs. [William C.] Preston in their tour to the North. We expect her about the 1st Sep[tembe]r.

The session [of Congress], in the main, terminated auspiciously. Many of the appropriation bills failed; and among them the Armory ["bill" *canceled*], & the light house bills. Our secretary [of the Senate, Walter Lowrie] informed me, that the aggregate appropriations would not much exceed $35,000,000. The disbursements I do not think will exceed $27,000,000, and the surplus will range between thirty & forty millions. The probability of its reaching the latter, is as great as that of falling to the former.

We experienced the good effect of the deposite act in cutting ["off" *canceled and then interlined*] useless expenditures the few last days of the session. It is to it, that we owe the failure of so many schemes of expenditure; and the reduction of others. The most important among the latter, was the Harbour bill, which by a system of log rolling ["in the House" *interlined*] was raised to about $2,000,000. It was met with sperit in the Senate on principle, and after a hard fought action the two last nights was reduced one-half. Every southern Senator present voted against it. The whole system was shacked [*sic*; shaken(?)] by the discussion to the centre, and I feel pretty confident, that under the influence of the deposite measure, ["that" *canceled*] it will be the last appropriation of the kind. I found that measure very popular with all parties on my route home, and, if I am not mistaken, such will be the fact throughout the Union, excepting, of course, the interest of the Deposite banks, the speculators & trading politicians. To them it is a death blow. If it be followed up, a complete political reform, which will give an ascendancy to our principles & doctrines, will be the result. It is in the mean time highly important, that our State should be kept as much united as possible. No step ought to be taken which ["our" *canceled*] would devide [*sic*], or distract the State. I cannot but think, that the tendency to discord and discontent which long continued ["and almost hopeless" *interlined*] opposition is ["app" *canceled*] apt to produce in all, but minds of the firmest texture, is passed; and that it will be found comparatively easy to preserve uni[o]n in our ranks hereafter, [*one word or part of a word canceled*] accompanied by a higher feelings [*sic*] of zeal & energy ["to" *canceled*] in asserting and maintaining our doctrine.

Make our kind respects to Mrs. [Eliza Simkins] Pickens, to your father & mother & Mrs. [Eldred] Simkins & family and believe me to be yours truely & since[re]ly, J.C. Calhoun.

ALS in ScU-SC, John C. Calhoun Papers.

From A[UGUSTIN] S. CLAYTON and Others

Athens [Ga.], 3rd August, 1836

Sir—As the organ of the Citizens of Athens and its vicinity, it has been made our pleasing duty to assure you that your visit among them is a source of high gratification, and besides the wish to offer you the civilities due to a stranger, they are anxious to afford you a testimony of the very great regard in which your distinguished public services, especially as relates to the question of Abolition and the distribution of the surplus revenue, are held by them, and to this end beg to tender you a public dinner at such time as will best suit your convenience. We earnestly request that you will not refuse this so favorable an opportunity of gratifying the wishes of a portion of your fellow-Citizens, who have not only greatly admired your political course, but who entertain for you personally the highest consideration. Very Respectfully, Your Ob[edien]t Serv[an]ts, A.S. Clayton, C[harles] Dougherty, S[eaborn] J. Mays, Geo[rge] H. Young, Asbury Hull, Geo[rge] R. Clayton, Hines Holt.

PC in the Augusta, Ga., *State Rights' Sentinel*, August 19, 1836, p. 3; PC in the Augusta, Ga., *Chronicle*, August 20, 1836, p. 2; PC in the Washington, D.C., *United States' Telegraph*, August 22, 1836, p. 3; PC in the Charleston, S.C., *Mercury*, September 5, 1836, p. 2. NOTE: Augustin S. Clayton was a former and Hines Holt a future Representative from Ga. Dougherty, Hull, and George R. Clayton were lawyers and members of the State legislature. Hull was, in addition, treasurer of the University of Ga. Mays was associated with the Athens Factory and the Bank of Athens. The occasion for the invitation was Calhoun's visit to Athens for the commencement exercises of the University.

Remarks at the University of Georgia, Athens, 8/3. In the morning of 8/3 Calhoun was initiated into the Phi Kappa Society. In the afternoon during the commencement exercises, accompanied by

Moses Waddel, he took his seat with the society as President for the day. An address was delivered by Howell Cobb [Jr., later a holder of a number of high political offices]. After further business, diplomas were conferred upon the graduates. "After the motion had been made for adjournment, Mr. Calhoun arose & said before he ["put" *canceled*] put the motion before Society, he deemed it his duty & privilege to make a few remarks; he accordingly enlarged upon the present state of our Country[,] touched upon the abolition question, now so much agitated. He then spoke of the great probability of some of the members of this Society being called to act in this scene with their talents & perhaps with their muskets, which last he said God Grant might never be; he then closed by assuring society of his sincere & eternal attachment to the body. Society then adjourned." From GU, University Archives, Phi Kappa Society Minutes, vol. for 1835–1853, pp. 41–42.

To A[UGUSTIN] S. CLAYTON
and Others, Athens, Ga.

Athens [Ga.], 5th August 1836
Gentlemen—If I could be induced to depart from a rule, which I adopted several years since, on the approach of a memorable crisis of our affairs, to decline all public demonstrations in approbation of my political course, I would with great pleasure accept the very kind and pressing invitation to a public dinner, which you have tendered me, in the name of the citizens of Athens and its vicinity. But the reasons, which induced me originally to adopt the rule, have not yet ceased to operate. Foreseeing, that the course, which a sense of duty impelled me to take on the occasion, to which I have referred, would give the ignorant and artful an opportunity to impute to me base and unworthy motives, I determined to forego (in order to repel, as far as possible such imputations,) all public honors, and to seek my reward in the difficult path which I purposed to tread, in the approbation of my conscience, and the approval of after times.

That my conduct in the difficult scenes, through which I have passed has met the approbation of yourselves and those you represent, is to me a source of much gratification. The two subjects, Abolition and the regulation of the public deposites, in reference to which, you have in particular approved my conduct, are of primary importance, and you could have selected none, on which your approbation would have been more acceptable.

Of all questions, which have been agitated under our government[,] abolition is that in which we of the South have the deepest concern. It strikes directly and fatally, not only at our prosperity, but our existence, as a people. Should it succeed, our fate would be worse, than the Aborigines, whom we have drove [*sic*] out, or the Slaves whom we command. It is a question, that admits of neither concession, nor compromise. The door must be closed against all interference on the part of the General Government in any form, whether in the District of Columbia, or in the States or territories. The highest grounds are the safest.

There is one point, in connection with this important subject, on which the South ought to be fully informed. From all, that I saw and heard during the Session, I am perfectly satisfied that we must look to ourselves and ourselves only for safety. It is perfectly idle to look to the non-slaveholding States to arrest the attacks of the fanatics. I readily admit that the great body of the enlightened citizens of all parties in these States are opposed to their wicked and dangerous schemes, but so intent are the two parties, which divide and distract all the non-slaveholding States, on getting, or retaining power, that neither will directly oppose the abolitionists on our account from the fear, that by incurring their displeasure they might lose their ascendency in their respective States, or defeat their prospect of rising to power. As strong as may be their sympathy for us, their regard for their party at home is still stronger. Of this we may be perfectly assured. Nor would it be less vain to look to Congress. The same cause, that prevents the non-slaveholding States from interfering in our favour at home, will equally prevent Congress. We must not forget, that a majority of Congress in both Houses are the Representatives of those States, and, of course, actuated by all the feelings and calculations which govern their respective States. But, if true to ourselves, we need neither their sympathy, nor aid. The Constitution has placed in our power ample means, short of secession, or disunion, to protect ourselves. All we want are harmony and concert among ourselves to call them into effectual action, when the necessity comes.

As to the act of regulating the public deposites, I consider it by far the most fortunate measure of the Session. And here let me say, which is due to truth and justice, that for the success of this great and beneficent measure, the Country is greatly indebted to the steady and firm co-operation of a majority of the friends of the

[Andrew Jackson] administration in both Houses, who proved by their acts that they preferred their Country and its Institutions to party attachment.

If I mistake not, the passage of the measure is the commencement of a new political era. It will be regarded in history as marking the termination of that long vibration of our system towards consolidation, which lately threatened the overthrow of our institutions & the loss of our liberty, and the commencement of its return to its true confederative character, as it came from the hands of its framers.

There is one view of this important subject highly interesting to the Southern Atlantic States[,] and especially to this, which deserves notice. It will afford the means, if properly applied, of opening our connection with the vast and fertile regions of the West[,] to the incalculable advantage of both them and us. We are far in the rear of the other sections in reference to internal improvement. Nature seemed to place an inseparable [*sic*] barrier between the Southern Atlantic ports, and the West; but a better knowledge of the geography of the Country, and the great advance of the means of communication between distant parts, by Rail Roads, have, in the last year, or two, opened new views of prosperity for our section. Instead of being cut off from the vast commerce of the West, as had been supposed, we find to our surprise that it is in our power with proper exertions to turn its copious stream to our own ports. Just at this important moment, when this new and brilliant prospect is unfolding to our view, the deposite bill is about to place under the control of the States interested ample means of accomplishing, on the most extended and durable scale, a system of rail road communication that, if effected, must change the social, political and commercial relations of the whole country, vastly to our benefit, but without injuring other sections. No State has a deeper interest in seeing the system executed than Georgia. Her position gives her great and commanding advantages in reference to rail roads; more so in my opinion, than any other State in the Union, and all that she wants to raise her prosperity to the highest point and place it on the most durable foundation is a wise and judicious application of her means. Tho' possessed of less advantages, I feel confident, I speak the sentiments of [South] Carolina in saying, that she feels no envy at the superior advantages of Georgia, and that she will rejoice to see them developed to the fullest extent. That there may be a generous rivalry and a hearty disposition between them to co-operate to the full extent, where their joint efforts may be of mutual advantage is my ardent desire; let us both bear in mind, that tho' each still may have its separate interest to a certain extent, yet as it regards other sections, they both have a common interest, and that interest is to unite the Southern Atlantic by *the nearest*[,] *cheapest* and *best routes with the great bosom of the Mississippi and its vast tributaries.* With great respect, I am &c. &c. J.C. Calhoun.

PC in the Augusta, Ga., *State Rights' Sentinel,* August 19, 1836, p. 3; PC in the Augusta, Ga., *Chronicle,* August 20, 1836, p. 2; PC in *Niles' Weekly Register,* vol. L, no. 26 (August 27, 1836), p. 432; PC in the Charleston, S.C., *Mercury,* September 5, 1836, p. 2; PEx in the Richmond, Va., *Whig,* August 26, 1836, p. 3; PEx's in the Washington, D.C., *Globe,* August 31, 1836, p. 3, and September 2, 1836, p. 3; PEx in the Washington, D.C., *Daily National Intelligencer,* September 5, 1836, p. 3. NOTE: The names of the committee addressed by Calhoun can be found above with the letter from Clayton and others of 8/3/1836. The issue of the Augusta, Ga., *Chronicle* that is cited above quoted two sharply contrasting accounts from Athens newspapers concerning Calhoun's reception on his visit to the commencement exercises of the University of Ga. According to the Athens *Banner,* Calhoun's reception was less than cordial due to his "recent attempt to continue the Indians upon our soil in defiance of the obligation of the General Government to remove them." Calhoun's "admirers," the *Banner* added, "were too 'few and far between.'" The Athens *Southern Whig,* on the other hand, called the *Banner* account as "false as it is possible to conceive." Calhoun, it reported, was greeted with "unus[u]al respect from all parties," and was cheered during the commencement exercises "by one universal plaudit from the time he rose till he ascended the stage."

Statement by the committee "to whom was referred the controversy between Mr. George O. White, and Mr. Benjamin C. Yancey," Athens, Ga., 8/5. The committee agrees unanimously that "there is no sufficient ground for an appeal to arms between the two gentlemen," [who are students in the University of Georgia]. Having examined the controversy, the signers "decide that the challenge & the preceding altercation between the parties, shall be considered as withdrawn" and that the controversy shall be terminated. DS (signed by Calhoun, J[oh]n Macpherson Berrien, Charles Dougherty, W[illiam] B[ellinger] Bulloch, and A[ugustin] S. Clayton) in NcU, Benjamin Cudworth Yancey Papers (published microfilm, roll 1, frames 220–221).

To a COMMITTEE at Pendleton, S.C.

Fort Hill, Aug. 10, 1836

Gentlemen—Believing that the course, which I have felt it my duty to take in the great crisis through which our State has passed, with so much honour and success, would expose me to the imputation of unworthy motives, I adopted the determination to decline all public demonstrations in approbation of my conduct, in order to repel, as far as possible, such imputations. But believing that I may, consistently with my past course, accept an invitation to a public dinner [on 8/12] coming from my immediate friends and neighbours, I do not feel myself at liberty to decline that which you have offered; and accordingly I accept it with those grateful feelings, which I have ever entertained for the kind regard of yourselves and those whom you immediately represent. With great respect, yours &c., J.C. Calhoun.

PC in the Pendleton, S.C., *Messenger*, August 12, 1836, p. 2; PC (reprinted from the Charleston *Courier*) in the Edgefield, S.C., *Advertiser*, September 1, 1836, p. 2. NOTE: The Pendleton newspaper's introduction of this letter reads, in part: "The following is the answer of Mr. Calhoun to the invitation to a public dinner to be given here on this day in compliment to him. . . ." The invitation to which Calhoun was replying and the names of his correspondents have not been found. However, the dinner in question was presided over by [militia] Col. Edward Harleston as president and [militia] Capt. Jacob Warley as vice-president, according to the Pendleton *Messenger*, August 19, 1836, p. 2.

SPEECH AT PENDLETON

[August 12, 1836]

The substance of Mr. Calhoun's Remarks at the Pendleton Dinner[:] After 25 years, fellow citizens, of uninterrupted service in the councils of the Union, in various capacities and during a most trying period of our history, that I should receive the cordial and unqualified approbation of my neighbors and immediate friends who had the best opportunities of judging of my motives and character, could not but be highly gratifying to me. In responding to the general approval of my public conduct, contained in the sentiment just offered, it would hardly be expected, that I should enter into a general recapitulation of my political course beginning with the second war of Independence, the first measure of importance in which I bore a prominent part, after I became connected with the General Government, and ending with the Deposite Bill, which has just received your warm approbation. But I may say of these measures, the first and last in which I had an effective agency, that as wide a-part as they stand in point of time, and as dissimilar as they might seem to be, yet in one important particular they are identical. They had a common object, the preservation of the constitution and liberty of the country, endangered at the former period by a foreign foe, and at the latter, by a domestic. And let me add, as great as the danger was in 1812, it was not half so formidable as at the present time. It is true, that then our ships were seized, our sailors impressed, our commerce recolonized; yes, as completely so as it was before the declaration of Independence, and this by the most powerful nation on earth, for such she proved to be in after events. To submit to such outrages, long continued and daily increasing, without any prospect of terminating, would have been followed by national degradation, and by consequence, contempt for our institutions, to the debasing effects of which such cowardly submission would have been attributed. This was seen and felt at the time. If such was the danger of longer submission, that of resistance to such a foe, under the circumstances in which the country was then placed, seemed not much less formidable. It was at this moment, when our affairs stood between these dangerous alternatives, I took my seat for the first time in the councils of the Union. The war session [of Congress], as it is called, was my first session. I then was a young man without experience, having never served previously excepting two short sessions in our own Legislature, in any deliberative body. Circumstances placed me at this critical juncture, young and inexperienced as I was, at the head of the Committee on Foreign Relations, the most important at the time of all the Committees. I saw to the full extent the danger and felt the responsibility, but did not hesitate. The country was unprepared; almost without ships, without fortifications, without munitions, without an army, and without a revenue, with a party powerful for talents, wealth and numbers, opposed to resistance; yet these difficulties did not intimidate. If to resist was full of danger, to submit was not less so; with this striking difference, which, with me was decisive, that if we failed in the former we would fail like men honorably and nobly resisting wrong, and struggling to maintain our independence and institutions, instead of basely sinking like slaves in humble submission, the scorn and contempt of the world. Fortunately for the country manly councils prevailed. The danger was met and surmounted, and a rich harvest of renown and prosperity followed. The peril of the contest was indeed great, but the danger was *without*. The country was free from corruption. The people were patriotic and the public morals untainted. However violent party spirit may have been at the time, no party, nor any public character of any party was suspected of corruption; but now the danger is *within*. The foe is in the bosom of the country, and in possession of the government. A powerful faction, (party it cannot be called,) held together by the hopes of public plunder, and marching under a banner whereon is written, "to the victors belong the spoils," has made successful war on our institutions, and converted all the power and influence of the government into instruments of gain. Ampler means for this purpose were scarcely ever placed in the hands of a dominant faction. With available means, five times greater than is required by the legitimate wants of the country; with the administration of a boundless public domain; with the unlimited control, till the passage of the Deposite Bill, over the public funds, and through them over the currency and banking institutions of the country; with 100,000 dependants on the bounty of the government; and, finally, with an organized, rigid and severe system of discipline, having its centre in Washington and extending in every direction over the wide circle of the country, a scene of speculation and corruption has been opened, reaching from the capitol to the extremities, embracing the high and the low, those in and those out of office, the like of which has scarcely ever existed under the most despotic and profligate governments. It is this powerful and corrupt combination, in actual possession of the government, against which the honest and patriotic have now to wage war. It is against them, that the Deposite Bill was levelled. I shall not venture to say, that the blow will be effectual. It may be, that corruption has struck its roots too widely and deeply to be eradicated; but I do assert, that without the measure, there would not be the slightest hope of reform. Leave the immense surplus in the hands of the government, with the means of controlling the circulation and the banking operations of the country, and of making whatever disbursements it pleased with the view to purchase States or individuals, and how idle would be the hope of reform! but as it is, divested of the surplus, with the public deposites and deposite banks placed under the protection of law and beyond the control of the Executive, the patriot may still hope. It is indeed a dawning—a gleam of light to those who love the country and its institutions. If we had no other evidence of its efficacy, the stern and bitter opposition, I will not say of the party, but of its more prominent leaders, headed by the President [Andrew Jackson] himself, and the loud and continued wailings of all the organs of the faction ever since the passage of the bill, would of themselves afford sufficient. With such an opposition it is wonderful that the measure was adopted; but let me add, as an act of justice, that the more wonderful the passage of the bill, the more honorable to the independent and sound portion of the administration party in both Houses, by whose co-operation it was effected. When I saw so many in the ranks of the party standing firm, and sacrificing party attachments to love of country, on this great occasion, under all the pressure which was brought to bear on them, new hope for our country and its institutions revived in my bosom.

But whatever may be the success of the measure, whether it be destined to open the way to a thorough and complete reform of our political system, or to prove by its failure that the disease is too far gone for medicine, there is one view of the subject that brings it home to us, and which cannot fail to excite an interest in the breasts of all who hear me. The act is the consummation of the Carolina doctrines, carried out in their practical consequences. It would be idle before such an audience, to discuss the nature of these doctrines and the object we had in view in their practical assertion. It is sufficient to say, that our leading object was to arrest the Tariff or protective system, with the view, first, to throw off an oppressive and unconstitutional burthen, which weighed down all the springs of our prosperity, and was rapidly reducing us to poverty; and, next, to reform the government by drying up the sources of a revenue, which we saw would so overflow the treasury on the payment of the public debt, as to corrupt the government and destroy our liberty, unless diminished by a great and decisive reduction of the Tariff. These were the motives which governed us—motives, let me say, worthy of our patriotic and gallant State. Fixed and resolved in our determination, we were in no haste to act. We waited patiently till it was announced the debt was paid, and till the act of 1832 was proclaimed on both sides, by the administration and the opposition, as a final adjustment of the Tariff in the new state of things consequent on the payment of the debt—an act, which we clearly saw at the time and which all must now acknowledge, fell far short of applying a remedy to the fatal disease against which this State contended. It was then and not till then, the State interposed its sovereign voice—wisely and patriotically interposed, as every impartial observer, enlightened by after events, must see, and as posterity will with one voice admit. But as powerful as was the remedy, it could not of itself at once arrest a disease so inveterate and deep. There is in the nature of things an interval—a convalescent state, between disease and health, both in the physical and political world. It is not in the power of the most potent medicine to restore the patient to instant health, nor of the most effective measure to restore the body politic, when diseased, at once to a sound condition. Time had to be allowed for the reduction of the duties to the point which the constitutional wants of the country might require. A sudden reduction would have prostrated the manufacturers with the loss of an immense amount of capital and skill, and the danger of a re-action that might prove fatal to the country. We intended no war against the manufacturers. We wished them no ill and were at all times, both then and before, willing to allow ample time for a reduction so gradual, as to avoid a shock, both to them and the coun-try. This was effected by the Compromise Bill [of 1833], which, while it repealed all the duties on articles which were thought to require no protection, allowed eight years for the reduction of the duties on protected articles.

I saw at the time, that notwithstandi[n]g the vast amount of the reduction, (as I shall hereafter shew,) there would be a considerable surplus, and that as much as it would comparatively be, yet it would be sufficient, to perpetuate power in the hands of those in possession of the government, and who had by their past acts left no doubt that it would be used for the corrupt and dangerous purpose to which it has since been perverted. I stated my impression to the distin-guished Senator from Kentucky [Henry Clay], who acted a part so honorable to himself and useful to the country on the occasion, with the view that in the adjustment of the details the evil might, as far as possible be guarded against. He was not insensible of the dan-ger; but could not, in his opinion, consistently with what was due to the interest he represented on the occasion, and without losing its support, do more than was done.

What I anticipated followed. It became apparent the next year there would be a surplus, and my attention was at an early period directed to the subject with the view of devising and applying some measure which might in its effects anticipate the action of the com-promise act, and thereby apply a remedy to a disease which, could not, be fully reached at once for the reasons stated, by a simple re-duction of the duties. With this view, I moved session before the last, for a special Committee on the subject of Executive patronage. A numerous and able Committee was appointed[,] selected from the three parties in the Senate, which, with other measures, reported [in 1835] a bill to regulate the deposite banks and a resolution to amend the Constitution, so as to authorise the distribution of the surplus revenue among the States during the operation of the com-promise act. It was too late in the session for definite action then.

I reviewed [*sic*; revived] both at the last session and had the good fortune to succeed in passing them in one bill in the form, which they finally assumed in the deposite act. The effect will be, to restore to the States, as the immediate representatives of the people, all the money not needed by the government; and of course, so far as the diseased state of the government depends on a surplus, at once eradicate the disease as effectually as if the duties had been at once reduced to the legitimate and constitutional wants of the government, and that without in the slightest degree injuriously affecting the manufacturing interest of the country. It does more —vastly more. It not only takes the surplus from the government, but by placing it in the custody of the States, puts it into the opposite scale. The effects will be to convert the State Governments into active and vigilant guardians of the common treasury, and to enlist them by their interests to become the advocates of economy and retrenchment in the general government, without which there can be no effectual reform. While accomplishing this important service, it will at the same time restore to the staple States a large portion of that excess, which they pay into the general treasury through the duties. To the extent of this difference between what we pay and what we receive back by the act, we will still be losers, in a money point of view, till the compromise bill completes the reduction. The difference is not large. It may be something more than a third of the excess of our contribution; but whether it be more, or less, I feel confident, that a fund applied in a manner so well calculated to enlist all of our copartners in the union in the great work of reform for which our gallant little State has so long contended almost alone, will be considered by you, as fully returned in the shape of the most substantial political benefits, particularly, if the share which may fall to us and the other States interested, shall be applied, to the construction of the magnificent work of connecting by Rail Road the Southern Atlantic Ports within [sic] the Mississippi and Ohio. Having thus by this last measure consummated the great object, for which our doctrines were called into action, it is time to pause and enquire what have we done? What good have we effected? Have we been compensated for our long and arduous struggle in defence of our interests and the liberty and constitution of the country?

That there has bursted on this and the other Southern States a tide of prosperity within the last three years, to which they had been for a long time strangers, none will deny. On whatever side we cast our eyes, we witness its effects in the improved condition of the country, and the easy and independent circumstances of the people. To what is this to be attributed? I doubt not that much may be traced to general causes growing out of a long peace and the vast improvement in all the arts, mechanical and chemical, which has distinguished the last 50 years, and the full benefit of which but begins now to be realized, in the increased prosperity of the civilized world. But how has it happened, that this growing, general prosperity, which has been so long visible in many portions of our country, as well as others with which we are commercially connected, has been scarcely felt in the Southern section of the Union till within the last three years? And how is it to be accounted for, that it broke in on us so suddenly about that time? How did it happen that we just then passed from a state of depression into one of prosperity, which has been ever since increasing? To these questions, but one sensible answer can be given; that it was then that the shackles of commerce, which had long bound our industry and pressed down the springs of our prosperity, were struck off. Yes, struck off, by the wise, bold and timely interposition of our State—by nullification, not only for her own benefit, but for the whole South; and, I may add, in a wider sense, looking to political consequences, the whole Union. Our prosperity as a great agricultural people, the producers of cotton, rice and tobacco, which depend for their consumption on the general market of the world, *must depend on a free exchange of our products with the rest of the world.* The protective system, in striking at this exchange, struck at the root of our prosperity, which felt the blow to its remotest branches. Under the Tariff of 1828, nearly one half of the back return of our exchanges with foreign nations, passed into the coffers of the General Government, to be disbursed, through its appropriations, almost exclusively on other sections. Hence the distress and poverty which weighed down the South, and hence the sudden prosperity which has followed the overthrow of the system.

I have been loooking [sic] over (said Mr. C[alhoun]) the commercial returns for the year 1835, since the adjournment of Congress, and comparing it [sic] with those of 1832, the year which immediately preceded the interposition of this State; not with the view of addressing you, but to keep myself informed of the progress which our commerce and prosperity have made since that important epoch in our history. The results are surprising. They more than realize what the most sanguine among us anticipated. I will state a few facts, beginning with the domestic exports of the country.

Our exports may be said to be the measure of our commercial prosperity. On them depend the imports, and on these the revenue of the country, with its commerce and navigation. How then stands [sic] the exports of domestic products at the two periods, '32 and '35, the year preceding the action of the State and the last year, with an interval of only three years between? That of '32 in round numbers amounted to $63,000,000, and that of '35 had increased in this short period to $101,000,000. But what is more striking still, of the sixty-three millions in '32, as near as can be ascertained, the exports from the staple States, I mean that portion that grows cotton, rice and tobacco, amounted to forty millions of dollars, and that from the rest of the Union to about twenty-three millions; while in '35 the former amounted to about eighty millions and the latter to but twenty-one millions, showing that the Southern exports had doubled in this short period, while that of the rest of the Union had rather fallen off. I doubt, if there be any thing on the record of history to be compared to this extraordinary commercial growth. To double in three years, and that not compared with a disastrous year, for that of '32 was a year of prosperity compared with those which preceded it. To increase more in three years than in the preceding forty-five, going back to the commencement of the government, and as much as through all the previous period from the first settlement of the country! Making every allowance that fairly can be made for other causes; the general prosperity of the world; a favourable commercial vibration, and others, if there be others, yet this result is too great to be attributed to them. Nothing but a burden taken off; commercial shackles removed; toll gates taken down; and freedom restored to our commerce and exchanges with the world, can adequately account for a prosperity so great and sudden, corresponding as it does, with the great change in our commercial code and the predictions of those who effected it.

If we return from the exports to the imports, we shall find, as might be anticipated, a corresponding increase. The imports for consumption in the year '32, that is the imports after deducting the re-shipments, amounted to $80,000,000 in round numbers, and that of '35 to $129,000,000. The duties levied on the former, if my memory serves me, was [sic] upwards of $35,000,000, (I speak of the gross revenue from the imposts, including the expense of collection and some other charges that do not come on the Treasury,) while that of '35 may be put down at about $22,000,000. You will ask how happens it, that so small a sum in the latter was collected on so large an amount of imports, when in the former so large was collected on comparatively so small. The commercial return will explain. In '32, out of $80,000,000 of imports but $8,500,000 in round numbers were free of duty, while in '35, out of $129,000,000, sixty-five millions were free of duty, rather more than half. This with the reduction of duties on protected articles already effected by the compromise act, explains the difference. If the act of 1828 had remained unmodified, the revenue on the imports of '35 instead of twenty-two millions, would not have been short of sixty millions, and the share that would have fallen on our portion of the foreign exchanges, estimated [*sic*; estimating], as I have stated, our exports at eighty millions, would not have been less than thirty-seven millions instead of thirteen, which may be estimated as the sum collected on our share of the foreign exchanges the last year. The difference shows what has been gained to us by the reduction of the Tariff of '28, and will account in no small degree for our present unexampled prosperity. I do not claim the whole of this reduction as the result of the interposition of this State. Some reduction had been made by previous acts; but more than two-thirds of the whole reduction may fairly be attributed to our exertions. In the mean time, the compromise act is gradually taking off the remaining protective duties, and will by the year 1842 remove the whole, if the act be left undisturbed, by which time from ten to twelve millions annually, in addition to the present reduction, will be taken off.

The result, my fellow citizens, on the whole is, that a reduction of $37,000,000 annually in the imposts has already been effected, being nearly two-thirds of the whole; and that in the next six years from ten to twelve millions more will be taken off under the compromise act, when only about one-sixth of those of '28 will remain.

We may see, said Mr. C[alhoun,] from these brief statements, the real cause of our great prosperity; and that the cause which has effected already so much, is still acting with increasing force. If we be but true to ourselves, and firmly maintain the position which we have acquired by such mighty exertions, I hazard nothing, in saying that without some unexpected disaster, resulting from the visitation of providence, or the calamity of war such as we were exposed to last winter, by the folly and vice of the administration, (which sought to involve the country in a war with France as anxiously as a wise and virtuous administration would have done to preserve peace,) that a degree of prosperity unexampled, awaits us. We may judge of what is to come, after all the causes are fully developed, and in full operation, when such fruits have followed a partial development, and the very commencement of their operation.

Here Mr. C[alhoun] noticed the proceedings of Congress on the abolition question and stated his impression, that though much was done by the discussion of the subject at the last session, to enlighten the public mind, both at the South and North, in relation to it, yet in conceding the right to abolish slavery in the District [of Columbia] and Territories, and establishing the principle that Congress was bound by the Constitution, to receive abolition petitions, every thing had been yielded to the incendiaries, for which they could have hoped. He saw in these concessions, the cause of increased activity and exertion or [*sic*; on] their part, and danger on ours. As yet, the enlightened of all parties at the North with little exception were sound but with the ample means possessed by the abolitionists—ample funds—complete organization—an energetic press—the young, the thoughtless, and the enthusiastic would receive the poison. The whole section, if nothing should be done to arrest the progress of the disease, must become infected, when consequences such as all must deplore, would follow. Mr. C[alhoun] stated also, as his impression, that we had nothing to hope from the North; that nothing effectual would be done there to arrest the danger; and that we must look to ourselves. Fortunately, he said, the constitution left ample means in our hands to protect ourselves, as had been fully shewn, during the session. All that we wanted, were union and concert, and spirit to apply them; and, in his opinion, the sooner applied the better, both for ourselves and the Union. He concluded this part of his remarks by saying, that the situation of the slave-holding States was new and extraordinary; that they were exposed to dangers of unexampled magnitude; but great and novel as they were, our means of meeting, and overcoming them were ample, provided we should prove to have the sagacity of seeing in time, the danger, with the remedy, and spirit to make the application. He said the destiny that awaits us is no ordinary one. If we successfully meet the perils that surround us, we would be among the first and greatest people of modern times; but if not, our lot would be worse than that of the savages we have driven out, or the slaves we command.

Mr. C[alhoun] resumed his remarks on the present prosperity of the country. I foresee, said he, in the midst of this prosperity a danger of no small magnitude, symptoms of which I fear are already visible. If we be not on our guard, the love of gain will overspread the land, to the absorption of every other passion and feeling. In the eager pursuit of wealth, we are in danger of forgetting the struggle by which our prosperity was won, as well as the principles on which it rests; and of forgetting almost that there is a government in existence, on whose movements our destiny so much depends. I rejoice to see the spirit of industry, activity and enterprize, now awake in the land. We of the South have had heretofore too little of this spirit. I shall say nothing to repress it when within proper bounds.

His object was to warn against its excess, to the neglect of higher objects, than the mere acquisition of wealth. In the spirit in which he made these remarks he would offer the following sentiment:

The people of the South: May they not forget in the midst of their ardent pursuit of gain, that virtue, patriotism[,] honor, and intelligence, and not wealth, are the only certain and durable foundation of national prosperity and greatness.

From the Pendleton, S.C., *Messenger*, August 26, 1836, pp. 2–3. Also printed in the Washington, D.C., *United States' Telegraph*, September 13, 1836, p. 2; the Charleston, S.C., *Mercury*, September 21, 1836, p. 2; *Niles' Weekly Register*, vol. LI, no. 5 (October 1, 1836), pp. 77–79. Printed partially in the Washington, D.C., *Daily National Intelligencer*, September 21, 1836, p. 3; the Richmond, Va., *Whig*, September 23, 1836, p. 4. NOTE: The *Messenger*, August 19, 1836, p. 2, gave an account of the dinner of 8/12 during which Calhoun, after being toasted, rose and addressed the company of about 100 persons "with great animation, for half an hour or more." In this issue the *Messenger* also reported: "We will not attempt to give even an outline of the speech, to which we would find it impossible to do justice. As Mr. C[alhoun] has promised to comply with the general request to furnish the substance of his remarks for publication, we hope to have the pleasure next week of laying them before our readers." This is the only evidence that exists as to the origin of the text that was published by the *Messenger* in its issue of 8/26. Because the above text switches inexplicably from first to third person near the end, it is possible that it is based upon some combination of material furnished by Calhoun and of material provided by the editor of the paper.

"Foederatus" to "His Grace the Duke of Pendleton," [published at Greenville, S.C., 8/13]. The author charges Calhoun with "childish petulance" in recent Senate speeches; this "indecorous conduct must have proceeded from the love of consistency." "In your efforts to discover and disseminate the elements of disunion . . . you felt the necessity of seducing prominent men, and making them the instruments of revolutionizing the opinion of the South as to the value of the Union." This is consistent with Calhoun's long-established "malignant policy of destroying all whom you cannot eclipse." The most notable example of this policy was Calhoun's vote that rejected [Martin] Van Buren's appointment as U.S. Minister to Great Britain. With this misguided act, "Foederatus" contends, Calhoun's "only and last hope for the Presidency was lost forever." He advises Calhoun on his return to Washington to assume a more "manly mien," as "the appearance of courage frequently confers the reputation of it," and not many people question the difference between appearance and reality. PC in the Greenville, S.C., *Mountaineer*, August 13, 1836, pp. 1–2.

To J[ames] Ed[ward] Colhoun, [Abbeville District, S.C.]

Fort Hill, Aug[us]t [*ca.* 15?,] 1836

Dear Sir, I am not able to answer your questions in referrence [*sic*] to Mrs. Tench. I would suppose, that the descent of the Virginia land bounty would be regulated by the laws of Virginia, till the land ["is" *canceled and* "warrant is" *interlined*] located, and that when located it would be in conformity to the laws of Ohio. If desirable, I could obtain information through some of my Virginia friends by letter, or obtain it when I go on next winter to Washington.

I have not heard from Col. [James] Gadsden yet, and I fear I may miss him altogether. The Gov[erno]r [George McDuffie] was with me a few days since; and I conversed freely with him. I think his views are sound. Your sister [Floride Colhoun Calhoun], with Andrew [Pickens Calhoun] & Margaret [Green Calhoun] think of starting to the ["sp" *canceled*] Warm Springs [of Va.] in a day, or two. As soon as they return, I will take my mountain trip, or sooner, if Col. Gadsden should come.

I had a conversation with Judge [Ezekiel?] Pickens in referrence to the negroes which were given to Mr. & Mrs. Milligan. He says there will be no difficulty in the recovery of them, or their value, if the gift was for life, either from Dr. Jones or the holder, if he has parted from them. He thinks the Doctor had better be sued, than even the holder, as there would be pretty strong presumptive evidence, that he knew that the right in the negroes was but for life. He thinks it would be advisable for you to obtain the proof from Rob[ert] Trimble and others that the gift was for life. The decleration [*sic*] of Milligan and his wife would be proof or even the beleif [*sic*] of the neighbours, or there may be some evidence among your mother's [Floride Bonneau Colhoun's] papers. If the knowledge of the fact could be brought home to Dr. Jones that it was but a life interest, it would make it but so much the stronger. He (the Judge) said, if you would transmit to him ["a statement" *interlined*], which could be proved he would attend to the case with pleasure. The value of the property is considerable and as your brother [John Ewing Colhoun] is very remiss, you had better, take it in hand yourself & without delay. It is said that delay is dangerous. It is eminently so at law. All are well & all desire their love. Affectionately, J.C. Calhoun.

ALS in ScCleA.

To Ja[me]s Ed[ward] Colhoun

Fort Hill, 17th August 1836

Dear Sir, I have received both of your letters and only wait the arrival of Col. [James] Gadsden to make the examination. I addressed a letter to him at Greenville immediately on my return from Georgia, which I requested the Postmaster there to deliver to him immediately on his arrival there; and in which I urged him by all means to make me a visit as I was exceedingly anxious to see him. I have not yet heard from him, but I understand that he is at flat rock [N.C.] superintending the surveys, and that ["the" *canceled*] gap creek gap[?] promises very favourably.

We are all well. I had a letter from Anna [Maria Calhoun] by the last mail dated at Niagara. She was delighted with that grand spectacle, as with her tour generally.

The fine season is bringing out my cotton crop surprisingly. All desire their love to you. Affectionately, J.C. Calhoun.

[P.S.] You do not state what you & John [Ewing Colhoun] agreed on in relation to the estate of your mother [Floride Bonneau Colhoun]. Let me know in your next, and when you will be up.

ALS in ScCleA.

To F[rancis] W. Pickens, Edgefield, S.C.

Fort Hill, 17th Aug[us]t 1836

My dear Sir, From what you write, my crop is a perfect contrast with yours. Instead of the best, it is about the worst I have ever had. Between hail storms, heavy and long continued falls of rain, cold weather and bad management in my absence, I cannot make much more than half a crop of cotton, and two thirds of corn. It is hard to get a good overseer any where, but doubly so here, where so few know any thing about planting. Your crop must indeed be fine; and I should be glad to see it; but it will be altogether out of my power to turn my ["face to"(?) *canceled and* "face" *interlined*] down the country, till I go to Washington, should I conclude to go.

I am sorry to see you so despondent and out with politicks. Among the worst symptoms of the times, I place the indif[f]erence to the political condition of the country of late so prevalent in this and the other Southern States, originating with the great mass in the eager pursuit of gain ["from" *canceled and* "caused by" *inter-lined*] the great prosperity of the country, [and; "in" *canceled and* "with" *interlined*] the intelligent, I fear, from despondency—a belief, that the system itself is unsound. No one can be more sensible than I am of the extent to which corruption has extended its roots, and the difficulty of reform, but I must say, that I regard the corruption, with less alarm, than the present indifference. We have made such advances, that I do not doubt, that with zeal & energy the Government may be reformed; but whether the people are not so much tainted, that the reform would be but temporary, I cannot venture to say. Experience can only decide that. But with a people careless of their fate, what can be done? You must permit me to say, that in my opinion you & many of our distinguished citizens yield too much to despondent feelings. True wisdom, it appears to me, ["to" *canceled and* "consist" *changed to* "consists"], in struggling against political disorders in a conservative sperit, without determining whether they be or be not incurable, till events themselves shall decide. If our efforts prove successful, we will have the consolation of having effected our object, short of the hazard of revolution; but, if not; if revolution must come, then we shall have much more decided control in shaping the course ["of events" *interlined*] under the new order of thing[s], by having done our duty under the old. In the direction, which I fear things are now taking in our State, I cannot but ["fear" *canceled and* "apprehend" *interlined*] the time is approaching, when the State will lose all its control, and that we will sink down to a level lower than Virginia itself; as our position and population are less commanding than hers. We have done much, and, if true to ourselves, can do much more to secure the country and to acquire honor & influence for the State; but to effect it, every feeling of despondency must be surpressed [*sic*]; and in its place a manly, & bold discharge of duty, be the [*partial word canceled*] consequence what it may, substituted. I, on my part, ["I" *canceled*] am not prepared to say, that the govcr[n]-ment & country can be regenerated, or that the Union can be preserved under the baneful influence of the abolition sperit at the North. I hold it rash to form a definitive opinion either way; and that the wise course is to act on the supposition, that the country & gover[n]ment may be regenerated and the Union saved; but at the same time to adopt the most effectual constitutional measure to arrest the progress of usurpation & corruption, and abolitionism, even tho' disunion should be the consequence. If possible, let us save the liberty of all; but, if not, our own at all events; and by aiming honestly & fairly at the former, we shall the more certainly, if we fail, succeed in the latter. If I differ from ["many of" *canceled*] our friends, it is not, that I am more certain of success in our political efforts to save the country and its institutions, ["as" *canceled and* "but" *interlined*] that I am less certain of defeat, ["and" *canceled and* "with" *interlined*] the conviction, that whether one, or the other shall befal[l] us, we shall be the more certain of effecting, what we must all desire, the ultimate security of the South & the honor and influence of our State, by pursuing the course, I have indicated.

I am sure that you will attribute ["bute" *canceled*] the freedom of these remarks to the entire confidence I have in your candour & friendship and the interest I feel, that one for whom I have so high a regard, should take the view in this great juncture of our affairs, ["wh" *canceled*] that would prove the most useful to the country & honorable to himself.

Floride [Colhoun Calhoun] & all the family join their love to you & Eliza [Simkins Pickens] & family, and also to your father [Andrew Pickens, Jr.] & ["family" *canceled*] mother.

The last letter [*sic*] brought me a letter from Anna [Maria Calhoun], dated at Niagara. She was well, and much pleased with her tour. She expects to be back about the 1st Sep[tembe]r. Sincerely, J.C. Calhoun.

ALS in ScU-SC, John C. Calhoun Papers.

To Ja[me]s Ed[ward] Colhoun

Fort Hill, 23d Aug[us]t 1836
My dear Sir, A Mr. Felix Green, appearently [*sic*] a substantial Farmer, called on me this morning to know whether you would sell your place on 26 [Mile Creek] and what was your price, with the terms of payment. I told him I would write to you and transmit your answer as soon as received. He lives in Greenville on the Enoree [River]. He is desireous [*sic*] of an early answer.

Col. [James] Gadsden has not yet reached Pendleton, nor have I heard from him. Whether he ["should" *canceled and* "come" *changed to* "comes"], or not, I am resolved to look at the pass myself; but as it would be much better to have him along, I think it better to wait till I hear from him.

We are all well except Patrick [Calhoun], who has suffered from a kick of a horse on his leg. He is getting will [*sic*]. The bone was not hurt. All desire their love to you. I am anxious to hear what agreement you & John [Ewing Colhoun] came too [*sic*] about the estate [of your mother, Floride Bonneau Colhoun]. Affectionately, J.C. Calhoun.

ALS in ScCleA.

From [James L. Edwards,] Pension Office, 8/27. Edwards returns a letter [*not found*] from "James Carlile" to Calhoun. Carlile's declaration was returned to James Wardlaw at Abbeville, S.C., on 8/23/1833, with a letter explaining why Carlile could not be granted a pension, and no additional evidence has been received since. FC in DNA, RG 15 (Records of the Veterans Administration), Letters Sent, 1831–1866.

"MANY STATE RIGHTS MEN"
to S.C. Members of Congress

[Published at Charleston, August 29, 1836]

Gentlemen—Mr. Henry L. Pinckney [Representative from S.C.], in his Address to the Electors of Charleston District, declares that he has been bitterly and unsparingly reviled and tyrannically doomed to destruction, by *certain individuals* acting under the influence of *vindictive malice,* because he refused to co-operate with them [in Congress] in "movements which he conscientiously believed to be disastrous to the South, destructive to the Union, and grossly violative of the Federal Constitution," and dared "to differ in opinion from them [on the question of the reception of abolition petitions], to reject invitations to resign his seat, and to disregard mandates to retrace his steps." Many of your fellow-citizens have received an impression from Mr. Pinckney's Address so strong, as almost to amount to positive assurance, that all or some of *you* are the individuals to whom he alludes.

We are unwilling to believe that you, or any of you are justly liable to these charges, and deem it due to you that we should suspend our judgment until you have been informed that we understand them as relating to you, and have had an opportunity of being heard in your own defence.

PC in the Charleston, S.C., *Mercury,* August 29, 1836, p. 2. NOTE: This letter was addressed to Calhoun and William C. Preston, Senators, and to William J.

Grayson, J[ohn] K. Griffin, Robert B. Campbell, Waddy Thompson, Jr., J[ames] H. Hammond, and Francis W. Pickens, Representatives. This included all the members of the S.C. Congressional delegation except for Pinckney and James Rogers. (Hammond had resigned in 2/1836.) Pinckney's "Address to the Electors of Charleston District" appeared in the *Mercury* for August 20, 22, 23, 24, 25, 27, 30, and 31, and September 1, 1836, and was issued as a pamphlet the same year.

To B[arkley] M. Blocker, D[aniel] Holland, W[illiam G.] Gallman, J[ohn] C. Allen, and J[esse?] Gomillion

Fort Hill, 5th Sept. 1836

Gentlemen, I have been honoured by your note of the 24th August, inviting me to attend a public dinner to be given to the Hon. F[rancis] W. Pickens, by the citizens of Edgefield [District, S.C., on 9/15], at the Central Springs, in testimony of the approbation of his constituents of his public conduct.

I regret, that the great distance, and engagements, with which I cannot dispense, forbid my acceptance of your invitation.

Your Representative richly merits this testimony of your respect, by the intelligence, abilities and zeal with which he discharged his public duties. No one could be more faithful to his trust. Permit me to add, without intending in any degree a compliment to myself, as having been your former representative, which I remember with proud satisfaction, that no portion of all this great Union better deserves to be faithfully served, than yourselves. Old Ninety-Six District has the distinction, and as far as I know, the solitary and proud distinction, of never having changed by her act, her representative in Congress from the beginning of the Government to this day. Every change of representative in the District has been caused by death or resignation. In 48 years and 25 elections you have never made a change, and now you are about to make the 26th by an unanimous vote; such has been the caution with which you have bestowed your confidence in the first instance, and such the steadiness with which you have preserved your confidence when once bestowed. If I had not the honour of having my name on the list of those whom you have distinguished with your confidence, I would add, that you have been served with a fidelity and ability no less honourable to you, than your representatives.

That such a constituency should remember my past services, and continue their confidence in me, after so many years of public service, in many and various stations of high responsibility, and during a most trying period of our history, is to me a source of great satisfaction. If it has been my fortune to render any service to the State and Union, the merit is yours, with the other portions of the District, which at an early period bestowed your confidence, and, by its continuance ever since, have cheered and sustained me in all the difficulties and trials, through which I have since passed. That you have thus afforded me an opportunity of serving our country, which, I trust, has not been entirely lost, and have sustained me in pursuing the course dictated, as I sincerely believed, by duty and patriotism, will ever be remembered by me with profound gratitude.

In conclusion, I take the liberty of offering the following sentiment:

Old Ninety-Six District. May she long retain her present proud distinction, of never having bestowed her confidence where it was not merited, and never having withdrawn it, when once bestowed.

With great respect, I am your humble serv[an]t, J.C. Calhoun.

PC in the Edgefield, S.C., *Advertiser*, September 29, 1836, p. 2; PC's in the Washington, D.C., *United States' Telegraph*, October 6, 1836, p. 3, and November 1, 1836, p. 3; PC in the Augusta, Ga., *Chronicle*, October 29, 1836, p. 4.

To a COMMITTEE in Anderson District, S.C.

Fort Hill, Sept. 5, 1836

Gentlemen—I have been favored by your note of the 27th ins[tan]t [*sic*; 8/27] inviting me in the name of the citizens in the vicinity of the Rock Mills to partake of a public [barbecue] dinner on the 16th of this month [in honor of Waddy Thompson, Jr., Representative from S.C.].

Seeking no reward for my public service, except the approbation of my own conscience, and the good opinion of the wise and virtuous, and wishing to avoid all imputation of improper motives in the course, which duty compelled me to pursue, I have, as you intimate, long declined all demonstrations of public opinion in my favour except on a recent occasion from my immediate neighbors and friends. On the principle, on which I accepted theirs, I would also accept the honor you have tendered, were I not prevented by engagements, with which I cannot dispense. I expect to be absent at the time on business, which will detain me from home for some time; and of course must ask you to excuse me for not accepting your very kind and hearty invitation.

So far from deserting the great principles, for which we have so long contended, time and experience but serve to raise them in my estimation. They have been put to the test and the result has more than realized our anticipations. Witness the sudden and unprecedented prosperity, which has bursted in on the South, and which continues to flow with a stronger and stronger current. Witness that respect for the State and its citizens, which is felt and expressed in every quarter, as the principles, which governed us are better understood, and the fruits of our long and arduous struggle are more clearly seen. I boldly venture the assertion, that in a few years, there will be but one opinion, that, if the liberty and institutions of our country shall be saved, it will have been, by the manly, bold and patriotic course of our State. Suppose the State had moved along with the corrupt current, that has overflowed the country for many years; suppose she had not resisted—had not interposed her sovereign authority to arrest the tide—to terminate the conflict between the North and South in relation to the Tariff—to stop the overflow of the revenue, which would have more than doubled the present enormous surplus, can any one doubt, but that the will of the Executive would have been absolute; that fraud, speculation, plunder and corruption would have pervaded the land, and that the institutions and liberty of the country would have sunk, never to rise again? If as it is, we have been scarcely able to save them, what would have been the case, if we had not acted?

To desert, or abate in our zeal for principles, which have diffused such prosperity throughout the land; which have given so much character to our State, and which have done already so much to save our liberty and institutions, and are destined to do so much more, if persevered in, would be as base, as unwise. Let us stand fast in the faith and persevere to the end, in the confident belief, that, if we but do our duty honestly and fearlessly, a righteous Providence will reward us in the end by the redemption and restoration of the Government to its primitive purity and the establishment of our liberty on a more solid foundation than ever. With great respect, I am, &c. J.C. Calhoun.

PC in the Pendleton, S.C., *Messenger*, September 30, 1836, p. 1. NOTE: According to the issue of the *Messenger* cited, some 1,200 people attended the event to which Calhoun sent the above message. The invitation to which Calhoun was responding and the names of his correspondents have not been found.

However, the officers of the meeting were J[esse] W[etheral] Norris, Dr. A[lexander] Evins, and Peter S. Vandiver.

From J[ohn] E[wing] Bonneau, Charleston, 9/6. As requested by Calhoun during his last trip to Charleston, Bonneau has procured from England "an oil Floor Cloth—21 feet 8 In[ches] by 15 feet—of grave colors, brown & green." He has forwarded the item to Pendleton by way of Hamburg [S.C.]. ALS in ScU-SC, John C. Calhoun Papers.

Deed executed by John D. Field, Sheriff of Lumpkin County, Ga., 9/10. This document indicates that as a result of a judgment in a suit of A.N. Baird against Pinkney Caldwell, Field had seized property of Caldwell, specifically "the undivided fourth part of lot number eight hundred & seventeen." After being duly advertised, this property was offered at public auction by the sheriff on 9/6 and was sold to John C. Calhoun for $12. (Caldwell had on 5/7/1835 executed a deed conveying the same property to Calhoun.) Field now conveys title to Calhoun to hold "in as full and ample a manner, as the said Pinkney Caldwell . . . did hold, or might have held, and enjoyed the same, had it not been seized and sold under Execution as aforesaid." The deed was witnessed by A[lfred] B. Holt and G[reen] K. Cessna and endorsed as having been recorded in the "Clerk's office of the Superior court of Lumpkin County" on 9/12. DS in ScCleA, Thomas Green Clemson Papers.

To J[AMES] ED[WARD] COLHOUN

Fort Hill, 19th Sep[tembe]r 1836

My dear Sir, I have just returned from a laborious examination of the country between this [place] and the mouth of Tuckyseege [*sic;* the Tuckasegee River in western N.C.] in company with Col. [James] Gadsden. We were nine days incessantly engaged. The result is eminently favourable; far more than I anticipated. I cannot state particulars now. You must come up immediately to concert measures to give the route [for the proposed railroad] the proper impulse to carry it through. I will come out with a statement of facts in the [Pendleton] Messenger on Friday next [9/23]. We will have a meeting the week after; and meetings must be had in Abbeville, Edgefield, & Orangeburgh. It has a decided preference over all other routes and nothing but suitable efforts are required to ensure its success.

While [you are] up, we must come to a settlement in reference to your mother's [Floride Bonneau Colhoun's] estate.

All send their love. Affectionately, J.C. Calhoun.

ALS in ScCleA; PC in Jameson, ed., *Correspondence*, p. 363; PC in [John B. Cleveland, compiler], *Controversy between John C. Calhoun and Robt. Y. Hayne as to the Proper Route of a Railroad from South Carolina to the West* [Spartanburg, S.C.: no publisher, 1913], p. 10.

To [FREDERICK W. SYMMES], Editor of the Pendleton *Messenger*

Fort Hill, Sept. 22, 1836

Dear Sir—Believing it to be the duty of every citizen to lay before the public such facts, as may come to his knowledge and which may contribute to the selection of the route for the contemplated Rail Road from Charleston, to Louisville, Lexington and Cincinnati, I have selected the *Messenger* as the medium of communicating some information that may not be unimportant, which I acquired in a recent visit, in company with Col. [James] Gadsden, to the portion of the Alleghany [*sic*] chain lying along the head waters of the Keowee River.

Concluding, as well from what I had heard as from the peculiar formation of the mountains in that quarter, that there was a favourable prospect of a gap, I determined to visit the region personally, in order to ascertain how far my impression might be correct. Knowing from a conversation with Col. Gadsden last fall, that he had similar impressions, I requested him by letter to join me, if his duties and convenience would permit, with which he readily complied, as well to test the truth of his own, as my impression. Mr. W[illiam] Sloan my neighbor at my request, accompanied us; and we were joined near the mountains by Mr. James M'Kinney, whose thorough knowledge of that section of the mountains was of the greatest service. We commenced our examination near his residence, and extended it to the gap in the mountain, in which the White Water, one of the Western branches of the Keowee, takes its source, and thence down the Tuckasiege [*sic*; Tuckasegee], which rises on the Western side of the same gap, to where it joins [the] Little Tennessee [River in Macon (later Swain) County, N.C.]; the distance about 45 miles by estimation. On our return, we examined the parts of the route that required further attention, and extended the examination from where we first commenced, across the Keowee River just below the old Fort [Prince George] along the old Indian path to Mr. Perry's. From thence to where the route would strike the dividing ridge between the waters of Saluda and Savannah [Rivers], about 8 or 10 miles below Pickensville [S.C.], there can be no difficulty, as there can be none from that point to Charleston.

Our entire examination then, extends from Mr. Perry's [in Greenville District?] to the mouth of the Tuckasiege; a line of about 84 miles, to which we devoted eight days of incessant labour, examining on foot the most difficult and inaccessible points. The result was satisfactory beyond expectation. I can only speak for myself. Col. Gadsden will of course reserve his opinion till it is his duty to speak officially [as one of three commissioners for the railroad].

In order to give any thing like a satisfactory view of the route, over which we passed, it will be necessary to divide it into sections, and to present the facts connected with each, separately. The first section, proceeding West, extends from Mr. Perry's to the point near Mr. M'Kinney's, at which we commenced our examination on our way out. Its length is about 10 miles. It is cut by the Keowee River, which as its banks are high in places and the river small, may be passed at a great elevation and moderate cost. The rise towards the mountain from the commencement to the termination of the section, can be conveniently overcome by gradually ascending the Eastern slope of the river ridge till it strikes some convenient point for crossing, and then ascending in like manner to the point where the section terminates, on the summit of the dividing ridge between Little River and Keowee. The rise, it is believed, will not any where exceed 25 feet in the mile. The next section, extends from the point where the last terminated to the top of the Alleghany. It terminates just at the point where the Chatuga [Chatooga] mountain joins the Alleghany. At this point, the White Water, one of the branches of the Keowee, which rises on the summit of the mountain, (a stream about the size of the 18 mile,) after cutting down and turning the Chatuga mountain, leaps from the top of the Alleghany in two perpendicular falls near to each other, about 45 or 50 feet, and then continues its rapid descent to the Valley below. The length of the section is about 29 miles; and from the best information we can obtain, the elevation to be overcome will not exceed 30 feet to the mile. The line of ascent may be conveniently lengthened or shortened to a considerable extent to suit the grading, so as to diminish the rise probably below what I have estimated; or if it should be thought advisable to reduce it to the lowest rate, it may be effected with little expense or delay, and without a stationary Engine, by using the power which the waters of the White Water afford, & which is more than sufficient to elevate the heaviest train.

The next section is on the top of the Alleghany, and extends from the termination of the last, where the White Water leaps from the top of the mountain to the East, to the point where the Tuckasiege makes a similar leap but to the West. The length of the line is about 16 or 17 miles. It passes through two Vallies of nearly equal length and extent, divided by a low[,] narrow ridge of about 150 feet high. The two Vallies are nearly on the same level. The one on the East of the ridge is called Cashier's [in what later became Jackson County, N.C.], and that on the West [is called] Yellow Valley, from the brownish yellow which the decayed fern gives to it. The Eastern extends from South-east to North-west, from the fall of the White Water [in what later became Oconee County, S.C.] where the Valley opens, about 8 miles; and from North-east to South-west, from the Chimney Top to the White Side mountains; two elevated peaks rising a thousand feet, or more, above the Valley. The White Water collects its waters in the Eastern and the Tuckasiege in the Western Valley. The sources of both are on the top of the low ridge that separates them, and but a few feet apart. The two Vallies form the gap, which we named the Carolina Gap, to distinguish it from the Rabun or Georgia Gap, which is 35 or 40 miles to the South-west of it.

The low ridge, or the crest of the Alleghany, as it may be called, that separates the Vallies, may be easily passed at a low angle by gradually ascending on the slopes on the South-west side of Cashier's to its summit, and descending in like manner on the opposite side, on the South-western slope of the Yellow Valley; but it would be both shorter and cheaper in the long run, to pierce the ridge with a tunnel, which would not exceed 200 yards, and which would give a beautiful run nearly level for 16 miles on the summit of the Alleghany, from fall to fall.

The next section extends from the termination of the last, at the head of the falls of the Tuckasiege, to some point down the River sufficiently distant to afford a gradual descent along the sides of the mountains through which it flows.

We examined this section carefully down the whole extent of the fall. The sight is beautiful. The volume of water is greater than that of the White Water. The falls consists of four perpendicular leaps in the space of about a mile. The first we estimated at 50 feet and the last at 70 or 80. The slope of the mountain on the West side of the stream was very favourable for grading, as far down as our examination extended, and we were informed, that it continued equally favourable all the way down.

The elevation of the fall may be overcome by a rise from below, certainly not greater than that to the top of the Alleghany, which I stated at 30 feet to the mile; or it may be turned, as we were informed, by passing up Shoal Creek, which enters the Tuckasiege on the East side, below the falls—a stream of considerable size, and which according to our information, rises in the Alleghany near the Eastern sources of the Tuckasiege, at a point where there would be no difficulty to pass from the one to the other, and passing round the ridge that limits the Yellow Valley on the East, descends with a rapid current, but without a leap, to where it joins the Tuckasiege. But, if a grading of still more gradual rise than could be effected by either of the routes, should be thought advisable, here, as well as on the Eastern slope of the Alleghany, there is the same cheap power to raise or let down gently the heaviest train.

The next and last section extends from the termination of the last to the mouth of Tuckasiege. It is difficult to imagine a pass through a mountain region finer than this section. The river is remarkably straight, and free from all sudden turns. The road would pass along its East side, two-thirds or more, of the way on level ground requiring but little expense in grading. A large portion of the residue, where the hills come in, would be on favorable slopes free from rocks. In the whole length there was not two hundred yards of rocky cliff to encounter; and through the whole length no walling in the river. We did not extend our examination farther, as the survey of Capt. Batche [*sic*; Hartman Bache] under the orders of the War Department gives ample information in relation to Little Tennessee from the junction of the Tuckasiege to the head of steamboat navigation on that river. It is sufficient to say, that there is no serious difficulty below.

Having now communicated briefly the information I collected during the examination, it will be proper to conclude with a few general remarks on the entire route, in order to bring its advantages, such as they are, before the public. The value of the gap must depend not simply on the facility of passing it, but its position; and that again on the fact, whether it be such that a road through it would be calculated to effect the great object in view, to connect Charleston commercially with the great region of the West and in particular the points at which it is proposed to terminate the road;

or in other words is the direction of the gap favorable to this great object? Is the route to and from it of easy approach? And is it favorable for branching to important points? I propose a few hasty remarks on these points.

The direction of the gap from Charleston is nearly North-west, and if a line be stretched from Charleston to the gap and continued in the same direction, it would strike the Mississippi near the mouth of the Missouri; cross the Ohio below the Wabash; pass on the ridge between Green and Cumberland rivers; cross the latter little above Carthage [Tenn.]; pass the Cumberland mountain at the Crab orchard gap; which Col. [Stephen H.] Long's survey shows to be practicable, pass the Great Tennessee near Kingston [Tenn.], and extend along Tuckasiege to the Carolina Gap. On this side, the line from the gap to Charleston, would take the old Indian trading path, which was used by the Cherokees west of the mountain before the Revolution, with little deviation throughout its entire course; passing through the forks of the Edisto and striking the Charleston and Hamburg Rail Road below Branchville. The line on this side of the gap would extend through the entire length of the State, 250 miles, from Southeast to North-west, and on the other side from the gap West, if extended[,] would divide into nearly equal parts, the great valley between the lakes and the Rocky mountain, through which the waters of the Mississippi and its tributaries flow.

As to its approach, it will be found, I am satisfied, very easy on both sides. The approach from Charleston on the East side, will be found remarkably so. There are two routes: the direct one through the forks on the Edisto, and up the dividing ridge between the forks, and thence along the dividing ridge between Saluda and Savannah [Rivers], to where the old Indian trail, to which I have referred, strikes that ridge, without crossing a drop of water after passing the North fork of the Edisto to that point. The other, bearing to the East, and keeping the main dividing ridge to the same point, without crossing a single stream, great or small, for 200 miles. This route, the longer by a few miles, possesses many advantages. What I have already said will supercede [*sic*] the necessity of any remark on the accessibility of the gap from the point where the Road would leave the ridge to the gap, except, that it will cross no other stream larger than a moderate sized Creek, but the Keowee, it being the only River on the route throughout the entire length of our State.

The gap is no less accessible on the Western side. In the whole extent of the direct line leading to the heart of the Continent, from the summit of the Alleghany to the Ohio, the Tuckasiege or perhaps

Little Tennessee, the Great Tennessee, and the Cumberland, would be the only Rivers to cross; and in the whole length, very few streams of any description, and no mountain or ridge, except the Cumberland.

The next point to be considered is, whether the line of route is favourable for branching and easy of approach from important points? A statement of facts will best answer the question. I will begin with Charleston and assume, that the Road will take the great dividing ridge to which I have frequently alluded. Keeping the ridge, it would approach within 8 miles of Mulberry castle on Cooper River, within 12 miles of the mouth of the Santee Canal, within 9 miles of Vance's Ferry, where there are bluffs on the Santee on both sides, and where a branch could be thrown out conveniently to Camden and Cheraw; within 12 miles of Orangeburgh, within the same distance from Columbia, through which a branch could be thrown out taking the ridge between Broad River and Catawba, and passing through Winnsborough, Chester, York, to the North Carolina line; within 14 of Edgefield, 25 of Newberry, 5 of Cambridge, 11 of Abbeville, 19 of Laurens, 8 of Anderson, 20 of Greenville, 8 or 10 of Pickensville, 7 of Pendleton, and 3 of Pickens.

On the West of the mountain it would strike Little Tennessee at the head of Steamboat navigation, about 80 miles from the gap and 340 from Charleston. The River would of course be, in effect, one important branch, leading to all the important places on navigable waters. At, or about that point, the main trunk, or a branch, as may be determined, would turn off to Knoxville, and one or the other to Kingston, on the Great Tennessee. I need not trace the route from Knoxville, as that is familiar to all. Which ever would take Kingston, would pass up Emory's River by the Crab Orchard gap over the Cumberland mountain, and striking the Cumberland River near Carthage, it would continue its route through a fine country, well calculated for Rail Roads, and having the advantage of throwing out frequent branches to important points at a short distance, through middle Tennessee and the Western parts of Kentucky. One of the most important points would be Nashville, about 60 miles below Carthage, on the same River.

But would the route in any degree sacrifice the immediate object of the road, to connect Charleston, with Louisville, Lexington and Cincinnati? That is a question, which I do not feel authorised to decide, nor have I the means, if I did. It belongs to others, whose duty it is to decide it. My object is simply to state facts and views, connected with a particular route, of which I happen to have some knowledge; and not to condemn, or disparage any other route—to enlarge the field of selection, so that the best possible should be selected. As favorably as I think of this, I shall heartily rejoice, if a better can be found—one shorter; capable of more favorable graduation, and cheaper construction, or better calculated to effect the great object in view—which must be so dear to every friend of his cou[n]try. Without intending comparison, I will simply give what I believe to be about the distance by the route to three important points with which it is intended to connect Charleston by the road. Supposing the road takes a course across the Cumberland mountain by Emory's river the distance to Cincinnati from Charleston would be about 635, to Lexington 565, and to Louisville 595; but what would be of great importance there would be a common trunk to the three places of about 525 miles and a common trunk to Lexington and Cincinnati of about 40 miles more, and what would be still more so, there would be a common trunk to Nashville and all the intermediate places between it and Cincinnati of about 415 miles.

I have now stated the information I possess; and the views I entertain in relation to the route in q[u]estion, in a very hasty and imperfect manner. My object it [*sic*; is] to draw public attention to it, and to have its advantages or disadvantages tested in a more satisfactory manner. I have not desired to under estimate the difficulties, whatever they may be; but no one can be more conscious than I am, how difficult it is to form a correct opinion of a route by the eye, particular[ly] through a mountain region, or any other mode, without an actual survey, which I doubt not will be ordered, if such should be the desire of this section of the State.

It may be asked how it can be explained, that a route, which on the examination I have given it, appears to possess so many advantages, has attracted, heretofore, so little attention?

The only reason that I can assign is, that the gap leads to a portion of North Carolina little known, and which has but lately been acquired from the Indians, and between the two established routes by Ash[e]ville [N.C.] and Rabun [County, Ga.], through one or the other of which, most persons going to the West pass. But it was not so obscure as not to be known by the neighborhood, and to attract the attention of those whose duty it was to explore the mountains, in order to find the best pass over it. Gen. [Robert Y.] Hayne, whose devotion to the great undertaking is so well known, undertook to examine the gap, but unfortunately his guide was not sufficiently well acquainted with the section of the mountains, to which so many ridges converge, and which on that account is so intricate, as to conduct him through the proper route. I was not at all surprised, when I looked at the route through which, I was told, he was taken, that he should have condemned it as utterly impracticable. He could not do otherwise. Learning that he was probably mis-conducted, and having a strong previous impression of the existence of a gap in that quarter, worthy of attention, induced me, as I have stated, to undertake the examination, of which I now communicate the result. With great respect, I am, &c. J.C. Calhoun.

PC in the Pendleton, S.C., *Messenger,* September 23, 1836, p. 2; PC in the Charleston, S.C., *Mercury,* October 4, 1836, p. 2; PC in the Charleston, S.C., *Southern Patriot,* October 4, 1836, p. 2; PC in the Washington, D.C., *Daily National Intelligencer,* October 6, 1836, p. 2; PC in the Edgefield, S.C., *Advertiser,* October 6, 1836, pp. 1–2; PC in the Washington, D.C., *United States' Telegraph,* October 7, 1836, p. 2; PC in *Niles' Weekly Register,* vol. LI, no. 6 (October 8, 1836), pp. 88–89; PC in the Columbia, S.C., *Southern Times and State Gazette,* October 14, 1836, p. 1. NOTE: The above cited issue of the *Messenger,* p. 2, announced: "We have been requested to call a meeting at this place on Friday next [September 30], on the subject of the Rail Road." Advertisements in the same issue solicited subscriptions to stock in the proposed Louisville, Cincinnati, and Charleston Rail Road at $100 per share, with a minimum down payment of $5. The Charleston *Mercury,* October 18, 1836, p. 2, gave an account of a public meeting held at Pendleton on 9/30 to consider the Carolina Gap route that had been the subject of Calhoun's letter. A committee, from which Calhoun asked to be excused, was appointed. The committee submitted a report and resolutions urging that a survey be made of the Carolina Gap route and that the selection of the route be free of "local bias." Robert Mills, *Statistics of South Carolina* (Charleston: published by Hurlbut and Lloyd, 1836; reprint edition, Spartanburg, S.C.: The Reprint Co., 1972), pp. 157, 688–689, described the Whitewater Falls region in terms as enthusiastic as were Calhoun's. Mills thought that a canal could be dug through the mountains in that region to connect the Tugaloo and Hiwassee Rivers (thus linking the Savannah and Tennessee Rivers).

To an UNIDENTIFIED TENNESSEAN

Fort Hill, 26th Sep[tembe]r 1836

Sir, Although I have not the pleasure of a personal acquaintance, I take the liberty of sending you the Pendleton Messenger [of 9/23], which you will find to contain a letter of mine to the Editor, stating some facts and taking some veiws [sic; "in relation" *interlined*] to our projected rail road, that may not be uninteresting to you.

I was anxious to extend my examination beyond the Smokey mountain, but time would not permit, with the veiw of tracing the route, and of seeing ["you" *interlined*] and other respectable citizens in your section. I would have been glad to have conversed fully with you and others in order to obtain your veiws and information.

I would judge, as well from what I heard, as well as from the formation of the country, that there would be no difficulty in turning the road off to Knoxville from some point on little Tennessee, say about Russel[l']s ferry, or going forward towards Kingston [Tenn.] and the Crab orchard Gap, or some other in that neighbourhood, over the Cumberland mountain. I would be glad to have your veiws, and such information as you may ["deep" *canceled and* "deem" *interlined*] interesting, on these points, particularly at what point the Cumberland mountain can be best ["cros" *canceled*] passed on the route, and what would be the probable difficulty. I cannot but think, the Emory River, must afford great facility for passing the Cumberland ["mountain" *interlined*].

As far as I know, I am very favourably impressed towards the route. It possesses many and great advantages, ["superior," *interlined*] as I am at present impressed, ["superior" *canceled*] to any other; but it is not to be disguised, that the publick mind has been turned to the route by the French Broad, as it is by far the best known. Measures will be taken to have this surveyed, so as to bring its claim fairly before the publick, in order that the best; ["that is" *interlined*] the shortest; cheapest of construction; of the lowest angle of grading, and that will draw the most travelling and trade, may be selected.

The subscription will be opened towards the end of next month. The directors will be chosen by the stock holders. To be a director, it is necessary to hold 50 shares at $100 the share; $5 the share to be paid at the time of subscribing, and the residue gradually, as may be needed. If the work should not go on, the subscription paid to be returned. On the directors, the selection of the route will mainly depend. The act of incorporation requires, that there shall be at least three in Tennessee. The charter is very liberal and gives ample privileges. It is perpetual. I cannot doubt, if the proper route be selected, and the work be placed in capable & faithful hands, the stock will be very profitable. It is desirable that your section ["of the State" *interlined*] should be represented in the direction; and for that purpose, I hope, that you, or some of your wealthy and respectable neighbours, ["should" *canceled and* "may" *interlined*] subscribe a sum requisite to qualify you for a place in the direction. Without it the interest, your quarter of the State may have in the work ["may" *canceled and* "would" *interlined*] be unrepresented in the board.

It is highly desirable, that every interest should be represented, in order to ensure the selection of the best route.

You will, I am sure, attribute this communication to the proper motive, the deep solicitude I feel for the success of the great work, and, for that purpose, to ensure the selection of the best route.

I would be glad to hear from you, as soon as it may be convenient. With respect I am & & J.C. Calhoun.

ALS in NcD, John C. Calhoun Papers. NOTE: In the ms. group in which the above letter is found is a related letter from C[ampbell] Wallace [President of the East Tennessee and Georgia Railroad] to "Judge [Edward] Frost" [of S.C.], dated at Knoxville, Tenn., on 7/26/1856. Wallace wrote: "During the time I was engaged in trying to get up some proper feeling about your great road, I came in possession of the enclosed interesting letter, written by the much lamented Calhoun, to an esteem[e]d friend of mine. I have carefully preserv[e]d it intending when some convenient opportunity offered to hand it over to some worthy South Carolinian who would properly appreciate the object and motive of the writer, engaged as you are now in carrying out practically Mr. Calhoun[']s ideas as given in this letter."

To J[AMES] ED[WARD] COLHOUN

Fort Hill, 2d Sep[tembe]r [*sic*; October] 1836

Dear James, I wrote you some time since and informed you, that I had made a satisfactory trip to the mountains, and at the same time expressed a desire to see you as soon, as you could possibly make it convenient to come up. As I have not heard from you, I conclude, that my letter has miscarried; and now write to repeat my desire to see you, as soon as you can possibly make us a visit; both in reference to the rail road, and the settlement of the estate. I am alarmed to think it is the 2d of October. It compels me to look to the time I must leave home for Washington.

The arrangement of my business must depend on the arrangement of the estate. It is the first thing to be done; and I must postpone my visit to the [gold] mines till that is done. It is so important to me to have ever[y]thing satisfactorily arranged before I leave home for the winter, that I do hope, you will lose no time in coming up. Bring with you a full list of the negroes with their age[s]. The will being invalid both as to the real & personal estate, I hope that there will be but little ["delay" *canceled and* "difficulty" *interlined*] in the settle[men]t.

I have just had a letter from Anna [Maria Calhoun], at Abington [*sic*; Va.]. We expect her this evening. If she should not come, I will go tomorrow morning to meet her at Greenville.

There is a good tone getting up here in reference to the rail road. I cannot doubt of the vast superiority of the route by the Carolina gap. You must make a movement at Abbeville. I wrote to Patrick Noble about it, but you know he wants energy. I also wrote to Francis Pickens to give the impulse at Edgefield. We have had a meeting at old Pendleton. It will be followed up by meetings at Pickens & Anderson. We must have able directors from this side. [George] McDuffie must be one. You ["& our friends" *interlined*] must insist on his subscribing the 50 shares to qualify himself for the place.

With proper efforts the road may be taken this way; and if it should, I do not doubt that it will be the best stock in the State. I feel confident, that $6,000,000 by the Carolina gap will carry it from Charleston to the Ohio such is the great facility of the route.

We are all well & all desire their love [to be sent to you]. Anna will be very glad to see you. Affectionately, J.C. Calhoun.

ALS in ScCleA; PEx in Jameson, ed., *Correspondence*, pp. 362–363; PEx in [John B. Cleveland, compiler], *Controversy between John C. Calhoun and Robt. Y. Hayne as to the Proper Route of a Railroad from South Carolina to the West* [Spartanburg, S.C.: no publisher, 1913], pp. 9–10.

Deed executed by John E[wing] Colhoun and J[ohn] C. Calhoun, Pickens District, S.C., 10/22. For the consideration of five dollars [and in settlement of the estate of Mrs. Floride Bonneau Colhoun] they release to J[ames] Edward Colhoun all rights to two tracts of land of approximately 1,000 acres and 621 acres. The deed was witnessed by A.H. Reese and J.D. Lewis. Attached is a statement sworn before Jacob Warley, one of the Justices of the Quorum of Anderson District, in which Floride [Mrs. John C.] Calhoun and M[artha] M[aria] Davis (Mrs. John Ewing)] Colhoun relinquish dower rights to the property thus conveyed. The deed was recorded by the Clerk of Court of Pickens District on 9/29/1840. Recorded copy (microfilm) in Sc-Ar, Pickens County Deeds, D-1:276–277.

Deed executed by John E[wing] Colhoun and J[ames] Edward Colhoun, Pickens District, S.C., 10/22. For the consideration of five dollars [and in settlement of the estate of Mrs. Floride Bonneau Colhoun] they release to John C. Calhoun all rights to the tract of land known as Fort Hill, "whereon said J.C. Calhoun now resides," containing 550 acres, and also a specified portion of a tract known as "Murphy Tract" containing 450 acres. The deed was witnessed by A.H. Reese and J.D. Lewis. Appended are a plat of the property and a statement by Martha M[aria Davis] Colhoun, "the wife of the within named John Ewing Colhoun," renouncing dower rights to the property. This statement was sworn before Jacob Warley. The deed was recorded on 8/22/1837 by the Clerk of Court of Pickens District. Recorded copy (microfilm) in Sc-Ar, Pickens County Deeds, C-1: 419–420.

Deed executed by J[ohn] C. Calhoun and J[ames] Edward Colhoun, Pickens District, S.C., 10/22. For the consideration of five dollars they release to John Ewing Colhoun all rights to "that tract of land, on which the late Mrs. Floride [Bonneau] Colhoun resided," containing 1,900 acres and known as Cold Spring. The deed was witnessed by A.H. Reese and J.D. Lewis. Attached are a plat of the property and a statement, sworn before Jacob Warley, by Floride [Colhoun (Mrs. John C.)] Calhoun, renouncing dower rights in the property. The deed was recorded by the Clerk of Court of Pickens District on 12/3/1836. Recorded copy (microfilm) in Sc-Ar, Pickens County Deeds, C-1:252–254.

Account between John C. Calhoun and H[enry] M. Clay, Dahlonega, Ga., 11/3. This document indicates that expenditures had been made by Clay on Calhoun's behalf on twelve occasions between 2/18 and 11/3/1836, totalling $2,618.25. Calhoun is indicated as having paid all amounts due to Clay up to 11/3 "except balance of meal[,] shoes and clothing [for slaves] for this fall." It is further indicated: "There is a balance due from Mr. R[obert] S. Patton to John C. Calhoun for balance of Gold 236 Dwts. 9 gr[ain]s which Mr. Clay is to bring to my Credit when he when he [*sic*] sees Mr. Patton." Ms. owned in 1961 by Mrs. Harold Colvocoresses of Litchfield, Conn.

To "Col." PATRICK NOBLE, Abbeville, S.C.

Fort Hill, 8th Nov[embe]r 1832 [*sic*; 1836]
My dear Sir, I was absent when your letter arrived, which will explain, why your request was not complied with. I now enclose a

general letter [*not found*] in favour of Samuel [Noble?, your nephew], which I hope may be of some use to him.

The proceedings at Columbia are of an extraordinary character, indeed, and certainly indicates a factious sperit, as well as a very selfish one. They have been well answered by our [Pendleton] Committee and delegation, which [answer] I hope you have seen.

I foresee a good deal of agitation ahead in relation to the rail road, which must distract and divide the State, unless there should be much prudence, and good management on the part of the Legislature. I hold as the first & indispensible [*sic*] step, to preserve the harmony of the State, to be, that the ["de" *canceled*] Legislature should come to a fixed determination before any subscription, or appropriation be made towards the work on its part, and as a condition of its aid and support, that the best route within the [*word fragment canceled*] limits of the charter shall be selected. The road must not bend to local or personal interest. Let it be fixed, that the two routes by the French Broad & Tuckasiege [valleys] shall be surveyed, and that the one which is the shortest, cheapest of construction, of the most favourable grading, and which shall from its direction command the greatest amount of trade and travelling shall be selected, and the whole State will acquiesce. Even the selfish would be ashamed to object. I answer for it, that the people in this quarter would cheerfully assent to such a course. It is the only one, that can unite all. In fact, I consider ["that" *interlined*] all the interests present at the Knoxville Convention [in 7/1836] have pledged themselves and those they represent expressly, to take the best route within the limits of the charter, and that it would be bad faith now to change the principle on which the selection ought to be made.

I do hope that you & the rest of the Representatives in the legislature on the south of the Santee will be vigillant [*sic*] and take care that justice shall be done to our section of the State. Heretofore all the appropriations for improvements have been in the other sections. It must not be repeated. It is time that justice should be done to this section.

I expect to be in Columbia early in the session [of the S.C. General Assembly which meets on 11/28] & will remain, as long as my Congressional duties will permit. The session will be an important one. Yours truely, J.C. Calhoun.

ALS in ScU-SC, John C. Calhoun Papers; PC (dated 11/8/1832) in Jameson, ed., *Correspondence,* pp. 321–322. NOTE: Calhoun erred in dating this letter as being of "1832." Internal evidence makes this plain. The letter must have been written after July, 1836, when the Knoxville Convention met, and before

October, 1838, when the directors of the proposed railroad decided in favor of the French Broad route. Calhoun wrote on 10/30/1837 to Noble that he would try to meet Noble in Abbeville soon; it seems likely that, if Calhoun wrote to Noble on 11/8 in 1837, he would have mentioned that expectation as having been consummated, as being then pending, or as having been postponed. By elimination, therefore, 1836 appears to have been the year in which the above letter of 11/8 was written. In 11/1836 Noble was a member and President of the S.C. Senate.

To Ja[me]s Ed[ward] Colhoun

Fort Hill, 11th Nov[embe]r 1836
My dear Sir, I was detained much longer at the [gold] mines than I anticipated, owing to the absence of Capt. [Henry M.] Clay, which, however, gave me some leisure ["wh" *canceled*] that was not lost. There are about Dahlonega many, who are familiar with the portion of our route ["by" *canceled*] beyond the mouth of the Tu[c]kaseige, where my examination ended. They all concur in giving the most favourable account of the route beyond, even ["beyond" *canceled and* "to exceed" *interlined*] my anticipation, and, in particular, of the Crab Orchard gap. Among others, I met with Maj[o]r [David?] Haynes, an intelligent gentleman who resides a few miles below Kingston [Tenn.], and who had come on to take a contract on the Georgia rail road, and has of course turned his attention some what to the subject of rail roads. He (and others concur with him) say[s] that our road ought to Cross at Casey's ferry, about six miles below Kingston, where the bluffs on both side[s] are high, so that a bridge of 50, or 60 feet ["high" *canceled and* "elevation" *interlined*] may be thrown over the Tennessee, and ought to run up White Creek, instead of the Emory river. He also states, that the gap is not more than 16 miles from the Crossing place, and the elevation not more than 200 feet above the river and ["would not (be) more than" *interlined*] 150 above the Bridge. On the west side, there is scarcely any de-[s]cent. The Sequachee [*sic;* Sequatchie River] bends in a large spring, just at the Gap, and affords along its valley every facility for a rail road to the Tennessee below the Suck.

I obtained some other information, which I consider highly interesting. I met with Dr. [C.B.?] Thomas, a very intelligent man, from Wetempka [*sic;* Wetumpka, Ala.], at the head of steam navigation on the Coosa, about 17 miles above Montgomery. He says (and others agree with him), that there is a beautiful level[?] route from Wetempka, which would intercept ours about Russel[l']s ferry, and that a rail road is already in contemplation in that direction. On calculation it is found, that the distance from Charleston to Wetempka, would be about ["520" *canceled*] 520 miles ["by the route" *interlined*]. He and others agree, that, if the road was completed, all mid[d]le and eastern Alabama would draw their supplies from Charleston. I also learn, that the Engineers who had been ordered to survey the route down the Tennessee and thence across to Athens & Macon [Ga.] from ["about" *canceled*] the Suck, had found the rout[e] between the Lookout & Allegany mountains impracticable, which must tend to throw the Athens and Augusta interest with us.

My information from Charleston is in the main favourable for our route, but a great effort will be required to succeed. I will leave here for Columbia about this day 2 weeks [hence], and would be glad you would go with us. Your presence there would be very useful.

Did you send my letter to [my] brother James [Calhoun]? It is important I should ["have" *canceled*] hear from him before I leave home.

All desire their love to you. Affectionately, J.C. Calhoun.

ALS in ScCleA; PC in Jameson, ed., *Correspondence*, pp. 364–365. NOTE: "The Suck" was an area of hazardous navigation on the Tennessee River below what later became Chattanooga.

From FARISH CARTER

Milledgeville, Ga., Nov[embe]r 14th 1836
My Dear Sir, I have your esteemed favour [of] the 3rd In[stan]t by the last Mail. It would have af[f]orded me great pleasure to have met you in Lumpkin County[;] indeed I went up at the time you ware [*sic*] expected as I was advised by Capt. [Henry M.] Clay. I agree with you as to the enourmous [*sic*] expences of the mines[;] the actual amount of gold dug is very good wages for hands but when you come to deduct the expence it almost or quite takes all[;] this at once determined me to remove all my hands. I agree with you that under a proper sistam [*sic*] it is and will be yet an excellent buisiness [*sic*;] for the presant [*sic*] I do not wish to increase my interest in the gold region as I cannot give it my personal attention. If I could I would yet be willing to make large investments in gold lands, as I believe still that it is excellent property, but you have to

watch it constantly to keep off the Swindlers and even then you have a large part of the gold abstracted by those rogues.

You state that it is possible you can make ar[r]angements to meet the demand I have against you before you leave for Washington by placeing [*sic*] the funds in one of the Charleston Banks[;] this ar-[r]angement will suit me as well or better than the money here[;] when you have made the ar[r]angements write me to whom I shall send the papers to have it adjusted.

My health has been for some time very feeble, which has in a great measure prevented me from attending to my ordinary buisiness.

Our [Ga.] Rail road convention closed its [*one word canceled and* "session" *interlined*] on Thursday last [11/10]. They have made large ar[r]angements provided the present Legislature will carry out their views. If I can lay my hands on the paper in which their proce[e]dings are published I will forward it to you by mail.

I am glad to see by your letter that you have been so fortunate as to have discovered so favourable a rout[e], for your rail road. It is really a great discovery for I was fearfull that by the rout[e] as originally proposed there would have been a failour [*sic*] at least as to the profits to the stock holders. I am rejoyced [*sic*] to see that the spirit of the times is for a fo[r]ward movement for internal improvement[;] it is all important for the South at this time.

We have not yet received all the returns for the election of [Presidential] electors, but from what has been rec[eive]d it is pretty clearly set down that the white Ticket [that is, the Electors for Hugh L. White] will prevail in this State. I am with great respect Your Ob[edient] Ser[vant,] Farish Carter.

ALS in ScU-SC, John C. Calhoun Papers. NOTE: *An AEU by Calhoun, doubtless related to the "demand" referred to in the second paragraph above, reads: "Paid by 30th May 1837[.] Directed J[ohn] E[wing] Bonneau to pay am[oun]t of the proceeds of my note discounted at the bank of the State [i.e., the Bank of the State of South Carolina]." As Carter predicted, Ga., previously a strong Jacksonian State, voted for White for President in preference to Van Buren.*

To F[RANCIS] W. PICKENS, Edgefield, S.C.

Fort Hill, 16th Nov[embe]r 1836

My dear Sir, I intended to answer your letter by the return mail, but received a note from Maj[o]r [Armistead] Burt [a member of the S.C.

House of Representatives for Abbeville District], that he would be up by the Tuesday's mail, which induced me to delay my answer till I should see him, & have the whole ground before me. I have seen & conversed fully with him, and I believe that he is satisfied, that the ground on which he thought of moving is an unsafe one. If it be proper to make a move, I have no doubt the view you take is the correct one. I intimated to the Maj[o]r that I had heard from you, without going into detial [*sic*], and advised him to see & converse with you fully & freely. He would have taken Edgefield on his route to Columbia ["for that purpose" *interlined*], but an engagement takes him by the way of Laurens. He will be at Columbia, at the first of the session, where you will see him, if ["he" *canceled*] you should take that in your way.

Whether any thing should be done is a question of great delicacy, and ought rather ["to" *interlined*] be determined by others than myself. There is certainly no reasons [*sic*], why I should interpose ["to prevent it" *interlined*], should the publick interest be thought to require it, and that the movement can be successfully made, of which I have no means of judging. An abortive attempt would be ["highly" *canceled*] unfortunate. It would seem to me, that the more ["discreet" *canceled*] prudent mode would be to postpone any determination till you reach Columbia, should you take that route, where you could see the whole ground, but you can best determine what ought to be done.

As to the rail road, I will converse fully with you, when I see you. All I can say in the mean time is that I have no other wishes on the subject, than that the best route should be selected and that its execution should be put in faithful hands. I would on no account touch it except on the principle of selecting the best route, after careful examination and survey, and then only on the condition, that ["it" *canceled*] it should be the decided wish of the company, and that it should not bring me in conflict, with any of our friends, who might be thought worthy of the place. I am no candidate [for president of the Louisville, Cincinnati, and Charleston Railroad], and regret that my name has been placed before the publick.

The defeat of [Martin] Van Buren is probable. It will have ["a tremendous effect" *canceled and* "a great effect" *interlined*] on party arrangements, and the aspect of affairs.

I ["hope" *canceled and* "expect" *interlined*] to be in Edgefield the last of next week, when I hope to see you. I take Columbia on my route. It is still doubtful whether, I can induce Mrs. [Floride

Colhoun] C[alhoun] to accompany me. I will go on by land, and will be very glad to have yours & Mrs. [Eliza Simkins] P[ickens's] company, to whom & yourself with your father & [step]mother [Andrew and Mary Harrison Pickens] all join their love. Sincerely, J.C. Calhoun.

ALS in ScU-SC, John C. Calhoun Papers.

DECEMBER 5, 1836–
MARCH 3, 1837

(24th Congress, 2nd Session)

▯

Probably hoping to influence the proceedings of the State in regard to the railroad from Charleston to the Ohio River, Calhoun spent a week in the South Carolina capital before departing for Washington. On December 14 he took his seat in the Senate for the last session of a Congress whose expiration coincided with that of Andrew Jackson's Presidency. The session was to involve much labor for little result.

First and last Calhoun worked to get rid of the Treasury surplus. Most desirable was to return it to the taxpayers from whose pockets it had come. This being impossible, the next best thing was to return it to the States. One of his first actions was to introduce a bill to extend the distribution that had been voted by the previous session. Jackson men, however, either denied there was a surplus or wished to expend it on national defense.

Calhoun's scorn was unrestrained. A party that had come to power on a platform of retrenchment was now spending more annually for the Navy than the entire budget under the derided John Quincy Adams. The Jacksonians had shown no hesitancy in distributing the Treasury deposits among favored bankers and the public lands among favored speculators. Why were they so averse to a distribution of the surplus back to the States? "Was it to prevent the people from being corrupted? Were the people alone capable of being corrupted? Were the Government and banks all pure, while the people, the people alone, were corrupt and corruptible?"

Throughout the first week of January Calhoun reverted to the comfortable role of political philosopher, exploring the delicate questions of sovereignty that had been raised by the irregular proceedings of the Congressional majority toward the Territory of Michigan. Congress had set aside a regularly elected convention of the people which had refused to agree to its demands in regard to boundaries and had recognized an irregularly elected body that presumed to give the consent of the State to those demands. If Michigan were a State, said Calhoun, Congress had no right to set aside her convention; if she were not, she had no right to participate in the Presidential election and send representatives to Congress.

The point of Calhoun's words was felt when Congress undertook to count the electoral votes on February 8. Nobody was sure whether the Michigan votes should be received or not. It was agreed to make up two sets of returns, one counting and one not counting the Michigan votes. In either case Van Buren would be elected. (When the Senate proceeded on the same day to select a Vice-President, by a strict party vote, Calhoun and his colleague from South Carolina, William C. Preston, did not even participate.)

These, with other recent events, like the President's naming his own successor through a convention and extra-constitutional proceedings in Maryland, "announce," said Calhoun, "the ascendency of the caucus system over the regularly constituted authorities of the country." Thus "the highest authority known to our laws and constitution, is gradually sinking to the level of those meetings which regulate the operation of political parties, and through which the edicts of their leaders are announced, and their authority enforced. . . ."

In the events of January 16 Calhoun could see only further confirmation of these dour forebodings. After three years of persistence, the President's friends now had the votes to "expunge," that is, to literally blot out of the Senate's official journal the 1834 censure of Jackson. This was consummated in a night session amidst tumult in the galleries and feasting in the Capitol by members of the victorious group. The act, said Calhoun, was not even covered by the usual tyrant's plea of necessity. It "originates in pure, unmixed personal idolatry. It is the melancholy evidence of a broken spirit, ready to bow at the feet of power."

A public land bill presented by the administration's friends as designed to benefit settlers was fought bitterly by Calhoun as a scheme to save the bacon of speculators. This unwholesome business he traced directly to the White House and to people not far from the President himself. These remarks brought a letter from Jackson demanding retraction. Calhoun, in response, rose in the Senate on February 9 and repeated his charges. And he brought in a bill to cede the public lands which remained unsold after a reasonable time on the market to the Western States in which they were situated. This would free the federal government from a major source of corruption and free the new commonwealths from vassalage. Further, it would be a gesture of generosity from the East to the

West that would help to restore some of the damaged bonds of Union.

On February 16, combatting administration efforts to enlarge the regular army and the permanent fortifications, the former Secretary of War made a survey of the past history and future needs of national defense. What "was needed to protect us from the Indians," he said, "was not more troops, but more faithful agents." The friends of Andrew Jackson "had made fortunes by treating those Indians in such a manner as fixed a stain on human nature." Send out men of integrity in their place and there would be no more Indian wars.

The Senate, as in the previous session, continued to dispose of abolition petitions by tabling the question of whether or not they should be received. The proceedings of the House of Representatives, however, were bitter and tumultuous on this matter. Opening still another aspect of the abolition question, Calhoun called the Senate's attention on several occasions to ramifications of the British Empire's recently undertaken role as world emancipator. Slaves on board American coasting vessels which had entered ports in British colonial islands had been set free. Need he remind Senators how recently they had been at war to controvert British presumptions of power over American vessels on the seas?

The end of Jackson and the coming of Van Buren was augured by changes in the Washington press. Duff Green, Calhoun's faithful ally at the United States' Telegraph *since 1826, published his last issue on February 21 and set off to devote more time to his interests as a coal and iron magnate. His place as Calhoun spokesman was taken by the Washington* Reformer, *published by William W. Moore and Company and edited by Richard K. Crallé. "We must have reform," declared the* Reformer, *true to its name. "The Government has been changed from a free representative democracy into a practical hereditary monarchy. . . . We shall labor to bring it back to what it was. . . ." The* Reformer *struggled along, saved itself for awhile by merger with the Baltimore* Merchant, *and expired in October. Calhoun was without an organ in the capital until January, 1838, when the* Chronicle *began. The* Daily National Intelligencer, *the Whigs' paper, continued along its sedate course. The* Globe *promised to support Van Buren as zealously as it had Jackson. But the* Globe *was challenged in August by the appearance of the* Madisonian, *a paper of dissident anti-Van Buren Democrats led by Senators William C. Rives of Virginia and Nathaniel P. Tallmadge of New York.*

As the session drew near an end Calhoun found himself in the strange position of opposing proposals to lower the tariff because such proposals would set aside the painfully-won Compromise of 1833 and subject the South to charges of bad faith. Speaking on this theme on February 23 gave him an opportunity to review the whole history of the tariff controversy and to detail in public for the first time the treacherous role that the man who would be President in little more than a week had played in the enactment of the 1828 "Tariff of Abominations."

⫿

To J A [ME] S E D [WARD] C O L H O U N, Terrysville, Abbeville District, S.C.

Columbia [S.C.], 9th Dec[embe]r 1836
My dear Sir, I have been here more than a week, and will take my departure tomorrow for Washington.

Mr. [Armistead] Burt will give you most of the news of this place, which will dispense with my detailing it.

I have had a pretty full conversation with him on the rail road, and have got him to assent to go to Knoxville, on the condition you will go, as one of the proxies. It is desirable that you both should be there, to see what is going on. I fear the game is in the hand of [Abram] Blanding, and that the enterprise will be so managed as to sink millions without any substantial advantage to the State. The push at this moment is to get banking priviledges [*sic*], and a sub-scription on the part of the State, without waiting the surveys. The object is to commit the State, so that she cannot recede, let the se-lection [of a route] be ever so objectionable. I fear both objects will succeed; and if they should, that the whole concern will terminate in little better than a mere Stock Jobbing affair.

[Capt. William George] Willia[m]s is here; and I learn, that the survey has been recommenced since I left home. I have no con-fidence in his impartiality & but little in his judgement. The route he has ordered ["on the east" *canceled*] to be surveyed on the east side of the gap is calculated to deceive, unless one should fully un-derstand the topography of the country. He proposes to terminate the line at Birche's ford on the Keowee, instead of terminating ["on" *canceled*] on little River, which is many hundred feet higher, or what would be still fairer, on the ridge at the foot of the mountain between

Nicholson's fork & Little River. The effect is to give a very high appeearent [*sic*] elevation to the gap, as the Keowee lies very deep. The elevation of the gap is probably greater than I estimated it, but unless it should exceed 1,500 feet above the mouth of 12 miles [that is, Twelve Miles Creek], after taking off the crest by a tunnel, which is not likely, the whole may be run down at an angle not exceeding 30 feet to the mile, by keeping along the side of the Chatuga Mountain, ["till" *canceled and* "round" *interlined*] the north fork of the Cheochee, then between the two ["forks of the" *canceled*] Cheochee, passing down near to Tomassee and on the ridge between Cane Creek & little River, and crossing the Keowee ["at a hi" *canceled*] on a high bridge below the mouth of 12 miles. Much the greater part of the route would be on ["one" *canceled*] one of the best ridges in the State. If a line still more developed ["should be required" *interlined*], it would be easy to give it a still farther developement to the west, so as to make the de[s]cent still more gentle. All I ask is an impartial survey when I am at home & can attend to it. I do not fear, but that the ["line" *canceled and* "route" *interlined*] will not only prove practicable, but the most so of any other.

As to the Presidency [of the proposed railroad company], I see so much that I do not approve, that I have concluded that I had better ["to" *canceled*] have nothing to do with it. The only terms on which I could accept would be that it should be tendered to me ["by the" *canceled*] without solicitation by the company, from a ["cofid" *canceled*] confidence in my capacity & integrity, and then only on condition that the best route should be selected, and I should not be brought into conflict with any of my friends. In a word, if I take it, it must be sole[l]y ["on" *canceled and* "from" *interlined*] a sense of duty. I cannot think there is the slightest prospect that it will be tendered on such condition[s], and my friends had better not bring my name forward. I read my letter to [Robert Y.] Hayne [*not found*] on this subject to Burt. He will tell you its contents.

The more I reflect, the more I am convinced, that the success of the road will depend on the direction, and that on striking steam navigation on the ["streams" *canceled*] intermediate streams between the Blue ridge & the Ohio at the nearest and most favourable ports. Steam navigation on the Western waters ["are" *canceled and* "is" *interlined*] many times cheaper than on rail roads; and, of course, the Tennessee, the Cumberland ["wo"(?) *canceled*] and Green Rivers, if struck where navigable for steam would be the best & cheapest extension of the rail road. Any route that overlooks this important advantage must fail.

If you go to Knoxville do not fail to write me from there. Affectionately, J.C. Calhoun.

ALS in ScCleA; PC in Jameson, ed., *Correspondence*, pp. 365–367; PC in [John B. Cleveland, compiler], *Controversy between John C. Calhoun and Robt. Y. Hayne as to the Proper Route of a Railroad from South Carolina to the West* [Spartanburg, S.C.: no publisher, 1913], p. 10.

To S[amuel] D. Ingham, [New Hope, Pa.]

Washington, 18th Dec[embe]r 1836

My dear Sir, It is is [*sic*] long since I have heard from you, and I now write to renew our correspondence. I have been here but a few days, and, of course, cannot speak with confidence, as to the tone of feeling here; but as far as I can judge, there is a fixed determination on the part of every branch of the opposition to wage war ag[ai]nst the Usurper [Martin Van Buren]. He certainly stands on a most uncertain foundation, and if he should maintain himself, he will not owe it to the strength of his position, nor the goodness of his cause, but exclusively to the character of the opposition. If the old national Republican leaders should change their principles, or withdraw, nothing would be more easy than to over turn the present power. It would not be the work of a year. I never saw my way clearer. The fact is, that the work is more than half done. Nullification, the compromise, and the deposite ["bill" *canceled and* "act" *interlined*] have nearly ["finish" *changed to* "finished"; "the work" *canceled and* "it" *interlined*]. They have demolished the ground on which the enemy stood, and cut off his supplies. The renewal of the deposite act, and an honest & firm assumption of the old Republican States rights doctrine would speedily finish the ["work" *canceled and* "reform" *interlined*]. It remains to be seen whether the leaders of the old national Republican party have the segacity [*sic*] & patr[i]otism to see and take the ground that ought to be assumed by the opposition. I, on my part, am resolved to maintain my position and will never consent to wage war on any other ground, ["on"(?) *canceled*] except that on which I now ["& ha" *canceled*] stand, and have stood for so many years. Our party, I believe to be strong—far stronger, than is believed, throughout the Union. ["Youths" *canceled and* "The rising generation" *interlined*] every where is with us. All we want is organization. Our friends have already an organization in Ohio, or rather ["a" *canceled and* "the" *interlined*] neucles [*sic*] of an organization. Would it be possible to organize in Pennsylvania? ["The" *canceled.*] Let the basis be the old Republican State rights doctrine of '98, and the object to put down extravagance & corruption, to rebuke executive interference in the election of a successor, to reverse the dangerous example of the last election; to preserve our liberty & institutions, and to restore the gover[n]m[e]nt to its primitive purity. Is there sound materials [*sic*] enough in your State to organize ["even" *canceled*] an honest and determined party on this basis, be it ever so small? If we could have an organized opposition on ["this" *changed to* "that" *and then canceled and* "the above" *interlined*] foundation, ["be it ever so" *canceled and* "however" *interlined*] small at first, ["that" *canceled*] the present power ["may" *canceled and* "might" *interlined*] be over thrown, and the gover[n]m[e]nt & country tho[ro]ughly reformed. The time has arrived, when with proper efforts much may be done for the country. I know how difficult ["it is" *interlined*] to rouse a country so bent on gain as ours; but let us not forget how worthless all ["of" *canceled*] the wealth of the world is without liberty & good political institutions.

I made an excursion during the summer to our mountain region, with the view of finding a passage, in what, I deem, the proper direction for our projected rail road. ["I deem" *canceled and* "the" *altered to* "The"] result of my examination ["to be" *canceled and* "was" *interlined*] highly successful. I found, what I consider, a good passage in the proper direction—one that would cut all the intermediate streams between the Blue ridge & ["Charleston" *canceled and* "the Ohio that is" *interlined*]; the little & great Tennessee, the Cumberland & Green rivers, where navigable for steam boats, which I hold to be indispensible to the success of any scheme of uniting the Ohio & Charleston by rail road. The competition ["will be" *canceled and* "is" *interlined*] between this route & one more easterly, which would cut all the intermediate streams above steam boat navigation. Should this route be taken, I fear the whole project would prove a total & ruinous failure. I can have no confidence in any road of 650 miles, without a single navigable stream to feed it, and without a branch save one short one; yet I fear that with all these disadvantages it will succeed, through the force of local interest.

In order to show the advantage of the Westerly route; it is important, that I should ["show" *canceled*] give a comparative statement of the cost of transportation on rail roads and ["on" *canceled and "by" interlined*] steam boats on the Western Waters. The latter I believe to be much the cheapest; and, if so, ought to be used wherever it can be in combination with our rail road. In order to make the comparison, it will be important to get an authentick statement, of the cost of transportation on the principal rail roads in the Union, and I must rely on you to obtain the information for me, ["I" *and a partial word canceled*] as to those of Pennsylvania. I would be glad to have it as soon as you can conveniently obtain it. I would be also glad to know the expense of your tunnels, of which I understand you have several—their length, their diameter, the materials through which they pass, and their cost per cubit [*sic*] foot, or yard and the relative costs of tunnelling through earth, and rocks, and also rocks of the several discription [*sic*] through which your tunnels have been carried. A Tunnel will be required on the route which I prefer of five, or six hundred yards through a stratified [*one illegible word and "or" canceled and "but hard" interlined*] slating[?] rock.

Among the peculiarities that marks [*sic*] the passage over the Blue Ridge, or Allegany mountain, on this route, is the fact, that two streams rise on the summit of the mountain, and ["discharge" *canceled*] precipitate themselves in opposite directions; one to the South East & the other to the North West, by perpendicular leaps at short intervals many hundred feet, to the level below. The streams afford ample water power, as a substitute for stationary steam power. The stream, that discharges to the N[orth] West falls in about a mile, in the manner stated, about 300 or 400 feet, which might be conveniently divided into two inclined planes. Have you any similar formations & water power, and has there been any instance in which such power has been used as a substitute for steam in like case?

I would be glad to hear from you at your early convenience on these and all other points you may deem of interest.

I am happy to hear of your good health by Mr. Rodman; but regret to hear, that your daughter[']s health is so delicate. Would not a Southern climate be of service to her? We live in a delightfully healthy climate near our mountains; and if you should think ["the" *canceled*] a change of air would be of any service, I would be much gratified to take charge of her on our return next spring. My daughter [Anna Maria Calhoun] is with me, who would be happy to have her company. She joins in kind respect & regard to yourself, Mrs. Ingham & your daughter. Truely & sincerely yours & & J.C. Calhoun.

ALS in ScU-SC, John C. Calhoun Papers.

Petition of fifty "Citizens of So[uth] Carolina and Georgia," presented by Calhoun to the Senate on 12/19. The petitioners request the establishment of a new post route between Athens, Ga., and Laurens Court House, S.C. They describe in detail a 107-mile route with 13 stops and argue the need for it. The signers were apparently mostly residents of the vicinity of Locust Grove, Laurens District, S.C. (The petition was referred to the Committee on the Post Office and Post Roads. On 3/3/1837 the committee was discharged from further consideration of the matter.) DS in DNA, RG 46 (Records of the U.S. Senate), 24A-G13.

Petition of Samuel Warren of S.C., presented by Calhoun to the Senate on 12/19. Warren, recipient of a pension under the law of 1828 for his period of active service as a Captain in the Revolutionary army, seeks additional compensation for time he spent as a disabled supernumerary officer after having been wounded and captured. (On 1/2/1837 the Senate Committee on Revolutionary Claims reported favorably on this petition, and a bill for Warren's relief passed the Senate on 1/9. The bill was also favorably reported on by the House Committee on Revolutionary Claims, but the House did not pass the bill.) Abs in Senate Document No. 39, 24th Cong., 2nd Sess.; jacket with endorsements (petition missing) in DNA, RG 46 (Records of the U.S. Senate), 24A-G16.

Remarks and motion on the reduction of the revenue, 12/19. Calhoun said that he would soon offer a bill to extend for another year the part of the deposit act passed at the previous session of Congress that provided for distribution of the surplus revenue. He then put a question to the Chairman of the Committee on Finance, Silas Wright. When Wright had moved on 12/15 to refer "so much of the President's [annual] message [to Congress] as relates to finance to the Finance Committee," had he intended to include "that part of the message which relates to the reduction of the revenue to the wants of the Government?" Wright was unsure whether the part referred to fell under the Committee on Finance or the Committee on Manufactures. "Mr. Calhoun said he would then move, in order to remove all doubts on the question, that the portion of the message to which he had alluded, be referred to the Committee on Finance. He made the motion, because of its having probably a stronger bearing on the action of this body, and on political events hereafter, than any other question which might be brought before the Senate." The motion was adopted. From *Register of Debates*, 24th Cong., 2nd

Sess., cols. 19–20. Also printed in the Washington, D.C., *Globe*, December 21, 1836, p. 2; *Congressional Globe*, 24th Cong., 2nd Sess., p. 29. Variant in the Washington, D.C., *United States' Telegraph*, December 19, 1836, p. 3. Another variant in the New York, N.Y., *Morning Courier and New-York Enquirer*, December 21, 1836, p. 2.

Further remarks on his motion in regard to the reduction of the revenue, 12/20. John M. Niles of Conn. objected that Calhoun's motion of yesterday slighted the Committee on Manufactures, of which he was chairman. He moved that so much of the President's annual message as referred to the reduction or repeal of duties be referred to the Committee on Manufactures. When Calhoun argued that the motion was out of order, Niles said that to avoid difficulty he would "confine his motion to so much of the message as related to the repeal of duties only." "Mr. Calhoun said this was included in his motion as much as the other. Whatever went to reduce the revenue he meant to refer to the Committee on Finance, as appropriately belonging to that committee. And he must be permitted to say that no committee in that body could represent more fully all the great interests concerned in such a subject. The chairman [Silas Wright of N.Y.] was connected extensively with one branch of Manufactures; the Senator from New York [*sic*; Daniel Webster of Mass.] with another; and the Senator from Louisiana [Robert C. Nicholas] represented the great sugar interest of the South; while he from Missouri [Thomas H. Benton] represented that of lead. As to the difficulty of the task, none could be more sensible of it than himself; none had felt it more deeply. The reduction, thus far, had been effected only by exertions such as he should be sorry to repeat." Niles's motion was then tabled. From *Register of Debates*, 24th Cong., 2nd Sess., col. 69. Also printed in the Washington, D.C., *Daily National Intelligencer*, December 21, 1836, p. 3. Variant in the Washington, D.C., *Globe*, December 22, 1836, p. 2; *Congressional Globe*, 24th Cong., 2nd Sess., p. 35. Other variants in the Washington, D.C., *United States' Telegraph*, December 20, 1836, p. 2; the New York, N.Y., *Morning Courier and New-York Enquirer*, December 22, 1836, p. 2.

Bill "to extend the provisions of certain sections" of the Deposit Act of 1836, introduced in the Senate on 12/21. This bill provided that any surplus in the Treasury on 1/1/1838 in excess of five million dollars should be deposited with the States in the same manner and under the same terms as the surplus distributed under the act of

6/23/1836 to regulate the public deposits. Draft in DNA, RG 46 (Records of the U.S. Senate), 24A-B3; PC in DNA, RG 46, 24A-B4; PC in DLC, Congressional Bills, 24th Cong., 2nd Sess., S-40.

REMARKS ON HIS BILL TO CONTINUE THE DISTRIBUTION OF THE SURPLUS REVENUE TO THE STATES

[In the Senate, December 21, 1836]

Mr. C[alhoun], in introducing the bill, observed that he had not asked leave to introduce this bill without satisfying himself that there would be a large surplus of the public revenue remaining in the Treasury at the termination of the next year, after allowing for very liberal appropriations on all proper subjects of expenditure. From the calculations he had made, he was convinced that the amount of this surplus would not fall short of eight millions of dollars.

He was fully aware that the Secretary of the Treasury [Levi Woodbury], in the report submitted by that officer to Congress, had taken a very different view; yet Mr. C[alhoun] thought he hazarded little when he said that on this subject the Secretary was certainly mistaken. He knew, indeed, that formerly such an assertion from a member of Congress, in relation to the highest fiscal officer of the Government, would have been deemed adventurous; but so vague, so uncertain, so conjectural, and so very erroneous, had been the report[s] from that Department for two or three years last past, that he could not be considered as risking much in taking such a position. That in this remark he did no injustice to the Secretary of the Treasury, (toward whom he cherished no personal hostility or unkind feelings whatsoever,) he would take the liberty of presenting to the Senate the estimates made by that officer for the present year, in December last, and comparing with it the actual result, as now ascertained from the Secretary's own report, made the present session. His estimate of the receipts from all sources, including the public lands and every other branch of the revenue, amounted to $19,750,000, whereas the report stated those receipts to have amounted to $47,691,898; presenting a difference in the estimate, for a single year, of $27,941,898. Thus the excess of the actual receipts had exceeded the estimate by more than one third of the whole amount of the estimate. Each of the great branches of the

314

revenue, the customs and the public lands, exceeded the estimate by millions of dollars.

Again: the Secretary had estimated the balance at the end of the year, then within four weeks of its termination, at $18,047,598, whereas the report showed that the balance actually amounted to $26,749,803, being an error of $8,702,250 [*sic*] for that short period. How these errors arose, whether from negligence or inattention, or whether they were made purposely to subserve certain political views, it was not for him to say; but they were sufficient to show that he ran no very formidable hazard in venturing to say that the views of the Secretary in respect to what was yet future might be erroneous.

But further: the Secretary, in his report last year, had estimated the available means of the Treasury for the current year at $37,797,598; they were now ascertained to have been $74,441,701, exhibiting the small error of $46,644,104 [*sic*]. We might search the fiscal records of all civilized nations, and would not find in the compass of history an error so monstrous. He stated this with no feelings of ill-will toward the Secretary, but with emotions of shame and mortification for the honor of the country. How must errors like these appear in the eyes of foreign nations? How would they look to posterity?

But he was not yet done. The Secretary estimated the expenditures of the year at $23,103,444, whereas they turned out to be $31,435,032, making a difference of $8,331,588. He estimates the balance in the Treasury at the end of this year at $14,500,000. He now admits that it will equal $43,005,669, making an error of $28,505,669, and this notwithstanding he had made an under-estimate of the expenditure of more than eight millions, which, if added, as it ought to be, would make a mistake of nearly thirty-seven millions.

The Secretary, however, had profited by the errors of last year. The estimates in the present report were somewhat nearer to the truth, but were still far removed from it. And indeed, so small was the amount in which he had profited, that he had risked an opinion that the expenditure would exceed the income, so that, of the sum which had been deposited with the States, a portion, amounting to between two and three millions, would have to be refunded. The Secretary held out language of this kind, when he acknowledged that the income of the year would be $24,000,000. Mr. C[alhoun] said he would be glad to see the administration, with such an income, venture to call upon the States to pay back the moneys they had received. No administration would venture to call, except in the case of a foreign war, in which case these deposites would prove a timely and precious resource. With proper management, they would enable the Government to avoid the necessity, at the commencement of a war, of resorting to war taxes and loans. All those gentlemen, and he saw several of them around him, who were here at the commencement of the last war, would well remember the difficulty and embarrassment which attended the operation of raising the revenue from a peace to a war establishment.

Assuming, then, that there would be a surplus, the question presented itself as to what should be done with it. That question Mr. C[alhoun] would not now attempt to argue. The discussion of it at this time would be premature and out of place. He proposed to himself a more limited object, which was to state the points connected with this subject, which he considered as established; and to point out what was the real issue at present. One point was perfectly established by the proceedings of the last session—that, when there was an unavoidable surplus, it ought not to be left in the Treasury, or in the deposite banks, but should be deposited with the States. It was not only the most safe, but the most just, that the States should have the use of the money in preference to the banks. This, in fact, was the great and leading principle which lay at the foundation of the act of last session—an act that would forever distinguish the 24th Congress—an act which will go down with honor to posterity, as it had obtained the almost unanimous approbation of the present day. The passage had inspired the country with new hopes. It had been beheld abroad as a matter of wonder, a phenomenon in the fiscal world, such as could have sprung out of no institutions but ours, and which went in a powerful and impressive manner to illustrate the genius of our Government.

He considered it not less fully established that there ought to be no surplus, if it could be avoided. The money belonged to those who made it, and Government had no right to exact it unless necessary. What, then, was the true question at issue? It was this: Can you reduce the revenue to the wants of the people?—he meant in a large political sense. Could the reduction be made without an injury that would more than countervail the benefit? The President thought it could be done; and Mr. C[alhoun] hoped he was correct in that opinion. If it be practicable, then, beyond all question, it was the proper and natural course to be adopted. It was under this impression that he had moved to refer this part of the President's message to the Committee on Finance. He not only considered that as the appropriate committee, but there were other reasons that governed him in making the reference. A majority of that committee were known to be hostile to the deposite bill, and would, therefore, do all in their power to avoid the possibility of having a surplus. If, then, that committee could not effect a reduction, then it might be safely assumed as impracticable. If they could agree on a reduction, the Senate no doubt would concur with them.

There was one point on which the committee need have no apprehension: that any reduction they might propose to make would be considered by the South as a breach of the compromise act [of 1833]. Her interest in that act is not against the reduction, but the increase of duties. If it be the pleasure of other sections to reduce, she will certainly not complain.

Mr. C[alhoun] said he would take this occasion to define with exactness the position he occupied in regard to the compromise. He stood, personally, without pledge or plighted faith, as far as that act was concerned. He clearly foresaw, at the time that bill passed, that there would be a surplus of revenue in the Treasury. He knew that result to be unavoidable, unless by a reduction so sudden as to overthrow our manufacturing establishments—a catastrophe which he sincerely desired to avoid. Whatever might be thought to the contrary, he had always been the friend of those establishments. He thought at the time that the reduction provided for in the bill had not been made to take place as fast as it might have been. But the terms of the bill formed the only ground on which the opposing interests could agree; and he, as representing in part one of the Southern States, had accepted it, believing it, on the whole, to be the best arrangement which could be effected; yet he saw (it did not, indeed, require much of a prophetic spirit) that there were those who were then ready to collect the tariff at the point of the bayonet, rather than yield an inch, who, when the injurious effects of the surplus should be felt, would throw the responsibility on those who supported the bill. Seeing this, Mr. C[alhoun] had determined that it should not be thrown upon him. He had, therefore, risen in his place [on 2/22 or 3/1/1833?], and, after calling on the stenographers to note his words, he had declared that he voted for that bill in the same manner, and no other, that he did for all other bills, and that he held himself no further personally pledged in its passage than in any other. Mr. C[alhoun] was therefore at perfect liberty to select his position, which he would now state. We of the South had derived incalculable advantage from that act; and, as one belonging to that section, he claimed all those advantages to the very last letter. That act had reduced the income of the Government greatly. Few, he believed, were fully aware of the extent to which it had operated. It was a fact, which the documents would show, that the act of 1828 arrested at the custom-house one half in value of the amount of the imports. The imports at that time, deducting reshipments, were about sixty-five millions of dollars in value, out of which the Government collected about thirty-two millions in the gross. The imports of last year, deducting reshipments, amounted to $120,000,000, which, if the tariff of 1828 had not been reduced, would have given an increase of $60,000,000, instead of something upwards of $21,000,000. He claimed not the whole difference for the compromise, but upwards of $20,000,000 may be fairly carried to its credit. Under this great reduction, we of the South began to revive. Our business began to thrive and to look up. But the compromise act had not yet fully discharged its functions. Its operation would continue until the revenue should be brought down till no duty should exceed 20 per cent. *ad valorem*, and the revenue be reduced to the actual wants of the Government. But, while he claimed for the South all these very important advantages, Mr. C[alhoun] trusted he was too honest, as well as too proud, while he claimed those benefits on her part, to withhold whatever advantage the North may derive from the compromise. His position, then, on the question of reduction, was to follow, and not to lead; and such he believed to be the true position of the South. If it be the wish of other sections to reduce, she will cheerfully follow; but I trust she will be the last to disturb the present state of things.

Having thus clearly defined his own position, Mr. C[alhoun] said he would venture a suggestion. If the manufacturing interests would listen to the voice of one who had never been their enemy, he would venture to advise them to a course which he should consider as wise on all sides.

It is well known, said Mr. C[alhoun], that the compromise act makes a very great and sudden reduction in the years [18]41 and [18]42. He doubted the wisdom of this provision at the time; but those who represented the manufacturing interest thought it was safer and better to reduce more slowly at first and more rapidly at the termination of the term, in order to avoid the possibility of a shock at the commencement of the term. He thought experience had clearly shown that there could be no hazard in accelerating the rate of reduction now, in order to avoid the great and rapid descent of [18]41 and [18]42; and in this view it seemed to him that it would be wise to distribute the remaining reduction equally on the six remaining years of the act. It was, however, but a suggestion.

Mr. C[alhoun] observed that, had not this been the short session of Congress, he should have postponed the introduction of the present bill, and awaited the action of the Committee on Finance. But it was possible that committee might find it impracticable to reduce the revenue, and as there were but about two months of the session left, if something were not effected in the mean time, a large surplus might be left in the Treasury, or rather in the deposite banks—left there to disturb and disorder the currency of the country; to cherish and foster a spirit of wild and boundless speculation, and to be wielded for electioneering purposes. A standing surplus in the deposite banks was almost universally condemned. The President himself had denounced it in his message, and Mr. C[alhoun] heartily agreed with him in every word he had said on that subject.

Before sending the bill to the Chair, he would take the liberty of expressing his hope that the subject would be discussed in the same spirit of moderation that had characterized the debates upon it last year. It was a noble example, and he hoped it would be followed. Let the subject be argued on great public grounds, and let all party spirit be sacrificed on this great question to the good of the country. Yet, he would say to the friends of the administration, that it was not from any fear, on party ground, that he uttered this sentiment; for he believed there was no subject which, in the hands of a skilful opposition, would be more fatal to power.

The bill was, by consent, read twice; when Mr. Calhoun moved that it be made the order of the day for Monday next [12/26]. He saw no necessity for its commitment [to a committee].

[*Henry Clay reaffirmed his support for the Compromise Tariff of 1833 which it would be a violation of public faith to disturb. He stated that his bill to distribute the proceeds of the sales of public lands was the proper remedy for the Treasury surplus and would have provided more money to the States than the Deposit Act. Robert J. Walker of Miss. moved the reference of Calhoun's bill to the Committee on Finance and accused Calhoun of being in favor of maintaining a Treasury surplus for purposes of distribution.*]

Mr. Calhoun, in reply, complained of having been entirely misstated by the Senator from Mississippi. He had not invoked the Senate to any such act, nor had he said any thing like it. But he had said that no administration could honestly plead any necessity for demanding back the deposites from the States, unless in contingency of a foreign war. So far from having expressed a desire to create and distribute a surplus, he had, on the contrary, expressly declared that he should greatly prefer a reduction of the revenue, if it could be safely effected; and he had expressed his willingness to send the bill to a committee opposed to his own views, that, if possible, this might be effected. Yet the gentleman accused him of a design to create a surplus.

The gentleman had again said that one of the arguments urged by him in favor of the distribution bill had been, that the deposite of the public money in banks was a great instrument of fraud and speculation. This was a great mistake. He had said no such thing. The President [Andrew Jackson], however, had undertaken to legislate on the subject, and had issued an order, [the Specie Circular of 7/11/1836,] which was much more like an act of Congress than an executive measure. The President deemed the evil so great, and the remedy so specific, that he had ventured on a great stretch of power to realize the object. Now, after what the President had said on this subject, any man who should vote to leave the public money in deposite banks stood openly convicted of being in favor of speculators.

Mr. C[alhoun] hoped the Senator would not persist in his motion to refer the bill to a committee which he knew to be utterly opposed to it. Nothing could be more unparliamentary. He hoped the gentleman would at least indulge him with a special committee.

[*James Buchanan and Walker supported the reference of Calhoun's bill to the Committee on Finance. Walker alluded to a previous occasion (on 3/16/1836?) when he had asked for a select committee for a bill of special importance to Miss., but at Calhoun's insistence the bill had been referred to the Committee on Public Lands.*]

Mr. Calhoun rejoined and explained, with a view to show that the case of which the gentleman from Mississippi complained was not parallel to the present, and still insisted on the propriety of allowing him a special committee. If, however, the Senate should resolve to send this bill to the Committee on Finance, he should not be at a loss to understand the movement. He had read the President's message attentively. It was an extraordinary document. He read with no less care the report of the Secretary of the Treasury: that, too, was an extraordinary document. The perusal had suggested some suspicions to his mind; and should the present bill be sent to the Finance Committee, those suspicions would be fully confirmed. Such a measure would go far to convince him that the policy of the administration was agreed upon, and that it would be to make a demonstration on a reduction of the revenue, but, in fact, to leave that revenue in the deposite banks. The end of this session was not far off, and that would tell whether he were not correct in his opinion. He would now, in his turn, venture to become a prophet, and he would predict that, if the present motion succeeded, the very thing which the President in his message had most decidedly condemned would be the thing actually realized. Notwithstanding the President's opposition to the collecting of the surplus revenue, and all he had said on its tendency to promote speculation and corrupt the public morals, that was the thing which would be done. He was sorry he did not see the Senator from New York (Mr. [Silas] Wright) in his place. On that gentleman, peculiarly, lies the obligation to provide for the reduction of the revenue. Mr. C[alhoun] well knew the difficulty of touching this subject. He had himself had a full and sound trial of that operation. He knew the efforts by which the existing reduction had been effected, and he felt very sure that the Senator from New York could not be sanguine in the expectation of effecting a reduction to any great amount. He had heard much said in private on that subject, and he could not but regret that the President, when alluding to it in his message, had not referred to the difficulties attending it. Mr. C[alhoun] thought he saw how things were to go, and he thus openly announced what his conviction was. He believed nothing would be done to reduce the revenue; that the money would still be collected, and would be left, not where it ought to be found, in the treasuries of the States, but in the deposite banks.

If the Finance Committee would report an adequate reduction of the revenue, Mr. C[alhoun] would consent to withdraw his bill. He should infinitely prefer a reduction to a distribution, provided the thing could be done. In the meanwhile the South claimed the execution of the compromise bill; it had not only closed a long and painful controversy, but had enabled them to make some feeble stand against the progress of executive influence. He concluded by moving for a special committee.

[*William C. Rives defended the Jackson administration against Calhoun's suggestion that it was making only a pretense at the reduction of the revenue. Rives further charged Calhoun with inconsistency in arguing on 12/19 and 12/20 that the reduction of the revenue should be referred to the Committee on Finance and in arguing now that his bill not be referred to that committee.*]

Mr. Calhoun repelled the charge of inconsistency. He had been in favor of sending the subject of a reduction of the revenue to the Committee on Finance, because he considered the subject as appropriate to their specific duties; but he was opposed to sending this bill to that committee, because they were known to be adverse to its object. In one case, he had gone on the great parliamentary principle that propositions were to be referred to committees favorable to the object proposed; and in the other case, he still had sent it to a committee at least not unfavorable to the measure. He was rejoiced to hear the honorable Senator from Virginia [Rives] declare so explicitly that he did not repent the course he had taken in reference to the compromise bill; he was confident the gentleman never would have reason to repent the able and honorable course he had pursued on that memorable occasion; and he trusted the gentleman would agree in sentiment with those who were opposed to leaving the public money in the deposite banks. Mr. C[alhoun] had given many evidences of his desire that a reduction should be made in the revenue; and had, on a former occasion [in 12/1835?], sent a bill to the Committee on Manufactures for that object, which afterwards had passed the Senate almost unanimously, and had been sent to the other House, after which it was never again heard of. He was not the man, however, to disturb the terms of the compromise, which had so happily been effected, unless it could be done by common consent. The South were prepared to assent to such a step, and if the North would also agree to it, there need be no difficulty in the case. The gentleman from Virginia seemed to suppose that, because it was the duty of the Finance Committee to consider the question whether there was likely to be a surplus revenue or not, therefore this bill ought to be sent to them. The argument was too wide: on the same principle, every proposition which related to the application of any portion of the public resources must be sent to that committee. It would swallow up almost all the business of the Senate. He concluded by demanding the yeas and nays on the question of commitment.

[*Rives spoke again. The vote on referring Calhoun's bill to the Committee on Finance was 22 to 22. By the casting vote of Vice-President Martin Van Buren the bill was so referred.*]

From *Register of Debates,* 24th Cong., 2nd Sess., cols. 79–89. Also printed in the Washington, D.C., *Daily National Intelligencer,* December 23, 1836, p. 2; the Washington, D.C., *United States' Telegraph,* December 28, 1836, p. 2; the Washington, D.C., *Globe,* July 19, 1837, p. 2; *Congressional Globe,* 24th Cong., 2nd Sess., Appendix, pp. 327–330; Crallé, ed., *Works,* 2:569–581. Variants in the Washington, D.C., *United States' Telegraph,* December 21, 1836, p. 3, and December 22, 1836, p. 3; the Washington, D.C., *Globe,* December 23, 1836, p. 2, and *Congressional Globe,* 24th Cong., 2nd Sess., pp. 39–41; the New York, N.Y., *Morning Courier and New-York Enquirer,* December 24, 1836, p. 2, and December 26, 1836, p. 2; the Charleston, S.C., *Mercury,* December 29, 1836,

p. 2. NOTE: Calhoun's bill was reported out of the Finance Committee on 12/26 without amendment and with a recommendation for its indefinite postponement. On 1/12/1837 the bill came up for consideration and was postponed. On 2/10 it was tabled on Calhoun's motion. (*Senate Journal*, 24th Cong., 2nd Sess., pp. 53, 63, 108, and 236.) The essential features of the bill subsequently were incorporated into a bill making appropriations for fortifications in the House of Representatives. Thus the distribution question came before the Senate again on 2/28.

MOTION TO ASCERTAIN THE REVENUE AND SURPLUS

[Submitted to the Senate, December 26, 1836]

Resolved, That the Secretary of the Treasury [Levi Woodbury] be directed to report to the Senate, as early as practicable after the first of January next, the amount of the exports for the year ending the 31st instant, ascertained and estimated, and distinguishing between the domestic and foreign, and the portion of the latter that is free and dutiable; the amount of the imports for the same period, estimated and ascertained, distinguishing in like manner the free and dutiable; the amount of duties accrued in the same period, ascertained and estimated, stating the portion paid into the Treasury during the year, and the amount outstanding at the end of the year; also, the amount of money that will be received in the year from the sales of lands, ascertained and estimated, distinguishing the receipts of each quarter; and, also the amount of public money in the Treasury at the end of the year, ascertained and estimated, and distinguishing what stands to the credit of the Treasurer [of the United States] from what stands to that of the disbursing officer[s].

PC in *Senate Journal*, 24th Cong., 2nd Sess., pp. 72–73; draft in DNA, RG 46 (Records of the U.S. Senate), 24A-B10. NOTE: This motion was agreed to by the Senate on 12/29.

REMARKS IN REPLY TO THOMAS H. BENTON ON THE TREASURY SURPLUS

[In the Senate, December 28, 1836]

[Benton spoke at length about a Treasury Department report which had been received by the Senate as a result of a motion made by

him previously. The report and Benton's remarks suggested that the money that would be in the Treasury at the end of the year was not really a surplus, but would be needed for appropriations. He deprecated the idea of a distribution of the surplus to the States and moved the printing of 1,000 extra copies of the report for distribution to governors, State legislatures, and the public.]

Mr. Calhoun rose to make a very few remarks on the very extraordinary motion of the Senator from Missouri, and to ask for the yeas and nays on the question. The sending out this paper in the manner proposed would make an erroneous impression on the minds of those to whom it would be sent, and would be an unusual departure from the ordinary practice of the Senate. Did not every Senator know that there was a large amount left in the Treasury, say five millions of dollars, by the deposite law of the last session, for the purpose of meeting these balances? Did not every Senator know that, by the report of the Secretary of the Treasury, there were three millions of dollars of these appropriations that would not be wanted, and were therefore transferred to the surplus fund in pursuance of a standing law? And was there not, besides, a large sum in the hands of the disbursing officers of the Government? He knew (Mr. C[alhoun] said) that every exertion would be made in order to defeat the deposite bill at this session. He knew well that the battle was yet to be fought—a battle in which the people would be on one side, and the office-holders and office-seekers on the other. While up, he would refer to the Committee on Finance, and make one remark in reference to the report of that committee on the bill introduced by him a few days since, and, much against his wishes, referred to them. They had reported against the bill, and it was not strange that they should do so, because a majority of that committee were three out of the six who voted against the deposite bill at the last session. But what he complained of was, that they had reported it without a single word of explanation; the chairman simply saying that he was instructed by the committee to move for its indefinite postponement. He would now ask the chairman on what grounds he had reported against this bill? Was it because the committee were satisfied that there would not be a surplus? If so, (said Mr. C[alhoun],) let us know it. I shall be glad to hear that such was their reason, because it is a debatable proposition. Was it because they would not have the surplus deposited with the States? If this was the case, it was directly contrary to the known sense of that body, expressed almost unanimously at the last session. He could scarcely believe that the committee reported against the bill on such grounds. With the denunciations of the President himself against the corrupting influence of a large surplus in the Treasury, and his declarations that the worst disposition that could be made of it was to let it remain in the deposite banks, he did suppose that the committee could not contemplate either result. He could not believe but that, from courtesy, the chairman would make such a report as would put the Senate in possession of the grounds on which the committee objected to the bill.

[*Silas Wright replied that he would discuss the committee's reasons when Calhoun's bill was before the Senate, and not now when another matter was under discussion.*]

Mr. Calhoun said, that although he very much regretted that they were not to have a detailed report, yet he must be permitted to say that he thought the course of the committee a very unusual one. A bill of acknowledged importance, if he might judge from the President's message and [the] report of the Secretary of the Treasury, together with the course of the Senate last session, was, after a full debate, referred to the Committee on Finance, because that committee was particularly constituted to advise on the subjects to which it related; yet that committee treated it as one of the most insignificant questions, and despatched it without a written report. This all might be very right, but it certainly was very extraordinary and unusual.

He had been here several years, both as presiding officer and as a member of the body, and he must say that this was the first time he had ever known a question to be put to the chairman of a committee, which he refused to answer. As a representative of one of the States of this Union, he must say that he had a right to an answer. The bill had gone to the committee, had received its disapprobation, and the committee ought to let them know the grounds on which they objected to it. If there was no surplus, let us (said Mr. C[alhoun]) hear the committee say so. If there was one, then, said he, let us hear what objections the committee have to depositing it with the States. He made no complaints; but he must say the course of the committee was very extraordinary.

[*Henry Hubbard of N.H. here made some remarks in opposition to the motion of Benton, as likely to mislead the State legislatures and the people. Benton replied at some length in defence of the report and his own course, when Calhoun again rose.*]

Mr. Calhoun remarked that he found the information which the gentleman from Missouri was so anxious to give the country was already before the Senate in a very authentic form. It was to be found in the table of estimates accompanying the report of the Secretary of the Treasury. He argued that, according to the assertion of the Secretary of the Treasury, who estimated the unexpended balances of appropriation at $14,636,062, the sum of $3,013,389 would not be wanted. The Senator, therefore, in sending out a document, setting forth that $14,500,000 were required for outstanding appropriations, would mislead the public, and make a false impression. Mr. C[alhoun] contended that, taking the five millions which must be left in the Treasury, on account of the deposite act, from the eleven and odd remaining of the fourteen millions, together with the money at present in the hands of the disbursing officers, there would be funds enough on hand, within a small amount, to meet the outstanding appropriations. Now, when it was admitted by every one that the surplus which would be on hand at the end of the next year would amount to at least twenty-five millions of dollars (and for himself he entertained no doubt that it would be thirty, unless the country should be disturbed by a war, or some other unforeseen catastrophe,) he would seriously ask, was there a Senator on that floor, of any party, who would say, in a time of profound peace, (for he would not call the Seminole war interrupting the peace of the Union,) and recollecting the fact that this administration came in as a reform administration, that a tax should be raised, or that the money distributed under the deposite bill should be refunded in order to make extravagant appropriations? He (Mr. C[alhoun]) could not believe it. He knew that attempts would be made to prevent the renewal of the deposite act, though he could not say that this was one of them. But let him tell gentlemen that these attempts would only produce a reaction, and end in their defeat.

Mr. C[alhoun], in conclusion, adverted to the subject of a reduction of the revenue, and the necessity of bringing it down to the legitimate wants of the Government. He insisted that the Committee on Finance, to whom was referred the consideration of this matter, were bound to show, in a satisfactory manner, either that there would be a surplus next year, or to admit the necessity of making an adequate reduction of the revenue.

[*Benton here again spoke at some length.*]

Mr. Calhoun said he had certainly made no complaint of inaccuracy on the part of the Secretary of the Treasury. He presumed that his calculations were perfectly accurate; but what he complained of was, that the Senator from Missouri proposed to send out a document which was not correct, with a view to show the outstanding appropriations remaining unsatisfied. He maintained that the document was entirely pernicious, for it set forth what was not really the truth of the case; and all that he desired was that the public should not be deceived on the subject.

From *Register of Debates*, 24th Cong., 2nd Sess., cols. 150–157. Also printed in the Washington, D.C., *Globe*, January 3, 1837, p. 2; *Congressional Globe*, 24th Cong., 2nd Sess., Appendix, pp. 39–41; Crallé, ed., *Works*, 2:581–586. Variant in the Washington, D.C., *United States' Telegraph*, December 28, 1836, p. 3; the Washington, D.C., *Daily National Intelligencer*, December 29, 1836, p. 3. Another variant (misdated as of 12/27) in the New York, N.Y., *Morning Courier and New-York Enquirer*, December 30, 1836, p. 2. NOTE: The above debate continued among a number of Senators. Calhoun spoke once more briefly. Benton's motion, after having been modified somewhat, was passed.

Remarks on his motion for ascertaining the revenue and surplus for 1836, 12/29. When the motion submitted by Calhoun on 12/26 was taken up, Calhoun "stated, that the design of the information called for was to aid in making an estimate for the coming year in reference to the public deposites, which he regarded as the great subject of the session, and liable to produce much debate." The motion was adopted. From the Washington, D.C., *Daily National Intelligencer*, December 30, 1836, p. 3.

REMARKS ON THE BILL FOR THE ADMISSION OF MICHIGAN INTO THE UNION

[In the Senate, December 29, 1836]
[Felix Grundy, from the Committee on the Judiciary, reported this bill, which was read twice. Grundy moved that the bill receive an immediate third reading. This aroused objections in which Calhoun joined.]

Mr. Calhoun had not looked much into the question; but assuming the facts to be correctly stated in the document which had been presented to the Senate, relative to the last convention held in Michigan, he must say that they presented questions of the gravest character for the consideration of Congress. There were facts and principles involved in this matter, which required the gravest examination and deliberation of the Senate, before it agreed to the admission of Michigan into the Union. He was sincerely desirous to look into the facts, and anxious to weigh the important principles which they embraced.

327

[*He therefore moved the postponement of further consideration
of the bill to 1/5/1837. Grundy replied that he was willing to grant
a postponement, but not one as long as requested. He wished Mich.
to be admitted to the Union in time to receive its share of the distribution of the surplus.*]

Mr. Calhoun said that no one could feel more anxious than he
did for the admission of Michigan, and he was desirous, too, that
she should have her full share of the deposits. And if, after this
question should have been disposed of, it was too late for the Secretary of the Treasury to give her the share of the surplus, to which
she would be entitled, some means would be devised by Congress
to effect that object. It was not his wish to delay her admission into
the Union; and, in order to meet the honorable Senator's [Grundy's]
wishes, he would change his motion to Tuesday [that is, 1/3]. According to the statement which the Senator had just made, he thought
that every one must see there was at the bottom of this matter something of the greatest importance. And, if his impression was not
incorrect, (for he did not wish to commit himself at this early stage,)
there were principles involved in this question of as great importance as those connected with the deposit act; indeed he would
rather see almost the withholding of the deposits from all the States,
than the admission of Michigan at this time. He wished time for
reflection, in order that he might be able to vote conscientiously for
the admission of Michigan.

[*After further debate the Senate agreed to motions by Calhoun
to put the bill on the calendar for 1/2 and to print the documents
related to it.*]

From *Congressional Globe,* 24th Cong., 2nd Sess., pp. 59–60. Also printed in
the Washington, D.C., *Daily National Intelligencer,* December 31, 1836, p. 3;
the Washington, D.C., *Globe,* January 5, 1837, p. 2. Variants in the Washington, D.C., *United States' Telegraph,* December 29, 1836, p. 3; the New York,
N.Y., *Morning Courier and New-York Enquirer,* January 2, 1837, p. 2; *Register
of Debates,* 24th Cong., 2nd Sess., cols. 167–168. PC's of motions in *Senate
Journal,* 24th Cong., 2nd Sess., p. 72.

To [Francis] Granger, Representative [from N.Y.]

[Washington, January, 1837]
D[ea]r Sir, I am much obliged to you for the printed statement of
the various articles, that passed through your [Erie] canal the last

season. It is quite interesting and will be useful in estimating the probable business on our [rail]road. May I ask you the favour not to forget my request for information of you? My object is to get information as to the r[e]lative expense of transportation by rail road, by canal & steam boat on rivers. Any authentick information as to the relative rate of ["these several kinds of" *interlined*] transpor[ta]tion will be very acceptable, and I rely on your kindness to furnish me with it as far as New York is concerned. With great respect I am & & J.C. Calhoun.

ALS in DLC, Gideon and Francis Granger Papers. NOTE: The date "Jan. 1837" was added to this undated letter in an unidentified hand some time after its writing.

FIRST SPEECH ON THE BILL FOR THE ADMISSION OF MICHIGAN

[In the Senate, January 2, 1837]
Mr. Calhoun [after the reading of the bill] then rose, and addressed the Senate as follows:

I have bestowed on this subject all the attention that was in my power, and, although actuated by a most anxious desire for the admission of Michigan into the Union, I find it impossible to give my assent to this bill. I am satisfied the Judiciary Committee has not bestowed upon the subject all that attention which its magnitude requires; and I can explain it on no other supposition why they should place the admission on the grounds they have. One of the committee, the Senator from Ohio on my left, (Mr. [Thomas] Morris,) has pronounced the grounds as dangerous and revolutionary. He might have gone farther, and with truth pronounced them utterly repugnant to the principles of the Constitution.

I have not ventured this assertion, as strong as it is, without due reflection, and weighing the full force of the terms I have used; and do not fear, with an impartial hearing, to establish its truth beyond the power of controversy.

To understand fully the objection to this bill, it is necessary that we should have a correct conception of the facts. They are few, and may be briefly told.

Some time previous to the last session of Congress, the Territory of Michigan, through its Legislature, authorized the people to meet in convention, for the purpose of forming a State Government. They met accordingly, and agreed upon a constitution, which they forthwith transmitted to Congress. It was fully discussed in this Chamber, and, objectionable as the instrument was, an act was finally passed, which accepted the constitution, and declared Michigan to be a State, and admitted into the Union, on the single condition, that she should, by a convention of the people, assent to the boundaries prescribed by the act. Soon after our adjournment the Legislature of the State of Michigan (for she had been raised by our assent to the dignity of a State,) called a convention of the people of the State, in conformity to the act, which met at the time appointed, at Ann Arbor. After full discussion, the convention withheld its assent, and formally transmitted the result to the President of the United States. This is the first part of the story. I will now give the sequel. Since then, during the last month, a self-constituted assembly met, professedly as a convention of the people of the State; but without the authority of the State. This unauthorized and lawless assemblage assume[d] the high function of giving the assent of the State of Michigan to the condition of admission, as prescribed in the act of Congress. They communicated their assent to the Executive of the United States, and he to the Senate. The Senate referred his message to the Committee on the Judiciary, and that committee reported this bill for the admission of the State.

Such are the facts out of which grows the important question, had this self-constituted assembly the authority to assent for the State? Had they the authority to do what is implied in giving assent to the condition of admission? That assent introduces the State into the Union, and pledges it in the most solemn manner to the constitutional compact which binds these States in one confederated body; imposes on her all its obligations, and confers on her all its benefits. Had this irregular, self-constituted assemblage the authority to perform these high and solemn acts of sovereignty in the name of the State of Michigan? She could only come in as a *State*, and none could act or speak for her without her express authority; and to assume the authority without her sanction is nothing short of treason against the State.

Again: the assent to the conditions prescribed by Congress implies an authority in those who gave it to supersede in part the constitution of the State of Michigan; for her constitution fixes the boundaries of the State as part of that instrument which the condition of admission entirely alters, and to that extent the assent would supersede the constitution; and thus the question is presented, whether this self-constituted assembly, styling itself a convention, had the authority to do an act which necessarily implies the right to supersede in part the constitution.

But further: the State of Michigan, through its Legislature, authorized a convention of the people, in order to determine whether the condition of admission should be assented to or not. The convention met; and, after mature deliberation, it dissented to the condition of admission; and thus again the question is presented, whether this self-called, self-constituted assemblage, this caucus—for it is entitled to no higher name—had the authority to annul the dissent of the State, solemnly given by a convention of the people, regularly convoked under the express authority of the constituted authorities of the State?

If all or any of these questions be answered in the negative—if the self-created assemblage of December had no authority to speak in the name of the State of Michigan—if none to supersede any portion of her constitution—if none to annul her dissent to the condition of admission regularly given by a convention of the people of the State, convoked by the authority of the State—to introduce her on its authority would be not only revolutionary and dangerous, but utterly repugnant to the principles of our constitution. The question then submitted to the Senate is, had that assemblage the authority to perform these high and solemn acts?

The chairman of the Committee on the Judiciary [Felix Grundy] holds that this self-constituted assemblage had the authority; and what is his reason? Why, truly, because a greater number of votes were given for those who constituted that assemblage than for those who constituted the convention of the people of the State, convened under its constituted authorities. This argument resolves itself into two questions—the first of fact, and the second of principle. I shall not discuss the first. It is not necessary to do so. But if it were, it would be easy to show that never was so important a fact so loosely testified. There is not one particle of official evidence before us. We had nothing but the private letters of individuals, who do not know even the numbers that voted on either occasion; they know nothing of the qualification of voters, nor how their votes were received, nor by whom counted. Now, none knows better than the honorable chairman himself, that such testimony as is submitted to us to establish a fact of this moment, would not be received in the lowest magistrate's court in the land. But I waive this. I come to the question of the principle involved; and what is it? The argument is, that a greater number of persons voted for the last convention than for the first, and therefore the acts of the last of right abrogated those of the first; in other words, *that mere numbers, without regard to the forms of law, or the principles of the constitution, give authority. The authority of numbers, according to this argument, sets aside the authority of law and the constitution.* Need I show that such a principle goes to the entire overthrow of our constitutional Government, and would subvert all social order? It is the identical principle which prompted the late revolutionary and anarchical movement in Maryland, and which has done more to shake confidence in our system of government than any event since the adoption of our constitution, but which happily has been frowned down by the patriotism and intelligence of the people of that State.

What was the ground of this insurrectionary measure, but that the Government of Maryland did not represent the voice of the numerical majority of the people of Maryland, and that the authority of law and constitution was nothing against that of numbers[?] Here we find, on this floor, and from the head of the Judiciary Committee, the same principle revived, and, if possible, in a worse form; for, in Maryland, the anarchists assumed that they were sustained by the numerical majority of the people of the State in their revolutionary movements; but the utmost the chairman can pretend to have is a mere plurality. The largest number of votes claimed for this self-created assemblage is 8,000; and no man will undertake to say that this constitutes any thing like a majority of the voters of Michigan: and he claims the high authority which he does for it, not because it is a majority of the people of Michigan, but because it [is] a greater number than voted for the authorized convention of the people that refused to agree to the condition of admission. It may be shown by his own witness, that a majority of the voters of Michigan greatly exceed 8,000. Mr. [John R.] Williams, the president of the self-created assemblage, stated that the population of that State amounted to nearly 200,000 persons. If so, there cannot be less than from 21,000 to 30,000 voters, considering how nearly universal the right of suffrage is under its constitution; and it thus appears that this irregular, self-constituted meeting, did not represent the vote of one-third of the State: and yet on a mere principle of plurality we are to supersede the constitution of Michigan, and annul the act of a convention of the people regularly convened under the authority of the Government of the State.

But, says the Senator from Pennsylvania, (Mr. [James] Buchanan,) this assembly was not self-constituted. It met under the authority of an act of Congress; and that act had no reference to the

State, but only to the people; and that the assemblage in December was just such a meeting as that act contemplated. It is not my intention to discuss the question whether the honorable Senator has given the true interpretation of the act, but, if it were, I could very easily show his interpretation to be erroneous; for, if such had been the intention of Congress, the act surely would have specified the time when the convention was to be held, who were to be the managers, who the voters, and would not have left it to individuals, who might choose to assume the authority to determine all these important points. I might also readily show that the word "convention" of the people, as used in law or the constitution, always means a meeting of the people regularly convened *by the constituted authority of the State*[s], in their high sovereign capacity, and that it never means such an assemblage as the one in question. But I waive this; I take higher ground. If the act be, indeed, such as the Senator says it is, then I maintain that it is utterly opposed to the fundamental principles of our Federal Union. Congress has no right whatever to *call a convention in a State*. It can call but one convention, and that is a convention of the United States to amend the Federal Constitution; nor can it call that, except authorized by two-thirds of the States.

Ours is a Federal Republic—a Union of States. Michigan is a State; a State in the course of admission, and differing only from the other States in her federal relations. She is declared to be a State in the most solemn manner by your own act. She can come into the Union only as a State; and by her voluntary assent, given by the people of the State in convention, called by the constituted authority of the State. To admit the State of Michigan on the authority of a self-created meeting, or one called by the direct authority of Congress, passing by the authorities of the State, would be the most monstrous proceeding under our constitution that can be conceived; the most repugnant to its principles, and dangerous in its consequences. It would establish a direct relation between the individual citizens of a State and the General Government, in utter subversion of the federal character of our system. The relation of the citizens to this Government is through the States exclusively. They are subject to its authority and laws only because the State has assented they should be. If *she dissents, their assent is nothing*; on the other hand, if she assents, their dissent is nothing. It is through the State, then, and through the State alone, that the United States Government can have any connexion with the people of a State; and does not, then, the Senator from Pennsylvania see, that if Congress can authorize a convention of the people in the State of Michigan, without the authority of the State, it matters not what is the object, it may in like manner authorize conventions in any other State, for whatever purpose it may think proper.

Michigan is as much a sovereign State as any other, differing only, as I have said, as to her federal relations. If we give our sanction to the assemblage of December, on the principle laid down by the Senator from Pennsylvania, then we establish the doctrine that Congress has power to call at pleasure conventions within the States. Is there a Senator on this floor who will assent to such a doctrine? Is there one, especially, who represents the smaller States of this Union, or the weaker section? Admit the power, and every vestige of State rights would be destroyed. Our system would be subverted, and, instead of a *confederacy of free and sovereign States,* we would have all power concentrated here, and this would become the most odious despotism. He, indeed, must be blind, who does not see that such a power would give the Federal Government a complete control of all the States. I call upon Senators now to arrest a doctrine so dangerous. Let it be remembered, that, under our system, bad precedents live forever; good ones only perish. We may not feel all the evil consequences at once but this precedent, once set, will surely be revived, and will become the instrument of infinite evil.

It will be asked, what shall be done? Will you refuse to admit Michigan into the Union? I answer no: I desire to admit her; and if the Senators from Indiana and Ohio will agree, am ready to admit her as she stood at the beginning of last session, without giving sanction to the unauthorized assemblage of December.

But if this does not meet their wishes, there is still another [way] by which she may be admitted. We are told two-thirds of the Legislature and people of Michigan are in favor of accepting the conditions of the act of last session. If that be the fact, then all that is necessary is, that the Legislature shall call another convention. All difficulty will thus be removed, and there will be still abundant time for her admission at this session. And shall we, for the sake of gaining a few months, give our assent to a bill fraught with principles so monstrous as this?

We have been told, that unless she is admitted immediately it will be too late for her to receive her proportion of the surplus revenue under the deposite bill. I trust that on so great a question a difficulty like this will have no weight. Give her at once her full share. I am ready to do so at once, without waiting her admission. I was mortified to hear on so grave a question such motives assigned for her admission, contrary to the law and constitution. Such considerations ought not to be presented when we are settling great constitutional principles. I trust that we shall pass by all such frivolous motives on this occasion, and take ground on the great and fundamental principle that an informal, irregular, self-constituted assembly, a mere caucus, has no authority to speak for a sovereign State in any case whatever; to supersede its constitution, or to reverse its dissent deliberately given by a convention of the people of the State, regularly convened under its constituted authority.

From *Speeches of Mr. Calhoun of S[outh] Carolina, on the Bill for the Admission of Michigan. Delivered in the Senate of the United States, January, 1837* (Washington: printed by Duff Green, 1837), pp. 3–7. Also printed in the Washington, D.C., *Daily National Intelligencer,* January 7, 1837, pp. 2–3; the Washington, D.C., *United States' Telegraph,* January 9, 1837, p. 2; the Washington, D.C., *Globe,* January 12, 1837, pp. 2–3; the Charleston, S.C., *Mercury,* January 18, 1837, p. 2; *Register of Debates,* 24th Cong., 2nd Sess., cols. 206–210; *Speeches of John C. Calhoun,* pp. 243–249; Crallé, ed., *Works,* 2:586–596. Variants in the Washington, D.C., *United States' Telegraph,* January 3, 1837, p. 2; the New York, N.Y., *Morning Courier and New-York Enquirer,* January 5, 1837, p. 2; *Congressional Globe,* 24th Cong., 2nd Sess., Appendix, pp. 64–65. NOTE: Earlier on the same day Calhoun spoke briefly three times in debate with Grundy. Calhoun attempted unsuccessfully to postpone consideration of the bill and to win from Grundy an abandonment of the preamble of the bill which recognized the authority of the second convention in Mich. to assent to Congressional conditions as to boundaries. If the Judiciary Committee would agree to drop the preamble, Calhoun "thought all difficulty would be at an end." His mind was made up that Mich. could not be admitted "on the ground of that second convention; but the Senate might set aside the whole of what had been done, and receive Michigan as she stood at the commencement of the last session." (*Register of Debates,* 24th Cong., 2nd Sess., cols. 204–205.) Late in the same day's session, when Robert J. Walker argued that Congress had frequently "called conventions to enable the people within certain territorial limits to establish State Governments," Calhoun replied that "he intended to say that Congress could call no convention in a State, and that Michigan was a State when this convention was called." (*Register of Debates,* 24th Cong., 2nd Sess., col. 227.)

Remarks on the bill for the admission of Michigan, 1/3. While speaking in favor of the bill, James Buchanan represented Calhoun as having argued that the convention which had accepted Congressional terms for the admission of that State to the Union was a nullity because it had not been authorized by the State legislature, which argument Buchanan said was untenable because the act of Congress had not (and Constitutionally could not have) stipulated that action of the State legislature was necessary to the calling of the convention. "Mr. Calhoun here explained. He said he would not here argue the question whether Congress meant to make a previous act of the State Legislature necessary; but if it did not, the act of Congress would itself be unconstitutional, because we had recognised Michigan as a State, and Congress have no right to call a convention in a State." Later in the same debate Calhoun made unreported remarks in support of a substitute preamble offered by Thomas Morris. From *Register of Debates*, 24th Cong., 2nd Sess., cols. 237–238, 267. Also printed in *Congressional Globe*, 24th Cong., 2nd Sess., Appendix, p. 73.

Amendment to the bill for the admission of Michigan, submitted to the Senate on 1/4. Calhoun moved to strike out of the preamble the following: "That the State of Michigan shall be one, and is hereby declared to be one of the United States of America, and admitted into the Union on an equal footing with the original States, in all respects whatever." He moved to substitute for those words the following: "That so much of the act of the 15th of June last, entitled 'An act to establish the northern boundary line of the State of Ohio, and to provide for the admission of the State of Michigan into the Union upon the conditions therein expressed,' as prescribes the condition of admission contained in the 3rd section of said act, be, and the same is hereby repealed; and that the State of Michigan be, and is hereby, admitted into the Union upon an equal footing with the original States, in all respects whatever." PC in *Senate Journal*, 24th Cong., 2nd Sess., p. 90.

Remarks on his amendment to the bill for the admission of Michigan, 1/4. After considerable debate Calhoun "offered an amendment proposing to strike out the preamble, and to amend the bill so as to divest it, of its obnoxious principles. His amendment proposed the immediate admission of the State into the Union. He expressed his solemn conviction that the bill, as it stood, was pregnant with most dangerous consequences; and with the view of expressing his opinions," he moved an adjournment to allow him an opportunity to speak on his amendment tomorrow. This motion failed 13 to 24. Calhoun then said, "I see, sir, that the majority have the power, and that they are determined to exercise it. I will not complain. I consider the amendment as of great importance, involving the most essential principles. But I will not speak at this late hour. Let them take their advantage." The question was then taken on Calhoun's amendment, which was lost 12 to 25. The bill was ordered to be engrossed for a third reading, 27 to 4. From the Washington, D.C.,

United States' Telegraph, January 5, 1837, p. 2. Variant in *Register of Debates,* 24th Cong., 2nd Sess., cols. 294–295; the Washington, D.C., *Globe,* January 6, 1837, p. 2; *Congressional Globe,* 24th Cong., 2nd Sess., p. 71. Other variants in the Washington, D.C., *Daily National Intelligencer,* January 5, 1837, p. 3; the Richmond, Va., *Whig and Public Advertiser,* January 10, 1837, p. 2 (from the Baltimore, Md., *Patriot*).

Second Speech on the Bill for the Admission of Michigan

[In the Senate, January 5, 1837]

Mr. [Felix] Grundy, chairman of the Committee on the Judiciary, having moved that the bill to admit the State of Michigan into the Union be now read a third time—

Mr. Calhoun addressed the Senate in opposition to the bill.

I have (said Mr. C[alhoun]) been connected with this Government more than half its existence, in various capacities, and during that long period I have looked on its action with attention, and have endeavored to make myself acquainted with the principles and character of our political institutions, and I can truly say that within that time no measure has received the sanction of Congress which has appeared to me more unconstitutional and dangerous than the present. It assails our political system in its *weakest point,* and where, *at this time, it most requires defence.*

The great and leading objections to the bill rest mainly on the ground that Michigan is a State. They have been felt by its friends to have so much weight, that its advocates have been compelled to deny the fact, as the only way of meeting the objections. Here, then, is the main point at issue between the friends and the opponents of the bill. It turns on a fact, and that fact presents the question—is Michigan a State?

If (said Mr. C[alhoun]) there ever was a party committed on a fact—if there ever was one estopped from denying it—that party is the present majority in the Senate, and that fact that Michigan is a State. It is the very party who urged through this body, at the last session, a bill for the admission of the State of Michigan, which accepted her constitution, and declared in the most explicit and strongest terms that *she was a State.* I will not take up the time of the

337

Senate by reading this solemn declaration. It has frequently been read during this debate, is familiar to all who hear me, and has not been questioned or denied. But it has been said there is a condition annexed to the declaration, with which she must comply, before she can become a State. There is, indeed, a condition; but it has been shown by my colleague [William C. Preston] and others, from the plain wording of the act, that the condition is not attached to the acceptance of the constitution, nor the declaration that she is a State, but simply to her *admission* into the Union. I will not repeat the argument, but, in order to place the subject beyond controversy, I shall recall to memory the history of the last session, as connected with the admission of Michigan. The facts need but to be referred to, in order to revive their recollection.

There were two points proposed to be effected by the friends of the bill at the last session. The first was to settle the controversy, as to boundary, between Michigan and Ohio, and it was this object alone which imposed the condition that Michigan should assent to the boundary prescribed by the act as the condition of her admission. But there was another object to be accomplished. Two respectable gentlemen, who had been elected by the State as Senators, were then waiting to take their seats on this floor; and the other object of the Bill was to provide for their taking their seats as Senators on the admission of the State, and for this purpose it was necessary to make the positive and unconditional declaration that Michigan was a State, as a State only could choose Senators, by an express provision of the constitution; and hence the admission was made conditional, and the declaration that she was a State was made absolute, in order to effect both objects. To show that I am correct, I will ask the Secretary to read the third section of the bill.

(The section was read accordingly as follows:

Sect[ion] 3. *And be it further enacted,* That, as a compliance with the fundamental condition of admission contained in the last preceding section of this act, the boundaries of the said State of Michigan, as in that section described, declared, and established, shall receive the assent of a convention of delegates elected by the people of said State, for the sole purpose of giving the assent herein required; and as soon as the assent herein required shall be given, the President of the United States shall announce the same by proclamation; and thereupon, and without any further proceedings on the part of Congress, the admission of the said State into the Union, as one of the United States of America, on an equal footing with all the original States in every respect whatever, shall be considered as complete, and the Senators and Representatives who have been elected by the said State as its representative in the Congress of the United States, shall be entitled to take their seats in the Senate and House of Representatives respectively, without further delay.)

Mr. Calhoun then asked—Does not every Senator see the two objects—the one to settle the boundary, and the other to admit her Senators to a seat in this body; and that the section is so worded as to effect both, in the manner I have stated? If this needed confirmation, it would be found in the debate on the passage of the bill, when the ground was openly taken by the present majority, that Michigan had a right to form her constitution, under the ordinance of 1787, without our consent; and that she was of right, and in fact, a State, beyond our control.

I will (said Mr. C[alhoun]) explain my own views on this point in order that the consistency of my course at the last and present session may be clearly seen.

My opinion was, and still is, that the movement of the people of Michigan in forming for themselves a State constitution, without waiting for the assent of Congress, was revolutionary, as it threw off the authority of the U[nited] States over the Territory; and that we were left at liberty to treat the proceedings as revolutionary, and to remand her to her territorial condition, or to waive the irregularity, and to recognise what was done as rightfully done, as our authority alone was concerned.

My impression was, that the former was the proper course; but I also thought that the act remanding her back should contain our assent in the usual manner for her to form a constitution, and thus to leave her free to become a State. This, however, was overruled. The opposite opinion prevailed, that she had a perfect right to do what she had done, and that she was, as I have stated, a State both in fact and right, and that we had no control over her; and our act accordingly recognised her as a State, from the time she had adopted her constitution, and admitted her into the Union on the condition of her assenting to the prescribed boundaries. Having thus solemnly recognised her as a State, we cannot now undo what was then done. There were, in fact, many irregularities in the proceedings, all of which were urged in vain against its passage; but the Presidential election was then pending, and the vote of Michigan was considered of sufficient weight to overrule all objections, and correct all irregularities. They were all accordingly overruled, and we cannot now go back.

Such was the course, and such the acts of the majority at the last session. A few short months have since passed. Other objects are now to be effected, and all is forgotten as completely as if they had never existed. The very Senators who then forced the act through on the ground that Michigan was a State, have wheeled completely round, to serve the present purpose, and taken directly the opposite ground! We live in strange and inconsistent times. Opinions are taken up and laid down, as suits the occasion, without hesitation, or the slightest regard to principle or consistency. It indicates an unsound state of the public mind, pregnant with future disasters.

I turn to the position now assumed by the majority to suit the present occasion; and, if I mistake not, it will be found as false in fact, and as erroneous in principle, as it is inconsistent with that maintained at the last session. They now take the ground that Michigan is not a State, and cannot, in fact, be a State till she is admitted into the Union; and this on the broad principle that a Territory cannot become a State till admitted. Such is the position distinctly taken by several of the friends of this bill, and implied in the arguments of nearly all who have spoken in its favor. In fact, its advocates had no choice. As untenable as it is, they were forced on this desperate position. They had no other which they could occupy.

I have shown that it is directly in the face of the law of the last session, and that it denies the recorded acts of those who now maintain the position. I now go further, and assert that it is in direct opposition to plain and unquestionable matter of fact. There is no fact more certain than that Michigan is a State. She is in the full exercise of sovereign authority, with a Legislature and a Chief Magistrate. She passes laws; she executes them; she regulates titles; and even takes away life—all on her own authority. Ours has entirely ceased over her; and yet there are those who can deny, with all these facts before them, that she is a State. They might as well deny the existence of this Hall! We have long since assumed unlimited control over the constitution, to twist, and turn, and deny it, as it suited our purpose; and it would seem that we are presumptuously attempting to assume like supremacy over facts themselves, as if their existence or non-existence depended on our volition. I speak freely. The occasion demands that the truth should be boldly uttered.

But those who may not regard their own recorded acts, nor the plain facts of the case, may possibly feel the awkward condition in which coming events may shortly place them. The admission of Michigan is not the only point involved in the passage of this bill.

A question will follow, which may be presented to the Senate in a very few days, as to the right of Mr. [John] Norvell and Mr. [Lucius] Lyon, the two respectable gentlemen who have been elected Senators by Michigan, to take their seats in this Hall. The decision of this question will require a more sudden facing about than has been yet witnessed. It required seven or eight months for the majority to wheel about from the position maintained at the last session to that taken at this, but there may not be allowed them now as many days to wheel back to the old position. These gentlemen cannot be refused their seats after the admission of the State by those gentlemen who passed the act of the last session. It provides for the case. I now put it to the friends of this bill, and I ask them to weigh the question deliberately—to bring it home to their bosom and conscience before they answer—can a Territory elect Senators to Congress? The constitution is express; *States* only can choose Senators. Were not these gentlemen chosen long before the admission of Michigan; before the Ann Arbor meeting, and while Michigan was, according to the doctrines of the friends of this bill, a Territory? Will they, in the face of the constitution, which they are sworn to support, admit as Senators on this floor those who, by their own statement, were elected by a Territory? These questions may soon be presented for decision. The majority, who are forcing this bill through, are already committed by the act of the last session, and I leave them to reconcile, as they can, the ground they now take with the vote they must give when the question of their right to take their seats is presented for decision.

A total disregard of all principle and consistency has so entangled this subject, that there is but one mode left of extricating ourselves without trampling the Constitution in the dust; and that is, to return back to where we stood when the question was first presented; to acquiesce in the right of Michigan to form a constitution, and erect herself into a State, under the ordinance of 1787; and to repeal so much of the act of the last session as prescribed the condition on which she was to be admitted. This was the object of the amendment that I offered last evening, in order to relieve the Senate from its present dilemma. The amendment involved the merits of the whole case. It was too late in the day for discussion, and I asked for indulgence till to-day, that I might have an opportunity of presenting my views. Under the iron rule of the present majority, the indulgence was refused and the bill ordered to its third reading; and I have been thus compelled to address the Senate when it is too late to amend the bill, and after a majority have committed themselves both as to its principles and details. Now [*sic*; New(?)] as such proceedings are in this body, I complain not. I, as one of the minority, ask no favors. All I ask is, that the constitution be not violated. Hold it sacred, and I shall be the last to complain.

I now return to the assumption that a Territory cannot become a State till admitted into the Union, which is now relied on with so much confidence to prove that Michigan is not a State. I reverse the position. I assert the opposite, that a Territory cannot be admitted till she becomes a State; and in this, I stand on the authority of the constitution itself, which expressly limits the power of Congress to admitting new States into the Union. But, if the constitution had been silent, he would indeed be ignorant of the character of our political system, who does not see that States, sovereign and independent communities, and not Territories, can only be admitted. Our is *a Union of States, a Federal* Republic. States, and not Territories, form its component parts, bound together by a solemn league, in the form of a constitutional compact. In coming into the Union, the State pledges its faith to this sacred compact; an act which none but a sovereign and independent community is competent to perform; and, of course, a Territory must first be raised to that condition before she can take her stand among the confederated States of our Union. How can a Territory pledge its faith to the constitution? It has no will of its own. You give it all its powers, and you can at pleasure overrule all her actions. If she enters as a Territory, the act *is yours, not hers. Her consent is nothing without your authority and sanction.* Can you, can Congress, become a party to the constitutional compact? How absurd.

But I am told, if this be so, if a Territory must become a State before it can be admitted, it would follow that she might refuse to enter the Union after she had acquired the right of acting for herself. Certainly she may. A State cannot *be forced* into the Union. She must come in *by her own free assent*, given in her highest sovereign capacity through a convention of the people of the State. Such is the constitutional provision; and those who make the objection must overlook both the constitution and the elementary principles of our Government, of which the right of *self government is the first*; the right of every people to form their own government, and to determine their political condition. This is the doctrine on which our fathers acted in our glorious revolution, which has done more for the cause of liberty throughout the world than any event within the record of history, and on which the Government has acted

342

from the first, as regards all that portion of our extensive territory that lies beyond the limits of the original States. Read the ordinance of 1787, and the various acts for the admission of new States, and you will find the principle invariably recognised and acted on, to the present unhappy instance, without any departure from it, except in the case of Missouri. The admission of Michigan is destined, I fear, to mark a great change in the history of the admission of new States; a total departure from the old usage, and the noble principle of self-government on which that usage was founded. Every thing, thus far, connected with her admission, has been irregular and monstrous. I trust it is not ominous. Surrounded by lakes within her natural limits, (which ought not to have been departed from,) and possessed of fertile soil and genial climate, with every prospect of wealth, power, and influence, who but must regret that she should be ushered into the Union in a manner so irregular and unworthy of her future destiny.

But I will waive these objections, constitutional and all. I will suppose, with the advocates of the bill, that a Territory cannot become a State till admitted into the Union. Assuming all this, I ask them to explain to me *how the mere act of admission can transmute a Territory into a State?* By whose authority would she be made a State? By ours? How can we make a State? We can form a Territory; we can admit States into the Union; but, I repeat the question, how can we make a State? I had supposed this Government was the creature of the States—formed by their authority, and dependent on their will for their [*sic*; its] existence. Can the creature form the creator? If not by our authority, then by whose? Not by her own, that would be absurd. The very act of admission makes her a member of the Confederacy, with no other or greater power than is possessed by all the others; all of whom, united, cannot create a State. By what process, then, by what authority, can a Territory become a State, if not one before admitted? Who can explain? How full of difficulties, compared to the long established, simple, and noble process which has prevailed to the present instant. According to old usage, the General Government first withdraws its authority over a certain portion of its territory, as soon as it has a sufficient population to constitute a State. They are thus left to themselves freely to form a constitution, and to exercise the noble right of self-government. They then present their constitution to Congress, and ask *the privilege* (for one it is of the highest character) to become a member of this glorious confederacy of States. The constitution is examined, and, if republican, as required by the federal constitution, she is admitted, with no other condition except such as may be necessary to secure the authority of Congress over the public domain within her limits. This is the old, the established form, instituted by our ancestors of the Revolution, who so well understood the great principles of liberty and self-government. How simple; how sublime! What a contrast to the doctrines of the present day, and the precedent which, I fear, we are about to establish! And shall we fear, so long as these sound principles are observed, that a State will reject this high privilege—will refuse to enter this Union? No; she will rush into your embrace, so long as your institutions are worth preserving. When the advantages of the Union shall have become a matter of calculation and doubt; when new States shall pause to determine whether the Union is a curse or blessing, the question which now agitates us will cease to have any importance.

Having now, I trust, established beyond all controversy, that Michigan is a State, I come to the great point at issue—to the decision of which all that has been said is but preparatory—had the self-created assembly which met at Ann Arbor the authority to speak in the name of the people of Michigan; to assent to the conditions contained in the act of the last session; to supersede a portion of the constitution of the State, and to overrule the dissent of the convention of the people, regularly called by the constituted authorities of the State, to the condition of admission? I shall not repeat what I said when I first addressed the Senate on this bill. We all, by this time, know the character of that assemblage; that it met without the sanction of the authorities of the State; and that it did not pretend to represent one third of the people. We all know that the State had regularly convened a convention of the people, expressly to take into consideration the condition on which it was proposed to admit her into the Union, and that the convention, after full deliberation, had declined to give its assent by a considerable majority. With a knowledge of all these facts, I put the question—had the assembly a right to act for the State? Was it a convention of the people of Michigan in the true, legal, and constitutional sense of that term? Is there one within the limits of my voice, that can lay his hand on his breast, and honestly say it was? Is there one that does not feel that it was neither more nor less than a *mere caucus* —nothing but a *party caucus*—of which we have the strongest evidence in the perfect unanimity of those who assembled? Not a vote was given against admission. Can there be stronger proof that it was a meeting got up by party machinery, for party purpose?

But I go further. It was not only a party caucus, for party purpose, *but a criminal meeting*—a meeting to subvert the authority of the State, and to assume its sovereignty. I know not whether Michigan has yet passed laws to guard her sovereignty. It may be that she has not had time to enact laws for this purpose, which no community is long without; but I do aver, if there be such an act, or if the common law be in force in the State, the actors in that meeting might be indicted, tried, and punished *for the very act on which it is now proposed to admit the State into the Union*. If such a meeting as this were to undertake to speak in the name of South Carolina, we would speedily teach its authors what they owed to the authority and dignity of the State. The act was not only in contempt of the authority of the State of Michigan, but a direct insult to this Government. Here is a self-created meeting, convened for a criminal object, which has dared to present to this Government an act of theirs, and to expect that we are to receive this irregular and criminal act as a fulfilment of the condition which we had prescribed for the admission of the State! Yet, I fear, forgetting our own dignity, and the rights of Michigan, that we are about to recognize the validity of the act, and quietly to submit to the insult.

The year 1836 (said Mr. C[alhoun]) is destined to mark the most remarkable change in our political institutions, since the adoption of the constitution. The events of the year have made a deeper innovation on the principles of the constitution, and evinced a stronger tendency to revolution than any which have occurred from its adoption to the present day. Sir, (said Mr. C[alhoun], addressing the Vice-President [Martin Van Buren],) duty compels me to speak of facts, intimately connected with yourself. In deference to your feelings as presiding officer of the body, I shall speak of them with all possible reserve, much more reserve than I should otherwise have done if you did not occupy that seat. Among the first of these events, which I shall notice, is the caucus at Baltimore; that too, like the Ann Arbor caucus, has been dignified with the name of the Convention of the people. This caucus was got up under the countenance and express authority of the President himself [Andrew Jackson]; and its edict, appointing you his successor, has been sustained, not only by the whole patronage and power of the Government, but by his active personal influence and exertion. Through its instrumentality he has succeeded in controlling the voice of the people, and for the first time the President has appointed his successor; and thus the first great step of converting our Government into a monarchy has been sustained. These are solemn and ominous facts. No one who has examined the result of the last election can doubt their truth. It is now certain that you are not the free and unbiassed choice of the people of these United States. If left to your own popularity, without the active and direct influence of the President, and the power and patronage of the government, acting through a mock convention of the people, instead of the highest, you would in all probability have been the lowest of the candidates.

During the same year, the State [Maryland] in which this ill-omened caucus convened has been agitated by revolutionary movements of the most alarming character. Assuming the dangerous doctrines that they were not bound to obey the injunctions of the constitution, because it did not place the powers of the State in the hands of an unchecked numerical majority, the electors belonging to the party of the Baltimore caucus who had been chosen to appoint the State senators refused to perform the functions for which they had been elected, with the deliberate intention to subvert the Government of the State, and reduce her to the Territory condition [sic], till a new Government could be formed. And now we have before us a measure, not less revolutionary, but of an opposite character. In the case of Maryland, those who undertook, without the authority of law, or constitution, to speak and act in the name of the people of the State, proposed to place her out of the Union by reducing her from a State to a Territory; but in this, those who in like manner undertook to act for Michigan, have assumed the authority to bring her into the Union without her consent, on the very condition which she had rejected by a convention of the people, convened under the authority of the State. If we shall sanction the authority of the Michigan caucus to force a State into the Union without its assent, why might we not here sanction a similar caucus in Maryland, if one had been called, to place the State out of the Union?

These occurrences, which have distinguished the past year, mark the commencement of no ordinary change in our political system. They announce *the ascendency of the caucus system over the regularly constituted authorities of the country.* I have long anticipated this event. In early life my attention was attracted to the working of the caucus system. It was my fortune to spend five or six years of my youth in the Northern portion of the Union, where unfortunately the system has so long prevailed. Though young, I was old enough to take interest in public affairs, and to notice the working of this odious party machine; and after reflection, with the experience then acquired, has long satisfied me that, in the course of time, the edicts of the caucus would eventually supersede the au-

346

thority of law and constitution. We have at last arrived at the commencement of this great change which is destined to go on till it has consummated itself in the entire overthrow of all legal and constitutional authority, unless speedily and effectually resisted. The reason is obvious: for obedience and disobedience to the edicts of the caucus, where the system is firmly established, are more certainly and effectually rewarded and punished, than to the laws and constitution. Disobedience to the former is sure to be followed by complete political disfranchisement. It deprives the unfortunate individual who falls under its vengeance of all public honors and emoluments, and consigns him, if dependent on the Government, to poverty and obscurity; while he who bows down before its mandates, it matters not how monstrous, secures to himself the honors of the State—becomes rich, and distinguished, and powerful. Offices, jobs, and contracts, flow on him and his connexions. But to obey the law and respect the constitution, for the most part, brings little except the approbation of conscience—a reward indeed high and noble, and prized by the virtuous above all others, but unfortunately little valued by the mass of mankind. It is easy to see what must be the end, unless indeed an effective remedy be applied. Are we so blind as not to see in this, why it is that the advocates of this bill—the friends of the system, are so tenacious on the point that Michigan should be admitted on the authority of the Ann Arbor caucus, and on no other? Do we not see why the amendment proposed by myself to admit her by rescinding the condition imposed at the last session should be so strenuously opposed? Why even the preamble would not be surrendered, though many of our friends were willing to vote for the bill on that slight concession, in their anxiety to admit the State.

And here let me say that I listened with attention to the speech of the Senator from Kentucky, (Mr. [John J.] Crittenden). I know the clearness of his understanding, and the soundness of his heart, and I am persuaded, in declaring that his objection to the bill was confined to the preamble, that he has not investigated the subject with the attention it deserves. I feel the objections to the preamble are not without some weight; but the true and insuperable objections lie far deeper in the facts of the case which would still exist were the preamble expunged. It is these which render it impossible to pass this bill without trampling under foot the rights of the States, and subverting the first principles of our Government. It would require but a few steps more to effect a complete revolution, and the Senator from North Carolina [Robert Strange] has taken the first. I will explain. If you wish to mark the first indications of a revolution, the commencement of the profound changes in the character of a people which are working beneath, before a ripple appears on the surface, look to the change of language; you will first notice it in the altered meaning of important words, and which, as it indicates a change in the feelings and principles of the people, become in turn a powerful instrument in accelerating the change, till an entire revolution is effected. The remarks of the Senator will illustrate what I have said. He told us that the terms "convention of the people" were of very uncertain meaning, and difficult to be defined, but that their true meaning was, *any meeting* of the people in their individual and primary character for political purpose. I know it is difficult to define complex terms; that is, to enumerate all the ideas that belong to them, and exclude all that do not; but there is always, in the most complex, some prominent idea which marks the meaning of the term, and in relation to which there is usually no disagreement. Thus, according to the old meaning, (and which I had still supposed was its legal and constitutional meaning,) a convention of the people invariably implied a meeting of the people, either by themselves, or by delegates expressly chosen for the purpose, *in their high sovereign authority*, in expressed contradistinction to such assemblies of individuals in their private character, or having only derivative authority. It is, in a word, a meeting of the people in the majesty of their power—in that in which they may rightfully make or abolish constitutions, and put up or put down Governments at their pleasure. Such was the august conception which formerly entered the mind of every American, when the terms "convention of the people" were used. But now, according to the ideas of the dominant party, as we are told on the authority of the Senator from North Carolina, it means any meeting of individuals for political purposes, and, of course, applies to the meeting at Ann Arbor, or any other party caucus for party purposes, which the leaders choose to designate as a convention of the people. It is thus the highest authority known to our laws and constitution, is gradually sinking to the level of those meetings which regulate the operation of political parties, and through which the edicts of their leaders are announced, and their authority enforced; or, rather, to speak more correctly, the latter are gradually rising to the authority of the former. When they come to be completely confounded; when the distinction between a caucus and the convention of the people shall be completely obliterated, which the definition of the Senator, and the acts of this body on this bill, would lead us to believe is not far distant, this fair political fabric of ours, erected by the wisdom and patriotism of our ancestors, and once the gaze [*sic*] and admiration of the world, will topple to the ground in ruins.

It has, perhaps, been too much my habit to look more to the future and less to the present, than is wise; but such is the constitution of [my] mind, that when I see before me the indications of causes calculated to effect important changes in our political condition, I am led irresistibly to trace them to their sources, and follow them out in their consequences. Language has been held in this discussion which is clearly revolutionary in its character and tendency, and which warns us of the approach of the period when the struggle will be between the *conservatives and the destructives*. I understood the Senator from Pennsylvania (Mr. [James] Buchanan) as holding language countenancing the principle that the will of a mere numerical majority is paramount to the authority of law and constitution. He did not indeed announce distinctly this principle, but it might fairly be inferred from what he said; for he told us the people of a State, where the constitution gives the same weight to a smaller as to a greater number, might take the remedy into their own hand[s]; meaning, as I understood him, that a mere majority might at their pleasure subvert the constitution and government of a State, which he seemed to think was the essence of democracy. Our little State [of South Carolina] has a constitution that could not stand a day against such doctrines, and yet we glory in it as the best in the Union. It is a constitution which respects all the great interests of the State, giving to each a separate and distinct voice in the management of its political affairs, by means of which the feebler interests are protected against the preponderance of the greater. We call our State a Republic—a Commonwealth, not a democracy; and let me tell the Senator it is a far more popular Government than if it had been based on the simple principle of the numerical majority. It takes more voices to put the machine of Government in motion, than in those that the Senator would consider more popular. It represents all the interests of the State, and is in fact the Government of the people, in the true sense of the term, and not that of the mere majority, or the dominant interests.

I am not familiar with the constitution of Maryland, to which the Senator alluded, and cannot, therefore, speak of its structure with confidence; but I believe it to be somewhat similar in its character to our own. That it is a Government not without its excellence, we need no better proof than the fact, that though within the shadow of Executive influence, it has nobly and successfully resisted all the seductions by which a corrupt and artful Administration, with almost boundless patronage, has attempted to seduce her into its ranks.

Looking, then, to the approaching struggle, I take my stand immovably. *I am a conservative in its broadest and fullest sense,* and such *I shall ever remain, unless, indeed, the Government shall become so corrupt and disordered that nothing short of revolution can reform it.* I solemnly believe that our political system is, in its purity, not only the best that ever was formed, but the best possible that can be devised for us. It is the only one by which free States, so populous and wealthy, and occupying so vast an extent of territory, can preserve their liberty. Thus thinking I can not hope for a better. Having no hope of a better, I am a conservative; and *because I am a conservative I am a State rights man.* I believe that in the rights of the States are to be found the only effectual means of checking the overaction of this Government; to resist its tendency to concentrate all power here, and to prevent a departure from the constitution; or, in case of one, to restore the Government to its original simplicity and purity. State interposition, or, to express it more fully, the right of a State to interpose her sovereign voice as one of the parties to our constitutional compact, against the encroachments of this Government, is the only means of sufficient potency to effect all this; and I am, therefore, its advocate. I rejoiced to hear the Senators from North Carolina (Mr. [Bedford] Brown) and from Pennsylvania (Mr. Buchanan) do us the justice to distinguish between nullification and the anarchical and revolutionary movements in Maryland and Pennsylvania. I know they did not intend it as a compliment; but I regard it as the highest. They are right. Day and night are not more different—more unlike in every thing. They are unlike in their principles, their objects, and their consequences.

I shall not stop to make good this assertion, as I might easily do. The occasion does not call for it. As a conservative, and a State rights man, or if you will have it, a nullifier, I have, and shall resist all encroachments on the constitution, whether it be the encroachment of this Government on the States, or the opposite: the Executive on Congress, or Congress on the Executive. My creed is to hold both Governments, and all the departments of each to their proper sphere, and to maintain the authority of the laws and the constitution against all revolutionary movements. I believe the means which our system furnishes to preserve itself are ample, if fairly understood and applied; and I shall resort to them, however corrupt and disordered the times, so long as there is hope of reforming the Government. The result is in the hands of the Disposer of events. It is my part to do my duty. Yet while I thus openly avow myself a conservative, God forbid I should ever deny the glorious right of rebellion and revolution. Should corruption and oppression become intolerable, and cannot otherwise be thrown off—if liberty must perish, or the Government be overthrown, I would not hesitate, at the hazard of life, to resort to revolution, and to tear down a corrupt Government that could neither be reformed nor borne by freemen; but I trust in God things will never come to that pass. I trust never to see such fearful times; for fearful, indeed, they would be, if they should ever befal[l] us. It is the last remedy, and not to be thought of till common sense and the voice of mankind would justify the resort.

Before I resume my seat, I feel called on to make a few brief remarks on a doctrine of fearful import, which has been broached in the course of this debate—the right to repeal laws granting bank charters, and, of course, of railroads, turnpikes, and joint stock companies. It is a doctrine of fearful import, and calculated to do infinite mischief. There are countless millions vested in such stocks, and it is a description of property of the most delicate character. To touch it is almost to destroy it. But, while I enter my protest against all such doctrines, I have been greatly alarmed with the thoughtless precipitancy (not to use a stronger phrase) with which the most extensive and dangerous privileges have been granted of late. It can end in no good, and, I fear, may be the cause of convulsions hereafter. We already feel the effects on the currency, which no one competent of judging but must see is in an unsound condition. I must say (for truth compels me) I have ever distrusted the banking system, at least in its present form, both in this country and Great Britain. It will not stand the test of time; but I trust that all shocks, or sudden revolutions, may be avoided, and that it may gradually give way, before some sounder and better regulated system of credit, which the growing intelligence of the age may devise. That a better may be substituted I cannot doubt, but of what it shall consist, and how it shall finally supersede the present uncertain and fluctuating currency, time alone can determine. All I can see is, that the present must, one day or another, come to an end, or be greatly modified, if that, indeed, can save it from an entire overthrow. It has within itself the seeds of its own destruction.

From *Speeches of Mr. Calhoun of S[outh] Carolina, on the Bill for the Admission of Michigan. Delivered in the Senate of the United States, January, 1837* (Washington: printed by Duff Green, 1837), pp. 7–13. Also printed in the Washington, D.C., *Daily National Intelligencer*, January 18, 1837, p. 2; the Washington, D.C., *United States' Telegraph*, January 19, 1837, p. 2; *Register of Debates*, 24th Cong., 2nd Sess., cols. 295–305; the Washington, D.C., *Globe*, May 18, 1837, p. 2; *Congressional Globe*, 24th Cong., 2nd Sess., Appendix, pp. 284–287; *Speeches of John C. Calhoun*, pp. 249–259; Crallé, ed., *Works*, 2:597–616; John M. Anderson, ed., *Calhoun: Basic Documents*, pp. 191–208. Variant in the Washington, D.C., *United States' Telegraph*, January 6, 1837, p. 3. Another variant in the Washington, D.C., *Globe*, January 16, 1837, p. 2; *Congressional Globe*, 24th Cong., 2nd Sess., Appendix, pp. 84–86. Still other variants in the New York, N.Y., *Morning Courier and New-York Enquirer*, January 7, 1837, p. 2; the Washington, D.C., *United States' Telegraph*, January 12, 1837, p. 2 (from the New York, N.Y., *Journal of Commerce*); the Washington, D.C., *United States' Telegraph*, January 14, 1837, p. 2 (from the Philadelphia, Pa., *United States Gazette*). NOTE: After further debate on this day, in which Calhoun took part, the bill passed the Senate 25 to 10. The House of Representatives approved the bill on 1/25 by a vote of 132 to 43.

Remarks in debate with Robert Strange of N.C. on the bill for the admission of Michigan, 1/5. Calhoun interrupted a speech by Strange "to explain himself, and said that he had not declared Congress competent to create a State, either in or out of the Union; but by withdrawing its jurisdiction from a given Territory, that Territory was then at liberty to form itself into a State." From *Register of Debates*, 24th Cong., 2nd Sess., col. 306. Also printed in *Congressional Globe*, 24th Cong., 2nd Sess., Appendix, p. 86.

REMARKS IN DEBATE WITH JAMES BUCHANAN ON THE BILL FOR THE ADMISSION OF MICHIGAN

[In the Senate, January 5, 1837]
[During his speech favoring the bill Buchanan represented Calhoun as having argued that the people of a State could not meet in convention without permission of the State authorities. This he declared to be in contradiction to the statement in the Declaration of

Independence in regard to the right of the people to alter or abolish governments and institute new ones.]

Mr. Calhoun, interposing, said: Certainly; it is a revolutionary right!

[*Buchanan continued discussing the American Revolution, remarking that "Our very rights to seats upon this floor rest upon what" Calhoun calls "revolutionary principles."*]

Mr. Calhoun. Certainly: I never denied the right of revolution: I contended for it. All our institutions rest on that right; they are the fruits of revolution. That was the very proposition which led to the revolutionary war. I said that a convention of the people had power to put up and to throw down any and every form of government; but that is, *per ex*, a revolution.

[*Buchanan continued, arguing that Calhoun had contended that the people of a State had no redress against a faulty organization of government except an act of the Legislature authorizing a convention or an open rebellion. Later in his remarks Buchanan alluded to nullification and offered Calhoun a bargain: if he would never mention the domestic concerns of Pa. in the Senate, Buchanan would do the same for S.C. Calhoun said he was agreeable to such a bargain. Later Buchanan said Calhoun should have raised his objections in regard to Mich. at the previous session of Congress rather than now.*]

Mr. Calhoun rose to explain. He reminded Mr. B[uchanan] of the late hour at which the bill had passed. He had spoken again and again, in the course of the debate, and felt reluctant again to occupy the floor; and the particular reason why he had not stated this point of objection was, that, according to his conception, the word *convention* signified a meeting of the people, duly convened through the action of their own constituted authorities. So he understood the law, and so the people of Michigan understood it, as their action showed.

Mr. Buchanan resumed. The bill, as it originally stood, required the assent of the Legislature of Michigan; but this clause was unanimously stricken out, and the consent of a convention of delegates elected by the people was substituted in its place, by a unanimous vote of the Senate. The bill, as it passed, contains no reference to any interposition by the Legislature.

Mr. Calhoun again explained. It was indeed certain that the Legislature could not give their assent to the conditions of that bill, because those conditions touched the State constitution on the question of boundary, and, therefore, no power could assent to those conditions, but a power which was equal to that which made the constitution. This could be done only by a convention; and, in point of fact, it had been a convention which considered it. A convention regularly called was competent to consider and decide upon it, and it is a great mistake to think otherwise. But surely, if a regular convention was incompetent to assent, and thereby change the State constitution, the meeting at Ann Arbor could not be competent.

[*Buchanan continued his speech for some time.*]

Mr. Calhoun here requested a few words of explanation, to which Mr. Buchanan signifying his assent, Mr. C[alhoun] proceeded. The Senator [Calhoun said] admits that Michigan is a State; that, waiving forms, she was a State as soon as we recognised her constitution. I wish, then, to ask the honorable Senator whether he holds that Congress has a right to call a convention within a State.

Mr. Buchanan. To that question I answer, no. Emphatically, no. Congress has no more right to call a convention in South Carolina than in the moon. But, before the State of Michigan has entered the Union, Congress possesses the power of proposing to her a condition, upon a compliance with which she shall be admitted. The proposition thus presented she may accept or reject, according to her will and pleasure; and she may accept it, if she thinks proper, by means of a convention of delegates elected for that purpose, in the manner proposed to her by Congress.

Mr. Calhoun. Then I would further ask the Senator, has Congress a right to offer a proposition to the people of a State without addressing their Legislature?

Mr. Buchanan. Under the circumstances in which Michigan stood, Congress, in my opinion, had the right to make the proposition which they did make at the last session, and it was for the people of Michigan, in their sovereign capacity, to assent or dissent, as they thought proper.

Mr. Calhoun. Congress has a right to make propositions to her constituted authorities, and the people of Michigan so understood our act.

Mr. Buchanan. The Senator will pardon me for contradicting him. The people of Michigan did not so understand our act. One of the very first acts of the first convention was to declare that the Legislature had no right to call that convention. The sovereign people of Michigan themselves objected to any interposition of their Legislature.

Mr. Calhoun. Then the whole matter amounts to this: when a State has provided a regular course for amending her own constitution, and the State does not choose to call a convention in conformity with that constitution, Congress may call a convention in that State to alter her State constitution.

Mr. Buchanan, (in an under tone.) This may be the gentleman's inference; it is not mine.

From *Register of Debates*, 24th Cong., 2nd Sess., cols. 313–317. Also printed in the Washington, D.C., *Daily National Intelligencer*, February 6, 1837, p. 1; the Washington, D.C., *Globe*, February 10, 1837, p. 2; *Congressional Globe*, 24th Cong., 2nd Sess., Appendix, pp. 148–150. Variant in the Richmond, Va., *Whig and Public Advertiser*, January 10, 1837, p. 2.

Motion to ascertain undrawn appropriations, 1/6. "Resolved that the Secretary of the Treasury [Levi Woodbury] be directed to report to the Senate as early as practicable the undrawn appropriations on the 1st day [of] January ["last" *canceled*] Inst[ant] with the date[s] of the acts making such appropriations." This motion was adopted on 1/6. ADU in DNA, RG 46 (Records of the U.S. Senate), 24A-B10; PC in *Senate Journal*, 24th Cong., 2nd Sess., p. 95.

Remarks on a memorial for the erection of U.S. public buildings in Philadelphia, 1/6. James Buchanan presented a memorial from the citizens of Philadelphia praying for an appropriation for a building to house the U.S. courts in that city and also for a U.S. penitentiary. Calhoun "said he had no objection to its being referred to the Committee on the Judiciary; but he hoped they would pause and weigh the question a long time before they would give their assent to our commencing a penitentiary system of the United States. There was patronage enough exercised by the General Government already—its powers were great and extensive, without their being introduced into a State. He objected to a State and General Government acting together. He merely threw out these suggestions to the committee, in the hope that they would pause a long time before they would give their sanction to the commencement of the proposed system." From *Register of Debates*, 24th Cong., 2nd Sess., col. 326. Also printed in the Washington, D.C., *Globe*, January 7, 1837, p. 3; *Congressional Globe*, 24th Cong., 2nd Sess., pp. 75–76. Variants in the Washington, D.C., *United States' Telegraph*, January 6, 1837, p. 3, and January 7, 1837, p. 3; the Washington, D.C., *Daily National Intelligencer*, January 7, 1837, p. 3.

To JOHN R. MATHEW[E]S, Charleston, S.C.

Washington, 7th Jan[uar]y 1837
My dear Sir, Previously to receiving your letter, I saw Mr. [George W.] Owens [Representative from Ga.] and requested his attention to our mail route; and also spoke to Mr. [Felix] Grundy [Senator from Tenn.], who was Chairman of the Post office Committee the last year. I could do nothing with the Post Master Gen[era]l [Amos Kendall] myself. Mr. Owens wrote me a note yesterday, saying that he had attended to the subject, and that ["the" *canceled*] a two horse coach would be put on the route, once a week; so that, I presume, it will go into operation in the spring.

I have no doubt our teacher, Mr. [Thomas] Wayland, is abundantly competent to teach all the ordinary branches of Mathematicks. He is an Englishman, and had the advantages in his education of some of their best schools. He is remarkably kind and attentive to his pupils, and the [Pendleton] school promises well. I think you will be pleased with it.

I am not aware, that Capt. [William George] Williams has reported against the practicability of the route by the Carolina Gap. He has, indeed, made a report, which no doubt was intended to make that impression; but he has not ventured to give such an opinion. It is easy to make an impression by a partial survey, that any route over the Allegany [Mountains] is impracticable. All that is necessary is to drop down from the summit by the shortest line to the basis [*sic*], and stop the survey there, without showing the means of overcoming the elevation by developing to the right, or left. Suppose a line to be dropped down from the Rabun gap by the nearest and steepest route to the Tugalo[o River] (an elevation of 14,500 [*sic*] feet) and the survey to stop there, all would pronounce it impracticable. That is just about what Capt. Williams has done at the Carolina gap.

I have read his report, and as far as the survey had gone at the time of making it, there is no doubt of the practicability, and that with a very favourable ascent, as much so as that stated in my letter [of 9/22/1836]; and I have no fear, ["but" *interlined*] that a full & impartial survey by Col. [Abbott Hall] Brisbane, or any other competent and ["skilful" *canceled and* "impartial" *interlined*] Engineer would confirm the statement throughout.

I have collected much information here, which goes to show in the clearest manner the vast importance that our great work should bear as far west as possible—as far at least as the route by the Carolina gap. I shall at the proper time present the whole in a digested form, so that if the Company is determined to make a ruinous selection, they shall do it with their eyes open.

The govern[me]nt is still verging more & more towards anarchy & revolution, of which we have strong proof in the ["mode" *canceled*] principle on which it is proposed to admit Michigan. I would call your attention to the debate, as I hope our papers will that of the State.

We will have the abolition question up on Monday [1/9], on petitions to be presented on that day.

I think the currency is in a critical condition. It is a bad period at which to enlarge our banking Capital and business. It is time to reef, not to spread sails.

My best respects to Mrs. [Elizabeth Jenkins Whaley] Mathew[e]s & your family. Yours truely & sincerely, J.C. Calhoun.

ALS in DLC, John C. Calhoun Papers. NOTE: The school referred to in the second paragraph was the recently-organized Pendleton Academy of which Calhoun was at this time a trustee and his son, John C. Calhoun, Jr., a student. Abbott Hall Brisbane (died 1861), a former officer of U.S. Army Topographical Engineers, was one of the commissioners appointed by S.C. to survey a route, along with James Gadsden and James G. Holmes. John Raven Mathewes (1788–1867) was a partner in Mathewes & Bonneau of Charleston and also a planter in St. Bartholomew's Parish, Colleton District. Apparently, also, like Calhoun, he had interests in northern Ga. where he spent much time. He signed himself "Mathewes" but was usually addressed by Calhoun and others as "Mathews."

From J[OHN] E[WING] BONNEAU

Ch[arle]sTon, S.C., 10th January 1837

D[ea]r Sir, Your two letters of 7th & 29th Ult[imo] I have received—the former enclosing a draft for $170 which has been carried to your credit—and a note of Mr. Gibbs Ag[en]t of the Vaucluse factory, which I have attended to & paid—say, $100. In regard to your obtaining a loan at one of the banks here for 4 or 5,000 dollars, with the understanding of an indulgence for one or two years, I see no difficulty in the way of your being accommodated. Should you require it, I think it can be obtained from the Bank of the State [of South Carolina]. I have seen & conversed with Judge [Charles Jones] Colcock the President of the Bank on the subject, & he says, that there is no doubt, but the bank will very readily accommodate you. Under these circumstances, as soon as you may require the money, you can send on to me, a blank with your signature, & I will fill it up for the amount & in the form required by the bank, and will then inform you as to the renewals, as I expect they will require the note to be renewed every 60 or 90 days.

Mrs. [Floride Colhoun] Calhoun's draft for $105 $\frac{38}{100}$ for her supplies for the ["present" *interlined*] year, purchased in Augusta, has been presented & paid. The white lead, paint oil & turpentine as directed in your letter of 29th Ult[imo] shall be forwarded immediately to Pendleton. Your enquiry as to the prospect of Cotton, whether, it will hold its own or decline, I confess, I feel some embarrasement [*sic*] in giving an opinion. The money concerns in Europe appear to be in such a deranged state, which must tend to effect [*sic*] the price—and added to which, the general impression both here & on the ["other" *interlined*] side of the water is, that the crop of last year will greatly exceed in *quantity* that of the preceeding [*sic*] year, leaves me in great doubt, as to any enhanced price. My own impression is, that it will be best, to take your own time in getting your Cotton into market; & to take the chances of the market.

Colo[nel John Ewing] Colhoun's wife [Martha Maria Davis Colhoun] & 4 children are now here & intend passing a month in Charleston. They are all well. The Colo[nel] is expected here about the 1st of the next month. We are all well. Do present our best respects to your daughters [Anna Maria Calhoun and Martha Cornelia Calhoun], and [I] remain D[ea]r Sir very respectfully Y[ou]r's &c. &c. J.E. Bonneau.

[P.S.] Judge Colcock is desirous of hearing from you, on the Deposite question.

ALS in ScU-SC, John C. Calhoun Papers.

REMARKS ON RESCINDING ANDREW JACKSON'S SPECIE CIRCULAR

[In the Senate, January 11, 1837]
[*Under consideration was a motion by Thomas Ewing to rescind the Treasury order designating what funds could be received in payment for public lands. John M. Niles moved to refer Ewing's proposal to the Committee on the Public Lands.*]

Mr. Calhoun briefly characterized the Treasury order, as unconstitutional, without law, without precedent, without any authority whatever. Its temporary character, under which refuge had been taken, was nowhere to be seen; on the contrary, it still continued in force, when the Executive himself ought to have repealed it, if it had been temporary. If it should be now referred, he could see no reason for referring it to the Committee on Public Lands. It partook wholly of a financial character, and its proper reference was, therefore, to the Committee on Finance. Mr. C[alhoun] said he depended on the action of that committee, whether there should be a recurrence of that state of things in the ensuing year, as well as the past, which had been used as the pretext for the Treasury order. The state of things, he urged, depended entirely on the accumulation of the surplus in the deposite banks, where it would not remain for nothing, but would be employed as it had been, in speculating on the public lands. To the Committee on Finance, he also looked for a reduction of duties, if that should be adopted as a preventive. The whole subject properly belonged to that committee, to which Mr. C[alhoun] would move to refer it if the motion of Mr. Niles should fail.

From the Richmond, Va., *Enquirer*, January 14, 1837, p. 2. Variant in the Washington, D.C., *United States' Telegraph*, January 12, 1837, p. 3. Another variant in the Washington, D.C., *Daily National Intelligencer*, January 12, 1837, p. 3, and *Register of Debates*, 24th Cong., 2nd Sess., cols. 375–376. NOTE: Niles's motion was approved 22 to 19.

Remarks on postponing the public land bill, 1/12. Robert J. Walker of Miss. was pushing consideration of a bill "to limit the sales of the public lands, except to actual settlers, and in limited quantities." Calhoun followed Henry Clay in arguing for postponement. "Mr. Calhoun regretted to hear that the chairman of the committee intended to go on with the bill. He had not the slightest idea that it would be taken up so soon, and had not, therefore, given any examination to the subject of it; he had not even had time to read the bill itself. He deemed it to be one of the most important subjects that could engage the attention of Congress, not only as regarded the revenue, but as it regarded the future policy of the country; and he hoped the Senate would not go on with it until every member had an opportunity of obtaining all the information necessary to a full understanding of the subject. He himself wished time for an examination, the better to enable him to understand the arguments that might be used either for or against the measure, and therefore proposed" postponement until 1/16. Later in the discussion Calhoun "remarked, that as one of the opposition, and being desirous of as little delay as possible, still he would tell gentlemen on the other side that he would afford them every opportunity of discussing the subject. But whilst he said this, he claimed from the majority that they should hear gentlemen of the opposition patiently, and give a reasonable time for discussion. He would not have asked the delay of one day, had it not been absolutely necessary; and he was not disposed to allow so important a subject as the present to be hurried through the Senate without bestowing on it all the attention it deserved." From *Register of Debates*, 24th Cong., 2nd Sess., cols. 378–379. Also printed in the Washington, D.C., *Globe*, January 13, 1837, p. 3; *Congressional Globe*, 24th Cong., 2nd Sess., p. 91. Variants in the Washington, D.C., *Daily National Intelligencer*, January 13, 1837, p. 3; the Richmond, Va., *Enquirer*, January 17, 1837, p. 2.

Remarks on reduction of the revenue, 1/12. Calhoun moved that the Senate postpone the order of the day and take up his bill to extend the distribution features of the deposit act of 1836. Felix Grundy remarked that a bill to regulate the sales of public lands was scheduled for consideration. This bill should be considered first, since its passage would affect whether there would be a surplus for distribution. Calhoun expressed his acquiescence. He was anxious to see what the Committee on Finance "intended to do in the way of a reduction of revenue. He wished to know from the chairman of that committee [Silas Wright], whether they proposed making a report on that subject; and if so, at what time. He desired to make the action on his own bill subordinate to that on the land bill, and to the report of the Committee on Finance." Wright replied that the subject was under consideration but he could not say when a report would be made. Calhoun said he was willing to postpone his bill for a week. "He wished for all the information possible, and greatly preferred a reduction of the revenue to depositing the surplus with the States. All gentlemen should have a fair opportunity of examining the subject. He must say that, when he looked at the state of things here, he felt but very little faith that a reduction would be made this session, as the time had now so far advanced that there would scarcely be an opportunity of acting on the subject." Calhoun further remarked that a call for information from the Secretary of the Treasury that had been made [on 1/6] by the Senate on his motion had not yet been answered. From *Register of Debates*,

24th Cong., 2nd Sess., cols. 376–377. Also printed in the Washington, D.C., *Globe*, January 13, 1837, p. 3; *Congressional Globe*, 24th Cong., 2nd Sess., p. 90. Variant in the Washington, D.C., *United States' Telegraph*, January 12, 1837, p. 3; the Washington, D.C., *Daily National Intelligencer*, January 13, 1837, p. 3. Another variant in the New York, N.Y., *Morning Courier and New-York Enquirer*, January 14, 1837, p. 2.

REMARKS ON THE MOTION TO EXPUNGE THE
SENATE'S CENSURE OF ANDREW JACKSON

[In the Senate, January 13, 1837]
[The proposal, introduced by Thomas H. Benton, to expunge the censure of Jackson that had been adopted in 1834 was under debate. A motion to adjourn had just failed 20 to 22.]

Mr. Calhoun then rose and addressed the Senate nearly as follows:

The gentleman from Virginia (Mr. [William C.] Rives) says that the argument in favor of this expunging resolution has not been answered. Sir, there are some questions so plain that they cannot be argued. Nothing can make them more plain; and this is one. No one, not blinded by party zeal, can possibly be insensible that the measure proposed is a violation of the constitution. The constitution requires the Senate to keep a journal; this resolution goes to expunge the journal. If you may expunge a part, you may expunge the whole; and if it is expunged, how is it kept? The constitution says the journal shall be kept; this resolution says it shall be destroyed. It does the very thing which the constitution declares shall not be done. That is the argument, the whole argument. There is no other. Talk of precedents? and precedents drawn from a foreign country? They don't apply. No, sir. This is to be done, not in consequence of argument, but in spite of argument. I understand the case. I know perfectly well the gentlemen have no liberty to vote otherwise. They are coerced by an exterior power. They try, indeed, to comfort their conscience by saying that it is the will of the people, and the voice of the people. It is no such thing. We all know how these legislative returns have been obtained. It is by dictation from the White House. The President himself, with that vast mass of patronage which he wields, and the thousand expectations he is able to hold up, has obtained these votes of the State Legislatures; and this, forsooth, is said to be the voice of the people. The voice of the people! Sir, can we forget the scene which was exhibited in this chamber when that expunging resolution was first introduced here? Have we forgotten the universal giving way of conscience, so that the Senator from Missouri [Benton] was left alone? I see before me Senators who could not swallow that resolution; and has its nature changed since then? Is it any more constitutional now than it was then? Not at all. But executive power has interposed. Talk to me of the voice of the people! No, sir. It is the combination of patronage and power to coerce this body into a gross and palpable violation of the constitution. Some individuals, I perceive, think to escape through the particular form in which this act is to be perpetrated. They tell us that the resolution on your records is not to be expunged, but is only to be endorsed "Expunged." Really, sir, I do not know how to argue against such contemptible sophistry. The occasion is too solemn for an argument of this sort. You are going to violate the constitution, and you get rid of the infamy by a falsehood. You yourselves say that the resolution is expunged by your order. Yet you say it is not expunged. You put your act in express words. You record it, and then turn round and deny it.

But what is the motive? What is the pretext for this enormity? Why, gentlemen tell us the Senate has two distinct consciences—a legislative conscience, and a judicial conscience. As a legislative body we have decided that the President has violated the constitution. But gentlemen tell us that this is an impeachable offence; and, as we may be called to try it in our judicial capacity, we have no right to express the opinion. I need not show how inconsistent such a position is with the eternal, imprescriptible right of freedom of speech, and how utterly inconsistent it is with precedents drawn from the history of our British ancestors, where the same liberty of speech has for centuries been enjoyed. There is a shorter and more direct argument in reply. Gentlemen who take that position cannot, according to their own showing, vote for this resolution; for if it is unconstitutional for us to record a resolution of condemnation, because we may afterwards be called to try the case in a judicial capacity, then it is equally unconstitutional for us to record a resolution of acquittal. If it is unconstitutional for the Senate to declare before a trial that the President has violated the constitution, it is equally unconstitutional to declare before a trial that he has not violated the constitution. The same principle is involved in both.

Yet, in the very face of this principle, gentlemen are here going to condemn their own act.

But why do I waste my breath? I know it is all utterly vain. The day is gone; night approaches, and night is suitable to the dark deed we meditate. There is a sort of destiny in this thing. The act must be performed; and it is an act which will tell on the political history of this country forever. Other preceding violations of the constitution (and they have been many and great) filled my bosom with indignation, but this fills it only with grief. Others were done in the heat of party. Power was, as it were, compelled to support itself by seizing upon new instruments of influence and patronage; and there were ambitious and able men to direct the process. Such was the removal of the deposites, which the President seized upon by a new and unprecedented act of arbitrary power; an act which gave him ample means of rewarding friends and punishing enemies. Something may, perhaps, be pardoned to him in this matter, on the old apology of tyrants—the plea of necessity. But here there can be no such apology. Here no necessity can so much as be pretended. This act originates in pure, unmixed, personal idolatry. It is the melancholy evidence of a broken spirit, ready to bow at the feet of power. The former act was such a one as might have been perpetrated in the days of Pompey or Caesar; but an act like this could never have been consummated by a Roman Senate until the times of Caligula and Nero.

[*A motion for adjournment was now carried.*]

From *Register of Debates*, 24th Cong., 2nd Sess., cols. 417–418. Also printed in the Washington, D.C., *Daily National Intelligencer*, March 20, 1837, p. 2; the Washington, D.C., *Reformer*, March 21, 1837, p. 2; the Pendleton, S.C., *Messenger*, May 12, 1837, p. 1; *Niles' Weekly Register*, vol. LII, no. 8 (April 22, 1837), p. 120.

To N[ATHAN] LOUGHBOROUGH

Senate Chamber, 16th Jan[uar]y 1837

My dear Sir, I have read the remonstrance with much satisfaction. It is strong, decorous & to the point.

I gave it to [Joseph] Kent [Senator from Md.], who will present it tomorrow, and have spoken to Mr. [Francis W.] Pickens [Repre-

sentative from S.C.] to attend to it in the House when presented by
Mr. [George C.] Washington [Representative from Md.]. Truely,
J.C. Calhoun.

ALS in DNDAR. NOTE: In the remonstrance referred to above the Washington County, D.C., grand jury called upon Congress "to arrest, and finally put a
stop to" the progress of petitions for the abolition of slavery in the District of
Columbia. The remonstrance was printed as Senate Document No. 75, 24th
Cong., 2nd Sess. Loughborough was foreman of the grand jury.

Remarks on the expunging motion, 1/16. During a long debate
by others, Calhoun "said that one of the amendments proposed was
to insert in the place of *'unconstitutional'* the words *'not warranted
by the constitution'* [in reference to the Senate's action of 3/28/1834
which was to be expunged]. He supposed that the latter words
meant no more nor less than the former." (At the end of the debate
the expunging motion was adopted by a vote of 24 to 19, and the
journal of 1834 was brought out and altered by the Secretary of the
Senate.) From the Washington, D.C., *United States' Telegraph,*
January 17, 1837, p. 2. Variant in the Washington, D.C., *Daily National Intelligencer,* January 18, 1837, p. 2.

Remarks on the arrest of a spectator for disorderly conduct, 1/17.
"On the reading of the Journal, Mr. Calhoun enquired whether the
proceedings at the conclusion of the sitting on yesterday in reference to the person arrested by the order of the Senate [in the tumult
which had followed the expunging of the journal], were legal, there
not being a majority of the body present. [The person had been
detained for a time and then released.] He thought that the constitution required a majority of the whole number, by which he
understood a majority, not only of the members who had taken their
seats, but of the whole number whose credentials had been received
and read." When William R. King disagreed, Calhoun said "he did
not intend to make the question *now.* He only wished to call the
attention of the body to the fact." From the Washington, D.C.,
United States' Telegraph, January 17, 1837, p. 3. Variant in the
Washington, D.C., *Daily National Intelligencer,* January 18, 1837,
p. 3. (According to another report of this occasion, Calhoun said
24 votes had been recorded "last night." He "had always understood
the Constitution to require a majority of the entire number of the
Senators to make a quorum, and he suggested that it is an important
question which ought now to be decided, whether 26 made a quorum
of the Senate, or 24, as had been understood last night." From the
Richmond, Va., *Enquirer,* January 21, 1837, p. 2.)

Remarks on the Petition from the Washington County Grand Jury against Receiving Abolition Petitions

[In the Senate, January 17, 1837]

[Joseph Kent of Md. presented a memorial from the grand jury of Washington County, D.C., opposing the reception by Congress of petitions for the abolition of slavery in the District of Columbia. It was moved to print extra copies of the petition for distribution.]

Mr. Calhoun said that he was pleased to see that the memorial took the proper ground. These petitions ought to be arrested at once, and the only course to adopt was to refuse to receive them. The subject was of the highest importance, and no countenance ought to be given by Congress to the machinations of a body of men, who seemed equally forgetful of the constitution and the rights and safety of a large portion of the people. He deprecated the introduction of these petitions when they were first thrown before Congress, and considered it an imperative duty to arrest them at once and forever.

[Garret D. Wall of N.J. argued against printing the extra copies because the petition would infringe the abolitionists' right of petition.]

Mr. Calhoun briefly replied, stating that the people of the District were, by the constitution, as fully secured in their rights as slaveholders, as any other citizens were to any other species of property. This was, to his mind, as clear as any proposition could be. The abolitionists petition Congress to divest these individuals of their rights in this kind of property. Had they any right to be heard in such a matter? Upon what ground can such a right be defended? On the other hand, the people of the District, whose rights were thus assailed, were entitled to be heard—had the right to demand that Congress should not receive the petitions, and to spread their reasons before the public. Their property, their peace, and their security, were put in jeopardy by the agitations produced by these petitions. Congress ought not to receive them, because they had no right to legislate on the subject, and the abolitionists no right to ask that they should.

[Bedford Brown of N.C. wished to avoid any implication that Congress could legislate on the subject and hinted that the purpose of the petition was to excite public opinion, which he deplored.]

Mr. Calhoun expressed his astonishment at the remarks of the Senator from North Carolina. Who *agitates* this question? The abolitionists or the slaveholders? Who keeps up the excitement? When the rights of the slaveholder are assailed, are they to sit quiet? Do they agitate the subject? And does the Senator mean to say that when the fanatics are organizing and concentrating their forces and means over a large portion of the Union—when they have already succeeded in a great measure, in bringing the public mind under their control in many of the States—that the slaveholder shall not be heard in defence of his property and fireside, lest it might *agitate* the public feelings? Are they to be denounced for defending themselves? Shall they be charged with a purpose of producing agitation?

[*After further debate the motion to print extra copies was approved 34 to 5.*]

From the Washington, D.C., *United States' Telegraph*, January 18, 1837, p. 3. Variant in *Register of Debates*, 24th Cong., 2nd Sess., cols. 507–511; *Congressional Globe*, 24th Cong., 2nd Sess., Appendix, pp. 110–112. Other variants in the Washington, D.C., *United States' Telegraph*, January 17, 1837, p. 3; the New York, N.Y., *Morning Courier and New-York Enquirer*, January 19, 1837, p. 2. NOTE: In the somewhat different and longer version of Calhoun's remarks in the *Register of Debates* he was reported as arguing, in addition to the above points, that "with respect to the people of the District of Columbia, when their rights were affected, they were compelled to look to Congress for protection. . . . As to the people of the States, they could be heard by their own Legislatures; and if they were not able to protect themselves, they would not receive protection from any quarter." He was also reported as saying that "slaves were as much the property" of the citizens of D.C. as "stocks, houses, or lands, were to those who would deprive them of their rights and property."

To J[ohn] K. Porter, C.M. Davidson, and T. Dodd, [Schenectady, N.Y.,] 1/18. Calhoun thanks them for an invitation from the three literary societies of Union College to address them at commencement next July. However, his "long absence from home . . . with my many engagements both publick & private" during the recess of Congress, make it impossible for him to meet the request. ALS in ScU-SC, John C. Calhoun Papers.

REMARKS ON THE BILL TO ANTICIPATE PAYMENT OF THE FRENCH AND NEAPOLITAN INDEMNITIES

[*In the Senate, January 18, 1837*]
[*Silas Wright, Chairman of the Committee on Finance, presented and argued for a bill which would loan $2,800,000 at four per cent*

interest to certain U.S. citizens who were claimants for indemnification for spoliations during the Napoleonic Wars. The Treasury was to be repaid the funds loaned when installments were collected under treaties that had been concluded with France and the Kingdom of the Two Sicilies.]

Mr. Calhoun expressed his utter astonishment at the course of the administration party, and the contradictions, gross and glaring, in their declarations. The members of the committee, the chairman himself, had said a short time since that there would be no surplus —that the deposite bill had robbed the Government of the means of meeting the outstanding appropriations. This was the language too, of the Treasury and the Executive. Now, there is a surplus— a surplus large enough to authorize a loan of two millions and a half to favored individuals at four per cent. per annum. One day the Treasury is empty—another it is full—and then again, it is empty. How are these contradictions to be reconciled? He was glad to hear now, from one whose opinion might influence the party, that there would be a surplus. It would show the necessity of reduction, and leave no pretext for leaving the excess in the banks. He expressed his opposition to the bill on constitutional grounds. The constitution gave no countenance to the system. It was not the first time the scheme had been before Congress. It was but another effort to extend the patronage of the Government. Is it not already great enough? It was a dangerous precedent, and he trusted the Senate would not, by regarding it as a party measure, give it any countenance. There was no telling where it would stop. The case of the bank deposites and this had no similarity whatever. The public money was deposited in the banks *for safe keeping*—but this was a *loan*, a gratuity to favored individuals. But he understood the motives, and saw the objects of gentlemen. This scheme of *private loans* was intended to get rid of the deposite bill, and place the surplus in the hands of Government. This was the object aimed at. It was now confessed that there would be a surplus.

[*Debate continued, and Wright once more defended the bill.*]

Mr. Calhoun said, in reply, that the Senator had failed to answer the constitutional objections. He had put the question on grounds of expediency only. And yet he pretended to be a *strict constructionist*. His party professed to be *strict constructionists*. Time was when men professing such principles looked to the constitution as a guide. A Senator from North Carolina (Mr. [Robert] Strange,) had said, a few days ago, in debate, that the constitution had "*no spirit in it*"; that he looked only to the "*words.*" Show, then, the words which authorize this extraordinary measure. No, sir, there is a different purpose now to answer. There is a *"spirit"* now, and *strict construction* is stale and unprofitable. He adverted to the charge that he was and had been in favor of creating a surplus, and desired to know whether he had understood the Senator correctly. (Mr. Wright remained silent.) He continued, and said that he had seen the charge published in a *"dirty sheet,"* [the Washington *Globe?*] as the Secretary of State [John Forsyth?] had called it, in this city, and also in another of the same character printed in the city (Albany) [the *Argus?*] where the Senator resided; but he had never expected to hear *the gross and palpable falsehood* uttered elsewhere. He had ever opposed the system from the time Gen. Jackson first recommended it until the present. The time would come, the occasion would shortly present itself, when he would justify his own course, and expose that of others high in office in regard to the subject. He knew, and *they* knew, who are obnoxious to the charge.

He implored the Senate to pause, and not give its sanction to this monstrous precedent. Our country is emphatically one of *precedents.* This was the commencement of a new system of Government patronage, under the countenance of those who *profess* to be *strict constructionists.*

From the Washington, D.C., *United States' Telegraph*, January 19, 1837, p. 3. Also printed in the Washington, D.C., *Daily National Intelligencer*, April 13, 1837, p. 2. Variant in the Washington, D.C., *Daily National Intelligencer*, January 20, 1837, p. 2; *Register of Debates*, 24th Cong., 2nd Sess., cols. 516–521. Another variant in the New York, N.Y., *Morning Courier and New-York Enquirer*, January 20, 1837, p. 2. NOTE: Calhoun spoke once more in this day's debate to refute again an implied accusation by Wright that Calhoun was in favor of accumulating a Treasury surplus for purposes of distribution. On the question of engrossment for a third reading the bill failed this day 19 to 22. In the fuller rendering of Calhoun's remarks in the *Register of Debates*, Calhoun was reported as contrasting ironically Wright's announcement of the availability of a surplus for this loan with Thomas H. Benton's attacks on the deposit bill as having depleted the Treasury to the point that needed appropriations could not be covered. Calhoun also described a loan at 4 per cent as "a pure gift" to "certain individuals" since the prevailing interest rate was "two and three per cent. a month."

REMARKS ON THE INDEPENDENCE OF TEXAS

[In the Senate, January 19, 1837]
[President Andrew Jackson had sent to the Senate copies of his recent correspondence with President Santa Anna of Mexico, who

asked for U.S. good offices in restoring peace between Mexico and Texas.]

Mr. Calhoun said he had always entertained the opinion that the people of Texas could never live under the Mexican Government in peace and happiness. He had thought, too, that it was our duty, at the earliest period practicable, to recognise the independence of Texas. He felt certain, from the events which had occurred in that country, that unless a speedy stop was put to what was going on there, the Rio del Norte [*sic*] would not be made the boundary of Texas. She would shake the Mexican empire to its very centre, if the controversy existing between her and Mexico should not instantly cease. He was ready to acknowledge her independence; and the sooner that was done the better.

From *Register of Debates*, 24th Cong., 2nd Sess., col. 528. Also printed in the Washington, D.C., *Globe*, January 21, 1837, p. 2; *Congressional Globe*, 24th Cong., 2nd Sess., p. 109. Variants in the Washington, D.C., *United States' Telegraph*, January 19, 1837, p. 3; the Washington, D.C., *Daily National Intelligencer*, January 20, 1837, p. 3; the Charleston, S.C., *Mercury*, January 25, 1837, p. 2.

ADVERTISEMENT BY THE TRUSTEES OF PENDLETON ACADEMY

Pendleton, Jan. 20 [1837]

The Trustees of this Institution deem it their duty to inform the public, that the Academy is now in operation under the direction of Mr. T[homas] Wayland. During the period he has been engaged, the Trustees have had reason to be satisfied with his qualifications, and hope the Institution may widely spread the benefits it is calculated to confer.

Price of Tuition ten dollars per q[uarte]r.

Good boarding can be had in the village and neighborhood on moderate terms. [Signed:] Fr[anci]s K. Huger, John C. Calhoun, J[oseph] N. Whitner, Sam[ue]l Cherry, J[oseph] V. Shanklin, James Stuart, Jesse P. Lewis, F[rederick] W. Symmes, Sam[ue]l Prioleau, Trustees.

PC in the Pendleton, S.C., *Messenger*, January 20, 1837, p. 3, and several subsequent issues.

From Levi Woodbury, [Secretary of the Treasury,] 1/20. In answer to Calhoun's inquiry of 1/19 [*not found*], Woodbury states that the Comptroller of S.C., [William] Laval, has complied with "the requisitions of law relative to the distributive share of that State of the surplus revenue." Two drafts have been issued in favor of S.C., one for $170,000 and one for $180,474.03, "the receipts for the sums being executed, a form of which was enclosed with the drafts." FC in DNA, RG 56 (General Records of the Department of the Treasury), Letters and Reports to Congress, Series E, 9:263; FC in DNA, RG 56, Letters to Individual Members of Congress, Series E, 1:237.

[To Mrs. Mary Barney, Baltimore, 1/24.] "If he [your son] will forward me suitable testimonials as to his capacity and skill as Engineer, I will give him a letter to Gen. [Robert Y.] Hayne, the president of our great railroad company. . . ." Abs of an ALS offered for sale by Anderson Galleries, New York City, in Catalogues No. 786 (1909), No. 904 (1911), and No. 1319 (1917).

Remarks on the bill for the relief of the executrix of Richard W. Meade, 1/25. Calhoun "thought it wrong to press the Bill until the new members should have had time to become informed as to its merits. Great diversity of opinion prevailed concerning this Bill among men of the greatest ability." After further discussion the bill "was amended and ordered to be engrossed." From the New York, N.Y., *Morning Courier and New-York Enquirer*, January 27, 1837, p. 2.

REMARKS ON THE AMERICAN COLONIZATION SOCIETY MEMORIAL

[In the Senate, January 27, 1837]
[Henry Clay presented a petition requesting Congress to grant a charter of incorporation to the American Colonization Society in D.C. so that it would be enabled to hold and convey real estate that had been donated to it. Clay moved the reference of the petition to the Committee on the District of Columbia.]

Mr. Calhoun regretted that the Senator from Kentucky had thought fit to present this memorial, and deprecated any discussion or agitation of the subject, which he thought would rather tend to increase than allay the excitement which had been produced by an injudicious interference with a question of much delicacy. He did not intend to oppose the reference of the memorial, but he indulged the hope that the committee would see the propriety of not acting on it during this session.

[*Clay defended his course.*]

Mr. Calhoun after some remarks in reply to Mr. Clay, said that from the first to the last he had been under the impression that any interference with the objects of this society by the General Government would not only be unconstitutional, but would have the most mischievous effects. He would remind the Senator from Kentucky, who had mentioned the late Mr. [James] Madison as one of the friends of the Colonization Society, that that great statesman was so strict in his notions as to the granting of charters by the General Government, that he had vetoed the act of Congress incorporating a church in Alexandria [D.C.]. The Senator from Kentucky must know that great diversity of opinion existed among the wisest and best men of the country as to the ultimate good to be effected by this society; and that the prevailing opinion of the great body of the people of the South was against it. Nine tenths of the Southern people at least, said Mr. C[alhoun], were opposed to any interference with the objects of this Society by the General Government.

[*Discussion continued among Clay, Robert J. Walker, and James Buchanan.*]

Mr. Calhoun conceived that the Senator from Pennsylvania [Buchanan] had taken the proper view of the question. He thought, too, that it should be referred to a select committee. The Senator from Kentucky and himself view the subject in a very different point of view. A mysterious Providence had brought the black and the white people together from different parts of the globe, and no human power could now separate them. The whites are an European race, being masters; and the Africans are the inferior race, and slaves. He believed that they could exist among us peaceably enough, if undisturbed, for all time; and it was his opinion that the Colonization Society, and all the other schemes which had been gotten up through mistaken notions of philanthropy, in order to bring about an alteration in the condition of the African, had a wrong foundation, and were calculated to disturb the existing relations between the races, and the relations between the North and the South. He knew the Senator from Kentucky viewed the subject in a very different light, for he had stated on many occasions the opinions he held. He (Mr. C[alhoun]) believed that the very existence of the South depended upon the existing relations being kept up, and that every scheme which might be introduced, having for its object an alteration in the

371

condition of the negro, was pregnant with danger and ruin. It was a benevolent object, and highly desirable that the blessings of civilization and Christianity should be introduced into benighted Africa; but this was a Government of limited powers, and had no more to do with free negroes than with slaves; and if Africa was to be Christianized and civilized, he hoped it would not be done by this Government acting beyond its constitutional powers. It was a matter of little importance to him, whether the memorial should be referred to a select committee, or to the Committee on the District of Columbia.

From *Register of Debates*, 24th Cong., 2nd Sess., cols. 564–567. Also printed in the Washington, D.C., *Globe,* January 30, 1837, p. 2; *Congressional Globe,* 24th Cong., 2nd Sess., p. 130. Variants in the Washington, D.C., *United States' Telegraph,* January 28, 1837, pp. 2–3, and February 2, 1837, p. 2; the Washington, D.C., *Daily National Intelligencer,* January 28, 1837, p. 3; the Charleston, S.C., *Southern Patriot,* February 1, 1837, p. 2.

Motion in Regard to the British Seizure of Slaves on Board the Brigs *Encomium* and *Enterprise*

[Submitted to the Senate, January 28, 1837]
Resolved, That the President [Andrew Jackson] be requested to communicate to the Senate, ["if not inconsistent with the public interest," *interlined*] a copy of the correspondence with the Government of Great Britain, in relation to the outrage committed on our Flag and the rights of our citizens, by the Authorities of Bermuda and New Providence, in seizing the slaves on board of the brigs Encomium and Enterprize, engaged in the coasting trade, ["but" *interlined*] which were forced by shipwreck and ["distress" *altered to* "stress of weather"] into the ports of those Islands.

CC in DNA, RG 46 (Records of the U.S. Senate), 24A-B10; slightly variant PC in *Senate Journal,* 24th Cong., 2nd Sess., p. 217. Note: The motion was agreed to by the Senate on 2/7 after Calhoun had accepted an amendment offered by Felix Grundy which is represented by the first interlineation above. The President replied on 2/13 with a report by the Secretary of State.

Remarks on a motion of thanks to the Vice-President, 1/28. Thomas H. Benton moved that the Senate reciprocate the farewell message that had been received that day from Vice-President [and

President-elect] Martin Van Buren with a motion congratulating Van Buren for the "impartiality, dignity, and ability" with which he had presided over the Senate. The motion required unanimous consent to be considered immediately. Calhoun objected and "inquired whether it was usual to pass a vote of this kind." When Benton quoted several precedents, Calhoun, "observing that it was a mere formality, withdrew his objection. . . ." From *Register of Debates*, 24th Cong., 2nd Sess., cols. 635–636. Also printed in the Washington, D.C., *Daily National Intelligencer*, January 30, 1837, p. 2.

Remarks on the bill to limit the sales of public lands to actual settlers, 1/30. "Mr. Calhoun and Mr. [Henry] Clay spoke with warmth against the unlimited pre-emptive rights conferred by the bill. . . ." From *Register of Debates*, 24th Cong., 2nd Sess., col. 645. Also printed in the Washington, D.C., *Daily National Intelligencer*, January 31, 1837, p. 3.

Remarks on the bill "to designate and limit the funds which shall be receivable for the public revenue," 1/30. Daniel Webster said that he approved the bill insofar as it attempted to resolve the confusion caused by the President's specie circular, but opposed it as giving too much discretion to the Secretary of the Treasury in determining what currency would be receivable. "Mr. Calhoun said that he agreed entirely with the view presented by the Senator from Massachusetts. This bill left that which should be the most stable of all, the most unstable. If the Senate would indulge him by postponing the subject till to-morrow, he would endeavor to present his views upon it." (Calhoun's wish to speak the next day was granted, but his remarks on that occasion were not reported. See *Congressional Globe*, 24th Cong., 2nd Sess., p. 142.) From *Register of Debates*, 24th Cong., 2nd Sess., col. 644. Also printed in the Washington, D.C., *Daily National Intelligencer*, February 1, 1837, p. 3. Variants in the Washington, D.C., *United States' Telegraph*, January 31, 1837, p. 3; the New York, N.Y., *Morning Courier and New-York Enquirer*, February 1, 1837, p. 2.

Remarks on the bill to prohibit the sale of public lands except to actual settlers, 1/31. Nathaniel P. Tallmadge offered an amendment to this bill that provided for its expiration on 6/30/1842. During discussion Calhoun said he "thought Mr. [William C.] Rives mistaken in supposing that citizens of the old States might obtain lands, under this bill, without personal occupation." Robert J.

Walker of Miss. disagreed with Calhoun. Calhoun "still thought that a man must occupy the land in his own right, and not in the right of another; but take the bill either way, it was equally objectionable. For if land might be occupied by an agent, then the whole domain was thrown open to the speculator; if not, then it was closed against the inhabitants of the old States. The friends of the bill might take either alternative." After further discussion Tallmadge modified his amendment by changing the expiration date from 1842 to 1840. Calhoun "thought that the only effect of this would be that, in 1842, a new swarm of pre-emptioners would present themselves, and the whole thing would have to be done over again." The amendment was then passed. From the Washington, D.C., *Daily National Intelligencer*, February 4, 1837, p. 2. Variant in the New York, N.Y., *Morning Courier and New-York Enquirer*, February 2, 1837, p. 2.

Remarks on the public land bill, 2/1. During discussion of a motion to strike out "the term of six months," Calhoun "expressed his astonishment at the declaration of the Senator from Mississippi [Robert J. Walker], that if the words were not stricken out, he would vote against the bill. It now came out that numbers had gone out in advance to settle on the lands, relying on the privileges conferred by this bill. At every step the iniquity of this bill became more apparent. There was to be no occupation or cultivation; the requisition of six months [occupancy] is to be stricken out, and the registers and receivers are to determine what is occupation and cultivation. He wished that even the word 'crop,' should be introduced after the word cultivation, and that the erection of a dwelling house should be accompanied by a provision that the individual shall reside in it." After further discussion, a motion to strike out six months and insert three months was agreed to. From the New York, N.Y., *Morning Courier and New-York Enquirer*, February 3, 1837, p. 2. Variant in the Washington, D.C., *Daily National Intelligencer*, February 4, 1837, p. 2.

MOTION TO ASCERTAIN REVENUES AND EXPENDITURES ON THE GREAT LAKES

[Submitted to the Senate, February 2, 1837]
Resolved, That the Secretary of the Treasury [Levi Woodbury] be directed to report to the Senate, as early as practicable, the aggregate

expense of collecting the duties on the Lakes during the year 1836, including the expense of revenue cutters; the net amount of duties collected, and the expenditure of the Government on the Lakes during the same period in constructing harbors, breakwaters, and Light houses, with the current expense attending the light houses on the lakes during the year.

Draft (partly in Calhoun's hand) in DNA, RG 46 (Records of the U.S. Senate), 24A-B10; PC in *Senate Journal*, 24th Cong., 2nd Sess., p. 194. NOTE: This motion was agreed to by the Senate.

Remarks on copyrights to foreigners, 2/2. Henry Clay presented to the Senate an address from certain living British authors, requesting the passage of a law to protect their rights to literary property in the U.S. "Mr. Calhoun said he was aware that the interest of booksellers in the United States was adverse to the object of this memorial; but he did not suppose that it was of a character or nature such as required its rejection. The works for which copy-rights would be secured in this country constituted but a small portion of the entire literature of Great Britain or this country; and of the works of the distinguished names on this memorial, the copy-right of a great portion had expired, which was, therefore, subject to free publication; and perhaps it would not be thought proper to revive the right in this country. By several living foreign authors, an attempt had been made to secure their property in this country, by designating the booksellers in the United States by whom alone their works were to be published. The attempt, however, proved impracticable, for other booksellers also published their works without license, so as entirely to deprive them of the benefit of such property in this country. Mr. C[alhoun] thought the proper committee was the Judiciary, though he would not object to a select committee." From *Register of Debates*, 24th Cong., 2nd Sess., col. 671.

REMARKS ON A PROPOSAL FOR THE RELIEF OF SICK AND DISABLED SEAMEN

[In the Senate, February 3, 1837]
[John Davis of Mass., Chairman of the Committee on Commerce, reported a bill that would eliminate the current tax of twenty cents per year on American seamen for a hospital fund and substitute an appropriation of $150,000 for one year. Along with the bill were

motions directing the Secretary of the Treasury to prepare a plan for the construction and operation of three seamen's hospitals.]

Mr. Calhoun, after hearing the resolutions read, said that he was decidedly opposed to the whole subject. Its tendency was to increase the prevailing disease of the Government, the accumulation of patronage and power in the hands of the Central Government. This was the commencement of a system which would lead, no one knew to what excess of patronage. He was solemnly impressed with the necessity of curtailing patronage, to arrest the tendency of all measures to increase the central power here. Reform must be pressed to the utmost. This Government was already surcharged with patronage, and it must be diminished; and he now entered his solemn protest against the system proposed by the bill. It is a proposition to change the old system, and tends directly to the increase of the corrupting patronage and power of this Government. Why should the Government pay the expenses of one class of men rather than another? Shall commerce and navigation be taken in favor, while other interests are left to their own resources? Why not pay the doctor[']s bills for the rice-growers, and cotton planters, as well as the class engaged in navigation? He was opposed to all such schemes. It was time to halt. The patronage and corruptions of the Government were rapidly undermining our liberties, and it is time to provide for our security, by cutting off the fatal courses of corruption and despotism.

From the Washington, D.C., *United States' Telegraph*, February 3, 1837, p. 3. Variant in the Washington, D.C., *Daily National Intelligencer*, February 4, 1837, p. 3; *Register of Debates*, 24th Cong., 2nd Sess., cols. 691–692. NOTE: In the variant report Calhoun was indicated as agreeing with Davis that seamen "were a meritorious class, and that they were not importunate upon Congress. They would not do the mischief, but the persons interested in erecting and conducting the hospitals." Calhoun also argued that the existing tax did not fall on the seamen themselves but "on the branch of business in which they were engaged; and the interest concerned ought to pay the expense."

SPEECH AGAINST THE RECOMMITMENT OF THE PUBLIC LAND BILL TO COMMITTEE

[In the Senate, February 4, 1837]
[*Robert J. Walker moved to recommit to the Committee on Public Lands the bill "to limit the sales of public lands to actual settlers"*

*which he had been managing in the Senate. The recommitment
would have the effect of dropping all amendments, a number of which
had been added by the Senate since Walker had first reported the
bill from committee on 1/2.]*

Mr. Calhoun addressed the Senate. I sincerely hope (said Mr.
C[alhoun]) that the motion for recommitment will not prevail. The
session is now far advanced; but a single month more remains, and
this bill has already occupied more than its due share of the time and
attention of the Senate. The discussion which it has undergone has
shown that there exists in this body a great diversity of opinion, not
on the details only, but on the principle of the bill. A large portion
of the Senate are under the impression that nothing ought to be
done; and among the residue who are in favor of some bill, the differences of opinion seem to be irreconcileable [*sic*]. If we recommit the bill, the inevitable consequence will be that we shall have a
new set of propositions to amend it, and a vast deal of time will be
wasted in vain attempts to reconcile things essentially irreconcileable. For myself, I believe the bill to be radically wrong; and that
no modifications which it is likely to assume can ever render it
right. I had intended to say something on the general subject, but
it is now late, and I forego much of what it was my purpose to have
submitted to the Senate. I will, however, as briefly as possible,
throw out one or two leading views in regard to it.

The professed object of this bill is to restrict the sales of the
public lands; to put down speculation, and to prevent the accumulation of a surplus revenue. Plausible objects, I admit, and such as
sound well to the ear; but the practical operation of the bill which
promises them will, as I apprehend, lead to results very different
indeed. So many and so subtle are the means by which those in
power are able to fleece the community without the people themselves being sensible of it, that the contemplation of it is almost
enough to make any lover of his country despair. I have long been
sensible of this; but if I was called upon to select an instance which
more than others forcibly illustrates the truth of the remark, I would
refer any one who doubted to the present bill. When we closely
examine its provisions, we shall perceive that, so far from repressing,
its effects will be to secure and consummate the most enormous
speculation which has ever been witnessed on this continent. This
speculation has been produced by those in power, and the large
profits they hope to realize are to be consummated by the passage
of this bill. The chairman of the committee himself [Walker] has
told the Senate that a body of the public lands, greater in extent

than the largest State in the Union, has been seized upon by speculators. The Senator from Georgia (Mr. [John P.] King) states the amount at from thirty to forty millions of dollars. This may be an over estimate, but at the lowest calculation the amount cannot be less than twenty-five millions. What has produced this vast investment? What has thus suddenly rendered the public lands an object of such enormous speculation? What but the state of the currency? Our circulating medium has nearly doubled in the space of three years. It has increased from an average of six and a half dollars per head, to an average of ten dollars. And what has been the natural and the inevitable effect? The rise in the price of every thing, the price of which is not kept down by some legal provision; the price of provisions and of labor have nearly doubled, while the price of land has continued fixed by force of law. Is it, then, any thing wonderful that land under this restraint should have become an object of speculation? There lies the root of the evil. This enormous augmentation of the circulating medium has filled all the channels of ordinary business to repletion, and the overflow finds an outlet in speculation. But who have been the authors of this state of things? Every Senator can answer the question. Every body knows that it has been the work of those in power. They began the experiment in 1833. They were distinctly told what would be the result. They were warned that bank capital would be increased, and with it the circulation of paper money; but in the face of all argument and all warning, the experiment went on. The only existing check [the Bank of the U.S.] which had power to control the excessive issue of bank paper was put down. The deposites of the public money were transferred from where the laws had put them, and placed in deposite banks, arbitrarily selected at the will of the Executive. The authors of the present state of things are the very men who come here and propose to us this bill as a remedy. These two facts should be put together, and should be kept together, in the mind of every Senator who will form a right judgment in this matter. The removal of the deposites was the first step. We are now come to the second step in the process. The men who accomplished the first have already profited by it politically, and, if rumor speaks true, in other ways also. Does any man here entertain a doubt that high officers of Government have used those deposites as instruments of speculation in the public lands? Is not the fact notorious? Is not one in the immediate neighborhood of the Executive among those the most deeply concerned? Will this be denied? Is it not well known that several officers in the Departments purchased lands to sell on speculation, with the funds officially under their own control? How the same combination of persons profited politically by the same movement, I shall show hereafter.

Assuming, then, what cannot be denied, that the excessive increase of the circulating medium produced by the experiment is the main cause of these speculations in the public lands, and assuming, on the authority of universal rumor, that high functionaries of the Government have availed themselves of the state of things thus produced, I come now to what is my main proposition, namely, that this bill is calculated to consummate these plans of speculation, and that without this measure, or something equivalent to it, they must end in loss.

(Here some explanation took place between Mr. Calhoun and Mr. Walker, as to the statements made by the latter in reference to the probable effect of the rejection of this bill.)

Well, sir, be it as the honorable chairman states. He says now that, if the bill shall not become a law, the purchases of public land will continue to go on as they have done for the last year. Admit it, and what must be the consequence? Cannot all men perceive that in this, as in all other cases, over supply must operate to reduce the price? The honorable chairman tells us that the amount of land required for fair and honest settlement, by the progress of the country, is five millions of acres annually; and that the amount taken upon speculation last year was thirty millions. If so, then there is already in the hands of the speculators a six years' supply. Should all the land offices be closed to-morrow, the amount these speculators hold would not be absorbed by the regular demands of the country in less than six years. Now, the greater part of these large purchases has been made upon loans; the interest is running on; and unless the sales shall be in proportion, do not all men see that the accumulation of unproductive land upon their hands must infallibly ruin those who are engaged in such speculations? Under such circumstances, the help of legislation is the only thing that can relieve them. I repeat it. This bill, or something like it, is indispensable. It puts a finish to the work. The land offices being left open, and no obstructions thrown in the way of the purchase for settlement, we may suppose that one half of the five millions annually required will be purchased from the Government. There will then remain but two and a half millions to take off the thirty millions stock which the speculators already hold; and at this rate it must be twelve years before that stock can be disposed of; and if the stock is to be augmented by new and large purchases during the present year, the speculation must end in inevitable ruin. The thing is plain; it cannot be denied; it admits of no demonstration.

What, then, is resorted to to prevent this disastrous catastrophe? The answer is found in the details of this bill. And I entirely concur with the Senator from Massachusetts (Mr. [John] Davis) in pronouncing them most odious in their character. No American citizen is to be left free to purchase a portion of the public domain, the property of the whole people of the United States, without a license. Yet, before he can buy the land which his own Government has offered for sale, he must first take out a license. Odious as I hold all licenses upon the press or licenses upon trade, I hold this to be fully as obnoxious as either. A license to purchase the public lands! I cannot buy myself a farm, though I have the money in my pocket, till I pay a dollar and a quarter per acre for a license, and then I do not get a title until I have complied with the most onerous conditions; and if, after I have paid my money, I see reason to change my mind, I cannot leave the land without forfeiting all I have paid, if I find the situation to be sickly. I cannot remain there without risking the lives of my family; I cannot sell it to one more accustomed to the climate, without incurring the pain of perjury as a speculator; nor can I remove without forfeiting the purchase money. But supposing the settler remains, he is required to consummate his title, not in a court of law or before a judicial officer, but before the register and receiver of the district. I do not know how Senators from the new States may feel, but this I know, that nothing under heaven shall induce me to place Carolinians in such circumstances. The registers and receivers of a land office to be judges in matters of real estate! Why, sir, these persons, for the most part, are political partisans. They have obtained their offices as a reward for services rendered at the election. Has not the doctrine of the spoils been openly avowed on this floor? Has it not been unblushingly maintained that the party which obtains a political victory has, as a thing of course, a right to all the offices of the State, and to the public money into the bargain, so that they may control it entirely for their own benefit? I have a right, therefore, to assume that, as a general thing, these registers and receivers will be political partisans. What, then, will be the condition of a large portion of our citizens? Allowing the consumption of public lands to be two and a half millions of acres a year, you will have about a hundred thousand voters, the title to whose earthly all will be in the hands of these registers and receivers. Can any thing be conceived more odious? Would the license of the press itself be a measure more hateful or dangerous? Sir, we have spent too much time considering so monstrous a proposition. I hope we shall not waste upon it another moment.

But, putting the political effects of this bill out of view, let us inquire what will be its moral influence. The Senator from New York (Mr. [Silas] Wright) told us that he considered the price of public land as already too high, and that he was averse to placing it still higher. Sir, these were his words; but let us look at the face of the bill; its practical effect will be an enormous increase in the price to be paid for the public domain; I put it to any man of sound common sense, whether he would not rather give two dollars an acre at once for his farm, and get a good title for his land without further difficulty? I would, most certainly. Consider the terms on which he must buy: the moment he enters his land under this bill, it becomes subject to State taxation; but if he buys from the speculators it will not be so. The entire mass of land purchased last year, and including some of the best parts of the public domain, is now held for sale free of taxation, while land purchased from the Government must immediately be taxed. What chance will the United States lands have against such a competition? None at all; the speculators will have the complete monopoly. This, then, is a question between the Government and the speculators. Our stock is one hundred and twenty millions, theirs is thirty millions; our land is at a dollar and a quarter, theirs is at not less than three dollars; and here is a fair competition. But this bill comes in, and throws the market into the hands of the speculators. In any other than these extraordinary times, one would suppose that these objections would be fatal to any bill. It is most obvious that unless you throw restrictions around the purchase of land from the United States, the object of the speculators must be defeated.

But we are asked, what is to be done with all this speculation? I answer, let it alone, and it will run down of itself. The times will react—the present state of things is artificial—it cannot possibly continue. Speculation, after it has run its course, will run down, and that with far less injury than will result from any attempt to put it down by legislation. If, however, you do legislate, there are many expedients besides that proposed in this bill. In the first place, you may raise the price of the public lands. This, to be sure, will confer a great benefit on those who have already purchased; but it will check future speculation. I have, however, no idea that any such measure will be resorted to; it would be very unpopular; and the object which gentlemen have in view must be secured without the loss of personal popularity. Then, in the second place, you may shut the land offices. This expedient, however, would be liable to the same objections with the other; for you can hit upon none which will not either be inoperative altogether, or of great advantage to those who have already purchased. My opinion, in regard to the public lands, has undergone a great change during the course of this debate. I thought there was a majority in this Senate who would resolutely object to all rash changes in our land system. I hoped, most confidently, that New England at least would have stood fast. I have been disappointed. I hoped that the public lands would not be drawn into our political contests. But in this, too, I have been entirely disappointed. I see that the era has arrived when our large capitalists are in a fair way to seize upon the whole body of the public lands. This has compelled a great change to take place in my mind. I greatly fear that we have reached the time when the public domain is lost to the Government for all useful purposes. We may, indeed, receive some amount of revenue from it, but it will be accompanied with such agitations, and so much trouble and political corruption, that the gain will not compensate for the evil incurred. I have made up my mind, if a fair concession can be made, to concede the whole to the new States, on some fixed and well considered condition[s]. I am for transferring the whole, on the condition that they shall pay us a certain per cent. of the proceeds, and submit to the necessary limitations as to the mode of bringing the lands into market. The present system of sale not to be disturbed for some years, and after that the principle of graduation to be prudently introduced. I have always felt the force of the argument that the new States are not now placed upon an equal footing with the other members of the confederacy. They are full of our land officers and of public officers under our control; and in regard to the soil within their limits, they sustain to us a relation which must ever be productive of discontent and agitation. Whether a thing of this kind can safely be done, I do not know; but of this I am fully persuaded, that such a measure would be infinitely better than the scheme proposed in this bill. The chairman of the Committee on the Public Lands has avowed his own earnest belief that the evils of the existing state of things are such that even a bill like this should be resorted to as a preferable alternative. He considers a surplus in the Treasury as a great evil; (and so do I, too, if it is to be permanent.) And his dread of a surplus is so great that it has prevented him from regarding the details of this bill as I am persuaded he would have done, but for the bias thus produced.

With these views, I conclude by expressing my hope that the bill will not be recommitted, but that we shall either reject it, or suffer it to sleep by laying it on the table.

[*The question was then taken on the recommitment of the bill and decided in the affirmative by 23 to 20.*]

From *Register of Debates*, 24th Cong., 2nd Sess., cols. 702–706. Also printed in the Washington, D.C., *Daily National Intelligencer*, April 8, 1837, pp. 2–3; the Washington, D.C., *Globe*, June 21, 1837, p. 2; *Congressional Globe*, 24th Cong., 2nd Sess., Appendix, pp. 321–322; Crallé, ed., *Works*, 2:617–625. Variant in the Washington, D.C., *Globe*, February 6, 1837, p. 3; *Congressional Globe*, 24th Cong., 2nd Sess., pp. 155–156. Other variants in the Washington, D.C., *United States' Telegraph*, February 7, 1837, p. 2; the New York, N.Y., *Morning Courier and New-York Enquirer*, February 6, 1837, p. 2.

Remarks on a petition concerning an obstruction in Lake Erie, 2/4. A petition presented by Thomas Morris of Ohio asked that Congress "remove the obstructions in the outlet at Black Rock, which had been built by their order." Calhoun said that he hoped this "case would be recollected when the subject of [appropriations for] harbors should come up." From the Washington, D.C., *Daily National Intelligencer*, February 6, 1837, p. 2.

Remarks on the Michigan electoral votes, 2/4. Felix Grundy introduced from a select committee a resolution providing that in counting the electoral votes for President and Vice-President the President of the Senate should announce the vote twice, once counting and once not counting the electoral votes of Mich. (The same candidate for President, Martin Van Buren, would have a majority in either case.) "Mr. Calhoun remarked that, notwithstanding what was said by gentlemen to the contrary, during the debate on the admission of Michigan, they would now see that she was a State *de facto*, at the time she formed her constitution. Now, if they applied the reason of that case to this, what was the result? Michigan was not a State in this Union when her Senators were elected, nor when she voted for President and Vice-President. The case was really a clear one, and any reason which would exclude these votes ought to have excluded her Senators [who were seated on 1/26] from taking their seats on this floor. He did not believe that doubtful questions of this kind should be waived; and this question should be settled at once. He should, therefore, feel himself bound to vote against the resolution." From *Register of Debates*, 24th Cong., 2nd Sess., col. 700. Also printed in the Washington, D.C., *Globe*, February 6, 1837, pp. 2–3; *Congressional Globe*, 24th Cong., 2nd Sess., p. 155.

Variant in the Washington, D.C., *Daily National Intelligencer,* February 6, 1837, p. 2.

To S[AMUEL] D. INGHAM, [New Hope, Pa.]

Washington, 5th Feb: 1837

My dear Sir, I am much obliged to you for the information, which you have given me in relation to rail roads. I fear, however, I am too late. The Knoxville meeting [of stockholders of the Louisville, Cincinnati, and Charleston Railroad on 1/9] have selected the route without waiting for the surveys, and without, I fear, taking into consideration the facts on which the success of the work must depend. It is astonishing how much can be done by a few active men on the spot to bend the most important work, to suit their private views.

The account you give of the abolition movement at Harrisburgh is at once disgusting and al[a]rming. I have long made up my mind, that the evil will progress till arrested by the South, which it can easily do, if united, but which if not done speedily can only be done at the expense of the Union. As to the state of things here, I can only say that political corruption is more open and less reserved than I have ever known. At no preceeding [*sic*] session could the journal have been expunged, or Michigan been admitted ["on" *canceled*] under the circumstance she was, or the attempt made, which I fear may succeed, of making the whole publick domain a subject of speculation and political influence. Yet I cannot but think the administration is weaker than it has ever been. As far as I can hear it gains no addition to its strength, while it seems certain that it is ["loosing" *altered to* "losing"] power in several quarters. What is wanted is concert of action on the part of the opposition. ["Attempts" *canceled*.] Efforts are making to effect a concert, and I hope it may be successful. It is ascertained that no paper can exist here without publick patronage unless it be sustained by the whole weight of the opposition. The proposition is to rear on the basis of the Telegraph a new paper to be called say the Reformer to become the organ of the opposition so far as the principles they hold in common are concerned, to be edited by Mr. [Richard K.] Crallé & Mr. Prentis [*sic*; George D. Prentice] of Louisville jointly. Should it succeed it would certainly add much to the strength of the opposition and do much to weaken the administration. There are, however, difficulties in effecting the object, which may defeat the move.

I send you my speech on the admission of Michigan in pamphlet form. I made yesterday a short speech aga[i]nst the land bill and should it be printed in pamphlet I will send ["it" *interlined*] to you.

I fear the session will be too short to renew the deposite bill, which I greatly regret, as it is worth all the other measures of reform. Had it not been for [Daniel] Webster I would have pressed it last year to continue in force till '42 which would have done the business for the administration. They have seen it and have done their best to defeat me this year, and I apprehend with success.

Anna [*partial word canceled*] with myself ["are" *canceled and* "is" *interlined*] much gratified to learn that the health of your daughter is improved so much. We would have been very glad of her company and I do trust, if a more southern climate should be found necessary to her complete restoration that you will without fear of putting us to the slightest inconvenience put her in our charge. Yours truly & since[re]ly, J.C. Calhoun.

ALS in ScU-SC, John C. Calhoun Papers.

To J[OHN] K. PORTER, [Union College, Schenectady, N.Y.?]

Washington, 5th Feb: 1837

Dear Sir, I would gladly comply with your request, but I have long since terminated my connection with the bar. I practised for a very brief period, not more than two years, and that more than 26 years since, so that I would be illy qualified to take direction of your *legal* studies.

The selfish and avaricious sperit of the age, which you so justly condemn is deeply to be deplored. I fear it is destined to subvert the noble institutions creeated[?] by the wisdom & patriotism of our fathers of the revolution. I look to the rising generation to reform the abuses of the present. With respect I am & & J.C. Calhoun.

ALS in ScU-SC, John C. Calhoun Papers. NOTE: A marginal comment written presumably by the recipient reads: "His [Calhoun's] subsequent letter containing the proposition to direct my political & supervise my legal studies was taken from my room at college, during my visit to Waterford." Porter, an 1837 graduate of Union College, was subsequently a N.Y. lawyer and judge and a delegate to the Whig national convention of 1844 and the N.Y. constitutional convention of 1846.

PRELIMINARY REMARKS ON THE QUESTION OF
RECEIVING ABOLITION PETITIONS

[In the Senate, February 6, 1837]
*[John Tipton of Ind. presented two petitions for the abolition of
slavery in the District of Columbia. He believed the prayer of the
petitioners to be unwise, unconstitutional, and unrepresentative of
his constituents, but he considered it his duty to present the petitions
and asked for their "respectful consideration."]*

Mr. Calhoun rose and asked the Chair [William R. King of Ala.,
recently elected President Pro Tempore of the Senate] whether the
petitions could be received before the preliminary question was put?
He was aware that the practice of the Senate was almost tantamount
to it; but, when it was known that the unanimous consent of the body
did not exist, the regular mode of proceeding was to propound this
question to the Senate: "Shall the petition be received?" The rule,
as laid down in page 140 of the Manual, was plain and express on
the subject. Now, he objected to receive this, or any similar petition. He was aware that last year a different rule was adopted, for
the question of reception was left to be made by Senators, instead
of the Chair putting the question to the Senate, as was formerly
done, thus changing the onus, and compelling Senators to make out
a case for reception, instead of the Presiding Officer. He trusted,
therefore, that the Chair would raise the question of reception.

The Chair would state the regular parliamentary rule. When
a petition is presented, the member who presents it shall state the
substance of it. It is required that this shall be done, in order that
the Senate may judge whether it is such a petition as ought to be
received. The practice has been to receive it as a matter of course,
there being no direct objection to it. The Chair is decidedly of
opinion, that whenever the question is made, either by a Senator
rising in his place, or objecting in his seat, to the reception of the
petition, this question must first be put, whether the petition shall
be received or not. This is the deliberate opinion of the Chair.

*[Tipton, Thomas Ewing of Ohio, and Benjamin Swift of Vt. ar-
gued that the receiving of all respectful petitions would help allay
excitement on the subject. Thomas Morris of Ohio said that if a
vote was to be taken on the reception, to save time all such petitions
should be presented at once. The Chair ruled "that no other petitions
could be received while the question was pending on the two already
presented, unless by unanimous consent."]*

Mr. Calhoun hoped that by unanimous consent the question

would be taken on the reception of all the petitions at once. He expressed his satisfaction at the decision of the Chair, but he thought the onus ought to be on those who presented the petitions to show that they were worthy of reception. He hoped that when Senators presented such petitions, they would make the proper motion that they be received.

[*Unanimous consent being given, a number of abolition petitions were presented by Ewing, Swift, Morris, Nehemiah R. Knight of R.I., Samuel Prentiss of Vt., and James Buchanan. A debate ensued during which Calhoun made the remarks below.*]

From *Congressional Globe*, 24th Cong., 2nd Sess., pp. 160–161. Variants in the Washington, D.C., *United States' Telegraph*, February 6, 1837, p. 3; *Register of Debates*, 24th Cong., 2nd Sess., cols. 706–708; the Washington, D.C., *Daily National Intelligencer*, February 7, 1837, p. 2.

Remarks on Receiving Abolition Petitions (First Report)

[In the Senate, February 6, 1837]

Mr. Calhoun said he thought it very desirable that the Senate and the South should know in what manner these petitioners spoke of Southern people. For this purpose he had selected, from the numerous petitions on the table, two, indiscriminately, which he wished the Secretary to read.

(These two petitions were read, and proved to be rather more moderate in their language than usual.)

Such is the language (said Mr. C[alhoun]) with which they characterize us and ours. That which was the basis of Southern institutions, and which could not be dispensed without blood and massacre, was denounced as sinful and outrageous on the rights of men. And all this was proclaimed, in the Senate of the United States, of States that were united together for the purpose of maintaining their institutions in a more perfect manner. Were Southern members to sit quietly and hear themselves denounced in this manner? And if they should speak at all under these circumstances, were they to be denounced as agitators? This institution existed when the constitution was formed; and yet Senators would not only sit and receive them, but were ready to throw blame on those who opposed them.

Mr. C[alhoun] said he did not belong to the school of those who

387

believe that agitations of this sort could be quieted by concessions; on the contrary, he maintained all usurpations should be resisted in the beginning; and those who would not do so were prepared to be slaves themselves. Mr. C[alhoun] knew, and had predicted, that if the petitions were received, it would not avail in satisfying the petitioners; but they would then be prepared for the next step, to compel action upon the petitions. Mr. C[alhoun] would ask Southern gentlemen if they did not see the second step prepared to be taken, not only that the petitions should be received, but referred.

Mr. C[alhoun] had told Mr. [James] Buchanan and his friends, last year, that they were taking an impossible position; and had said that these men would, at this session, press a reference. Were we now to be told that this second concession would satisfy this incendiary spirit? Such was the very position (a reference) at which the other House arrived at the last session. Had they at all quieted the spirit of abolition? On the contrary, it had caused it to spread wider and strike its roots still deeper. The next step would be to produce discussion and argument on the subject. Mr. C[alhoun] insisted that the South had surrendered essentially by permitting the petitions to be received. He said it was time for the South to take her stand and reject the petitions. He conscientiously believed that Congress were as much under obligation to act on the subject as they were to receive the petitions; and that they had just as good a right to abolish slavery in the States as in this District.

Mr. C[alhoun] said that the decision of the Chair settled the question that the Senate had a right to refuse to receive the petitions; for if they had a right to vote at all on the subject, they had the right to vote in the negative; and to yield this point was to yield it for the benefit of the abolitionists, at the expense of the Senate. But it was in vain to argue the subject. Mr. C[alhoun] would warn Southern members to take their stand on this point without concession. He had foreseen and predicted this state of things three years ago, as a legitimate result of the force bill. All this body were now opposed to the object of these petitions. Mr. C[alhoun] saw where all originated—at the very bottom of society, among the lowest and most ignorant; but it would go on, and rise higher and higher, till it should ascend the pulpit and the schools, where it had, indeed, arrived already; thence it would mount up to this and the other House. The only way to resist was to close the doors; to open them was virtually to surrender the question. The spirit of the times (he said) was one of dollars and cents, the spirit of speculation, which had diffused itself from the North to the South. Nothing (he said) could resist the spirit of abolition but the united action of the South. The opinions of most people in the North and South were now sound on this subject; but the rising generation would be imbued by the spirit of fanaticism, and the North and South would become two people[s], with feelings diametrically opposite. The decided action of the South, within the limits of the constitution, was indispensable.

[*Here John Tipton called for the recording of the yeas and nays on the question of receiving the petitions. Then Richard H. Bayard of Del. moved that the question of the reception be tabled, a motion that was carried 31 to 13. John Davis of Mass. presented about forty abolitionist petitions and moved their reference to committee. The Chair stated that the question before the Senate was on reception. Bayard again moved to table the question of reception, which was agreed to. After further discussion John P. King of Ga. said that Calhoun was wrong in thinking there was any material difference between the policy of the Senate during the last session and that now adopted on Bayard's motion.*]

Mr. Calhoun said he, for one, was extremely pleased with the decision of the Chair, (that a mere objection required a vote on the reception of the petitions.) But he ought to go further, and put the question of reception, whether the petition were objected to or not. According to the rule, he said, the burden of making a motion to receive should fall on those presenting the petitions. Mr. C[alhoun] had formerly pressed the Chair twice on this point, but was then overruled. The question was whether we are bound to receive the petitions by the constitution. That question the Chair had now yielded, and had admitted that it was in the power of the body itself to say whether or not the petitions should be received.

Mr. C[alhoun] again argued that, if Congress were bound to receive petitions, they were equally bound to refer and act upon them.

[*Discussion continued among seven Senators, during which William C. Rives of Va, said that he "had no objection that Senators should present their petitions, but he protested against the gratuitous exhibition of these horrid pictures of misery which had no existence. He was not in favor of slavery in the abstract. On that point he differed with the gentleman from South Carolina. . . ." When Rives concluded:*]

Mr. Calhoun explained, and denied having expressed any opinion in regard to slavery in the abstract. He had merely stated, what was a matter of fact, that it was an inevitable law of society that one portion of the community depended upon the labor of another portion, over which it must unavoidably exercise control. He had not spoken of slavery in the abstract, but of slavery as existing where two races of men, of different color, and a thousand other particulars, were placed in immediate juxtaposition. Here the existence of slavery was a good to both. Did not the Senator from Virginia consider it as good?

Mr. Rives said, no. He viewed it as a misfortune and an evil in all circumstances, though, in some, it might be the lesser evil.

Mr. Calhoun insisted on the opposite opinion, and declared it as his conviction that, in point of fact, the Central African race (he did not speak of the north or the east of Africa, but of its central regions) had never existed in so comfortable, so respectable, or so civilized a condition, as that which it now enjoyed in the Southern States. The population doubled in the same ratio with that of the whites—a proof of ease and plenty; while, with respect to civilization, it nearly kept pace with that of the owners; and as to the effect upon the whites, would it be affirmed that they were inferior to others, that they were less patriotic, less intelligent, less humane, less brave, than where slavery did not exist? He was not aware that any inferiority was pretended. Both races, therefore, appeared to thrive under the practical operation of this institution. The experiment was in progress, but had not been completed. The world had not seen modern society go through the entire process, and he claimed that its judgment should be postponed for another ten years. The social experiment was going on both at the North and the South—in the one with almost a pure and unlimited democracy, and in the other with a mixed race. Thus far, the results of the experiment had been in favor of the South. Southern society had been far less agitated, and he would venture to predict that its condition would prove by far the most secure, and by far the most favorable to the preservation of liberty. In fact, the defence of human liberty against the aggressions of despotic power had been always the most efficient in States where domestic slavery was found to prevail. He did not admit it to be an evil. Not at all. It was a good—a great good. On that point, the Senator from Virginia and himself were directly at issue.

[*Rives spoke again. Then:*]

Mr. Calhoun complained of having been misrepresented. Again [he] denied having pronounced slavery in the abstract a good. All he had said of it referred to existing circumstances; to slavery as a practical, not as an abstract thing. It was a good where a civilized race and a race of a different description were brought together.

Wherever civilization existed, death too was found, and luxury; but did he hold that death and luxury were good in themselves? He believed slavery was good, where two races coexisted. The gentleman from Virginia held it an evil. Yet he would defend it. Surely if it was an evil, moral, social, and political, the Senator, as a wise and virtuous man, was bound to exert himself to put it down. This position, that it was a moral evil, was the very root of the whole system of operations against it. That was the spring and wellhead from which all these streams of abolition proceeded—the effects of which so deeply agitated the honorable Senator.

Mr. C[alhoun] again adverted to the successful results of the experiment thus far, and insisted that the slaveholders of the South had nothing in the case to lament or to lay to their conscience. He utterly denied that his doctrines had any thing to do with the tenets of Sir Robert Filmer, which he abhorred. So far from holding the dogmas of that writer, he had been the known and open advocate of freedom from the beginning. Nor was there any thing in the doctrines he held in the slightest degree inconsistent with the highest and purest principles of freedom.

From *Register of Debates*, 24th Cong., 2nd Sess., cols. 710–719. Also printed in the Washington, D.C., *Daily National Intelligencer*, February 7, 1837, p. 2, and February 10, 1837, pp. 1–2. NOTE: Directly below in this volume appears a different report of Calhoun's remarks on this day. The version below is probably that reviewed and approved by Calhoun himself. The two versions presented do not disagree in substance but vary considerably in language, tone, and in the emphasis they give to various points. The two versions provide an extremely informative example of the variations in published reports of Congressional speeches, in this case between an early report and a later, probably polished and expanded version. Still other variant reports of this day's remarks are cited in the footnote to the version which follows.

REMARKS ON RECEIVING ABOLITION
PETITIONS (Revised Report)

[In the Senate, February 6, 1837]
If the time of the Senate permitted, I would feel it to be my duty to call for the reading of the mass of petitions on the table, in order that we might know what language they hold towards the slaveholding States and their institutions; but as it will not, I have selected, indiscriminately from the pile, two: one from those in manuscript, and the other from the printed, and without knowing

their contents will call for the reading of them, so that we may judge, by them, of the character of the whole.

(Here the Secretary, on the call of Mr. Calhoun, read the two petitions.)

Such, resumed Mr. C[alhoun], is the language held towards us and ours. The peculiar institutions [*sic*] of the South, that on the maintenance of which the very existence of the slave-holding States depends, is pronounced to be sinful and odious, in the sight of God and man; and this with a systematic design of rendering us hateful in the eyes of the world, with a view to a general crusade against us and our institutions. This too, in the legislative halls of the Union; created by these confederated States, for the better protection of their peace, their safety and their respective institutions; and yet we, the representatives of twelve of these sovereign States against whom this deadly war is waged, are expected to sit here in silence, hearing ourselves and our constituents day after day denounced, without uttering a word—if we but open our lips, the charge of agitation is resounded on all sides, and we are held up as seeking to aggravate the evil which we resist. Every reflecting mind must see in all this, a state of things deeply and dangerously diseased.

I do not belong, said Mr. C[alhoun], to the school which holds that aggression is to be met by concession. Mine is the opposite creed, which teaches that encroachments must be met at the beginning, and that those who act on the opposite principle are prepared to become slaves. In this case in particular I hold concession or compromise to be fatal. If we concede an inch, concession would follow concession—compromise would follow compromise, until our ranks would be so broken that effectual resistance would be impossible. We must meet the enemy on the frontier, with a fixed determination of maintaining our position at every hazard. Consent to receive these insulting petitions, and the next demand will be that they be referred to a committee in order that they may be deliberated and acted upon. At the last session we were modestly asked to receive them simply to lay them on the table, without any view of ulterior action. I then told the Senator from Pennsylvania, (Mr. [James] Buchanan) who strongly urged that course in the Senate, that it was a position that could not be maintained; as the argument in favor of acting on the petitions if we were bound to receive, could not be resisted. I then said that the next step would be to refer the petition to a committee, and I already see indications that such is now the intention. If we yield, that will be followed by another, and we would thus proceed step by step to the final consummation of the object of these petitions. We are now told that the most effectual mode of arresting the progress of Abolition is to reason it down, and with this view it is urged that the petitions ought to be referred to a committee. That is the very ground which was taken at the last session in the other House, but instead of arresting its progress it has since advanced more rapidly than ever. The most unquestionable right may be rendered doubtful, if once admitted to be a subject of controversy, and that would be the case in the present instance. The subject is beyond the jurisdiction of Congress—they have no right to touch it in any shape or form, or to make it the subject of deliberation or discussion.

In opposition to this view it is urged that Congress is bound by the Constitution to receive petitions in every case and on every subject, whether within its constitutional competency or not. I hold the doctrine to be absurd, and do solemnly believe, that it would be as easy to prove that it has the right to abolish slavery, as that it is bound to receive petitions for that purpose. The very existence of the rule that requires a question to be put on the reception of petitions, is conclusive to show, that there is no such obligation. It has been a standing rule from the commencement of the Government, and clearly shows the sense of those who formed the Constitution on this point. The question on the reception would be absurd, if as is contended we are bound to receive; but I do not intend to argue the question; I discussed it fully at the last session, and the arguments then advanced neither have nor can be answered.

As widely as this incendiary spirit has spread, it has not yet infected this body, or the great mass of the intelligent and business portion of the North; but unless it be speedily stopped, it will spread and work upwards till it brings the two great sections of the Union into deadly conflict. This is not a new impression with me. Several years since, in a discussion [on 2/26/1833] with one of the Senators from Massachusetts, (Mr. [Daniel] Webster,) before this fell spirit had showed itself, I then predicted that the doctrine of the proclamation and the force bill—that this Government had a right in the last resort to determine the extent of its own powers, and enforce it at the point of the bayonet, which was so warmly maintained by that Senator, would at no distant day arouse the dormant spirit of abolitionism; I told him that the doctrine was tantamount to the assumption of unlimited power on the part of the Government, and that such would be the impression on the public mind in a large portion of the Union. The consequence would be inevitable—a large portion of the Northern States believed slavery to be a sin, and would believe it to be an obligation of conscience to abolish it, if they should feel themselves in any degree responsible for its continuance, and that his doctrine would necessarily lead to the belief of such responsibility. I then predicted that it would commence as it has with this fanatical portion of society, and that they would begin their operation on the ignorant, the weak, the young, and the thoughtless, and would gradually extend upwards till they would become strong enough to obtain political control, when he and others holding the highest stations in society, would, however reluctant, be compelled to yield to their doctrine, or be driven into obscurity. But four years have since elapsed, and all this is already in a course of regular fulfilment.

Standing at the point of time at which we have now arrived, it will not be more difficult to trace the course of future events now than it was then. Those who imagine that the spirit now abroad in the North, will die away of itself without a shout [*sic*; shock?] or convulsion, have formed a very inadequate conception of its real character; it will continue to rise and spread, unless prompt and efficient measures, to stay its progress, be adopted. Already it has taken possession of the pulpit, of the schools, and to a considerable extent of the press; those great instruments by which the mind of the rising generation will be formed.

However sound the great body of the non-slaveholding States are at present, in the course of a few years they will be succeeded by those who will have been taught to hate the people and institutions of nearly one half of this Union, with a hatred more deadly than one hostile nation ever entertained towards another. It is easy to see the end. By the necessary course of events, if left to themselves, we must become, finally, two people[s]. It is impossible under the deadly hatred which must spring up between the two great sections, if the present causes are permitted to operate unchecked, that we should continue under the same political system. The conflicting elements would burst the Union asunder as powerful as are the links which hold it together. Abolition and the Union cannot co-exist. As the friend of the Union I openly proclaim it, and the sooner it is known the better. The former may now be controlled, but in a short time it will be beyond the power of man to arrest the course of events. We of the South will not, can not surrender our institutions. To maintain the existing relations between the two races, inhabiting that section of the Union, is indispensable to the peace and happiness of both. It cannot be subverted without drenching the country in blood, and extirpating one or the other of the races.

Be it good or bad, it has grown up with our society and institutions, and is so interwoven with them, that to destroy it would be to destroy us as a people. But let me not be understood as admitting even by implication that the existing relations between the two races in the slave-holding States is an evil—far otherwise; I hold it to be a good, as it has thus far proved itself to be to both, and will continue to prove so if not disturbed by the fell spirit of abolition. I appeal to facts. Never before has the black race of Central Africa, from the dawn of history to the present day, attained a condition so civilized and so improved, not only physically, but morally and intellectually. It came among us in a low, degraded, and savage condition, and in the course of a few generations it has grown up under the fostering care of our institutions, as reviled as they have been, to its present comparative civilized condition. This, with the rapid increase of numbers, is conclusive proof of the general happiness of the race in spite of all the exaggerated tales to the contrary.

In the mean time, the white or European race has not degenerated. It has kept pace with its brethren in other sections of the Union where slavery does not exist. It is odious to make comparison; but I appeal to all sides whether the South is not equal in virtue, intelligence, patriotism, courage, disinterestedness, and all the high qualities which adorn our nature. I ask whether we have not contributed our full share of talents and political wisdom in forming and sustaining this political fabric; and whether we have not constantly inclined most strongly to the side of liberty, and been the first to see and first to resist the encroachments of power. In one thing only are we inferior—the arts of gain; we acknowledge that we are less wealthy than the Northern section of the Union, but I trace this mainly to the fiscal action of this Government, which has extracted much from, and spent little among us. Had it been the reverse, if the exaction had been from the other section, and the expenditure with us, this point of superiority would not be against us now as it was not at the formation of this Government.

But I take higher ground. I hold that in the present state of civilization, where two races of different origin, and distinguished by color, and other physical differences, as well as intellectual, are brought together, the relation now existing in the slave-holding States between the two, is, instead of an evil, a good—a positive good. I feel myself called upon to speak freely upon the subject where the honor and interests of those I represent are involved. I hold then, that there never has yet existed a wealthy and civilized society in which one portion of the community did not, in point of fact, live on the labor of the other. Broad and general as is this assertion, it is fully borne out by history. This is not the proper occasion, but if it were, it would not be difficult to trace the various devices by which the wealth of all civilized communities has been so unequally divided, and to show by what means so small a share has been allotted to those by whose labor it was produced, and so large a share given to the non-producing classes. The devices are almost innumerable, from the brute force and gross superstition of ancient times, to the subtle and artful fiscal contrivances of modern. I might well challenge a comparison between them and the more direct, simple, and patriarchal mode by which the labor of the African race is among us commanded by the European. I may say with truth, that in few countries so much is left to the share of the laborer, and so little exacted from him, or where there is more kind attention to him in sickness or infirmities of age. Compare his condition with the tenants of the poor houses in the most civilized portions of Europe—look at the sick, and the old and infirm slave, on one hand, in the midst of his family and friends, under the kind superintending care of his master and mistress, and compare it with the forlorn and wretched condition of the pauper in the poor house. But I will not dwell on this aspect of the question; I turn to the political; and here I fearlessly assert that the existing relation between the two races in the South, against which these blind fanatics are waging war, forms the most solid and durable foundation on which to rear free and stable political institutions. It is useless to disguise the fact. There is and always has been in an advanced stage of wealth and civilization, a conflict between labor and capital. The condition of society in the South exempts us from the disorders and dangers resulting from this conflict; and which explains why it is that the political condition of the slave-holding States has been so much more stable and quiet than those of the North. The advantages of the former in this respect will become more and more manifest if left undisturbed by interference from without, as the country advances in wealth and numbers. We have in fact but just entered that condition of society where the strength and durability of our political institutions are to be tested; and I venture nothing in predicting that the experience of the next generation will fully test how vastly more favorable our condition of society is to that of other sections for free and stable institutions, provided we are not disturbed by the interference of others, or shall have sufficient intelligence and spirit to resist promptly and successfully such interference. It rests with ourselves to meet and repel them. I look not for aid to this

Government, or to the other States; not but there are kind feelings towards us on the part of the great body of the non slave-holding States; but as kind as their feelings may be, we may rest assured that no political party in those States will risk their ascendancy for our safety. If we do not defend ourselves none will defend us; if we yield we will be more and more pressed as we recede; and if we submit we will be trampled under foot. Be assured that emancipation itself would not satisfy these fanatics—that gained, the next step would be to raise the negroes to a social and political equality with the whites; and that being effected, we would soon find the present condition of the two races reversed. They and their northern allies would be the masters, and we the slaves; the condition of the white race in the British West India Islands, bad as it is, would be happiness to ours;—there the mother country is interested in sustaining the supremacy of the European race. It is true that the authority of the former master is destroyed, but the African will there, still be a slave, not to individuals but to the community—forced to labor, not by the authority of the overseer, but by the bayonet of the soldiery and the rod of the civil magistrate.

Surrounded as the slave-holding States are with such imminent perils, I rejoice to think that our means of defence are ample, if we shall prove to have the intelligence and spirit to see and apply them before it is too late. All we want is concert, to lay aside all party differences, and unite with zeal and energy in repelling approaching dangers. Let there be concert of action, and we shall find ample means of security without resorting to secession or disunion. I speak with full knowledge and a thorough examination of the subject, and for one see my way clearly. One thing alarms me—the eager pursuit of gain which overspreads the land, and which absorbs every faculty of the mind and every feeling of the heart. Of all passions avarice is the most blind and compromising—the last to see and the first to yield to danger. I dare not hope that any thing I can say will arouse the South to a due sense of danger; I fear it is beyond the power of mortal voice to awaken it in time from the fatal security into which it has fallen.

From *Remarks of Mr. Calhoun, of South Carolina, on the Reception of Abolition Petitions, Delivered in the Senate of the United States, February 1837* (Washington: printed by William W. Moore & Co., 1837). Also printed in the Washington, D.C., *Reformer*, April 6, 1837, p. 2; *Register of Debates*, 24th Cong., 2nd Sess., cols. 2184–2188; *Speeches of John C. Calhoun*, pp. 222–226; John S. Jenkins, *The Life of John Caldwell Calhoun*, pp. 330–336; Crallé, ed., *Works*, 2:625–633. Variant printed above in this volume as the immediately preceding document. Still other variants in the Washington, D.C., *United*

States' Telegraph, February 7, 1837, p. 3, and February 8, 1837, p. 2; the New York, N.Y., *Morning Courier and New-York Enquirer,* February 8, 1837, p. 2; the Washington, D.C., *Globe,* February 8, 1837, p. 3, and February 11, 1837, p. 2; *Congressional Globe,* 24th Cong., 2nd Sess., pp. 161–163; *ibid.,* Appendix, pp. 154–155. NOTE: An interesting application of Calhoun's remarks above on class conflict was made by Benjamin E. Green, son of Duff Green, in support of the post-Civil War Greenback movement. See a draft ms. entitled "Civil War at the North & West" in NcU, Duff Green Papers (published microfilm, roll 17, frames 427–431).

BILL TO CEDE UNSOLD PUBLIC LANDS TO THE STATES IN WHICH THEY ARE SITUATED

[Introduced in the Senate, February 7, 1837] Strike out all after the word That, in the first line, [that is, strike out of the public land bill now pending all except *"Be it enacted by the Senate and House of Representatives of the United States of America in Congress assembled,* That"] and insert:

["That" *canceled*] all the public lands within the States of Alabama, Mississippi, Louisiana, Arkansas, Missouri, Illinois, ["Indiana" *interlined,*] Ohio, and Michigan, with the exceptions of the sites of fortifications, navy and dock yards, arsenals, magazines, and all other public buildings, be ceded to the States, within the limits of which they are respectively situated, on the following conditions:

First, That the said States shall severally pass acts, to be irrevocable, that they will annually pay to the United States, thirty-three and one third per cent on the gross amount of the sales of such lands, on or before the first day of ["May" *canceled and* "February" *interlined*] of each succeeding year.

Secondly, That the minimum price as now fixed by law [$1.25 per acre], shall remain unchanged until the first day of January, eighteen hundred and forty two; after which time, the price of all lands heretofore offered at public sale, and then remaining unsold ten years or upwards preceding the first day of January aforesaid, may be reduced by said States to a price not less than one dollar per acre; and all lands that may have been offered at public sale, and remaining unsold fifteen years or upwards preceding the first day of January, eighteen hundred and forty seven, may thereafter be reduced by said States to a price not less than seventy five cents per acre; and all lands that may have been offered at public sale and remaining unsold twenty years or upwards, preceding the first day of January, eighteen hundred and fifty two, may then be reduced by said States to a price not less than fifty cents per acre; and all lands that may have been offered at public sale and remaining unsold twenty [*sic*] years or upwards, preceding the first day of January, eighteen hundred and fifty seven, may thereafter be reduced by said States to a price not less than thirty-five cents per acre; and all lands that may have been offered at public sale and remaining unsold thirty years or upwards preceding the first day of January, eighteen hundred and sixty two, may thereafter be reduced by said States to a price not less than twenty cents per acre; and all lands that shall have been offered at public sale and remaining unsold thirty five years or upwards, shall be ceded immediately to the States in which said lands are situate: Provided, That all lands which shall remain unsold after having been offered at public sale for ten years ["preceding said first of January, eighteen hundred and forty two" *canceled and* "and which does (*sic*) not come under the above provisions" *interlined*] shall be subject to the provisions of graduation and cession aforesaid at the respective periods of ten, fifteen, twenty, ["and" *canceled*] twenty-five, thirty, and thirty-five ["years" *interlined*] after ["dating" *canceled and* "said sale, commencing" *interlined*] from the expiration of ten years after the same had been offered at public sale.

Thirdly. That the lands shall be subject to the same legal subdivisions in the sale and survey as is now provided by law, reserving for each township the sixteenth section, or the substitute, as heretofore provided by law; and the land not yet offered for sale, shall be first offered by the State at public auction and be sold, for cash only, in the manner now provided by law: and any land now or hereafter remaining unsold after the same shall have been offered for sale at public auction, shall be subject to entry for cash only according to the graduation which may be fixed by the States respectively under the provisions of this act.

Fourth. This cession, together with the portion of the sales to be retained by the States respectively under the provisions of this act shall be in full of the five per cent fund [to be distributed among the States from the Treasury surplus according to the Deposit Act of 1836] or any part thereof, not already advanced to any State, and the said States shall be exclusively liable for all charges that may hereafter accrue from the surveys, sales, and management of the public lands ["in" *canceled and* "and" *interlined*] extinguishment of Indian title within the limits of said States respectively.

Fifth, That on a failure to comply with any of the above condi-

399

tions, or a violation of the same on the part of any of the said States, the cession herein made to the State failing to comply with, or violating, said conditions, shall be thereby rendered null and void, and all grants or titles thereafter made by said State, for any portion of the public lands within the limits of the same ceded by this act, shall be and is hereby declared to be null and void, and of no effect whatever.

Sec[tion] 2. And be it further enacted, that whenever the President of the United States shall be officially notified that any of the said States has passed an act in compliance with the above conditions, it shall be his duty forthwith to adopt such measures as ["he" *interlined*] shall think proper ["proper" *canceled*], to close the land offices, including the surveying department, within the limits of said ["States" *altered to* "State"]; and that the commissions of all officers connected therewith shall expire on a day to be fixed by him, ["but" *canceled*] which day shall not be beyond six months from the day he received the official notification of the passage of said act.

Sec[tion] 3. And be it further enacted, That on such notification being made, the said State shall be relieved from all compacts, act[s] or ordinance[s], imposing restrictions on the right of said State to tax any lands by her ["authority subsequent to the sale thereof" *interlined*] ceded by this act; and all maps, titles, records, books, ["and" *canceled*] documents and papers, in the General Land Office at Washington, relative to said lands, shall be subject to the order and disposition of the Executive of said State.

Sec[tion] 4. And be it further enacted, That all lands of the United States within the limits of the State of Tennessee, with the exceptions enumerated in the first section of this act, shall be and and [*sic*] the same are hereby, ceded to said State.

CC in DNA, RG 46 (Records of the U.S. Senate), 24A-B4; PC in *Senate Journal*, 24th Cong., 2nd Sess., pp. 223–224; PC in *Register of Debates*, 24th Cong., 2nd Sess., cols. 729–731. NOTE: The ms. copy that is transcribed above is the earliest known version of Calhoun's "land bill." On 12/14/1836 Thomas Morris of Ohio had introduced a bill (S-20) "to prohibit the sale of public lands, except to actual settlers, in limited quantities." By 1/2/1837, when that bill was reported out of the Committee on the Public Lands, it had been amended so that there was an entirely new text written by Robert J. Walker. Walker's bill was vigorously debated in the Senate for some weeks and many amendments were proposed as to details. On 2/7 Calhoun offered the above proposal as an "amendment"—actually a substitute. Calhoun's proposal was defeated the same day, 7 to 28. It reappeared, however, on 2/9 as a new bill for the same purpose. The public land bill managed by Walker, much amended, was passed by the Senate on 2/10 by 27 to 23, Calhoun voting in the negative. It failed in the House of Representatives. Morris's and Walker's bills, with many of the amendments, can be found in DLC, Congressional Bills, 24th Cong., 2nd Sess., S-20.

REMARKS ON HIS PROPOSITION TO CEDE THE PUBLIC LANDS TO THE STATES

[In the Senate, February 7, 1837]

Mr. Calhoun said that the [public land] bill [now before the Senate], especially since it had been reduced to its present shape, was beneficial neither to the new nor to the old States, and very oppressive to actual settlers. He should infinitely prefer ceding the lands entirely to the States in which they lie; and, with that view, he had prepared an amendment in the shape of a substitute for the present bill, and which he now moved.

[*The amendment was sent to the Secretary's table and read. An extended discussion among nine Senators ensued. Then a motion by John M. Robinson of Ill. that Calhoun's bill be printed was defeated 16 to 17.*]

Mr. Calhoun then said that he wished the Senate to be assured that, in offering the proposition he had presented, he had no indirect or concealed purpose. He was perfectly sincere in proposing and advocating it, and that on the highest possible ground. When the Senate entered upon the present discussion, he had had little thought of offering a proposition like this. He had, indeed, always seen that there was a period coming when this Government must cede to the new States the possession of their own soil; but he had never thought till now that period was so near. What he had seen this session, however, and especially the nature and character of the bill which was now likely to pass, had fully satisfied him that the time had arrived. There were at present eighteen Senators from the new States. In four years there would be six more, which would make twenty-four. All, therefore, must see that in a very short period those States would have this question in their own hands. And it had been openly said that they ought not to accept of the present proposition, because they would soon be able to get better terms. He thought, therefore, that, instead of attempting to resist any longer what must eventually happen, it would be better for all concerned that Congress should yield at once to the force of circumstances, and cede the public domain. His objects in this movement were high and solemn objects. He wished to break down the vas-

401

salage of the new States. He desired that this Government should cease to hold the relation of a landlord. He wished, further, to draw this great fund out of the vortex of the presidential contest, with which it had openly been announced to the Senate there was an avowed design to connect it. He thought the country had been sufficiently agitated, corrupted, and debased, by the influence of that contest; and he wished to take this great engine out of the hands of power. If he were a candidate for the presidency, he would wish to leave it there. He wished to go further: he sought to remove the immense amount of patronage connected with the management of this domain—a patronage which had corrupted both the old and the new States to an enormous extent. He sought to counteract the centralism, which was the great danger of this Government, and thereby to preserve the liberties of the people much longer than would otherwise be possible. As to what was to be received for these lands, he cared nothing about it. He would have consented at once to yield the whole, and withdraw altogether the landlordship of the General Government over them, had he not believed that it would be most for the benefit of the new States themselves that it should continue somewhat longer.

These were the views which had induced him to present the amendment. He offered no gilded pill. He threw in no apple of discord. He was no bidder for popularity. He prescribed to himself a more humble aim, which was simply to do his duty. He sought to counteract the corrupting tendency of the existing course of things. He sought to weaken this Government by divesting it of at least a part of the immense patronage it wielded. He held that every great landed estate required a local administration, conducted by persons more intimately acquainted with local wants and interests than the members of a central Government could possibly be. If any body asked him for a proof of the truth of his positions, he might point them to the bill now before the Senate. Such were the sentiments, shortly stated, which had governed him on this occasion. He had done his duty, and he must leave the result with God and with the new States.

After a remark or two from Mr. [Lewis F.] Linn and Mr. [Thomas H.] Benton,

Mr. Calhoun was understood to say that he had sincerely presented the motives of his course. He had in view but one object only, which was the benefit of the new States; although he believed the old States were as much interested to get rid of these lands as the new States to receive them. He thought the amendment contained provisions which would prevent any contest between the new States for this territory. But, provided the great principles of the amendment were adopted, he was not at all solicitous about the details. He should be very willing to submit them to a committee composed of individuals in part from the new and in part from the old States.

The question was now taken on Mr. Calhoun's amendment, and decided in the negative [by a vote of 7 to 28].

From *Register of Debates*, 24th Cong., 2nd Sess., cols. 729–736. Also printed in the Washington, D.C., *Daily National Intelligencer*, February 14, 1837, p. 2. Printed partially in the Washington, D.C., *Reformer*, March 1, 1837, p. 2; *Remarks of Mr. Calhoun, of South Carolina, on His Proposition to Cede the Public Lands to the New States Upon the Payment of One-Third of the Gross Amount of the Sales. In Senate of the United States, February 7, 1837* (Washington: printed by William W. Moore & Co., 1837), pp. 3–6; Crallé, ed., *Works*, 2:636–638. Variant in the Alexandria, D.C., *Gazette*, February 16, 1837, p. 2. Another variant in *Congressional Globe*, 24th Cong., 2nd Sess., pp. 167–168.

From [President] ANDREW JACKSON

Washington, February 7, 1837

Sir: In the [Washington, D.C.,] Globe of the 6th instant I find the report of a speech made by you on the 4th, upon the land bill, which contains the following passages, viz.:

"Was it not notorious that the President of the United States himself had been connected with the purchase of the public lands? Yes, the 'experiment' (Mr. Calhoun delighted in the word) was the cause of speculation in public lands; and if this bill should not be passed, speculations could not go on, and the price of the public lands must consequently be reduced. He contended that every man could not but see that it would be utter ruin to those who had borrowed money to speculate in lands, if the system was not to go on." In a former part of your speech, as reported, you say: "The speculation, which a particular state of things had given rise to, had been produced by those in power. They had profited by that state of things; and, should this bill be passed, it would only consummate their wishes," &c.

Knowing the liabilities of reporters to err, in taking down and writing out the speeches of members of Congress, I have made enquiry in relation to the accuracy of this report, and have been furnished with certificates of gentlemen who heard you, affirming that it is substantially correct.

You cannot but be aware, sir, that the imputations which your language conveys are calculated, if believed, to destroy my character as a man, and that the charge is one which, if true, ought to produce my impeachment and punishment as a public officer. If I caused the removal of the deposites for the base purpose of enriching myself or my friends by any of the results which might grow out of that measure, there is no term of reproach which I do not deserve, and no punishment known to the laws which ought not to be inflicted upon me. On the contrary, if the whole imputation, both as to motive and fact, be a fabrication and calumny, the punishment which belongs to me, if guilty, is too mild for him who wil[l]fully makes it.

I am aware, sir, of the constitutional privilege under which this imputation is cast forth, and the immunity which it secures. That privilege it is in no degree my purpose to violate, however gross and wicked may have been the abuse of it. But I exercise only the common right of every citizen, when I inform you that the imputations you have cast upon me are false in every particular, not having for the last ten years purchased any public land, or had any interest in such purchase. The whole charge, unless explained, must be considered the offspring of a morbid imagination or of sleepless malice.

I ask you, sir, as an act due to justice, honor, and truth, to retract this charge on the floor of the Senate in as public a manner as it has been uttered; being the most appropriate mode by which you can repair the injury which might otherwise flow from it.

But in the event that you fail to do so, I then demand that you place your charge before the House of Representatives, that they may institute the necessary proceedings to ascertain the truth or falsehood of your imputation, with a view to such further measures as justice may require.

If you will neither do justice yourself, nor place the matter in a position where justice may be done me by the representatives of the people, I shall be compelled to resort to the only remedy left me, and, before I leave the city, give publicity to this letter, by which you will stand stigmatized as one who, protected by his constitutional privilege, is ready to stab the reputation of others, without the magnanimity to do them justice, or the honor to place them in a situation to receive it from others. Yours, &c. Andrew Jackson.

P.S. I herewith enclose you the copies of two notes [by Arthur Campbell and W.E. Drake], verifying the correctness of the report of your speech in the Globe of the 6th instant. A.J.

PC with Ens in *Register of Debates*, 24th Cong., 2nd Sess., cols. 753–755; PC with Ens in the Washington, D.C., *United States' Telegraph*, February 10, 1837, p. 3; PC with Ens in the Alexandria, D.C., *Gazette*, February 13, 1837, p. 2; PC in the Columbia, S.C., *Southern Times and State Gazette*, February 17, 1837, p. 3; PC in the Charleston, S.C., *Mercury*, February 22, 1837, p. 2; PC with Ens in the Pendleton, S.C., *Messenger*, March 31, 1837, p. 1; PC with Ens in Crallé, ed., *Works*, 3:1–3. NOTE: Arthur Campbell's brother John Campbell, [Treasurer of the U.S. by Jackson's appointment,] wrote another brother in regard to this incident that Jackson's supposed friends had played upon his passions, instigating him to demand the "mortifying" statement from Arthur. "The truth is the poor old Gen[era]l ought to have been at the Hermitage four years ago." (ALI, undated, in NcD, Campbell Family Papers.)

REMARKS ON HIS MOTION IN REGARD TO BRITISH SEIZURES OF SLAVES

[In the Senate, February 7, 1837]

Mr. Calhoun said that he considered the cases referred to in the resolution [he had submitted to the Senate on 1/28] as among the greatest outrages that had ever been committed by any foreign power on the flag and the rights of the citizens of the United States.

The facts connected with the Encomium, which was the first in point of date, are these: She sailed from Wilmington, North Carolina, in the spring of 1834, having on board forty-five slaves belonging to Mr. [Hugh] Waddell, a citizen of high respectability, and who is now Speaker of the House of Commons of North Carolina, and who intended to settle a plantation in Mississippi, or some one of the Southwestern States. The vessel was wrecked upon the False Keys —the passengers and crew taken by a wrecker into New Providence, [Bahamas,] where the slaves were forcibly seized and detained by the local authorities of the island. The case of the Enterprise is similar. She sailed in the spring of 1835, from Alexandria [D.C.] for Charleston, South Carolina, and was forced, by stress of weather, into Bermuda, where the slaves on board were in like manner seized and detained.

I hold, said Mr. Calhoun, the principle to be unquestionable, that, according to the laws of nations, a vessel on the high seas is in fact an extension of the territory of the nation to which it belongs, and is not in time of peace liable to be molested or interfered with by any power whatever. I also hold that this principle, if possible, was stronger and more sacred as applied to the coasting trade, which may be fairly regarded as sacred as the coastwise communication inland. I also hold that when a vessel or crew is forced, by stress of weather or shipwreck, into the port of another power, she loses none of the rights which belong to her on the ocean; but, on the contrary, she has superadded the rights imposed by the laws of humanity, which all civilized people hold sacred; and that neither vessel nor crew, under such circumstances, are subject to the laws of the country, except so far as may be made necessary by the police of the country during their continuance there.

I regard these principles so sacred that I am quite at a loss to conjecture how it has happened that the outrages committed by the local authorities on our flag and the rights of our citizens have remained so long unredressed. I can hardly believe that the Administration has neglected its duty, by failing to press the case home to the attention of the British Government in the pointed manner which its magnitude demands. On the other hand, it appears to be equally difficult to believe that the Government of Great Britain, which has been distinguished for its justice and magnanimity, should refuse for a moment to make ample acknowledgment and compensation, if the case has, in fact, been pressed on its attention in the manner it deserves. My object (said Mr. C[alhoun]) in moving the resolution is to ascertain the state of the facts, and to know how it has happened that the slaves have not been restored, or ample compensation made to our citizens who have been injured.

From the Washington, D.C., *United States' Telegraph*, February 15, 1837, p. 3. Also printed in the Alexandria, D.C., *Gazette*, February 18, 1837, p. 2. Variant in *Register of Debates*, 24th Cong., 2nd Sess., col. 725; the Washington, D.C., *Globe*, February 9, 1837, p. 2; *Congressional Globe*, 24th Cong., 2nd Sess., p. 167.

"A Bill to Cede the Public Lands within the Limits of the New States, on Certain Conditions therein Mentioned," introduced in the Senate on 2/9. This bill was nearly identical with the proposal that had been offered by Calhoun on 2/7 as an amendment to the public land bill then pending. This new bill differed only in that blanks were left in the second section where minimum prices had been set forth in the earlier version. (This new bill was tabled on its second reading on 2/11 by a vote of 26 to 20. It was also, fairly unusually, ordered to be printed on a motion of Ambrose H. Sevier of Ark.) CC in DNA, RG 46 (Records of the U.S. Senate), 24A-B3; PC in DNA, RG 46, 24A-B4; PC in DLC, Congressional Bills, 24th Cong., 2nd Sess., S-207; PC in Crallé, ed., *Works*, 2:634–636.

SPEECH ON HIS BILL TO CEDE THE PUBLIC LANDS TO THE STATES IN WHICH THEY ARE SITUATED

[In the Senate, February 9, 1837]

Mr. Calhoun introduced as a substantive proposition, and in form of a bill, the amendment he had the day before [*sic*; on 2/7] moved to the land bill; which proposes a cession of the public lands, on certain conditions therein specified, to the States, respectively, in which they lie. It was read once, and, by unanimous consent, received its second reading.

Mr. Calhoun said that he wished it to be referred to the Committee on Public Lands, or to a select committee, as the Senate might choose.

[*After discussion by several Senators Daniel Webster moved that the Senate reconsider the second reading that had just been approved. Though opposed to the bill, he thought it an important one, and he wished that the yeas and nays be recorded on the vote for a second reading.*]

Mr. Calhoun hoped the vote would not be reconsidered. The subject was obviously of great moment; and, at a period very shortly to come, it must press itself home on the consideration of every Senator. It was in vain to expect, on a bill of this magnitude, a naked vote by yea and nay. He should himself desire to be fully heard in its behalf, as he doubted not other gentlemen would, from both the new and the old States. It was a matter of perfect indifference to him in what form his views should be presented, whether by a speech on the floor, or through the report of the committee. A reference and report were the usual course, and he hoped that a bill of this character would not be treated with less courtesy than others.

[*Discussion continued. Henry Clay mentioned his own public land distribution bill which had been vetoed by Andrew Jackson and declared that the land bill before the Senate and the substitute offered by Calhoun were both equally objectionable to him.*]

Mr. Calhoun observed, in reply, that he had come there with a fixed resolution to resist all attempts at innovation upon our system in relation to the public lands; and, he might add, with no small hope that he should be successful.

Mr. C[alhoun] said he took it as rather unkind, though he was sure it had not been so intended, that the Senator from Kentucky should say that there was any analogy between this bill and that from the Committee on the Public Lands, which Mr. C[alhoun] had strenuously opposed. This measure, reluctantly forced upon him by the necessity of the case, had been introduced with a desire to terminate great political evils. He did assure that honorable Senator, whatever might be the obligation of duty which he felt in opposing this measure, a no less imperative obligation urged Mr. C[alhoun] to bring it forward. There is, said Mr. C[alhoun], too much power here; the tendency of this Government to centralism is overpowering; and among the many powerful instruments which can be and are brought to bear on the securing and extending of executive power, this control of the public lands is one of the greatest and most effectual. It now gives to any administration disposed so to use it control over nine States (eight, certainly) of this Union. Those States, so far as this regulation of the public lands is concerned, are the vassals of this Government. We are in the place of a great landlord, and they of tenants; we have the ownership and control over the soil they occupy. Can there be any doubt as to how such an ascendency will be used in the present corrupt state of the country? Is there any doubt as to how it has been used, or that the influence derived from it is a growing influence? We must find some remedy for such a state of things, or sink under it. It is in vain to tell us that the Senators from the new States are as capable of giving an independent vote on measures connected with the public lands as those from the old States. It is impossible, in the nature of things. Their constituents have that feeling of ownership which is naturally inseparable from the occupation of the soil; and it must and will control the action of their representatives.

And now I put it to the bosom of every Senator, whether the mere moneyed income derived from the public domain is to be compared for one moment to the great advantage of putting these Senators on the same independent footing with ourselves? I look with sympathy upon their condition, and I feel very sure they will be liberated from it with joy. Such, I am very sure, would be my feelings in the like circumstances. So long as there was no attempt to use the control of the public lands for purposes of a political character, their condition was very different; but since this has been swept into the great vortex of political influence, their situation is wholly changed. I am for knocking off their chains. Sir, said Mr. C[alhoun], I have, on a deliberate view of the whole case, entered upon this course, and I am resolved to go for this measure with all my power. I seek not its popularity or influence. I had rather that some other individual had moved in it, as more than one Senator here can bear me witness; but none would have, and I have therefore determined to proceed. I believe the time has arrived, and I am resolved to go on in the face of all the imputations to which my motives may be liable. I have often done my duty under very difficult circumstances, as all who hear me well know. As to popularity, I despise it. I would not turn on my heel to obtain it. It is a fleeting shadow, unworthy of the pursuit of an upright man. No, sir, I move here on a conscientious conviction of high and imperious duty; and I shall therefore go forward until I have effected my object, if it can be effected. I believe it will prove, in its practical results, a great blessing to the country. I am convinced no stronger measure can be devised for withdrawing the public lands from the great game of political scrambling and gambling for the presidency.

As to the details of the bill: I am under the impression that the sum demanded from the new States for the cession of these lands should be moderate, especially considering that they will be charged with the whole trouble and expense of their administration; and that, from the nature of the human mind, they will necessarily have the feeling that they possess a better right to these lands than others, from the fact of their occupancy. The next reason is, that we may prevent any disturbance from a feeling of discontent, but that the arrangement we make may be viewed as a liberal one, even by the new States themselves. So desirous am I to effect this object, that I will consent to modify this feature of the bill, by inserting almost any rate per cent. which the new States shall, on the whole, deem most prudent and advisable. Another reason why I have set the bonus at a low rate is a desire that the plan should operate as a benefit to the new States. I wish to counteract the tendency to running down of the price of land, and to secure its sale at prices calculated for the benefit of all parties. To secure this, I have inserted a provision, that if there shall be any departure from this condition of the cession, the grant itself shall be void, so as to make it a judicial question.

This measure is not, as has been said, a surrendering of the public domain to a few States of the Union. The lands are not surrendered; they are ceded, on terms by which this Government will make the most of them, even on a mere calculation of money. But I hope all such considerations will be held as entirely secondary and subordinate to greater and higher interests. All, I am confident, feel that there must be some remedy devised for the existing evils connected with this subject. There is too much action here; how it enures, and to whose advantage, we have fully seen. It is the great evil of patronage, which, if not limited and curtailed, will render perfectly futile all efforts to preserve the liberties of the country. My ideas on this subject are well known. It is the law of our political situation that, as our territory spreads, and our population is augmented, that action of the centre of the system must be diminished more and more. It should be confined merely to the sustaining of a harmonious intercourse of the several portions of the confederacy; a harmony of parts throughout the great and wide-spread system. I solemnly believe that a knowledge of this great fundamental law, and a steadfast adherence to it, are the only means by which our freedom can be preserved. We must watch the stealthy advance of power, and resist it, step by step. We must not suffer every power of this Government to be perverted into an engine for President making. Let us apply, at once, the axe to the root.

These are my motives in bringing forward this important measure, and not a grovelling desire of popularity, or any reserved hope of personal benefit to be enjoyed hereafter; I hold all such things light as air. I seek to do my duty, and to preserve, so far as I can, the liberties of my country.

[*Webster insisted on his motion to reconsider. If Calhoun did not consent, he would move to table, which would shut off discussion.*]

Mr. Calhoun expressed his regret that the bill should be opposed at this early stage, and in so unusual a manner. As long as I have been a member of this and the other House, (said Mr. C[alhoun],) I cannot recollect more than three or four instances, before the present, in which a bill has been opposed at its second reading, and then under very peculiar circumstances. And why, may I ask, is the usual course departed from on the present occasion? Why not let this bill receive its second reading and be referred, as other bills are, to a committee, to be considered and reported on? The reply is, to prevent agitation; that is, as I understand it, to prevent the feelings of the public from being excited and its attention directed to this highly important subject. If that be the intention, I tell gentlemen they will fail in their object. The subject is already before the public; and, if my life be spared, I shall keep it there—shall agitate it till the public attention shall be roused to a full and thorough investigation of a measure that I firmly believe is not less essential to the interest of the whole Union than it is to that of the new States. I tell them more: that the very unusual and extraordinary course they have adopted, in opposition to this bill, will but more deeply agitate the public mind, and the more intensely attract its attention to the subject. It will naturally excite the inquiry, why not let this bill take the ordinary course? Why not let it go to a committee, to investigate its provisions, and present all the arguments for and against it, fully and fairly, so that its merits and demerits, such as they are, may be clearly understood? Opposition to so reasonable a course will make the impression that the object is to suppress investigation, whatever may be the motive of gentlemen, and will naturally excite suspicion and more diligent inquiry.

In making these remarks, I am not ignorant that the merits of the bill are fully open to discussion on the pending question [that is, the motion to reconsider]; but it is impossible that a hasty discussion, at this last stage of the session, and when the time of the Senate is so fully engrossed with other subjects, can be so satisfactory as would be a report, in which the views of the majority of the committee, after a full consultation, might be calmly and deliberately spread at large before the public. And why not adopt so natural a course? Besides being more favorable to investigation, it would consume less time; a point of no small importance at the present stage of the session. If referred, the committee would doubtless be so constituted as to comprehend both friends and opponents of the measure. Among the latter, if my wishes should be consulted, I would be glad to see the name of the Senator from Massachusetts, (Mr. Webster,) who is so capable of doing full justice to whatever side he undertakes to defend. It is thus that the whole merits of the measure would be fully presented; and if it be so liable to objections as is supposed, the result might be to satisfy the new States themselves that it ought not to be adopted. But if, on the other hand, the argument should prove to be decidedly in its favor, as I firmly and conscientiously believe, the very agitation which gentlemen seem so much to dread would be promptly terminated by the adoption of the measure. Thus regarding the subject, I cannot but regret that this bill has not been permitted to take the usual course, and that I am compelled, in this hasty manner, without premeditation, to reply to the arguments of the Senator from Massachusetts, (Mr. Webster,) which, after mature deliberation, he has urged with all his force against the measure. I shall begin with my reply to his constitutional objections. He holds that the measure is unconstitutional, because we have no authority to give away the public lands.

I do not feel myself obliged to meet this objection. It is not true in fact. The bill makes no gift. It cedes the public lands to the States within which they are respectively situated, subject to various conditions, and, among others, that they shall pay over one third of the gross amount of the sales to the United States; that they shall surrender all their claims against the Government under the two and three per cent. funds, and take the whole trouble and expense of the management of the land, including the extinguishment of the Indian titles. But I waive this decisive answer. I meet the Senator on his own ground, and with a conclusive argument, as far at least as he is concerned. He admits that it would not be a violation of the constitution for Congress to make a donation of land to an individual; and what, I ask, is there to prevent it from making a donation to two; to an hundred; or to a thousand? and if to them individually, why not to them in the aggregate, as a community or a State? He, indeed, admits, that Congress may make a donation of public lands to a State, for useful purposes. If to one State, why not to several States—to the new States, if the measure should be thought to be wise and proper? If there be a distinction, I acknowledge my intellect is too obtuse to perceive it; but as the bill makes no gift, I feel under no necessity of pressing the argument further.

The Senator's next position is, that we have no right to delegate the trust of administering the public domain, confided to us by the constitution, to the States. Here, again, I may object, that the argument has no foundation in truth. The bill delegates no trust. It makes a concession—a sale of the public lands to the new States; and what the Senator calls trusts are but conditions annexed to the sales—conditions alike beneficial to them and to the old States. The simple question, then, is, can Congress sell public lands to a State? Suppose the State of Ohio were to offer to pay $1.25 an acre for the remnant of the public lands within her limits, could not Congress sell it to her? And if it may sell for $1.25, may it not for a dollar, for 75 cents, or a less sum, if it should be deemed the true value? Again: if Congress can make an absolute sale, may it not make a conditional one? And if so, why may it not make the disposition proposed in this bill? That is the question, and I would be glad to have it answered. If I ever had any constitutional scruples on the subject, the arguments of the Senator would have satisfied me that they were without the shadow of foundation. His reasoning faculties are well known; and if these are the strongest constitutional objections that he can advance, we may be assured that the bill is perfectly free from all objections of that description.

Having now dispatched the objections against the constitutionality of this bill, I shall next consider the arguments which the Senator urged against its expediency. He says that I placed the necessity of this bill on the fact of the passage of the land bill

412

reported by the Committee on Public Lands; and, as it was still uncertain whether it would become a law, the ground on which the necessity of this bill was based may yet fail. The Senate will remember the remarks I made on asking leave to introduce this bill, and that I was far from placing it on the simple fact of the passage of that bill. I took broader ground, and rested my motion on the character of the bill and the circumstances which attended its passage through this body. From these, I concluded that the period we all acknowledge must sometime come had actually arrived, when the public lands within the new States should on proper conditions be ceded to them. I do not deem it necessary now to go into a discussion of the character of the bill, nor the history of its passage through the Senate. We all have, no doubt, formed our opinion in relation to both. From all I saw and heard, I am satisfied that the bill had not the hearty assent of its supporters, whether from the new or old States; and I doubt very much whether there was an individual who voted for it, that gave it his hearty approbation. Many who had uniformly opposed all measures of the kind, and who represented portions of the Union which had ever been vigilant on all questions connected with the public lands, were found in the ranks of those who supported the bill. The explanation is easy. It assumed the character of a party measure, to be carried on party grounds, without reference to the true interests of either the new or old States; and, if we are to credit declarations made elsewhere, to fulfil obligations contracted anterior to the late presidential election. From all this, I inferred we had reached the period when it was no longer possible to prevent the public domains from becoming the subject of party contention, and being used by party as an engine to control the politics of the country. It was this conviction, and not the mere [probable] passage of the bill, as the Senator supposes, that induced me to introduce this bill.

I saw, clearly, it was time to cut off this vast source of patronage and power, and to place the Senators and Representatives from the new States on an equality with those from the old, by withdrawing our local control, and breaking the vassalage under which they are now placed. The Senator from Massachusetts objects to the term, and denies that Congress exercises any local control over those States. I used it to express the strong degree of dependence of the new States on this Government, whose power and patronage are ramified over their whole surface, and whose domains constitute so large a portion of their territory. I certainly did not anticipate that the Senator from Massachusetts, or any other, would deny the ex-

413

istence of this dependence, or the local control of the Government within their limits. Can any thing be more local than the lands of a State? and can any State be said to be free from dependence on a Government, when that Government has the administration of a large portion of its domain? Is it no hardship that the citizens of the new States should be compelled to travel nine or ten hundred miles to this place, and to wait our tardy justice on all claims connected with the public lands; a subject, in its own nature, the most local of all, and which ought, above all others, to be under the charge of the local authorities of the States? I ask him if he would be willing to see Massachusetts placed in the same relation to this Government? and, if it were, whether it would not destroy its independence? I ask him if it must not give a great and controlling influence wherever it exists? Through its lands, [the] authority and action of the Government pervades [*sic*] the whole territory of the new States, and their citizens become claimants at your doors, session after session, either for favor or justice. I do not say that all this is incompatible with the sovereignty of those States, but I do aver that it is in derogation of their sovereignty.

The Senator next objects to this measure, that it would not free Congress from its present difficulties, in reference to the public domain. He says that we should soon have the new States here, besieging us with memorials to alter the conditions of cession, with all the dependence and difficulties of which we now complain. My impression is very different. Make the terms liberal, and they will be satisfied. They will relieve Congress from the whole burden of business, as far as the lands are concerned, which now occupies so much of its time; and the public councils will no longer be under the dangerous influence inseparable from their management. If hereafter a new state of things should arise, and the arrangement proposed in the bill should require reversion, it will be for those who come after us to apply a remedy; and I have no fear but they will do their duty.

The Senator next insists that the acquisition of these lands will prove no benefit to the new States, and predicts that it would involve them in incessant agitation and trouble. Such might be the case, if the cession was absolute; but the bill contains provisions which will prove an effectual check against these difficulties. To place its provisions beyond alteration or attack, it is expressly provided that, if they should be violated by the States, the cession itself should be void, and all grants made subsequent thereto shall be null and of no effect. They are thus placed under the safeguard of the

Judiciary, and the courts of the Union will determine on questions growing out of their infraction. For this purpose, the cession has assumed the form of a compact, and I feel confident that, under its provisions, the new States would administer the land without agitation or any serious trouble or difficulty. If this can be effected, I appeal to the Senators, whether the land within their limits ought not to be under their local administration? I, for one, feel that we of the old States have not, and cannot have, that full and accurate local knowledge necessary for their proper management. Of all the branches of our business, it is that which I least understand. From this defect of information, the Land Committee has it almost exclusively under its sole control, whenever it is so constituted as to attract in any degree the confidence of the House. This has been the case from the first. I well remember, that when I first took my seat in the other House, Jeremiah Morrow, a member from Ohio, a man of great integrity and good sense, was the chairman of the Committee on Public Lands, and was, in fact, the sole legislator on all subjects connected with them; and in this body we have almost invariably yielded our judgment to the committee, from a conscious want of information. The difficulty is growing from year to year, with the vast increase of the new States and Territories, and the growing complication of our land code; and the consequent increase of business is such that we already have scarce time to despatch it with due attention. In a short time the increase will be doubled; and what shall we then do? By passing this bill, we will be wholly relieved from this burden, and the questions we are now compelled to determine without adequate knowledge will then be settled by those whose local knowledge will make them familiar and well acquainted with the subject.

But we are told by the Senator that the public lands have been well administered by the General Government, and that he cannot surrender his belief but that they will continue so to be. That they were well administered in the early stages of the Government, while they were not an object of much pecuniary or political interest, I am ready to admit; but I hold it not less certain, that as the number and population of the new States increase, and with them, the value of the public lands and the political importance of those States, we must become year by year less and less competent to their management, till finally we shall become wholly so. I believe that we are not now far from that period. Does not the Senator see the great and growing influence of the new States, and that it is in the power of any unprincipled and ambitious man from one of them to wield that influence at his pleasure? Should he propose any measure in relation to the public lands, be it ever so extravagant and dangerous, the members from the new States dare not vote against it, however adverse to the measure. It is useless to disguise the fact that our possession of so much land in the new States creates and cherishes an antagonist feeling on their part towards the Government, as to every measure that relates to them. They naturally consider your policy as opposed to their interest, and as retarding their growth and prosperity, as great as they are. We must take human nature as it is, and accommodate our measures to it, instead of making the vain attempt to bend it to our measures. We must calculate that the means of control, which this state of things puts into the hands of the ambitious and designing, will not be neglected; and, instead of idly complaining, let us remove the cause by wise and timely legislation. The difficulties and dangers are daily on the increase. Four years more will probably add three more new States, and six additional Senators, with a great increase of members in the other House; and, what is more important, a corresponding increase of votes and influence in the electoral college. Can you doubt the consequences? The public lands, with their immense patronage, will be brought to bear more and more on the action of Congress; will control the presidential elections; and the result will be, that he who uses this vast fund of power with the least scruple will carry away the prize.

The Senator himself sees and acknowledges the approach of this dangerous period, and agrees that, when it does come, we must surrender the public lands within the new States; but is for holding on till it shall have actually arrived. My opinion is the reverse. I regard it as one of the wisest maxims in human affairs, that when we see an inevitable evil, like this, not to be resisted, approaching, to make concessions in time, while we can do it with dignity, and not to wait until necessity compels us to act, and when concession, instead of gratitude, will excite contempt. The maxim is not new. I have derived it from the greatest of modern statesmen, Edmund Burke. He urged its adoption on the British Government, in the early stages of our Revolution; and if the obstinate and infatuated statesman, Lord North, then at the head of affairs, had listened to his warning voice, it may be doubted whether our Revolution would have taken place; but events were ordered otherwise. The voice of wisdom was unheeded, and the Revolution followed, with all its consequences, which have so greatly changed the condition of the world.

I have thus hastily, and without the advantage of previous re-flection, replied to the arguments of the Senator from Massachusetts. I would have been much gratified if a course better suited to the magnitude of the subject and more favorable for full and deliberate discussion, had been adopted; but, as it is, I have passed over no arguments, as far as I can remember, which he advanced, and, I trust, have replied to none which I have not successfully refuted.

I shall now conclude with a few remarks, in reply to the Senator from New Jersey, (Mr. [Samuel L.] Southard.) He tells us that he will not bid for the new States. (I regret, said Mr. C[alhoun], that I do not see him in his place.) Does he mean to intimate that, in introducing this bill, I am bidding for them? If he does, I throw back the injurious imputation. I indignantly repel the charge. No, sir, I am not a bidder. What I have done has been from an honest conviction of duty, and not less for the benefit of the old than the new States. The measure I conscientiously believe would be alike serviceable to both.

(Mr. Southard, who had been absent, here returned to the cham-ber. Mr. C[alhoun], seeing him, repeated his remarks; on which Mr. S[outhard] disclaimed having said any thing like what Mr. C[al-houn] understood him to have said. On which, Mr. C[alhoun] re-sumed:)

I am happy to hear it. I felt confident that the Senator could not intend to cast so injurious an imputation on me, and I rejoice to hear from his own lips the frank and honorable disclosure he has made.

But I not only believe the measure to be beneficial and expedient, but I firmly believe it to be indispensable, in order to restore the Government to a sound and healthy condition.

The tendency of our system to centralism, with its ruinous con-sequences, can no longer be denied. To counteract this, its patron-age must be curtailed. There are three great sources to which its immense patronage may be mainly traced, and by which the Gov-ernment is enabled to exert such an immense control over public opinion—the public lands, the post office, and the currency. The first may be entirely removed. This bill will cut it up root and branch. By a single stroke we would not only retrench this growing and almost boundless source of patronage, but also free ourselves from the pressure of an immense mass of business, which encumbers our legislation, and divides and distracts our attention; and this would be done without impairing, in the long run, our pecuniary resources. In addition, the measure would place the Senators from

417

the new States on the same equal and independent footing in this chamber with ourselves. In such results who would not rejoice? The Senators from the new States would especially have cause to rejoice in the change. Relieve them from the dependent condition of their States, and they would be found in the front ranks, sustaining the laws and the constitution against the encroachments of power.

But the Senator from New Jersey tells us that we have no power to pass this bill, as it would be in violation of the ordinance which makes the public land a common fund for the benefit of all the States; and that we, as trustees, are bound to administer it strictly in reference to the object of the trust. In reply, I might ask the Senator how he can reconcile his construction of the ordinance with the constant practice of the Government, in which, if I mistake not, it has been sustained by his vote? How many grants have been made out of the public domain to colleges, academies, asylums for the deaf and dumb, and other institutions of like character? If such concessions be consistent with provisions of the ordinance, what prevents this bill from being so also? But I rest not my reply on that ground. I meet the Senator according to his interpretation of the ordinance. I assert boldly that the disposition this bill proposes to make of the portion of the public domain within the new States is the very best, under existing circumstances, that can be made, regarding it in reference to the common interest of all the States. Let it be borne in mind, that all sides agree the new States will soon be able to command their terms, when others less favorable to the common interest may be imposed. If we of the old States make it a point to hold on to the last, they will, by a necessary reaction, make it a point to extort all they can when they get the power. But if we yield in time, a durable arrangement may be made, mutually beneficial and satisfactory to both parties.

The Senator further objects, that if this bill should pass, its provisions would be extended, from necessity, to all States which may hereafter be admitted into the Union. I must say, I see no such necessity; but my present impression is, that such would be the course that wisdom would dictate. According to my mode of thinking, all the revenue we may derive from the sales of lands in a State, after its admission, is not to be compared in importance to its independence as a sovereign member of the Union; for there is no danger of the falling of our institutions for the want of pecuniary means, while there is no small danger of their overthrow from the growing and absorbing attraction of this central power.

[*Debate continued. Webster maintained his position, and Thom-*

as H. Benton declared himself opposed to any further proceedings on Calhoun's bill. Henry Hubbard also opposed Calhoun's bill. All the opponents stressed that they did not wish the impression to become widespread that there was any likelihood that Congress would seriously entertain such a proposal. Hubbard moved that Webster's motion be laid on the table.]

Mr. H[ubbard] withdrew the motion, on request of

Mr. Calhoun, who again pressed for a select committee. The time for action had arrived. The measure had already been presented to the public, and could not be unpresented; and he wished the country to hear and consider the arguments both for and against it.

[The Senate then voted 29 to 22 for Webster's motion to reconsider the second reading, leaving the bill before the body on its first reading.]

From *Register of Debates*, 24th Cong., 2nd Sess., cols. 739–753. Printed partially in the Washington, D.C., *Daily National Intelligencer*, February 14, 1837, pp. 2–3; the Washington, D.C., *Reformer*, March 1, 1837, p. 2; *Remarks of Mr. Calhoun, of South Carolina, on His Proposition to Cede the Public Lands to the New States Upon the Payment of One-Third of the Gross Amount of the Sales. In Senate of the United States, February 7 [sic], 1837* (Washington: printed by William W. Moore & Co., 1837), pp. 6–14; Crallé, ed., *Works*, 2:638–652. Variant in the Washington, D.C., *Globe*, February 14, 1837, p. 2; *Congressional Globe*, 24th Cong., 2nd Sess., Appendix, pp. 155–157. Another variant in the New York, N.Y., *Morning Courier and New-York Enquirer*, February 11, 1837, p. 2.

REMARKS ON ANDREW JACKSON'S LETTER

[In the Senate, February 9, 1837]

[Calhoun's land bill having been disposed of for the time, the bill "to prohibit the sale of public lands, except to actual settlers, in limited quantities," which was being managed by Robert J. Walker, came up.]

Mr. Calhoun said: I have received, within the last forty-eight hours, a communication from the Chief Magistrate, connected with the bill now before the Senate, of such a nature that duty to myself, as well as to this body, renders it necessary that I should lay it before the Senate.

[Here the Secretary of the Senate, upon request, read the letter from Andrew Jackson to Calhoun, dated 2/7, and its supporting

affidavits, in regard to Calhoun's remarks in the Senate on 2/4 during discussion of the land bill.]

I do not intend, (said Mr. C[alhoun],) in what I propose to say, to comment on the character or the language of this extraordinary letter. It has excited in my bosom the mingled feelings of pity for the weakness of its author, contempt for his menace, and humiliation that one occupying the office which he does should place himself in a situation so unworthy of his exalted station. Nor do I intend to invoke the interposition of the Senate to protect the privilege attached to a Senator from one of the sovereign States of this confederacy, which has been outraged in my person. I seek no aid to defend my own privileges; and, so far from being intimidated, I shall be emboldened to express myself with greater freedom, if possible, to denounce the corruption of the administration, or the violation of the laws and of the constitution, in consequence of this attempt to restrain the free exercise of the right of expressing my opinions upon all subjects concerning the public interests, secured to me by the constitution. I leave to the Senate to determine what measures the preservation of their own privileges demands.

Much less do I intend to comply with the request or demand made of me; demand has no place between equals; and I hold myself, within my constitutional privilege, at least equal to the Chief Magistrate himself. I, as a legislator, have a right to investigate and pronounce upon his conduct, and to condemn his acts freely, whenever I consider them to be in violation of the laws and of the constitution. I, as a Senator, may judge him; he can never judge me.

My object is to avail myself of the occasion to reiterate what I said, as broadly and fully as I uttered them on a former occasion, here in my place, where alone I am responsible, and where the friends of the President will have an opportunity to correct my statement if erroneous, or to refute my conclusions if not fairly drawn. I spoke without notes, and it may be that I may omit something which I said on the former occasion that may be deemed material, or express myself less full and strong than I then did. If so, I will thank any Senator to remind me, so that my statement now may be as strong and as full as then.

If my memory serves me, I opened my remarks, when I spoke formerly, by stating that so many and so subtle were the devices by which those who were in power could, in these times, fleece the people, without their knowing it, that it was almost enough to make a lover of his country despair of its liberty. I then stated that I knew of no measure which could better illustrate the truth of this remark than the one now before us. Its professed object is to restrict the sales of public land, in order, as is avowed, to prevent speculation; and, by consequence, the accumulation of a surplus revenue in the Treasury. The measure is understood to be an administration measure. I then stated that, so far from preventing speculation, it would, in fact, but consummate the greatest speculation which this country had ever witnessed—a speculation originating in a state of things of which those in power were the authors; by which they had profited; and which this measure, should it become a law, would but complete. I then asked what had caused such an extraordinary demand for public land, that the sales should have more than quintupled within the last three years? and said that, to answer this question, we must look to the state of the currency. That it was owing to the extraordinary increase of bank paper, which had filled to repletion all the channels of circulation. The Secretary had estimated this increase, within that period, at from six dollars and fifty cents per individual to ten dollars. I believe the increase to be much greater; the effects of which have been to double the price of every article which has not been kept down by some particular cause. In the mean time, the price of public land has remained unaltered, at one dollar and twenty-five cents the acre; and the natural consequence was, that this excessive currency overflowed upon the public land, and has caused those extraordinary speculations which it is the professed object of this bill to prevent.

I then asked, what had caused this inundation of paper? The answer was, the experiment, (I love to remind the gentleman [Jackson?] of the word,) which had removed the only restrictions that existed against the issue of bank paper. The consequence was predicted at the time; it was foretold that banks would multiply almost without number, and pour forth their issues without restriction or limitation. These predictions were at the time unheeded; their truth now begins to be realized.

The experiment commenced by a transfer of the public funds from where they were placed by law, and where they were under its safeguard and protection, to banks which were under the sole and unlimited control of the Executive. The effect was a vast increase of executive patronage, and the opening [of] a field of speculation, in describing which, in anticipation, I pronounced it [in 1834] to be so ample, that Rothschild himself might envy the opportunity which it afforded. Such it has proved to be.

The administration has profited by this vast patronage, and the prejudice which it has excited against the bank [of the U.S.], as the means of sustaining themselves in power. It is unnecessary to repeat the remarks in illustration of this. The truth of the statement is known to all the Senators who have daily witnessed the party topics which have been drawn from this fruitful source. I then remarked that, if rumor were to be trusted, it was not only in a political point of view that those in power had profited by the vast means put in the hands of the Executive by the experiment; they had profited in a pecuniary as well as in a political point of view. It has been frequently stated, and not contradicted, that many in high places are among the speculators in public lands; and that even an individual connected with the President himself, one of his nephews, was an extensive adventurer in this field of speculation. I did not name him, but I now feel myself called upon to do so. I mean Mr. [John C.] McLemore.

Having established these points, I next undertook to show that this bill would consummate those speculations, and establish the political ascendency which the experiment had given to the administration. In proof of the former, I availed myself of the declaration of [Robert J. Walker] the chairman of the Committee on Public Lands, who had stated that the speculators had already purchased and held a vast amount of public land, not less, as I understood him, than twenty-five or thirty millions of acres; and that, if this bill did not pass, the scenes of the last two years would be repeated in this and the coming year. I then undertook to show, from the showing of the chairman himself, that these speculations would prove ruinous without the aid of this bill. He had stated that the annual demand for public land, resulting from our increased population, could not exceed five millions of acres.

Now, assuming that the quantity on hand is thirty millions of acres, there would be six years' supply in the hands of speculators, even if the land offices of the United States be closed; and that if the bill did not pass, according to his showing, it would take double or treble the time to dispose of the lands which, in that case, will be in the hands of speculators. All must see the certain ruin, in that event, of those who have borrowed money to speculate in land; particularly if the sales of public land should be free and open to every one, as it now is, to purchase to the extent of his means. I next showed that the contest was between the Government, as a dealer in public land, and the speculators; that they held in market at least an equal quantity in value to that which the Government now has offered for sale, and that every restriction imposed upon the sales of Government land must, of necessity, increase the advantages of its rival dealers.

I then showed that very onerous and oppressive restrictions, of an odious character, upon the sales of the public lands, would be imposed if the bill should pass. No one thereafter could purchase land of the Government without a license—a license, in my opinion, as offensive and odious as would be a license on the press. To obtain this license, the oath of the applicant was required, and then it could only be obtained on payment of one dollar and twenty-five cents per acre, for which the citizen may now receive a grant in fee simple. After he had made his purchase, under the authority of his license, the purchaser has to comply with the condition of settlement and cultivation, and must, within the period of five years, prove to the satisfaction of the register and receiver [of a Land Office], who are made high judicial officers, a compliance with these conditions, before he can receive his title; and if he failed to comply, by accident or otherwise, he forfeits both his money and the land. I stated that this was a virtual increase of the price of the public lands to the actual settler; so much so, that any sober-minded man would prefer to give the speculators two dollars per acre for land of the same quality, to giving the Government one dollar and twenty-five cents for a license with these oppressive conditions.

Having established this point, I then undertook to show that it would increase vastly the power of the Government in the new States, if they chose to exercise this patronage for political purposes. That they would so use it, we have ample proof in the past conduct of the administration, and in the principles which have been openly avowed by its friends. A former Senator from New York [William L. Marcy], high in the confidence of the party, and now Chief Magistrate of that State, has openly avowed, in his place on this floor, that to the victors belong the spoils; for which he was reprimanded at the time by the Senator from Massachusetts (Mr. Webster) in a manner worthy of his distinguished talents. Assuming, then, that the power would be exercised with a view to political influence, I showed that it would place a vast number of citizens of the new States, probably not less than one hundred thousand, in a condition of complete dependence on the receivers, and of vassalage to the Government.

These are the sentiments which I delivered on a former occasion, and which I now reiterate to the full extent—omitting nothing that is material, as far as connected with the letter of the President; and for the delivery of which, my privileges as a Senator, and those of this body, have been so grossly outraged.

[*Felix Grundy regretted the "long continued and unhappy differences" between the President and the Senator from South Carolina; said that Calhoun had spoken nothing on 2/4 "directed against the President, personally or individually"; and stated that John Mc-Lemore was not a blood relative of Jackson but had married the daughter of Jackson's brother-in-law, John Donelson.*]

Mr. Calhoun made some remarks. He was understood to say that he had not read the report of his remarks in the Globe, or in any other paper; he had often done so, and generally found them very incorrectly given. Nor was this surprising; the situation of the reporters, and the noise in the chamber, rendered it almost impossible that they should distinctly hear all that was said. The reporter who had certified in this case sat, he believed, immediately behind him; and the reporters of the Globe were never in the habit of submitting to him any of their reports for revision.

Mr. C[alhoun] did not impute any blame for what had been reported in the Globe. The President, however, had thought proper to take up that report, and, in commenting upon it, had used language which no gentleman was in the habit of employing to another, and which, indeed, was more worthy of the purlieus of Billingsgate than of the manner of the Chief Magistrate of a great nation.

[*Walker defended himself against the implication that the present land bill was related to the removal of the deposits and to "the system of speculation."*]

Mr. Calhoun here interposed, and disclaimed any imputation whatever on the motives of the honorable gentleman in introducing the bill; he had never doubted for a moment that they were honest and patriotic, and that the honorable Senator's whole course in the matter was prompted by his zeal for what he understood to be the interests of the new States.

[*Walker said the present land bill did not originate with the administration and was not related to the removal of the deposits, which he had opposed.*]

Mr. Calhoun would merely observe that, if he had been led into error in supposing that the funds derived from banks had been used for purposes of speculation in the public lands, he had been led into it by the President himself, who had said so in his [annual] message.

[*Henry Clay here took the floor to denounce Jackson's letter and to regret that the administration majority in the Senate prevented that body from making a response "that would make the throne shake on which he sits."*]

From *Register of Debates*, 24th Cong., 2nd Sess., cols. 753–759. Also printed in the Washington, D.C., *United States' Telegraph*, February 10, 1837, p. 3, and February 17, 1837, p. 2; the Washington, D.C., *Daily National Intelligencer*, February 14, 1837, p. 3. Printed partially in the Pendleton, S.C., *Messenger*, March 31, 1837, p. 2; Crallé, ed., *Works*, 3:1–9. Variant in the Washington, D.C., *Daily National Intelligencer*, February 10, 1837, p. 3; the Alexandria, D.C., *Gazette*, February 11, 1837, p. 2; the Richmond, Va., *Enquirer*, February 14, 1837, p. 2. NOTE: Later in this day's proceedings Walker's land bill was approved on third reading by 27 to 23.

To S[AMUEL] D. INGHAM

Senate Chamber, Feb. [10; "1837" *written over* "1836"] My dear Sir, We are so incessantly engaged in our Congressional duties, that I have but little more time than to say that I wrote to you a few days since [on 2/5], and addressed to New Hope [Pa.], where I supposed you would be before it could reach there, and that I have since received your letter of the 7th Ins[tan]t.

I do not anticipate that any thing will be done with the Tariff this session. There is no sincerity in the movements that have been made to reduce. It is mere humbug, as most of the acts of the ["parties" *altered to* "party"] are. The position which I take in regard to reduction you will find in the enclosed remarks in the Telegraph.

The occur[r]ences here are full of profound interest, and indicate any thing, rather than a stable condition of our institutions. Yesterday while in the House [of Representatives] they were discussing the right of Congress to receive petitions from slaves, in the Senate ["we were engaged in" *interlined*] a case of outrageous violation of my right ["as and that" *canceled*] as a Senator, and that of the body ["by the President" *interlined*]. The Telegraph which I enclose will give you an account of this outrage & how I met it. The deliberation of the House ended in a recognition of the right to receive the petitions of our slaves. The excitement is prof[o]und. A meeting of the Southern delegation is called for tomorrow 10 o[']clock A.M. It is difficult to say what will be done.

I have ["moved" *canceled and* "introduced" *interlined*] a bill to

425

["rec" *canceled*] cide [*sic*] the publick lands to the new States on certain equitable condition[s], impelled by a deep conviction from what I have seen during the session, that hereafter they are to constitute a fund for speculation, and political influence if they remain under our control.

What I have said will give you some idea of the corrupt state of things here & how rapid the tendency is to a general catastrophy, unless the course of events should be speedily arrested. Yours truely, J.C. Calhoun.

ALS in ScU-SC, John C. Calhoun Papers.

Remarks on "the bill making appropriations for fortifications, &c. for the year 1837," 2/10. Calhoun, "remarking on the impropriety of haste on such a measure," moved to table the bill until tomorrow. He "said that this bill was so unexpected, and the hour so late, that he should decline making the observations which he intended to make, unless further time should be allowed." This motion failed and the bill was ordered to a third reading. From *Register of Debates*, 24th Cong., 2nd Sess., col. 779. Also printed in the Washington, D.C., *Daily National Intelligencer*, February 13, 1837, p. 2.

Remarks on "the bill to designate and limit the kinds of funds receivable for the public revenue," 2/10. When this bill, which was a response to Andrew Jackson's "Specie Circular," was under consideration, Calhoun "said he had been very anxious to express his opinions somewhat at large upon this subject. He put no faith in this measure to arrest the downward course of the country. He believed the state of the currency was almost incurably bad, so that it was very doubtful whether the highest skill and wisdom could restore it to soundness; and it was destined, at no distant time, to undergo an entire revolution. An explosion he considered inevitable, and so much the greater, the longer it should be delayed. Mr. Calhoun would have been glad to go over the whole subject; but as he was now unprepared to assign his reasons for the vote which he might give, he was unwilling to vote at all." The bill then passed by a vote of 41 to 5. From *Register of Debates*, 24th Cong., 2nd Sess., col. 778. Also printed in the Washington, D.C., *Daily National Intelligencer*, February 11, 1837, p. 3.

FURTHER REMARKS ON HIS BILL TO CEDE THE PUBLIC LANDS TO THE NEW STATES

[In the Senate, February 11, 1837]
[*The bill was under consideration on its second reading. It had been vigorously debated by eight Senators, several of whom favored tabling it without further consideration.*]

Mr. Calhoun observed that [during debate on 2/9] one of the reasons assigned against reading the bill a second time was, that it would prevent agitation. The subject had already been agitated; and he, for one, so long as he should have a seat on that floor, would continue to agitate it, until public attention should be thoroughly aroused. He contended that this attempt to prevent the bill from being again read and referred would only cause the subject to be the more deeply agitated. The provisions and principles of the bill could not be so well tested as if sent to a committee, where they would be deliberately examined. They would then make a report on the bill, which would go out to the country, and the people would have an opportunity of forming a deliberate judgment respecting it, and the effect might be to convince the new States themselves that the measure was wrong; and if so, an early termination would be put to it. Then, why should this not be done? He felt a profound regret that Senators did not think fit to permit the bill to take the usual course. He had not risen for the purpose of advancing a new argument, but merely to reply to the constitutional objections of the Senator from Massachusetts [Daniel Webster]. If it were necessary, he could at least present an argument *ad hominem* [*sic*].

If Congress possessed the right to make donations to individuals of eighty acres of land, as was remarked by the Senator from Mississippi, (Mr. [Robert J.] Walker,) had they not equally, on the same principle, the power to make donations of hundreds, or one hundred thousand? If there were any distinction, he (Mr. C[alhoun]) was not able to see it. Congress had a right, as was said by the Senator from Massachusetts, to make donations to States for certain purposes. Now, if they could make a donation for any purpose—for a deaf and dumb asylum, for an infirmary, or for any purpose whatever—he would ask, why not make a gift of the public lands? He repeated, that if there were a distinction, he, for one, was incapable of perceiving it.

The Senator from Massachusetts had said Congress had no right to give up the trust delegated to them. The object of the bill was to make a sale, and not a trust. It was a series of conditions of sale, which were intended to be beneficial to the new States as well as to the old; and the question was, "Can you make a sale of the public lands?" Congress could dispose of lands to individuals: then, why not to a State? If they could make an absolute sale, could not they make a conditional sale? That was the simple question. If they could not, then all he could say was, that he did not understand the argument. He must say that if he ever did entertain any constitutional scruples on the subject, the Senator's argument had satisfied him that there were none. He knew that the gentleman was capable of presenting (if there were any) objections in the strongest possible light; but he had not succeeded in convincing him (Mr. C[alhoun]) that there were any. But the Senator had said that the grounds upon which he (Mr. C[alhoun]) had put his bill at this time was the passage of the land bill, objectionable as it was, and which he (Mr. Webster) said might not yet become a law. Now, that was not so; he did not place the bill upon the naked fact of the land bill having passed this body. It was the character of the bill which had satisfied his mind that we had reached the time when something must be done on the subject. He would not characterize the bill, for he had already expressed his opinions on it. He asked whether every Senator opposed to the administration had not opposed the land bill? Did gentlemen not see there were political causes in operation? The time had arrived when the corrupt tendency of such bills should cease, which was controlling, to a certain extent, the action of Senators on that floor. These were the indications which induced him to introduce this bill.

But the Senator from Massachusetts said that what he (Mr. C[alhoun]) proposed to effect could scarcely be effected by this measure, or rather that the evil did not exist; that the present condition of things did not affect the sovereignty of the new States, or that they are in a state of vassalage. He admitted that this was a strong term, and he had used it in the heat of debate. He begged gentlemen to look at the fact. Could any thing be more local than the territory of a State? And was there no small state of dependency in a people being obliged to come here from a distance of eight hundred or a thousand miles?

He would ask the Senator from Massachusetts, whether this was not giving the General Government an unreasonable control over the new States? Their officers were diffused every where, creating a state of dependence, which did not exist in the other States of the Union. People were obliged to come here, session after session, to get what they claimed to be just. If the control at present exercised by the General Government was not inconsistent with the sovereignty of a State, it was at least a derogation.

The Senator remarked that this bill would not stop agitation, and that the new States would come here before long, and ask that the conditions should be altered. He (Mr. C[alhoun]) did not think it improbable that they would do that, but it would probably be eight or ten years first; and in the mean time our councils would be free from the control under which they at present suffered, and from political agitation, growing out of the discussion of questions connected with the public lands.

And if, at the end of that time, any of these conditions should be found burdensome, it would remain for those who might be here to apply the proper remedy. But the Senator argued that the bill would prove of no benefit to the new States; that they were small in population, and would be subject to agitation themselves, and might not fulfil the conditions of this bill. The bill, however, provided certain restrictions, which could not be overcome. Should any one of them be violated, the grant would be null and void. After some further remarks, in explanation and defence of the provisions of the bill, he concluded by an expression of his hope that Senators would permit it to be read a second time and referred; so that an opportunity would be given the country to examine and deliberate on the report which would be spread before it, in relation to this important measure.

[*Debate continued until, on a motion of James Buchanan, the bill was tabled by 26 to 20.*]

From *Register of Debates*, 24th Cong., 2nd Sess., cols. 790–792. Also printed in the Washington, D.C., *Globe*, February 15, 1837, pp. 2–3; *Congressional Globe*, 24th Cong., 2nd Sess., Appendix, p. 159.

To J[OHN] R. MATHEW[E]s, Clark[e]sville, Ga.

Washington, 12th Feb. 1837

My dear Sir, I am not surprised that you have taken the view you have of Cambrelleng's [*sic*; Churchill C. Cambreleng's] report & bill [in the House of Representatives, on tariff reduction], but you may rest assured that it is all a humbug, never intended to be carried into effect. The only object is to weaken and devide [*sic*] the South.

In the Telegraph ["you" *canceled*] enclosed, you will see the grounds on which I place myself on the question of reduction [in my speech of 12/21/1836?]. Before I shall surrender the advantages we have in the act of '32 [*sic*; 1833], I must be satisfied that the measure of reduction proposed will become a law, and that it secures to us advantages at least equal to those under that act. I cannot but regret, that our papers [in S.C.?] have not done me the justice to publish what I said on a subject ["that" *canceled*] in relation to which they have so deep an interest. The state of feebleness & lethargy into which our press has fallen is lamentable.

Nothing can be worse than the state of things here. The Telegraph of yesterday contains a letter from the President [Andrew Jackson] to me, grossly violating my priviledges [*sic*] and that of the body, wi[th] my remarks on it; yet as gross as is this outrage the majority when called on by Mr. [Henry] Clay to vindicate the rights of the Senate sat silent. Their expunging resolution had ["tied the" *canceled*] stiffled [*sic*] their voice.

While this was going on in the Senate, the House was deliberating on the right of slaves to petition Congress, and as wonderful as it may seem passed a resolution, which by strong implication affirms the right. Yesterday a deceptive attempt was made and succeeded to undo the work of of [*sic*] the preceeding [*sic*] day, which I fear leaves things still in a worse condition. I fear there is not sperit enough in the Southern delegation to meet the crisis. Something must be done and ["in" *interlined*] my opinion that something is a Southern convention, and yet it will be impossible to get the Southern members I fear to agree to a call. The people at home must take the work in hand. If we can submit to this, we can submit to any thing. I have not time to say more. I write not, you know, for the press. Truely, J.C. Calhoun.

ALS in DLC, John C. Calhoun Papers. NOTE: Calhoun's last paragraph refers to the complicated and heated proceedings in the House of Representatives on 2/9 and 2/11 that had been provoked by John Quincy Adams's offering of what purported to be a petition from slaves in favor of slavery. The House overwhelmingly passed resolutions on 2/11 refusing to receive the petition and affirming that "slaves do not possess the right of petition secured to the people of the United States by the Constitution." This "deceptive attempt" was unacceptable to Calhoun because it implied indirectly that a Constitutional right of petition against slavery did exist. This position was stated in the House by Henry A. Wise of Va., who refused to vote on the second resolution on the ground that "he held that Congress had no power to interfere, in any way, with the subject of slavery." (*Register of Debates*, 24th Cong., 2nd Sess., col. 1734.)

From [James L. Edwards,] Pension Office, 2/13. He returns papers concerning the late Maj. Thomas Farrar, which he has examined at Calhoun's request. Farrar's name would be eligible to be placed on the Revolutionary pension list under a law of 1832, provided proof is presented of six months' service and of his having left a widow or child. Payment cannot be made to an executor or administrator. (Calhoun had perhaps made inquiry on behalf of the attorney for Farrar's heirs, to whom he wrote [*not found*] on 2/16, according to a letter from David McCaleb to Calhoun dated 1/14/1838.) FC in DNA, RG 15 (Records of the Veterans Administration), Letters Sent, 1831–1866.

Petitions from citizens of Sevier County, Tenn., presented to the Senate by Calhoun on 2/13. These three petitions, with 123 signatures, ask that a postal route be established between Sevierville, Tenn., and Pendleton Courthouse, S.C., on a route suggested by them which they call the most direct route between Knoxville and the "Southern Commercial Cities." (Endorsements indicate that the matter was referred to the Committee on the Post Office and Post Roads and that the Committee was discharged from consideration of it on 3/3.) DS's in DNA, RG 46 (Records of the U.S. Senate), 24A-G13.

REMARKS ON THE ARMORY BILL

[In the Senate, February 13, 1837]
[Under consideration was a bill "to establish a foundry, an armory in the West or Southwest, arsenals in the States in which none have yet been established, and depots for arms in certain States and Territories."]
Mr. Calhoun observed that he had looked at the provisions of the bill, and that nothing in this world could be more useless than the expenditure it proposed. The country had already on hand about 800,000 stands of arms—an amount almost equal to that provided by Great Britain for her immense military establishment. The mere interest on such an investment was itself a heavy charge upon the Treasury; besides which, there was the liability to have the whole superseded by the invention of a better species of arms. The Government had already two large armories, capable of furnishing arms much faster than they were needed; and there was a necessity rather for retrenching than extending the means of supply. These arguments had all been urged at the last session; but he supposed it was

vain to repeat them. They had not been answered, and could not be. But the money was to be expended on something, and perhaps it might as well be on this as on any thing else. The Government must get clear of it in some way; it must not go back to the States; and ways and means must be devised to expend it. The bill had no other object on the face of the earth. Mr. C[alhoun] appealed to the majority of the Senate, entreating them to economize the public expenditure. He reminded them of the strong denunciations which had been poured on a previous administration [John Quincy Adams's] for its alleged extravagance, and that it was on the plea and promise of economy that the present party had come into power. Yet no sooner had they got control of the Treasury, than they went on to expend beyond all previous example. The moral effect of this state of things had been most pernicious. It had led the nation to conclude that the professions of no party could be believed. They were not believed; and the result of this incredulity in the public mind would always tend to place in the hands of an existing administration a vast amount of power.

[*Thomas H. Benton here spoke in favor of the bill.*]

Mr. Calhoun was very happy to hear so frank an avowal from the Senator from Missouri of the truth of what he had observed when last up, that the object of the bill was to get rid of a part of the surplus revenue in the Treasury. As to the argument derived from the fact that the Government obtained a portion of its supply from private factories, all that was easily explained. These factories were old establishments, which had been gotten up by their proprietors expressly on the faith of the Government; and they were in practice as really public establishments as the armories of the Government. The Government had been obliged to take enough from these individuals to keep their establishments from ruin, and that was the sole reason for the item quoted by the Senator from the returns. The two armories we already possessed were capable of turning out 20,000 stands of arms a year; and now it was proposed to erect a third, while the actual consumption was but between one and two thousand stands annually. There was one source of consumption which could not be avoided; but, instead of being an argument for the manufacture, it was a strong argument against the unnecessary multiplication of arms; and that was, their decay while lying in boxes. The larger the amount on hand, the greater was this source of decay. The country had already between 700,000 and 800,000, which had cost it ten millions of dollars, besides a large amount of capital invested in magazines; so that the total annual interest was little, if any thing, short of a million of dollars. As to the arming of our people, this bill did not propose to put a single gun into the hands of a single man. But for what purpose was so large an amount needed? It must be either to arm the Government against the people, or to fight some foreign enemy. He trusted our people did not want them to cut each other's throats. He repeated that the expenditure was useless; that it went to produce an accumulation of what was already accumulated, and was merely a contrivance to keep the money from the States.

The debate was further continued by Messrs. Benton and Calhoun, each of them insisting on the ground already taken, and endeavoring further to strengthen their respective positions.

From *Register of Debates*, 24th Cong., 2nd Sess., cols. 798–800. Also printed in the Washington, D.C., *Daily National Intelligencer*, February 15, 1837, pp. 1–2. Variant in the New York, N.Y., *Morning Courier and New-York Enquirer*, February 15, 1837, p. 2. NOTE: After further debate, the Senate, by a vote of 26 to 11, ordered the bill to be engrossed for a third reading.

To A[RMISTEAD] BURT, Abbeville, S.C.

Washington, 15th Feb. 1837

My dear Sir, So laborious has [*sic*] been our sittings in the Senate, that I have been compelled for some weeks past to suspend almost entirely my private correspondence, which I hope you will accept as an apology for not answering immediately your letter from Knox-Ville.

The course you adopted at the meeting was judicious & meets my entire approbation. Capt. [William George] Williams has sent me his report, in full, but I have not yet read it, for the want of time, and of course am not prepared to say how far his condemnation of the Carolina Gap [as a route for the proposed Louisville, Cincinnati, and Charleston Railroad] has been warranted by the state of the facts. If it rests on no better foundation than his statement to the Legislature it is worth nothing. That was perfectly deceptious [*sic*]. In fact, I cannot doubt its condemnation was taken in advance, and that it would share the fate it has[,] had it been the best imaginable.

I have collected a great deal of valuable information in relation to the route since my arrival here. On my return home I intend to take up the whole subject, and determine after full consideration, what is proper to be done.

Things are in a sad state here. The Telegraph will give you [Andrew] Jackson's letter [of 2/7] to me, and the manner I met it. Friends & foes condemn him & sustain me in my course. It is a perfect triumph over him. While this scene was before the Senate, the House had under ["the" *canceled*] discussion the right of slaves to petition Congress and dreaderful [*sic*], as it may appear, have actually by strong implication affirmed the right!! An effort has since been made to smooth over the ["affair" *canceled*] vote, but in my opinion it has left it in the worse [*sic*] possible condition. The papers will give you the account of the whole proceedings.

I must say the Southern delegation showed a lamentable want of sperit. They could be brought to no firm, or consistent stand. I never have been so deeply mortified.

The people must take the subject in hand. Something must be done. [Henry L.] Pinckney [Representative from S.C.] gave the first blow aga[i]nst us, and now we are reaping the bitter fruits. If no stand be taken, I fear the worse [*sic*]. My impression is, that there ought to be a meeting of delegates from the slave holding States say at Athens [Ga.] in August during commencement week. See [George] McDuffie and other friends, and converse freely. I do hope McDuffie's health is fully restored. He & our ["publick" *canceled*] other prominent men must not abstract themselves so much from publick affairs. I wrote him [*not found*] yesterday and hope he has my letter.

I have much to say, but will delay it till we meet, which I hope will be on my return home.

Anna [Maria Calhoun] joins her love to you & Martha [Calhoun Burt]. Remember me kindly to all friends. Sincerely, J.C. Calhoun.

ALS in NcD, John C. Calhoun Papers. NOTE: The "meeting" referred to in Calhoun's second paragraph was the gathering of stockholders of the Louisville, Cincinnati, and Charleston Railroad at Knoxville on 1/9. This meeting elected Robert Y. Hayne president of the company. A committee on surveys was appointed, headed by Abram Blanding of Columbia, S.C., which made a report in favor of the French Broad route. Among the corporate directors elected were, for S.C., Calhoun, Blanding, Benjamin T. Elmore, James Hamilton, Jr., Charles Edmondston, Mitchell King, John W. Simpson, and Robert G. Mills. (Pendleton, S.C., *Messenger*, January 27, 1837, pp. 2, 4.)

REMARKS ON THE BILL TO INCREASE THE MILITARY ESTABLISHMENT

[In the Senate, February 16, 1837]
[The bill was being considered on its third reading, the question before the Senate being its passage.]

Mr. Calhoun addressed the Senate at length in opposition to the bill, not, however, as he said, with the least hope of preventing its passage; there was money in the Treasury, and it must be spent; and this he knew would prove, with many gentlemen, a reason why the bill must pass. Yet, bearing a certain relation to this branch of our establishment, he felt called upon to say a few words, and they should be very few. He could not assent to the bill. The object it proposed was useless, and a good deal more than useless. The bill proposed to increase our existing military establishment, as a peace establishment, too, by the addition of 5,500 men, making the aggregate amount of the army over 12,000 men, and augmenting the [annual] expense of its maintenance by a million and a half or two millions of dollars. Was this necessary? He contended that it was not, and that there never was a time when there was so little necessity for a measure of this character. Abroad we were at peace with all the world; and as to Mexico, he believed no gentleman seriously contemplated that we were to go to war with her. Never had there been a time when so little force was necessary to put our Indian relations upon the safest footing. Our Indian frontier had, within a few years, been contracted to one half its former dimensions. It had formerly reached from Detroit all the way round to the mouth of the St. Mary's in Georgia; whereas, at present, its utmost extent was from St. Peter's [later in Minn.] to the Red River [in western La. and Ark.]. To guard this frontier, the Government had nine regiments of artillery, seven of infantry, and two of dragoons. He would submit to every one to say whether such a line could not be amply defended by such a force. Supposing one regiment to be stationed at St. Louis, and another at Baton Rouge, there still remained seven regiments to be extended from St. Peter's to Red River. Supposing one of them to be stationed at St. Peter's, one upon the Missouri, one in Arkansas, and one upon the Red River, there were still three left at the disposal of the Government. He contended that this force was not only sufficient, but ample. He should be told that there was a very large Indian force upon this frontier. That was very true. But the larger that force was, the more secure did it render our position; provided the Government appointed among them faithful Indian agents, who enjoyed their confidence, and who would be sustained by the Government in measures for their benefit. Of what did this vast Indian force consist? In the first place, there were the Choctaws, who had removed beyond the Mississippi with their own consent; a people always friendly to this Government, and whose boast it was that they had never shed, in a hostile manner, one drop of the white man's blood. Their friendship was moreover secured by heavy annuities, which must at once be forfeited by any hostile movement. Whenever this was the case, the Government possessed complete control, by the strong consideration of interest. Next came the friendly Creeks, who had all gone voluntarily to the west bank of the river. Then came the friendly Cherokees, who had done the same thing; and next the Chickasaws, whom we also held by heavy annuities. All this vast body of Indians were friendly toward the United States, save a little branch of the Creeks [that is, the Seminoles]; and it would be easy for any prudent administration, by selecting proper agents, and sustaining them in wise measures, to keep the whole of these people peaceable and in friendship with this Government, and they would prove an effectual barrier against the incursions of the wild Indians in the prairies beyond. But to increase largely our military force would be the most certain means of provoking a war, especially if improper agents were sent among them—political partisans and selfish land speculators. Men of this cast would be the more bold in their measures, the more troops were ready to sustain them; every body knew that [an] Indian force, when fairly opposed to white in the field, was as nothing. Where there were no swamps and fastnesses, but they had to contend in the open field, they were not more formidable than buffalo.

Mr. C[alhoun] then proceeded to denounce the bill as a measure of extravagance, designed chiefly to expend the money in the Treasury for objects not only unnecessary but pernicious. He went into some general observations on the corrupting tendency of the present course of policy, and then observed that every change that had been made in the army had gone to destroy its *morale*. He had not the confidence that the proper *materiel* would be selected in the bestowment of the many prizes which this bill proposed to create. All must remember what had been the history of the regiment of dragoons in this respect. Who had been appointed to command in that corps? In many instances cadets who had been discharged for misconduct in the Military Academy. Persons of this cast had been set over those who had gone through the whole course in that institution in a manner most highly creditable. The effect had been demoralizing, and he feared that the results of this bill would prove still more so. Mr. C[alhoun] then proceeded in a course of general objection to all measures calculated to increase the powers of the General Government; dwelt on the central tendency of our system; the necessity of diminishing and generalizing the action of this Government, as our population increased. He compared the Government to a partnership. While there were but few partners, the regulations might be minute and particular; but when they were numerous, and amounted to hundreds, the system must be more general.

Our chief arm of defence was the navy. This was exterior in its character, and less dangerous on the ground of patronage; and it would be his policy to increase this arm of the national force, and to render it respectable in the eyes of foreign nations. Then, this Government needed a sound Judiciary and a well-regulated Post Office; and beyond this he would not advance one inch. He concluded by remarks of a general character on the state of the Treasury, and the determination to expend the surplus, that it might not be returned to the people.

[*Thomas H. Benton defended the bill, stating that his task was easy because the report made to Congress on 12/11/1818 by Calhoun as Secretary of War (upon which Benton expounded at length) provided a complete answer for the speech just made by Calhoun as Senator from South Carolina.*]

Mr. Calhoun said he was much gratified with the opportunity of showing that there was not the slightest inconsistency between his course at this time and that to which the Senator from Missouri had triumphantly alluded. Mr. C[alhoun] then went on to recapitulate the grounds of objection he had before stated, as to the reduction of the Indian frontier, &c. And how had the Senator met these objections? By reading a report made by him when Secretary of War, in opposition to a proposed reduction of the army. Mr. C[alhoun] alluded to the different state of the country at the two periods of time. We had just emerged from the exasperation of a recent war, in which numbers of the Indians had been engaged, and many cruelties committed. There still remained much hostile feeling on both sides. A large force remained at Rouse's Point [N.Y., on Lake Champlain], and another at Sackett's Harbor [N.Y., on Lake Ontario]. Our fortifications were dilapidated. There were 100,000 hostile Indians in the interior of the country, in the very midst of us, besides a vast body still more hostile on the frontier. The South

American States had recently been liberated from the yoke of Spain, and the Holy Alliance were meditating an armed interference in that contest, and were with difficulty dissuaded from the attempt. Under these circumstances, he had been of opinion that the proposed reduction of our military establishment should not take place. The Senator from Missouri, however, had forgotten to tell the Senate one thing: that he himself had been opposed to the report, and had voted against it.

(Mr. Benton. I was not here.)

Mr. C[alhoun] said, perhaps he was mistaken in the date, but the Senator from Missouri had certainly aided in the reduction, and voted for it in 1821; and yet he accuses me of inconsistency in now opposing its increase. Mr. C[alhoun] said that, when the reduction did take place, he had been almost the only man who was in favor of fixing the number of the army at 10,000. Mr. Dashiell [*sic*; Joseph Desha, then Representative from Ky.], a member of the other House, had proposed 6,500; to which Mr. C[alhoun] had replied that he would assent to that number but for the large British force still remaining in Canada. The same principles which actuated him then governed him now; and he was happy in being able to show that there was no inconsistency in his course. The man who was upright in his intentions, and who desired only to do his duty, need not fear falling into inconsistency. The report which the gentleman had quoted Mr. C[alhoun] prided himself in. He had been urged by parties on both sides, but he had stood firm and kept his ground, objecting to the reduction on the principle that the establishment of the army should be the most stable thing in the Government. As to the charge of having been in favor of fortifying the Gulf and the Chesapeake, and now being opposed to fortifications, Mr. C[alhoun] had urged those measures when he was in the House of Representatives; and afterwards, when Secretary of War, he had used his utmost exertions to have the objects effected. The Senator charged him with opposing the defence of Baltimore, but the charge was not fairly stated. The fortification of Baltimore formed but one item in a bill which went to lavish millions, and his opposition had been directed against the bill in general, on account of its extravagance. He never had been in favor of fortifying all the exposed points in the Chesapeake bay, because they were so numerous. His plan had been to fortify thoroughly below, and to combine the defence by forts with that from floating batteries and the navy.

Besides, the expenditures of the Government in 1818 had been very different from what they are now. The whole expenditure then, exclusive of the public debt, had not exceeded ten millions. It was now twenty-five or twenty-six millions, and yet Mr. C[alhoun] was accused of inconsistency in opposing, under circumstances so different, an uncalled for extension of our military establishment. The Senator had referred to our experience in the Black Hawk war, as demonstrating an increase of the army to be indispensable. Our experience in that war demonstrated a very different thing. It proved that we should appoint among the Indians faithful agents, who would not stand by and suffer the Indians to be trampled in the dust. And, as to the Florida war, he had recently conversed with a gentleman from the spot, who assured him that nothing occasioned that contest but the very grossest neglect on the part of the Government. General [Wiley] Thompson [of Ga.], our Indian agent, and formerly a member of the other House, when a certain order of the [War] Department in respect to the purchase of negroes had been received by him, had warmly remonstrated, and had even refused to execute the order, warning the Department that it would inevitably provoke a war. The order, however, had been enforced by the authority of the President [Andrew Jackson] himself, as Mr. C[alhoun] understood. In like manner, General [Duncan L.] Clinch had again and again apprized the Government that there would be hostilities on that frontier, unless additional forces should be despatched to strengthen his position. And, as to the miserable Creek war, he believed that the Senators from Georgia [John P. King and Alfred Cuthbert] themselves would both admit that frauds and oppression, beyond all human endurance, had been the real cause of that contest. It was more than human nature would endure. The reptile itself would turn when it was trampled on.

(Mr. Cuthbert here interposed with some warmth. He was understood to deny the charge, as applied to Georgia, and to refer it to the treatment of Indians in Alabama.)

Mr. C[alhoun] insisted on the truth of the charge. The facts were open and palpable, and notorious as our own existence. Men had made fortunes by treating those Indians in such a manner as fixed a stain on human nature. Mr. C[alhoun] again said that what was wanted to protect us from the Indians was not more troops, but more faithful agents. The remnants of these native tribes were now a disheartened and broken down people. They had once esteemed themselves the greatest nations on the earth, but they had now become convinced of our strength and their own weakness. The half-bloods among them were partially civilized. They were sensible of the value of property, and very desirous to acquire it. The heavy annuities accruing to their tribes, by treaties with the Government, afforded ample security for their remaining peaceable, unless oppressed beyond endurance. Send them fit agents, and you will hear no more of Indian wars.

Mr. C[alhoun] briefly recapitulated the grounds of argument he had advanced, and observed, in conclusion, that, while the navy was our great arm of defence, all that we needed in the army was to keep up our military science, and to preserve a well-organized staff. On the latter subject, he had not particularly examined this bill. It was very possible that there might be some necessity in increasing the staff of the army; and if, on further investigation, he should be convinced of this, and a separate bill should be introduced for that purpose, he would very cheerfully yield it his support; but for the present bill he could not vote.

[*Debate continued during which several Senators spoke for and against the bill, and Calhoun made some unreported remarks. Lewis F. Linn of Mo. dwelled upon the need of the Western people for protection from Indian depredations.*]

Mr. Calhoun [again rose and] referred to an apparent inconsistency in the estimates of the Secretary of the Treasury [Levi Woodbury], in which Mr. C[alhoun] was understood to say the Secretary had fixed the expense of 5,500 men at about $3,000,000; and of 7,000 men at only $3,800,000. Mr. C[alhoun] inquired how both these estimates could be correct.

The Senator from Missouri, (Mr. Linn,) Mr. C[alhoun] said, claimed protection for the people of that State. It was Mr. C[alhoun]'s object to give them protection; and if Mr. L[inn] would join him in procuring the appointment of honest, skilful, and faithful Indian agents, such protection might be secured, or at least rendered unnecessary. And in an open country (he said) a very small white force, with artillery and cavalry, could overthrow any Indian force that might be brought against them.

It had been mentioned as a difficulty, that the regiments of the army would not be kept full enough. Mr. C[alhoun] thought it a much better remedy for this difficulty to increase the pay of the troops, rather than to increase the nominal number. These measures of this Government, he said, had disturbed and embarrassed the currency of the country, raised the prices of the means of living, and the wages of such as might be employed in the army; and now, in order to obviate all this, it was proposed to increase the army with 5,500 men. Mr. C[alhoun] insisted that this was no adequate remedy. The cause of the evil lay deeper—in the past measures of the

Government, and the consequent increase of banks, which would still increase and swell the currency, till an explosion would be inevitable, without a timely remedy.

Mr. C[alhoun] deemed the troops already in service as ample to defend that frontier. The Indians, he said, were a poor, broken down, dissipated people, and all that was wanted was faithful and skilful Indian agents. He thought they ought to be left to themselves in relation to wars between them and the Indians further west. If not allowed to go to war when they thought proper, they would all die of drunkenness. He would let them go to war, and drive the wild Indians still further west. In every view of the bill, Mr. C[alhoun] regarded it as objectionable, and hoped it would not pass.

[*Debate continued, during which Linn spoke again, denying that Indians were as harmless as Calhoun had suggested.*]

Mr. Calhoun made some remarks in rejoinder. He was understood as saying that his remarks had been intended to refer only to the southern Indians, and not to those of our Northwestern border. The Senator from Missouri had represented the Indians in his neighborhood as far advanced in civilization, yet was demanding troops to protect his constituents against their ravages.

[*Debate continued until the question was taken, and the bill passed 26 to 13.*]

From *Register of Debates*, 24th Cong., 2nd Sess., cols. 807–840. Also printed in the Washington, D.C., *Daily National Intelligencer*, February 20, 1837, pp. 1–2; Crallé, ed., *Works*, 3:28–36. Variant in the Washington, D.C., *Globe*, February 22, 1837, p. 2, and February 23, 1837, p. 2; *Congressional Globe*, 24th Cong., 2nd Sess., Appendix, pp. 177–184. Another variant in the New York, N.Y., *Morning Courier and New-York Enquirer*, February 18, 1837, p. 4. NOTE: The first variant report cited indicates that Calhoun said he was a friend of the army; that "a well regulated currency," in addition to the Navy, judiciary, and post office, was a proper activity of the federal government; that the people were much less likely to be corrupted by receiving the treasury surplus than were officeholders; and that "it was a maxim of our ancestors that a standing army was dangerous to liberty—dangerous not only as to the means of force it put into the hands of a corrupt administration, but dangerous from the patronage which was necessarily put at its disposal. . . ."

Remarks on the bill to relieve the sufferers by fire at New York City, 2/17. When this bill, which would cancel tariff duties assessed on goods that had been destroyed, was under consideration, Calhoun inquired of Silas Wright "if he could state about the amount of the claims which would be presented under the bill?" Wright replied at length, estimating the amount at about $500,000. From *Register of Debates*, 24th Cong., 2nd Sess., col. 848. Also printed in *Congressional Globe*, 24th Cong., 2nd Sess., p. 208. (A variant report in the New York, N.Y., *Morning Courier and New-York Enquirer*, February 20, 1837, p. 2, states: "Mr. Calhoun, after a brief statement from Mr. Wright, expressed his willingness, considering it to be a very hard case, to vote for the bill, adding, that in this shape the act of last session ought to have passed.")

To J[AMES] H. HAMMOND [in Europe]

Washington, 18th Feb. 1837

My dear Sir, I avail myself of the favourable opportunity by Col. [Joseph M.] White to acknowledge your letter of August last [from England?], which I read with much pleasure, and I may add with information. Many of the facts you stated are new to me. I had no conception, that the lower class had made such great progress to equality and independence. Such change of condition and mode of thinking on their part indicates great approaching changes in the political & social condition of the country, the termination of which is difficult to be seen. Modern society seems to me to be rushing to some new & untried condition.

With us great changes have occurred, as short as has been the period of your absence. You have of course read the papers and have kept up with the general march of events in this quarter. The Presidential election terminated, as was anticipated, when you left us; but far less decisively, than was anticipated by friend, or foe. It is quite certain, that the President elect [Martin Van Buren] did not receive a majority of [popular] votes, and that, if the opposition had known their strength, he could have been defeated easily. The general impression is, that he cannot maintain himself. The opposition show no indication of yielding, while his own party is agitated ["with" *canceled*] by conflicts within. The more decent portion under [William C.] Rives, [James] Buchanan and others are making war aga[i]nst their more filthy associates under [Thomas H.] Benton, Kendel [that is, Amos Kendall], [Francis P.] Blair & [Richard M.] Johnson. Thus far victory leans in favour of the latter. In the mean time, the outrage[ou]s acts of the party, forced on them by Jackson and Benton with his associates are shocking the feelings of the country corrupt and debased as it is. No act within my recollection has excited such disgust & loathing as the expunging resolutions. The party Senators, in voting it, looked more like culprits, ["and" *canceled and* "than" *interlined*] victorious leaders. That has been followed by repeated breaches of priviledges [*sic*] of the members of the two Houses by the President. The last & most violent was in my own case. You will of course have seen his letter to me, and the manner in which I met it. My triumph was complete. His friends in the Senate hung their heads in dum[b] silence.

This is a sad picture of the state of things on this side of the water; and yet with my [*one word canceled and* "non" *interlined*] dispa[i]ring disposition, I am disposed to regard it as the precursor of a general & thor[o]ugh reform. The principle of stability and regeneration is wonderful strong in our country & ["under our" *interlined*] political system. We have for the last 12 years been going through a great & dangerous juncture. The passage is almost made, and, if no new cause of difficulty should intervene, it will be successfully made. I, at present, see none, but the abolition question, which, however, I fear is destined to shake the country to its centre. It has made great progress since you left us. Its advocates are more numerous and audacious than ever, and have taken higher ground, at this, than the last session. For the first time the bold ground has been taken, that slaves have a right to petition Congress; and what is wonderful, a vote of the House of Representatives, has by strong implication, sustained the ground, which has neither been re[s]cinded, nor superceded, and we are about to adjourn leaving ["the" *altered to* "this"] question, which involves directly the right to emancipate in this uncertain condition; or rather to express myself more strongly, and at the same time more truely, the act of emancipation; for ["I must" *canceled*] the right to petition Congress is itself emancipation. It would make the masters but overseers, aga[i]nst whom the slave would have a right to appeal to Congress, as the absolute master of all. Such is the present posture of this, to us, all important question. How it is to end time can alone disclose. I have ever had but one opinion on the subject. Our fate, as a people, is bound up in the question. If we yield we will be exterpated [*sic*]; but, if we successfully resist, we will be the greatest & most flourishing people of modern time. It is the best substratum of population in the world; and ["one" *interlined*] on which great & flourishing com[mon]wealths may be most easily & safely reared.

I trust yours & Mrs. [Catherine Fitzsimons] Hammond[']s health is greatly improved, and that you have both enjoyed yourselves in your long absence from your country. Your numerous friends will heartily welcome your return.

443

Anna [Maria Calhoun] is with me and joins her best respects to you both, and requests me to say that she almost ["envy" *canceled and "*envies*" interlined*] you the pleasure you must have experienced in passing over the old & renowned regions of the old world.

I enclose a copy of my speech on the admission of Michigan which is the ["only" *canceled and then interlined*] one, that has [yet] been printed in pamphlet form this session.

I will be much gratified to hear from you. Yours truely & since[re]ly, J.C. Calhoun.

ALS in DLC, James Henry Hammond Papers, vol. 6; PC in Jameson, ed., *Correspondence*, pp. 365–367.

REMARKS ON THE PROPOSED PURCHASE OF JAMES MADISON'S NOTES ON THE PHILADELPHIA CONVENTION

[In the Senate, February 18, 1837]
[*Under consideration was a joint resolution "authorizing the purchase of the manuscripts of the late President Madison" relating to the proceedings of the Constitutional Convention of 1787.*]

Mr. Calhoun said that he had listened with pleasure and delight to the venerable gentleman from Rhode Island, (Mr. [Asher] Robbins,) and he coincided in opinion with him, that we were indebted to Mr. Madison, at least as much as to any other man, for the form of government under which we live. Indeed, he might be said to have done more for our institutions than any man now living, or that had gone before him.

A great and efficient aid he was, undoubtedly, in forming the Government. But there was another great act, which would immortalize him in the eye of posterity—the profound and glorious views which he took of our Government in his celebrated Virginia report [of 1799]. In his opinion, that was by far the ablest document that issued from the pen of Mr. Madison—one from which Mr. C[alhoun] had derived more information, and a profounder insight into our Government, than all the other documents he had perused.

Now, if he understood the object in view, it was in direct opposition to the great and fundamental principles of Mr. Madison himself, an adherence to which, he (Mr. C[alhoun]) solemnly believed, would give durability to the Government, under which we were now living.

444

He wished at some other time (as he was not prepared at this time) to be heard on the subject, when he would endeavor to satisfy the Senate that, in giving our assent to the appropriation asked for, we should not honor the name of Madison. Mr. C[alhoun] would postpone what he had to say until the third reading of the resolution; and, in the mean time, Senators would have an opportunity of coming to a full understanding of the subject.

From *Register of Debates*, 24th Cong., 2nd Sess., cols. 849–852. Also printed in the Washington, D.C., *Globe*, February 20, 1837, p. 3; *Congressional Globe*, 24th Cong., 2nd Sess., p. 218. Variants in the Washington, D.C., *Daily National Intelligencer*, February 20, 1837, p. 3; the Charleston, S.C., *Southern Patriot*, February 22, 1837, p. 2.

REMARKS ON THE PROPOSAL TO PURCHASE JAMES MADISON'S NOTES ON THE CONSTITUTIONAL CONVENTION

[In the Senate, February 20, 1837]
[*Under consideration on third reading was a resolution authorizing the Congressional Joint Committee on the Library to purchase from his widow the manuscript of James Madison's notes on the proceedings of the Philadelphia Convention, reserving to Mrs. Madison the rights to publication in foreign countries.*]

Mr. Calhoun said this resolution from the Committee on the Library proposed to appropriate $30,000 to accomplish the object proposed. The facts, he said, were these: Mr. Madison, under the impression that these papers would be favorably received by the public and by publishers, had levied several legacies upon them, one of some thousands of dollars to the Colonization Society, and some smaller ones to other public charities, in addition to some private bequests. But, so far from his anticipations having been realized, it seemed that Mrs. [Dorothea Payne Todd] Madison was unprepared to run the risk of publishing them at all, and on this account had applied to the President [Andrew Jackson] in relation to them. He had recommended to Congress to purchase them; and the Committee on the Library had consequently made this report.

Every one (Mr. C[alhoun] said) was ready to render to the memory of Mr. Madison all possible respect. But the questions involved in this case were of a constitutional character, and it was therefore impossible for Mr. C[alhoun] to vote for the proposition.

445

The question was, have Congress the right to make this appropriation? The constitution gives Congress the power to lay and collect taxes, to pay the debts of the Government, and to provide for the common defence and general welfare. It was under this provision of the constitution that Mr. C[alhoun] understood this appropriation was to be made.

In reference to this clause of the constitution there had long been a diversity of opinion. From the very commencement of the Government, the two great parties in the country were divided upon it. One of these parties conceived that, by these words in the constitution, Congress had the right, in promoting the general welfare, to appropriate money to any and every object which they believed would be conducive to the promotion of the general welfare. The other party, at the head of which was Mr. Madison himself, believed this power was limited by the constitution, and that Congress have no right to make an appropriation, unless authorized to do so by a specific provision of the constitution. These two schools had existed from an early stage of the Government to the present time. Mr. Madison, in his celebrated report of 1799, had given his views on the subject, in the most clear and conclusive language, which required not one word from Mr. C[alhoun]. He would ask the Secretary to read the passage on the 23d, 24th, 25th, 26th and 27th pages of the report.

(The Secretary then read the passage indicated by Mr. Calhoun.)*

Here, Mr. C[alhoun] said, Mr. Madison, by a very able argument, had proved, beyond all controversy, that Congress has the power only to make specific grants, and that no more than specific powers are vested in them by that clause of the constitution. The opposite doctrine involved unlimited power in the possession of Congress. Mr. C[alhoun] would not repeat the argument. Mr. Madison had also predicted what Mr. C[alhoun] feared he should see fulfilled, that the opposite argument would lead to consolidation, or was consolidation itself, and that the consequent effect would be a monarchy. What was predicted in 1799, was already, Mr. C[alhoun] said, in part

---

*Editor's note: The page numbers seem to refer to the version of Madison's report that is printed in *The Resolutions of Virginia and Kentucky; Penned by Madison and Jefferson in Relation to the Alien and Sedition Laws* (Charleston, S.C.: printed by A.E. Miller, 1828). In that pamphlet the pages cited contain a detailed argument against a broad construction of the "common defence" and "general welfare" statements in the preamble of the Constitution as tending to lead to consolidation and monarchy.

realized. We had not yet arrived at the stage of monarchy, but the executive department was in a fair way of absorbing the whole powers of the system.

Mr. C[alhoun] held it to be due to the memory of Mr. Madison and to the powerful argument just read in his report, that questions of this kind should be considered with all possible caution. He had given his views of this portion of the constitution in the prime of his life and vigor of his manhood; and such views elevated Mr. [Thomas] Jefferson to the chief magistracy in the political revolution of 1800, and afterwards elevated Mr. Madison himself. The fame of this illustrious man, and the debt which we owed him for all he did for our institutions, demanded that we should do nothing on the present occasion to show a want of respect for him or his sentiments.

The question now before the Senate, Mr. C[alhoun] said, was whether Congress had the power to purchase the copy-right to Mr. Madison's papers, which, in the present state of political feelings, were regarded of little or no value in the money market. Mr. C[alhoun] regarded it as truly deplorable, that these invaluable papers, which threw a light upon the constitution which had never been shed upon it before, should be deemed of no value by the public, absorbed with party politics and the low love of gain, so that such a work could not be published. But where, Mr. C[alhoun] asked, was the special power in the constitution for Congress to publish such a work? This was a solemn question, the answer to which should be shown not by precedent, but by the constitution. The practice of Congress, Mr. C[alhoun] said, had been most loose on this and all other points. But the real question was, whether there was such a power in the constitution. The chairman of the committee [Asher Robbins] had not rested his argument on this, but on the broad general principle, that these papers would throw a new and brilliant light upon our institutions, and constitute a new era in their history, and in the progress of the human mind; thus promoting the general welfare by the diffusion of intelligence, for which Congress had no authority in the constitution. Mr. C[alhoun] felt that his position in opposition to this resolution was a painful one; but the opinions of Mr. Madison, which were the text-book of Mr. C[alhoun], and of those with whom he acted, demanded that he should not abandon it. He had spoken as briefly as possible, and wished chiefly for the opportunity of recording his vote against the proposition.

[*Here several Senators, including William C. Preston of S.C., argued for the expediency and constitutionality of the purchase.*]

Mr. Calhoun rejoined, and further insisted upon the ground he had before taken. There was no diversity of opinion as to the value of these manuscripts, nor with regard to the great character of Mr. Madison, nor as to its being a very desirable object that this work should be published; but whether it should be published by the agency of Congress was a different question. The work, however, would be published at all events. Mrs. Madison had been offered $5,000 for it. That was sufficient to secure the publication. If Congress wished any copies for the library, they could furnish themselves with as many as might be necessary. Why must they purchase the copy-right? Would this application ever have come here if Mrs. Madison had been offered by the booksellers enough money to cover the legacies in her husband's will?

(Mr. [John J.] Crittenden [of Ky.] interposed, and said he presumed it would. The reverence in which that distinguished woman held her husband's memory would naturally induce her to desire to dispose of this manuscript rather to the Government of this country than to the booksellers. As to purchasing the copy-right, so precious did he hold the manuscript itself, that, did he possess it, he would not take the $30,000 for it.)

Mr. Calhoun resumed, and insisted that, let gentlemen twist and turn the question as they pleased, it amounted to neither more nor less than this: an appropriation by Congress to pay the legacies in Mr. Madison's will. Mr. C[alhoun] profoundly regretted that those legacies had ever been charged upon the avails of this manuscript. Mr. Madison had died childless, and had left his wife in easy circumstances. How much better would it have been had he left this work, free of all cost, as a legacy to the American people? And he no less regretted that Mrs. Madison had ever made the present application to Congress; and his regret was yet heightened, because a compliance with her request involved a plain and palpable violation of that rule in the interpretation of the constitution which Mr. Madison himself had laid down. The rule was full of the profoundest political wisdom and foresight, and evinced in the mind of that great man a just foreboding as to the fate of this Government. It would honor the memory of Madison far more to regard this rule than to purchase this manuscript. And if the manuscript itself was esteemed so valuable, there was no doubt that the printer, after the edition was worked off, would very gladly give the original to Congress. He then went on in a course of argument to show that the appropriation involved a violation of the principles laid down by Mr. Madison with respect to limited powers, and would, if carried out, leave it in the power of the Government to perform any act whatever which it might deem conducive to the general welfare. In reply to the inquiry of Mr. Crittenden as to the erection and decoration of the Capitol, he observed that the case was very plain. They were a legislative body, and must have a house in which to assemble; and whether the building were small or large, more or less expensive, did not vary the constitutional question. As to its profuse decoration, there had been many politicians of the old school who doubted its expediency, and thought that much plainer buildings would have been more consistent with our republican simplicity. As to the exploring expedition, Mr. C[alhoun] greatly doubted the right of Congress to sanction any such measure. But thus we proceeded, step by step; one departure was made to sanction another, until at length they came down to the great question which had originally separated the two parties in this Government. Mr. C[alhoun] admitted that when a young man, and at his entrance upon political life, he had inclined to that interpretation of the constitution which favored a latitude of powers, but experienced observation and reflection had wrought a great change in his views; and, above all, the transcendent argument of Mr. Madison himself, in his celebrated resolutions of 1798, had done more than all other things to convince him of his error. The opposite course tended to a government of unlimited powers, and in such a government the executive department must inevitably swallow up all the rest. The Senator from Kentucky (Mr. Crittenden) had warred nobly against executive encroachments, but that warfare would be all in vain unless the money power of the Government should be closely watched. He had been struck with the sagacity and foresight of Mr. Jefferson, in a remark of that great statesman, that legislative usurpation would always precede executive, but that executive would always succeed it. Yet there would be a thousand cases which so strongly appealed to the hearts and sympathies of legislators, that these salutary restraints and warnings were all in danger of being swept away; and he who should oppose appeals of that nature would come to feel little in his own eyes, and to accuse himself of a want of the noblest feelings of the heart. He concluded by once more asserting that the naked question before the Senate was, whether they would vote an appropriation to pay the legacies in Mr. Madison's will. As he could not in conscience vote in the affirmative, he desired that the question should be taken by yeas and nays.

[*William C. Rives of Va. spoke at considerable length in support of the resolution, suggesting that Calhoun's position tended, whether deliberately or not, to cast censure on Madison.*]

Mr. Calhoun explained. He had cast no censure on the legacies of Mr. Madison. On the contrary, he considered them as all very proper, and he must be allowed to say that he was not a little surprised at the nature and tone of the remarks of the Senator from Virginia. That which had called forth the expression of his regret had been simply this: that the legacies charged on the avails of these manuscripts should have had the effect of bringing this application before Congress. What he had said was, that if an arrangement could have been made with the booksellers that would have covered those legacies, this application never would have been made; and there was nothing in the language of the will to show the contrary. Mr. C[alhoun], after a brief recapitulation of the ground he had taken, concluded by observing that not one of the cases quoted by the Senator from Virginia availed in the least against the constitutional objection he had advanced; nor had he said any thing which any friend of Mr. Madison had the least right to take exception to.

From *Register of Debates,* 24th Cong., 2nd Sess., cols. 858–871. Also printed in the Washington, D.C., *Daily National Intelligencer,* February 23, 1837, p. 2; the Washington, D.C., *Globe,* April 18, 1837, p. 2; *Congressional Globe,* 24th Cong., 2nd Sess., Appendix, pp. 250–254; Crallé, ed., *Works,* 3:36–42. Variants in the New York, N.Y., *Morning Courier and New-York Enquirer,* February 22, 1837, p. 2; the Charleston, S.C., *Southern Patriot,* February 24, 1837, p. 2. NOTE: The Senate this day approved the resolution by a vote of 32 to 14 and sent it to the House of Representatives, which took no action during the session. Pertinent documents can be found in Senate Document No. 9, 24th Cong., 2nd Sess.

From N[ICHOLAS] B[IDDLE]

Phil[adelphi]a, Feb[ruar]y 21, 1837
My dear Sir, The interest you have always felt in the Bank [of the United States], which in truth owes its existence to you, makes me desire that you should perceive, that to the last hour of its existence it has been faithful to its trust, and both willing & able to close its connexion with the Gov[ernmen]t in the most liberal & honorable manner. The report of the Secretary of the Treasury [Levi Woodbury] is calculated to mislead the country, & we have thought it proper to place the Institution in its proper light before the country by a memorial which goes by this mail & of which I inclose a printed copy (printed merely for convenience but not published) intended in a few words to state ["that" *interlined*] the Bank is perfectly willing

to settle on any terms proposed by the Gov[ernmen]t but that it never will be driven from its clear constitutional rights by any denunciations from the Executive. I beg you to believe me, with high respect, Very truly y[ou]rs, N.B.

FC in DLC, Nicholas Biddle Papers, President's Letterbooks, 1:139–140. NOTE: The "memorial" enclosed was doubtless a reply to Woodbury's report to Congress in 12/1836 on the closing of the accounts of the government with the Bank of the United States. The report can be found in Senate Document No. 2, 24th Cong., 2nd Sess., pp. 42–74.

REMARKS ON THE BILL TO REDUCE CERTAIN TARIFF DUTIES

[In the Senate, February 21, 1837]
[Silas Wright of N.Y. moved that the Senate set aside the scheduled business and take up the bill he was sponsoring for the reduction of tariff duties on certain specified goods. Calhoun spoke briefly several times during debate, favoring the motion to take up the bill, and then, apparently, opposing a motion to strike certain chemical and medicinal articles out of the bill. The discussion turned toward the relation between the bill in question and the Compromise Tariff of 1833, as to whether this bill would or should interfere with the compromise.]

Mr. Calhoun observed that the South had a deep interest in the compromise bill, the terms of which were, that all the duties were to be gradually reduced down to the year 1842. According to his calculation at the time, if the imports did not increase, there should be a reduction of two millions annually. He would tell Senators, on all sides, that for no little or paltry consideration, as the reduction of duties to the amount of fifty or one hundred thousand dollars, should induce him to give up the advantages which the South had in the compromise bill. And let him tell southern gentlemen, their interests were greatly involved in pursuing this course, and they would injure themselves if they gave up the strong hold they had upon that bill. The Senators from the southern States would find, before this small bill would be got through, how difficult it was to take off duties.

He remembered that when he first came to Congress, an old and sagacious friend told him that he would see that it was much more difficult to repeal than to lay on taxes. He (Mr. C[alhoun]) was astonished at the time, but he had long since found the remark to be strictly correct. He was persuaded that if gentlemen should commit the egregious folly of yielding the advantages they possessed by this compromise bill, they would pay for it hereafter.

Gentlemen opposite [that is, Whig supporters of protection] called upon southern gentlemen to respect the bill. For his own part, he would say that he would not disturb the compromise act. When it passed, he voted for it, as he would have done for any other bill, and in doing so he did not feel himself governed by any pledge, in case there should be an excess of revenue. I stand here (continued Mr. C[alhoun]) upon the advantages which have been given me. I, for one, will not act in any manner calculated to disturb the advantages which the people of the northern States have now, but I do claim that they shall not disturb the advantages which we shall have hereafter. Going upon that ground, all that I ask, is taking into full consideration the tariff interests, that all duties, which may be deemed desirable of more than twenty per cent. shall be taken off. But duties of less than twenty per cent. (unless some special reason can be assigned to the contrary) I will vote to repeal. I have taken my position, and I believe it to be perfectly strong, and such as my constituents demand, and, with due deference to other southern Senators, what their constituents would approve.

[*Alfred Cuthbert of Ga. complained that the Compromise Tariff stood in the way of duties being reduced. "He cared not what the Senators from Massachusetts and Kentucky (Daniel Webster and Henry Clay) said as to the necessity of not violating the compromise. Nor did he admit at all, as the Senators from South Carolina and Tennessee (Calhoun and Felix Grundy) seemed to do, the binding force of the compromise act."*]

Mr. Calhoun explained that he had used no such expression as "binding force." Mr. C[alhoun] had said that he would only take that part which was but fair and honorable to the North, while he at the same time looked forward to the advantages which would arise, and which were decidedly in favor of the South. Therefore it was that he would not disturb the compromise.

From *Congressional Globe*, 24th Cong., 2nd Sess., pp. 239–240. Also printed in the Washington, D.C., *Globe*, April 6, 1837, pp. 2–3; the Washington, D.C., *Daily National Intelligencer*, April 6, 1837, pp. 2–3. Variant in *Register of Debates*, 24th Cong., 2nd Sess., cols. 872–882. Another variant in the Washington, D.C., *Reformer*, February 22, 1837, p. 3.

Remarks on the Indian appropriations bill, 2/22. Along with three Western Senators Calhoun participated in discussion of an amendment reported by the Committee on Indian Affairs to appropriate funds "to remove the Indians beyond the Mississippi." Calhoun said he "thought the whole of our Indian system required to be renewed. The present system would lead to great evils. The accumulation of Indians on the frontier, would lead to the concentration of our military force there; lands would rise, and speculation increase. He wished more time to be given to the subject, and therefore moved the postponement of the further consideration of the bill till next session, but withdrew it." The amendment was later agreed to. From the New York, N.Y., *Morning Courier and New-York Enquirer*, February 24, 1837, p. 2.

From W[illia]m Glover

Elizabeth City [N.C.], Febr[uar]y 23d. 1837

Sir, A vacancy having been occasioned in the office of Collector of this port by the death of Stephen Charles Sen[io]r Esquire there will be numerous applicants for the situation. Among others who will apply from this place is one *Abner Williams* who has been a warm supporter of the present administration & at the late elections for Electors for President & Vice President was the leader of the Van Buren & Jackson Party in this section. Having acted upon the well known principle of that party & as it has been succes[s]ful he now expects his reward. It is more than probable that his name will be presented to your Hon[ora]ble body for confirmation. The office of collector of this port altho small is one of respectability & therefor[e] should at least be filled by an Honorable man no matter what be his political way of thinking.

Mr. Williams being I presume an entire stranger to the members of the Senate, and at the departments altho personally unknown his services have been recorded—I conceive it my imperious duty as a member of the community in which Mr. Williams resides to present his true character to your Hono[ra]ble Body, so that you may be able to judge whether he is such a person as deserves to fill an office the duties of which have been heretofore discharged by a [Isaac] Gregory, [Enoch] Sawyer & Charles in a manner alike hono[ra]ble to themselves & satisfactory to the government. As I have not the Honor of an acquaintance with you I beg leave to refer you to the Hon[ora]ble William B. Shepard our respected representative who is acquainted with me & with the particulars of the enclosed transcript from the

Records of the Superior Court of this (Pasquotank) County—and I
hope should the said *Abner Williams* be nominated to your Hon[ora]-
ble Body you will make known to it his character. That part of
his sentence relating to standing in the Pillory was remitted by Mont-
fort Stokes then I believe Gov[erno]r of our State. With great respect Sir, I have the honor to be Your ob[e]d[ien]t Serv[an]t, Wm.
Glover.

P.S. I have since writing the above learnt it was Gov[erno]r
[James] Iredell [Jr.] who remitted the Pillory part of the sentence.

ALS with En in DNA, RG 46 (Records of the U.S. Senate), 27B-A5, Williams.
NOTE: The En referred to was an authenticated copy (dated 2/23/1837) of
the proceedings in the case of North Carolina vs. Jasper Pickett, William Griggs,
and Abner Williams, who were convicted of falsifying papers relative to the
ownership of a vessel. Williams was sentenced to a short jail term, an hour
in the pillory, and a fine of $100. The Senate journals do not indicate that
Williams's nomination was ever sent to that body.

SPEECH ON THE BILL TO REDUCE THE DUTIES ON CERTAIN IMPORTS

[In the Senate, February 23, 1837]
Mr. Calhoun rose and addressed the Senate as follows:

The annunciation by the chairman of the Committee on Finance
[Silas Wright], that this bill was framed and introduced on the assumption that the act of 1833 was no longer to be respected, gave to it
an importance which demanded the most serious consideration. That
act closed the tariff controversy between the North and the South;
and the question now presented is, shall it again be opened? Shall
we reopen a controversy which, during the long period from 1821 to
1833, agitated the country, governed its legislation, controlled the
presidential elections, and finally shook its institutions to the centre?
Shall we of the South, in particular, assent to open this formidable
controversy—we who are, on this subject, in a permanent minority?
Shall we agree to surrender our share of interest in the act of 1833—
an act which has already repealed from twenty to twenty-five millions
of duties annually, and which, if left undisturbed, will in a few years
take off ten more, and reduce the duties to the constitutional and
legitimate wants of the Government? Will we agree to surrender all
of these advantages, which were extorted from the adverse interest
at the hazard of civil conflict, and take our chance in the renewed

conflicts which must follow, if the controversy be again opened? This the chairman of the Committee on Finance asks you to do; and what is the compensation he holds out to you for such great sacrifices?

The whole may be summed up in the repeal of the duty on salt, amounting annually to about $550,000. It is true, this bill goes further, and provides for a reduction to the amount of $2,400,000 annually; but of these the larger portion are duties under twenty per cent. ad valorem, which by the act may be repealed without disturbing the compromise; and the residue, with the exception of salt, and perhaps one or two other articles, are either of a doubtful character, or can be repealed by common consent of all the interests involved. Here, then, is the great boon which is proffered by the Senator, (Mr. Wright,) to induce us to sacrifice our interest in the act of 1833, to magnify which, he has pronounced an eulogium on the magnanimous course of the State of New York, in assenting to the repeal of the duty on salt; of which article, he tells us, she manufactures more than any other State, while he forgets to inform us that she has little or no interest in the repeal, as she has secured a monopoly in favor of her manufacture by the imposition of an enormous duty on the transportation of salt on her canals, through which channel only the imported can come in competition with the manufactured salt. The question now to be decided is, shall we accept the boon, and make the sacrifice?

I acknowledge the duty to be odious and unequal, but I must think, as much so as it may be, we should purchase its repeal too dearly by the sacrifice we are asked to make. Regarded as a mere pecuniary transaction, and laying aside all political considerations, we would not be justified. The duty on salt amounts, as I have stated, to upwards of half a million annually, while the average reduction of duties under the act of 1833 will not be less than two millions annually, for the next five years, all of which we may reasonably expect will be taken off, if, on our part, we firmly adhere to the act. But this is altogether too strong a statement of the case on the side of repeal.

The Senator, in his eagerness to magnify the oppressive character of the duty on salt, stated it to be ten cents the bushel, overlooking the fact that the act of 1833 has already reduced it below eight cents, and that it will in a short time reduce it below three, if it be left undisturbed; so that the real question is not between a repeal and a permanent continuance of the duty at ten cents, as the Senator would have us believe, but between a sudden repeal of eight cents, and a gradual reduction, in the course of a few years, to the low rate of duty I have stated. It is, in fact, substantially a question between a sudden and a gradual repeal; and, regarded in that light, I would submit to the judicious of all parties which is the preferable, viewed in the abstract, without regard to the act of 1833[?] The chairman states the present duty at an average of about eighty-six per cent. ad valorem; I would ask, would it be wise to repeal at once so high a duty? Can it be done without ruinous losses, as well to the dealers in the article, as the manufacturer? Even [South] Carolina, in the heat of her contest against the protective system, never contemplated allowing less than six or seven years for the reduction of the protective duties to the revenue point; and shall we [that is, the Senate] now, by a sudden and total repeal of so high a duty, prove ourselves less considerate in relation to existing investments than a State so decidedly opposed to the whole system in the midst of the greatest excitement?

But, whichever may be preferable, it is certain that the practical difference, as far as the South is concerned, is too small to warrant the sacrifice of the great interest which she has in maintaining inviolably the act of 1833, particularly when we consider that, as small as is the difference, we have no assurance of ever receiving this inconsiderable boon. Let us not forget that, if we of the South vote for this bill, we not only give much where we can receive but little, but we also give a certainty for an uncertainty. By the vote itself, whether the act passes or not, we surrender our position. We cannot, after disregarding the interest of others in the act, insist that they shall respect ours, when they become the subject of discussion. If we should now vote to repeal or reduce duties more rapidly than the act provides, how can we complain if the manufacturing interest should hereafter increase the duties, or retard or arrest the reduction provided by the act? Fair and honorable dealing has ever distinguished the Southern character; and I trust we have too much self-respect to complain, if the measure we now mete to others should hereafter be measured to ourselves. Our vote, then, for this measure would release the opposite interests from all obligation to respect the act of 1833, whatever may be the fate of this bill. Now, I ask, what assurance have we that this bill will pass? Is it not almost certain that it cannot? We are now within seven days of the end of the session. The bill is in Committee of the Whole, and cannot pass the Senate in less than two days; and what prospect is there that it can pass the other House in so short a time as remains, with the great diversity of opinion which must exist there as to this measure? It is next to impossible.

But suppose it to be practicable, have we any assurance that those who have introduced the bill are sincere in their desire to pass it?

Have we no cause to apprehend that it is a mere political manoeuvre, without regard to the interest of North or South, and which the contrivers would rather see defeated than passed? I must say that, to me, it seems to wear that appearance. Why has this bill been delayed to this late period? It is now more than three weeks since it was reported, and why were measures of little importance, and, to say the least, of doubtful policy, permitted to occupy the time of the Senate, in preference to this, which we are now told is so important? Why such contradictory declarations as to the state of the Treasury? At one time we are told that there will be no surplus, and that the duties must be raised; and at another that the revenue will be so excessive as to call not only for the passage of this bill, but the extraordinary one which has passed this body in relation to the public lands. With all these indications, gentlemen must not be surprised that I am somewhat incredulous as to their zeal or sincerity, which is not a little increased when I look to the source from which it comes. Have you forgot the tariff of 1828, that bill of abominations so execrated by the South, and which has brought so many disasters on the country? I have (looking at Mr. Wright) its author in my eyes, and he knows the fact. He well remembers the part he bore in the passage of that act, and the means by which it was effected. It was passed by a breach of faith. We were deceived then. It will not be my fault if we be deceived now. To guard against that, I must ask the indulgence of the Senate while I give a brief narrative of the passage of that oppressive act, and the part which the Senator acted at the time. I have no intention to wound his feelings. My object is not personal. That would be unworthy of the occasion, and, I trust, of myself. Far different motives actuate me. From the past we learn to anticipate the future. We then followed his lead. We know the result. He now invites us again to follow him on the same subject, though apparently in an opposite direction. Shall we follow? His course on the former occasion will best enable us to decide that question. I was a witness of the events of the day, and feel called upon to give the history of the transaction, in order to guide our decision now.

The tariff of 1828 was as much a political movement as a measure of protection. The protective policy had triumphed in Congress by the passage of the Tariff Act of 1824, which was followed by the election of Mr. [John Quincy] Adams to the presidency the next year, by which the protective system gained an ascendency in the executive, as it had previously in the legislative department of the Government. Emboldened by this success, an attempt was made in the session of 1826–'27 to increase the duty on wool and woollens, which was rejected by my casting vote as presiding officer of this body. These interests, not finding themselves strong enough to force their way through Congress, determined, in the spirit of the system, to unite with other interests, so that by their joint influence they might secure a majority. With this view, a combined movement was made by the manufacturing interests, which met at Harrisburg [Pa.], and agreed on a new tariff, to be laid before Congress at the next session, and containing a long list of articles, with a great increase of duties. This movement was understood to have the countenance and support of the then administration. In the mean time, the anti-tariff interest of the South had selected General Jackson as the candidate against Mr. Adams for the presidency. His principal strength in the tariff States lay in Pennsylvania, New York, and Ohio. They were thoroughly in favor of the protective system, and his supporters there were not a little alarmed at the movement at Harrisburg. The battle was to be fought in Congress, and thus the presidential election came to be blended with the subject of the tariff, as it will ever be when an open question.

On the meeting of Congress, the [Adams] administration proved to be in a minority in the House of Representatives, and their opponents elected Mr. [Andrew] Stevenson (now Minister at the court of St. James) Speaker; and then, as now, a devoted friend of the President elect [Martin Van Buren]. It was apparent that the movements of the session would be governed by the tariff question, and the Committee on Manufactures was so organized as to give the control to the friends of Mr. Van Buren in the Middle and Western States. Mr. [Rollin C.] Mallary, [then Representative from Vt.,] who had long been chairman, was continued, but the present chairman of the [Senate] Committee on Finance (Mr. Wright) who was then a member of the other House, Mr. [Thomas P.] Moore of Kentucky, afterwards minister to Colombia, and Mr. Stephenson [that is, James S. Stevenson] of Pittsburg, were placed on the committee, who, with one member from the South, gave a majority against the administration. Representing, as the committee did, the interests of the Middle and Western States, which were thoroughly tariff, without opposing or conflicting interests of any kind, they reported a bill with much higher duties and far more comprehensive in its items than the Harrisburg project, which was predicated on the joint interests of the whole tariff party, comprehending New England, where industry was divided between manufacturers on one side and commerce and navigation on the other. The staple States were wholly opposed to the protective system; and their representatives, being in a minority, had no alternative but to choose between the two projects; and the question was then presented, what ought to be done? One of two courses might be taken: to join the New England interest, and vote such amendments to the bill as would make it acceptable to them, or to resist all such amendments, and take the chance of the members from New England joining those of the South, to defeat the bill in its passage in one or the other House. By the former course they would certainly defeat the bill as reported by the Committee on Manufactures, but they would as certainly insure its passage in a mitigated form, as the members from the Middle and Western States would take any tariff, however small the increase of duty, rather than have none. The former would have fixed the system on the country more firmly than ever, particularly as it would have involved, in all probability, the re-election of Mr. Adams, the acknowledged candidate of the tariff interests. The latter afforded a reasonable prospect of defeating the whole system, as well as the re-election of Mr. Adams. The difficulty in this course was the possible reunion of the two tariff interests by mutual concession in the last stage, in order to insure the passage of the bill. To guard against that result, assurances were given which placed the representatives of the South at ease on that point. I speak not of my own personal knowledge. It was generally so understood at the time; and I was informed by individuals who had a right to know, and who consulted with me what course, under the pressing difficulties of our situation, ought to be adopted, that such was the fact. Our friends accepted the assurance, and accordingly resisted all amendments that would make the bill acceptable to the Eastern interests, as the only possible means of defeating an odious and oppressive system.

The bill passed the House, but in so obnoxious a form to the New England States, that a large portion of their Representatives joined those of the South in voting against it. When sent to the Senate, it was soon ascertained that, in this body, where the Southern and Eastern States had a much larger representation in proportion, there was a decided majority against it in the form it came from the House. Every New England Senator, with the exception of one or two, was understood to be decidedly opposed; and, relying on the assurance on which our friends acted in the House, we anticipated with confidence and joy that the bill would be defeated, and the whole system overthrown by the shock. Our hopes were soon blasted. A certain individual, then a Senator, but recently elected to the highest office in the Union, was observed to assume a mysterious air in relation to the bill, very little in accordance with what there was every reason to believe would have been his course. The mystery was explained when the bill came up to be acted upon. I will not give in detail his course. It is sufficient to say that, instead of resisting amendments, as we had a right to expect, he voted for all which were necessary to secure the votes of New England; particularly the amendments to raise the duties on woollens, which were known to be essential for that purpose. All these amendments, with one or two exceptions, were carried by his votes, as appears from the journal, now on my table, which I have recently examined. If his name had been recorded on the opposite side, they would have been lost, and with them the bill itself. He held, at this critical juncture, the fate of the country in his hands. Had he acted in good faith, the bill of 1828 never would have become a law; and the responsibility of its defeat would have fallen on those who first moved on the subject, and would have prostrated the administration which gave that movement its support. With the prostration of the administration would have followed that of the protective system itself, and thus all the consequences which followed that disastrous act would have been averted. Why a course which good faith as well as the public interest so obviously dictated was avoided, and the opposite pursued, has never been explained. It is certain that the instructions of the New York Legislature did not require it; but it may be that those by whose agency the bill was passed, and who owe their present ascendency to it, then, as now, saw the advantage, in a party view, in having the tariff an open question, however much the country might be the sufferers.

Having traced the tariff of 1828 to the chairman of the Committee on Finance and the President elect, as its authors, I next propose to trace, very briefly, what followed, down to the passage of the act of 1833, which settled the controversy that grew out of the former, and which this bill, originating with its authors, is intended to unsettle, in order that the Senate may have a connected view of the whole series of events connected with this deeply important subject, and of which the present measure forms the last.

I have already stated, that General Jackson had been selected by the opposition, as the candidate against Mr. Adams; and it now becomes necessary to add what were the motives which governed the opposition, as far as myself and friends were concerned, in making this selection. They were altogether political. There never was any intimacy, at any time, between him and myself. Our relations were simply friendly, without being in any degree confidential. The leading objects were to reverse the precedent that brought Mr. Adams into power, to arrest the protective system; to overthrow the principle in which it originated, and to restore the old republican doctrines, from which the Government had so greatly departed.

After a long and arduous struggle, the protective system had completely triumphed, as has been stated, in the election of Mr. Adams. Successful opposition to [*sic*; by] an anti-tariff candidate was hopeless; and the opponents of the system were, accordingly, compelled to elect some one whose position, in relation to the tariff, was not well defined; and who had a popularity in the States friendly to the protective system, unconnected with politics. General Jackson united these advantages, to which he added others, which recommended him to the confidence of the South. He was a cotton planter and a slaveholder; and as such, it was believed, would use his power and influence to arrest the further progress and to correct the excesses of a system so oppressive to the staple States. Circumstances connected with the passage of the act of 1828 first weakened that confidence. I refer in particular to the course of one of the Senators from Tennessee at the time, who was known to be in the entire confidence of General Jackson. I mean not him (Judge [Hugh L.] White) who sits at my right; his conduct throughout was above all suspicion; and let me here add, as an act of justice, that, at a subsequent period, when the bill of 1833 was pending, the country owes much to his upright and firm conduct, as the presiding officer of the Senate, in effecting the passage of that measure, which closed the controversy and saved the country from a civil conflict. The course of Mr. [John H.] Eaton, the individual to whom I allude, was well calculated, on the occasion, to excite doubts as to the views and intentions of General Jackson in relation to the protective policy. Without going into detail, it is sufficient to say that he voted for the bill; and that on one or two decisive questions, on which the fate of the bill depended, it was saved by his votes. These indications shook our confidence in General Jackson; and that, at the critical moment when the passage of the bill cast so deep a gloom over the South, and menaced with so much danger the liberty and institutions of the country.

With the decline of our confidence in General Jackson, it became necessary to seek some efficient remedy that could not deceive, should he fail to fulfil the object for which we selected him as our candidate. That remedy we found in State interposition, and every effort was made without delay to revive the doctrines of the Kentucky and Virginia resolutions of 1798, which formed the original basis of the republican party, but which had so long lain dormant, or neglected, as furnishing means of arresting the fatal consequences of the act of 1828, in the event that all others should fail.

In the mean time, the opposite interest was not idle. Measures were taken without delay to secure and perpetuate the advantages already acquired. With this view, the first movement was made by Mr. [Mahlon] Dickerson, then a member of the Senate [from N.J.], but now Secretary of the Navy, who was then, as now, a decided friend of the President elect. At the next session he introduced a bill for the distribution of the surplus revenue, as a permanent measure, intended to perpetuate and protect the system. This was the origin of the measure, now so frequently and loudly denounced by the Senator from New York, and those who act with him. Whatever evil may flow from it, the responsibility is on him and his political associates, who originated and supported the tariff of 1828. As to us, we saw at once the design and tendency of the measure, and without delay opposed it so decidedly as to defeat its passage. I am gratified to perceive that the Senator, with whom the act of 1828 (the cause of the surplus) originated, is now compelled to acknowledge by his acts our foresight, and the correctness of the course which we pursued; but he must permit me to say that it is unkind in him, who was the author of the evil, to hold us up as the friends of distribution—a measure originating with his party, and introduced in order to perpetuate an act of which he is the author. Instead of censure, he ought to give us some credit for sagacity in foreseeing those evils which he so often denounces, and for our patriotism in raising our warning voice against the measure in which they originated. He might surely, in our past conduct, find some apology for us, in the fact that we, who have been opposed to distribution, should now, when the surplus is in a regular course of reduction by the act of 1833, prefer depositing an unavoidable surplus with the States, rather than leave it to the deposite banks, for the benefit of stockholders and political partisans. It is not exactly just that they who have done the mischief should escape the blame, and that censure should fall on those who have in every stage been opposed to distribution, and have done all in their power to prevent a surplus.

The failure of Mr. Dickerson's movement in Congress, to perpetuate the tariff of 1828 by distributing the surplus revenue, did not deter the party from pursuing their favorite scheme. The next movement was at the Hermitage, and with so much success that General Jackson was secured in its favor before he arrived in this place to assume the duties of Chief Magistrate. As short as was his inaugural address, it contained, as originally draughted, a recommendation in favor of distribution, which he was induced, with great difficulty, to take out. I speak not of my own knowledge, but on authority on which I implicitly rely. The scheme was not abandoned, though taken out of his inaugural address. He strongly recommended it to Congress in his first and second annual messages, in direct opposition to the opinion of several of the ablest members of his cabinet; and this, too, before the reduction of the tariff of 1828, when, according to his confession in his last [annual] message, it would have tended powerfully to perpetuate that oppressive and disastrous measure.

That he acted in concert, in all this, with the authors and supporters of the tariff of 1828, we have conclusive evidence in the corresponding movements of the New York Legislature. Governor [William L.] Marcy, of that State, followed up the message of the President by a strong recommendation in favor of the distribution of the surplus, to which the Legislature responded by a vote of approval, with a decisive majority; but the measure was too repugnant to the feelings of the community to be forced through Congress, even by the aid of party machinery, backed by the influence and popularity of the President.

In the mean time, the period of the final payment of the public debt was rapidly approaching, when, without a very great reduction of duties, there must be an immense surplus revenue, which could not be absorbed by the legitimate objects of expenditure; and yet the administration then, as at all times, under the control of the party to which the Senator belongs, were too much engrossed in the paltry politics of the day to make the least preparation to meet a juncture so full of embarrassment and danger. Our course was different. We clearly saw what was coming, and prepared in time for this crisis. We saw that if the tariff of 1828 was perpetuated, the staple States would be reduced to poverty and ruin, and accordingly opposed, with all our might, every attempt of the Senator and his party to perpetuate that odious and oppressive measure. We saw, with equal clearness, that without reduction there would be an immense surplus, and, at the same time, that there was not the slightest prospect of such reduction from those in power, who were either blind to the danger or too indifferent to the interests of the country to bestow a moment's attention on the subject. Above all, we saw the danger of so large a surplus; the vast increase, in consequence, of the power and patronage of the executive; the corruption and speculation that would follow, with the loss of all responsibility on the part of those in power. In all this we could not but see the overthrow of our institutions, and, with them, of the liberty of the country, unless some effectual remedy should be applied. This remedy, as I have stated, was to be found in State interposition; and we accordingly spared no exertion in preparing our State to meet coming danger, under the banner of State sovereignty. In the mean time, we patiently waited the final payment of the public debt, when, if a sufficient reduction of the duties was not made, by which only the approaching calamity could be averted, it was resolved to interpose the sovereign voice of the State, as the last and only efficient remedy.

At the opening of the session of 1831–'32, the President in his annual message, announced that the public debt might be considered as extinguished, as there was sufficient money in the Treasury to meet the remnant unpaid; and then, for the first time, the administration began to move on the reduction of the protective duties; but even then, when forced by necessity to act, so absurd and inefficient were the schemes proposed for reducing the duties, that it may well be doubted, even now, whether their desire to keep open the dangerous and vexed question of the tariff did not preponderate over all other motives. Instead of proposing a system of gradual reduction, which would bring down the duties in a limited period to the wants of the Treasury, after the discharge of the debt, without the overthrow of the manufacturing establishments of the country, which was obviously the only practicable and wise course, a partial and inefficient bill was introduced, which provided a limited reduction, without any regular plan. It received the sanction of Congress, and was officially announced to be a final adjustment of the tariff between the conflicting interests. The amount of the reduction of the revenue under its provisions was estimated not to exceed three or four millions of dollars, and yet it was seriously maintained that this inconsiderable reduction would bring down the revenue to the wants of the Government; and such was the force of party delusion at the time, that gentlemen of intelligence returned home and staked their reputation and re-election on that issue. But we were not deceived then, as we do not intend to be now. We clearly saw through the deception, and took our stand at once, with a fixed determination to close the dangerous controversy, and throw off the oppressive and unconstitutional burden which weighed so heavily upon the energy and prosperity of the South. The time for action had arrived. The debt was paid, and yet the tariff of 1828, the offspring of the Senator from New York and his party, remained almost in full energy. After a warm canvass, the State of South Carolina, as one of the sovereign members of this Union, met in convention, declared the act to be unconstitutional, and, as such, null and void. In a word, we nullified. Then followed the proclamation and force bill, as the ultimate means of prolonging the existence of the odious and unconstitutional act of

1828, which the party of which the Senator is a member had attempted to fix on the country by a scheme of permanent distribution; and which, when the issue was made, they were ready to sustain at the hazard of civil war. But, thanks to a kind Providence which had watched so constantly over our destinies, their counsel did not prevail. The spirit of conciliation and compromise overruled that of violence and force. The memorable bill of 1833 was introduced by the Senator from Kentucky, (Mr. Clay,) and became a law of the land, in despite of the protective and force-bill party. It closed the conflict between the North and the South, which, if not revived by the arts of those who passed the tariff of 1828, will, I trust and believe, remain closed for ever.

Such is the train of events which led to the act of 1833, and the circumstances under which it passed; and we are now called on to decide whether we shall adhere to its provisions or not. The Senator from New York invites us to surrender our interest in it, and to open anew the tariff controversy; and, with a view to test our determination, has inserted in this bill the repeal of the duty on salt. He signifies his dissent. I am glad of it. It proves that he dreads a direct issue on the subject, which is not surprising after the statement made; but I must tell him that it is immaterial whether it was so intended or not. Salt is among the articles comprehended in the act, and, if we may touch one item, we may all. To vote for the repeal of a single item, unless with common consent, as effectually surrenders the compromise as to vote for the repeal of all.

The Senator from New York must excuse me. I feel it my duty to speak plainly where the interest of my constituents and the whole country is so deeply concerned. I must tell him I lack confidence in him. I see in his bill a design, under the show of reduction, to revive the tariff controversy, by which he and his party have so much profited at the expense of the country. It is an artful and bold stroke of party policy, calculated to distract and divide the opposition, and place almost unlimited control over the capital and labor of the country in the hands of those in power. It affords the means of appealing to the hopes and fears of every section and interest, while the distraction and division which must follow would prevent the possibility of united efforts to arrest the abuses and encroachments of power. Experience has taught us to understand the game, and to be on our guard against those who are playing it. We cannot close our eyes to the fact that the party which is now so intent to disturb the compromise is the very party that was the author of the tariff of 1828; and which, after using every effort to render it permanent, was ready to shed our blood rather than surrender the act. Their devotion to a measure, of which they are the authors, and to which they owe their present elevation, prepared us to expect that deep hostility to the act which gave their favorite a mortal blow, and opened the way for an united, and, we trust, ere long, a successful resistance to power, acquired by deception, and retained by delusion and corruption. The entire South may well apply to the Senator, as the author of the tariff of 1828, the reply which a distinguished Senator (Mr. [Littleton W.] Tazewell of Va.) gave, after its passage, to one who now occupies a higher station than he then did, and who undertook to explain to him his vote on the occasion; "Sir, you have deceived me once; that was your fault; but if you deceive me again, the fault will be mine." Alas, for Virginia! that once proud and patriotic State; she has dismissed her honest and enlightened son, who served her with so much fidelity, and has elevated to the highest office him who betrayed her and trampled her interest in the dust.

I know full well the attempts that will be made to misrepresent my position on this occasion, and to weaken me in the confidence of the public. I fear them not. I know well those whom I represent. They have too clear a conception of their true interest, and place too high an estimate on truth and honor, to withhold their confidence from him who fearlessly follows their dictates. They will scorn the miserable boon proffered by the Senator from New York, and the hand that offers it, and will cling to the act which they so proudly wrung from this Government. Were I to listen to the voice of the Senator from New York, they would hold me blind to their interests, and indifferent to their honor. I shall firmly maintain the position I have taken. I shall not assent to disturb the act of 1833, in the slightest degree, so long as the manufacturing interests shall adhere to its provisions, be the conduct of politicians what it may. Thus far they have firmly adhered. Not a murmur has been heard, or a petition offered, from that quarter, against it, from its passage to the present day; while the memorials of the Legislatures of the two great tariff States—Massachusetts and Pennsylvania—which pledged themselves to abide by the provisions of the act, give strong additional assurance that, if we do not disturb it on our part they will not on theirs.

From *Register of Debates*, 24th Cong., 2nd Sess., cols. 902–911. Also printed in the Washington, D.C., *Reformer*, March 14, 1837, p. 2; the Pendleton, S.C., *Messenger*, April 7, 1837, pp. 1, 4; the Charleston, S.C., *Mercury*, April 21, 1837, p. 2; the Edgefield, S.C., *Advertiser*, April 27, 1837, pp. 1–2; the Richmond, Va., *Whig and Public Advertiser*, May 9, 1837, p. 4; Crallé, ed., *Works*, 3:43–59. Variant in the Washington, D.C., *Globe*, March 4, 1837, p. 3; *Congressional Globe*, 24th Cong., 2nd Sess., Appendix, pp. 209–210. Other variants in the

Washington, D.C., *Reformer,* February 25, 1837, p. 3; *Niles' Weekly Register,* vol. LII, no. 1 (March 4, 1837), p. 1.

FURTHER REMARKS ON THE BILL TO REDUCE CERTAIN TARIFF DUTIES

[In the Senate, February 23, 1837]
[When Calhoun had finished his speech on this bill, Bedford Brown of N.C. rose and condemned Calhoun for "an uncalled for and unwarrantable denunciation against those of their Northern friends who had come forward as the advocates of a reduction of duties on this occasion." He also remarked that Calhoun was contributing to keeping up the tariff system and "therefore, that the relative positions of gentlemen had undergone some change in the progress of events." Calhoun queried: "Am I to understand the Senator to say that I have changed my sentiments in relation to the tariff?" Brown continued his remarks. When he had finished Calhoun rose.]

Mr. Calhoun observed in reply, that the mode in which the Senator from North Carolina reasoned went to hold up Mr. C[alhoun] to the country as being opposed to the reduction of the tariff. Mr. C[alhoun] protested against such an interpretation of his course. He was, and always had been, decidedly in favor of a reduction, and he voted against the present motions expressly from his utter aversion to the whole tariff system. He believed that the small reductions now proposed, by unsettling the compromise, would bring back the system in its whole extent; but he had not the slightest faith on earth that the party who had brought forward this bill ever intended to pass it. If they had really been in earnest in desiring that a bill of this character should become a law, why had these disputed items been put into the bill? The great body of the reductions in the bill were without dispute, and might have been passed in ten minutes; why, then, had these others been put in? Was not the design plain and palpable? Who expected that there would be any reduction in the revenue? And because he would not give a vote which, while it would tell on nothing at all, would go to commit his State to break the compromise, was he to be held up as opposed to the reduction of the tariff? The Senator from North Carolina himself could not but see that Mr. C[alhoun]'s position showed and proved that he was as much opposed to the tariff as he had ever been. He had never retrograded a single inch.

[*Brown spoke again, insisting that those who opposed the bill were voting to perpetuate the tariff, which was "the honest truth." He further referred to "contemptible vanity and overweening egotism which was sometimes displayed on that floor."*]

Mr. Calhoun observed, in reply, that the Senator from North Carolina had fully satisfied him of one thing. The Senator continued to assert that Mr. C[alhoun] was in favor of the tariff, because he was opposed to taking off this duty on salt. All he could say was, that a gentleman who could think or say so, after the two distinct explanations and admonitions which Mr. C[alhoun] had given, would not hereafter receive any notice from him. Mr. C[alhoun] regretted that his appeal to the good sense of the Senator had not been met. He had expressly asked him whether he meant to affirm that Mr. C[alhoun] was not opposed to the tariff. From the reply he had received, he had learned a lesson; and it was, not in the future to respond to any remarks which might fall from that Senator.

[*Brown spoke again, referring to Calhoun's position on the bill in question as a "miserable subterfuge," a remark of which Calhoun said he "threw it back with indignation." Debate resumed, a number of Senators, including Wright, taking part.*]

Mr. Calhoun said he had heard so much of promise, and had seen so little of performance, since he came into public life, that the Senator from New York must really excuse him for not giving that implicit faith to all he heard, which he might, at an earlier period of life, have been disposed to yield. If any one looked at the indisposition of men in power to yield any portion of the power they held, he would readily become convinced that it was a most difficult task to get rid of existing duties. This was not the first time he had been led to make this remark. At the very outset of this session he had said that there would be no reduction of the revenue, and no deposite bill; nor had he uttered this prophecy from any peculiar trait of suspicion which belonged to his character, but from the teachings of experience. Why was the Senate not agreed on this measure? Here was a dominant majority held as closely bound by party ties as he had ever seen a set of men in his life; and yet they could not get along in a bill to reduce the revenue, without the votes of his colleague and himself. It was manifest that the reigning party were divided on the tariff, and equally obvious that that difference did not divide them politically. The tariff was one of those open questions on which men of both sides were left at liberty to vote as they pleased. The party would never get Northern Senators to vote for repealing the protective duties. Mr. C[alhoun] did, therefore, want faith in the sincerity of the present effort. The Senator from New York (Mr. Wright) had disclaimed all unnecessary delay in reference to the present bill; but did not all know that it was not until two weeks after the land bill that this bill had been brought forward? What hindered its earlier consideration? Gentlemen had suffered the new fortification bill to be taken up, and then a bill to enlarge the army, and then an armory bill; all these consumed time; and, under such circumstances, he must doubt the zeal of gentlemen in pushing, as they might have done. And why was it discussed now, when there was not the remotest chance of its becoming a law? It might produce political agitation, but no reduction of the revenue. If gentlemen had been sincere and earnest in their anxiety to accomplish that object, why were not the items in this bill divided into two distinct classes, and reported in two different bills? In regard to many of them there was no dispute; and if these had been classed together, the bill containing them would have been passed at once by common consent. From the mixing up of these with other items which were sure to produce great controversy, Mr. C[alhoun] was justified in believing, and time would show the correctness of the opinion, that they would have much talk and no action. Mr. C[alhoun] was not opposed to those who in good faith desired to reduce the revenue. Those who professed to have this desire had the majority. Let that majority be brought together, and let the declaration be made in a certain quarter that all who oppose the measure would be considered as out of the true faith, and then Mr. C[alhoun] would believe gentlemen to be in earnest; otherwise he could not. But the Senator from New York (Mr. Wright) had declared that, if there was any secret understanding in regard to the tariff of 1828, he knew nothing of it.

I was (said Mr. C[alhoun]) consulted at the time, to know how the South would go, and whether the South would sustain the bill as it came from the Middle States? We did so sustain it, but refused to agree to such amendments as would suit the members from the Eastern States. The internal history of the bill shows what was our calculation. Can any man believe that Southern men would ever have voted for such a bill as the tariff of 1828, unless they believed that by so voting they would insure its ultimate defeat? Do not all the world know that we of the Southern States were for free trade, and looked upon all these protecting duties as neither more nor less than sheer oppression? We surely had an ordinary measure of common sense; and would we vote to resist all amendments to such a bill as was ultimately passed, unless we felt ourselves assured of a contingent advantage? We saw that the system might be pushed too far to suit New England; that it might be made to affect injuriously the interests of navigation and commerce; and that in that case they would go against the bill. Surely we must have had some assurance that in the final vote New England would join us. We took our hazard on this issue. We resisted all amendments, and kept the bill in such a shape that we were assured they never could vote for it. Our great inducement was a hope of being able to prostrate the administration, and aiding New England in the defeat of the bill; but the very men who had the most warmly denounced the bill suddenly wheeled round, and, on the final question, took ground against us. If, after all this, I am a little suspicious that gentlemen may be acting here a political part, with the intention of again bringing the whole industry of the country under the action of Congress, and thus gain for their party an unlimited control of its affairs, is it to be wondered at? Is it marvellous that I, who have seen and mingled with and been an actor in such a scene as passed here in 1828, should suspect the entire sincerity of the same gentlemen in 1837?

But the honorable Senator says that salt is not the only article selected by the Finance Committee as an object of reduction; but that others, on which the existing duty is over 20 per cent., have also been inserted in this bill. It is very true. But as the act of 1833 was an adjustment of the tariff, by way of compromise between the manufacturing and agricultural interests of the country, some duties included in it may be reduced by common consent of both parties. Thus, the duties on wines and vinous spirits may be lowered, without interfering with the tariff system, because they are in a manner open articles; but this cannot be said of this duty on salt. This is a test question, and the only article in the bill which presents a fair test, whether the compromise is to be respected or not. On that view of the subject I take my ground. The difference between reducing this salt duty all at once, and reducing it gradually, presents no temptation to me. I neither can nor will be caught in such a trap. In 1840 and 1841 the duties go off rapidly. I shall then claim the benefit of our side of the arrangement; and shall I not be stronger then if I concede now? I put it to all Southern men, whether, even allowing that the compromise has no absolutely binding force, it will not be our wisest policy to hold to it? Whether we shall not thereby render ourselves stronger in 1841 and 1842? Most certainly we shall. When Senators on the other side sit silent while we thus explain our understanding of the agreement, I hold it to be an acquiescence in our view; for surely it is a most unmanly course if they mean otherwise.

We are told that the President elect [Martin Van Buren] is most wonderfully attached to the Southern States and the advancement of Southern interests; and the evidence is the speech he delivered in New York previous to the vote he gave to fix the tariff upon us in 1828; and the vote is not permitted to explain the speech. He voted for the duty on wool and woollens, and for the whole bill of 1828—one of the most oppressive measures to the South that ever was devised; and yet gentlemen have faith in his deep attachment to Southern interests. I am much disposed to look back. Perhaps it is constitutional in my mind; but I feel a strong proneness to retrospection. I well remember the constitution of the first cabinet of General Jackson. There was Mr. [John M.] Berrien, a stout anti-tariff man, and stoutly opposed to the tariff of 1828, (which was passed by the vote of Mr. Van Buren.) Then there was Mr. [John] Branch, decidedly opposed to it. Mr. [Samuel D.] Ingham, who acted a manly, open part in that business. All these were General Jackson's warm friends. With them were Mr. [Mahlon] Dickerson, of New Jersey, a most thorough tariff man, and Mr. [Levi] Woodbury, of New Hampshire, who (to do him justice) acted not badly in 1828. At bottom, he was opposed to the bill. He acted a very different part from Mr. Van Buren. Mr. Van Buren, if we may judge by his vote, was most thoroughly tariff. Yet it seems extraordinary to the Senator from New York that, with that thoroughly tariff man for President, I should be unwilling to have the compromise disturbed! Let us have some proof that Mr. Martin Van Buren is as hostile to the tariff as the Senator from North Carolina [Bedford Brown] says he is. Until I have proof on that point, I, for one, can never consent to have the tariff question opened, because I am very sure, the moment it is, we in the minority are sure of being sacrificed. Whatever surplus may be left in the Treasury, it is infinitely safer to return it to the States, until a gradual reduction of the revenue shall have dried up the sources from which it is derived. I have determined, under present circumstances, not to call up the deposite bill. I am well persuaded, if the Government shall go on in future as extravagantly as it has lately done, there will soon be complaint heard about a surplus in the Treasury. I have no faith in the present state of the country. It is unsound. There is a plethoric, bloated state of apparent prosperity; but the slightest reverse will throw our whole money concerns into irretrievable confusion. The currency, both of Great Britain and America, was never before in so critical a condition.

Mr. C[alhoun] concluded by reiterating the declaration that he had taken his stand upon the advantages to be derived to the South from an adherence to the compromise.

From *Register of Debates*, 24th Cong., 2nd Sess., cols. 914–928. Also printed in the Washington, D.C., *Daily National Intelligencer*, April 18, 1837, pp. 2–3. Variant in *Congressional Globe*, 24th Cong., 2nd Sess., Appendix, p. 211. Another variant in the New York, N.Y., *Morning Courier and New-York Enquirer*, February 25, 1837, p. 2.

SPEECH DURING FINAL CONSIDERATION
OF THE BILL TO REDUCE
CERTAIN TARIFF DUTIES

[In the Senate, February 25, 1837]

Mr. Calhoun said he was fully apprized of the impatience of the Senate, and regretted to detain them at so late an hour; but he could not avoid saying a few words before the question should be put upon the passage of this bill. It now appears (said Mr. C[alhoun]) that the administration party did not intend to respect the provisions of the compromise law. The people of the North seem, with but little exception, to be disposed to adhere to it. The question then arises, what course ought to be pursued by me, and by those who act with me, on this subject? The course, as I apprehend, is an obvious one. So far as the manufacturing interests are concerned, they concur in the arrangement; not a petition has been presented, not an effort has in any shape been made, to disturb it. The present is the first attempt which we have witnessed in any wise to interfere with it. And this attempt is not made by manufacturers, but by politicians; and by politicians from the manufacturing region of the Union. I regret exceedingly that the South, which has so deep a stake in the observance of the compromise, should give any countenance to such a design. This bill does not violate our share of that arrangement; not an article of it; the violation is of that part of the bargain which belongs to the North. It rests, therefore, with the Northern interest to say whether they will sustain their public men in such an attempt or not. I leave it to them to settle the question.

As to myself, I care not how many duties are taken off, provided it be done by gentlemen from that section of the Union; but, in the mean time, I shall do my duty. We of the South, it is always to be remembered, are the weaker interest; in this sort of contest it is we who are to be the sufferers. I therefore, for one, will not vote to disturb the compromise of 1833.

I am not, however, much surprised that the friends of the administration from the Southern States should be tempted to give their votes for this bill. We have long warred against the tariff; and when a proposition is made for repealing any portion of it, it is not wonderful that they should seize upon it with avidity. But let me tell them to beware. Will you, for the trifling benefit now held out to you, establish the principle that the act of 1833 is to be disregarded? You may now make a small reduction in violation of its provisions; but do you forget that, if that act remains inviolate, in 1842 six tenths of the whole protective duties will go off? Let me tell my Southern friends that I know the men with whom we have to deal. Abandon the compromise, and they will be among the first to resist all future reduction. We see the bait, but we do not perceive the hook that lies under it. We see a proposition to repeal the duty on salt; the motion, coming from a New York Senator [Silas Wright], has the appearance of great magnanimity; but we did not remember, till we were reminded of it, that New York has laid a State tax of six cents a bushel on all salt ascending her canals. This salt duty is the bait; and for the sake of this small gain we are invited to disturb the arrangements of the compromise. But I can tell these fishers, they shall not catch me. I was caught once by following the same lead. I am not to be caught a second time. Wait till 1842, and you will find that which I say is true.

We have been told that the Senators in the opposition have given no pledges to observe the compromise law; but I ask, have either the chairman of the Committee on Finance, or other gentlemen of the same party, given any pledge that they will not violate that compromise when the year 1842 comes? They are now for reducing duties; but will they not then be for arresting the reduction provided by the act? Rely upon it, that is the very thing that they have in view. Their professed object is to get rid of the surplus, and they talk of making war upon the protective system, and even of its entire overthrow.

When men make professions, I am called upon to judge of their sincerity; I am in the habit of looking at the measures they pursue, and whether these measures are the fit and appropriate means toward the end they profess to have in view; and if I perceive that they are not, I hold it proper to be on my guard. I admit that these gentlemen are opposed to having a surplus in the Treasury, and I perceive that they have given a pledge to the South that they mean to make war upon the protective system. Such being their aim, what is the mode which they ought to take to attain it? Is not that mode obvious?

Should they pick out the article of salt, to accelerate the reduction proposed by the compromise of 1833? It was one defect of that arrangement that the reduction proposed by it was to be too rapid towards the close, and too slow in the beginning. The obvious rule of proceeding would rather have been to make it swift at first, and slow afterwards. It would have been perfectly easy to say that the amount of all protective duties should have been reduced one fifth on the 1st of January, in every year, for the five years. That would have reduced a greater amount than the whole of what is proposed by this bill, and would have given a sure pledge to the South that gentlemen were sincere in their professions and promises. I should then have believed them. But when I see them proceed to select articles not made in the States where they have the majority, and see them opposing the reduction on articles made in States where they have not, I am naturally led to predict that, in 1842, they will come here and tell us that the reduction proposed by the compromise act is too rapid.

Our friends of the South (I speak now of such as are friends of the administration, who are all deeply interested in the articles of cotton and tobacco, and who, in relation to those articles, move all together, and must be sincere) found their course on the declaration of the Senator from Virginia, (Mr. [William C.] Rives,) who comes forward here as the personal friend and political organ of the President elect. That Senator tells us that Mr. Van Buren is a "practical politician." And when he is asked what Mr. Van Buren proposes to do, his reply is, that he intends to reduce the tariff in such a manner as that it shall not be injurious to any great interest of the country. And what, I pray you, is this but the old song which has been sung in our ears a thousand times? It is neither more nor less than the old story of a "judicious tariff." The Senator from Kentucky [Henry Clay], the Senator from Massachusetts [Daniel Webster], and all the friends of the protective policy, are for a tariff which shall not be injurious to any of the great interests of the country. They have never asked for any thing else, if you take their account of it; and yet for this vague declaration, made at second hand by the Senator from Virginia, we of the South are asked to surrender the immense advantages secured to us by the act of 1833—an act which explicitly provides that the duties shall come off at a certain specified rate until the whole are gone. Sir, this word *practical* is a very important word. We call a man a practical man who is a man of business, who is practical in his business. Mr. Van Buren is a politician. That is his business, and we are told that he is a practical politician. Now, sir, what sort of an animal is a practical politician? I will endeavor to describe it. It is a man who considers the terms *justice, right, patriotism,* &c., as all being so many abstractions, mere vague phrases, which it is very well to use, but which are to be shaped wholly by circumstances. It is a man who acts in each peculiar juncture as expediency may require; who studies the men about him with great care, with a view to a given end; who studies especially their assailable points, and who uses them as instruments for the accomplishment of his own purposes. If, for example, there be near him a Chief Magistrate distinguished by strong passions, a very determined will, and a good deal of personal vanity, he will touch that vanity, and, by skilfully playing upon it, will get hold of the mind and will of its possessor; and having once obtained a firm hold upon the Chief Magistrate, he will employ the power and influence of such an individual to an object eminently practical, viz: the attainment of his own political ends. The same thing he does with all other men around him. He uses them all, he turns them all to practical use, for he is himself "practical." He looks at particulars, and considers all propositions of a general nature as mere abstractions, with which a wise man will not too much concern himself. A practical politician judges of all actions by the event. If they are successful, he is in favor of them; if not, not. He adopts precisely the policy that was pursued in the Italian republics, and weighs every principle of morals and patriotism by the degree in which it will conduce to a certain given purpose which is to be gained. This is a practical politician. And now I will tell you how such a politician is likely to act in regard to the tariff question. He sees in the opening of that question again the means and prospect of a great increase of power; by rightly managing the different States, and displaying them off in a skilful manner against each other, and standing ready to make the most of every result, he will hope to get into his hands an entire control. By putting all things afloat, he calculates to bring them all under the Government to be managed; and this, let that management result as it may to them, must be promotive of his interest. Now, the South, as we all know, has an interest in the principles of free trade. What is likely to be her fate under such a system of things it is easy to tell. She brings him the least weight, and her interest will therefore be the soonest disposed of, in whatever way it can be made the most of.

Entertaining these views, I cannot consent to change my position. I am for adhering to the compromise. I think that the act holds out to us of the South great advantages, while, at the same time, the manufacturers of the country flourish under it; (and whatever may have been said or thought, I am no enemy to the manufacturing interest, nor ever have been.) I think they will go through the reduction uninjured, provided we can but have a sound currency; for nothing can be so injurious to the protective principle as a currency that is unsound. We all desire that the manufacturers may get through the descent safely; and with a sound currency they may do it. Calculating on the same rate of importation as now exists, the amount of duties in 1842 will not exceed ten millions. I say, therefore, let the country remain quiet; disturb not this long-vexed question. He who shall deliberately disturb it will give evidence either that he disregards the public interest, or that he misunderstands it. I regret that a single article has been inserted in this bill going to disturb the arrangements of the compromise. I am sorry that the Senator from Kentucky (Mr. Clay) did not succeed in his motion to recommit the bill with instructions. Had these disputed articles been stricken from it, the bill would have passed the House of Representatives almost unanimously. It is now late in the session, and it is exceedingly doubtful whether the bill in its present shape can pass that body. I hope that some gentleman who voted with the majority will yet move a reconsideration, and let us have the bill in such a shape that we can pass it unanimously.

From *Register of Debates*, 24th Cong., 2nd Sess., cols. 975–978. Also printed in the Washington, D.C., *Daily National Intelligencer*, April 25, 1837, p. 2. Variant in the New York, N.Y., *Morning Courier and New-York Enquirer*, February 27, 1837, p. 2. NOTE: At the conclusion of the day's debate the bill was passed by the Senate 27 to 18; it did not come to a vote in the House of Representatives.

Remarks on a bill concerning pilots, 2/28. When this bill was under final consideration Calhoun "objected to it, as relating to a subject which required considerable attention, and as one which he was rather disposed to think properly belonged to the several States." After explanation by two supporters the bill was passed. From *Register of Debates*, 24th Cong., 2nd Sess., cols. 1008–1009.

Remarks on an amendment to the lighthouse bill, 2/28. When the bill for appropriations for navigational aids for 1837 came under final consideration, John Davis of Mass. offered an amendment requiring the Board of Navy Commissioners "to examine the premises before any appropriations shall be applied." Calhoun "expressed his high approbation of this amendment, objecting, however, to the whole system, and especially to the practice of making appropriations before the examinations are actually made." From *Register of*

Debates, 24th Cong., 2nd Sess., col. 1009. Also printed in the Washington, D.C., *Daily National Intelligencer*, March 2, 1837, p. 2.

REMARKS ON THE DISTRIBUTION OF THE SURPLUS REVENUE

[In the Senate, February 28, 1837]
The Senate proceeded to the consideration of the fortification bill; and the question being on the amendment reported by the Committee on Finance, viz: to strike out the second section of the bill [originating in the House of Representatives], which contains the provision for distribution among the States of any surplus which may remain in the Treasury on the 1st of January, 1838—

Mr. Calhoun regretted that the committee had not made a written report on so important a recommendation.

Mr. [Silas] Wright explained that the second section of the bill being neither more nor less than the bill formerly introduced [on 12/21/1836] by the Senator from South Carolina himself, the case was fully understood by all the Senate, and needed no consumption of time to explain it. As to a written report, there had been no time to prepare one, even had the committee deemed it necessary.

Mr. Calhoun reminded the Senate of the triumphant majority by which the deposite bill had been adopted at the last session; and as there had occurred nothing since then to change the principle of the measure in any respect, he was content to rest the present question on the principles then so unanswerably established, and the discussion by which they had been defended at the last session.

[*After a debate in which at least nine Senators took part, Calhoun resumed the floor.*]

Mr. Calhoun said the question was now brought to the single point, of what discrimination there was between this bill and the other, and whether this was unwise and that a wise one. Gentlemen admitted that the situation of the banks last year and now was precisely the same. The next point of [James Buchanan] the Senator from Pennsylvania (for others had followed almost exactly in the track which he had stricken out) was, that when the law of last year passed, there was a large surplus in the Treasury, while now there was none. But (said Mr. C[alhoun]) notwithstanding the distribution on the 1st of January last, our Treasury is as full now as it was at that time.

477

Mr. C[alhoun] here went into the details of various statements and estimates, to prove this assertion. He made the sum in the Treasury now $42,000,000. The income of the customs last year he said was $21,000,000; which differed by $2,000,000 from his estimate for the present year. The imports, he said, were regulated by the exports, which were now known. The exports of cotton were greater than in the year preceding, and the price was now rising, and would probably continue to rise. The rice crop, also, was rather better, though the tobacco was not quite as much; so that the products for export in 1837 might be fairly put down to equal those of 1836. The profits of trade were never higher, and the customs would probably not be less than $25,000,000 or $30,000,000, though in his estimate he had made the customs rather less than last year.

In relation to the revenue from the public lands, Mr. C[alhoun] had been guided more by the opinions of others who had more experience, and he had set it down at eight or nine millions of dollars. To this was to be added the stock in the United States Bank, which would make an aggregate, for the year, of $42,000,000.

The question now, whether there would or would not be a surplus, depended (he said) on the answer to the question whether Congress would appropriate all this money. Would politicians of the Jefferson school, who had expelled the old [John Quincy Adams] administration, partly on account of its prodigality in an annual expenditure of some $12,000,000, would they go so far as to appropriate even $27,000,000? At this Mr. C[alhoun] would place the expenditure, though he thought the extreme ought not to exceed fifteen or sixteen millions, and the average not more than twelve or fourteen millions. There would then be a surplus of some fifteen or seventeen millions with the enormous expenditure which he admitted might be made.

Last year, the reiterated predictions that there would be no surplus had proved to be false. This year they would be equally so. There was a heavy surplus now and, without extraordinary expenditures, there would be at the end of the year. There were two reasons which he thought decisive in urging at this time the measure of distribution. One was, that if they made no disposition of the surplus, the scenes of last year would be renewed; the banks would loan extravagantly, relying on the surplus as banking capital, and would extend speculation every way and to every thing. This state of things the President [Andrew Jackson] himself had denounced, and yet, notwithstanding past experience and these denunciations of the President, we were now told to omit this measure for preventing such a result. The opposite course (Mr. C[alhoun] said) was the true one. Pass this law now, and it would check extravagance and speculation, and remedy the very disordered state of the currency, which would otherwise be still more disordered. This would meet fully and decisively the two first objects of the Senator from Pennsylvania and of every Senator.

The next argument was, that the passage of the bill would familiarize us to a system of distribution, which might thus be permanently ingrafted on the administration of the Government; whereas distribution ought to be an exception, and not the rule. To this latter proposition Mr. C[alhoun] agreed most heartily; and no man urged it more than he. He was the first to denounce such a system, and his opinion on this point had undergone no change whatever. It ought to be an exception, and not the rule. His own language was, that it was to be used as medicine, and not as food; and the provisions of this very bill were founded on the disordered condition of the republic. It was in the congestive state, and this bill was intended to remove the obstructions. But the dose must be repeated till the system should become healthy. In Mr. C[alhoun]'s opinion, the measure ought to be repeated while the revenue should be going down, till the time of its reduction to the economical wants of the Government. It might require repetition again and again; while the scheme, as a permanent one, would be perfectly absurd. As such, there was not the smallest reason to fear that the people would ever come into it. General Jackson, in two of his messages, had strongly recommended it; but, with all his popularity and power even he could not carry it; and nothing but absolute necessity had ever effected the passage of the former bill, or could effect the passage of this; and that this had already passed the House was decisive proof that it was a measure of necessity.

The Senator from Pennsylvania was in favor of reducing the revenue; and so was Mr. C[alhoun]. Early in the session, the Senator from New York and himself passed some words on the subject, and Mr. C[alhoun] then told him that he had no faith in a reduction at this session, which was difficult at all times, but was now attended with insuperable difficulty. There were then two measures in view, one of which was to reduce the tariff of 1833. Mr. C[alhoun] thought then there was very little prospect of the passage of such a law, or of a law reducing the revenue from the public lands. Yet, if they would and could reduce, he said, go on and do so. It was now the last day but one, and there was no hope that the bill for reducing could pass. The administration majorities in both Houses had failed of reduction. Would they now leave the money in the hands of the banks? Mr. C[alhoun] trusted they would not. There were now but three alternatives, one of which was to leave the money in the banks. Would Congress do this, receiving only two per cent., and that not on the whole, but only a part of the amount, when it was well known that with them it was at least worth six per cent.? Were they to leave it with the banks, as an instrument for political purposes? Why should gentlemen recommend so extraordinary a course, so unequal, so partial, to avoid returning it to the people to whom it belonged? Why were they so averse to such a distribution? Was it to prevent the people from being corrupted? Were the people alone capable of being corrupted? Were the Government and banks all pure, while the people, the people alone, were corrupt and corruptible? Mr. C[alhoun] however, would not argue in regard to the State Governments, as he thought they of course must be perfectly safe.

The second alternative (Mr. C[alhoun] said) was to expend this enormous amount. That had already been contemplated as a dangerous error. In 1828, the income of the Government was raised enormously. We were now about in the commencement of the operation of raising the expenditure, and at the very time when the revenue was going down at about an annual average of $2,000,000 till 1842. Mr. C[alhoun] thought $12,000,000 or $15,000,000 a most ample provision; especially as the fortifications and other defences being nearly completed, the expenses must be nearly limited to the civil list. The administration of Mr. Monroe was called extravagant in the expenditure of $10,000,000, which was the extreme annual amount. The appropriations then for fortifications and the army were called most extravagant. But now gentlemen could not be contented with less than $20,000,000 or $30,000,000; and at this rate the expenditure would very soon overrun the income. We must then raise the tariff or cut down the expenditure. These sudden vibrations (Mr. C[alhoun] said) were all wrong. This want of looking forward, this wilful blindness to the future, was wholly unworthy of those who had the management of the republic. The responsibility and the danger was great, if either this bill should be lost, or if a resort should be had to extravagant expenditures.

The last and only remaining alternative was a deposite of the surplus with the States. It was now late in the session, and Mr. C[alhoun] would not further consume the time; but what he had said was ample to show that there was no material distinction between the case now and that of the year preceding.

From *Register of Debates*, 24th Cong., 2nd Sess., cols. 992–1001. Also printed in the Washington, D.C., *Daily National Intelligencer*, March 2, 1837, p. 2; the Richmond, Va., *Enquirer*, March 4, 1837, p. 2. Variant in the New York, N.Y., *Morning Courier and New-York Enquirer*, March 2, 1837, p. 2. NOTE: During a speech following Calhoun's, Buchanan remarked that he had voted for Calhoun's deposit bill during the previous session, but at that time he had heard nothing from Calhoun "which would authorize us to infer that he intended to make the extreme medicine of the constitution its daily bread." Calhoun explained "that the bill introduced by him at the last session contained a distribution for several years." (*Register of Debates*, 24th Cong., 2nd Sess., col. 1006.) At the end of the debate the motion to strike out the distribution portion of the fortification bill was carried 26 to 19.

Remarks on the bill making appropriations for the Naval service for 1837, 3/1. When this bill was under final consideration Calhoun "remarked that the balances on hand for the naval service amounted to about $4,800,000. This, with the appropriations of this bill, would make the whole a very large sum, rather greater than the whole expenditure of Government under Mr. [James] Monroe, and about equal to the highest entire expenditure under Mr. [John Quincy] Adams." Later in the debate Calhoun "said he would now say to the Senate that this bill, in connexion with previous appropriations, would put under the control of the Navy Department something like $12,000,000." (The bill passed. Shortly after, Calhoun made an unsuccessful effort to table a bill making appropriations for river and harbor improvements.) From *Register of Debates*, 24th Cong., 2nd Sess., col. 1014. Also printed in the Washington, D.C., *Daily National Intelligencer*, March 3, 1837, p. 2.

Remarks on the motion to supply Senate committee rooms with various publications, 3/1. When this proposal was under final consideration Calhoun "joined the opposition to the measure, as but the commencement of a system of expense, &c." The motion was tabled. From *Register of Debates*, 24th Cong., 2nd Sess., col. 1010.

Remarks on the resolution for recognition of the independence of Texas, 3/1. As a substitute for Robert J. Walker's resolution for immediate recognition, John Norvell of Mich. offered a proposal stating that it would be expedient for the President of the U.S. to extend recognition when he received word of the "successful operation of a civil Government" in Texas. Walker objected to the amendment. "Mr. Calhoun also opposed the amendment, and spoke for a short time in support of Mr. Walker's resolution." (Later in the day Walker's resolution was adopted 23 to 19.) From *Register of Debates*, 24th Cong., 2nd Sess., col. 1012.

Further remarks on the distribution of the surplus revenue, 3/2. A message was received that the House of Representatives disagreed with the Senate action in striking out the section of the fortification bill providing for a distribution of the surplus revenue. Calhoun spoke briefly twice in the debate that followed the receipt of the House message. First, "he expressed his hope that the Senate would recede, and not resist an expression of the will of the Representatives of the people, given by so decided a majority as was said to have voted in the other House." Later he "said the naked question was, whether the surplus revenue should be left in the deposite banks, or should be returned to the people to whom it belonged." By a vote of 28 to 22 the Senate agreed to insist upon its previous decision. From *Register of Debates*, 24th Cong., 2nd Sess., cols. 1019–1021. Also printed in the Washington, D.C., *Daily National Intelligencer*, March 3, 1837, p. 2.

Remarks on a proposed reconsideration of a vote, 3/2. Senator John Ruggles of Me. moved a reconsideration of the resolution for recognizing the independence of Texas so that he could change his vote, "which was given, under misapprehension." Calhoun joined Robert J. Walker in arguing that this motion violated the spirit of a Senate rule. From *Register of Debates*, 24th Cong., 2nd Sess., col. 1019. Also printed in *Congressional Globe*, 24th Cong., 2nd Sess., p. 274.

REMARKS ON THE CORRESPONDENCE WITH
GREAT BRITAIN CONCERNING THE BRIGS
Comet, Encomium, AND *Enterprise*

[In the Senate, March 2, 1837]
Mr. Calhoun said that it would be remembered that on his motion a resolution was adopted [on 2/7] requesting the President to communicate to the Senate the correspondence between this Government and that of Great Britain in relation to the case of the brigs Encomium and Enterprise. He held in his hand the message of the President [received on 2/14] in answer to the resolution, from which

he found there was another case (that of the Comet) of a similar character, of which he was not aware when he made his motion, and which occurred as far back as 1832. He had read with care the correspondence, but he must say with very little satisfaction—it was all on one side. Our Executive has been knocking—(no, that is too strong a term)—tapping gently at the door of the British Secretary [of State for Foreign Affairs, Lord Palmerston], to obtain justice for these five years, without receiving an answer, and this in the plainest case imaginable. It was not his intention to censure those who had been intrusted with the correspondence on our part. They had written enough, and more than enough; but truth compelled him to say the tone was not high enough, considering the injustice to our citizens, and the outrage on the flag and honor of the Union. His remarks were intended more especially for the latter part of the correspondence, after the long delay without an answer from the British Government. At first, in so plain a case, little more could be thought necessary than a plain statement of the facts, which was given in a very clear and satisfactory manner in the letter of the President elect [Martin Van Buren, then Minister to Great Britain] in the case of the Comet.

Without repeating what he said on the introduction of the resolution, he would remind the Senate of the facts of the case in the briefest manner possible. The three brigs were engaged in the coasting trade, and among other passengers, had slaves on board, belonging to our citizens, who were sending them to the southwestern States with a view to settlement. The Enterprise was forced, by stress of weather, into Port Hamilton, Bermuda, where the slaves on board were forcibly seized and detained by the local authorities. The other two were wrecked on the Keys belonging to the Bahama Islands, and the passengers and crew taken by wreckers, contrary to their wishes, into Nassau, New Providence, where the slaves shared the same fate as at Bermuda.

These were the essential facts of the case. He did not intend to argue the questions that grew out of them. There was, indeed, little or no ground for argument. No one in the least conversant with the laws of nations can doubt that those vessels were as much under the protection of our flag, while on their voyage, proceeding from one port of the Union to another, as if they were in port, lying at the wharves, within our acknowledged jurisdiction. Nor is it less clear that, forced as the Enterprise was by stress of weather, and taken under the circumstances that the passengers and crews of the other two were, into the British dominions, they lost none of the rights which belonged to them while on their voyage on the ocean. So far otherwise, so far from losing the protection which our flag gave them while on the ocean, they had superadded, by their misfortunes, the additional rights which the laws of humanity extend to the unfortunate in their situation, and which are regarded by all civilized nations as sacred. It follows, as a necessary consequence, that the municipal laws of the place could not divest the owners of the property which, as citizens of the United States, they had in the slaves who were passengers in the vessels; and yet, as clear as is this conclusion, they were forcibly seized and detained by the local authorities of the islands, and the Government of Great Britain, after five years' negotiation, has not only withheld redress, but has not even deigned to answer the often-repeated applications of our Government for redress. We are thus left by its silence to conjecture the reasons for so extraordinary a course.

On casting his eyes over the whole subject, he could fix on but one that had the least plausibility, and that resting on a principle which it was scarcely credible that a Government so intelligent could assume: he meant the principle that there could not be property in persons. It was not for him to object that Great Britain, or any other country, should assume that or any other principle it might think proper, as applicable to its subjects; but he must protest against the right to adopt it as applicable to our country or citizens. It would strike at the independence of our country, and would not be less insulting than outrageous, while it would ill become a nation that was the greatest slave-holder of any on earth, notwithstanding all cant about emancipation, to apply such a principle in her intercourse with others. It is time to speak out boldly on this subject, and to expose freely the folly and hypocrisy of those who accuse others of what, if there be guilt, they are more guilty themselves. Ours is not the only mode in which man may have dominion over man. The principle which would abrogate the property of our citizens in their slaves would equally abrogate the dominion of Great Britain over the subject nations under her control. If one individual can have no property in another, how can one nation, which is but an aggregate of individuals, have dominion, which involves the highest right of property, over another? If man has, by nature, the right of self-government, have not nations, on the same principle, an equal right? And if the former forbids one individual from having property in another individual, does not the other equally forbid one nation holding dominion over another? How inconsistent would it be in Great Britain to withhold redress for injustice and injury to our citizens committed in the West Indies, on the ground that persons could not be property, while in the East Indies she exercised unlimited dominion over more than a hundred millions of human beings, whose labor she controls as effectually as our citizens do that of their slaves? It is not to be credited that she will venture to assume, in her relations with us, a principle so utterly indefensible, and which could not but expose her to imputations which would make her sincerity questionable. This she must see, and to the fact that she does he attributed her long and obstinate silence.

But it may be asked, why, then, does she not make reparation at once in so clear a case? why not restore the slaves, or make ample compensation to their owners? He could imagine but one motive. She had among her subjects many whose fanatical feelings on this subject she was unwilling to offend; but while respecting the feelings of her subjects, blind and misdirected as they are, she ought not to forget that our Government is also bound to respect the feelings of its citizens. Let her remember that, if to respect the rights which our citizens have over their slaves be offensive to any portion of her subjects, how much more so would it be to our citizens for our Government to acquiesce in her refusal to respect our right to establish the relation which one portion of our population shall have to another, and how unreasonable it would be for her to expect that our Government should be more indifferent to the feelings of its citizens than hers to any portion of her subjects. He, with every lover of his country on both sides, desired sincerely to see the peace and harmony of the two countries preserved; but he held that the only condition on which they could possibly be preserved was that of perfect equality, and a mutual respect for their respective institutions; and he could not but see that a perseverance in withholding redress in these cases must, in the end, disturb the friendly relations which now so happily exist between the two countries.

He hoped, on resuming the correspondence, our Government would press the claim for redress in a manner far more earnest and becoming the importance of the subject than it has heretofore done. It seemed to him that a vast deal too much had been said about the decision of the courts and the acts of the British Government than ought to have been. They have little or nothing to do with the case, and can have no force whatever against the grounds on which our claims for justice stand. However binding on her own subjects, or foreigners voluntarily entering her dominions, they can have no binding effect whatever, where misfortunes, such as in these cases, placed our citizens within her jurisdiction.

If they be properly presented, and pressed on the attention of the British Government, he could not doubt but that speedy and ample justice would be done. It could not be withheld but by an open refusal to do justice, which he could not anticipate. As to himself, he should feel bound, as one of the representatives from the slaveholding States, which had a peculiar and deep interest in the question, to bring this case annually before Congress, so long as he held a seat on the floor, if redress shall be so long withheld.

From *Congressional Globe*, 24th Cong., 2nd Sess., Appendix, p. 327. Also printed in the Washington, D.C., *Daily National Intelligencer*, March 10, 1837, p. 2; the Charleston, S.C., *Mercury*, March 17, 1837, p. 2; the Washington, D.C., *Globe*, July 17, 1837, p. 2; *Register of Debates*, 24th Cong., 2nd Sess., cols. 1016–1018; Crallé, ed., *Works*, 3:9–14. Variants in the Washington, D.C., *Reformer*, March 2, 1837, p. 2; the Washington, D.C., *Daily National Intelligencer*, March 3, 1837, p. 2; the New York, N.Y., *Morning Courier and New-York Enquirer*, March 4, 1837, p. 2. NOTE: On Calhoun's motion the President's message and accompanying documents were ordered by the Senate to be printed. They can be found in Senate Document No. 174, 24th Cong., 2nd Sess., where they fill 58 printed pages. The date of these remarks is somewhat problematic. Crallé assigned a date of February 14, the day Jackson's message was received in the Senate. Careful comparison of contemporary newspapers and records of Congressional proceedings leaves a predominant but not conclusive impression that March 2 is the correct date.

FINAL REMARKS ON THE DISTRIBUTION OF THE SURPLUS REVENUE

[In the Senate, March 3, 1837]
[The House of Representatives refused to concur in the Senate amendment striking out the section of the fortifications bill providing for a distribution of surplus revenue. A conference committee was unable to resolve the difference. Silas Wright moved that the Senate adhere to its position.]

Mr. Calhoun observed that this was a very important amendment indeed, and one which he deeply regretted the committee had deemed it proper to report. He could not consent to sit by in silence, and suffer the question to be taken, without at least requesting to hear some reason why an amendment of this character had been reported. If there should be a large surplus in the Treasury, as there was every reason to expect there would be, the natural and proper distribution of it was obviously to return it to the people. He could not but express his surprise that the committee should expect the Senate to strike out an amendment of this importance, simply on their recommendation.

[*Wright offered an explanation for the lack of a committee report in that the issue was a familiar one.*]

Mr. Calhoun said he now understood the Senator from New York to rest the question of concurrence in the amendment on the discussion which had taken place at the last session. To this he could have no objection; for, so triumphant had been the argument last year in favor of the distribution bill, that the gentleman had been left in a minority of six against the whole Senate. As no reason had since intervened to change the circumstances of the case, Mr. C[alhoun] was content to rest the issue as it had then been made. A more triumphant argument he had never listened to; and, such had been its irresistible force, that it had broken through the bonds of party discipline, and compelled gentlemen to leave their party and vote for the bill. He would not repeat it, but he would ask those Senators who had at the last session felt and admitted its force, and had voted for the distribution bill, whether they would now change their ground, without a single argument having been urged in reply. Surely the Senator from New York was bound to show some difference in the case, which should induce those who had voted for distribution last year to vote against it now. The Senator from New York owed this to gentlemen of his own side, if he expected them thus to turn about in the face of the world.

From *Register of Debates*, 24th Cong., 2nd Sess., cols. 1022–1023. Also printed in the Washington, D.C., *Daily National Intelligencer*, April 25, 1837, p. 2; the Washington, D.C., *Globe*, July 13, 1837, p. 2; *Congressional Globe*, 24th Cong., 2nd Sess., Appendix, p. 319. Variant in the New York, N.Y., *Morning Courier and New-York Enquirer*, March 6, 1837, p. 1. NOTE: At the conclusion of a debate following Calhoun's remarks the Senate voted 27 to 23 to adhere to its decision to strike out the distribution feature. The two houses failing to concur, the bill was lost.

Remarks on the bill making appropriations for the civil and diplomatic service, 3/3. "After a few words from Mr. Calhoun and Mr. [Silas] Wright, relative to the amendments [by the House of Representatives] allowing an additional compensation to clerks in some of the departments—the first contending against it, and the latter for it—this and all the other amendments were concurred in by the Senate." From *Congressional Globe*, 24th Cong., 2nd Sess., p. 277.

MARCH 4–SEPTEMBER 3
1837

⬚

When Martin Van Buren was inaugurated on March 4 there were already signs of economic distress. The price of cotton was at less than half of what it had been earlier and the unemployed had recently rioted at New York City. Calhoun took little part in the special session of the Senate that sat until March 10 to receive the messages and nominations of the new Chief Magistrate. He had other business in Washington: hosting a dinner for Memucan Hunt, lately arrived representative of the Republic of Texas, for one thing. For another, securing the appointment of his second son, Patrick, to West Point. "He is 16 years of age, of good constitution and well advanced in his education," Calhoun told the Secretary of War. "He is very desireous of receiving his education at West Point, and as this is the first favour I have ever asked in relation to an institution I cherished not a little, I would be pleased if his wishes could be gratified."

On March 9 Calhoun left for home. On March 17 he addressed Charlestonians on the subjects of Martin Van Buren's prospects, the nation's economic difficulties, and abolition. By the 27th he was at home and deeply embroiled in the life of a planter, struggling with the problem of getting his cotton down river to market.

The break from political life afforded opportunity, unfortunately limited, for intellectual pursuits. Calhoun corresponded with Francis Lieber and Albert Gallatin on the history of languages. "I have occasionally turned my thoughts to the subject," he wrote, "and have been struck with its richness & variety. It opens a new volume of the history of our race, in which many discoveries will be made, as geology does of the history of our planet, but I have had neither leisure nor opportunity to do more, than to take a few glances." To Lieber he deplored "the taste of the age for trashy works. . . . There never was a period less given to serious reading & reflection. There is a vast amount of mental activity, but it is either devoted to gain, or arts connected with gain, or amusement. . . ." And he confessed that his understanding of the affairs of Europe was hampered by a lack of knowledge of the central and eastern parts.

The banks of New York City suspended specie payments on May

10 and those of New Orleans on May 13. None could doubt that the "panic," long anticipated, had arrived. Calhoun feared the social and political consequences. "Our gover[nment]," he wrote, "by its folly & vice has lost all control for good over the banks and currency." He greatly feared, considering the degeneracy that had been exhibited in the past decade, that some "master sperit" would arise among the capitalists of the North to convert disaster and dismay into dictatorship. Perhaps, however, the bad times would turn the minds of Northerners back from the pursuits of gain to republican principles and to the realization of "the deep stake they have in the proper management of publick affairs."

In July he once more explored the Appalachian passes, as he had the previous summer, and in August went to Georgia to supervise his gold mine, where things had not been going as well as hoped. Personal pressure from hard times was evident in concern over the mine and in efforts to sell Bonneau's Ferry, the Low Country plantation which Calhoun and his brothers-in-law had inherited. He had also to decide whether the spinal deformity of his second daughter, Martha Cornelia, could be helped by sending the thirteen-year-old girl to New York City to undergo extended treatment. But there was time to write fatherly advice to Patrick who had entered West Point: "Take care, my dear son, of your health; be attentive to your studies, respectful to your teachers, courteous to your companions & correct in your deportment. Avoid the idle & vicious and cultivate the acquaintance of the worthy & studious."

Writing on July 27 to his old friend Duff Green, who was trying to make a go as an industrialist, Calhoun was unusually frank and self-revealing. "Of all things in the world, I have the least taste for money making, and the poorest capacity for success in it. . . . My highest ambition as to money is to be independent, in a moderate and plain mode of living." If forced by necessity to give up the life of a planter, he was far better fitted to become an engineer than a capitalist, he said.

During the Congressional recess, Calhoun undertook as a duty to give the whole matter of panic, banks, and currency "in all its bearings & ramifications the fullest investigation." To close associates he gave indications of the trend of his thinking. Despite previous compromises with necessity, he had always been averse to a national bank, he told his colleague William C. Preston. And he did not believe that the way for those who viewed the republic in his light to go was with the Whigs. "The wors[t] thing that could befal[l] us and the country would be for us to bring in a party hostile to our doctrines and principles. The present state of things is greatly to be preferred to that." In the present state of things, presumably the government of Van Buren and the Democratic party, "there is some hope . . . there would be none in the other." On August 25 he departed on the Pendleton stage to take his seat in the emergency session of Congress that had been called by "the present state of things."

〖〗

To [W ILLIE P.] M ANGUM, [former and future Senator from N.C., Red Mountain?, N.C.]

Washington, 8th Feb: [*sic*; March] 1837
My dear Sir, I had intend[ed] to write you long since, but one of the most busing [*sic*; busy and pressing?] sessions I have ever witnessed has nearly suspended all my private correspondence till now, when I am on the eve of my departure.

The papers have kept you informed of the current of events here, and I shall limit my communication to what I believe to be the general result ["of the session" *interlined*] and the state of things at ["the" *altered to* "this"] time. In the main the former is not unsatisfactory. Most of the projects of the [Jackson] administration have been defeated; the land bill, the increase of the army, the ererction[?] of new arsenals and Armory, new fortification bill & & and [*sic*] the appropriations generally are far below those of last year, and will not, I think, exceed much those of the preceeding [*sic*]. We failed in carry[ing] the deposite [bill], but under circumstances, looking to the future ["it is" *interlined*] calculated to embarrass & weaken the administration.

The defeat of the administration in all the above measures was in the House [of Representatives]. They have full control of the Senate, tho' I do not think the party adheres so closely together even there, as formerly. In the House they have lost much of their control, as the results of the session shows [*sic*].

As to the state of things at this time, I cannot doubt, that the administration is losing power, and is now in a minority in the Union. The tone of the House is no weak evidence of this. It is perhaps the best test on that point. When an administration is going down,

490

they first lose their control ["usually" *canceled*] in the House, and hence on a change of party, the new administration is supported by the House, and opposed by the Senate. The change of language on the part of those in power is remarkable in relation to the two Houses. It is no longer the factious Senate. That epithet is now applied to the other House, while the Senate is regarded as the prop of power.

This is not the only indication, that the administration is losing. The language of discontent is of late often heard in their ranks, and from those you would not expect, and a sc[h]ism begins to show itself between those who would set up as the [*one word, possibly* "genteel," *canceled*] decent portion, and the [Thomas H.] Benton & [Amos] Kendal[l; "portion" *canceled and* "party" *interlined*], which will be hard to ["control" *canceled*] close and difficult to control. Another source of discord is between the ins and outs of the party. Those in office are anxious to hold on, while those seeking office are equally anxious to have them turned out. So much for the side of the administration.

As to the opposition, as far as my knowledge extends, it stands firm. I know of no loss, and there is visibly a greater tendency of its various elements to come together, just as the basis of the national [republican] portion, wears out, and ours, which is the true opposition ground[?], strengthens. I have, as you will have seen, taken a far more active part, than at preceeding sessions; and this because I saw & felt our position was gaining strength, and that of our associates in the opposition was losing. At the next session, this will be more visible than ever. The materials of opposition will then be more abundant than ever, but they will all be such as belongs to us, and not the national branch.

On the whole there is no cause of dispair [*sic*]. Things are certainly improving. The only thing to be dreaded is that we may become tired of so long a struggle, and in consequence too many of our best and ablest men, of the most experience and influence with the country may yield to the current in dispair. This I would profoundly regret, and, I trust, that such will not be your feelings in particular. Remember, that we and ours [are] on board and must share the fate of the vessel, let who will be at the helm.

The House now is the field of action; and we greatly lack experienced and able men there. You must offer from your district, and come in. Let nothing dissuade you. We may make with proper efforts a thorough reform the next four years, and now is the time, or never. Never before could we have a victory worth having. One now would be permanent & glorious. Not only start yourself, but let a strong man be started in every district in the State on our side, particularly in the Warren [County district], whether defeated or not. A meeting of young men would be desirable; to give an impulse. Should you ["be" *canceled*] succeed, which I do not doubt, if you will try, you must join [Francis W.] Pickens & myself, who mess together, with a portion of our families. Anna [Maria Calhoun] is now at my elbow, and she requests me to say to you, that she misses you much and would be glad to see you again in Congress. With ["a" *canceled*] vigorous efforts our friends are sanguine, that the administration will be in a minority in the next House.

I enclose you three speeches (the only ones in pamphlet form) delivered [by me] this winter.

I leave this in the morning and you must be sure to write to me on receiving ["it" *canceled and* "this" *interlined*]. Direct to Pendleton[,] South Carolina. Yours truly, J.C. Calhoun.

ALS in NcD, Willie Person Mangum Papers; variant PC in Henry Thomas Shanks, ed., *The Papers of Willie Person Mangum*, 2:490–492. NOTE: The date of this letter has been corrected from February to March on the grounds of Calhoun's statement in the first sentence that he was on the eve of his departure from Washington. Mangum had received the electoral votes of S.C. for President in 1836. Warren County, the home of Nathaniel Macon, was perhaps the most politically influential county of the State.

To J[OEL R.] POINSETT, [Secretary of War]

Washington, 9th March 1837

My dear Sir, Our delegation placed the name of my son Patrick [Calhoun] on the list of applicants for West Point. He is 16 years of age, of good constitution and well advanced in his education. He is very desireous [*sic*] of receiving his education at West Point, and as this is the first favour I have ever asked ["of" *canceled and* "in relation to" *interlined*] an institution I cherished not a little, I would be ["gratified" *canceled and* "pleased" *interlined*] if his wishes could be gratified.

We start [for S.C.] in the course of an hour, and my daughter [Anna Maria Calhoun] & myself regret that our incessant engagement has deprived ["us" *interlined*] of the pleasure of calling on yourself & Mrs. [Mary Izard Pringle] P[oinsett].

This will be handed ["to" *altered to* "by"] Capt. [William Haywood] Bell of the Ordnance, an excellent officer, ["to" *canceled and* "with" *interlined*] whom I take pleasure in making you acquainted.

If you can give my son a warrant with propriety address [it] to Pendleton, So[uth] Carolina. With great respect I am & & J.C. Calhoun.

ALS in PHi, Poinsett Papers; PC in Jameson, ed., *Correspondence*, pp. 369–370. NOTE: Calhoun was not precisely accurate in stating that Patrick's appointment would be the first favor he had asked in regard to West Point. His oldest son Andrew Pickens Calhoun had been appointed to the Military Academy in 1827. However, since Andrew had not accepted the appointment, Patrick's would be the first favor Calhoun received.

REMARKS ON THE CONDITION
OF THE CURRENCY

[Washington, *ca.* March 9, 1837]
[*In an article praising Calhoun's stand on banking questions and in particular his speeches on that subject in 1834, Richard K. Crallé, editor of the Baltimore, Md.,* Merchant, *included the following:*]

In connection with the subject, and to show how fully he comprehended the state of affairs, we will give the substance of a conversation between a gentleman, who felt much interest in the question, and Mr. Calhoun, on the day of his departure from this city [Washington] after the adjournment of the last Congress. The gentleman called on him, and desired that he would communicate his views in reference to the condition of the currency; and to point out the remedy, if any, for evils which he himself apprehended.

MR. CALHOUN. There is no remedy, sir. It is too late. You cannot prevent the catastrophe. The aspect of things is entirely delusive, and in a much briefer space than is commonly supposed the crash will come. It cannot be arrested. The currency is in the most critical and dangerous situation. I have thought of it much, but can see no remedy for the calamity which is at hand.

GENTLEMAN. Would not a repeal of the specie circular tend to relieve the banks, and give time to correct the alarming expansion of the currency?

MR. CALHOUN. No, sir, it is too late. That measure has done much mischief, but its repeal cannot repair the mischief. It has hastened the catastrophe, and its repeal now can have but little if any effect. The banking system in this country has been, for years, running into greater and greater excesses. It has now reached a

493

point where no remedy can operate. Had my recommendations in 1834, been adopted, we might have been able to have reformed the system without much suffering. My plan was to arrest the over-action of the system then, and gradually to restore a healthy currency, by restricting issues and enlarging the specie basis. This might have been done without producing any sensible shock. But the violence of both sides defeated the plan. In the war of the Executive [Andrew Jackson] against the Bank [of the United States], the Administration party would listen to nothing short of an immediate and absolute extermination, while the friends of the Bank, occupying the other extreme, would countenance no proposition short of an entire restoration of all its powers. Between the two, the only practicable and sure alternative was crushed. The Bank went by the board, and instead of adopting measures to restrain the natural tendencies of the system to excessive action, the Administration immediately and most unwisely stimulated that action by gorging the State banks with the enormous revenues of the country. From that time to the present I have looked on in despair. The system became like a man delirious with fever, and the Government administered incessant doses of the strongest stimulants. The system has thus become absolutely insensible to the action of remedies. The deposite bill operated in some degree to diminish the over-action, but not enough to restore sensibility to the system. I have done all I could to forestall the calamity, and wash my hands of the mischiefs that must ensue.

GENTLEMAN. But if Mr. [Martin] Van Buren should adopt the currency bill, or act upon its recommendations, might it not tend to put off the evil day, and give time to correct the over-action in the system?

MR. CALHOUN. No, sir, the time is past. These are mere expedients, and might have had very salutary effects, if adopted sooner. Now they can only alleviate the symptoms, they cannot heal the disease. I see no remedy. There will be a terrible revulsion, and what it will lead to I know not. I should not be surprised if it were to produce a radical change in the entire banking system, and substitute a different medium of exchange. There is no telling to what results it may finally lead. The excesses of the system in this country have been, for years, approaching that point not more fatal to the prosperity of the public than to its own existence. It has reached that point now, and no man can tell what is in the future.

GENTLEMAN. What then is to be done?

MR. CALHOUN. Nothing can be done. The evil must correct

itself, and the system work out its own cure. I can see no other result. Live, sir, economically, pay the debts you owe, if any, and contract no new ones—for I tell you that the present state of things cannot last. It is impossible. A revulsion, sudden and desolating, must come, and that at no distant day. Depend upon it, that he who owes money had better sell his property immediately and pay. Let those who can, get out of debt as soon as possible, and take care to avoid all liabilities. When the revulsion comes, I fear the state of the country will not be propitious for the adoption of wise remedies. The times are as unsound as the currency, and the excitements of party are little calculated to qualify us for the emergency. The wildest schemes will, probably, be the most successful, and party ends will take place of the public interests.

PC in the Baltimore, Md., *Merchant*-Washington, D.C., *Reformer*, July 17, 1837, p. 3; PC in the Charleston, S.C., *Mercury*, July 22, 1837, p. 2; PC in the Pendleton, S.C., *Messenger*, August 4, 1837, p. 1. NOTE: "Such, in substance, was the conversation, as well as we can detail it," Crallé noted.

From J[OHN] H. EUSTACE and Others

[Richmond, *ca.* March 10, 1837?]
Dear Sir, We the undersigned Merchants in the City of Richmond, having in the course of our business, to remit large sums of money by mail, and frequently in Bank notes, the anxiety always great, under the best mail arrangements, has been most painfully increased by the present circuitous, dangerous, and uncertain arrangement[.]

The comfort, peace, ["and" *canceled*] happiness, & prosperity, of the people, should always be the object of good government[.] From the grievances under which we labour, we confidently appeal to you for redress[.] You have ever been ready to rebuke oppression, nor have you ever allowed party trammels, to bias your course, when the rights and best interests of the people were at stake[.] We take no part in any controversy, between the Post Master Gen[era]l [Amos Kendall] and any corporation—we understand it costs the Government more under the present, than under the former arrangement —but of that we profess to know nothing[.] We want our representatives in the National Councils to give us, as we think we are entitled to, the best, quickest, and safest mail arrangement. With Considerations of high resp[ec]t We remain Y[ou]r fr[ien]ds & ob[e]-

495

d[ien]t S[e]r[van]ts, J.H. Eustace, W[illia]m Williams, John Thompson, Neal[?] & J.J. Fry & Co., W.S. & J. Dorman, [and] Dunlop, Moncure & Co.

ALS in ScCleA. NOTE: This undated letter was postmarked in Richmond on 3/11, [no year], and bears Calhoun's AEU: "Several Merchants of Richmond. Relates to mail arrangement."

REMARKS AT CHARLESTON

[March 17, 1837]

In responding to the second toast, Mr. Calhoun addressed the meeting, and after some introductory remarks, pertinent to the occasion, proceeded to give a perspicuous and rapid sketch of that series of corrupt measures, by which the Government of the United States had arrived at the present height of disorder and iniquity. He dwelt upon the removal of the Deposites, by which the whole treasure of the nation came under the control of the Executive, to be employed, as it was employed, in corrupting the Press, and buying the people. He showed that the vast speculations in public Lands, the mad outpouring of the East into the West, the feverish eagerness of our capitalists to chalk out Romes and Londons, on every brook in the vale of the Mississippi, originated in the depositing great sums of the public money in the Western Banks—and consequently, that the surplus Revenue, against which the late President and his party exclaimed so furiously, was the direct effect of [Andrew] Jackson's own favorite measure: He remarked upon the Compromise Act [of 1833], that its object was not to exterminate the manufactures of the North, but to deliver the South from a system of unequal and unjust taxation —to confer a great good, with the least possible evil. He fully exculpated the manufacturing interest from any share in the late attempt to shake the compromise—he said that attempt was the work of politicians alone, with the purpose of re-embroiling the North and South—he showed the necessity of that act—the completeness of its final operation, to reduce the Revenue to the wants of Government, and in the meantime, the necessity of distributing the surplus among the States, to whom it belonged. He pointed out the motives of the dominant party, in opposing the distribution, and showed, that in spite of their momentary and miserable triumph, the measure would yet prevail—interest, patriotism, and every good principle, he said, would unite to carry it into effect.

He alluded to Mr. [Robert J.] Walker's Land Bill, by which was attempted to be introduced and legalized, more than the present mischiefs of Western speculation and Executive patronage.

After having given a true and unvarnished picture of the present disorders, he proceeded to express a strong confidence in the ultimate triumph of the good over the evil—the Reform of the Government and the restoration of the Constitution. He said he saw his way through the present confusion—the Distribution measure would prevail—he believed that the Public Lands would be given up to the States—the [Martin Van Buren] Administration must yield to these measures or fall before them. He had the strongest assurance that the Government would be reformed and that Reform must come from the South—the North never had, and in the nature of things could not reform the Government: the South had never united for Reform without effecting it—there had been but two Administrations of *four years*—the two Adams[es]' had both been swept out of power by the union of the South—the present incumbent was immeasurably inferior to either of them in talent and dignity of character—he had none of the despotic popularity of his immediate predecessor, that he lacked his audacity, his promptitude, his inflexibility—all those striking and stern qualities which had conducted the latter through his astonishing career of usurpation—Van Buren must stand by conciliation—if he failed in that he was ruined.

He then alluded to abolition—he considered it the mightiest evil that had ever threatened our Government, and the only cause now in operation sufficiently powerful to effect a dissolution of the Union —he believed the great body of the Northern people to be sound on this question; but we must remember that the Northern States were themselves divided upon great principles, full of parties, and agitated with sharp and absorbing controversies—all their local interests lay between us and cut off or chilled their sympathy with the South—the Abolitionists were strong, active, uncompromising—their support was an object of sufficient importance to enforce the silence —in many cases to buy the voices of those who wished us well—we could not depend upon the North—we could not depend upon the Government—we could only depend upon ourselves. He left it to the people of the South to determine the time and mode of action on this momentous subject, but it was his opinion that to be successful, it must be prompt, energetic, and universal.

He spoke of Texas, and at that name was interrupted with long and loud cheering, and his concluding words on that topic, pronounced with deep emotion, that "Texas must be annexed to the Union!" were answered with a universal burst of applause that showed how glowing was the sympathy of the people of South Carolina with the heroes of San Jacinto. He pointed out clearly the vital importance to the South of the annexation, and after a few other remarks, concluded, amid great cheering with a toast, which, owing to his early departure from Charleston, we are sorry to say, we could not obtain.

From the Charleston, S.C., *Mercury*, March 20, 1837, p. 2. Also printed in the Augusta, Ga., *Chronicle and Sentinel*, March 22, 1837, p. 1; the Washington, D.C., *Reformer*, March 28, 1837, p. 2; the Edgefield, S.C., *Advertiser*, March 30, 1837, p. 2; the Richmond, Va., *Whig and Public Advertiser*, March 31, 1837, p. 4. Note: Calhoun, Senator William C. Preston, and Representative William J. Grayson arrived in Charleston from Washington on 3/13. A public dinner honoring them was held at the Carolina Hotel on 3/17. Calhoun's speech followed a toast to him by Robert Y. Hayne: "While Carolina is justly proud of his high talents and excellent character, his heroic efforts to *reform* the Government—restore the Constitution—support our Institutions—and thereby preserve public *Liberty*, and establish a *perpetual Union* among the States, entitle him to the admiration and gratitude of the *whole country.*"

To J[ames] Ed[ward] Colhoun

Abbeville [S.C.], 22d March 1837

My dear James, Anna [Maria Calhoun] & myself are thus far on our return home. We were detained yesterday by the bad weather, and were in great hopes of that [*sic*] would have the pleasure of meeting with you. We are just on the eve of setting out for Pendleton; and we hope that you will as soon as you can make it convenient ["to" *interlined*] make us a visit ["shortly" *interlined*]. I am very desirous of seeing you and [*sic*; on] many accounts.

I attended to your business at Washington, and have collected a good deal of information in relation to the manufacture of the cotton seed oil, of the success of which I have very flattering accounts.

I was detained several days in Charleston to partake of a publick dinner ["and have" *canceled*]. It was fully attended and went off exceedingly well. I will give the particulars when we meet.

On the whole, I think the last session [of Congress] went off well. The administration lost every measure they had at heart, and were for the last 8 or 10 days of the session in a minority in the House of Representatives. [Martin] Van Buren goes in very weak and may be easily crushed with any ["think" *canceled*] thing like a vigorous effort. There is a great & growing change in our favour.

I have not time to add more, and must conclude with expressing the hope that you will come up as soon as you can.

Anna joins her love to you, with the request that I would say to you how much she was disappointed in not meeting you ["have"(?) *canceled*] here and how much she wants to see you. Affectionately, J.C. Calhoun.

ALS in ScCleA; PEx in Jameson, ed., *Correspondence*, p. 370.

To Ja[me]s Ed[ward] Colhoun, Terrysville, Abbeville District, S.C.

Fort Hill, 27th March 1837

My dear James, I find it very difficult, if not impossible to get my cotton taken down to Hamburgh, and I see no other chance unless you can undertake it with your boats. Myself, Mr. [William?] Sloan and Mr. [Elisha?] Lawrence have between us two full boat loads, and if you can possibly send up your boats, or, if not both, ["even" *canceled and then interlined*] one, we would give you ["even" *canceled*] as high as a dollar a hundred [pounds], rather than not have our cotton taken down. Should you consider Boatman's shoals a serious obstacle, which I am told [it] is not, we would send our cotton below the shoals to meet your boats, but would greatly rather send from our landings. Mr. Lawrence would send down his to mine, or Mr. Sloan's. Do not fail to let me know by ["the" *interlined*] return mail whether you can take our cotton, and, if so, when, and at what price.

I wrote you from Abbeville. I hope you have got my letter and that ["you" *canceled*] we may ere long expect you.

We had the pleasure to find the family all well and they all join their love to you. Affectionately, J.C. Calhoun.

ALS in ScCleA.

To [Joel R. Poinsett, Secretary of War, *ca.* 4/2]. John C. Calhoun assents to his son Patrick's "signing articles binding himself to five years service as Cadet unless sooner discharged." (On the same paper is a letter from Patrick to Poinsett of 4/2/1837 accepting conditional appointment as Cadet in the U.S. Military Academy.) ADS in DNA, RG 94 (Records of the Adjutant General's Office), Application Papers of Cadets, 1805–1866, 1837, 65 (M-688:108, frame 167).

To "Prof[esso]r [Francis] Lieber," [South Carolina College]

Fort Hill, 8th April 1837

Dear Sir, I am under much obligation to you for the [March, 1837] mumber [*sic;* "in" *altered to* "of"] the Southern Literary Messenger containing your letter to Mr. [Albert] Gallatin on the importance of stud[y]ing foreign languages, which I have read with pleasure & instruction.

Your remarks place the subject in a new and interesting point of view. It opens a wide field of comparison between the genius & character of various languages, which if followed up in all of its details, would present many curious and important results.

I shall be gratified when we next meet to renew our conversation on the subject of languages, not with the view of giving, but of receiving information. I have occasionally turned my thoughts to the subject, and have been struck with its richness & variety. It opens a new volume of the history of our race, in which many discoveries will be made, as geology does of the history of our planet, but I have had neither leisure nor opportunity to do more, than to take a few general glances.

Mr. Gallatin was so kind as to send me a copy of the work to which you refer in your note. I received it, with the one directed to yourself, just before I left Washington. Your's [*sic*] I forwarded through the mail, under the Frank of the Secretary of the Senate [Asbury Dickins], as I could not take Columbia in my route, and I am glad you have received it, as I felt some anxiety lest it should share the fate, which occasionally befal[l]s, what is transmitted by that conveyance. I forwarded my own in a box of books by water and have not yet received it. I am anxious to peruse it, and shall devote my first leisure moment after its arrival to that object. With great respect I am yours truely, J.C. Calhoun.

ALS in CSmH, Francis Lieber Papers; PEx in Frank Freidel, *Francis Lieber: Nineteenth-Century Liberal,* p. 181. NOTE: Gallatin's work referred to in the fourth paragraph was his synopsis of North American Indian tribes to which Calhoun had contributed information and which was published as vol. II of the *Transactions of the American Antiquarian Society* in 1836. An AEU by Lieber reads: "J.C. Calhoun. About my article on Comp. Philology."

To [FRANCIS] LIEBER, [Columbia, S.C.]

Fort Hill, 25th April 1837

Dear Sir, A work such as you refer to is much needed, and I do hope, notwithstanding the taste of the age for trashy works, you will be able to find a publisher. There never was a period less given to serious reading & reflection. There is a vast amount of mental activity, but it is either devoted to gain, or arts connected with gain, or amusement; but this must change ere long. Publick affairs, and the higher objects and pursuits of life, cannot be long neglected, without being followed in the end by fearful calamities, which must in turn rouse the attention and give a more serious cast to thoughts & pursuits. Already we see the germs of many calamities both here and ["in" *interlined*] all the western states of Europe. I am not so familiar with the affairs of the more central and eastern, as to venture an opinion ["as"(?) *canceled and* "in relation" *interlined*] to them. These in their developement will give a new direction to the reflection and the reading of ["the" *canceled*] coming years. Already the disorganized state of the currency, over the greater part of the commercial world begins to affect all the relations of life, which must powerfully attract the attention of the reflecting. The cause of the disorder lies very deep, so much so, that I would not be at all surprised, if the present embarrassment should prove to be the begin[n]ing of an entire revolution in the system of the currency. With great respect I am & & J.C. Calhoun.

ALS in CSmH, Francis Lieber Papers. NOTE: An AEU by Lieber reads: "Calhoun about general pecun[iary] distress." The work referred to in the first sentence cannot be identified with certainty, although in 1837 Lieber published a treatise on legal hermeneutics.

To RICHARD PETERS, [U.S. Supreme Court Reporter], Philadelphia

Fort Hill, 25th April 1836 [*sic*; 1837]

My dear Sir, I am under much obligation to you for the cuttings of the Multicilis [*sic*; Multicaulis?] which I have planted with care, and with a fair prospect that some of them will take.

As great as is the ["existing" *interlined*; "disaster" *altered to* "disasters" (*sic*)], I fear it is but the begin[n]ing of the evils from the disordered state of our currency. When & what will be the end no one can conjecture. I would not be surprised, if it should prove to be the begin[n]ing of an entire revolution in the system of the currency. Nothing can save us from untold disasters, but the profoundest wisdom, if even that can now save us. One good, I hope may come, to teach all, the deep stake they have in the proper management of publick affairs. The intelligence of the North, in particular, has been too much absorbed in the pursuit of gain; so much so as almost to forget the first principles of our Gover[n]ment.

The movements in the Mass[achuset]ts Legislature ["is" *changed to* "on"] the abolition subject is [*sic*] deeply to be deplored, in every view. The intelligent portion of the South has had a stra[n]ge [*or* strong(?)] attachment to that State, notwithstanding the difference in our political principles, and what has occurred in her Legislature will do more to shake the confidence of the South in the North in reference to that all important subject, than any thing which has ever occurred.

Miss Anna [Maria Calhoun] was much gratified with your kind remembrance and begs me to assure ["you that" *interlined*] your place in her memory and regard is too strongly occupied to be easily dispossessed. With great respect I am yours truly, J.C. Calhoun.

ALS in MH. NOTE: While Calhoun clearly wrote "1836" as the year of this letter, it has been assigned a date of 1837 because Calhoun on 4/25 in 1836 was not at Fort Hill but in Washington and because the recipient endorsed the letter as received on 5/1/1837. On 3/29/1837 the upper house of the Mass. legislature unanimously adopted a resolution asserting that Congress had the power to abolish slavery and the slave trade in D.C. and that an "early exercise" of such right was demanded by world opinion, humanity, and the principles of the Revolution.

To G[EORGE] W. FEATHERSTONHAUGH, Greenville, S.C.

Fort Hill, 3d May 1837

My dear Sir, I learn from Mr. William Green, that you had left Washington for the South and that a letter would probably reach you at Greenville, as he understood from what he heard, that your operations for some time would be in the vicinity of the survey of the rail road route. I fear from what he says, that we will not have the pleasure of your society at Pendleton as we anticipated, which, if such should be the fact, we would very greatly regret. We hope, however, if we should not have your headquarters with us, that we shall have at least a portion of your time.

I write now to say, that it is my intention to make an excursion to the mountains in our neighbourhood and thence along the general direction, of the mountains to the mines in Georgia which will keep close to the gold belt all the way some time this month; and if you ["could" *canceled*] can possibly make your arrangement to join me, it would be a source of great gratification. I would be glad to know as soon as convenient whether I may expect you, and, if so, at what time. I will make my arrangement to suit your's [*sic*], but would prefer some time before the 20th, if equally conven[ien]t to you. With great respect I am & & J.C. Calhoun.

ALS in PHi, Gratz Collection. NOTE: Featherstonhaugh was an English geologist who subsequently published two books about his American travels. Endorsements indicate that this letter was forwarded from Greenville to Washington and was not received until 10/11.

To J[OHN] R. MATHEW[E]S, Clark[e]sville, Ga.

Fort Hill, 7th May 1837
My dear Sir, The last mail brought yours of the 25th[?] April. I shall see that the subject receives prompt attention in this quarter.

The whole affair is a great outrage. At the request of Mr. [George W.] Owen[s, Representative from Ga.], I moved the resolution in the Senate to establish the route from Pendleton [S.C.] to Dahlonega [Ga.] by the way of Clark[e]sville and had it referred to the Committee on Post offices & post roads. I spoke to Mr. [Felix] Grundy, the Chairman and had his assurance, that he would take special charged [*sic*] of it and in consequence bestowed no further attention on the subject, except to enquire whether the action of the Committee had been favourable which he informed [me it] had been, knowing that with the support of the Chairman & the Committee its passage was certain. On examin[in]g the act, when I went on last winter[,] to my surprise, I found the name of Greenville [S.C.] substituted for Pendleton, but when or by whom the change was made I know not. I have just got the the [*sic*] printed journals and shall examine them to ascertain, if possible. I again spoke to Mr. Grundy, knowing his influence with the [Post Office] Department and intended to move an amendment to some ["one" *interlined*] of the post office bills to have Pendleton substituted, as in the ["first" *canceled and* "original" *interlined*] resolution. He examined the map with me and seeing ["the" *canceled*] Pendleton in all most [*sic*] a direct line with the route with a stage between it & Greenville, he assured me, that no alteration would be necessary, that the discretion of the Postmaster General [Amos Kendall] would reach the case and that the thing was so plain there was no doubt, but that the ori[gi]nal object would be carried into effect by uniting at Pendleton, and that he would see the Postmaster General & explain it to him which I afterwards understood him that he had done and that there would be no difficulty. I remained under the impression, that all was as it should be till I returned home.

We ["have"(?) *canceled and* "here" *interlined*] can do but little; but a spirited Movem[e]nt at Clark[e]sville & Dahlonega seconded by Mr. Owen[s] can yet correct, what has been done. Every thing with the administration goes by party; and in the present state of things in Georgia, they would be averse to weak[en]ing themselves in two such important points. I am not certain but a move here would tend to defeat our wishes, but as it is desired we will make it, and forward the remonstrance without delay.

I will probably make a visit to Dahlonega in the course of the month & should I, will make a point to spend a night with you. With great respect I am & & J.C. Calhoun.

ALS in DLC, John C. Calhoun Papers.

To J A [M E] S E D [W A R D] C O L H O U N, Terrysville, Abbeville District, S.C.

Fort Hill, 12th May 1837

My dear James, I can hear nothing of Scipio. I saw Mr. Murphy myself and spoke to him to keep a look out. I do not think he made this way. Andrew [Pickens Calhoun] says, that he knows not who was his former master. He bought him at vendue. If you have not got him; he will write down and learn, and let you know.

My box, in which I supposed, I left Maj[o]r Miller's memorandum has arrived; but after careful search, I cannot find it. I cannot conjecture how I ["have" *canceled*] lost it; but I will get any information you desire by writing to him through some of my Mississippi friends. Let me know the points on which you desire to be informed.

I am glad that you have been able to effect so satisfactory and advantageous [a] change of land. If you go on, you will own half of the District.

I enclose the [Pendleton] Messenger, containing an article signed Amicus, recommending the Southern Review to the patronage of the slave holding States. Such a work is indispensable to our character & safety; and I hope you will take charge of Abbeville. I know no one so well calculated to give an impulse to the work in the District as yourself. See Maj[o]r [Armistead] Burt, Col. [Patrick] Noble, Mr. [David L.] Wardlaw, Mr. [George] McDuffie and others and on some sale day, or other publick occasion have a meeting and give the impulse to the subscription. It is all important. No man, who can spare $5 ought to withhold his name. We ought to get in the South at least 6,000 subscribers.

The difficulties of the times increase ["and" *canceled*]. I see not ["when" *canceled*] the end. Unless the British Government should interpose and arrest the progress of the Disorder, I would not be surprised, that it should end in the overthrow [of] the banking system. Our gover[nment] by its folly & vice has lost all control for good over the banks and the currency.

We are all well and all join in their love to you. Affectionately, J.C. Calhoun.

ALS in ScCleA; PEx in Jameson, ed., *Correspondence*, p. 370. NOTE: In the Pendleton *Messenger* of May 12, 1837, p. 2, there appeared for the first time a letter from "Amicus" addressed "to the Citizens of the Slave-holding States" and endorsing a prospectus, also printed, for a new "Southern Review." This review was to be published at Washington by William W. Moore & Co. and edited by Abel P. Upshur. The *Southern Review* of Charleston had folded in 1832. Apparently the attempted revival was unsuccessful. The *Messenger* of June 30, 1837, p. 2, quoted the Baltimore *Merchant's* lamentation that the journal would probably not be published due to lack of subscribers. The *Messenger* of November 3, 1837, p. 4, printed an appeal from Duff Green, dated Washington, October, 1837, for any undispatched subscriptions to be forwarded immediately so that it could be determined whether there was enough support to publish.

To ALBERT GALLATIN,
[President, National Bank of New York City]

Fort Hill, 25th May 1837
Dear Sir, I received the second vol. of the transactions of the American Antiquarian Society which you were so kind as to send me just

at the close of the last session, with one for Mr. [John L.] Miller & another for Prof[esso]r [Francis] Lieber, both of which I forwarded immediately.

My engagements since my return home have so engrossed my time, as to prevent me till now from perusing your synopsis of our Indian tribes, which will explain, why I have not at an earlier period acknowledged the obligation, I am under to you for transmitting the volume.

I read your synopsis with much pleasure and information; and I do hope, that your life may be spared, and that you may be induced to resume your labours till you have completed the work according to your original plan. The labour you have already bestowed will make it comparatively an easy task; and you will add greatly to the obligation, under which you have already placed, ["all" *interlined*] who take any interest in so curious & important a portion of the history of our race, as the medium of communicating their thoughts & feelings by language.

I have long thought, that the analogy of languages is destined to ["add" *canceled*] recover much of the lost history of nations, just as geology has of the globe, we inhabit. If I do not mistake, the changes both of sound and the meaning of words are subjected to a great extent to ["fixed" *canceled*] laws of a very general character, which will one day, or another be traced out, and which will throw much light on the history of the race. The same remark will be found applicable to the structure of languages and the changes, which ["take" *interlined*] place by the blending of languages, either by conquest, commerce, or other intercourse. I have no doubt, for instance, the more primitive the language, the more concrete; and the more it has been blended and mixed with other languages, the more it will be broke up into small auxiliary words. To this investigation, it is of great importance that no language should be lost, and your synopsis will hereafter be prized, as contain[in]g a most curious & valuable body of materials. Few works of the age will out live it.

The conquest of the five nations [of Iroquois] extended farther to the south west, than you appear to be informed. The stream, on which I reside, is called the Senaca [*sic*], and the place of my residence (20 miles above the junction with the Tugaloo) was called Senaca old town, and is said to be the extreme point, to which their conquest extended in this direction. The original name of the stream was Keowee, which it still retains, above the juncture[?] of 12 miles [Creek], its main branch on the east side. The Senacas had been expelled, or abandoned the country before the arrival of the whites, at which time it was held by the Cherokees. With great respect I am & & J.C. Calhoun.

ALS in NHi, Albert Gallatin Papers (published microfilm, roll 42, frames 322–323).

To S[AMUEL] D. INGHAM, N[ew] Hope, Pa.

Fort Hill, 25th May 1837
My dear Sir, The late occur[re]nce takes my recollection back with yours to 1816 and the part we acted then & since; the review of which and the downward tendency of our system, in spite of all of our exertions ["then & since," *canceled*] secon[d]ed by the virtue & intelligence of the country, ["excite" *canceled*] are far from exciting hope for the future. There is no instance on record of so sudden a degeneracy of a people, as ["that of ours" *interlined*] within the last 12 years. I hold it doub[t]ful, whether a reformation be ["practicle" *changed to* "practic(a)ble"], so deep and general is the corruption. My hope is that the cause of this sad change is not to be traced to ["our" *canceled*] the character of our institutions, but a gross misconception of their true character & nature. If the principles of our system had been adhered to, and consequences such as we now witnessed [*sic*] had followed, I should have utterly dispaired [*sic*] of ["our" *canceled*] preserving our liberty. With all the reflection, I can bestow on the subject, aided by the experience of more than 25 years, I am satisfied, a more admirable system—one better calculated to preserve our liberty & add to ourr [*sic*] prosperity could not be devised; and my hope is, that we shall come to understand its real character, and return to its principles before anarchy & despotism shall have fixed for ever their dominion over us. If we should not, the present disordered & wretched condition of our country is but the begin[n]ing of our woes. It would be difficult to extricate ourselves from the existing difficulties, with all the wisdom & virtue of the country; but utterly hopeless ["with" *canceled*] under the control of those in power. The most effective and appropriate remedy, in their hands would be but the instrument of new mischief, by being converted into the means of party power & control. Were it even possible to apply successfully a remedy, while the control ["was" *canceled*] is in their hands, it would, but confirm & perpetuate the principles by which they rose to power, and *effectually resist all*

efforts at Reform; and the end would be the certain loss of liberty. The expulsion from power, then, of the authors of the mischief is the first & necessary step, not only to arrest the progress of corruption, ["but" *interlined*] to extricate the country from its present difficulties; and to that point, all the patriotism & virtue left in the country ought to be instantly directed. If I could see the wise & virtuous, roused into action, instead of sinking down into dispair [*sic*], my hopes would be bright; but as it is, ["I can do but" *canceled*] little ["can be done" *interlined*], but to watch the moment, when the growing disorders & difficulties shall bring them into action, if they ever ["should" *canceled and* "will be brought" *interlined*]. But to return to the immediate cause of our difficu[l]ties, the suspension of specie payment. There can, in my opinion, be no remedy unconnected with an United States bank, in some form, or another. The curr[e]ncy ["whatever it is in fact" *interlined*] must be ["in fact" *canceled*] under the control of the General Governm[en]t or its disorder will be innevitible [*sic*]. Of all the subjects of Legislation, it is that ["by" *canceled and* "through" *interlined*] which the action of the parts can most effect [*sic*] the whole, and in the exercise of which the parts have the deepest interest, (I mean immediate & temporary interest) in producing disorder by over issue or debasement of the currency. What the General Govern[me]nt receives and pays away as money will in fact constitute ["a part of" *canceled*] the currency, and unless it be under the official control of that Govern[me]nt will according to the rule I have stated, fall into disorder. Hence I, who have ever had great objections to the banking system, have been compelled to yield them, to the irresi[s]table [*sic*] necessity of controlling the issues of the ["State" *interlined*] banks, which from the begin[n]ing of our Govern[me]nt have in its receipts & disburs[e]ments been considered as cash. But I must say, that my objection to Banks of any discription [*sic*] and in particular to a national bank, as it is called is greatly increased, and that nothing but the necessity of the case can compel me to vote for another, ["&" *canceled*] and even that necessity shall not, but with the most regid [*sic*] restrictions and then only for a short period and as the means of unbanking the banks to the extent that the ["phi"(?) *canceled*] financial & commercial wants of the country will admit. In a word, my views, as expressed on the currency question in 1833 remain unchanged, excep[t] with an increased want of confidence in the whole banking system. I have no doubt, but that a currency made up of gold & silver, and the notes of the Govern[me]nt itself, without car[r]ying interest and for large [a]mounts, say not less than $50 would be a far better currency, if limited to an amount, not exceeding, or much exceeding at furthest, ["the" *interlined*] average receipts of the Government, and provided the Governm[en]t would receive & ["pay away" *interlined*] nothing but its notes & gold & silver. My apprehension is, that in practise no limitation that could be imposed would, in the present state of the publick intelligence on the subject, be respected.

But what ought to be done and what will ["be" *interlined*] are very different questions. The administration will try to make the most of ["it" *canceled and* "the crisis" *interlined*], unless their sperit should be broke entirely by the extent of the difficulty. The existing banking interest will doubtless endeavour also to make the most of it, after the first panick is over, both for their profit & power, and ["should" *canceled and* "if" *interlined*] any master sperit should rise among that interest, capable of commanding their confidence, and combining the whole in an efficient organization, they will obtain an irres[is]tible control over the destiny of the country. By moderating the bank issues, and permitting specie to be freely shipped, till the equilibrium between this country & England be restored, which would take less than a year under a free shippment [*sic*], a confidence might be created in the banking system, greater than ever existed before, and which with address and moderation might be turned into an opposition to a return to specie payment, and in favour of a mere paper system. The difficulty is in the number & dispersed situation of the banks, and above all their avarice, which would with infinite[?] reluctance submit to any arrangement which stood in the way of their immediate gains.

I have given you my first impressions, just as they presented themselves, without regard to arrangement. As I shall be called on to act on the subject officially in my place in the Senate, I shall of course give the whole subject in all its bearings & ramifications the fullest investigation. It is possible some ["distinct" *canceled*] view distinct from any I have suggested may present itself, which will carry me through ["the juncture" *interlined*], in the performance of my duty, more ["satisfactory" *changed to* "satisfactoryly"; *sic*] than [any], which I have been yet able to take.

I would be glad in the mean time to hear fully from you and [*sic*] the subject and will be obliged to you for any suggestion you may make.

We regret to learn, that your da[u]ghter still remains indisposed;

509

and hope that the approach of summer may act beneficially on her system. Make our kind respects to her & Mrs. Ingham & believe me to be yours truely & sincerely, J.C. Calhoun.

ALS in ScU-SC, John C. Calhoun Papers.

From J[OHN] E[WING] BONNEAU

Charleston, 26th May 1837

Dear Sir, Your letter of 20th Inst[ant], I received yesterday. As in all probability it will not be convenient for me to become the purchaser of Bonneau's Ferry, I think it necessary to enable me to find a purchaser, that the place be offered for a certain price, with *the conditions as to the payment.* Therefore, I would suggest that yourself, the Colo[nel, John Ewing Colhoun], & James Edward [Colhoun] determine what would be the lowest price, you would agree to take (at private sale) & authorise me accordingly—or have the property offered at Public Sale in Decem[be]r next. In offering ⅓ or ⅔ of the Plantation for sale, it is not likely I shall succeed in getting a purchaser. I have seen Judge [Charles Jones] Colcock [President of the Bank of the State of S.C.] on the subject of your being accommodated with a loan of $5,000 & he has assured me, that your note for that amount will be done as soon as it is offered. Consequently, I send you enclosed, Three Blank Notes for your signature. *Two* of which, are intended as renewals. The original note, you will find, I have drawn, payable at 6 months after date. The bank requires the interest in advance. With great respect I remain D[ea]r Sir yours &c. &c. J.E. Bonneau.

ALS in ScU-SC, John C. Calhoun Papers. NOTE: Calhoun's AEU indicates that on 5/30 he directed Bonneau "to apply the proceeds of the note to the take up [of] my note in the hands of Col. [Farish] Carter of Georgia[,] all the balance to be applied to the interest of the note in bank."

To JA[ME]S ED[WARD] COLHOUN

Fort Hill, 29th May 1837

My dear Sir, I have written to Maj[o]r Miller agreeably to your request, through a friend in Mississippi and as soon as I get his answer will forward it to you.

Patrick [Calhoun] left us this morning for West Point. He was anxious to see you before his departure, but I could not make the arrangement conveniently to send him down.

[John Ewing] Bonneau has declined taking the [Bonneau's] ferry owing to the times; I have, however, written to him since the suspension of specie payment repeating the offer, and as an inducement stated, that I had no doubt but that you would let him have your share on the same condition.

I ["wold" *canceled and* "would" *interlined*] with pleasure do what you request in relation to the tract on 26 [Miles Creek], but do not remember the name or address of the Greenville man. If you will find my letter to you and give me his name and residence, I will attend to it immediately.

Congress you see is called to meet the 1st Monday of Sep[tembe]r. There will be much distraction & confusion. It is hard to say, what ought to be done. You must come up and see me before I set out, say the 20th August.

Andrew [Pickens Calhoun] has a fine son, and Margaret [Green Calhoun] is doing well.

All join their love to you. Affectionately, J.C. Calhoun.

ALS in ScCleA. NOTE: The "fine son," the first child of Andrew P. and Margaret Green Calhoun, was named John Caldwell and died around Christmas, 1837.

To Ja[me]s Ed[ward] Colhoun

Fort Hill, 30th May 1837

My dear Sir, I have just heard from John [Ewing] Bonneau. He declines taking the Ferry, but will undertake the sale of the place provided yourself, your brother [John Ewing Colhoun] & myself will fix a price. I am willing to take $5,000 for my share, retaining the rent of the year, if your self & brother will take the same, and you can get his assent in writing (there is no intercourse between us). I will write to Mr. Bonneau to make sale of the place for $15,000, retaining the rent, ["at one" *canceled and* "one" *interlined*] half down, and the balance in a year with interest, and secured by bond & Mortgage.

Let me hear from you on the subject.

I wrote you day before yesterday, and hope you have got my letter.

We are all well and all join in their love to you. Affectionately, J.C. Calhoun.

ALS in ScCleA.

To W[ILLIAM] C. PRESTON,
[Senator from S.C., Columbia]

Fort Hill, June 1837

My dear Sir, I hold the present juncture to be one of extreme difficulty and danger. It is hard to say what can or ought to be done. I have long believed, that the banking system was destined to run down by its intrinsick defects, and I am not certain, that the time is not near at hand. The present state of the currency in the commercial world looks, as if it was the begin[nin]g.

My aversion is, & has been ever, strong ["aganst" *canceled and* "to" *interlined*] a U[nited] States Bank. Necessity, & that alone, ever compelled me to vote for one. I hope some devise [*sic*] may be fallen on to free us from it in the present instance; but, I am of the impression, that the disease is not yet so fully developed, as to enable us to form a just opinion of its extent and the remedy, that may be demanded. We must hear from the other side of the Atlantick first, and especially from England. We cannot move safely without taking into consideration the state of things there.

But as great as the difficulty is intrinsickly, it is made vastly more so by the utter incompetency & destitution of principle of those who have the control of our affairs. What can be done with those at the helm, who were either too blind to see, or too indifferent to the fate of the country to prevent the present disaster? The best and most effecent [*sic*] remedy in such hands ["I fear" *canceled*] must fail from vice, or folly, which renders it hazardous even to propose any measure of relief, however wise or efficient. In England, or even France they would be instantly expelled; but here we must bear with them, I suppose, 'till '41 or even longer, if suff[ici]ent patronage be left in their hands to purchase the mercenary. If such be the case, it matters little what is done, as the ruin of our institutions & the country would be inevitable.

I fear from what I see, and what you mention of the state of publick feelings even in Columbia, that the Southern Review is destined to fail, which I ["would" *interlined*] regret profoundly. If we of the South be not roused in time to the sense of the danger that surrounds us, we have a sad fate before us. It seems to me, that such blindness & indifference never before befel[l] a people. I see the [Columbia Southern] Times does not even republish Amicus. I did not receive the last [Columbia] Telescope. I hope it has not been as indifferent.

My family join their regard[s] to yourself & family. I am with great respect your ob[edient] s[ervan]t, J.C. Calhoun.

ALS in DLC, John C. Calhoun Papers.

From THO[MA]S P. JONES

Washington, June 3rd 1837

Dear Sir, Mrs. Reed has forwarded to you a pamphlet containing some account of Mr. J.K. Casey's Dormant Balance, and in accordance with a wish expressed by that Lady I now offer such further information concerning it as may appear to me of importance. I had occasion to use the instrument in my own family, and this was done with great advantage to my Daughter. It will be manifest to you that the balance alone will not contribute towards the cure of the disease of debility in the patient, but that its use is to arrest the progress of the distortion, and thus to afford an opportunity of giving tone to the system by appropriate exercise and regimen. Upon the persevering, judicious, and unremitting use of these depends every well founded hope of permanent advantage. Many who have had the balance, and have been instructed in its use have failed of success from that want of energy and perseverance which so frequently render chronic complaints incurable. My advice, therefore, would be that, for a time at least, you place your daughter [Martha Cornelia Calhoun] under the special care of Mrs. Casey, who now resides in New York, and who, I presume, still undertakes the care of young Ladies with distorted spine.

I was formerly on terms of much intimacy with Mr. Casey's family, but from considerations entirely personal all intercourse between me and Mr. Casey ceased about two or three years since, and I do not, therefore, know any thing of the domestic arrangements of the family. Mrs. Casey is a Lady of very great worth, talented, energetic, and kind. She has manifested a particular aptitude in the business referred to, and nearly all the good that has been done to those who have used the balance has had her for its author. They have daughters residing at home, who are well educated, and amiable.

Should you, Sir, wish to make any enquiries which it is in my power to answer, be assured that you will gratify me by affording me an opportunity of doing so. I am with great esteem your obed[ien]t Serv[an]t, Thos. P. Jones.

ALS in ScU-SC, John C. Calhoun Papers.

To S[AMUEL] D. INGHAM, New Hope, Pa.

[Pendleton, June 5, *ca.* 1837]
. . . . subject touched on in your last, I agree with you som[e]thing efficient must be done. Experience has [proved], and will continue to prove, that mere subscription, cannot support an independent press, against the existing power, which constitutes a great weakness in our system. The result is, that the centinel [*sic*] of liberty becomes its enemy, and instead of resisting the encroachment of despotick power, lulls to security, while it saps the foundation of liberty. There is but ["one" *interlined*] remedy, and that the minions of power, who can ["cheaply" *interlined*] bribe[?] *by the people's* ["p"(?) *canceled*] *money*, will always endeavour to render odious, but which I would not hesitate openly to avow, as being right and even commendable in r[es]isting usurped authority. You may calculate that in this particular we will do our duty, but others ought not to let the weight fall on us in undue proportion.

Mrs. Calhoun desires her best respects to you and Mrs. I[ngham]. With sincere regard, I am & & J.C. Calhoun.

[Marginal P.S.] That this may reach you more certainly I do not frank.

ALS (incomplete) in ScU-SC, John C. Calhoun Papers. NOTE: This letter was postmarked at Pendleton, S.C., on June 5. The year has been conjectured.

From J[OHN] E[WING] BONNEAU

Cha[rle]ston, 7th June 1837
D[ea]r Sir, Your two letters of 28 & 29 Ult[imo] by your Son Patrick [Calhoun], I received. He left this [city] on Friday last for Norfolk in the Steam Boat So[uth] Carolina. He was quite well when he left here. I have also received your letter of 30 Ult[imo], enclosing 3 Blank Notes, with your signature, together with a Statement of a Note of yours held for Colo[nel] Farish Carter, amounting with interest to 20 April last to $4,873.33, which shall be attended to & paid as directed in your letter, as soon as the Note is presented to me. I shall not discount your Note until I am called upon for the money. Your Cotton has not yet arrived, although I received yesterday the Rail Road receipt dated 3d Inst[ant] for 28 Bales of your Cotton from J[oseph] F. Benson of Hamburg [S.C.]. I have no doubt but it will be here in the course of a day or two. Our Cotton market is still dull

& prices very low. I see no prospect of its being better. On 2d Inst[ant] I forwarded by the Rail Road to Hamburg to the care of Mr. Robert Anderson, A Bale of Cotton Osnaburgs containing 384¼ yards, for you—and at the same time wrote to Mr. Anderson, requesting him to forward it to Pendleton with as little delay as possible. In future, I will forward all articles for you to your factor, Mr. J.F. Benson of Hamburg. I have not been able as yet to trace any thing in relation to the stolen articles of Jewellery [*sic*], belonging to your daughter [Anna Maria Calhoun?]. With great respect I remain D[ea]r Sir Y[ou]rs &c. &c. J.E. Bonneau.

ALS in ScU-SC, John C. Calhoun Papers.

To "Col." C[HARLES] P. GREEN

Fort Hill, 7th June 1837
My dear Sir, Such is the uncertainty of the mail, as far as my correspondence is concerned, and the hazard of this reaching you, that I will not venture to say much, that I feel inclined to do, in answer to yours of the 20th June. I agree in most of your views. If we wish to save the country and our institutions, it is high time for the State rights party to organize. There is no hope of salvation, but through ["the hope" *canceled*] their ascendancy. Till then, things will go on from bad to worse; and will become so disordered, that it will be beyond the power of wisdom and patriotism to restore them. What we want is for the active & zealous young men of our party to come into action. The old are too timid & cautious and too anxious to save themselves, to save the country. I regret your absence from N[orth] Carolina at this time, and hope you will return sufficiently early to be at the election. She is a most important State & can do much, if she goes right. Few States have more in their power.

As to the present ["difficulty," *canceled*] disorder in the currency, the difficulty is not so much to devise a remedy, as great as that is, as to apply it with the present weak & corrupt rulers in power. The wisest & most efficient would in their hands be converted into the instrument of party power. The first step to ["th" *canceled*] remedy the disorder is their expulsion from power. Till then, all that can be be [*sic*] done, I fear, will prove mere palliatives.

You must be sure to take this on your return. We would be very glad to see you, and you would find it, at this season, the most pleasant & healthy route. Let me know about what time you expect to be here, and I will make my arrangement to be home at the time. With great respect I am & & J.C. Calhoun.

ALS in ScU-SC, John C. Calhoun Papers. NOTE: Charles Plummer Green was a native of Warren County, N.C., who had edited the Boydton, Va., *Virginia Expositor and Southern Advocate* during 1835–1836, and had subsequently led a group of volunteers to fight in Texas.

To DUFF GREEN, [Baltimore?]

Fort Hill, 26th June 1837
Dear Sir, It will be impossible to form a definitive opinion, as to the proposed convention, to which you refer, till we see the objects distinctly stated, and the motives, which actuate those who propose it fully developed. If it is intended under the general name of Whigs to call all the opposition together in order to ascertain, which section is the strongest, with an understanding, that all shall rally under him, who may be the choice of the strongest, without regard to his political principles, or views of policy, I do not see, how we could go into such a meeting without an unqualified surrender of our principles and the policy we deem the best for the country. We are in a minority of the opposition, and would be sure to be voted down and be compelled to vote for [Henry] Clay or [Daniel] Webster, or to violate the pledge implied in going into the convention. If we do the former, [we] would be merged in the national Republican party, and leave the whole States rights ground open to be seized on by those in power; if the latter, we would be weakened, and disgraced in the eyes of the community.

But, if the object be to harmonize the two sections of the opposition, the States rights, and the national, it seems to me, it would fail and leave us in a worse condition than ever. On what grounds can we compromise? How can the consolidation party and the anti-consolidation; the abolition and anti-abolition, the retrenchment, and the expenditure parties compromise? Where is the mid[d]le ground? I must say I can see none. If they should come together, it must be by concession, or surrender. One or the other must yield. At all events, if compromise be the object, it is clear, that there should be a previous understanding among the leaders, before the convention meets; and that can only be done after the meeting of Congress; or all will be in confusion. And hence I am clearly of the opinion, no countenance should be given to the move at the present time. If the object be to select a candidate, it is too soon; and if to harmonize, I would say, that all attempts at harmonizing faster, than experience and reflection may bring the heterogeneous mass together, will prove worse than useless, and will certainly defeat the object in view.

My impression has been and is, that we occupy the strong ground of truth and principle, and ought not to surrender it on any account; that it is the only ground on which the administration can be defeated, and on which defeat would be of any value to the community. On none other can the country and its institutions be saved, and there is no hope of its being made available but by our adhering to it with inflexible tenacity. The wors[t] thing that could befal[l] us and the country would be for us to bring in a party hostile to our doctrines and principles. The present state of things is greatly to be preferred to that. There is some hope in the present: there would be none in the other.

Let us then stand fast, do our duty firmly, and maintain kind relations with all, except the rogues, who have got hold of power; and show much more solicitude to redeem the country, than to advance ourselves. The crisis is too great and dangerous for a display of ambitious feelings. It is the time for the patriot; one who cares more for the publick, than himself; and, if I mistake not, all, who push forward to get an advantage in the hope of getting the start will be defeated. They at least ought to be. The difficulties and dangers are destined to increase, and the people to be saved must look to the wise, the resolute and patriotick. Be kind to all, but commit to none; and distrust any opining, that does not lead in the direction of a rigid adherence, to our principles and doctrines. If we stand firm, the national [republican] party must become extinct; and till it becomes so the country cannot be saved. Time and experience have decided against them. We cannot save them by uniting with them; but would only identify our fate with theirs. I see my way clearly. The past is in our favour. We have nothing to correct or repent of.

Let me hear from you often. I greatly rejoice, that the prospect of your paper [the Baltimore *Merchant?*] is so good. It is of vast importance that it should hold its ground.

PC in Jameson, ed., *Correspondence*, pp. 372–374. NOTE: During 7/1837 what appears to have been a slightly modified excerpt from this letter or (less likely) a similar letter to another person appeared in newspapers. This excerpt went as follows: "Let us do our duty firmly, maintaining kind relations with all except those who have so much abused their power, and show much more solicitude to redeem the country than to advance ourselves. The crisis is too great and dangerous for a display of ambitious feelings. This is the course for the patriot—the man who cares more for his country than for himself." The excerpt apparently was first published in the New York, N.Y., *Evening Chronicle*, a short-lived paper that appeared in May and disappeared in July. It was reprinted widely; for instance, in the Baltimore, Md., *Merchant*-Washington, D.C., *Reformer*, July 17, 1837, p. 2, and July 25, 1837, p. 3, and in *Niles' Weekly Register*, vol. LII, no. 21 (July 22, 1837), p. 321. The publication, it may be surmised, was inspired by Green.

Anna [Maria Calhoun], Fort Hill, to [Cadet] Patrick Calhoun, West Point, N.Y., 7/6. Anna acknowledges the receipt of a letter from Patrick and explains why she was late in replying to it. The family "all got home safe from the Mountains a few days ago." "Pa [John C. Calhoun] had been a little indisposed since his return. He is however quite well again." James [Edward Calhoun] has acquired "a beautiful grey hound which he called 'Zip.' " Anna also mentions the expected visit of Eliza [Simkins Pickens], Francis [W. Pickens], and Maria [Simkins] next week, her upcoming trip to Athens for the commencement exercises at the University of Ga., and the receipt of an invitation to the wedding of William Henry [Calhoun, son of John C. Calhoun's brother James, to Jane Stewart Orr,] on 7/28. ALS in ScU-SC, John C. Calhoun Papers.

To [JAMES EDWARD COLHOUN?]

Fort Hill, 7th July 1837
My dear Sir, I have just returned from an excursion from the mountains to look at a gold lot in which Andrew [Pickens Calhoun] has an interest in that quarter. I availed myself while there to review carefully the ascent to the Carolina Gap from this side. Mr. [William] Sloan and myself timed our travelling in ascending the Chatuga [*sic*; Chattooga] mountain, and [*one interlined word canceled*] descending from its summit to the valley of the White water, noting the time and the ["estimated" *interlined*] angles of ascent & descent at every point, and I feel the utmost confidence that my original estimate is correct, and that the mountain can be ascended at as low an Angle, as I stated. There is beyond all doubt a prodigious error in the survey. Now that I am familiar with the mountains, I can in a clear day distinctly trace the point where the Chatuga mountain is cut by the White water, a comparison of which with the gen[era]l elevation of the mountains ["would" *canceled*] clearly of itself proves that there must be an error. With a suitable instrument, the elevation might be

taken from my door. The distance on an air line does not exceed 25½ miles.

Gen[era]l [James] Hamilton [Jr.] writes ["me" *interlined*] that Col. [William Gibbs] McNeil[l] is to be here shortly to ["see"(?) *canceled*] examine this route for himself. I trust he comes in a right sperit, and, if he ["do" *canceled*] should, I fear not the result. ["Be" *canceled.*] Be that as it may, I feel it due to myself, the company & stockholders to correct the error that has been made. I believe it to exceed 1,000 feet. Can you not come, and bring with you your instruments, if you have any suitable to take distant elevation? It is now a leisure season, and I would be glad that you would come immediately so as to be hear [*sic*] before McNeill. Besides, I expect Mr. [George W.] Featherstonhaugh here shortly to explore our mountains, as a mineralogist, in which you may take some interest, which may be some inducement to you to come up. Affectionately, J.C. Calhoun.

ALS in ScCleA.

From W[illia]m Gibbs McNeill, "Eng[inee]r"

Flat Rock [N.C.], July 10th 1837
My Dear Sir, As I desired Gen[era]l [James] Hamilton [Jr.] to say to you where I was, as then, unable myself to write, "If there be any one person whom I desired more particularly to meet than another, & whom I certainly shall visit, it is Mr. Calhoun," & I added, that it really seemed as if some fatality had thwarted my several efforts to meet you. Such had been the case when that untoward accident befel[l] me by which I have been confined, or very much limited in my movements for the last six weeks, until it has become necessary that I should no longer delay visiting the several parties west of this, indeed between this and Lexington [Ky.]. My desire ["to see" *interlined*] you [had] well nigh given place to the conviction of the necessity I allude to, when just now I was favored with the receipt of yours of the 7th but I was not for the moment mindful that positive instruction from the President [of the Louisville, Cincinnati, and Charleston Railroad, Robert Y. Hayne,] urge[d] me at once to visit Tennessee & Kentucky & my visit to Pendleton must be postponed until my return. I now purpose to proceed direct from Knoxville, on my return from Lexington til I intersect the route you have proposed,

& by it reach Pendleton, and I therefore should be obliged if you would address me at Lexington, advising me respecting the route you would desire me to examine. I should of course at once reply, & possibly thereby it might be arranged that we should meet—at all events I could notify you with much exactness when I should be at Knoxville; I should be delighted should your convenience permit me the pleasure of your company thence to Pendleton.

I am this moment about to proceed on my journey—indeed was on the point of mounting my horse when your letter was handed [to me]. I am Dear Sir Ever Your Ob[edien]t S[er]v[an]t, Wm. Gibbs McNeill, Eng[inee]r &c.

FC in ScU-SC, William G. Williams Letterbook, pp. 94–95. NOTE: The signature appended to the document transcribed above has been added by a slip of paper glued into the letterbook. In 1837 McNeill resigned his commission as Bvt. Maj. in the U.S. Army Topographical Engineers to become a civil engineer employed by various railroads. In 3/1837 he had assumed duties as Chief Engineer of the Louisville, Cincinnati, and Charleston Railroad. The Pendleton *Messenger*, March 10, 1837, p. 3, stated that McNeill "has constructed more Rail Roads, and with more success than any man in America, and perhaps in the world."

From D[UFF] GREEN

Baltimore, July 11th 1837

Sir, I wrote to you yesterday under a state of fealings [*sic*] to which I seldom give way—the truth is I fear I shall be compelled to suspend the publication of the paper [the Baltimore *Merchant*]—I shall not do it if I can command the means to keep it up. I have been so miraculously sustained even against hope that I will not despair so long as I have room to labour.

But to Business—By a word you can render my family and your own independently rich and you have lived long enough to know the value of money[.] Will you say that word?

The present commercial revolusion [*sic*] has been produced by the effect of the Bank of England to compel a reflux of the precious metals drawn from her vaults by ["some" *canceled*] Gen[era]l [Andrew] Jackson[']s experiment[;] the depression in the price of our great Staples was necessary as part of the opporation [*sic*], the refusal to sustain the holders of Cotton was to compel the shipment of Specie.

Under my Charter [for the Union Potomac Company] we can hold 50,000 acres of the best Coal land in the United States[.] Coal and Iron constitute the best basis ["for" *interlined*] our Credit in

Europe. The consumption of the Coal cannot be less than 500,000 [tons] and will grow to millions, say one million at $7 gives us a disposal of seven Millions in the East, New York and New England to sustain the credit, which will enable us to pay for the Labour in the notes of our Bank. Under the charter we can buy up the stock of the Bank of Maryland, which is perpetual and unlimited or un-restricted in its issues.

So much for the Coal and Iron, by the Charter we are autherised [*sic*] to ["]purchase[,] transport to market and sell goods[,] wares and merchandise[.]" We are also autherised to issue our bonds for any am[oun]t and to make all kinds of Contracts which involve the in-terest of ["mony" *altered to* "money"] or the casualties of Life[.]

I hope to organise the Company, so as to create a Credit, that will command any amount of foreign Capital[.]

We are autherised to establish such agenencies [*sic*] and branches as we please, and buy and issue of our bonds Conditioned that the holder shall be autherised to receive a semi annual rate of Int[erest] equal to the semi annual dividend on the stock of the Company and that the bonds [are] to run with the institution and that the holder shall share his rata [*sic*] of its assets. These bonds will create new stock and we may increase the Capital to any definite sum. We can establish branches in all the Southern and Western and Northern Cities. The purpose of issuing this stock is to create a Credit in Europe that will enable us to become the shippers on Commission of the Cotton and Tobacco of the United States. If the parties to whom we issue these bonds are not able to pay for them let them give us their notes for the amount secured by real estate to twice the amount[,] payable in ten annual instal[l]ments[.] A sale to the amount of fifty millions of our bonds[,] secured by real estate with one Hundred Millions[,] may be made in the United States[.] Such a sale would enable us to make large shipments of Cotton and Tobac-co which with our American Credit would enable us to command what funds we want in Europe to be bound in this Country in a pledge of real estate and advanced shipments of Cotton & Tobacco[.]

This is a splended [*sic*] scheme. It is your own to car[r]y it into effect. You will do more to save this Country than you could do in any other situation and with the command of the resourses [*sic*] which the plan will give you[,] you could command any ["political" *interlined*] position. The experiment which Mr. [Nicholas] Biddle has made with his Credit in Europe proves what we could do—the Command of the Cotton and Tobacco, which would of necessaty [*sic*] fall into our hands, would enable us to command any amount

521

of Europe[a]n Capital; and the fact that we could lend at so much higher interest in this Country than in Europe would Constitute our agents the great money dealers of Europe. Having the Command of the Cotton and Tobacco the value of the Imports must pass through our hands and our Commissions upon the Sales, Interest upon the advances and profits on our bills of exchange would give to our Company a greater profit than any other moneyed institution of the Country. The times a[re] pecul[i]arly favourable to this operation. Think of it and write to me[.]

I believe that you have a Copy of my Charter[.] Yours, D[uff] Green.

FC in NcU, Duff Green Papers, vol. 9, pp. 293–295 (published microfilm, roll 24, frames 887–888). NOTE: Documents found in NcU, Duff Green Papers, dated in early 1837 (published microfilm, roll 2), outline Green's plans for the Union Potomac Company and indicate that he projected Calhoun as one of the Directors.

From J[ohn] E[wing] Bonneau, Charleston, 7/15. He encloses two papers related to Calhoun's business with Mathew[e]s & Bonneau, one accounting for the firm's sale of Calhoun's cotton and the other showing the balance of his accounts with the firm for all purposes. "The Sale I have made of your Cotton was the best, that it was in my power to effect," Bonneau reports. "The Cotton was inferior." Calhoun's 28 bales of cotton were sold for $711.45. After deducting charges for weighing, storage, railroad freight, drayage, and the sales commission, the net proceeds were $642.95. The second enclosure includes ledger entries for all debits and credits to Calhoun's account since last year's account was closed on 7/12/1836. This account indicates a net balance of $1,618.87 owed by Calhoun to the firm. ALS with Ens in ScU-SC, John C. Calhoun Papers.

Deed executed by John C. Calhoun, Anderson District, S.C., 7/19. For $5,000, Calhoun sells to Turner [H.] Richardson of Laurens District 640 acres of land "lying on Both Sides of Twenty Six mile Creek waters of Savan[n]ah River." This deed was witnessed by Asa Clinkscales and Joseph N. Whitner; it was recorded on 12/10/1838. Recorded copy in Sc-Ar, Anderson County Deeds, W:144–145.

To J[AMES] ED[WARD] COLHOUN

Fort Hill, 22d July 1837

My dear Sir, I have sold my 26 Miles [Creek] tract, and on searching the clerk's office at Anderson, for your conveyance to me (where it had been left to be recorded) it could not be found. The clerk was of the impression he had delivered it to Andrew [Pickens Calhoun]. On enquiry of Andrew, I find he is mistaken, and my hope is that it was delivered to you. Instead of the conveyance to you, I find in the office, the original grant, which I suppose must have been left ["there" *interlined*] by you for me, but without the conveyance ["of" *canceled*] from the original grantor to your father [John Ewing Colhoun, Sr.]. I hope you will be able to give me some ["explanation" *canceled and* "information" *interlined*] in relation to it and your conveyance to me. If you are not coming up shortly (which I hope you are) write me on the subject.

We are all well. My crop is very good notwithstanding a long & severe drought. The season is now good, and if it continues, and there be no accident, it will be very fine.

I expect Mr. [George W.] Featherston[h]augh about the 1st Aug[us]t to explore our mountain region; and I would be glad that you would ["visit(?) him" *canceled and* "meet" *interlined*] and accompany him in his exploration.

Your brother [John Ewing Colhoun] is in very bad health. I have not seen him, but the Doctor thinks it a general decline, which if not attended to may prove fatal. He speaks, I understand of going to the [Va.] springs.

All desire their love to you. Affectionately, J.C. Calhoun.

ALS in ScCleA. NOTE: In regard to Calhoun's first paragraph above, he and James Edward Colhoun had in 11/1834 made an exchange of lands by which Calhoun had received 640 acres on Twenty-Six Mile Creek. (Recorded deeds in Sc-Ar, Anderson County Deeds, U-322:322–323, and Pickens County Deeds, C-1:22.)

Willis Hall, New York [City], to Duff Green, Baltimore, 7/[26]. Hall expresses his regret at the recent nomination of Daniel Webster for President, made in spite of great opposition within the Whig Party. Calhoun's name is heard in N.Y. much more often than one would think in connection with the Presidency. "I am aware that private friendship as well as political principle lead you to look forward to the elevation of Mr. Calhoun to the Presidency as an event ["of" *canceled*] at once gratifying to you as an individual and important to the welfare of the country. I agree with you, and can truly say that although not entirely coinciding with him, in every point I have always had the highest admiration of his tallents [*sic*] and the most unbounded confidence in his patriotism. In a few words and with frankness allow me to say our wishes can be attained. Let a national convention be held at a proper time & place—previous to that convention let South Carolina recommend Mr. [Henry] Clay to the favorable consideration of that convention. And as sure as Mr. Clay is elected so sure will Mr. Calhoun be his successor after four years. By this single act will Mr. Calhoun not simply regain the ground he once occupied in the north & West, his magnanimity will place him higher than ever in the admiration & affections of the people." Hall is a member of the corresponding committee of Clay's supporters; he solicits Green's views in this matter and promises to hold as confidential any communication that may be forthcoming. ALS in ScCleA, John C. Calhoun Papers.

To Cadet PATRICK CALHOUN, [West Point, N.Y.]

Fort Hill, 27th July 1837

My dear Patrick, We receive your letters regularly, and are much gratified to learn[?] that you are becoming[?] more and more pleased with your situation, notwithstanding the severity of its duties. You will hereafter know how to appreciate the good effect of early rising, sound[?] exercise, and close attention. You will feel the good of it through life. We were all particularly gratified to learn [*or* "hear"] how correctly you behaved and how soberly you conducted yourself on the 4th July, when there was so much [*one word or partial word canceled*] riot. You did well not to respond to the toasts to one, who stood opposed to us in arms so lately.

Mr. Ingoldsby & Street[?] will advance you the funds you may need till the return of Mr. [James Edward] Boisseau [to New York City], who will ["then" *interlined*] furnish you with what you may need. I trust however you will need but little after you get settled[?] down. Your pay ought to support[?] you handsomely.

You will find the first quarter the most severe; but I have no fear of your going through with the attention which I know you will bestow on your studies. After a while you will find all comparatively easy.

You continue to improve in your correspondence [*or* "composition"; *two or three words illegible*] but you must pay some more attention to your spelling. Keep a small dictionary about you, and you will soon acquire a habit of spelling correctly.

Anna [Maria Calhoun] & the other children write to you often and give all the news. Your brother Andrew [Pickens Calhoun] has not yet had a letter from you. You must write to him & your Uncle James

[Edward Colhoun]. They will both be glad to hear from you & ["will" *interlined*] write back in turn.

Your Uncle William [Calhoun] is very unwell and I [*one word canceled*] fear will not ["survive" *canceled and then interlined*]. His case is the Dyspepsia. Your Uncle John [Ewing Colhoun] is also in bad health with the [*one word illegible*] disease.

We are all well. Your little nephew [John Caldwell Calhoun] grows finely. All join their love. Willy [that is, William Lowndes Calhoun] has got a sheet of paper from me to write to you tomorrow or next day.

Take care, my dear son, of your health; be attentive to your studies, respectful to your teachers, courteous to your companions & correct in your deportment. Avoid the idle & vicious[?] and cultivate the acquaintance of the worthy & studious. Your affectionate father, J.C. Calhoun.

ALS in ScU-SC, John C. Calhoun Papers. Note: The above transcription is of a manuscript that is so faded as to render the reading of many words less than certain.

To W. A. Graham

Fort Hill, 27th July 1837

Dear Sir, Absence from home has prevented me from acknowledging at an earlier date your letter of the 4th Inst[ant].

The object you propose to effect is one of vast magnitude and the agent you have selected for the purpose, very powerful; but how far the difficulties in the way of its application can be overcome, I do not feel competent to judge. There can, however, I suppose be no doubt, that the subject is one for which a patent can be obtained. If you should determine to apply and will send on your specifications to me during the extra session, I will cheerfully lay it before the Superintendent of the patent office. With respect I am & & J.C. Calhoun.

ALS in ScSpW. Note: Calhoun's correspondent in this letter has not been identified. No patents were granted to a person of his name during 1837–1839.

To Duff Green

Fort Hill, July 27th 1837

Dear Sir, Absence from home has prevented me from acknowledging your several letters from the 12th to the 15th Inst[ant] both inclusive till now.

I am distressed to hear of your difficulties with the paper and would do anything in my power, to which I could by any possibility bring my feelings, that would afford relief; but I must say, after full reflection, that I cannot think the acceptance of the place you propose would have the effect, that you suppose, and that it would be difficult for me to get my consent to undertake it.

So far from aiding, its effects as it appears to me, would be to bring a weight of opposition, originating in political considerations, against you. It would be viewed and regarded as a political move-ment, and would rouse both national and administrative forces to thwart it. But placing this consideration out of sight, and regarding it personally, as it relates to myself, I see great difficulties. The business would be entirely new to me, and to one at my time of life, few things are more formidable. Rare are the instances of the success of one in a new undertaking so late in life. It is difficult to acquire a taste for a new pursuit, when our habits are all fixed. This in my case would especially apply to the duties attached to the place in question. Of all things in the world, I have the least taste for money making, and the poorest capacity for success in it, and in particular the branch connected with stock, exchange, or banking, to which I have a pecu-liar aversion. My highest ambition as to money is to be independent, in a moderate and plain mode of living. I have just about sufficient for that purpose and it is all I want. I know, that Mammon is the idol of the times, but, I cannot get my consent to worship at his Shrine. Thus feeling and thinking, you must see how illy qualified I am for the task you propose, and how exceedingly irksome its duties would be me [*sic*] to me: I would infinitely prefer, if I was compelled to choose to take the place of chief Engineer, at the head of the mining Department of your concern, for which I would have much more capacity and inclination. To develope the resources of so fine a deposite would at least require so much reflection and energy as to absorb the attention.

As to the other topics you touched of a political character, and which you seemed to think might be offensive to me, it would be difficult for any one, whose friendship to me has been so severely tested as yours has been, to say anything, which I would regard in that light; but I must say, that tho' your remarks gave no offense, they deeply mortified my feelings. I am sure, that if your letters would fall into the hands of those who are to come after us, they would infer from the topics you urge on me to adopt the course you recommend, and the remarks with which you accompany them, that

I was a vain, light headed, ill judging and ambitious man, ignorant alike of the nature of the times, and my own strength, and constantly leading myself and those who follow me, into false positions, and aiming constantly at the Presidency and destined constantly to be defeated. I know you do not and cannot so think of me. No one knows better than yourself, that in the heat of youthful years, I never sought, or desired the Presidency, but through a faithful discharge of my duty, and as an instrument of high usefulness and distinguished service; and that when the alternative was presented between truth and duty on one side, and personal ag[g]randizement on the other, I never hesitated for a moment. You also well know, I never held out office, or emoluments to those who followed me; nor have ever asked or sought the support of any; and that for years I have, in obedience to what I believed to be my duty, knowingly pursued a course, that would sacrifice my popularity. How then can you say, that I more over rate my strength than any other publick man? I who have resisted every attempt of my friends to bring forward my name, on the express ground that I did not suit the times, nor the times me, and that I would not accept the Presidency, unless my services were demanded by the country to reform the government from top to bottom. So far from overestimating, I have no doubt, that the very services, which ought to recommend me to the country, and the qualities, which ought to give confidence, constitute insuperable objections to my election. Nothing can raise me short of saving the country from convulsions; which gives me not a moment of grief. I would rather, to use your own expression, stand alone in my glory, seeing what is coming, raising an honest and fearless voice of forewarning, untainted and untouched by the times, than to be President of these States, on any other condition, than through a discharge of my duty, which I know is your own opinion of me. This I wish my friend [*sic*] to know; and that there is very little prospect of honor, or emoluments in following me. But enough of this.

As to my taking [a] place on the [William Henry] Harrison ticket, I am sure it could be no more than a momentary impulse with you. How could I who am anti national, take a place under a prominent national Republican? How can I, who am anti abolition, go on a ticket, headed by one, who has expressed an opinion in favour of appropriating money to emancipate our slaves by purchase; and whose main support is in a State [Pa.?] chiefly tainted by abolitionism, and by the Gov[erno]r of that State [Joseph Ritner] who has come out an open abolitionist? I touch not other topicks, the danger of elevating a weak, vain man with no fixed principles, and having such men as [Francis] Granger, and others of like discription [*sic*] as my competitors, and being defeated by them.

As to the convention of the Whigs, I intend for one to have nothing to do with it. I am not of the same party with [Daniel] Webster and others, and do not intend to go into any move, that may be controlled by abolitionists, consolidationists, colonizationists. I speak as an individual. If my friends think differently, I shall not complain: but shall regard it as a signal, that they are tired of being in a hopeless minority, and that it is time for me to step of[f] the stage. I believe the sound portion of the country, if there be one, that is left, is to be found in the original [Andrew] Jackson party; I mean those who rallied under him [in 1828] to put down Mr. [John Quincy] Adams, and his administration, and that the true policy is to reorganize the old party. Such of our friends, who take a different view will be woefully disappointed in the end. They may sacrifice their principles in going with others, but their reward will be scorn and contempt. Mr. L. has taken the true view, and no one can do more to effect it both in and out of the administration party, than himself, and if he succeeds, he will deserve and receive the lasting praise of the country. He also selects the proper State in which to commence action, and can do more there, than any other man. He has taken, the common sense and patriotick view, which opens a glim[p]se of light, coming from that quarter, in the midst of darkness that surrounds us.

PC in Jameson, ed., *Correspondence*, pp. 374–377. NOTE: The "Mr. L." mentioned by Calhoun cannot be identified with certainty. A possibility is Benjamin W. Leigh, a former Senator from Va. This conjecture is supported by circumstantial evidence. We know from Calhoun's letter of 7/31 to James Iredell, Jr., below, that Duff Green was about that time travelling southward from Baltimore to Raleigh. Therefore, he might have easily visited Leigh in Richmond and written Calhoun about their interview.

To [JAMES] IREDELL, [JR., former Senator from N.C.], Raleigh, N.C.

Fort Hill, 31st July 1837

My dear Sir, I wrote Gen[era]l [Duff] Green day before yesterday [*sic*; 7/27?] and addressed him at Raleigh. Should he have passed through before my letter reached there, I would be much obliged to you, if you forward my letter to him, if you can ascertain w[h]ere it will find him.

If he should be in Raleigh when you receive this, or afterwards, I will thank you to say to him, that I received his several letters as late as July the 24th, and that it will be impossible for me to leave home more than 10 or 12 days before the beginning of the session, and that my route will remain uncertain, till I hear from N[ew] York, which will not be for some time yet.

We are all looking on with great interest as to the result of your election. Few States are more important at this moment than N[orth] Carolina. A decided victory in the coming election in your State, would go far to settle the question with the Administration. I see clearly there must be a reorganization of parties. The ranks both of the administration & opposition are full of discord. It seems to me, that the time is approaching, when there ought to be a rally called of the old [Andrew] Jackson party; those who elevated him to put down the [John Quincy] Adams administration. After all, most of the same materials are to be found in their ranks; and there are thousands of them, who now rank with the [Martin] Van Buren party, who would gladly leave him, if they saw where to go. They are committed against nullification (the name) and cannot join the nationals. The effects of such a rally would do much to unite the South—a point of vital importance to us & the whole Union.

You must consider these reflections as intended for yourself. They are based not on the actual state of things, but what I believe will be in the course of a few months. Sincerely, J.C. Calhoun.

ALS in NcD, James Iredell Papers.

To G[EORGE] W. FEATHERSTONHAUGH, Dahlonega, Ga.

Fort Hill, August [*ca.* 12,] 1837
My dear Sir, I received your letter from Gain[e]s Ville [Ga.] yesterday, and intended to set out tomorrow for Dahlonega, but I will, I fear, be prevented by the state of the weather. It has been blowing a ["perfectly" *altered to* "perfect"] equinoxial gale for the last 15 hours, without any prospect of its immediate termination. I propose to s[t]art as soon as the weather will permit, and hope to have the pleasure of meeting you at Dahlonega early next week, and of ac-

compan[y]ing you to my residence. We will keep a large portion of the way nearly in ["a" *changed to* "the"] line of the gold belt.

I crossed ["lately" *interlined*] what I believe to be the belt in this State near our mountains, and, if I do not mistake, it will be found to be very strongly marked in our mountain region between where it crosses the Chatuga [Chattooga] river, and cuts the Allegany [*sic*] chain, near the Hog back mountain. It cuts the chain at [an] angle of about 45 degrees, which runs from where the belt intercepts it to its termination in Georgia nearly east & west.

Your tour must have been a very interesting ["and" *canceled*] one, and, when we meet, I shall be very happy to go over it with you. The information, which you have collected will no doubt furnish much light on the geological st[r]ucture of our country. I think you will find no portion of the mountain region more marked, or interesting, than that immediately back of me. More of this when we meet. With very great respect I am & & J.C. Calhoun.

ALS in MH. NOTE: This letter was postmarked at Pendleton on 8/12.

To the Rev. B [ASIL] MANLY, [Charleston, S.C.]

Fort Hill, 21st Aug[us]t 1837

My dear Sir, Absence from home prevented the immediate acknowledgement of your note of the 3d Inst[ant].

A great multiplicity of business, prevented an early perusal of the book of President [Francis] Wayland [of Brown University] on the elements of Political Economy, which you were so kind as to leave at my lodgings, on the eve of my departure from Charleston.

I have read it with the attention due to the high standing of its author & the importance of the subject of which it treats, and I take pleasure in adding with great satisfaction. It is marked throughout with great good sense and perspicuity of style, and there are very few of the conclusions, in which I do not concur. With great respect I am & & J.C. Calhoun.

ALS in RPB. NOTE: Manly was pastor of the First Baptist Church of Charleston, 1826–1837, and President of the University of Alabama, 1837–1855. Wayland's *The Elements of Political Economy* was published in 1837.

From Edward Harleston, Pendleton, 8/27. He requests Calhoun's favorable influence in securing a warrant as Cadet at West

Point for Tho[ma]s Cordes Harleston, his nephew. Thomas has been studying privately for a year at West Point to prepare himself. Would Calhoun also speak to [Francis W.] Pickens and [John K.] Griffin about the appointment? ALS in DNA, RG 94 (Records of the Adjutant General's Office), Application Papers of Cadets, 1805–1866, 1837, 128 (M-688:109, frames 315–324).

To [HENRY M. CLAY]

Fort Hill, Aug[us]t 1837

D[ea]r Sir, I have written you twice since my return from Washington in March last addressed at Nashville and have not yet had an answer. During my late visit to Dahlonega I was informed you were daily expected there, and I have left my papers with Mr. [J.] Hansell with authority to settle with you. It appears by a copy of my note to Mr. [Robert S.] Patton, which was sent me by Mr. Collins, that you have made no payment on it since our settlement on the 3d Nov[embe]r last, and as you have made no payment to me, nor any one authorised to receive payment for me, you are of course indebted to ["my" *canceled*] me for my share of the proceeds of the operation on our lotts [*sic*] on Cane Creek from the 3d Nov[embe]r till the time my hands were withdrawn, on the evening of the 7th January last, as will appear by a statement of my son [Andrew Pickens Calhoun] in the hands of Mr. Hansell. In addition to this you have not accounted for my share of the Tools, machines, cooking utensils, hogs, stock, except two cows, which as it appears by my son's statement was all that he received; to which must be added the toll paid for gold taken out of the vein, and my share of the toll out of your operation, subsequent to the time of my withdra[wa]l.

I greatly regret, that you did not settle with my son as he passed through. I had authorised him to settle in full, and informed him that there would be no difficulty, as our last settlement on the 3d Nov[embe]r [1836] included the provisions, which were on hand and which you had assured me would be sufficient to the end of the year, and all other expenses except such as were referred to in the final settlement. When he called on you for a settlement he understood you, that you would bring to my credit whatever was due me on my note to Mr. Patton. This not having been done, I have requested Mr. Hansell to make the settlement with you. All I want is to bring to my credit on the note all that is due me, including the

236 dwt. & 9 grains of gold due from Mr. Patton to me on an old settlement, and which you promised to bring to my credit in our last settlement in Nov[embe]r last. I left with him ["(Mr. H.)" *interlined*] a list of my hands and of yours ["since" *canceled*] that were present on the 3d Nov[embe]r, from which it can be determined in what proportion the gold that was taken up should be divided, provided your hands that were then present remained the same till mine were withdrawn. I learn that only a part of my hands received their ["cloth" *canceled*] winter clothing. Of course the clothing they received with the shoes, and the meal purchased & supplied for the use of the mine subsequent to the 3d Nov[embe]r are to be deducted, according to the terms of the settlement. They make the only deduction.

I am very anxious to have this business closed, and to ["make" *canceled*] know, what I owe on Mr. [*here this fragment ends.*]

Autograph letter (incomplete) in ScCleA.

SEPTEMBER 4–OCTOBER 16
1837

(25th Congress, 1st Session)

〇

Political optimism characterized Calhoun for the first time in many a day. "Things are doing well here," he wrote home shortly after his arrival in Washington for the special session. President Van Buren "has been forced by his situation and the terror of Jackson to play directly into our hands and I am determined, that he shall not escape from us." The South had "now a fair opportunity to break the last of our commercial shackles; I mean the control which the North through the use of government credit acting through the banks, have exercised over our industry & commerce." The fair opportunity was the program Van Buren had requested Congress to enact to deal with the emergency created by the financial panic. He proposed that the government henceforward operate its own fiscal system (soon dubbed the Subtreasury), collecting, transferring, and disbursing funds without making use of any banks.

"How wonderful," commented Calhoun privately, "that the author of the safety fund system and the favourite of New York (the State above all others the most benefitted by the union of bank & state) should be forced by circumstances, which he could not control, to give the fatal blow to his own offspring and supporters! Into what situation may not an artful but short sighted politician be forced!"

When an administration bill was brought in on September 11 to suspend the distribution of surplus funds that Calhoun had labored for, he expressed willingness to acquiesce, asking only that it not be enacted alone but be considered along with other proposals for relief. In a major speech on September 18 Calhoun made his stand public and clear. He reviewed the history of American currency and banking and took high ground in defense of the administration's general program. It was time that the government undertook its Constitutional responsibility for a stable currency and separated itself from private profit and privilege.

This was the moment of reform he had been waiting for. Ameri-

cans had arrived at an important turning point. The day of executive and legislative encroachment, tariff and surplus, bank privileges, debts, and extravagant spending was over. "The Government stands in a position disentangled from the past, and freer to choose its future course than it ever has been since its commencement. We are about to take a fresh start. . . . I seize the opportunity thoroughly to reform the Government; to bring it back to its original principles. . . ."

On September 20 he did the administration one better by offering an amendment to the Subtreasury bill which would begin the gradual elimination of the government's acceptance of bank notes. The amendment was received cordially by Van Buren's friends, expounded by Calhoun in a major speech on October 3, and adopted by a narrow vote. The Senate then passed the Subtreasury 26 to 21. It did not come to a vote in the House of Representatives before the session expired, however.

Calhoun for the first time since it had come into existence received kind words from the Washington Globe. On October 2 that paper commended Calhoun's September 18 speech "to the attentive consideration of all parties." The Whigs, however, excoriated the traitor in unrestrained terms. Resumption of personal relations with the President and a real merger with his party were still a considerable distance in the future. "In taking his course," Calhoun declared, "he was neither an administration man nor an opposition man, and much less any man's man. He belonged to no party but the States rights, and wished to be considered nothing more than a plain, and an honest nullifier."

Optimism did not mean that there were not serious problems yet to be faced. South Carolina's second Senator, William C. Preston, declined to follow Calhoun. Of the State's Representatives only Francis W. Pickens and Robert Barnwell Rhett were enthusiastic, though Calhoun's Virginia friends were delighted. Consternation and incipient mutiny had been created in the ranks at home, the full extent of which Calhoun perhaps did not realize until he reached there. On October 15 he prepared to depart on a hurried trip to South Carolina to take care of vital farming business before Congress reassembled in December.

Whatever problems lay ahead, Calhoun's course had been carefully chosen and he was not to be turned aside from it. With his favorite daughter Anna Maria, now twenty years old, he discussed public affairs as frankly and maturely as he would with an old and trusted adviser. His new political course, he had written her early in the session, "causes much speculation; but I think I see my way clearly. It puts me in a position much more congenial to my feelings, than that which I have occupied for the last few years. It was impossible for me to go with the leaders of the nationals. We disagreed on almost all points except resistance to Executive usurpation. We could not part on a point better for me, than the one on which we now separate."

Ⅲ

To W[illiam] O. Niles, [Editor, *Niles' National Register*, Baltimore,] 9/4. "I will thank you to furnish me in addition to the number you desire me to distribute a sufficient number of your Register to make 200." ALS in NHpR, Autograph and Miscellaneous Historical Manuscripts Collection.

To J[AMES] ED[WARD] COLHOUN

Washington, 7th Sep[tembe]r 1837

My dear Sir, Things are doing well here. [Martin] Van Beuren [*sic*] has been forced by his situation and the terror of [Andrew] Jackson to play directly into our hands and I am determined, that he shall not escape from us. We have now a fair opportunity to break the last of our commercial shackles; I mean the control which the North through the use of government credit acting through the banks, have exercised over our industry & commerce. How wonderful, that the author of the safety fund system and the favourite of New York (the State above all others the most benefitted [*sic*] by the union of bank & state) should be forced by circumstances, which he could not control, to give the fatal blow to his own offspring & supporters! Into ["such" *canceled and* "what" *interlined*] situation may not an artful but short sighted politician be forced!

I have taken my stand. I go against the chart[er]ing of a United States bank, or any connection with [Nicholas] Biddle[']s, or any other bank. I go in a word for a complete seperation [*sic;* "of" *canceled and* "from" *interlined*] the whole concern. So far, I have come to a fix[ed] determination. Beyond that, I wait for developement; and shall come to no conclusion, till I see the whole ground. We will divide. My colleague [William C. Preston], as I understand him, goes for Biddle's bank and will probably take a portion of the

Representatives [from S.C.] with him. Like divisions will probably run throughout all the States, and I would not be surprised, ["that" *canceled and* "if" *interlined*] an entirely new organization of parties should rise out of the present state of things.

In the mean time, it is of vast importance, that the meeting in Augusta [Ga.] should be fully attended. Now is the time. Abbeville [District] must send her delegates. You & [George] McDuffie ought to be two of them. Let a meeting be called at the court House and the nomination be made. It is of little importance whether it be fully attended or not. Some body must move in the affair; and I know of no [one] better calculated to give the impulse than yourself.

I had a long letter yesterday from [William Gibbs] McNeil[l], on his Western tour of exploration. He writes me that he is determined not to hasten a final decision on the route [for a railroad to the Midwest]; and I have no doubt from the tone of his letter he will do his duty. I trust, I may get off in time to attend the meeting of directors. There is, I think, a fair prospect that the work may yet take the proper direction. If you can, you ought to attend.

Let me hear from you & believe me to be affectionately yours & & J.C. Calhoun.

ALS in ScCleA; PEx in Jameson, ed., *Correspondence*, pp. 377–378. NOTE: In a message to the two houses of Congress delivered on 9/5 Van Buren had reviewed in detail the fiscal problems facing the government and people and, in effect, had left it to Congress to devise legislation to meet the situation— legislation which, he suggested, should be along lines that would "separate the fiscal operations of the Government from those of individuals or corporations." The meeting in Augusta, Ga., referred to by Calhoun was a Merchants' and Planters' Convention which met for a week beginning 10/16 to promote direct trade between the South and Europe. Among those attending were George McDuffie and James Gadsden of S.C.

To Miss A[NNA] M[ARIA] CALHOUN, Pendleton

Washington, 8th Sep[tembe]r 1837
My dear Anna, On the day of my arrival here, I wrote to your mother [Floride Colhoun Calhoun], and since then to Andrew [Pickens Calhoun]. I hope both letters have been received.

We expected, when I first wrote, to change our lodgings, but Col. [Francis W.] Pickens, and myself both concluded, after looking about, that we could not better ourselves, and have determined to remain with Miss Coc[h]ran for the session. Our Mess is a mixed concern. It consists of Col. Pickens, myself, Mr. [Abraham] Rencher [Representative] of N[orth] Carolina, the Philadelphia and the Rhode Island Representatives, and is of course too discordant to be very social on political subjects. In other respects it is agreeable enough; but contrasted with the mess of last winter, which was like a family party, it is ["like" *canceled*] solitude compared to a social circle of friends. The consolation is, that we have the prospect of a short session. Every one seems to think that it will adjourn by the mid-[d]le of next month; and some suppose earlier. It cannot be too short for me. There is no prospect of doing much. There are now four parties; the two great divisions of Administration and opposition, each divided in itself; the former into administration proper & the conservatives, and the latter into the States['] rights & Nationals. The division is such that neither of these subdivisions can move without the other. What is to grow out of all this time alone can disclose; but I see clearly it must end in a complete reorganization of the political elements of the country.

I stand on my old position and have avowed my determination, ["to" *canceled*] not to go for the chartering of a United States bank, nor for [Nicholas] Biddle[']s, or any other State bank, or combination of banks, reserving to myself the right to determine on other propositions, as they may be presented. I see clearly that [Martin] Van Buren has been compelled to play into our hands (no thanks to him, he had no choice) and I am resolved to use my position, to re-form the Government, and to throw off the last of our commercial shackles. In the meantime my position is one of great delicacy, and will require consummate prudence with decision & boldness. It causes much speculation; but I think I see my way clearly. It puts me in a position much more congenial to my feelings, than that which I have occupied for the last few years. It was impossible for me to go with the leaders of the nationals. We disagreed on almost all points except resistance to Executive usurpation. We could not part on a point better for me, than the one on which we now seperate [*sic*]. I stand now on my own bottom, with no influence acting on me but a rigid adherence to those great principles, for which I have made so many sacrafices [*sic*].

I have not had a letter from home since I left, tho it has been a week since my arrival here. I hope to hear soon. My love to all & tell the children they ["must" *interlined*] write me. I shall be very impatient to get home. Your affectionate father, J.C. Calhoun.

[P.S.] As usual I have had a bad cold since my arrival, but am better.

ALS in ScCleA; slightly variant PC in Jameson, ed., *Correspondence*, pp. 378–379; PEx in Harriet Hefner Cook, *John C. Calhoun—The Man*, p. 47.

To Dr. F[RANCIS] LIEBER, [Columbia, S.C.]

Washington, 11th Sept[embe]r 1837

My dear Sir, I regret the complete engrossment of my time at this moment has left me so little leisure, as to confine me to a rapid glance over only two chapters of your manuscript; the one on the state, and the other ["on" *interlined*] absolutism.

They are both subjects of deep importance; and are treated in a new & very interesting manner. With some, not important exceptions, I am disposed to concur in the views, which you take.

I hope you will present the work to the publick at an early day. It would be quite an acquisition to our literature, and do much to call publick attention to subjects in which all have so great an interest. With great respect I am & & J.C. Calhoun.

ALS in CSmH, Francis Lieber Papers; PEx in Frank Freidel, *Francis Lieber: Nineteenth-Century Liberal*, p. 164. NOTE: The work referred to was probably Lieber's *On Civil Liberty and Self-Government* . . . , 2 vols. (Philadelphia: Lippincott, Grambo and Co., 1853).

Remarks on the bill to suspend distribution of the surplus, 9/11. Silas Wright, Chairman of the Committee on Finance, brought in a bill for this purpose (as had been recommended by President Martin Van Buren in a message at the beginning of the session). Wright promised a committee report later. "Mr. Calhoun hoped that the bill would not be pressed upon the Senate immediately. He thought it due to the body and to the occasion to say that whatever views the committee might entertain, that they should all be laid before us before we acted on this important subject. However disconnected in their nature they might be, still they had all grown out of a common calamity, and were all so intimately connected, that we could not act well on one part of the subject, without having the other before us. He therefore hoped that the bill would not be acted upon until the committee should have reported all their views." When Daniel Webster supported his sentiments, Calhoun added that he "fully concurred with the Senator from Massachusetts, that it was due to the country that there should be a full and early consideration of the measures of relief to be proposed. But it was highly important that the whole ground should be presented, so that each measure might be discussed not only upon its particular merits, but upon the general merits of the plan." Later in the proceedings, after several Senators presented petitions, Calhoun "hoped that all the ordinary business would be laid on the table. He trusted that the course would be pursued in regard to these petitions." From *Congressional Globe*, 25th Cong., 1st Sess., pp. 17–18. Also printed in the Washington, D.C., *Globe*, September 11, 1837, p. 3. Variant in the Washington, D.C., *Daily National Intelligencer*, September 12, 1837, p. 2; *Register of Debates*, 25th Cong., 1st Sess., cols. 7–8. Other variants in the Baltimore, Md., *Merchant*-Washington, D.C., *Reformer*, September 11, 1837, p. 2; the Washington, D.C., *Madisonian*, September 12, 1837, p. 3.

From B[ENJAMIN] W. LEIGH, [former Senator from Va.]

Richmond, Sept. 13, 1837
My dear sir[,] Read the correspondence between Dr. [Miles S.] Watkins of Huntsville [Ala.] and me, published in the [Richmond] Whig of this morning (I send you the paper) and then hand it to Mr. [Richard K.] Crallé and get him to publish it [in the Baltimore, Md., *Merchant*]. Yours truly (in haste) B.W. Leigh.

ALS in DLC, Richard K. Crallé Papers. NOTE: The correspondence referred to, published in the *Merchant* of September 19, 1837, p. 2, concerned Calhoun's old enemy William Smith, former Senator from S.C. Watkins had inquired of Leigh about the accuracy of a statement made by Smith, now a resident of Huntsville. Smith had alleged that the judicial support of the late Chief Justice John Marshall for the Bank of the United States had been the result of corruption by virtue of his alleged ownership of seventeen shares of stock in the Bank. Leigh in several replies to Watkins defended Marshall and refuted Smith's imputations.

Remarks on the bill to suspend the fourth installment of the distribution of the surplus to the States, 9/13. "Mr. Calhoun said he hoped this bill would not now be acted upon. It was his wish that no action should be had on any of these measures proposed by the Committee on Finance until a report had been made. He hoped, therefore, that the chairman of the committee (Mr. [Silas] Wright) would consent to a postponement until all the contemplated measures should have been reported." Wright acquiescing, the Senate agreed to postpone the bill until tomorrow. From *Register of Debates*, 25th Cong., 1st Sess., col. 10. Also printed in the Washington, D.C., *Daily National Intelligencer*, September 14, 1837, p. 2. Variant in *Congressional Globe*, 25th Cong., 1st Sess., p. 23. Another variant in the Baltimore, Md., *Merchant*-Washington, D.C., *Reformer*, September 14, 1837, p. 2.

Remarks on the Bill to Suspend Distribution of the Surplus to the States

[In the Senate, September 14, 1837]
[*Under consideration was the bill reported by the Committee on Finance which would suspend payment of the fourth installment of the Treasury surplus to the States under a provision of the deposit act of 1836, which provision had been originated by Calhoun. William C. Rives of Va. moved to postpone the bill until the Committee reported on other fiscal proposals it had under consideration.*]

Mr. Calhoun was deeply impressed with the magnitude and danger of the present emergency. It, however, had not taken him by surprise, nor was it unlooked for by him. In his humble opinion, of the many difficulties through which the country had passed within the last five-and-twenty years, this was by far the most distressing and overwhelming. Seeing and believing this, he had come here with a full and fixed determination to do his duty, despite of all personal considerations and party feeling; for, when his country was in danger, he knew but one impulse, and that was to perform his duty. He had been looking forward with the most intense anxiety for the remedy which would be proposed. Fixing two great points in his mind, he had observed the most strict reserve until he saw the plan of the administration. Having now seen it, he felt that the only feature in the [President's] message, and in the report of the Secretary of the Treasury [Levi Woodbury], which gave character to the present bill, was to be abandoned. For himself, while he was ready to act on this understanding, he must say that, with regard to the other measures, he regarded them as nothing—as perfectly immaterial. And he would tell gentlemen that this was not a crisis for weak action. They had a difficult scene to go through, and, if they did not meet it with promptness and boldness, they would find it no easy matter to overcome. He professed himself prepared to act immediately on the bill before the Senate.

[*The efforts to postpone the bill failed, and Daniel Webster, Silas Wright, and James Buchanan spoke at length.*]

Mr. Calhoun said that he was decidedly of the impression that, under the circumstances of the case, this postponement [of the distribution] ought to be made. The object of the deposite law was to draw the revenue out of the grasp of the Government, and restore it to those to whom it ought to be restored. And now, when there was no surplus, it was not contrary to the purpose of that law to withhold it. But the responsibility of doing so would rest on gentlemen of the administration and those of the opposition who made last year the extravagant appropriations of thirty-two millions, exceeding the estimate of the Secretary of the Treasury. They were then told of the folly of raising the revenue, and of raising the disbursements. The result now was, that the Government was bankrupt. Were they never to look ahead, and see the difficulties that threatened them?

Another era had now arisen. They had got through with the surplus, and Mr. C[alhoun] trusted they were through with extravagant appropriations. If they did not economize and retrench, he saw a new age commencing—perhaps that of Treasury notes—when the compromise act [of 1833] would be annulled, and the high tariff revived. But Mr. C[alhoun] would agree that the fourth deposite should be withheld, since that law had fulfilled its main purpose, and since a new series of extravagances was now to arise unless they kept a good lookout.

[*Buchanan proposed an amendment by which any call upon the States for repayment of the first three installments would have to be made by Congress and not by the Secretary of the Treasury.*]

Mr. Calhoun said he fully concurred in the proposed amendment. It was due to the States in their sovereign capacity not to subject themselves to be called upon for the money by any other authority than Congress.

[*The Senate adopted Buchanan's amendment by a vote of 33 to 12, and ordered the bill to be engrossed for a third reading by a vote of 27 to 18.*]

From *Register of Debates*, 25th Cong., 1st Sess., cols. 14–15, 29–30. Also printed in the Washington, D.C., *Daily National Intelligencer*, September 15,

1837, p. 2, and September 19, 1837, p. 2; the Washington, D.C., *Globe*, September 20, 1837, p. 2; *Congressional Globe*, 25th Cong., 1st Sess., Appendix, pp. 9, 14. Variant in the Baltimore, Md., *Merchant*-Washington, D.C., *Reformer*, September 16, 1837, p. 2; the Charleston, S.C., *Mercury*, September 23, 1837, p. 2; the Pendleton, S.C., *Messenger*, September 29, 1837, p. 2. Other variants in *Congressional Globe*, 25th Cong., 1st Sess., pp. 28, 30; the Washington, D.C., *Madisonian*, September 16, 1837, p. 3; the Charleston, S.C., *Southern Patriot*, September 20, 1837, p. 2. NOTE: In the first variant report cited, perhaps the only one that was reviewed by Calhoun before publication, he was recorded as prefacing his approval of the suspension of distribution with a regret for the difficulty which the suspension would cause the States. "They had just reason to expect it; and many of them, he believed, had made such disposition of it, in advance, as might subject them to much inconvenience should they not receive it." Nevertheless, the main object of distribution, to remove the surplus from corrupting control of the federal executive, had been accomplished.

Further remarks on the bill to suspend distribution of the surplus to the States, 9/15. William C. Preston of S.C. spoke at length against the bill. He thought it would be damaging to the States and without benefit to the Treasury, which could be relieved in other ways. "Mr. Calhoun said he thought it would be better for his colleague (Mr. Preston) to make a motion at once for the repeal of unexpended appropriations to the amount of nine millions of dollars, the amount of the [fourth] instalment [of the distribution]. If Mr. P[reston] felt unwilling at this stage of the bill to make such a motion, he (Mr. C[alhoun]) would agree to the laying of the bill on the table in order to give time. He confessed that the idea had occurred to him which his colleague had just stated; but he did not see any probability of such a proposition being attended with success. He had done his utmost to stop the extravagant course pursued at former sessions in granting the appropriations. His efforts had been unsuccessful, and now he thought there was still less chance of getting back that which it had not been possible to prevent from being legislated away. He agreed with his colleague that it was entirely useless to lock up this money. It would do no good to the Government; when, if let go, it would do good to the States." From *Register of Debates*, 25th Cong., 1st Sess., col. 34. Also printed in the Washington, D.C., *Globe*, September 22, 1837, p. 2; the Washington, D.C., *Daily National Intelligencer*, September 22, 1837, p. 2; *Congressional Globe*, 25th Cong., 1st Sess., Appendix, p. 15. Variants in the Baltimore, Md., *Merchant*-Washington, D.C., *Reformer*, September 16, 1837, p. 2; the Washington, D.C., *Madisonian*, September 16, 1837, p. 3.

Remarks on the bill for the issuance of Treasury notes, 9/15. "At this [early] stage of the bill, Mr. Calhoun expressed a wish that a postponement of the bill until to-morrow might be allowed, for an examination into some points." From *Register of Debates*, 25th Cong., 1st Sess., col. 47.

To [EDGAR SNOWDEN], Editor of the Alexandria, D.C., *Gazette*

[Published on September 15, 1837]
.... On the highly important subject on which Congress has been called to deliberate, I shall express my views and opinions in my place in the Senate.

As to the calumnies which may be circulated to my prejudice, they are not unexpected. It is my rule to pass them unnoticed, leaving it to my conduct to put them down.

How strange that any man who knows me, should imagine it possible for me to be driven or seduced from my position! I live but to carry out the great principles for which I have been contending since 1824, and which I have maintained under every danger and difficulty. In their defence I have acted with and against every party, without blending with any. Mr. [Martin] Van Buren has been driven into a position favorable to their advancement; and shall I not avail myself of the opportunity which it affords me to accomplish my object? Shall I permit him to drive me from my position because he has been driven on it? All I ask is to be heard. My confidence, in every juncture, is in the force of truth and integrity.

PEx in the Baltimore, Md., *Merchant*-Washington, D.C., *Reformer*, September 16, 1837, p. 2; PEx in the Washington, D.C., *Globe*, September 16, 1837, p. 2; PEx in *Niles' National Register*, vol. LIII, no. 3 (September 16, 1837), p. 33; PEx in the Richmond, Va., *Whig and Public Advertiser*, September 19, 1837, p. 1; PEx in the Columbia, S.C., *Southern Times and State Gazette*, September 22, 1837, p. 3; PEx in the Pendleton, S.C., *Messenger*, September 29, 1837, p. 1. NOTE: No copy of the issue of the Alexandria *Gazette* of September 15 which contained the first printing of this letter has been located. The excerpt above was probably all that was originally printed, because all the numerous reprintings were nearly identical with it. The *Southern Times and State Gazette* headed its printing of the excerpt with the notice: "The various letters and publications which have lately appeared in the public journals, have doubtless produced the following letter, which we find in the Alexandria Gazette."

REMARKS ON THE BILL AUTHORIZING AN ISSUE OF TREASURY NOTES

[In the Senate, September 16, 1837]
[Under consideration was a bill from the Committee on Finance. The bill directed the President of the U.S. to authorize issuance of $10,000,000 in Treasury notes, redeemable in a year at no more than six per cent interest. The notes, limited to denominations of over $100, would be transferable and receivable in government dues. Thus presumably the bill would relieve the empty Treasury and provide a currency.]

Mr. Calhoun said he had turned his attention to the bill, but had found great difficulty in bringing his mind to a satisfactory conclusion respecting it. The very point which the Senator from Massachusetts [Daniel Webster?] so much approved (allowing interest) was one which constituted an objection to the bill, in the view of Mr. C[alhoun]. Neither was he satisfied to give up his opinion to any one scheme, till he understood what was to be done on the great point involved in the subject of this bill, namely, the separation of Government from all banks. All ought to verge to this point, even if considered as a measure of relief. As the law now was, the Secretary of the Treasury was compelled to receive the notes of all specie-paying banks. Of course, when specie payments should be resumed, all would be received. If this should occur, and if Congress should adjourn without altering the law, the result would be, that the Government would, under the sub-treasury system, have the custody of the money, but would collect it in bank-notes. If it was intended to restore the connexion between the Government and the banks, this bill ought to be different; and if it was not so intended, it still ought to be different. Mr. C[alhoun] could support it as it was, in neither alternative.

But he designed to move an amendment to this bill, which would serve as a testing question, whether it was the object or not to make a separation between the banks and the Treasury. If it was intended to make such separation, now was the acceptable time. And if it was not done now, it would perhaps never be done. The question was one of great magnitude; and Mr. C[alhoun] therefore hoped that the subject would be postponed till Monday, by which time he hoped to be prepared to offer the amendment which he had indicated.

On this great point Mr. C[alhoun]'s opinion had been long made up; and he believed, firmly, that the only alternative was a separation from all banks, or a Bank of the United States. He had so declared it in the debate of 1834, and he had never seen any reason to change his opinion. On the contrary, the catastrophe at the present time had greatly confirmed that opinion. In his view, it was one of the greatest questions that had been, or that could be presented to this body. And, further, it was due to the country, to themselves, and to posterity, that gentlemen on all sides should meet this question openly, boldly, and decidedly. He entreated them to show their hands, as Mr. C[alhoun] would show his, and go on with the question. He moved to postpone the bill till Monday [that is, 9/18].

[*Silas Wright, Chairman of the Committee on Finance and sponsor of the bill, spoke against postponing the bill, stating that the Treasury would not be able to satisfy its creditors for another twenty days without help from Congress.*]

Mr. Calhoun said it was impossible for him to say what ought to be done on this bill till he could know how the Executive would shape its course. Mr. C[alhoun] was willing to grant the relief, (to the Treasury,) but he would not do it in the dark. The great point was the one to which he had alluded, and to that all kindred measures ought to have a reference. If time should not be given him, Mr. C[alhoun] would vote against this bill, and would forever disconnect himself from all responsibility as to the result. He knew that all ought to feel a proper sensibility for the embarrassments of the Government, but he felt still more for those of the country; and he thought it infinitely more important that all should be well, rather than speedily, done; and as far as his voice had any power, it should be done well. On this question, as the chairman of the committee was opposed to a postponement, Mr. C[alhoun] called for the yeas and nays; which were ordered.

[*Robert J. Walker supported Calhoun. Thomas H. Benton and William R. King opposed postponement.*]

Mr. Calhoun said that this unexpected opposition required that he should go a little into detail. If it was the intention of the Senate, or rather of the administration, to restore gradually the connexion between the Government and the banks, in that event, instead of issuing Treasury notes, they ought at once to resort to a provisional loan, made in notes of the State banks, and then pay off the loan as the means should come in; or, otherwise, they should issue Treasury notes so as to constitute a currency. No Senator could properly know how to act, unless he knew the course to be pursued on the principal point. There never had been a better time to separate the Treasury and the banks; and, if to be done at all, it ought to be done at once. Mr. C[alhoun] wished to be put in a position that he might vote understandingly on measures for the relief of the country. The demands of the Treasury he considered as trifling, compared with the settlement of this great question.

[*After further debate the Senate voted 28 to 18 to postpone.*]

From *Register of Debates*, 25th Cong., 1st Sess., cols. 47–49. Also printed in the Washington, D.C., *Daily National Intelligencer*, September 18, 1837, p. 2. Variant in the Washington, D.C., *Globe*, September 16, 1837, p. 2; *Congressional Globe*, 25th Cong., 1st Sess., pp. 35–36. Other variants in the Washington, D.C., *Madisonian*, September 19, 1837, p. 3; the Richmond, Va., *Whig and Public Advertiser*, September 19, 1837, p. 1; the Charleston, S.C., *Southern Patriot*, September 19, 1837, p. 2; *United States Magazine and Democratic Review*, vol. IV ("Historical Register"), p. 16.

Remarks on the bill "to authorize merchandize to be deposited in the public stores" [in lieu of tariff duties], 9/1. "Mr. Calhoun said it appeared to him that the bill [aimed at the relief of merchants] required more consideration, and that it ought to be postponed to the regular session. He moved, therefore, to postpone it to the first Monday in December." James Buchanan argued against the postponement. "Mr. Calhoun said the situation of himself and the Senator differed. He (Mr. Buchanan) had studied the subject, and had satisfied himself that the bill would be beneficial; and for him there might be sufficient reason for such a conclusion. But Mr. C[alhoun] hoped that he would not, therefore, call upon others to vote without understanding the subject. He thought the request to postpone perfectly reasonable, that others might be as well informed on the subject as the Senator from Pennsylvania." William R. King of Ala. moved a postponement until 9/25, which Calhoun accepted, "though he still thought it ought not to be acted on till the next session. . . ." From *Register of Debates*, 25th Cong., 1st Sess., cols. 76–77. Also printed in the Washington, D.C., *Daily National Intelligencer*, September 19, 1837, p. 3. Variant in *Congressional Globe*, 25th Cong., 1st Sess., p. 38.

Speech on the Bill Authorizing an Issue of Treasury Notes

[In the Senate, September 18, 1837]

The bill for the issue of Treasury notes having been postponed to this day, in order to give Mr. Calhoun an opportunity of preparing an amendment, and of offering his sentiments generally upon the subject, was now resumed by the Senate.

Mr. Calhoun rose and addressed the Chair as follows:

Mr. President: An extraordinary course of events, with which all are too familiar to need recital, has separated, in fact, the Government and the banks. What relation shall they bear hereafter? Shall the banks again be used as fiscal agents of the Government—be the depositories of the public money—and, above all, shall their notes be considered and treated as money, in the receipts and expenditures of the Government? This is the great and leading question; one of the first magnitude, and full of consequences. I have given it my most anxious and deliberate attention; and have come to the conclusion that we have reached the period when the interest both of the Government and the banks forbids a reunion. I now propose to offer my reasons for this conclusion. I shall do it with that perfect frankness due to the subject, to the country, and to the position I occupy. All I ask is, that I may be heard with a candor and fairness corresponding to the sincerity with which I shall deliver my sentiments.

Those who support a reunion of the banks and the Government have to overcome a preliminary difficulty. They are now separated by operation of law, and cannot be reunited while the present state of things continues, without repealing the law which has disjoined them. I ask, who is willing to propose its repeal? Is there any one who, during the suspension of specie payments, would advocate their employment as the fiscal agents of the Government, who would make them the depositories of the public revenue, or who would receive and pay away their notes in the public dues? If there be none, then it results that the separation must continue for the present, and that the reunion must be the work of time, depending on the contingency of the resumption of specie payments.

But suppose this difficulty to be removed, and that the banks were regularly redeeming their notes: from what party in this body can the proposition come, or by which can it be supported, for a reunion between them and the Government? Who, after what has happened, can advocate the reunion of the Government with the league of State banks? Can the opposition, who for years have been denouncing it as the most dangerous instrument of power, and efficient means of corrupting and controlling the Government and country? Can they, after the exact fulfilment of all their predictions of disastrous consequences from the connexion, now turn round and support that which they have so long and loudly condemned? We have heard much from the opposite side of untried experiments on the currency. I concur in the justice of the censure. Nothing can be more delicate than the currency. Nothing can require to be more delicately handled. It ought never to be tampered with, nor touched, until it becomes absolutely necessary. But if untried experiments justly deserve censure, what condemnation would a repetition of an experiment that has failed deserve?—an experiment that has so signally failed, both in the opinion of supporters and opponents, as to call down the bitter denunciation of those who tried it[?] If to make the experiment was folly, the repetition would be madness.

But if the opposition cannot support the measure, how can it be expected to receive support from the friends of the administration, in whose hands the experiment has so signally failed as to call down from them execrations deep and loud?

If, Mr. President, there be any one point fully established by experience and reason, I hold it to be the utter incompetency of the State banks to furnish, of themselves, a sound and stable currency. They may succeed in prosperous times, but the first adverse current necessarily throws them into utter confusion. Nor has any device yet been found to give them the requisite strength and stability, but a great central and controlling bank, instituted under the authority of this Government. I go farther. If we must continue our connexion with the banks—if we must receive and pay away their notes as money, we not only have the right to regulate and give uniformity and stability to their value, but we are bound to do so, and to use the most effective means for that purpose. The constitution makes it our duty to lay and collect the taxes and duties uniformly throughout the Union; to fulfil which, we are bound to give the highest possible equality of value, throughout every part of the country, to whatever medium it may be collected in; and, if that be bank-notes, to adopt the most effective means of accomplishing it, which experience has shown to be a Bank of the United States. This has been long my opinion. I entertained it in 1816, and repeated it in my place here on the deposite question in 1834. The only alternative then is, disguise it as you may, between a disconnexion and a Bank of the United States. This is the real issue to which all must come, and ought now to be openly and fairly met.

But there are difficulties in the way of a national bank, no less formidable than a reconnexion with the State banks. It is utterly impracticable, at present, to establish one. There is reason to believe that a majority of the people of the United States are deliberately and unalterably opposed to it. At all events, there is a numerous, respectable, and powerful party—I refer to the old State rights party—who are, and ever have been, from the beginning of the Government, opposed to the bank; and whose opinions, thus long and firmly entertained, ought at least to be so much respected as to forbid the creation of one, without an amendment of the constitution. To this must be added the insuperable difficulty, that the Executive branch of the Government is openly opposed to it, and pledged to interpose his veto, on constitutional grounds, should a bill pass to incorporate one. For four years, at least, then, it will be impracticable to charter a bank. What must be done in the mean time? Shall the treasury be reorganized to perform the functions which have been recently discharged by the banks; or shall the State institutions be again employed until a bank can be created? In the one case, we shall have the so much vilified and denounced sub-treasury, as it is called; and, in the other, difficulties insurmountable would grow up against the establishment of a bank. Let the State institutions be once reinstated, and reunited to the Government as their fiscal agents, and they will be found the first and most strenuous opponents of a national bank, by which they would be overshadowed and curtailed in their profits. I hold it certain, that, in prosperous times, when State banks are in full operation, it is impossible to establish a national bank. Its creation, then, should the reunion with the State banks take place, will be postponed until some disaster, similar to the present, shall again befall the country. But it requires little of the spirit of prophecy to see that such another disaster would be the death of the whole system. Already it has had two paralytic strokes—the third would prove fatal.

But, suppose these difficulties were overcome, I would still be opposed to the incorporation of a bank. So far from affording the relief which many anticipate, it would be the most disastrous measure that could be adopted. As great as is the calamity under which the country is suffering, it is nothing to what would follow the creation of such an institution under existing circumstances. In order to compel the State institutions to pay specie, the bank must have a capital as great, or nearly as great, in proportion to the existing institutions, as the late bank had, when established, to those of that day. This would give it an immense capital—not much less than one hundred millions of dollars, of which a large proportion (say twenty millions) must be specie. From what source is it to be derived? From the State banks? It would empty their vaults, and leave them in the most helpless condition. From abroad, and England in particular? It would reproduce that revulsive current which has lately covered the country with desolation. The tide is still running to Europe, and if forced back by any artificial cause before the foreign debt is paid, cannot but be followed by the most disastrous consequences.

But suppose this difficulty overcome, and the bank re-established; I ask what would be the effects under such circumstances? Where would it find room for business, commensurate with its extended capital, without crushing the State institutions, enfeebled by the withdrawal of their means in order to create the instrument of their oppression? A few of the more vigorous might survive; but the far greater portion, with their debtors, creditors, and stockholders, would be involved in common ruin. The bank would, indeed, give a specie currency, not by enabling the existing institutions to resume, but by destroying them and taking their place.

Those who take a different view, and so fondly anticipate relief from a national bank, are deceived by a supposed analogy between the present situation of the country and that of 1816, when the late bank was chartered, after the war with Great Britain. I was an actor in that scene, and may be permitted to speak in relation to it with some little authority. Between the two periods there is little or no analogy. They stand almost in contrast. In 1816, the Government was a debtor to the banks—now, it is a creditor; a difference of the greatest importance, as far as the present question is concerned. The banks had overissued, it is true, but their over-issues were to the Government—a solvent and able debtor, whose credit, held by the banks in the shape of stock, was at par. It was their excessive issues to the Government on its stock which mainly caused the suspension; in proof of which, it is a remarkable fact, that the depreciation of bank paper under gold and silver was about equal to the proportion which the Government stock held by the banks bore to their issues. It was this excess that hung on the market and depressed the value of their notes. The solution is easy. The banks took the Government stock, payable in twelve years, and issued their notes for the same, payable on demand, in violation of the plainest principles of banking. It followed, of course, that when their notes were presented for payment, they had nothing but Government stock to meet them. But its stock was at par, and all the banks had to do was to go into market with the stock they held, and take up their notes; and thus the excess, which hung upon the market, and depressed their value, would have been withdrawn from circulation, and the residue would have risen to par, or nearly par, with gold and silver; when specie payments might be easily resumed.

This they were unwilling to do. They were profiting every way—

by drawing interest on the stock, by discounting on it as capital, and by its continued rise in the market. It became necessary to compel them to surrender these advantages. Two methods presented themselves: one a bankrupt law, and the other a national bank. I was opposed to the former then, as I am now. I regarded it as a harsh and unconstitutional measure, opposed to the rights of the States. If they have not surrendered the right to incorporate banks, as is conceded, its exercise cannot be controlled by the action of this Government, which has no power but what is expressly granted, and no authority to control the States in the exercise of their reserved powers. It remained to resort to a national bank as the means of compulsion. It proved effectual. Specie payments were restored; but even with these striking advantages, it was followed by great pressure in 1818, [18]19 and [18]20, as all who are old enough to remember that period must recollect. Such, in fact, must ever be the consequence of resumption, when forced, under the most favorable circumstances; and such, accordingly, it proved even in England, with all her resources, and with all the caution she used in restoring a specie circulation, after the long suspension of 1797. What, then, would be its effects in the present condition of the country, when the Government is a creditor instead of a debtor—when there are so many newly-created banks without established credit—when the over-issues are so great, and when so large a portion of the debtors are not in a condition to be coerced? As great as is the tide of disaster which is passing over the land, it would be as nothing to what would follow were a national bank to be established as the means of coercing specie payments.

I am bound to speak without reserve on this important point. My opinion then is, that, if it should be determined to compel the restoration of specie payments by the agency of banks, there is but one way; but to that I have insuperable objections—I mean the adoption of the Pennsylvania Bank of the United States as the fiscal agent of the Government. It is already in operation, and sustained by great resources and powerful connexions, both at home and abroad. Through its agency specie payments might undoubtedly be restored, and that with far less disaster than through a newly created bank; but not without severe pressure. I cannot, however, vote for such a measure. I cannot agree to give a preference and such advantages to a bank of one of the members of this confederacy over those of others —a bank dependent upon the will of a State, and subject to its influence and control. I cannot consent to confer such favors on the stockholders, many of whom, if rumor is to be trusted, are foreign capitalists, and without claim on the bounty of the Government. But, if all these and many other objections were overcome, there is still one which I cannot surmount.

There has been, as we all know, a conflict between one of the departments of the Government and that institution, in which, in my opinion, the department was the assailant; but I cannot consent, after what has occurred, to give to the bank a triumph over the Government—for such its adoption as the fiscal agent of the Government would necessarily be considered. It would degrade the Government in the eyes of our citizens and of the world, and go far to make that bank the Government itself.

But if all these difficulties were overcome, there are others, to me, wholly insurmountable. I belong to the State-rights party, which, at all times, from the beginning of the Government to this day, has been opposed to such an institution as unconstitutional, inexpedient, and dangerous. They have ever dreaded the union of the political and the moneyed power, and the central action of the Government to which it so strongly tends; and at all times, have strenuously resisted their junction. Time and experience have confirmed the truth of their principles; and this, above all other periods, is the one at which it would be most dangerous to depart from them. Acting on them, I have never given my countenance or support to a national bank, but under a compulsion which I felt to be imperious, and never without an open declaration of my opinion as unfavorable to a bank.

In supporting the bank of 1816, I openly declared that, as a question *de novo*, I would be decidedly against the bank, and would be the last to give it my support. I also stated that, in supporting the bank then, I yielded to the necessity of the case, growing out of the then existing and long-established connexion between the Government and the banking system. I took the ground, even at that early period, that so long as the connexion existed, so long as the Government received and paid away bank-notes as money, they were bound to regulate their value, and had no alternative but the establishment of a national bank.

I found the connexion in existence and established before my time, and over which I could have no control. I yielded to the necessity, in order to correct the disordered state of the currency, which had fallen exclusively under the control of the States. I yielded to what I could not reverse, just as any member of the Senate now would, who might believe that Louisiana was unconstitutionally admitted into the Union, but who would, nevertheless, feel compelled to vote to extend the laws to that State, as one of its members, on the ground that its admission was an act, whether constitutional or unconstitutional, which he could not reverse.

In 1834 I acted in conformity to the same principle, in proposing the renewal of the bank charter for a short period. My object, as expressly avowed, was to use the bank to break the connexion between the Government and the banking system gradually, in order to avert the catastrophe which has now befallen us, and which I then clearly perceived. But the connexion, which I believed to be irreversible in 1816, has now been broken by operation of law. It is now an open question. I feel myself free, for the first time, to choose my course on this important subject; and, in opposing a bank, I act in conformity to principles which I have entertained ever since I have fully investigated the subject.

But my opposition to a reunion with the banks is not confined to objections limited to a national or State banks. It goes beyond, and comprehends others of a more general nature, relating to the currency, which to me are decisive. I am of the impression that the connexion has a most pernicious influence over bank currency; that it tends to disturb that stability and uniformity of value which is essential to a sound currency; and is among the leading causes of that tendency to expansion and contraction, which experience has shown is incident to bank-notes as a currency. They are, in my opinion, at best, without the requisite qualities to constitute a currency, even when unconnected with the Government; and are doubly disqualified by reason of that connexion, which subjects them to sudden expansions and contractions, and exposes them to fatal catastrophes, such as the present.

I will explain my views. A bank-note circulates not merely on account of the credit of the institution by which it is issued, but because Government receives it like gold and silver in all its dues, and thus adds its own credit to that of the bank. It, in fact, virtually endorses on the note of every specie-paying bank, "receivable by the Government in its dues." To understand how greatly this adds to the circulation of bank-notes, we must remember that Government is the great money-dealer of the country, and the holder of immense public domains; and that it has the power of creating a demand against every citizen, as high as it pleases, in the shape of a tax, or duty, which can be discharged, as the law now is, only by bank-notes or gold and silver. This, of course, cannot but add greatly to the credit of bank-notes, and contribute much to their circulation, though it may be difficult to determine, with any precision, to what extent.

It certainly is very great. For why is it that an individual of the first credit, whose responsibility is so indisputable that his friend of equal credit endorses his note for nothing, should put his name with his friend's, being their joint credit, into a bank, and take out the notes of the bank, which is, in fact, but the credit of the bank itself, and pay six per cent. discount between the credit of himself and his friend and that of the bank? The known and established credit of the bank may be one reason, but there is another and powerful one: the Government treats the credit of the bank as gold and silver in all its transactions, and does not treat the credit of individuals in the same manner. To test the truth: let us reverse the case, and suppose the Government to treat the joint credit of the individuals as money, and not the credit of the bank; and is it not obvious that, instead of borrowing from the bank, and paying six per cent. discount, the bank would be glad to borrow from them on the same terms? From this we may perceive the powerful influence which bank circulation derives from the connexion with the credit of the Government.

It follows, as a necessary consequence, that to the extent of this influence the issues of the banks expand and contract with the expansion and contraction of the fiscal action of the Government; with the increase of its duties, taxes, income, and expenditure; with the deposites in its vaults, acting as additional capital, and the amount of bank-notes withdrawn, in consequence, from circulation; all of which must directly affect the amount of their business and issues, and bank currency, and must, of course, partake of all those vibrations to which the fiscal action of the Government is necessarily exposed, and, when great and sudden, must expose the system to catastrophes such as we now witness. In fact, a more suitable instance cannot be selected to illustrate the truth of what I assert than the present, as I shall proceed to show.

To understand the causes which have led to the present state of things, we must go back to the year 1824, when the tariff system triumphed in Congress—a system which imposed duties not for the purpose of revenue, but to encourage the industry of one portion of the Union at the expense of the other. This was followed up by the act of 1828, which consummated the system. It raised the duties so extravagantly, that out of an annual importation of sixty-four millions, thirty-two passed into the Treasury; that is, Government took one-half for the liberty of introducing the other. Countless millions were thus poured into the Treasury beyond the wants of the Government, which became in time the source of the most extravagant expenditures. This vast increase of receipts and expenditures was followed by a corresponding expansion of the business of the banks. They had to discount and issue freely, to enable the merchants to pay their duty bonds, as well as to meet the vastly-increased expenditures of the Government. Another effect followed the act of 1828, which gave a still further expansion to the action of the banks, and which is worthy of notice. It turned the exchange with England in favor of this country. That portion of the proceeds of our exports, which, in consequence of the high duties, could no longer return with profit in the usual articles which we had been in the habit of receiving principally from that country in exchange for our exports, returned in gold and silver, in order to purchase similar articles at the North. This was the first cause which gave that western direction to the precious metals, the revulsive return of which has been followed by so many disasters. With the exchange in our favor, and consequently no demand for gold and silver abroad, and the vast demand for money attendant on an increase of the revenue, almost every restraint was removed on the discounts and issues of the banks, especially in the northern section of the Union, where these causes principally operated. With their increase, wages and prices of every description rose in proportion, followed, of course, by an increasing demand on the banks for further issues. This is the true cause of that expansion of the currency, which began about the commencement of the late administration, but which was erroneously charged by it to the Bank of the United States. It rose out of the action of the Government.

The bank, in increasing its business, acted in obedience to the condition of things at the time, and in conformity with the banks generally in the same section. It was at this juncture that the late administration came into power; a juncture remarkable in many respects, but more especially in relation to the question of the currency. Most of the causes which have since terminated in the complete prostration of the banks and the commercial prosperity of the country were in full activity.

Another cause, about that time (I do not remember the precise date,) began to produce powerful effects. I refer to the last renewal of the charter of the Bank of England. It was renewed for ten years, and, among other provisions, contained one making the notes of that bank a legal tender in all cases except between the bank and its creditors. The effect was to dispense still further with the use of the precious metals in that great commercial country, which, of course, caused them to flow out in every direction throughout the various channels of its commerce. A large portion took their direction hitherward, and served still further to increase the current which, from causes already enumerated, was flowing in this direction; and which still further increased the force of the returning current, on the turn of the tide.

The administration did not comprehend the difficulties and dangers which surrounded it. Instead of perceiving the true reason of the expansion of the currency, and adopting the measures necessary to arrest it, they attributed it to the Bank of the United States, and made it the cause or pretext of waging war on that institution. Among the first acts of hostility, the deposites were removed, and transferred to selected State banks; the effect of which, instead of resisting the tendency to expansion, was to throw off the only restraint that held the banking institutions of the country in check; and, of course, gave to the swelling tide, which was destined to desolate the country, a powerful impulse. Banks sprung up in every direction; discounts and issues increased almost without limitation; and an immense surplus revenue accumulated in the deposite banks, which, after the payment of the public debt, the most extravagant appropriations could not exhaust, and which acted as additional banking capital. The value of money daily depreciated; prices rose; and then commenced those unbounded speculations, particularly in public lands, which were transferred, by millions of acres, from the public to the speculators for worthless bank-notes, till at length the swelling flood was checked, and the revulsive current burst its barriers, and overspread and desolated the land.

The first check came from the Bank of England, which, alarmed at the loss of its precious metals, refused to discount American bills, in order to prevent a further decrease of its cash means, and cause a return of those which it had lost. Then followed the execution of the deposite act, which, instead of a remedial measure, as it might have been made if properly executed, was made the instrument of weakening the banks at the point of pressure, especially in the great commercial metropolis of the Union [New York City], where so large a portion of the surplus revenue was accumulated. And, finally, the Treasury order [that is, Jackson's "Specie Circular"], which still further weakened those banks, by withdrawing their cash means to be invested in public lands in the West.

It is often easy to prevent what cannot be remedied, which the present instance strongly illustrates. If the administration had formed a true conception of the danger in time, what has since happened might have then been easily averted. The near approach of the expiration of the charter of the United States Bank would have afforded ample means of staying the desolation, if it had been timely and properly used. I saw it then, and purposed [on 3/21/1834] to renew the charter, for a limited period, with such modifications as would have effectually resisted the increasing expansion of the currency, and, at the same time, gradually and finally wear out the connexion between the bank and the Government. To use the expression I then used, "to unbank the banks"; to let down the system easily, and so to effect the separation between the bank and the Government as to avoid the possibility of that shock which I then saw was inevitable without some such remedy. The moment was eminently propitious. The precious metals were flowing in on us from every quarter, and the vigorous measures I purposed to adopt in the renewal of the charter would have effectually arrested the increase of banks, and checked the excess of their discounts and issues; so that the accumulating mass of gold and silver, instead of being converted into bank capital, and swelling the tide of paper circulation, would have been substituted in the place of bank-notes, as a permanent and wholesome addition to the currency of the country.

But neither the administration nor the opposition sustained me, and the precious opportunity passed unseized. I then clearly saw the coming calamity was inevitable; and it has neither arrived sooner, nor is it greater, than I anticipated.

Such are the leading causes which have produced the present disordered state of the currency. There are others of a minor character, connected with the general condition of the commercial world, and the operations of the Executive branch of the Government, but which, of themselves, would have produced but little effect. To repeat the causes in a few words: the vast increase which the tariffs of 1824 and 1828 gave to the fiscal action of the Government, combined with the causes I have enumerated, gave the first impulse to the expansion of the currency. These, in turn, gave that extraordinary impulse to overtrading and speculation (they are effects, and not causes) which has finally terminated in the present calamity. It may thus be ultimately traced to the connexion between the banks and the Government; and it is not a little remarkable that the suspension of specie payments in 1816 in this country, and that of 1797 in Great Britain, were produced by like causes.

There is another reason against the union of the Government and the banks, intimately connected with that under consideration, which I shall next proceed to state. It gives a preference to one portion of citizens over another, that is neither fair, equal, nor consistent with the spirit of our institutions.

That the connexion between the banks and the Government, the receiving and paying away their notes as cash, and the use of the public money from the time of the collection to the disbursement, is the source of immense profit to the banks, cannot be questioned. It is impossible, as I have said, to ascertain with any precision to what extent their issues and circulation depend upon it, but it certainly constitutes a large proportion. A single illustration may throw light upon this point. Suppose the Government were to take up the veriest beggar in the street, and enter into a contract with him that nothing should be received in payment of its dues or for the sale of its public lands in future except gold and silver and his promissory notes, and that he should have the use of the public funds from the time of their collection until their disbursement: can any one estimate the wealth which such a contract would confer? His notes would circulate far and wide over the whole extent of the Union; would be the medium through which the exchanges of the country would be performed; and his ample and extended credit would give him a control over all the banking institutions and moneyed transactions of the community. The possession of a hundred millions would not give a control more effectual. I ask, would it be fair, would it be equal, would it be consistent with the spirit of our institutions, to confer such advantages on any individual? And if not on one, would it be if conferred on any number? And if not, why should it be conferred on any corporate body of individuals? How can they possibly be entitled to benefits so vast, which all must acknowledge could not be justly conferred on any number of unincorporated individuals?

I state not these views with any intention of bringing down odium on banking institutions. I have no unkind feeling towards them whatever. I do not hold them responsible for the present state of things. It has grown up gradually, without either the banks or the community perceiving the consequences which have followed the connexion between them. My object is to state facts as they exist, that the truth may be seen in time by all. This is an age of investigation. The public mind is broadly awake upon this all-important subject. It affects the interests and condition of the whole community, and will be investigated to the bottom. Nothing will be left unexplored, and it is for the interest both of the banks and of the community that the evils incident to the connexion should be fully understood in time, and the connexion be gradually terminated, before such convulsions shall follow as to sweep away the whole system, with its advantages as well as its disadvantages.

But it is not only between citizen and citizen that the connexion is unfair and unequal. It is as much so between one portion of the country and another. The connexion of the Government with the banks, whether it be with a combination of State banks or with a national institution, will necessarily centralize the action of the system at the principal point of collection and disbursement, and at which the mother bank, or the head of the league of State banks, must be located. From that point the whole system, through the connexion with the Government, will be enabled to control the exchanges both at home and abroad; and with it, the commerce, foreign and domestic, including exports and imports.

After what has been said, these points will require but little illustration. A single one will be sufficient; and I will take, as in the former instance, that of an individual.

Suppose, then, the Government, at the commencement of its operation, had selected an individual merchant, at any one point in the Union, (say New York,) and had connected itself with him, as it has with the banks, by giving him the use of the public funds from the time of their collection until their disbursement, and of receiving and paying away, in all its transactions, nothing but his promissory notes, except gold and silver: is it not manifest that a decisive control would be given to the port where he resided over all the others? that his promissory notes would circulate everywhere, through all the ramifications of commerce? that they would regulate exchanges? that they would be the medium of paying duty bonds? and that they would attract the imports and exports of the country to the port where such extraordinary facilities were afforded? If such would clearly be the effects in the case supposed, it is equally clear that the concentration of the currency at the same point, through the connexion of the Government with the banks, would have equal, if not greater, effects; and that, whether one general bank should be used as an agent, or a league of banks, which should have their centre there. To other ports of the country, the trifling advantages which a branch or deposite bank would give, in the safekeeping of the public revenue, would be as nothing, compared to the losses caused to their commerce by centralizing the moneyed action of the country at a remote point. Other gentlemen can speak for their own sections; I can speak, with confidence, of that which I have the honor in part to represent. The entire staple States, I feel a deep conviction, banks and all, would, in the end, be great gainers by the disseverance, whatever might be the temporary inconvenience. If there be any other section in which the effects will be different, it would be but to confirm the views which I have presented.

As connected with this, there is a point well deserving consideration. The union between banks and Government is not only a main source of that dangerous expansion and contraction in the banking system which I have already illustrated, but is also one of the principal causes of that powerful and almost irresistible tendency to the increase of banks, which even its friends see and deplore. I dwelt on this point on a former occasion, (on Mr. [Daniel] Webster's motion to renew the bank charter in 1833,) [*sic*; on 3/21/1834] and I will not repeat what I then said. But, in addition to the causes then enumerated, there are many others very powerful, and among others the one under consideration. They all may be summed up in one general cause. We have made banking too profitable—far, very far, too profitable; and I may add, too influential. One of the most ample sources of this profit and influence may be traced, as I have shown, to the connexion with the Government; and is, of course, among the prominent causes of the strong and incessant tendency of the system to increase, which even its friends see must finally overwhelm either the banks or the institutions of the country. With a view to check its growth, they have proposed to limit the number of banks and the amount of banking capital by an amendment of the constitution; but it is obvious that the effects of such amendment, if it were practicable, would but increase the profits and influence of bank capital; and that, finally, it would justly produce such indignation on the part of the rest of the community against such unequal advantages, that in the end, after a long and violent struggle, the overthrow of the entire system would follow. To obviate this difficulty, it has been proposed to add a limitation upon the amount of their business; the effects of which would be, the accommodation of favorites, to the exclusion of the rest of the community, which would be no less fatal to the system. There can be, in fact, but one safe and consistent remedy—the rendering banking as a business less profitable and influential; and the first and decisive step towards this is a disseverance between the banks and the Government. To this may be added some effectual limitation on the denomination of the notes to be issued, which would operate in a similar manner.

I pass over other important objections to the connexion—the corrupting influence and the spirit of speculation which it spreads far and wide over the land. Who has not seen and deplored the vast and corrupting influence brought to bear upon the Legislatures to obtain charters and means necessary to participate in the profits of the institutions? This gives a control to the Government which grants such favors, of a most extensive and pernicious character; all of which must continue to spread and increase, if the connexion should continue, until the whole community must become one contaminated and corrupted mass.

There is another and a final reason which I shall assign against the reunion with the banks. We have reached a new era with regard to these institutions. He who would judge of the future by the past, in reference to them, will be wholly mistaken. The year 1833 marks the commencement of this era. That extraordinary man [Andrew Jackson], who had the power of imprinting his own feelings on the community, then commenced his hostile attacks, which have left such effects behind, that the war then commenced against the banks, I clearly see, will not terminate, unless there be a separation between them and the Government, until one or the other triumphs—till the Government becomes the bank, or the bank the Government. In resisting their union, I act as the friend of both. I have, as I have said, no unkind feeling toward the banks. I am neither a bank man, nor an antibank man. I have had little connexion with them. Many of my best friends, for whom I have the highest esteem, have a deep interest in their prosperity, and, as far as friendship or personal attachment extends, my inclination would be strongly in their favor. But I stand up here as the representative of no particular interest. I look to the whole, and to the future, as well as the present; and I shall steadily pursue that course which, under the most enlarged view, I believe to be my duty. In 1834 I saw the present crisis. I in vain raised a warning voice, and endeavored to avert it. I now see, with equal certainty, one far more portentous. If this struggle is to go on—if the banks will insist upon a reunion with the Government against the sense of a large and influential portion of the community—and, above all, if they should succeed in effecting it, a reflux flood will inevitably sweep away the whole system. A deep popular excitement is never without some reason, and ought ever to be treated with respect; and it is the part of wisdom to look timely into the cause, and correct it before the excitement shall become so great as to demolish the object, with all its good and evil, against which it is directed.

The only safe course for both Government and banks is to remain, as they are, separated—each in the use of their own credit, and in the management of their own affairs. The less the control and the influence of the one over the other, the better. Confined to their legitimate sphere—that of affording temporary credit to commercial and business men, bank-notes would furnish a safe and convenient circulation in the range of commerce and business within which the banks may be respectively situated, exempt almost entirely from those fluctuations and convulsions to which they are now so exposed; or, if they should occasionally be subject to them, the evil would be local and temporary, leaving undisturbed the action of the Government, and the general currency of the country, on the stability of which the prosperity and safety of the community so much depend.

I have now stated my objections to the reunion of the Government and the banks. If they are well founded; if the State banks are of themselves incompetent agents; if a Bank of the United States be impracticable, or, if practicable, would, at this time, be the destruction of a large portion of the existing banks, and of renewed and severe pecuniary distress; if it would be against the settled conviction of an old and powerful party, whose opposition time cannot abate; if the union of Government and banks add to the unfitness of their notes for circulation, and be unjust and unequal between citizen and citizen, and one portion of the Union and another; and, finally, if it would excite an implacable and obstinate war, which could only terminate in the overthrow of the banking system or the institutions of the country, it then remains that the only alternative would be permanently to separate the two, and to reorganize the Treasury so as to enable it to perform those duties which have heretofore been performed by the banks as its fiscal agents. This proposed reorganization has been called a sub-treasury—an unfortunate word, calculated to mislead and conjure up difficulties and dangers that do not really exist. So far from an experiment, or some new device, it is only returning to the old mode of collecting and disbursing public money, which, for thousands of years, has been the practice of all enlightened people till within the last century.

In what manner it is intended to reorganize the Treasury, by the bill [recently] reported ["imposing additional duties as depositories, in certain cases, on public officers,"] I do not know. I have been too much engaged to read it; and I can only say that, for one, I shall assent to no arrangement which provides for a Treasury bank, or that can be perverted into one. If there can be any scheme more fatal than a reunion with the banks at this time, it would be such a project. Nor will I give my assent to any arrangement which shall add the least unnecessary patronage. I am the sworn foe to patronage, and have done as much and suffered as much in resisting it as any one. Too many years have passed over me to change, at this late day, my course or principles. But I will say, that it is impossible so to organize the Treasury for the performance of its own functions as to give to the Executive a tenth part of the patronage it will lose by the proposed separation, which, when the bill for the reorganization comes up, I may have an opportunity to show. I have ventured this assertion after much reflection, and with entire confidence in its correctness.

But something more must be done besides the reorganization of the Treasury. Under the resolution of 1816, bank-notes would again be received in the dues of the Government, if the banks should resume specie payments. The legal as well as the actual connexion must be severed. But I am opposed to all harsh or precipitate measures. No great process can be effected without a shock, but through the agency of time. I accordingly propose to allow time for the final separation; and, with this view, I have drawn up an amendment to this bill, which I shall offer at the proper time, to modify the resolution of 1816, by providing that after the 1st of January next, three-fourths of all sums due to the Government may be received in the notes of specie-paying banks; and after the 1st of January next following, one-half; and after the 1st of January next subsequent, one-fourth; and after the 1st of January thereafter, nothing but the legal currency of the United States, or bills, notes, or paper issued under their authority, and which may by law be authorized to be received in their dues. If the time is not thought to be ample, I am perfectly disposed to extend it. The period is of little importance in my eyes, so that the object be effected.

In addition to this, it seems to me that some measure of a remedial character, connected with the currency, ought to be adopted, to ease off the pressure while the process is going through. It is desirable that the Government should make as few and small demands on the specie market as possible during the time, so as to throw no impediment in the way of the resumption of specie payments. With this view, I am of the impression that the sum necessary for the present wants of the Treasury should be raised by a paper, which should at the same time have the requisite qualities to enable it to perform the functions of a paper circulation. Under this impression, I object to the interest to be allowed on the Treasury notes which this bill authorizes to be issued, on the very opposite ground that the Senator from Massachusetts bestows his opposition [*sic*; approbation]. He approves of interest, because it would throw them out of circulation into the hands of capitalists, as a convenient and safe investment; and

I disapprove, because it will have that effect. I am disposed to ease off the process; he, I would suppose, is very little solicitous on that point.

But I go farther. I am of the impression, to make this great measure successful, and secure it against reaction, that some stable and safe medium of circulation, to take the place of bank-notes in the fiscal operations of the Government, ought to be issued. I intend to propose nothing. It would be impossible, with so great a weight of opposition, to pass any measure without the entire support of the administration; and, if it were possible, it ought not to be attempted where so much must depend on the mode of execution. The best measure that could be devised might fail, and impose a heavy responsibility on its author, unless it met with the hearty approbation of those who are to execute it. I, then, intend merely to throw out suggestions, in order to excite the reflection of others on a subject so delicate, and of so much importance—acting on the principle that it is the duty of all, in so great a juncture, to present their views without reserve.

It is, then, my impression, that, in the present condition of the world, a paper currency, in some form, if not necessary, is almost indispensable in financial and commercial operations of civilized and extensive communities. In many respects it has a vast superiority over a metallic currency, especially in great and extended transactions, by its greater cheapness, lightness, and the facility of determining the amount. The great desideratum is, to ascertain what description of paper has the requisite qualities of being free from fluctuation in value, and liability to abuse, in the greatest perfection. I have shown, I trust, that the bank-notes do not possess these requisites in a degree sufficiently high for this purpose. I go farther. It appears to me, after bestowing the best reflection I can give the subject, that no convertible paper—that is, no paper whose credit rests upon a promise to pay—is suitable for currency. It is the form of credit proper in private transactions between man and man, but not for a standard of value, to perform exchanges generally, which constitute the appropriate functions of money or currency. The measures of safety in the two cases are wholly different. A promissory note, or convertible paper, is considered safe so long as the drawer has ample means to meet his engagements; and, in passing from hand to hand, regard is had only to his ability and willingness to pay. Very different is the case in currency.

The aggregate value of the currency of a country necessarily bears a small proportion to the aggregate value of its property. This proportion is not well ascertained, and is probably subject to considerable variation in different countries, and at different periods in the same country. It may be assumed, conjecturally, in order to illustrate what I say, at one to thirty. Assuming this proportion to be correct, (which probably is not far from the truth,) it follows that, in a sound condition of the country, where the currency is metallic, the aggregate value of the coin is not more than one in thirty of the aggregate value of the property. It also follows, that an increase in the amount of the currency, by the addition of a paper circulation of no intrinsic value, but increases the nominal value of the aggregate property of the country in the same proportion that the increase bears to the whole amount of currency; so that, if the currency be doubled, the nominal value of the property will also be doubled. Hence it is, that, when the paper currency of a country is in the shape of promissory notes, there is a constant tendency to excess. We look for their safety to the ability of the drawer; and so long as his means are ample to meet his engagements, there is no distrust; without reflecting that, considered as currency, it cannot safely exceed one in thirty in value, compared to property; and the delusion is farther increased by the constant increase in value of property, with the increase of the notes in circulation, so as to maintain the same relative proportion. It follows that a Government may safely contract a debt many times the amount of its aggregate circulation; but, if it were to attempt to put its promissory notes in circulation in amount equal to its debts, an explosion in the currency would be inevitable. And hence, with other causes, the constant tendency to an excessive issue of bank-notes in prosperous times, when so large a portion of the community are anxious to obtain accommodation, and who are disappointed when negotiable paper is refused by the banks; not reflecting that it would not be safe to discount beyond the limits I have assigned for a safe circulation, however good the paper offered.

On what, then, ought a paper currency to rest? I would say on demand and supply simply, which regulates the value of every thing else—the constant demand which the Government has on the community for its necessary supplies. A medium resting on this demand, which simply obligates the Government to receive it in all of its dues, to the exclusion of every thing else except gold and silver, and which shall be optional with those who have demands on Government to receive or not, would, it seems to me, be as stable in its value as those metals themselves, and be as little liable to abuse as the power of coining. It would contain within itself a self-regulating power. It could only be issued to those who had claims on the Government, and to those only with their consent, and, of course, only at or above par with gold and silver, which would be its habitual state; for, so far as the Government was concerned, it would be equal in every respect, to gold and silver, and superior in many, particularly in regulating the distant exchanges of the country. Should, however, a demand for gold and silver from abroad, or other accidental causes, depress it temporarily, as compared with the precious metals, it would then return to the Treasury; and as it could not be paid out during such depression, its gradual diminution in the market would soon restore it to an equality, when it would again flow out into the general circulation. Thus there would be a constant alternate flux and reflux into and from the Treasury, between it and the precious metals; but, if at any time a permanent depression in its value be possible from any cause, the only effect would be to operate as a reduction of taxes on the community, and the only sufferer would be the Government itself. Against this its own interest would be a sufficient guaranty.

Nothing but experience can determine what amount and of what denominations might be safely issued; but it may be safely assumed that the country would absorb an amount greatly exceeding its annual income. Much of its exchanges, which amount to a vast sum, as well as its banking business, would revolve about it, and many millions would thus be kept in circulation beyond the demands of the Government. It may throw some light on this subject to state that North Carolina, just after the Revolution, issued a large amount of paper, which was made receivable in dues to her. It was also made a legal tender, but which, of course, was not obligatory after the adoption of the federal constitution. A large amount—say between four and five hundred thousand dollars—remained in circulation after that period, and continued to circulate for more than twenty years, at par with gold and silver during the whole time, with no other advantage than being received in the revenue of the State, which was much less than $100,000 per annum. I speak on the information of citizens of that State, on whom I can rely.

But, whatever may be the amount that can be circulated, I hold it clear that, to that amount, it would be as stable in value as gold and silver itself, provided the Government be bound to receive it exclusively with those metals in all its dues, and that it be left perfectly optional with those who have claims on the Government to receive it or not. It will also be a necessary condition that notes of too small a denomination should not be issued, so that the Treasury shall have ample means to meet all demands, either in gold or silver, or the bills of the Government, at the option of those who have claims on it. With these conditions, no further variation could take place between it and gold and silver than that which would be caused by the action of commerce. An unusual demand from abroad for the metals would, of course, raise them a little in their relative value, and depress relatively the Government bills in the same proportion, which would cause them to flow into the Treasury, and gold and silver to flow out; while, on the contrary, an increased demand for the bills in the domestic exchange would have the reverse effect, causing, as I have stated, an alternate flux and reflux into the Treasury, between the two, which would at all times keep their relative values either at or near par.

No one can doubt that the fact of the Government receiving and paying away bank-notes in all its fiscal transactions is one of the principal sources of their great circulation; and it was mainly on that account that the notes of the late Bank of the United States so freely circulated all over the Union. I would ask, then, why should the Government mingle its credit with that of private corporations? No one can doubt but that the Government credit is better than that of any bank—more stable and more safe. Why, then, should it mix it up with the less perfect credit of those institutions? Why not use its own credit to the amount of its own transactions? Why should it not be safe in its own hands, while it shall be considered safe in the hands of 800 private institutions scattered all over the country, and which have no other object but their own private profits, to increase which they almost constantly extend their business to the most dangerous extremes? And why should the community be compelled to give six per cent. discount for the Government credit blended with that of the banks, when the superior credit of the Government could be furnished separately, without discount, to the mutual advantage of the Government and the community? Why, let me ask, should the Government be exposed to such difficulties as the present, by mingling its credit with the banks, when it could be exempt from all such, by using by itself its own safe credit? It is time the community, which has so deep an interest in a sound and cheap currency, and the equality of the laws between one portion of the citizens of the country and another, should reflect seriously on these things—not for the purpose of oppressing any interest, but to correct gradually disorders of a dangerous character, which have insensibly, in the long course of years, without being perceived by any one, crept into the state.

The question is, not between credit and no credit, as some would have us believe; but in what form credit can best perform the functions of a sound and safe currency. On this important point I have freely thrown out my ideas, leaving it to this body and the public to determine what they are worth. Believing that there might be a sound and safe paper currency founded on the credit of Government exclusively, I was desirous that those who are responsible and have the power should have availed themselves of the opportunity of a temporary deficit of the Treasury, and the postponement of the fourth instalment intended to be deposited with the States, to use them as the means of affording a circulation for the present relief of the country and the banks, during the process of separating them from Government; and, if experience should justify it, of furnishing a permanent and safe circulation, which would greatly facilitate the operations of the Treasury, and afford, incidentally, much facility to the commercial operations of the country. But a different direction was given; and when the alternative was presented, of a loan, or the withholding of the fourth instalment from the States, I did not hesitate to give a decided vote for withholding it. My aversion to a public debt is deep and durable. It is, in my opinion, pernicious, and is little short of a fraud on the public. I saw too much of it during the late war [of 1812] not to understand something of the nature and character of public loans. Never was a country more egregiously imposed on.

Having now presented my views of the course and the measures which the permanent policy of the country, looking to its liberty and lasting prosperity, requires, I come finally to the question of relief. I have placed this last—not that I am devoid of sympathy for the country in the pecuniary distress which now pervades it. No one struggled earlier or longer to prevent it than myself; nor can any one more sensibly feel the widespread blight which has suddenly blasted the hopes of so many, and precipitated thousands from affluence to poverty. The desolation has fallen mainly on the mercantile class—a class which I have ever held in the highest estimation. No country ever had a superior body of merchants—of higher honor, of more daring enterprise, or of greater skill and energy. The ruin of such a class is a heavy calamity, and I am solicitous, among other things, to give such stability to our currency as to prevent the recurrence of a similar calamity hereafter. But it was first necessary, in the order of things, that we should determine what sound policy, looking to the future, demands to be done at the present juncture, before we consider the question of relief, which, urgent as it may be, is subordinate, and must yield to the former. The patient lies under a dangerous disease, with a burning thirst and other symptoms, which distress him more than the vital organs which are attacked. The skilful physician first makes himself master of the nature of the disease, and then determines on the treatment necessary for the restoration of health. This done, he next alleviates the distressing symptoms as far as is consistent with the restoration of health, and no further. Such shall be my course. As far as I possibly can, consistently with the views I entertain, and what I believe to be necessary to restore the body politic to health, I will do every thing in my power to mitigate the present distress. Further I cannot go.

After the best reflection, I am of the opinion that the Government can do but little in the way of relief, and that it is a case which must be mainly left to the constitution of the patient, who, thank God, is young, vigorous, and robust, with a constitution sufficient to sustain and overcome the severest attack. I dread the doctor and his drugs much more than the disease itself. The distress of the country consists in its indebtedness, and can only be relieved by the payment of its debts. To effect this, industry, frugality, economy, and time, are necessary. I rely more on the growing crop—on the cotton, rice, and tobacco, of the South—than on all the projects or devices of politicians. I am utterly opposed to all coercion by this Government. But Government may do something to relieve the distress. It is out of debt, and is one of the principal creditors both of the banks and of the merchants, and should set an example of liberal indulgence. This I am willing to give freely. I am also prepared to vote freely the use of Government credit in some safe form, to supply any deficit in the circulation during the process of recovery, as far as its financial wants will permit. I see not what more can be safely done. But my vision may be obtuse upon this subject. Those who differ from me, and who profess so much sympathy for the public, seem to think that much relief may be afforded. I hope they will present their views. I am anxious to hear their prescriptions; and I assure them, that whatever they may propose, if it shall promise relief, and be not inconsistent with the course which I deem absolutely necessary for the restoration of the country to perfect health, shall cheerfully receive my support. They may be more keen-sighted than I am as to the best means of relief, but cannot have a stronger disposition to afford it.

We have, Mr. President, arrived at a remarkable era in our political history. The days of legislative and executive encroachments, of tariffs and surpluses, of bank and public debt, and extravagant expenditure, are past for the present. The Government stands in a position disentangled from the past, and freer to choose its future course than it ever has been since its commencement. We are about to take a fresh start. I move off under the State rights banner, and go in the direction in which I have been so long moving. I seize the opportunity thoroughly to reform the Government; to bring it back to its original principles; to retrench and economize, and rigidly to enforce accountability. I shall oppose strenuously all attempts to originate a new debt; to create a national bank; to reunite the political and money power—more dangerous than that of church and state—in any form or shape; to prevent the disturbances of the compromise, which is gradually removing the last vestige of the tariff system; and, mainly, I shall use my best efforts to give an ascendency to the great conservative principle of State sovereignty, over the dangerous and despotic doctrine of consolidation. I rejoice to think that the Executive department of the Government is now so reduced in power and means, that it can no longer rely on its influence and patronage to secure a majority. Henceforward it can have no hope of supporting itself but on wisdom, moderation, patriotism, and devoted attachment to the constitution, which I trust will make it, in its own defence, an ally in effecting the reform which I deem indispensable to the salvation of the country and its institutions.

I look, sir, with pride to the wise and noble bearing of the little State-rights party, of which it is my pride to be a member, throughout the eventful period through which the country has passed since 1824. Experience already bears testimony to their patriotism, firmness, and sagacity; and history will do it justice. In that year, as I have stated, the tariff system triumphed in the councils of the nation. We saw its disastrous political bearings; foresaw its surpluses and the extravagances to which it would lead. We rallied on the election of the late President [Jackson] to arrest it, through the influence of the Executive department of the Government. In this we failed. We then fell back on the rights and sovereignty of the States, and by the action of a small but gallant State, and through the potency of its interposition, we brought the system to the ground, sustained as it was by the opposition and the administration, and by the whole power and patronage of the Government. The pernicious overflow of the Treasury, of which it was the parent, could not be arrested at once. The surplus was seized on by the Executive, and, by its control over the banks, became the fruitful source of Executive influence and encroachment. Without hesitation, we joined our old opponents on the tariff question, but under our own flag, and without merging in their ranks, and made a gallant and successful war against the encroachments of the Executive. That terminated, we part with our late allies in peace; and move forward, lag, or onward who may, to secure the fruits of our long but successful struggle, under the old republican flag of 1798, which, though tattered and torn, has never yet been lowered, and, with the blessing of God, never shall be with my consent.

From *Register of Debates*, 25th Cong., 1st Sess., cols. 50–66. Also printed in the Baltimore, Md., *Merchant*-Washington, D.C., *Reformer*, September 27, 1837, p. 2; the Washington, D.C., *Daily National Intelligencer*, September 29, 1837, pp. 1–2; the Washington, D.C., *Globe*, October 2, 1837, p. 3, and November 11, 1839, p. 2; the Charleston, S.C., *Mercury*, October 2, 1837, p. 2; the Augusta, Ga., *Chronicle and Sentinel*, October 6 and 9, 1837; *Niles' National Register*, vol. LIII, no. 6 (October 7, 1837), pp. 83–87; the Edgefield, S.C., *Advertiser*, October 12 and 19, 1837; the Columbia, S.C., *Southern Times and State Gazette*, October 13, 1837, pp. 1–3; the Pendleton, S.C., *Messenger*, October 13, 20, and 27, 1837; *Congressional Globe*, 25th Cong., 1st Sess., Appendix, pp. 32–37; *Remarks of Mr. Calhoun, on the Bill Authorizing an Issue of Treasury Notes. Delivered in the Senate of the United States, September 19 [sic], 1837* (Washington: Blair and Rives, 1837), published in two different editions with nearly identical title pages, one of 12 and one of 16 pages; *Remarks of Mr. Calhoun, in the Senate of the United States, on the Bill Authorizing an Issue of Treasury Notes, on the 19th September, 1837* (No place: no publisher, no date); *Speeches of John C. Calhoun*, pp. 259–275; Crallé, ed., *Works*, 3:60–92. Variant in the Baltimore, Md., *Merchant*-Washington, D.C., *Reformer*, September 19, 1837, p. 2. Another variant in the Washington, D.C., *Globe*, September 18, 1837, p. 3; *Congressional Globe*, 25th Cong., 1st Sess., pp. 36–37. Still another variant in the Washington, D.C., *Madisonian*, September 19, 1837, p. 3, and the New York, N.Y., *Morning Courier and New-York Enquirer*, September 20, 1837, p. 2. Partially printed in *De Bow's Review*, vol. XXXI, nos. 4 and 5 (October and November, 1861), pp. 437–438. NOTE: Many of the later printings of this speech erroneously dated it as having been delivered on 9/19. When Calhoun had concluded, Thomas H. Benton rose and said he agreed with the object of Calhoun's proposal and offered some amendments of his own for the same purpose. It was not until 9/20 that Calhoun actually introduced in the Senate his proposal, and when he did so it was as an amendment to S-6, "a bill imposing additional duties, as depositories in certain cases, on public officers," and not to the bill (S-2) authorizing an issue of Treasury notes. During the debate that followed his speech of 9/18 on the Treasury note bill, Calhoun spoke briefly three more times. He rose during a speech by Robert J. Walker "to move that the bill be so amended as to prevent the allowance of interest on the notes to be issued by the Treasury; but yielded the floor to Mr. Walker, who said he had all along intended to offer a similar amendment, and would now (by leave of Mr. C[alhoun]) do so." Later Calhoun "said he thought it not a desirable thing that these notes should be equal to gold and silver." Still later, when John P. King argued that the public creditors could not be induced to take the Treasury notes unless they bore interest, Calhoun remarked, "If the banks resume, these notes will be equal to gold and silver." *Register of Debates,* 25th Cong., 1st Sess., cols. 72–73, 75.

From "Roscoe," published at Charleston, 9/18–22. In four public letters addressed to Calhoun, the pseudonymous "Roscoe" questions the fiscal policies of the Van Buren administration. He opposes the sub-treasury system and specie payments and tells Calhoun, "you suppose that the sub-treasury system is to operate an emancipation of the South from its commercial vassalage to the North. Depend on it, this is sheer fallacy. Our commercial dependence on the North depends on the laws of trade, and certain physical and moral causes on which the Government Deposites would have no more effect than the feeble current which the Tiber pours into the Potomac would have on the entire volume of the Ocean." "Roscoe" proposes as a remedy to the financial crisis the incorporation of a new Bank of the U.S. and a Constitutional amendment preventing States from excessive issuance of paper money. PC's in the Charleston, S.C., *Mercury,* September 18, 20, 21, and 22, 1837.

AMENDMENT TO THE BILL IMPOSING ADDITIONAL DUTIES AS DEPOSITORIES ON CERTAIN PUBLIC OFFICERS (Subtreasury Bill)

[In the Senate, September 20, 1837]
[*On 9/14 the Committee on Finance had reported a bill of nine sections evidently designed to separate the government's collections and disbursements from banks, which had suspended specie payments. The bill, soon referred to as the "subtreasury" proposal, outlined ways in which the Treasurer of the U.S., officers of the U.S. Mint, Collectors of Customs, Receivers of Public Moneys, and Postmasters would keep and transfer public funds. On 9/20 this bill came up in Committee of the Whole.*]

Mr. Calhoun rose, and moved the amendment of which he had given notice on Monday [9/18] he should offer to this bill [an amendment which would modify a joint Congressional resolution of 1816 permitting the receipt of government dues in the notes of specie-paying banks]; which having been stated to the Senate, it was, at the instance of Mr. [Silas] Wright, with the consent of Mr. Calhoun, modified to read as follows, the passages enclosed in [ ] being those added by Mr. W[right].

Sec. — *And be it further enacted,* That from and after the first day of January, eighteen hundred and thirty-eight, three-fourths of the amount due to the Government for duties, taxes, sales of public lands, or other debts, may be received in the notes of specie-paying banks; and that from and after the first day of January, eighteen hundred and thirty-nine, one-half may be so received; and from and after the first day of January, eighteen hundred and forty, one-fourth; and from and after the first day of January, eighteen hundred and forty-one, all sums due for duties, sales of public lands, or other debts to the Government, [and all payments to the General Post Office Department, shall be paid in gold and silver coin only,] or in such notes, bills, or papers issued under the authority of the United States, as may be directed to be received by law; [and from and after the first day of January, eighteen hundred and forty-one, all officers or agents engaged in the making disbursements for the United States or General Post Office Department, shall make all payments in gold and silver only, or in such notes or papers as shall be authorized by law; and any receiving or disbursing officer neglecting so to do, shall be dismissed from his office, and forfeit all compensation which shall then be due.]

PC in *Register of Debates,* 25th Cong., 1st Sess., col. 105; drafts in DNA, RG 46 (Records of the U.S. Senate), 25A-B1 and 25A-B2; variant PC in DLC, Congressional Bills, 25th Cong., 1st Sess., S-6, amendments. NOTE: Calhoun's amendment received extended consideration by the Senate and underwent some modification before it was approved. For instance, changes suggested by Thomas Morris on 9/26 and 9/27 and by Henry Hubbard on 9/27 were incorporated with Calhoun's consent during Committee of the Whole deliberations. Calhoun's proposal, as modified, was incorporated into the bill on 10/3 by a vote of 24 to 23. Further modified, it became Section 10 of the bill which was passed by the Senate on 10/4 by a vote of 26 to 21. The text of the bill and section as passed can be found in *Congressional Globe,* 25th Cong., 1st Sess., pp. 96–97. The bill did not come to a vote in the House of Representatives. The revisions in Calhoun's proposal included changing the date for beginning the specie requirement from 1/1/1838 to 12/1/1838; providing that the notes of banks that did not accept "in payment and deposite, at par with gold and silver, such Treasury notes, or bills, as Congress shall authorize to be received by law, in the public dues," should not be received; and providing that no bank note of denomination less than ten dollars or which was not payable at the time issued would be received. There is considerable error and confusion in the published accounts of the history of this amendment. For instance, the *Register of Debates* for 9/26, 25th Cong., 1st Sess., col. 283, gives a text of a proposal by Morris that it erroneously states to have been substituted for Calhoun's.

REMARKS ON THE SUBTREASURY BILL

[In the Senate, September 22, 1837]
Mr. Calhoun rose and made some observations in relation to the two measures now before the Senate. He contended that it would have to choose between them. If he understood the plan of the Senator from Virginia, (Mr. [William C.] Rives) [in his bill introduced on 9/19 "to designate the funds receivable in payment of the revenues of the Government"] he said, there appeared to him to be an insuperable objection to its adoption. He proposed to receive the notes of all banks in discharge of the public dues, provided they shall resume specie payments by a given day in the year 1838; and all those banks which shall not resume by that period, shall be excluded. Now, a most serious question was presented for the decision of this body. We were, by this proposition, about to make a compact with the banks. It was an offer, an inducement held out, to them to comply with a certain requisition; and, if they should accept it, it would constitute an unlimited compact between them and the Government. The effect of the proposition was, to endorse the credit of the Government for ever upon the notes of such banks as resumed specie payments by a certain time. He would ask the gentleman from Virginia, himself, whether he was willing to enter into such a compact. It could not be misconstrued. We were dealing with corporations, some of which were great and powerful, and we must be on our guard. What was the argument advanced here only the other day? Why, that the deposite act constituted a compact between us and the banks. He however, did not think so. But, even if it were, then how irresistible was the conclusion that the bill involved a perpetual compact with the banks. A consideration must be given in order to make a compact; and in this instance, a great sacrifice would have to be made. The Government was now holding it out; and when once made, honor, justice, every thing, demanded that it should be faithfully and religiously complied with on our part. Mr. C[alhoun] proceeded to argue that the benefit of this compact would be enjoyed only by the large banks, which would combine together to obtain the prize held out to them, and to put down the little banks. In fact, the bill of the honorable Senator was, in effect, nothing more nor less than an offer to the Pennsylvania Bank of the United States to come forward and fulfil the condition. Now, that bank had the means of doing it, and this would be an inducement to it. In order to comply with the offer, it would be worth while for that institution to make a great sacrifice; ay[e], a

sacrifice of millions! It has strong and powerful connections, not only in this country, but in Europe also, who would rally to its aid, and enable it to accomplish its objects; to resume specie payments, and to put down feebler institutions. Supposing that the bank should comply with the offer made by this bill, what would be our condition? Why, in my opinion, it would be the worst that could possibly be imagined. We should then have a bank of the United States, in the most objectionable form—in a local form, and combined with other banks. He would regard such a consequence as going far to destroy the liberties of the country, and it would create great discontent and heart-burnings among the people. It seemed to him impossible that gentlemen would prefer the Senator's proposition to his.

He was averse to using coercion towards the banks, to compel them to resume specie payments; for the consequence would be, to produce difficulties as great as those which had already taken place. The resumption of specie payments must be the work of time, and after the payment of our debts.

Mr. C[alhoun] replied to the objections urged by Mr. Rives to his proposition, in reference to its having the effect of creating two currencies; one of paper and the other of specie. He then asked what sort of a currency we had now? Was not the whole country flooded with currencies of all kinds; with shin-plasters of all sorts, sizes, and shapes? Nothing could possibly be worse. He said that the proposition of the Senator from Virginia involved a departure from the principles that gentleman contended for, and argued as being lost sight of in his (Mr. C[alhoun]'s) own proposition. The principle of equality was not observed in it; and the consequence would follow that the people would be compelled to receive one description of notes, and the Government another. The large notes were for the rich, and the small notes for the poor. Mr. C[alhoun] adverted to his own scheme, and added that he entertained very great doubt whether the Government could receive in the payment of its dues any thing but gold and silver, and notes issued on its own credit. He remarked that he had no confidence in the scheme of the Senator from Virginia, because he regarded it as inefficient. He concluded by answering some of the objections urged against the Sub-Treasury scheme. He maintained that the notes which would be issued would not produce any thing like the evils arising from the existence of so much paper as was now afloat, issued by an immense number of banks.

[*Rives spoke. In defending his proposal he argued that if his bill was a compact with the banks, so was the joint resolution of 1816 permitting the receipt of the notes of specie paying banks by the government. Calhoun asked for the reading of that resolution.*]

Mr. Calhoun explained what was the state of things existing when the Bank of the United States was chartered in 1816, and contended that Congress was perfectly independent of the State banks, and that there was no reason for holding out any inducement to them to resume specie payments. His colleague [William C. Preston] had stated the other day that he considered there was a compact between the States and the General Government, and that it was imperative on us to pay the fourth instalment of deposite to the States. Now, he (Mr. Calhoun) differed in opinion from his friend. Notwithstanding that the gentleman from Virginia, (Mr. Rives,) did not intend to favor the bank by his proposition, he (Mr. C[alhoun]) thought that such was its tendency. Whatever might be the impression of the Senator as to this being a compact, he (Mr. C[alhoun]) felt assured that the legal advisers of the bank would consider it a compact, and would establish that fact in the Supreme Court of the United States.

Mr. Rives here made some remark (not heard by the reporter) which Mr. Calhoun answered by saying that the immediate [and main] object of the resolution of 1816 was not to compel the [State] banks to resume specie payments.

[*Rives spoke again, denying Calhoun's suggestion that banks and particularly the Pennsylvania Bank of the United States would avail itself of the provisions in Rives's bill.*]

Mr. Calhoun said that the Bank of the United States held, at this time, a most remarkable attitude. He spoke of Mr. [Nicholas] Biddle as being a very able financier; as distinguished for talent and ability, in that respect, as any other in this country, or in Europe. Mr. C[alhoun] concurred with the Senator from Virginia, that the bank was not at present disposed to resume specie payments; and the reason was on account of its strength, having more credit than any other, and being capable of turning these times to advantage. Mr. Biddle knew what he was about. Pass the bill of the gentleman from Virginia, and we would very soon see Mr. Biddle change his policy. He would be glad to see that bill become a law, for it would go to increase his power immensely. Mr. Biddle's solicitude was lest a separation should be made of the Government from the banks. He knew full well that a Bank of the United States was now out of the question. Until a separation of the Government from the banks took place, the whole game would be in his hands. But while Mr.

Biddle (concluded Mr. C[alhoun]) struggles with great determination and fidelity for the stockholders of the bank, I am determined to struggle with no less zeal against that institution; for I believe the interests of the people are antagonistical to its existence; and I will resist the introduction of his bank in any form, as much so as I would resist the creation of a bank by the Government itself. I will do my duty, unguided by party attachment. I shall act as a Senator of South Carolina upon this important occasion, looking to the welfare and interests of my own State, and to the whole Union.

From *Congressional Globe*, 25th Cong., 1st Sess., pp. 54–55. Also printed in the Washington, D.C., *Globe*, September 23, 1837, p. 2; the Charleston, S.C., *Mercury*, October 6, 1837, p. 2. Variant in the Washington, D.C., *Daily National Intelligencer*, October 3, 1837, p. 2; the Baltimore, Md., *Merchant*-Washington, D.C., *Reformer*, October 5, 1837, p. 2; *Register of Debates*, 25th Cong., 1st Sess., cols. 184–188. Another variant in the Washington, D.C., *Madisonian*, September 23, 1837, p. 2, and the New York, N.Y., *Morning Courier and New-York Enquirer*, September 25, 1837, p. 2. NOTE: In the first variant report cited above Calhoun was reported as saying of Biddle that he "respected the man, for he knew he had done his duty well, and with great fidelity on behalf of the two institutions over which he had presided. He was worthy of the high destinies which he had attained; but Mr. C[alhoun] would resist him now more than if he were certain there would be a new Bank of the United States. . . ."

Memorial from citizens of Mobile, Ala., presented by Calhoun to the Senate on 9/23. More than 800 signers request Congress to charter a specie-paying national bank. DS in DNA, RG 46 (Records of the U.S. Senate), 25A-H2; PC in Senate Document No. 22, 25th Cong., 1st Sess.

REMARKS ON A MOTION TO
POSTPONE THE SUBTREASURY BILL

[In the Senate, September 23, 1837]
Mr. Calhoun rose and said that he greatly regretted that the Senator from Georgia [John P. King] had thought proper to make the motion to postpone the bill [to the next session of Congress]. Its effect, should the motion succeed, would be highly injurious to the country generally, and especially to the South. It was conceded that there was a vast amount of capital locked up, waiting the decision of Congress on this highly important subject; not less, probably,

than from sixty to one hundred millions; which would flow into the business channels of the country as soon as the decision was made. This, he would remind the Senator, was the commencement of the business season for the great staples of the South. The cotton and rice would soon be prepared for market, and the tobacco would follow them. The entire machine of commerce, by which these great products were to be exchanged with the world, is deranged, he might say broke, and would not be reconstructed until it is ascertained what was to be done here. If the question is postponed till the regular session, there will be no final action till the spring; during all of which time, comprehending the almost entire business season, things would remain in their present uncertain and deranged condition. The consequences would be a very heavy loss to the planting interest of the South, not to mention other portions; a loss, he would venture to say, of many millions to the planters alone; which would be of vast detriment to that great interest, embarrassed as it now is by heavy debts. After full reflection, he did not think the loss on the coming crop of cotton alone, from delay of action here, would be less than one or two cents the pound, and more than a million and a half on the whole crop. But there was another reason, to his mind, still more powerful against the postponement. We are on the eve of a great revolution in regard to the currency. The first step in that revolution is the separation of the Government and the banks, which he sincerely believed the good of both required. That once made, and each left to move in its own proper sphere, unembarrassed by the other, the change in the credit system, which he held to be inevitable, would, in all probability, be gradual, and without a shock, or injury to any of the great interests of the community. But, if the question of separation be left open; if it is to run into the politics of the country, and be made an engine to act on the presidential election, there is no answering for consequences. A direct issue will be made; and, when passions were roused, there would ensue a conflict between the Government and the banks, which may become violent and convulsive, and shake our system to the centre. For these reasons he deemed it highly desirable, on all sides, that the motion to postpone should not succeed.

The Senator [King] made a remark which had a personal bearing, which he (Mr. C[alhoun]) could not pass unnoticed. He expressed great abhorrence at the declaration that he (Mr. C[alhoun]) would not (if there were not other and powerful reasons against it) agree to employ Mr. [Nicholas] Biddle's bank as our fiscal agent, because it would give that institution a triumph over the Government, and go far to make it the Government itself.

There was (said Mr. C[alhoun]) no disputing about taste. We were so dissimilarly constituted, that what was sweet to one was sometimes bitter to another. But he was inclined to think that in this case the difference did not result so much from any organic dissimilarity between him and the Senator, as from the different aspect under which they regard the controversy between General Jackson and the bank. The Senator regards it, as is manifest from the whole tenor of his remarks, as a mere personal affair between General Jackson and the president of the bank; or, at best, between the Executive branch of the Government and the bank; in which, let which side prevail that might, it would be but the triumph of one individual over another, or of the bank over the Executive, or the reverse. Thus regarding it, he was not at all astonished that the Senator should indulge himself in the strong expression that he did; but he must say, that he was not a little astonished that the Senator, knowing him and his past course, as he did, could for a moment suppose that he (Mr. C[alhoun]) regarded it under that aspect. When did he ever utter a sentiment, or do an act, which could by possibility give countenance to the attributing such a sentiment to him, as to consider General Jackson, or the whole House, or the Executive department, as the Government? He would suppose that he was the last man to whom such a sentiment could be attributed. In making the declaration he did, he viewed the subject far more comprehensively. He regarded the controversy under all its circumstances, and looked to results as testing the relative strength of the Government and the banks. He saw the most popular and powerful President that ever filled the chair of State, with boundless patronage, and sustained by a well-formed and compact majority in the Union, and both Houses, (of which the Senator was one,) waging war against the bank, and striving, with all his energy and power, to put it down. Whether right or wrong, (wrong he believed him to be, and still believed,) he was backed by the entire power of the Government, and a great majority of the people. Now, sir, I ask if, after all this, that bank should prove to be so indispensable to the Government as to force itself on it, notwithstanding all these powerful opposing obstacles, greater than can ever again be arrayed against any similar institution, would it not prove that the bank had become stronger than both Government and people? And would it not go far, as he confessed himself, to make the bank the Government? It was under this aspect that he obviously regarded the struggle; and he must say, that, if the Senator, looking on it in the same light, did not regard it with similar sentiments, he could neither envy him his feelings nor his patriotism.

From *Register of Debates,* 25th Cong., 1st Sess., cols. 243–244. Also printed in the Washington, D.C., *Daily National Intelligencer,* October 17, 1837, p. 2; the Charleston, S.C., *Mercury,* November 1, 1837, p. 2; the Washington, D.C., *Globe,* November 2, 1837, p. 3; *Congressional Globe,* 25th Cong., 1st Sess., Appendix, pp. 195–196; Crallé, ed., *Works,* 3:93–96. Variant in the Washington, D.C., *Globe,* September 25, 1837, pp. 2–3; *Congressional Globe,* 25th Cong., 1st Sess., p. 62. NOTE: The Senate adjourned without voting on King's motion. It came to a vote on 9/25 and was defeated 19 to 27.

REMARKS IN REPLY TO WILLIAM C. RIVES ON THE SUBTREASURY BILL

[In the Senate, September 23, 1837]
[*As debate progressed, William C. Rives of Va. rose to reply to several critics of his bill to designate the funds receivable in payment to the government. These critics included Thomas H. Benton and Calhoun.*]

Mr. Calhoun said this attack of the Senator is very extraordinary. Yesterday, in the course of my argument, I endeavored to show that his proposition would inure to the benefit of the Pennsylvania Bank of the United States, and I stated my reasons. I believed he did not contemplate it in that light, but I did; and I said to the Senator, you hold out a powerful temptation to the banks. I stated that the strong banks, and they alone, would take the benefit of this measure, with the United States Bank at their head. Their predominating influence over every other bank was inevitable; and if they got it, they would hold it in *perpetuo.* They would make the necessary sacrifice in the resumption of specie payments, and this bill would serve as the motive; and, if Mr. [Nicholas] Biddle tried, he would get it. And now, twenty-four hours afterwards, I am surprised at the storm of passion and personal attack, when I acquitted the gentleman of all improper intentions.

The gentleman says that in 1834 I was in favor of restoring the deposites. I was so; and I now, as then, think they were unnecessarily and illegally removed, and that it was one of the accelerating

580

causes of the catastrophe which he so much laments. New zeal! A new convert! I never made stronger declarations in my life of the banking system than at that time. I said the whole system was hostile to liberty. I was then in favor of the Bank of the United States; but not so as to qualify my position relative to banking. I went farther, and told the Senator and others, your system will fail if you retain a connexion with the banks; there must be a Bank of the United States. With me the question of bank or no bank had reference to the whole banking system. Has he any foundation on which he can now call me a convert? No, sir, I have seen, not for four, but fourteen years, that the issue must be that the banks will be the Government, or the Government the banks; that, by the constant tendency to increase the issues of paper, the banks or the Government must be prostrated. I hardly expected to see that issue in my day; but come I knew and declared it would, sooner or later; and when the question should arise, it would be the greatest of modern times. I would lay a hundred to one, if the Senator's bill should pass, the United States Bank will monopolize its benefits. Of his remarks I will only say that they were unworthy of him, and of the State from which he comes.

From *Register of Debates*, 25th Cong., 1st Sess., col. 250. Also printed in the Washington, D.C., *Daily National Intelligencer*, October 3, 1837, p. 2. Variant in *Congressional Globe*, 25th Cong., 1st Sess., pp. 62–63.

REMARKS ON HIS COURSE IN REGARD TO THE
PETITIONS FOR A NATIONAL BANK

[In the Senate, September 26, 1837]
[*Silas Wright, Chairman of the Committee on Finance, to which had been referred numerous petitions praying for the establishment of a national bank, moved "That the prayer of the respective petitions ought not to be granted." Henry Clay, Daniel Webster, and William C. Preston of S.C. asked for further consideration of the question. Clay moved a substitute report, "That it will be expedient to establish a Bank of the United States whenever it shall be manifest that a clear majority of the people of the United States desire such an institution." Nathaniel P. Tallmadge of N.Y. moved a substitute for Clay's motion, "That in the opinion of the Senate a clear majority of the people of the United States are opposed to a national bank, and that it is inexpedient to grant the prayer of the petitioners."*]

Mr. Calhoun said that the course which he intended to pursue was, first to vote against the amendment to the amendment, and, if that succeeded, to vote against the amendment itself, so as to bring the question nakedly on the report of the Committee on Finance, that the prayer of the petitioners ought not to be granted. He was not prepared to say what the opinion of the people of the United States is at this time in relation to a bank; and much less was he prepared to commit himself in favor of one in contingencies contemplated by the amendment to the amendment. Where the Constitution or important principles are involved, his only guide was his judgment and his conscience, and not the popular voice.

If there was any trick or management in bringing forward the report, to entrap any Senator who may not have made up his opinion definitively as to the necessity of a bank, as my colleague [Preston] supposes, he was wholly ignorant of it. He did not know that the Committee on Finance had reported until this morning, nor that it was intended to take up the report, till a short time before it was called up; but he did not doubt the propriety of taking the sense of the Senate upon the subject of the bank. The memorialists had petitioned to establish a national bank, and it was due to them, as well as to the country at large, that there should be an explicit declaration of the sense of the Senate on the subject. He considered it, in fact, among the measures of relief, that the sense of Congress should be fully known as to what ought and what ought not to be done; there is a vast amount of capital now locked up awaiting our decision, which would flow out, as soon as it was known, to stimulate business, and relieve the money pressure, at this important season, when the fall trade is about to commence.

Mr. C[alhoun] then said that his colleague [Preston] had made some remarks which he could not pass unnoticed. He understood him to say that to assent to any important part of the [President's] Message was to support the whole, and that it was, in fact, to become a partisan of the administration.

(Here Mr. Preston dissented, and stated that what he did say was, that *according to his impression,* the support of the leading measure of the administration *seemed to him,* as necessarily involving an entire support of the administration.)

Mr. C[alhoun] resumed, that he was gratified to receive the explanation of his colleague; and that he now understood him as merely stating his impression of what ought to be the effects of supporting any of the prominent measures recommended in the Message. He must say that his (Mr. C[alhoun]'s) impression[s] were wholly different. No one knew better than his colleague, that he never acted but in relation to an object, and that object usually one somewhat remote; and that he advanced towards it with a steady step, regardless of the difficulties and the party combinations about him. He was master of his own move, and acknowledged connections with no party but the State rights party and the small band of nullifiers; and acted either with or against the administration or the national party, just as it was calculated to further the principles and policy which we of that party regarded [as] essential to the liberty and institutions of the country. It was thus he acted in the present instance. He knew his latitude and longitude; he had not neglected his log-book, and had kept an exact reckoning, and knew the precise point where he was, and in what direction he was moving. The object for which he and those with whom he had acted had united with the nationals had been *accomplished*. Executive usurpation had been arrested. The Treasury was empty, and the administration had scarcely a majority in either House, or the Union. But the event which had separated us and the nationals, had at the same time put an end to the *Jackson party—they had run out*. That remarkable man had formed a personal party, held together by his great influence, and the immense patronage placed in his hands. He was off the stage now, and the gorged Treasury had been turned into empty boxes. The cohesive principle of his party was destroyed, and it had dissolved into its elements. It had no option but to reunite on the old principles which brought it into power, and fall back on the ground where it stood in 1827, and where he and his friends had continued to stand all along. It was that or utter destruction. In the meantime, the Government itself had been brought back by a series of decisive moves, almost to where it stood at its commencement in 1798 [*sic*; 1789]; no bank, no tariff, nor almost any of those measures to which they were the fruitful parent. This was the point we had reached: Executive encroachments arrested from its [*sic*] own weakness, and Legislative encroachments by the overthrow of the system which it had builded up in a long course of years. Could he, a member of the State Rights party, hesitate what course he should pursue in so remarkable a juncture? It was as clear as the noonday sun. We are the sworn enemy both of Executive and Legislative usurpation; and of the two, more opposed, if possible, to the latter than the former; because, in the nature of things, it must take precedence in the order of time. Without the Legislative, there could be no Executive usurpation. Congress must first encroach on the powers of the State, before the Executive can be strong enough to encroach on its powers; but as soon as they do, the benefit enures, not to them, but the President. Reason and experience both prove this. Now, sir, while the national party have shown themselves the foes of Executive encroachments, they have been, and he feared were still, the advocates of a liberal construction of the Constitution—the supporters of delegated against reserved powers. To it, then, may be traced most of those acts which have gone so far to convert this into a consolidated Government, and to which they still cling. On the contrary, a very large portion of the Jackson party, then drawn off from their principles, by his extraordinary influence and power, still professed, and, I doubt not, sincerely, the opposite principle, notwithstanding their frequent, and, he must say, great departure from their practice in many particulars. Now, he would ask, what course ought he to pursue under such circumstances? He, the opponent of all encroachments, from whatever quarter, Executive or Legislative? Was it for him to join the friends of the tariff, of a national bank, and the whole system of congressional usurpation, and utterly break down his old allies of 1827, who had sheltered under his position, and thus give a complete and final victory to his old opponents of that period, and with it a permanent ascendancy to them and their principles and policy, which he honestly believed could not but end in consolidation, with the loss of our liberty and institutions? Or rather was it not his duty, thinking as he did, and with the objects he had been long pursuing, to prevent such a result, and to call a rally of his old allies on the ground where he stood, and where they did in 1827, in order to arrest the final triumph of the principles to which he and they were then both opposed? But my colleague seems to think that the danger of Executive usurpation is not yet over, and that that Department is not so prostrated as he (Mr. C[alhoun]) supposed. Instead of this, he thinks they are still meditating schemes of power. Be it so. He was not more confiding than his colleague. Experience had taught him distrust of power; and if his apprehensions should prove correct, he stood ready to rally with his recent allies against executive usurpation, with all the zeal and energy which had ever impelled him.

He was prepared to go much further, and hoped to have the aid of those with whom he so lately acted, to push forward and guard, by prudent and wise enactments, guided by our recent experience, against the recurrence hereafter of the danger of the encroachments of the Executive. We now know the great danger from that quarter, and he was prepared to do his duty in providing effectual guards.

He saw that this was the moment to reap the fruit of the double victory which had been achieved, mainly by the small party to which he belonged, both against the encroachment of Congress on the rights of the States, and the President on the rights of Congress, and thereby place the liberty and institutions of the country on a durable basis, which he hoped to effect by uniting with the nationals in providing effectual guards against the future usurpations of the Executive, and his old friends and allies of [18]27, in resisting the usurpation of Congress on the States; and as the first step in the discharge of this important duty, he joined them in opposing a bank and a reunion of the Government with the banking system, and was prepared to act throughout with them against Congressional encroachment in every form and shape. He trusted he had now defined his position so as to leave no possibility of mistake as to where he was, where he was going, and under what flag he sailed. In taking his course, he was neither an administration man nor an opposition man, and much less any man's man. He belonged to no party but the States rights, and wished to be considered nothing more than a plain, and an honest nullifier.

From *Congressional Globe*, 25th Cong., 1st Sess., pp. 73–74. Also printed in the Washington, D.C., *Globe*, September 28, 1837, p. 2; the Baltimore, Md., *Merchant-*Washington, D.C., *Reformer*, October 2, 1837, p. 2; the Charleston, S.C., *Mercury*, October 10, 1837, p. 2; Crallé, ed., *Works*, 3:96–101. Variant in the Washington, D.C., *Daily National Intelligencer*, October 24, 1837, p. 2; *Register of Debates*, 25th Cong., 1st Sess., cols. 271–272, 275–276. Another variant in the Baltimore, Md., *Merchant-*Washington, D.C., *Reformer*, September 27, 1837, p. 3.

To J[OHN] R. MATHEW[E]S, [Clarkesville, Ga.?]

Washington, 27th Sep[tembe]r 1837

My dear Sir, I have barely time to enclose you my speech [of 9/18?] and to say that the Postmaster Gen[era]l [Amos Kendall] has agreed to give a direct mail from Pendleton to Dahlonega [Ga.] by the way of Clark[e]sville.

My time is completely engross[ed] by the great & pressing business before us, than which none can be more vital to the South. Should I have leisure during the short period that the session is to last, as I hope, I will write you fully. ["But" *interlined*] let me, however, as pressed as I am for time say, that we have given, I think, a mortal blow to the Union of the political and money power; and that we have a fairer prospect to unite & liberate the South, provided the States right party shall be true to itself & its principles. Yours truely & Sincerely, J.C. Calhoun.

ALS in DLC, John C. Calhoun Papers.

Remarks on the adjournment of Congress, 9/27. Thomas Morris proposed changes to Calhoun's amendment to the "Subtreasury bill." Calhoun said that the Senate ought to adjourn [for the day] "in order that Senators might give to the amendment of the Senator from Ohio (Mr. Morris) some little reflection. Besides, this body was far advanced in the business before them." James Buchanan declared the need for haste in completing the business of the special session. "Mr. Calhoun disapproved of the time for the adjournment of Congress being fixed at so early a day [as 10/9, as yesterday recommended by the Senate to the House of Representatives]. An early decision on the matters before Congress was important, but still it was necessary that discussion should be had on them. He said he was willing to remain here till December or January next, rather than leave this important question unsettled. He would vote for an adjournment [for the day] for the reasons which he had stated." From *Congressional Globe*, 25th Cong., 1st Sess., p. 80. Also printed in the Washington, D.C., *Globe*, September 27, 1837, p. 3. Variant in the Washington, D.C., *Madisonian*, September 28, 1837, p. 3.

Motion by Calhoun to amend the 47th rule, submitted to the Senate on 9/28. "Resolved, That the 47th rule [of the Senate, concerning those who are entitled to be admitted to the floor] be amended, as follows: After the word 'Union,' insert judges of the supreme courts of law and equity of any State." (This motion was agreed to by the Senate.) PC in *Senate Journal*, 25th Cong., 1st Sess., p. 47; draft in DNA, RG 46 (Records of the U.S. Senate), 25A-B12.

Remarks during Daniel Webster's speech on the "Subtreasury bill," 9/28. During a long argument against the bill, Webster referred to Calhoun's speech of [2/26]/1816 "as an able argument" and a "high authority," which set forth the position Webster was now taking. "Mr. Calhoun here rose to make an explanation. He said that he never saw the reporter's notes of his speech on that occasion, and, therefore, what he did say, may not have been what he would have said. There were points of omission in that speech[,] which occupied a column and a half of the National Intelligencer. Mr. C[alhoun] said, that he took care then, as now, to fortify himself, and leave a road open to oppose, at any coming time, a national bank. He then said that he was opposed to a bank, but that he submitted to the necessity of the case. There was then a connexion between the Government and the banks; and, if the Government had a right to regulate the currency, there was no means of doing it but by a national bank. He had, both then, and since then, contended, that Government had no right to have any connexion with any banks. In his opinion, the United States Bank (which he then advocated, and assisted to establish) was not established according to the Constitution. Congress had no right to establish such a bank. He acted contrary to his own impressions of right. Many people may do things which they do not believe to be lawful, from necessity. He acted from necessity." Webster remarked that he recalled Calhoun as saying in 1816 that the question of the constitutionality of the bank had been closed. "Mr. Calhoun again explained: He (Mr. C[alhoun]) thought the connexion between Government and banks was now broken, and that set him at liberty; so that now he could oppose what he had then, and since, earnestly advocated." From *Register of Debates*, 25th Cong., 1st Sess., col. 326. Also printed in *Congressional Globe*, 25th Cong., 1st Sess., Appendix, p. 172.

Motion on the reception of abolition petitions, 9/29. Samuel McKean presented two petitions from citizens of Montrose, Pa., praying for the abolition of slavery in D.C. "Mr. Calhoun having objected to the receiving of these petitions, they were, on his motion, laid on the table." From *Congressional Globe*, 25th Cong., 1st Sess., p. 85.

To Miss A [NNA] M [ARIA] CALHOUN, Pendleton

Washington, 30th Sep[tembe]r 1837

I was quite refreshed, my dear Anna, with the account you gave me of the wedding & wedging [*sic*] parties and the gray [*sic*] hours, which you and Maria [Simkins] have spent. It was quite a contrast of my life for the last month, which has been one of incessant toil & labour, without relaxation, or amusement of any discription [*sic*] whatever. I have to stand in the breach in this great conflict, and bear the brunt of the action. My situation was extraordinary. I held the fate of the country, by the confession of all in my hand, and had to determine in what direction I should turn events hereafter. I did not hesitate. Acting on long established conceptions, I could not array myself under the flag of the banks and by so doing lay the foundation ["of" *canceled and* "for" *interlined*] restoring the very system of plunder, which has cost me so much ["labour" *interlined*] to pull down. The decision has embittered the national Republican party against ["me" *interlined*], but for that I care little. We hold no principle scarcely in common, and neither I, nor my section had any thing to expect from them. As I acted with them to put down executive usurpation on Congress, I now act with the opposite side to repel theirs on the State, and such is the force [of] my position, that I hope to accomplish both.

I regret that my colleague [William C. Preston] has not thought fit to go with me. I think both he & Gen[era]l [Waddy] Thompson [Jr.] have acted ["badly" *interlined*], but I leave it to them and their constituents.

I can say nothing about the gayety [*sic*] of Washington. I have not heard of a party; tho the city is full of strangers. Our gallery is daily crow[d]ed, & with a large portion of ladies. The debate is drawing to a close, & I expect to conclude it on Tuesday. The dicision [*sic*] is doubtful, but I think the seperation will pass by a few votes.

Mr. [John M.] Felder is here on his way [from Orangeburg District, S.C.] to the north for his neice [*sic*]; and I am glad he brings so favorable account of the state of publick sentiment in his quarter of the State. Col. Nisbit called on me last evening, just from West Point, and says that he saw Patrick [Calhoun]. He is well, looks well & stands well in the institution. He is quite pleased, the Col. says with the place. All this was highly gratifying.

I received William[']s [William Lowndes Calhoun's] letter & say to him he may expect an answer by the next mail.

I wrote to your mother [Floride Colhoun Calhoun] a few days since, and to Andrew [Pickens Calhoun] by this mail. I enclosed a copy of my speech [of 9/18?] in pamphlet to you & him. I hope you have each received your copy.

Give my love to Maria [Simkins], Mrs. Yates, if with you, to your mother and all the family.

I hope to be home by the 25th Oct[obe]r and I look impatiently for the time.

My health is pretty good. I need exercise & relaxation. Your affectionate father, J.C. Calhoun.

ALS in ScCleA; slightly variant PEx in Jameson, ed., *Correspondence*, pp. 379–381.

Mahlon Dickerson, [Secretary of the Navy,] to Calhoun and R[obert] B[arnwell] Rhett, [Representative from S.C.,] 9/30. Dickerson acknowledges their letter of "yesterday" recommending R[ichard?] M. Cunningham of Charleston for appointment as Midshipman. The application will be filed for consideration, "but from the fact that So[uth] Carolina has seven or eight more than her due proportion of Mid[shipme]n at this time" there is no prospect of its early success. FC in DNA, RG 45 (Naval Records Collection of the Office of Naval Records and Library), Miscellaneous Letters Sent by the Secretary of the Navy, 1798–1886, 24:76 (M-209:9).

From [Ebenezer S. Thomas]

[Cincinnati] Written July [*sic*; October?], 1837
Sir: No circumstance, that has occurred in these days of political misdoings, is calculated to cause so much grief to the breasts of real patriots, and true friends of their country, as your recent political tergiversation. Know, sir, that *six* years ago, you could not have numbered *six* political friends in this city; but that, since that period, your political ERRORS have been forgiven, and in a great measure, forgotten, by a large portion, I believe I may safely say majority, of the voters of this large and growing city; and that many of them already have, with others who were continually joining them, fixed their eyes upon you, as one of those destined to redeem our common country from that thraldom into which it has been brought by wicked and unprincipled rulers—with a view, ultimately, of elevating you to the highest situation in the gift of man. Judge, then, of their astonishment and regret, at beholding you "*return like the dog to his vomit, and the sow that was washed, to her wallowing in the mire.*" Yes, sir, you have come out alike in boastful defiance of your foes, and regardless of the feelings of your friends. Sir, does such a reckless course become the great statesman—the "man of gigantic mind,"—to whom all have at times looked up with fear, or respect? Permit me to say, sir, it does not; for by it you have be-

trayed the good opinion of your friends, and gladdened the hearts of your foes.

In your recent letter to the Editor of the Alexandria [D.C.] Gazette, there is this paragraph:

"How strange, that any man who knows me, should imagine it possible for me to be driven, or seduced from my position! I live but to carry out the great principles for which I have been contending since 1824; and which I have maintained under every danger and difficulty."

Now, sir, will you have the goodness to tell the American people what these "GREAT PRINCIPLES" are, for which you have been contending so long? I for one, sir, have looked in vain for them in your speeches, spoken before, or since you wrote the letter. The next paragraph, or, more properly, a part of the same just quoted, is in these words:

"In their defense, I have acted with, and against, every party, *without blending with any*. Mr. [Martin] Van Buren has been driven into a position favorable to their advancement, and shall I not avail myself of the opportunity which it affords me to accomplish my object? Shall I permit him to drive me from my position, because he has been driven on it? All I ask is to be heard."

Sir, I speak of what I know, when I say that the people of this Union have been divided into parties ever since the organization of the federal government; and when those parties have been nearly equally divided, as they frequently have been, and are at present, the individual who sets himself up in DIRECT opposition to both of them, even if it be John C. Calhoun, does little good for himself, and less for his country. A deceased Virginia (I was going to say statesman) orator [John Randolph], afforded as striking an evidence of the folly of such a course, as is to be found in the history of politics. I pray you, sir, adopt it not.

Although, sir, you have never told us what those "*great principles*" are, for which you contend, I thank you, that through your own acknowledgment, and the agency of Mr. Van Buren, we are likely to arrive at a pretty tolerable knowledge of them, inasmuch as you admit that he (Mr. Van Buren,) "*has been driven into a position favorable to their advancement*"; and you proceed, "*shall I not avail myself of the opportunity which it affords me to accomplish my object?*" Now, sir, I understand you; you have become jealous of Mr. Van Buren, and will not permit him to "*drive you from your position, because he has been driven on it.*" Now, Mr. Van Buren has broached, distinctly, but one subject in, I had almost said, his interminable message; and what is that, which has thus driven him upon your position? *An increase of executive power, by adding the purse to the sword.* In doing this, it seems he treads upon your toes, I beg pardon, *"is driven upon your position."* This, then, is the "great principle" which you have been contending for since 1824. It is well, sir, that the American people have, at length, arrived at a knowledge of this fact, for which, it appears, they are indebted to Mr. Van Buren, and the more to be estimated on that account, as it is, probably, the only obligation they will ever be under to him.

PC in E[benezer] S[mith] Thomas, *Reminiscences of the Last Sixty-Five Years, Commencing with the Battle of Lexington; Also, Sketches of His Own Life and Times* (2 vols. Hartford: printed by Case, Tiffany and Burnham for the author, 1840), 2:144–147. NOTE: Thomas, a native of Mass., was a former editor of the Charleston, S.C., *City Gazette.* He was later associated with the Cincinnati *Daily Evening Post,* for which the above may have been penned.

Remarks in reply to Richard H. Bayard, 10/2. In a speech against the "Subtreasury bill" Bayard quoted from Calhoun's speech of 3/21/1834 as indicating that Calhoun then regarded "a disconnexion between the Government and the banks as an evil to be dreaded." "Mr. Calhoun here desired to know whether the Senator from Delaware read that extract from his speech for the purpose of convicting him of inconsistencies in his opinions and course of conduct on this subject; for he wished to observe that he could not admit that his opinions were to be gathered from one extract from a single speech, when he had delivered several others, which, if all taken together, would show that his opinions were unchanged in relation to the propriety of disconnecting the Government from the banks." Calhoun made further unreported remarks at the end of Bayard's speech. From *Register of Debates,* 25th Cong., 1st Sess., cols. 437, 440. Also printed in *Congressional Globe,* 25th Cong., 1st Sess., Appendix, p. 222.

Amos Kendall, [Postmaster General,] to Calhoun, [Felix] Grundy, Senator [from Tenn.], and [George W.] Owens, Representative [from Ga.], 10/3. "Your proposition for Stage service between Pendleton & Pickens C[ourt] H[ouse, S.C.,] has been considered, and is declined on the ground that the revenue of the route [less than $100 annually] will not justify the requisite expenditure [of more than $500 annually]." In 1838 a stage connection between those two places will be reconsidered. FC in DNA, RG 28 (Records of the Post Office Department), Letters Sent by the Postmaster General, D.2:128.

Amos Kendall to Calhoun, [Felix] Grundy, and [George W.] Owens, 10/3. Kendall has considered their letter "of the 28th inst[ant] desiring a two horse Coach mail line to be run from Pendleton [S.C.] by Clarkesville [Ga.] to Dahlonega [Ga.]." Under the statute of 7/2/1836 a route from Greenville [S.C.] via Clarkesville to Dahlonega is in operation via Pickensville and Pickens Courthouse but not via Pendleton, which is served by an old route from Greenville to Pendleton. No law justifies the route they propose. FC in DNA, RG 28 (Records of the Post Office Department), Letters Sent by the Postmaster General, D.2:129–130.

SPEECH ON HIS AMENDMENT TO SEPARATE THE GOVERNMENT AND THE BANKS

[In the Senate, October 3, 1837]

The Senate resumed the consideration of the bill to provide for the collection and keeping of the public money, with the amendment offered by Mr. Calhoun.

Mr. Calhoun rose and said that, in reviewing this discussion, he had been struck with the fact that the argument on the opposite side had been limited, almost exclusively, to the questions of relief and the currency. These are, undoubtedly, important questions, (said Mr. Calhoun,) and well deserving the deliberate consideration of the Senate; but there are other questions involved in this issue, of a far more elevated character and commanding control, and which more imperiously demand our attention. The banks have ceased to be mere moneyed incorporations.

They have become great political institutions, with vast influence over the welfare of the community; so much so, that a highly distinguished Senator (Mr. [Henry] Clay) has declared, in his place, that the question of the disunion of the Government and the banks involved in its consequences the disunion of the States themselves. With this declaration sounding in our ears, it is time to look into the origin of a system which has already acquired such mighty influence; to inquire into the causes which have produced it, and whether they are still on the increase; in what they will terminate, if left to themselves; and, finally, whether the system is favorable to the permanency of our free institutions, to the industry and business of the country, and, above all, to the moral and intellectual development of the community. I feel the vast importance and magnitude of these topics, as well as their great delicacy. I shall touch them with extreme reluctance, and only because I believe them to belong to the occasion, and that it would be a dereliction of public duty to withhold any opinion which I have deliberately formed on the subject under discussion.

The rise and progress of the banking system is one of the most remarkable and curious phenomena of modern times. Its origin is modern and humble, and gave no indication of the extraordinary growth and influence which it was destined to attain. It dates back to 1609, the year that the Bank of Amsterdam was established. Other banking institutions preceded it, but they were insulated, and not immediately connected with the systems that have since sprung up, and which may be distinctly traced to the Bank of Amsterdam. That was a bank of deposite, a mere store-house, established under the authority of that great commercial metropolis, for the purpose of safe-keeping the precious metals, and facilitating the vast system of exchanges which then centered there. The whole system was the most simple and beautiful that can be imagined. The depositor, on delivering his bullion or coin in store, received a credit, estimated at the standard value on the books of the bank, and a certificate of deposite for the amount, which was transferable from hand to hand, and entitled the holder to withdraw the deposite on payment of a moderate fee for the expense and hazard of safe-keeping. These certificates became, in fact, the circulating medium of the community, performing, as it were, the hazard and drudgery, while the precious metals, which they in truth represented, guilder for guilder, lay quietly in store, without being exposed to the wear and tear, or losses incidental to actual use. It was thus a paper currency was created, having all the solidity, safety, and uniformity, of a metallic, with the facility belonging to that of paper. The whole arrangement was admirable, and worthy of the strong sense and downright honesty of the people with whom it originated.

Out of this, which may be called the first era of the system, grew the bank of deposite, discount, and circulation—a great and mighty change, destined to effect a revolution in the condition of modern society. It is not difficult to explain how the one system should originate in the other, notwithstanding the striking dissimilarity in features and character between the offspring and the parent. A vast sum, not less than three millions sterling, accumulated and remained habitually in deposite in the Bank of Amsterdam—the place of the returned certificates being constantly supplied by new depositors. With so vast a standing deposite, it required but little reflection to perceive that a very large portion of it might be withdrawn, and that a sufficient amount would be still left to meet the returning certificates; or, what would be the same in effect, that an equal amount of fictitious certificates might be issued, beyond the sum actually deposited. Either process, if interest be charged on the deposite withdrawn, or the fictitious certificates issued, would be a near approach to a bank of discount. This once seen, it required but little reflection to perceive that the same process would be equally applicable to a capital placed in bank as stock; and from that, the transition was easy to issuing bank notes, payable on demand, or bills of exchange, or promissory notes having but a short time to run. These combined constitute the elements of a bank of discount, deposite, and circulation.

Modern ingenuity and dishonesty would not have been long in perceiving and turning such advantages to account; but the faculty of the plain Belgian was either too blunt to perceive, or his honesty too stern to avail himself of them. To his honor, there is reason to believe, notwithstanding the temptation, the deposites were sacredly kept; and that, for every certificate in circulation, there was a corresponding amount in bullion or coin in store. It was reserved for another people, either more ingenious or less scrupulous, to make the change.

The Bank of England was incorporated in 1694, eighty-five years after that of Amsterdam, and was the first bank of deposite, discount, and circulation. Its capital was £1,200,000, consisting wholly of government stock, bearing an interest of eight per cent. per annum. Its notes were received in the dues of the government, and the public revenue was deposited in the bank. It was authorized to circulate exchequer bills, and make loans to Government. Let us pause for a moment, and contemplate this complex and potent machine, under its various characters and functions.

As a bank of deposite, it was authorized to receive deposites, not simply for safe-keeping, to be returned when demanded by the depositor, but to be used and loaned out for the benefit of the institution, care being taken always to be provided with the means of returning an equal amount when demanded. As a bank of discount and circulation, it issued its notes on the faith of its capital stock and deposites, or discounted bills of exchange, and promissory notes backed by responsible endorsers, charging an interest something greater than was authorized by law to be charged on loans; and thus allowing it for the use of its credit, a higher rate of compensation than what individuals were authorized to receive for the use and hazard of money or capital loaned out. It will, perhaps, place this point in a clear light, if we should consider the transaction in its true character, not as a loan, but as a mere exchange of credit. In discounting, the bank takes, in the shape of a promissory note, the credit of an individual so good that another, equally responsible, endorses his note for nothing, and gives out its credit in the form of a bank note. The transaction is obviously a mere exchange of credit. If the drawer and endorsers break, the loss is the bank's; but if the bank breaks, the loss falls on the community; and yet this transaction, so dissimilar, is confounded with a loan, and the bank permitted to charge, on a mere exchange of credit, in which the hazard of the breaking of the drawer and endorser is incurred by the bank, and that of the bank by the community, a higher sum than the legal rate of interest on a loan; in which, besides the use of his capital, the hazard is all on the side of the lender.

Turning from these to the advantages which it derived from its connexion with the government, we shall find them not less striking. Among the first of those in importance is the fact of its notes being received in the dues of the government, by which the credit of the government was added to that of the bank, which added so greatly to the increase of its circulation. These again, when collected by the government, were placed in deposite in the bank; thus giving to it not only the profit resulting from their abstraction from circulation, from the time of collection till disbursement, but also that from the use of the public deposites in the interval. To complete the picture, the bank, in its capacity of lending to the government, in fact paid in its notes which rested on the faith of the government stock, on which it was drawing eight per cent.; so that, in truth, it but loaned to the government its own credit.

Such were the extraordinary advantages conferred on this institution, and of which it had an exclusive monopoly; and these are the causes which gave such an extraordinary impulse to its growth and influence, that it increased, in a little more than a hundred years, from 1694 to 1797, (when the second era of the system, commenced with the establishment of the Bank of England, terminated,) from £1,200,000 to nearly £11,000,000; and this mainly by the addition to its capital by loans to the government above the profits of its annual dividends. Before entering on the third era of the system, I pause to make a few reflections on the second.

I am struck, in casting my eyes over it, to find that, notwithstanding the great dissimilarity of features which the system had assumed in passing from a mere bank of deposite to that of deposite, discount, and circulation, the operation of the latter was confounded throughout this long period, as it regards the effects on the currency, with the bank of deposite. Its notes were universally regarded as representing gold and silver, and as depending on that representation exclusively for their circulation; as much so as did the certificates of deposite in the original Bank of Amsterdam. No one supposed that they could retain their credit for a moment after they ceased to be convertible into the metals on demand; nor were they supposed to have the effect of increasing the aggregate amount of the currency; nor, of course, of increasing prices. In a word, they were in the public mind as completely identified with the metallic currency as if every note in circulation had laid up in the vaults of the bank an equal amount, pound for pound, into which all its paper could be converted the moment it was presented.

All this was a great delusion. The issues of the bank never did represent, from the first, the precious metals. Instead of the representatives, its notes were in reality the substitute for coin. Instead of being the mere drudges, performing all the out-door service, while the coins reposed at their ease in the vaults of the banks, free from wear and tear, and the hazard of loss or destruction, as were the certificates of deposites in the original Bank of Amsterdam, they substituted, degraded, and banished the coins. Every note circulated became the substitute of so much coin, and dispensed with it in circulation, and thereby depreciated the value of the precious metals, and increased their consumption in the same proportion; while it diminished in the same degree, the supply, by rendering money less productive. The system assumed gold and silver as the basis of its circulation; and yet, by the laws of its nature, just as it increased its circulation, in the same degree the foundation on which the system stood was weakened. The consumption of the metals increased, and the supply diminished. As the weight of the superstructure increased, just in the same proportion its foundation was undermined and weakened. Thus, the germ of destruction was implanted in the system at its birth; has expanded with its growth, and must terminate, finally, in its dissolution, unless, indeed, it should, by some transition, entirely change its nature, and pass into some other and entirely different organic form. The conflict between bank circulation and metallic (though not perceived in the first stage[s] of the system, when they were supposed to be indissolubly connected) is mortal; one or the other must perish in the struggle. Such is the decree of fate; it is irreversible.

Near the close of the second era, the system passed the Atlantic and took root in our country, where it found the soil still more fertile, and the climate more congenial, than even in the parent country. The Bank of North America was established in 1781, with a capital of $400,000, and bearing all the features of its prototype, the Bank of England. In the short space of a little more than half a century, the system has expanded from one bank to about eight hundred, including branches, (no one knows the exact amount, so rapid the increase,) and from a capital of less than a half million to about $300,000,000, without apparently exhausting or diminishing its capacity to increase. So accelerated has been its growth with us, from causes which I explained on a former occasion, [in my speech of 3/21/1834,] that already it has attained a point much nearer the assigned limits of the system in its present form than what it has in England.

During the year 1797, the Bank of England suspended specie payments; an event destined by its consequences to effect a revolution in public opinion in relation to the system, and to accelerate the period which must determine its fate. England was then engaged in that gigantic struggle which originated in the French Revolution, and her financial operations were on the most extended scale, followed by a corresponding increase in the action of the bank, as her fiscal agent. It sunk under its overaction. Specie payments were suspended. Panic and dismay spread through the land—so deep and durable was the impression that the credit of the bank depended exclusively on the punctuality of its payments. In the midst of the alarm, an act of Parliament was passed, making the notes of the bank a legal tender; and, to the surprise of all, the institution proceeded on, apparently without any diminution of its credit. Its notes circulated freely as ever, and without any depreciation, for a time, compared with gold and silver; and continued so to do for upwards of twenty years, with an average diminution of about one per cent. per annum. This shock did much to dispel the delusion that bank notes represented gold and silver, and that they circulated in consequence of such representation, but without entirely obliterating on that point the old impression which had taken such strong hold on the public mind. The credit of its notes during the suspension was generally attributed to the tender act, and the great and united resources of the bank and the Government.

But an event followed of the same kind, under circumstances entirely different, which did more than any preceding to shed light on the true nature of the system, and to unfold its vast capacity to sustain itself without exterior aid. We finally became involved in the mighty struggle that had so long desolated Europe, and enriched our country. War was declared against Great Britain in 1812, and, in the short space of one year, our feeble banking system sunk under the increased fiscal action of the Government. I was then a member of the other House, and had taken my full share of responsibility in the measures which had led to that result. I shall never forget the sensation which the suspension, and the certain anticipation of the prostration of the currency of the country, as a consequence, excited in my mind. We could resort to no tender act; we had no great and central regulating power like the Bank of England; and the credit and resources of the Government were comparatively small. Under such circumstances, I looked forward to a sudden and great depreciation of bank notes, and that they would fall speedily as low as the old Continental money. Guess my surprise when I saw them sustain their credit, with scarcely any depreciation for a time, from the shock. I distinctly recollect when I first asked myself the question what was the cause? and which directed my inquiry into the extraordinary phenomenon. I soon saw that the system contained within itself a self-sustaining power; that there was between the banks and the community mutually the relation of debtor and creditor, there being, at all times, something more due from the banks to the community than from the latter to the former. I saw, in this reciprocal relation of debt and credit, that the demand of the banks on the community was greater than the amount of their notes in circulation could meet and absorb, and that, consequently, so long as their debtors were solvent, and bound to pay at short periods, their notes could never fail to be at or near a par with gold or silver. I also saw, that as their debtors were principally the merchants, they would take bank notes to meet their bank debts, and that which the merchant and the Government, which are the great money-dealers, take, the rest of the community would also take. Seeing all this, I clearly perceived that self-sustaining principle which poised and impelled the system, self-balanced in the midst of the heavens, like some celestial body, [moving] with scarcely a perceptible deviation from its path, from the concussion it had received.

Shortly after the termination of the war specie payments were coerced with us by the establishment of a national bank, and a few years afterwards in Great Britain, by an act of Parliament. In both countries the restoration was followed by wide-spread distress, as it always must [be] when effected by coercion, for the simple reason that banks cannot pay unless their debtors first pay; and that to coerce the banks compels them to coerce their debtors before they have the means to pay. Their failure must be the consequence, and this involves the failure of the banks themselves, carrying, in their consequences, universal distress. Hence I am opposed to all kinds of coercion, and am in favor of leaving the disease to time, with the action of public sentiment and the States, to which the banks are alone responsible.

But to proceed with my narrative. Although specie payments were restored, and the system apparently placed where it was before the suspension, the great capacity it proved to possess of sustaining itself without specie payments was not forgotten by those who had its direction. The impression that it was indispensable to the circulation of its notes that they should represent the precious metals was almost obliterated, and they were regarded rather as restrictions on the free and profitable operation of the system, than as the means of its security. Hence a feeling of opposition to gold and silver gradually grew up on the part of the banks, which created an *esprit du corps*, followed by a moral resistance to specie payments, if I may so express myself, which in fact suspended in a great degree, the conversion of their notes into the precious metals long before the present suspension. With the growth of this feeling, banking business assumed a bolder character, and its profits were proportionably enlarged; and, with it, the tendency of the system to increase kept pace. The effect of this soon displayed itself in a striking manner, which was followed by very important consequences, which I shall next explain.

It so happened that the charters of the Bank of England and the late Bank of the United States expired about the same time. As the period approached, a feeling of hostility, growing out of the causes just explained, which had excited a strong desire in the community, who could not participate in the profits of these two great monopolies, to throw off their restraint, began to disclose itself against both institutions. In Great Britain it terminated in breaking down the exclusive monopoly of the Bank of England, and narrowing greatly the specie basis of the system, by making the notes of the Bank of England a legal tender in all cases, except between it and its creditors. A sudden and vast increase of the system, with a great diminution of the metallic basis in proportion to banking transactions, followed, which have shocked and weakened the stability of the system there. With us the result was different. The bank fell under the hostility. All restraint on the system was removed, and banks shot up in every direction almost instantly under the growing impulse which I have explained, and which, with the causes I stated when [on 9/18/1837] I first addressed the Senate on this question, is the cause of the present catastrophe.

With it commences the fourth era of the system, which we have just entered—an era of struggle, and conflict, and changes. The system can advance no further in our country, without great and radical changes. It has come to a stand. The conflict between metallic and bank currency, which I have shown to be inherent in the system, has, in the course of time, and with the progress of events, become so deadly, that they must separate, and one or the other fall. The degradation of the value of the metals, and their almost entire expulsion from their appropriate sphere, as the medium of exchange and the standard of value, have gone so far, under the necessary operation of the system, that they are no longer sufficient to form the basis of the widely extended system of banking. From the first, the gravitation of the system has been in one direction—to dispense with the use of the metals; and hence the descent from a bank of deposite to one of discount; and hence, from being the representative, their notes have become the substitute, for gold and silver; and hence, finally, its present tendency to a mere paper engine, totally separated from the metals. One law has steadily governed the system throughout—the enlargement of its profits and influence; and under that operation, through which metallic currency became insufficient for circulation, it has become, in its progress, insufficient for the basis of banking operations; so much so, that, if specie payments were restored, it would be but nominal, and the system would in a few years, on the first adverse current, sink down again into its present helpless condition. Nothing can prevent it but great and radical changes, which would diminish its profits and influence, so as effectually to arrest that strong and deep current which has carried so much of the wealth and capital of the community in that direction. Without that, the system, as now constituted, must fall, unless, indeed, it can form an alliance with the Government, and through it establish its authority by law, and make its credit, unconnected with gold and silver, the medium of circulation. If the alliance should take place, one of the first movements would be the establishment of a great central institution; or, if that should prove impracticable, a combination of a few selected and powerful of the State banks, which, sustained by the Government, would crush or subject the weaker, to be followed by an amendment of the constitution, or some other device, to limit their number and the amount of capital hereafter. This done, the next step would be to confine and consolidate the supremacy of the system over the currency of the country, which would be in its hands exclusively, and, through it, over the industry, business, and politics of the country; all of which would be wielded to advance its profits and power.

The system having now arrived at this point, the great and solemn duty devolves on us to determine this day what relation this Government shall hereafter bear to it. Shall we enter into an alliance with it, and become the sharers of its fortune and the instrument of its aggrandizement and supremacy? This is the momentous question on which we must now decide. Before we decide, it behooves us to inquire whether the system is favorable to the permanency of our free republican institutions, to the industry and business of the country, and, above all, to our moral and intellectual development, the great object for which we were placed here by the Author of our being. Can it be doubted what must be the effects of a system whose operations have been shown to be so unequal on free institutions whose foundation rests on an equality of rights? Can that favor equality which gives to one portion of the citizens and the country such decided advantages over the other, as I have shown it does in my opening remarks? Can that be favorable to liberty which concentrates the money power, and places it under the control of a few powerful and wealthy individuals? It is the remark of a profound statesman [Edmund Burke], that the revenue is the state; and, of course, those who control the revenue control the state, and those who control the money power can [control] the revenue, and through it the state, with the property and industry of the country, in all its ramifications. Let us pause for a moment, and reflect on the nature and extent of this tremendous power.

The currency of a country is to the community what the blood is to the human system. It constitutes a small part, but it circulates through every portion, and is indispensable to all the functions of life. The currency bears even a smaller proportion to the aggregate capital of the community, than what the blood does to the solids in the human system. What that proportion is, has not been, and perhaps cannot be, accurately ascertained, as it is probably subject to considerable variations. It is however probably between twenty-five and thirty-five to one. I will assume it to be thirty to one. With this assumption, let us suppose a community whose aggregate capital is $31,000,000; its currency would be, by supposition, one million, and the residue of its capital thirty millions. This being assumed, if the currency be increased or decreased, the other portion of the capital remaining the same, according to the well known laws of currency, property would rise or fall with the increase or decrease; that is, if the currency be increased to two millions, the aggregate value of property would rise to sixty millions; and, if the currency be reduced to $500,000, it would be reduced to fifteen millions. With this law so well established, place the money power in the hands of a single individual, or a combination of individuals, and, by expanding or contracting the currency, they may raise or sink prices at pleasure; and by purchasing when at the greatest depression, and selling at the greatest elevation, may command the whole property and industry of the community, and control its fiscal operations. The banking system concentrates and places this power in the hands of those who control it, and its force increases just in proportion as it dispenses with a metallic basis. Never was an engine invented better calculated to place the destiny of the many in the hands of the few, or less favorable to that equality and independence which lie at the bottom of all free institutions.

These views have a bearing not less decisive on the next inquiry —the effects of the system on the industry and wealth of the country. Whatever may have been its effects in this respect in its early stages, it is difficult to imagine any more mischievous on all the pursuits of life than the frequent and sudden expansions and contractions to which it has now become so habitually subject, that it may be considered its ordinary condition. None but those in the secret know what to do. All are pausing and looking out to ascertain whether an expansion or contraction is next to follow, and what will be its extent and duration; and if, perchance, an error be committed—if it expands when a contraction is expected, or the reverse, the most prudent may lose by the miscalculation the fruits of a life of toil and care. The effects are to discourage industry, and to convert the whole community into stock-jobbers and speculators. The evil is constantly on the increase, and must continue to increase just as the banking system becomes more diseased, till it shall become utterly intolerable.

But its most fatal effects originate in it[s] bearing on the moral and intellectual development of the community. The great principle of demand and supply governs the moral and intellectual world no less than the business and commercial. If a community be so organized as to cause a demand for high mental attainments, they are sure to be developed. If its honors and rewards are allotted to pursuits that require their development by creating a demand for intelligence, knowledge, wisdom, justice, firmness, courage, patriotism, and the like, they are sure to be produced. But, if allotted to pursuits that require inferior qualities, the higher are sure to decay and perish. I object to the banking system, because it allots the honors and rewards of the community, in a very undue proportion, to a pursuit the least of all others favorable to the development of the higher mental qualities, intellectual or moral, to the decay of the learned professions, and the more noble pursuits of science, literature, philosophy, and statesmanship, and the great and more useful pursuits of business and industry. With the vast increase of its profits and influence, it is gradually concentrating in itself most of the prizes of life—wealth, honor, and influence—to the great disparagement and degradation of all the liberal and useful and generous pursuits of society. The rising generation cannot but feel its deadening influence. The youths who crowd our colleges, and behold the road to honor and distinction terminating in a banking-house, will feel the spirit of emulation decay within him [sic], and will no longer be pressed forward by generous ardor to mount up the rugged steep of science, as the road to honor and distinction, when perhaps, the highest point he could attain in what was once the most honorable and influential of all the learned professions, would be the place of attorney to a bank.

Nearly four years since [on 1/13/1834], on the question of the removal of the deposites, although I was opposed to the removal, and in favor of their restoration, because I believed it to be unconstitutional and illegal, yet, foreseeing what was coming, and not wishing that there should be any mistake as to my opinion on the banking system, I stated here in my place what that opinion was. I declared that I had long entertained doubts, if doubts they might be called, which were daily increasing, that the system made the worst possible distribution of the wealth of the community, and that it would ultimately be found hostile to the further advancement of civilization and liberty. This declaration was not lightly made; and I have now unfolded the grounds on which it rested, and which subsequent events and reflection have matured into a settled conviction.

With all these consequences before us, shall we restore the broken connexion? Shall we again unite the Government with the system? And what are the arguments opposed to these high and weighty objections? Instead of meeting them and denying their truth, or opposing others of equal weight, a rabble of objections (I can call them by no better name) is urged against the separation: one currency for the Government, and another for the people; separation of the people from the Government; taking care of the Government and not the people; and a whole fraternity of others of like character. When I first saw them advanced in the columns of a newspaper, I could not but smile, in thinking how admirably they were suited to an electioneering canvass. They have a certain plausibility about them which makes them troublesome to an opponent, simply because they are merely plausible, without containing one particle of reason. I little expected to meet them in discussion in this place; but since they have been gravely introduced here, respect for the place and company exacts a passing notice, to which of themselves they are not at all entitled.

I begin with that which is first pushed forward, and seems to be most relied on—one currency for the Government and another for the people. Is it meant that the Government must take in payment of its debts whatever the people take in payment of theirs? If so, it is a very broad proposition, and would lead to important consequences. The people now receive the notes of non-specie-paying banks. Is it meant that the Government should also receive them? They receive in change all sorts of paper, issued by we know not whom. Must the Government also receive them? They receive the notes of banks issuing notes under five, ten, and twenty dollars. Is it intended that the Government shall also permanently receive them? They receive bills of exchange. Shall Government, too, receive them? If not, I ask the reason. Is it because they are not suitable for a sound, stable, and uniform currency? The reason is good, but what becomes of the principle that the Government ought to take whatever the people take? But I go further: it is the duty of Government to receive nothing in its dues but which it has the right to render uniform and stable in its value. We are by the constitution made the guardian of the money of the country. For this the right of coining and regulating the value of coins was given, and we have no right whatever to receive or treat any thing as money, or the equivalent of money, the value of which we have no right to regulate. If this principle be true, and it cannot be controverted, I ask what right has Congress to receive and treat the notes of the State banks as money? If the States have the right to incorporate banks, what right has Congress to regulate them or their issues? Show me the power in the constitution. If the right be admitted, what are its limitations, and how can the right of subjecting them to a bankrupt law in that case be denied? If one be admitted, the other follows as a consequence; and yet those who are most indignant against the proposition of subjecting the State banks to a bankrupt law, are the most clamorous to receive their notes, not seeing that the one involves the right of the other. I am equally opposed to both as unconstitutional and inexpedient. We are next told, to separate from the banks is to separate from the people. The banks, then, are the people, and the people the banks—united, identified, and inseparable; and as the Government belongs to the people, it follows, of course, according to this argument, it belongs also to the banks, and of course is bound to do their biddings. I feel on so grave a subject, and in so grave a body, an almost invincible repugnance in replying to such arguments; and I shall hasten over the remaining one of the fraternity, which I shall condescend to notice with all possible despatch. They have no right of admission here; and, if I were disposed to jest on so solemn an occasion, I should say they ought to be driven from this chamber, under the 47th rule [which regulates admission to the chamber of the Senate]. The next of these formidable objections to the separation from the banks is, that the Government, in so doing, takes care of itself, and not of the people. Why, I had supposed that the Government belonged to the people; that it was created by them for their own use, to promote their interest, and secure their peace and liberty; that, in taking care of itself, it takes the most effectual care of the people; and, in refusing all embarrassing, entangling, and dangerous alliances with corporations of any description, it was but obeying the great law of self-preservation. But enough; I cannot any longer waste words on such objections. I intend no disrespect to those who have urged them; yet these, and arguments like these, are mainly relied on to countervail the many and formidable objections, drawn from the highest considerations that can influence the action of Government or individuals, none of which have been refuted, and many not even denied.

The Senator from Massachusetts (Mr. [Daniel] Webster) [in his speech on 9/28] urged an argument of a very different character, but which, in my opinion, he entirely failed to establish. He asserted that the ground assumed on this side was an entire abandonment of a great constitutional function conferred by the constitution on Congress. To establish this, he laid down the proposition, that Congress was bound to take care of the money of the country. Agreed: and with this view the constitution confers on us the right of coining and regulating the value of coins, in order to supply the country with money of proper standard and value; and is it an abandonment of this right, to take care, as this bill does, that it shall not be expelled from circulation, as far as the fiscal action of this Government extends? But, having taken this unquestionable position, the Senator passed (by what means he did not condescend to explain,) from taking care of the money of the country to the right of establishing a currency, and then to the right of establishing a bank currency, as I understood him. On both of these points, I leave him in the hands of the Senator from Pennsylvania, (Mr. [James] Buchanan,) who, in an able and constitutional argument, completely demolished, in my judgment, the position assumed by the Senator from Massachusetts. I rejoice to hear such an argument from such a quarter. The return of the great State of Pennsylvania to the doctrines of rigid construction and State rights, sheds a ray of light on the thick darkness which has long surrounded us.

But we are told that there is not gold and silver enough to fill the channels of circulation, and that prices would fall. Be it so. What is that compared to the dangers which menace on the opposite side? But are we so certain that there is not a sufficiency of the precious metals for the purpose of circulation? Look at France, with her abundant supply, with her channels of circulation full to overflowing with coins, and her flourishing industry. It is true that our supply is insufficient at present. How could it be otherwise? The banking system has degraded and expelled the metals, driven them to foreign lands, closed the mines, and converted their products into costly vases, and splendid utensils and ornaments, administering to the pride and luxury of the opulent, instead of being employed as the standard of value, and the instrument of making exchanges as they were manifestly intended mainly to be by an all-wise Providence. Restore them to their proper functions, and they will return from their banishment; the mines will again be opened; and the gorgeous splendor of wealth will again reassume the more humble, but useful, form of coins.

But, Mr. President, I am not driven to such alternatives. I am not the enemy, but the friend of credit—not as the substitute, but the associate and the assistant of the metals. In that capacity, I hold credit to possess, in many respects, a vast superiority over the metals themselves. I object to it in the form which it has assumed in the banking system, for reasons that are neither light nor few, and that neither have been nor can be answered. The question is not whether credit can be dispensed with, but what is its best possible form—

the most stable, the least liable to abuse, and the most convenient and cheap? I threw out some ideas on this important subject in my opening remarks. I have heard nothing to change my opinion. I believe that Government credit, in the form I suggested, combines all the requisite qualities of a credit circulation in the highest degree; and also that Government ought not to use any other credit but its own in its financial operations. When the Senator from Massachusetts made his attack on my suggestions, I was disappointed. I expected argument, and he gave us denunciation. It is often easy to denounce, when it is hard to refute; and when that Senator gives denunciations, instead of arguments, I conclude that it is because the one is plenty, and the other scarce.

We are told the form I suggested is but a repetition of the old continental money—a ghost that is ever conjured up by all who wish to give the banks an exclusive monopoly of Government credit. The assertion is not true; there is not the least analogy between them. The one was a promise to pay when there was no revenue; and the other a promise to receive in the dues of Government when there is an abundant revenue.

We are also told that there is no instance of a Government paper that did not depreciate. In reply, I affirm that there is none, assuming the form I propose, that ever did depreciate. Whenever a paper receivable in the dues of Government had any thing like a fair trial, it has succeeded. Instance the case of North Carolina, referred to in my opening remarks [of this session on 9/18]. The drafts of the Treasury at this moment, with all their incumbrance, are nearly at par with gold and silver; and I might add the instance alluded to by the distinguished Senator from Kentucky [Henry Clay], in which he admits that, as soon as the excess of the issues of the Commonwealth Bank of Kentucky were reduced to the proper point, its notes rose to par. The case of Russia might also be mentioned. In 1827 she had a fixed paper circulation, in the form of bank notes, but which were inconvertible, of upwards of $120,000,000, estimated in the metallic ruble, and which had for years remained without fluctuation, having nothing to sustain it, but that it was received in the dues of the Government, and that, too, with a revenue of only about $90,000,000 annually. I speak on the authority of a respectable traveller. Other instances, no doubt, might be added; but it needs no such support. How can a paper depreciate which the Government is bound to receive in all payments to it, and while those to whom payments are to be made are under no obligation to receive it? From its nature, it can only circulate when at par with gold and silver; and if it should depreciate, none could be injured but the Government.

But my colleague [William C. Preston] objects that it would partake of the increase and decrease of the revenue, and would be subject to greater expansions and contractions than bank notes themselves. He assumes that Government would increase the amount with the increase of the revenue, which is not probable, for the aid of its credit would then be least needed; but if it did, what would be the effect? On the decrease of the revenue, its bills would be returned to the Treasury, from which, for the want of demand, they could not be re-issued; and the excess, instead of hanging on the circulation, as in the case of bank notes, and exposing it to catastrophes like the present, would be gradually and silently withdrawn, without shock or injury to any one. It has another and striking advantage over bank circulation, in its superior cheapness as well as greater stability and safety. Bank paper is cheap to those who make it, but dear, very dear, to those who use it, fully as much so as gold and silver. It is the little cost of its manufacture, and the dear rates at which it is furnished to the community, which gives [*sic*] the great profit to those who have a monopoly of the article. Some idea may be formed of the extent of the profit, by the splendid palaces which we see under the name of banking houses, and the vast fortunes which have been accumulated in this branch of business; all of which must ultimately be derived from the productive powers of the community, and of course adds so much to the cost of production. On the other hand, the credit of Government, while it would greatly facilitate its financial operations, would cost nothing, or next to nothing, both to it and the people, and of course would add nothing to the cost of production, which would give every branch of our industry, agriculture, commerce, and manufactures, as far as its circulation might extend, great advantages both at home and abroad.

But there remains another and great advantage. In the event of war, it would open almost unbounded resources to carry it on, without the necessity of resorting to what I am almost disposed to call a fraud—public loans. I have already shown that the loans of the Bank of England to the Government were very little more than loaning back to the Government its own credit; and this is more or less true of all loans, where the banking system prevails. It was pre-eminently so in our late war. The circulation of the Government credit, in the shape of bills receivable exclusively with gold and silver in its dues, and the sales of public lands, would dispense with the necessity of loans, by increasing its bills with the increase of taxes. The increase of taxes, and, of course, of revenue and expenditures, would be followed by an increased demand for Government bills, while the latter would furnish the means of paying the taxes, without increasing, in the same degree, the pressure on the community. This, with a judicious system of funding, at a low rate of interest, would go far to exempt the Government from the necessity of contracting public loans, in the event of war.

I am not, Mr. President, ignorant, in making these suggestions, (I wish them to be considered only in that light,) to what violent opposition every measure of the kind must be exposed. Banks have been so long in the possession of Government credit, that they very naturally conclude they have an exclusive right to it, and consider the withdrawal of it, even for the use of the Government itself, as a positive injury. I have some experience on this subject. It was my fortune to take a stand on the side of the Government against the banks during the most trying period of the late war—the winter of 1814 and 1815—and never in my life was I exposed to more calumny and abuse—no, not even on this occasion. It was my first lesson on the subject. I shall never forget it. I propose to give a very brief narrative of the scenes through which I then passed; not with any feeling of egotism, for I trust I am incapable of that, but to illustrate the truth of much I have said, and to snatch from oblivion not an unimportant portion of our financial history. I see the Senators from Massachusetts, (Mr. Webster,) and from Alabama, (Mr. [William R.] King,) who were then members of the House of Representatives [from N.H. and N.C.], in their places, and they can vouch for the correctness of my narrative, as far as the memory of transactions so long passed will serve.

The finances of the country had at that time fallen into great confusion. Mr. [George W.] Campbell had retired from the head of the Treasury, and the late Mr. [Alexander J.] Dallas had succeeded —a man of talents, bold and decisive, but inexperienced in the affairs of the Department. His first measure to restore order, and to furnish the supplies to carry on the war, was to recommend a bank of $50,000,000, to be constituted almost exclusively of the new stocks which had been issued during the war, to the exclusion of the old, which had been issued before. The proposed bank was authorized to make loans to the Government, and was not bound to pay specie during the war, and for three years after its termination.

It so happened that I did not arrive here till some time after the commencement of the session [of 9/19/1814–3/3/1815], having been

detained by an attack of bilious fever. I had taken a prominent part
in the declaration of the war, and had every motive and disposition
to sustain the administration, and to vote every aid to carry on the
war. Immediately after my arrival, I had a full conversation with
Mr. Dallas, at his request. I entertained very kind feelings towards
him, and assured him, after he had explained his plan, that I would
give it my early and favorable attention. At that time I had reflected
but little on the subject of banking. Many of my political friends
expressed a desire that I should take a prominent part in favor of
the proposed bank. Their extreme anxiety aroused my attention,
and, being on no committee (they had been appointed before my
arrival,) I took up the subject for a full investigation, with every
disposition to give it my support. I had not proceeded far before
I was struck with the extraordinary character of the subject; a bank
of $50,000,000, whose capital was to consist almost exclusively of
Government credit in the shape of stock, and not bound to pay its
debts during the war and for three years afterwards, to furnish the
Government with loans to carry on the war! I saw at once that the
effect of the arrangement would be, that the Government would
borrow back its own credit, and pay six per cent. per annum for what
they had already paid eight or nine. It was impossible for me to
give it my support under any pressure, however great. I felt the
difficulty of my situation, not only in opposing the leading measure
of the administration at such a crisis, but, what was far more responsible, to suggest one of my own, that would afford relief to the embarrassed Treasury. I cast my eyes around, and soon saw that the
Government should use its own credit directly, without the intervention of a bank; which I proposed to do in the form of Treasury
notes, to be issued in the operations of the Government, and to be
funded in the subscription to the stock of the bank. Treasury notes
were, at that time, below par, even with bank paper. The opposition
to them was so great on the part of the banks, that they refused to
receive them on deposite, or payment at par with their notes; while
the Government, on its part, received and paid away notes of the
banks at par with its own. Such was the influence of the banks,
and to such degradation did the Government, in its weakness, submit.

All this influence I had to encounter, with the entire weight of
the administration thrown into the same scale. I hesitated not. I
saw the path of duty clearly, and determined to tread it, sharp and
rugged as it was. When the bill came up, I moved my amendment,
the main features of which were, that, instead of Government stock
already issued, the capital of the bank should consist of funded

Treasury notes; and that, instead of a mere paper machine, it should be a specie paying bank, so as to be an ally instead of an opponent in restoring the currency to a sound condition on the return of peace. These were, with me, indispensable conditions. I accompanied my amendment with a short speech [on 11/16/1814] of fifteen or twenty minutes; and so overpowering was the force of truth, that, notwithstanding the influence of the administration, backed by the money power, and the Committee of Ways and Means, which was unanimous, with one exception, as I understood, my amendment prevailed by a large majority; but it, in turn, failed, the opposition [Federalists], the adherents of the administration, and those who had constitutional scruples, combining against it. Then followed various but unsuccessful attempts to charter a bank. One was vetoed by the President [James Madison], and another was lost by the casting vote of the Speaker, (Mr. [Langdon] Cheves). After a large portion of the session was thus unsuccessfully consumed, a caucus was called, in order to agree on some plan, to which I and the few friends who still adhered to me, after such hard service, were especially invited. We of course attended. The plan of compromise was unfolded, which approached much nearer to our views, but which was still objectionable in some features. I objected, and required further concessions, which were refused, and was told the bill could be passed without us; at which I took up my hat and bade good night. The bill was introduced in the Senate, and speedily passed that body. On the second reading [in the House] I rose and made a few remarks, in which I entreated the House to remember that they were about to vote for the measure against their conviction, as had been frequently expressed; and that, in so doing, they acted under a supposed necessity, which had been created by those who expected to profit by the measure. I then reminded them of the danger of acting under such pressure, and I said that they were so sensible of the truth of what I uttered, that if peace should arrive before the passage of the bill, it would not receive the support of fifteen members; I concluded by saying that I would reserve what I intended to say on the question of the passage of the bill, when I would express my opinion at length, and appeal to the country. My objections had not gone to the people, as nothing that I had said had been reported—such was my solicitude to defeat the bill, without extending our divisions beyond the walls of the House, in the then critical condition of the country. My object was to arrest the measure, and not to weaken confidence in the administration.

In making the supposition, I had not the slightest anticipation of peace. England had been making extensive preparations for the ensuing campaign, and had made a vigorous attack on New Orleans, which had just been repelled; but, by a most remarkable coincidence, an opportunity (strange as it may seem) was afforded to test the truth of what I said. Late in the evening of the day, I met Mr. [Lewis Burr] Sturges, then a member of Congress from Connecticut. He said that he had some information which he could not withhold from me; that a treaty of peace had been made, and that it had actually arrived in New York [City], and would be here the next day; so that I would have an opportunity of testing the truth of my prediction. He added, that his brother, who had a mercantile house in New York, had forwarded the information to him by express, and that he had forwarded the information to connected houses in the Southern cities, with directions to purchase the great staples in that quarter, and that he wished me to consider the information as confidential. I thanked him for the intelligence, and promised to keep it to myself. The rumor, however, got out, and the next day an attempt was made to pass through the bill; but the House was unwilling to act till it could ascertain whether a treaty had been made. It arrived in the course of the day, when, on my motion, it was laid on the table, with less than fifteen votes against the motion; and I had the gratification of receiving the thanks of many for defeating the bill, who, a short time before, were almost ready to cut my throat for my persevering opposition to the measure. An offer was then made to me to come to my terms, which I refused, declaring that I would rise in my demand, and would agree to no bill which should not be formed expressly with the view to the speedy restoration of specie payments. It was afterwards postponed, on the conviction that it could not be so modified as to make it acceptable to a majority. This was my first lesson on banks. It has made a durable impression on my mind.

My colleague [Preston], in the course of his remarks, said he regarded this measure as a secret war waged against the banks. I am sure he could not intend to attribute such motives to me. I urge no war, secret or open, against the existing institutions. They have been created by the legislation of the States, and are alone responsible to the States. I hold them not answerable for the present state of things, which has been brought about under the silent operation of time, without attracting notice, or disclosing its danger. Whatever legal or constitutional rights they possess, under their charters, ought to be respected; and, if attacked, I would defend them as resolutely as I now oppose the system. Against that I wage, not secret, but open and uncompromising hostilities, originating not in opinions recently or hastily formed. I have long seen the true character of the system, its tendency and destiny, and have looked forward for many years, as many of my friends know, to the crisis in the midst of which we now are. My ardent wish has been to effect a gradual change in the banking system, by which the crisis might be passed without a shock, if possible; but I have been resolved for many years, that, should it arrive in my time, I would discharge my duty, however great the difficulty and danger. I have, thus far, faithfully performed it, according to the best of my abilities, and, with the blessing of God, shall persist, regardless of every obstacle, in performing it, with equal fidelity, to the end.

He who does not see that the credit system is on the eve of a great revolution, has formed a very imperfect conception of the past, and anticipation of the future. What changes it is destined to undergo, and what new form it will ultimately assume, are concealed in the womb of time, and not given us to foresee. But we may perceive in the present many of the elements of the existing system which must be expelled, and others which must enter it in its renewed form.

In looking at the elements at work, I hold it certain that in the process there will be a total and final separation of the credit of Government and that of individuals, which have been so long blended. The good of society, and the interests of both, imperiously demand it, and the growing intelligence of the age will enforce it. It is unfair, unjust, unequal, contrary to the spirit of free institutions, and corrupting in its consequences. How far the credit of Government may be used in a separate form, with safety and convenience, remains to be seen. To the extent of its fiscal action, limited strictly to the function of the collection and disbursement of its revenue, and in the form I have suggested, I am of the impression it may be both safely and conveniently used, and with great incidental advantages to the whole community. Beyond that limit I see no safety, and much danger.

What form individual credit will assume after the separation is still more uncertain; but I see clearly that the existing fetters that restrain it will be thrown off. The credit of an individual is his property, and belongs to him as much as his land and houses, to use it as he pleases, with the single restriction, which is imposed on all our rights, that they are not to be used so as to injure others. What limitations this restriction may impose, time and experience will show; but, whatever they may be, they ought to assume the character of general laws, obligatory on all alike, and open to all; and, under the provisions of which all may be at liberty to use their credit, jointly or separately, as freely as they now use their land and houses, without any preference by special acts, in any form or shape, to one over another. Every thing like monopoly must ultimately disappear before the process which has begun will finally terminate.

I see, not less clearly, that, in the process, a separation will take place between the use of capital and the use of credit. They are wholly different, and, under the growing intelligence of the times, cannot much longer remain confounded in their present state of combination. They are as distinct as a loan and an endorsement; in fact, the one is but giving to another the use of our capital, and the other the use of our credit; and yet so dissimilar are they that we daily see the most prudent individuals lending their credit for nothing, in the form of endorsement or security, who would not loan the most inconsiderable sum without interest. But, as dissimilar as they are, they are completely confounded in banking operations, and which is one of the main sources of the profit, and the consequent dangerous flow of capital in that direction. A bank discount, instead of a loan, is very little more, as I have shown, than a mere exchange of credit—an exchange of the joint credit of the drawer and endorser of the note discounted for the credit of the bank in its own note. In the exchange, the bank insures the parties to the note discounted, and the community, which is the loser if the bank fails, virtually insures the bank; and yet, by confounding this exchange of credit with the use of capital, the bank is permitted to charge an interest for this exchange rather greater than an individual is permitted to charge for a loan, to the great gain of the bank and loss of the community. I say loss; for the community can never enjoy the great and full benefit of the credit system, till loans and credit are considered as entirely distinct in their nature, and the compensation for the use of each be adjusted to their respective nature and character. Nothing would give a greater impulse to all the business of society. The superior cheapness of credit would add incalculably to the productive powers of the community, when the immense gains, which are now devised by confounding them, shall come in aid of production.

Whatever other changes the credit system is destined to undergo, these are certainly some which it must; but when and how the revolution will end—whether it is destined to be sudden and convulsive, or gradual and free from shock—time alone can disclose.

Much will depend on the decision of the present question, and the course which the advocates of the system may pursue. If the separation takes place, and is acquiesced in by those interested in the system, the prospect will be that it will gradually and quietly run down, without shock or convulsions, which is my sincere prayer; but if not—if the reverse shall be insisted on, and, above all, it should be effected through a great political struggle, (it can only be so effected,) the revolution would be violent and convulsive. A great and thorough change must take place. It is wholly unavoidable. The public attention begins to be roused throughout the civilized world to this all-absorbing subject. There is nothing left to be controlled but the mode and manner, and it is better for all that it should be gradual and quiet than the reverse. All the rest is destiny.

I have now, Mr. President, said what I intended, without reserve or disguise. In taking the stand I have, I change no relation, personal or political, nor alter any opinion I have heretofore expressed or entertained. I desire nothing from the Government or the people. My only ambition is to do my duty, and shall follow wherever that may lead, regardless alike of attachments or antipathies, personal or political. I know full well the responsibility I have assumed. I see clearly the magnitude and the hazard of the crisis, and the danger of confiding the execution of measures in which I take so deep a responsibility, to those in whom I have no reason to have any special confidence. But all this deters me not, when I believe that the permanent interest of the country is involved. My course is fixed. I go forward. If the administration recommend what I approve on this great question, I will cheerfully give my support; if not, I shall oppose; but, in opposing, I shall feel bound to suggest what I believe to be the proper measure, and which I shall be ready to back, be the responsibility what it may, looking only to the country, and not stopping to estimate whether the benefit shall enure either to the administration or the opposition.

From *Register of Debates*, 25th Cong., 1st Sess., cols. 469–485. Also printed in the Washington, D.C., *Globe*, October 10, 1837, p. 2; the Baltimore, Md., *Merchant*-Washington, D.C., *Reformer*, October 17, 1837, p. 2; the Charleston, S.C., *Mercury*, October 18 and 19, 1837; the Washington, D.C., *Daily National Intelligencer*, November 9, 1837, pp. 2–3; *Congressional Globe*, 25th Cong., 1st Sess., Appendix, pp. 121–126; *Speech of the Hon. John C. Calhoun, on His Amendment to Separate the Government from the Banks. Delivered in the Senate of the United States, October 3, 1837* (Washington: printed at the Globe Office, 1837); *Speeches of John C. Calhoun*, pp. 275–290; John S. Jenkins, *The Life of John Caldwell Calhoun*, pp. 337–361; Crallé, ed., *Works*, 3:102–133. Partially printed in the Pendleton, S.C., *Messenger*, November 11 and December

1, 1837; E.L. Magoon, *Living Orators in America,* pp. 216–217. Variant in the Baltimore, Md., *Merchant*-Washington, D.C., *Reformer,* October 5, 1837, p. 2. Another variant in the Washington, D.C., *Madisonian,* October 5, 1837, p. 2, and the New York, N.Y., *Morning Courier and New-York Enquirer,* October 5, 1837, p. 2. NOTE: After Calhoun's speech, Webster replied. In two footnotes to its report of Webster's remarks (cols. 486 and 487) the *Register of Debates* (published by Gales and Seaton, opponents of the Subtreasury plan,) stated that Calhoun's printed speech differed so much, at those points, from his spoken remarks that Webster's reply (which was directed to the spoken remarks) was unintelligible. In the first point footnoted Webster was reported as saying that he disagreed with Calhoun's contention that in 1797 when the Bank of England suspended specie payments, "the suspension produced no great shock." In the second place so noted, Webster argued that Calhoun had contended (wrongly) that "the banking system is full of dangers: 1st, to civil liberty; 2dly, to industry; and, 3dly, to the moral and intellectual development of mankind." When the day's debate concluded, Calhoun's amendment was approved 24 to 23. The bill itself passed the Senate the next day, 26 to 21, but never came to a vote in the House of Representatives.

From "T"

[Published at Richmond, October 6, 1837]
Sir—I have read your speech delivered in the Senate of the United States on the 19th [*sic*; 18th] ult[imo], and with many parts of it am highly pleased. I am a strict constructionist, and always have been, belonging to that school at the present day who are called Nullifiers. I perceive, among other projects, you advise a large emission of Treasury notes—first, to relieve the Government; secondly, to aid in facilitating exchanges, and thereby restoring uniformity in the currency. I wish to ask you, with all respect, if you have maturely considered the power of Congress to emit Treasury notes such as you describe? You know that when the Convention was called in 1787, its object was, as defined at the time, "to amend the articles of confederation," which had carried our country through the war of the revolution—but that illustrious assemblage presented the result of their labors in a new Constitution. Under the articles of confederation, you find this distinct clause—Congress shall have authority "to borrow money, or emit bills, on the credit of the United States." In the Constitution as recommended by the Convention, and adopted by the States, and which now exists, the second clause, in the enumeration of the powers of Congress, is the following: Congress shall have power "to borrow money on the credit of the U. States." The copy is exact from the articles of confederation, with the omission of the

words "or bills of credit." Now, did the Convention intend nothing by this omission? or rather, does it not irresistibly prove that the power "to emit bills on the credit of the U. States" granted by the articles of confederation, was expressly withheld in the Constitution? This conclusion is farther established by the fact that "the Federal Constitution contains a grant of limited powers by the State sovereignties—and therefore, unless the power is given, it is withheld. But to make this restriction, which resulted from the nature of the grant, doubly sure, that most sagacious of men, Patrick Henry, introduced an amendment which was adopted, declaring that the powers not delegated to the U. States by "the Constitution, nor prohibited by it to the States, are reserved to the States respectively, or to the People." Now, Sir, I ask you[,] have Congress the power to emit "bills of credit?" And if you answer in the negative, as I think you must, then I beseech to know what are these Treasury notes which you propose, but "bills of credit," to all intents and purposes? From the parts of the Constitution which I have quoted, if they were all, the power would remain to the States to "emit bills of credit"; but the wise framers of that instrument provided against this, and, as they believed, against "paper Money," in the 10th section of the 1st article of the Constitution, where it says—"No State shall coin money, emit bills of credit," &c. The conclusion is irresistible to my mind, that the framers of the Constitution never intended that either the State or Federal Governments should emit bills of credit; and here, according to my views, lies the true argument against the power to establish any bank, either State or Federal. Neither Government has power to emit "bills of credit." It is (as I think has been already proven) withheld from the one, and prohibited to the other. Are Bank notes bills of credit? Certainly, to all intents and purposes, and nothing else. But the reply is, neither Government, State nor Federal, emits Bank notes—they only incorporate and give being to the companies by law, which do emit the bills, and hence these are not the "Bills of Credit" contemplated by the Constitution. I rejoin, in the legal adage, *Quod facit per alium, facit per, &c.* Is not the converse equally true—what you have no rightful power to do yourself, you have no rightful power to authorize others to do? I then perfectly agree with Mr. [Benjamin W.] Leigh [former Senator from Va.], in the opinion expressed in his letter in 1834, "that the framers of the Constitution had no thought of any Bank agency whatever, State or Federal, &c." and I will add, still less thought of any "Treasury Notes," alias "Bills of Credit" to be issued and circulated by either Government. To give to the Federal Government the power to emit Bills of Credit, alias Treasury Notes, at its option, in peace and in war, will be in effect, to make that Government Banker General of the whole Union. It will, indeed, "unbank all other banks." I will only add, that, although a pretty attentive observer of the times and the signs of the times, of public men and their public course, for hard upon forty years, I do not remember to have noticed your warm State Rights notions, as early as 1816 on the Bank question or any other; and if any such opinions as you say you openly expressed at that time, were contained in any of your public speeches, they have totally escaped my recollection. With very high respect, Your obedient servant, T.

PC in the Richmond, Va., *Whig and Public Advertiser*, October 6, 1837, p. 1.

Remarks on "the bill regulating the fees of [U.S.] district attorneys," 10/9. Under discussion was whether and under what circumstances District Attorneys should receive fees in matters concerning the renewal or non-payment of bonds given by merchants for payment of customs duties. "Mr. Calhoun was averse to any charge on the parties, or subjecting the Government to any." From *Register of Debates*, 25th Cong., 1st Sess., col. 514. Also printed in the Washington, D.C., *Globe*, October 10, 1837, p. 3; *Congressional Globe*, 25th Cong., 1st Sess., p. 116. Variant in the Washington, D.C., *Daily National Intelligencer*, October 10, 1837, p. 3.

Remarks on the "Warehouse Bill," 10/9. Under discussion was a bill which would allow "the deposite of merchandise in the public stores" [in lieu of paying tariff duties] and also affect the system of credit previously granted merchants in the payment of duties. "Mr. Calhoun agreed with the Senator from Alabama [William R. King], that it was better to postpone it to" the next session of Congress "when it could be fully acted on, and all its features maturely considered. He was not prepared at this time to enter on any discussion, and he was aware that there was a great diversity of opinion on the subject." Henry Clay argued that his understanding of the Compromise Tariff of 1833 barred his support for the bill, for the Compromise Act provided that credits for duties were to be allowed until 1842, when credits were to be abolished and all duties were to be collected in cash. "Mr. Calhoun thought the view taken by the Senator from Kentucky was correct. There was no subject which could be touched on which could excite greater contention; and he submitted to the Senators on all sides whether there was any necessity for agitating this question now. If it met the wishes of the chairman of the Committee on Finance [Silas Wright] to have the bill passed without the clause which violated the compact, it might do very well; but if not, he would move to postpone the bill to the first Monday in December next." After further discussion, the bill was postponed till the next day. From *Register of Debates*, 25th Cong., 1st Sess., cols. 516–517. Also printed in the Washington, D.C., *Globe*, October 10, 1837, p. 3; *Congressional Globe*, 25th Cong., 1st Sess., pp. 116–117. Variant in the Richmond, Va., *Enquirer*, October 13, 1837, p. 2.

Amendment to the "Warehouse Bill," submitted to the Senate on 10/10. "Add to the first section the following proviso: '*Provided always,* That in all cases where, by the existing laws, credits are allowed for duties, and bonds to secure the payment of the same are receivable by the collectors of the customs, it shall be at the option of the importer, his factor, agent, or consignee, until the first day of July, which will be in the year of our Lord one thousand eight hundred and forty-two, to place the goods upon which such duties are chargeable, in store, pursuant to the provisions of this act, or to give the bonds for the duties allowed by the existing laws, and for the periods of time provided for in those laws: but the election shall in all cases be made at the time of importation, and before the goods have been placed in store, as allowed by this or any other existing law.'" (This amendment was defeated 23 to 14 the same day it was offered.) PC in *Senate Journal*, 25th Cong., 1st Sess., p. 59.

Remarks on his amendment to the "Warehouse Bill," 10/10. "Mr. Calhoun said he had not given this bill so thorough an examination as he could desire; but, as far as his vote was concerned, he would be happy to give it, if certain objections could be removed, related to the compromise bill [that is, the tariff act of 1833], respecting which he had felt, and should still feel, a difficulty. It was important, he said, that that act should remain undisturbed, till its objects should have been accomplished in 1842; and he should certainly not disturb it. With a view to remove the difficulty on this point, he offered a proviso to be annexed to the first section of the bill, which, he said, would remove all the difficulty as far as it related to Southern interests; and he would then cheerfully give the bill his vote, provided gentlemen who represented the manufacturing and commercial interests of the North were satisfied with the bill. The whole effect of this proviso was to leave it optional with the importer either to avail himself of the provisions of this bill, or to refuse and conform to existing laws. The choice, however, was required to be made before the goods should be deposited in the public stores." When Henry Clay objected, Calhoun "repeated his declaration, that he did not present the amendment as an exclusive representative of the South, without regard to the interest of other sections of the Union; but there were able and intelligent gentlemen now present, particularly representing those sections, and he would go for the bill when amended, only on the condition that it should be agreeable to them." From *Register of Debates*, 25th Cong., 1st Sess., cols. 518–519. Also printed in the Washington, D.C., *Daily National Intelligencer*, October 11, 1837, p. 2. Variant in the Washington, D.C., *Globe*, October 12, 1837, p. 1; *Congressional Globe*, 25th Cong., 1st Sess., p. 120. Another variant in the Washington, D.C., *Madisonian*, October 12, 1837, p. 3, and the New York, N.Y., *Morning Courier and New-York Enquirer*, October 12, 1837, p. 2.

Remarks on the Treasury note bill, 10/10. The Senate received a bill passed by the House of Representatives authorizing an issue of Treasury notes. Daniel Webster indicated that he preferred the House bill to the one passed by the Senate, which he regarded as "irregularly originated" in violation of the Constitutional requirement that revenue measures begin in the House. "Mr. Calhoun said he had not made up his mind on this point, in relation to this bill; but it was his impression that it did not come within the scope of the revenue bills, which were required by the constitution to originate in the other House." From *Register of Debates*, 25th Cong., 1st Sess., col. 518. Also printed in the Washington, D.C., *Daily National Intelligencer*, October 11, 1837, p. 2.

Further remarks on the "Warehouse Bill," 10/11. When Henry Clay urged that the bill be postponed until the next session of Congress, "Mr. Calhoun followed on the same side, and hoped the bill would be postponed. It had many points, and might be viewed in many aspects, all requiring more time and more information, with which he hoped the Senate would be indulged." The efforts to postpone failed. From *Register of Debates*, 25th Cong., 1st Sess., col. 524. Also printed in the Washington, D.C., *Daily National Intelligencer*, October 13, 1837, p. 2.

From Mahlon Dickerson, [Secretary of the Navy,] 10/12. He acknowledges Calhoun's note of 10/9 enclosing [former Representative from Va.] John S. Barbour's recommendation of Dr. John E. Shackelford for appointment as Assistant Surgeon. "It will give me great pleasure to take this case into respectful consideration when selections are about to be made for the next Medical Board." FC in DNA, RG 45 (Naval Records Collection of the Office of Naval Records and Library), Miscellaneous Letters Sent by the Secretary of the Navy, 1798–1886, 24:98 (M-209:9).

To J[ames] M[ontgomery] Calhoun, [Decatur, Ga.?]

Washington, 13th Oct[obe]r 18[3]7

Dear Sir, I enclosed yesterday Niles['] Register [of 10/7] containing my remarks [on 9/18] on opening the discussion of the great question of the day and now enclose my concluding remarks [of 10/3]; and at the same time avail myself of the opportunity of congratulating you on your election to the legislature. I have received the intelligence of your success with much pleasure and hope it is but the commencement of your career of usefulness and honor.

The subject, which has occupied us this session is one of deep importance, and in which the South has a profound interest. The contcentrating [*sic*] of the currency in the Northern section has been one of the most efficient means by which that section has governed our commerce; and we accordingly see them making a death struggle against it. I cannot doubt, but the whole South will come to take the same view of it that ["as" *canceled*] I do. I should regret exceedingly if our State rights friend[s] in Georgia should take a different view of it. It ["would" *interlined*] lose them the advantage ground of principle on which they now stand, and throw them into the hands of the national Republicans, with all their heretical opinions. In fact, I trust, that all parties to the South will harmonize in the measure. It would give us vast strength. It is time that all party divisions should ["cease" *interlined*] where our interest is at stake. It requires united councils and united exertions to defend our rights, assailed as they openly are in the other section.

I had to venture much; but I did not doubt, but I would be fully sustained, when my motives and reasons came to be fully understood at the South. I never saw my way more clearly.

Remember me kindly to your brother Ezekiel & believe [me] to be with affectionate regard yours & J.C. Calhoun.

ALS in GAHi.

To [Joel R.] Poinsett, Secretary of War, 10/14. Calhoun encloses a letter [dated 8/27] "from my neighbour, Mr. [Edward] Harleston, who is desireous of having his Nephew Tho[ma]s Cordes Harleston appointed a Cadet [at West Point]." Calhoun requests that Harleston's application, which will be supported by other members of Congress from S.C., be put on file. (Endorsements by C[harles] Gratiot on Calhoun's letter indicate that S.C.'s only vacancy in the Military Academy had already been offered to R[ichard] H[eron] Anderson.) ALS with En in DNA, RG 94 (Records of the Adjutant General's Office), Application Papers of Cadets, 1805–1866, 1837, 128 (M-688:109, frames 315–324).

To [Joel R.] Poinsett, 10/14. Calhoun recommends Patrick [Calhoun] Noble, a son of "Col." [Patrick] Noble [President of the S.C. Senate], for appointment as a Cadet at West Point. ALS offered for sale on 6/5/1970 by the Mercury Stamp Co.

To A[RMISTEAD] BURT, [Abbeville, S.C.]

Washington, 15th Oct[obe]r 1837

My dear Sir, I have bearly [*sic*] time to say, that I will leave this [city] tomorrow, and unless I meet the Lincolnton [N.C.] Stage at Salisbury which is doubtful, I shall proceed direct to Abbeville, where I expect to be on the 22d or 23d Ins[tan]t and where I shall be very glad to see you. I postpone ["mu"(?) *canceled*] what I have to say till I meet you. If I should not meet you at Abbeville, you must be sure to make me a visit on my return. I have much to say. Do not fail & bring Mar[tha Calhoun Burt] with you. I wrote to [George] McDuffie that I would probably be in Abbeville by the 22 or 23d and and [*sic*] that I would be glad that he would meet me. I trust, that he is right. A national bank *now* would seal our fate at the South.

I would have written you but I have had scarcely a moment's leisure during the session.

My love to Martha and believe me to be yours truely, J.C. Calhoun.

ALS in NcD, John C. Calhoun Papers.

To JAMES LYNAH, [Charleston]

Washington, 15th Oct[obe]r 1837

My dear Sir, In the midest [*sic*] of my preperation [*sic*] to return, I have bearly [*sic*] time to acknowledge your letter of the 10th which has afforded ["me" *interlined*] much pleasure. I trust in God that our beloved State will see her true interest at this great juncture. If she should, all that we have ever contended for will be fully realized; but if not, we shall lose all and be crushed under Northern domination. Never did I see the future more clearly and what our ["interest," *interlined*] honor, and safety demand. I would be greived [*sic*] to think, that the State rights party should falter at such a moment. I cannot believe it, tho' every attempt has been made here to devide [*sic*] & distract us.

I sent you a copy of my opening and concluding remarks in pamphlet form by yesterday['s] mail. I hope they get safe to hand. Truely & sincerely, J.C. Calhoun.

ALS in NcU, James Lynah Papers.

From J[oel] R. Poinsett, [Secretary of War,] 10/16. He replies to Calhoun's letter of 10/14 concerning the appointment of [Patrick Calhoun] Noble as a Cadet. The appointment is not possible because the one appointment to which S.C. is entitled next year has already been conferred on R[ichard] H[eron] Anderson. LS in ScU-SC, Noble Family Papers; FC in DNA, RG 107 (Records of the Office of the Secretary of War), Letters Sent by the Secretary of War Relating to Military Affairs, 1800–1861, 18:57 (M-6:18); FC in DNA, RG 94 (Records of the Adjutant General's Office), Records Relating to the U.S. Military Academy, 1812–1867, 6:370 (M-91:6).

From J[oel] R. Poinsett, 10/16. In reply to Calhoun's letter of 10/14 concerning the appointment of [Thomas Cordes] Harleston as a Cadet, Poinsett states that the appointment cannot be made for the reason pointed out in his previous letter today to Calhoun. FC in DNA, RG 107 (Records of the Office of the Secretary of War), Letters Sent by the Secretary of War Relating to Military Affairs, 1800–1861, 18:58 (M-6:18); FC in DNA, RG 94 (Records of the Adjutant General's Office), Records Relating to the U.S. Military Academy, 1812–1867, 6:370 (M-91:6).

OCTOBER 17–DECEMBER 3
1837

◫

When Calhoun reached home on October 24 both personal and political sorrows awaited him. One of those fever epidemics that were an unavoidable part of life in the South had been raging. There had been extensive sickness at Fort Hill. Calhoun's young overseer, the best he had ever had, had died, and most of the family was convalescent. Plantation affairs were in disarray and efforts to raise needed funds ran into obstacles.

Politics was just as bad. Old friends on every hand were in revolt. Calhoun had an unsatisfactory conversation with former Governor James Hamilton, Jr., on banking questions, and a long, politely disagreeing letter from former Governor George McDuffie on the same matter. McDuffie regretted parting with Calhoun: "We must be content to regulate & restrain the banks as far as we can, but I cannot believe either in the wisdom or practicability of any measure which looks to their destruction." The Columbia Telescope, *organ of Calhoun's Senatorial colleague Preston, rumbled in discontent. Waddy Thompson, Jr., the Representative from Calhoun's home district, openly condemned the Subtreasury. These discontents Calhoun combatted with a public letter to friends in Edgefield District on November 3.*

All the news was not bad, however. Patrick Calhoun was doing well at West Point, and Calhoun and Duff Green shared a new grandson who seemed a healthy child.

For the time being Senator Calhoun had to take a back seat to farmer Calhoun. On December 2, two days before Congress convened, he was still at Fort Hill, deeply involved in the unfinished harvesting of cotton and corn. It promised to be a good crop. "I shall make upwards of 4,000 bushels of corn, and about 65,000 pounds of cotton off of 90 acres." The prospect was satisfying enough, perhaps, to push aside, at least for a time, contemplation of the trials and challenges of public life.

◫

From E[LIZUR] WRIGHT, JR., "Ed[itor], Quart[erly] Anti-S[lavery] Mag[azine]"

New York [City], Oct. 18, 1837

Sir, You are well aware that the number is constantly increasing at the North of those who regard slave holding as the highest social crime. Whatever evil this fact may portend, either to the South or the Country at large, you as well know is only to be averted by the power of argument addressed to the people. Calumny, clamor, ["mob" *canceled*] lynch law & "Incendiary publication Bills," are not to be relied on, as the nation must by this time be well nigh convinced, to do any thing else than ["to" *canceled*] arrest the attention of men and predispose them to take the side which shows the least faith in argument. Hence, as you are sincere in your defense of slavery, and as you value the integrity of the Country and the unanimity of its citizens, you will be desirous of meeting the abolitionists on the field of argument. Speaking in behalf of those especially with whom I have the honor to act, it is no less the desire of the abolitionists to put their cause to the test of a full & fair encounter with the ablest defenders of slavery. If it cannot be sustained in the light of truth, if the great measure at which they aim ["is" *canceled*; "cannot be proved to the satisfaction of reasonable and unprejudiced men to be" *interlined*] not ["only" *interlined*] the wisest policy for ["the South even" *canceled*] the slave holders of the South, ["as well as" *canceled and* "but" *interlined*] the happiest for the slaves, they are willing to abandon their enterprise. They hold themselves open to conviction, even to the extent of believing, if proof should require it, ["what they now look upon with horror," *interlined*] that slavery is the best condition of ["any" *canceled and* "a" *interlined*] laboring population. As a proof of this disposition, allow me to say that the small [*two or three words canceled*] publication under my care, entitled the Quarterly Anti-Slavery Magazine, will, from the commencement of the next volume, be enlarged to the size of our large Reviews, and will be freely opened to the ablest of our opponents to the extent of 100 pages of each number. That there may be no occasion for the complaint of unfair play, the replies, when we see fit to make any, will be limited to the same space & type as the respective articles that ["shall" *interlined*] have called them forth. Here then we offer to those who deprecate the effect of our agitation, access to the same readers—the power of sending the antidote along with the poison. It will be the ["ful" *canceled*] fault of their courage or their arguments, if they do not make our Magazine a pro-slavery instead of an Anti-slavery engine. Most cheerfully ["sir" *interlined*] shall we welcome an article from your pen, ["sir," *canceled*] either with or without your name. Should you prefer to write anonymously, you may depend ["on our" *canceled*] upon the incog[nito] being honorably observed so far as we are concerned. Or, should ["your" *canceled*] any ["reason" *canceled*] cause prevent your writing at all, we will admit any champion of your selecting on the same terms as yourself, confiding in the seriousness of your purpose to put us down by a fair & manly defence of southern institutions, or by a logical exposure of our own absurdity.

I cannot believe, sir, that you will treat this overture lightly. However strongly you may be disposed to set[?] down some of us, who have staked all on the abolition ["die" *interlined*] and *written our books*, as incorrigible, you cannot but think more favorably of ["the candor of our" *interlined and* "the" *canceled*] large and constantly increasing circle of ["our" *canceled*] readers, embracing ["a large portion" *canceled and* "many" *interlined*] of our most influential professional men, and especially those who in our educational institutions are giving character to the youth both of the north & the south. The opportunity of influencing such minds, if I am not greatly mistaken, cannot be a matter of indifference to one whose prospects of political elevation and honorable fame in the history of our Country are ["so flattering" *canceled*] like yours. Since the discussion must ["in some shape" *interlined*] proceed, why not let the north & the south understand ["one an" *canceled and* "each" *interlined*] other at once? Let us, who are so much shocked at your conclusions in regard to the practical application of our great political axioms, be made familiar with the reasonings by which you arrive at them. Perhaps our aversion to your institutions ["would be" *canceled and* "will" *interlined*] thus ["be" *interlined*] removed, and the bond of brotherhood, which nature has made no geographical provision for sundering, will be strengthened. Do not allow yourself to suppose, that even those of us who regard slaveholders as criminals ["of th" *canceled*; "regard them as" *changed to* "think them"] the worst of men, or hopelessly malevolent. ["No," *canceled and* "On the contrary," *interlined*] we find much to honor and love in Southern character, and our abhorrence of slavery shall not blind us to it. It is upon this we found our hopes. We well know, we are not understood at the South. But we doubt not the day is coming when we shall be, and shall be numbered among the best of your northern friends.

A line informing me whether we may expect any thing from you for our first enlarged number which we hope to issue by the first of March, 1838, or for any subsequent one, will be esteemed a favor by, Sir, your respectful & most ob[edien]t serv[an]t, E. Wright, Jr.

FC in DLC, Elizur Wright Papers, 4:597–598. NOTE: If Calhoun ever received this letter, it is likely he did not reply to it.

Mortgage by Turner H. Richardson to John C. Calhoun, Anderson District, S.C., 10/21. Richardson acknowledges his indebtedness to Calhoun for three promissory notes totalling $4,000. As security for the payment of these he mortgages 640 acres of land on Twenty-Six Mile Creek [that he had purchased from Calhoun on 7/19]. This document was witnessed by Joseph N. Whitner and William H. Harrison. It was recorded on 11/11/1838. Recorded copy in Sc-Ar, Anderson County Deeds, W:145–146.

To J[ames] Ed[ward] Colhoun, [Abbeville District, S.C.]

Fort Hill, 27th Oct[obe]r 1837

My dear Sir, I returned home on the 24th & had the pleasure of finding the sick all on the recovery. Maria [Simkins] & Anna [Maria Calhoun] are free from all disease and only require the Cook and time to restore them to their usual health & strength.

Andrew [Pickens Calhoun] will set out west in a week, or ten days and is much obliged to you for your information of the mill seat on the Phillibody, which he will certainly visit.

I could not get off in time to be at Flat Rock [N.C.], but I learn, that things took a proper turn. I saw Gen[era]l [James] Hamilton [Jr.] for a short time at Abbeville on his return from there and I learn from him, that the F[rench] Broad route is in fact abandomned [*sic*]; and that the intention is to purchase the Hamburgh [rail]road and to unite with the Augusta & Athens interest to extend their road to meet the Georgia main track from the Suck to the Chattahoochee. This is as it should be. They now take the very route, which I recommended three years since, and [for] which I could not get a single man in Charleston to join me. All the movements about the French Broad, at the late meeting, was [*sic*] but to cover a retreat. A branch will probably be made to Columbia, to gratify the interest in that quarter, to which there can be no great objection. Thus far, Charleston has a fair prospect, to consum[m]ate which only requires, that the Compromise act [of 1833] shall be rigidly adhered to and that the monied & commercial power shall not be concentrated by an act of Congress in the North.

On this point I did not find the General so sound. He expressed himself decidedly opposed to a national bank but equally as much so to the divorce. His plan is a union of ten of the strongest of the State banks to be selected by the general government and to be maid [*sic*; made] their fiscal agent and the instrument of restoring specie payment, [Nicholas] Biddle[']s bank of course to be one—a plan in my opinion still more objectionable, than a national bank. He professed great personal regard, but, I infer, from his conversation that there will be a vigorous effort made in this State in favour of his views, and against the divorce, which must be counteracted, and in which you must take an active part.

The first point will be to carry & secure the members of the legislature. Every one of your members ought to be seen and secured on the opposite side. You must be at Abbeville on sale day next and see and converse with all of them, who may be out and the rest ought to be written to.

The next will be ["to" *interlined*] secure prominent and influential individuals, and [George] McDuffie in particular. They are making great efforts to secure him. He was perfectly sound when I saw him at my house, a short time before I sat [*sic*] out for Washington, and I hope is still so; but he is liable to be acted on by men inferior to himself; and I must request you to see him as early as convenient to confirm him in the faith, if sound, and if not to bring him right.

I am gratified to learn that all in this neighbourhood are right as far as my information extends; and that such is also the case as far as I could learn through the entire line of my route home with the State rights party. There never was so favourable an opportunity to break the last shackles on our industry and to unite the entire South. It must not be lost.

I sent you a copy of each of my speeches, which I hope you got. I also sent a copy to each member of the Legislature.

If I can possibly leave home, I intend to be at Anderson ["at" *canceled*] on sale day and the day after at Abbeville. I wish to make a visit to my brothers Patrick [Calhoun] and William [Calhoun] and will return by your residence. I would be glad to meet you at Abbeville.

All join their love to you. Affectionately, J.C. Calhoun.

ALS in ScCleA; PC in Jameson, ed., *Correspondence*, pp. 381–382; PEx in [John B. Cleveland, compiler], *Controversy between John C. Calhoun and Robt.*

Y. Hayne as to the Proper Route of a Railroad from South Carolina to the West [Spartanburg, S.C.: no publisher, 1913], p. 11.

To DUFF GREEN, [Baltimore?]

Fort Hill, 27th Oct[obe]r 1837

My Dear Sir, I arrived here day before yesterday after a safe and pleasant journey with the exception of the Dust, which was very troublesome throughout the whole way.

The little opportunity I had of ascertaining publick sentiment has brought me to the conclusion, that the indications are not unfavorable, but that the publick sentiment is still in a course of formation. I am of the impression, that the party opposed to seperation [of the government from the banks] in this State intend a rally. Columbia will be the centre of their hostility. The attack will be made on the [Washington] Reformer, under the pretex[t] of repelling its alledged [*sic*] attacks on Col. [William C.] Preston, but with the real design of attacking me through its sides. You will see the line of operation in the [Columbia] Telescope, and the use they intend to make of your supposed enmity to Col. Preston and relation to me. It appears to me, that the most effectual mode of cutting this line of hostile operation is, in the first place for Mr. [Richard K.] Crallé to come out in a temperate article denying that the Reformer has gone one inch beyond the defensive, and stating at the same time that he fully understands the real object of the Telescope, and his determination not to afford it the pretex[t] for its insidious and indirect attack on me through the Reformer. I have written him to this effect. In the next place, it does seem to me, that you ought at an early day to announce your withdrawal from the editorial department entirely, and that the establishment has been transferred to trustees. I think it due to yourself and Mr. Crallé both, that the responsibility of the editorial department should be clearly understood. Any confusion on that point, must be unpleasant to you both and injurious to the establishment, by giving an unfair advantage to its enemies, as in the case of the Telescope; and I feel convinced, that both you and Mr. Crallé must desire, that whatever may be the merit, or demerit of any article, which may appear in the paper, should be attributed to the proper source. I do hope that you have been able to make some arrangement that will free you from all future charges on account of the paper, and leave you to attend exclusively to your domestick concerns. The times, I think, must improve, and the completion of the [Chesapeake and Ohio] canal to Cumberland [Md.] will give you a fair prospect, if you should succeed in making the arrangement you contemplated, when I left Washington. Your property must be invaluable, if you can only hold out; and your activity and experience, if directed exclusively to your private interest, ought soon to put you at your ease.

We have had more sickness than ever has been known on the place; but all are well, or on the recovery now. Andrew [Pickens Calhoun], Marg[a]ret [Green Calhoun] and the child [John Caldwell Calhoun] have had uninterrupted health throughout. The child has grown much in my absence and is really a fine boy.

All join their love to you, Mrs. Green, Mrs. Reed and the family.

PC in Jameson, ed., *Correspondence*, pp. 383–384.

From J[ohn] E[wing] Bonneau

Charleston, 28th October 1837

D[ea]r Sir, I wrote you on 26 May last, that it would not be convenient for me to purchase the [Bonneau's] ferry tract on Cooper river, now owned by yourself & others—since then, I have concluded, to become the purchaser, provided, the place can be got for what I consider a liberal & fair market price. You are no doubt aware, that there is not a single building on the place, that will not require entire new buildings to be erected in their stead—added to which, the river banks, which are very long for the size of the place, are much washed & very much out of order & which will require a vast deal of labor to make them secure—many of the trunks are old & must be replaced by new ones—so that, whoever may become the purchaser, these things will be taken into consideration. I am disposed to give for the place *$13,000*, provided, the terms of payment will suit me. I should however, prefer the place being put up at public sale, to the highest bidder, or for you to appoint two persons, who are well acquainted with the plantation & altogether disinterested, to say, what is the value of it. In short, I am willing to give for the place as much I think as any other person will, & for this plain & simple reason, that the place adjoins my own, & will be of more value to me than any one else. The planting lands of *both* tracts, being not over 200 acres[,] I mean of rice Land, the places generally are too small. I gave for my own place $15,000, but it was in excellent order & had more rice land than the Ferry tract & had every necessary building upon it at the time & all of them as good as new—with the exception of ["the" *canceled and* "a" *interlined*] dwelling house. I have thus given you my candid views, & will be glad to hear from you fully on the subject, as early as it may suit your convenience, after seeing the other parties interested [that is, John Ewing Colhoun and James Edward Colhoun]. The present lease of the Ferry expires on the first of January next. I hope this may find you safe[ly] returned home & yourself & family in good health. With great respect I remain D[ea]r Sir Yours &c&c J.E. Bonneau.

ALS in ScU-SC, John C. Calhoun Papers. Note: Calhoun's AEU indicates that he received a note from Col. [John Ewing] Colhoun [on the same subject] and that Calhoun wrote answers to Bonneau and Colhoun on 11/13. Neither of these answers has been found.

From Geo[rge] McDuffie, [former Governor of S.C.]

Cherry Hill [Abbeville District, S.C.], 29th Oct. 1837
My dear Sir, I have received your letter from Washington written just before the adjournment, with your last Speech [that of 10/3]. Though all must admit that you have made a profound & masterly exposition of the subject of banking, I regret to be constrained to differ with you as to the expediency of *overthrowing* it, by any process however gradual. We must be content to regulate & restrain the banks as far as we can, but I cannot believe either in the wisdom or practicability of any measure which looks to their destruction. The measure of exacting specie in payment of all government dues, though harsh in my opinion, and at this period of distress, most untimely, even if it were just & wise in the abstract, would not be half so objectionable but for the avowed & open hostility to the whole banking system in which it originates, and of which it is the incipient belligerent measure. If I understand the issue presented, it is *banks or no banks*. On this issue I must prefer to "bear the ills we have ["that" *canceled and* "than" *interlined*] fly to others that we know not of." The banking system as it now exists has not been the creation of a day. In a slow progress of half a century, it has "grown with our growth & strengthened with our strength," gradually accommodating itself to the wants of society, and stimulating industry & *enterprize*. It has thus become inseparably connected with every interest in the community, & however you may suppose it to be

631

diluted, it is the actual blood which invigorates our social system. Now, weak & insufficient as this blood may be, I should think it extremely hazardous to open the veins of the body politic by way of invigorating the patient. I solemnly believe it would expire under the operation, or more probably, would use the strength it has left to resist it. I am sure this country could not & would not endure the protracted spasm of passing from our present to a metallic currency. If every bank had come into existence by a public fraud, and if every bill issued were an act of swindling, it would be no reason for destroying those extended interests, which are now inseparably identified with the system, and which so far from participating in the supposed fraud & swindling, have grown up under the ["plighted" *canceled*] faith of the States, plighted by the several laws of incorporation. In fact the process of destroying, or unbanking the banks, would in my opinion, produce one hundred times as much suffering, and ten times as much injustice, as that of their creation, estimating the latter as highly as even you do.

A short analysis will make this evident. Without pretending to strict accuracy in statistical details, in which I am now but little conversant, I will assume our whole currency to be 150 millions, one hundred consisting of paper & fifty of specie. I will also assume the amount due the banks, on discounted notes & bills to be 400 millions. In this state of things the transition to a metallic currency would produce the following effects: It would reduce the currency from 150 to 50 millions; This would enhance the value of that portion of the national wealth which consists of money ["300" *canceled and* "200" *interlined*] per cent, & diminish all other descriptions of wealth in a corresponding degree, *as between these two classes.* That is to say, the money holders could command ["three times" *canceled and* "twice" *interlined*] as much property, as they could before the transition. This would be simply transferring property to the amount of 100 millions from the great mass of the enterprizing & productive classes to the money holders, and not the least of these would be the bank stock holders themselves. But the operation would be still more unjust & ruinous between the debtor & creditor classes, the latter again composed principally of the banks. For recollect that these institutions ["would" *interlined*] have during the proposed transition, to collect 400 millions of dollars from the community, which would have to be paid in a currency continually growing scarcer & more valuable, and after the 100 millions of bank notes should be called in, would have to be paid in specie, that is to say, 300 millions of debt would have to be discharged with 50 millions of specie! This it is obvious could not be done. The debtors of the bank, after giving up all their property, would ["be" *interlined*] insolvent to the amount of millions. The whole tendency of the proposed change is to increase the value of money & depreciate the value of all other descriptions of property, concentrating the wealth of the country in the hands of the most unproductive class & the one least entitled to favor.

I know you will say this process will be slow & gradual, but it will nevertheless produce the relative changes I have stated not the less certainly for being slow. If the operation should extend over twenty years, it would cause a continually decreasing ["amount" *canceled and* "proportion" *interlined*] of currency, as compared with the wealth to be measured & circulated by it—a state of things of all others the most paralizing [*sic*] to national industry & enterprize. If it be said that the exaction of specie in payment of all government dues, will not break down the banks nor lead to a metallic currency, but leave the banking system as we now have it, I can only say that your main argument in favor of the change—the unsoundness & corrupting tendency of the banking system—would entirely fail. For why should we increase the general distress, by making the government play Shylock, if it is to end in giving the officers & contractors of the federal government, their salaries & dues in specie, leaving us not only the ["supposed" *interlined*] curse of the banking system, but that system cut loose from its moorings? The federal government, by agreeing to receive the bills of such banks only as will redeem their notes in specie, can present a very strong motive to the leading banks to resume payment, as soon as the state of the foreign exchange will permit—probably in three months. But if it refuse their bills in all cases, it can present no such motive. On the contrary it will, by drawing from five to ten millions of specie into its vortex, permanently withdraw that much of the ["specie" *canceled and* "means" *interlined*] which would enable the banks to resume payment, diminishing at the same time their motives & their ["means for doing so" *canceled and* "ability to do so" *interlined*].

Now I cannot perceive what benefit the country or any class of its citizens, except the office holders, the money holders & the manufacturers, would derive from a curtailment of banking operations, *produced by a previous curtailment of their specie basis.* If the government takes the specie & keeps it (to a certain amount) permanently employed in its fiscal operations, the operations of the banks will not be any sounder or safer, though limited in their extent, than they would have been in their original extent, with a proportionably larger amount of specie to sustain them. If the discounts & issues of the banks could be diminished, *without* diminishing their specie means, it might give some additional safety to their operations. But the proposed measure will diminish their means, and at the same time take away the only motive the federal government can fairly offer to them, to [*one word canceled*] limit their issues. If only five millions of specie should be taken from the banks, while the government should refuse to receive their paper, these causes combined would render a curtailment of at least twenty millions in the bank circulation necessary. Now it seems to me that the process of curtailment will be severe enough without any artificial causes to increase it. Although I think this the very time for separating the government from the banks as depositories, it does seem to me the most unsuitable time that could have been selected for refusing to receive the bills of specie paying banks in discharge of the public dues.

Finally I believe this war against the banks urged by the federal government, will either break down the banks and produce the disasters I have described, or what is more probable ["at first" *canceled*], will create such a sympathy with the banks as will lead substantially to a mere paper system, by causing such a change in public opinion, as to sustain the banks in permanently suspending specie payments from a conviction of its impossibility.

I have thus presented my opinions fully & frankly, that you may distinctly understand that they are not hastily formed. The strong language in which I denounced [Thomas H.] Benton's gold scheme in my last speech on the removal of the deposites, & the uniform current of my published opinions on the subject of banking & currency, place me distinctly on the ground I now occupy. I cannot change that position, & should deplore any attempt to make an organization of political parties on this question. I think the [Washington] Reformer has been imprudent & hasty in denouncing [William C.] Preston, & the [Columbia] Telescope not much less so in defending him.

I will conclude my objections to the exaction of specie in payment of the dues of the government, by one peculiar to the South. It will certainly enhance the tariff, in the degree that specie may be more valuable than our common state currency, and God knows how much that may be.

Upon the whole, then, I think the separation from the banks as depositories—standing by itself—would be a salutary, practicable &

popular measure, and that it never can succeed coupled with the other.

I have had more sickness than usual at my plantation & regret to learn that you have had a great deal. My ["cotton" *interlined*] crop with a uniformly unfavorable season, & the loss of 30 or 40 bales by the storm, will turn out seven bales to the hand, with a large surplus of corn. I have made 46 bushels per acre on an old field ["(100 acres)" *interlined*] that would not have brought 12 bushels this very dry year without manure. By this system, with large oat crops, I can make as much cotton as I can pick out the worst of seasons. Yours sincerely, Geo[rge] McDuffie.

ALS in ScCleA; slightly variant PC in Boucher and Brooks, eds., *Correspondence*, pp. 155–158.

To P[ATRICK] N OBLE, Willington, [Abbeville District], S.C.

Fort Hill, 30th Oct[obe]r 1837

My dear Sir, I had the happiness on my return to find my family all convalescent. We have had much sickness on the [Seneca] River, but thanks to ["the" *canceled*] a kind Providence, but few deaths.

I am gratified in having it [in] my power to say, that ["I" *interlined*] have found the tone of publick sentiment, as far as the ["States" *altered to* "State"] Right party is concerned, sound as far as I had an opportunity of judging, from Washington to this place on the route by which I returned. I am exceedingly anxious to see you and have a full conversation before ["I" *canceled and* "you" *interlined*] leave home for Columbia. I intend to make a visit to see my brother Patrick, if possible, the begin[n]ing of week after next; say to be at Abbeville the day after sale day in Nov[embe]r where I would be very glad to meet you & [George] McDuffie; and I would be ["very"(?) *canceled*] glad, if you would inform him of my arrangement, if he is at home and [of] my desire to see him. We never had such an opportunity to break the last shackle on our commerce and industry, and to consimate [*sic*] the great objects, for which we have so long contended. All that is wanting is union in this State.

I enclose a letter [of 10/16] from Mr. [Joel R.] Poinsett [Secretary of War] in relation to the application ["of" *canceled and* "for" *interlined*] your son [to be a Cadet]. I still hope when the time for the regular appointments come to be made out, there may be a vacancy. If so, nothing shall be wanting to secure his appointment.

Mrs. [Floride Colhoun] Calhoun & the family join ["in" *canceled*] their affectionate regards to your self & family. Truely, J.C. Calhoun.

ALS in ScCleA; variant PC in Alice Noble Waring, ed., "Letters of John C. Calhoun to Patrick Noble, 1812–1837," *Journal of Southern History,* vol. XVI, no. 1 (February, 1950), p. 73. NOTE: Patrick Calhoun Noble (born 1821) received an appointment as Cadet in 1838.

To J[OHN] BAUSKETT and Others, Edgefield District, S.C.

Fort Hill, Nov. 3rd, 1837

Gentlemen, It is with very great reluctance I decline your kind invitation to partake of a public dinner. From no quarter and on no occasion could an expression of approbation be more acceptable, but so short is the interval between this [time] and the next regular session of Congress, and so indispensible [*sic*] is it, that I should devote it exclusively to my domestic concerns, preparatory to my long absence from home, that I am compelled to decline the honor intended.

In saying that on no occasion could the expression of your confidence be more welcome, I intend no unmeaning common place. During the long period of my public service, never have I seen a more important crisis, than the present, and in none have I ever been compelled, in the discharge of my duty, to assume a greater responsibility. I saw clearly on my arrival at Washington, at the commencement of the late extra session, that our affairs had reached the point, when, according to the course we might take, we should reap the full harvest of our long and arduous struggle against the encroachments and abuses of the General Government, or lose the fruits of all our labour. I clearly saw, that our bold and vigorous attacks had made a deep and successful impression. State interposition had overthrown the protective Tariff and with it the American System, and put a stop to Congressional usurpation; and the joint attacks of our party and that of our old opponents, the National Republicans, had effectually brought down the power of the Executive, and arrested its encroachments for the present. It was for that purpose, we had united. True to our principle of opposition to the encroachment of power, from whatever quarter it might come, we did not hesitate, after overthrowing the protective system and arresting legislative usurpation, to join the authors of that system, in order to arrest the encroachments of the Executive, although we differed as widely as the poles on almost every other question, and regarded the usurpation of the Executive, but as a necessary con-sequence of the principles and policy of our new allies. In joining them, we were not insensible to the embarrassment of our position. With such allies, success was difficult, and victory itself, without a change of principles and policy on their part, dangerous; and, ac-cordingly, while we united with them against the Executive, we refused all participation in the Presidential contest. But, with all its embarrassments, it was the only practicable course left us, short of abandoning our principles, or the country, by retiring altogether from the field of contest. In this embarrassing position, we waited the development of events, with the fixed determination, that let what might come, we would inflexibly pursue the course, which a regard to our principles, and the success of our cause demanded.

Such was the position we occupied, from 1833, when our contest with the General Government terminated, to the commencement of the late Extra session, when it became manifest a great change had been effected, which could not but have a powerful influence over our future course. It soon became apparent after the meeting of Congress, that the joint resistance of ourselves and our late allies in conjunction with the course of events in reference to the currency, had brought down the lofty pretensions of the Executive Depart-ment. The union between the Government and the money power, which had so greatly strengthened those in authority at first, had not only ceased, but they were forced to take ground against the reunion of the two, and to make war against those very banks, which had been instruments of their power and aggrandizement. Forced to take this position, and divested in a great measure of patronage and influence from the exhausted state of the Treasury, they were compelled to fall back, as the only means of saving themselves, on the principles of 1827, by which, we had ejected from office the National Republican party, and to which our portion of the old party of '27 have inflexibly adhered, but from which, the other, adhering to the A[d]ministration, had so greatly departed in practice. As soon as I saw this state of things, I clearly perceived, that a very important question was presented for our determination, which we were compelled to decide forthwith; shall we continue our joint attack, with the Nationals, on those in power, in the new position, which they have been compelled to occupy? It was clear, with our joint forces, we could utterly overthrow and demolish them, but it was not less clear, that the victory would inure, not to us, but exclusively to the benefit of our allies and their cause. They were the most numerous and powerful, and the point of assault on the position, which the party to be assaulted had taken in relation to the banks, would have greatly strengthened the settled principles and policy of the National party, and weakened in the same degree ours. They are, and ever have been, the decided advocates of a national bank, and are now in favor [of] one, with a capital so ample, as to be sufficient to controul the State institutions, and to regulate the currency and exchanges of the country. To join them, with their avowed object in the attack, to overthrow those in power, on the ground they occupied against a bank, would, of course, not only have placed the Government and country in their hands without opposition, but would have committed us, beyond the possibility of extrication, for a bank, and absorbed our party in the ranks of the National Republicans. The first fruits of the victory, would have been an overshadowing national bank, with an immense capital, not less than from fifty to an hundred millions, which would have centralized the currency and exchanges, and with them, the commerce and capital of the country, in whatever section the head of the institution might be placed. The next would be the indissoluble union of the political and money power in the hands of our old political opponents, whose principles and policy are so opposite to ours, and so dangerous to our institutions as well as oppressive to us.

Such clearly would have been the inevitable result, if we had joined in the assault on those in power, in the position they had been constrained to occupy; and he must indeed be blind—all past experience must be lost on him, who does not see, that so infatuated a course would have been fatal to us and ours. The connection between the Government and the bank would, by necessary consequence in the hands of that party, have led to a renewal of that system of unequal and oppressive legislation, which has impoverished the staple States, and from which we have escaped with such peril and difficulty. The bank, when united with the Government, is the natural ally of high duties and extravagant expenditure. The greater the revenue and the more profuse the disbursements, the greater its circulation and the more ample its deposites. This tendency on the part of that institution, and the known principles and views of policy of the party, would have co-operated, with irresistible force, to renew the system we have pulled down with so much labour, with an aggravation of its oppression far beyond any thing we have ever yet experienced, and thus the fruits of all our exertions and struggles against the system, would have been lost—forever lost.

By taking the opposite course, the reverse of all this will follow, if our States Rights party be but firmly united and true to their principles. Never was there before, and never probably will there be again, so fair an opportunity to carry out fully our principles and policy, and to reap the fruits of our long and arduous struggle. By keeping the banks and the Government separated, we effectually prevent the centralization of the currency and exchanges of the country at any one point, and, of course, the commerce and the capital, leaving each to enjoy that portion, which its natural advantages, with its industry and enterprise may command. By refusing to join our late allies in their attack on those in power, where they have sheltered themselves, we prevent the complete ascendency of the party and their principles, which must have followed, and gain the only opportunity we could have of rallying anew the old States Rights Party of 1827, on the ground they then occupied, as an opposing power, to hold in check their old opponents, the National Republican Party. It would also give us the chance of effecting, what is still more important to us, the union of the entire South. The Southern division of the Administration party must re-occupy the old State Rights ground. They have no alternative; and unless we, who have so long and under so many difficulties adhered to it, shall now desert our stand, the South must be united. If once united, we will rally round the old State Rights party all in every section, who are opposed to consolidation, or the overaction of the Central Government; and the political parties will again be formed on the old and natural division of State Rights and National, which divided them at the commencement of the Government, and which experience has shown is that division of party most congenial to our system, and most favorable to its successful operation.

As obvious as all this must appear, I felt, that I assumed a heavy responsibility in taking the course I did. It was impossible, that all the circumstances and motives, under which I acted, could at once be generally understood, and, of course, the part I was compelled to take was liable to be misconceived and grossly misrepresented. We had been so long contending against the abuses and encroachments of the Executive power, as to forget, that they originated in the prior abuses and encroachments of Congress, and were accordingly exclusively intent on expelling from office, those who had acquired and exercised their authority in a manner so dangerous, without reflecting into whose hands the power would go, and what principles and policy would gain the ascendency. With this state of feelings on the part of our friends, I saw it was impossible to take a position, which, by consequence was calculated to cover those in power, however urgent the cause, without occasioning a shock, in the first instance, and the imputation of unworthy motives, to meet which, however transient the misapprehension might be, required some resolution and firmness. But there were other, and far greater causes of responsibility, to which this was as nothing. Of all the interests in the community, the banking is by far the most influential and formidable—the most active, and the most concentrated and pervading; and of all the points, within the immense circle of this interest, there is none, in relation to which the banks are more sensitive and tenacious, than their union with the political power of the country. This is the source of a vast amount of their profits, and of a still larger portion of their respectability and influence. To touch their interest on this tender point is to combine all in one united and zealous opposition, with some exceptions in our portion of the community, where the union of the two powers acts injur[i]ously to the banking, as well as to the commercial and other great interests of the section. To encounter so formidable an opposition, supported by a powerful political party with whom I had been acting for some years against entire [*sic*; executive?] power, and who regarded the union of the Government and the banks as essential to the union of the States themselves, was to assume a heavy responsibility, under the most favorable circumstances; but to back and sustain those in such opposition, in whose wisdom, firmness and patriotism, I have no reason to confide, and over whom I have no control, is to double that responsibility. This responsibility, I have voluntarily assumed. Desiring neither office, nor power, and having nothing to hope personally from the movement, no motive, but the disastrous political consequences, which I clearly saw must follow from any other course, to the country and its institutions generally, and our section in particular, and a deep sense of duty, could have induced me to take the step I did. That it has met the approbation of so respectable a portion of my old constituents and friends, to whose early and steadfast support, under every trial and difficulty[,] I am so much indebted, is a source of deep gratification which I shall long remember and acknowledge. With great respect, I am &c., J.C. Calhoun.

PC in the Edgefield, S.C., *Advertiser,* November 16, 1837, p. 2; PC in the Augusta, Ga., *Chronicle and Sentinel,* November 20, 1837, p. 1; PC in the Charleston, S.C., *Mercury,* November 21, 1837, p. 2; PC in the Charleston, S.C., *Southern Patriot,* November 22, 1837, p. 2; PC in the Columbia, S.C., *Southern Times and State Gazette,* November 28, 1837, p. 3; PC in the Alexandria, D.C., *Gazette,* November 30, 1837, p. 2; PC in the Pendleton, S.C., *Messenger,* December 1, 1837, p. 2; PC in *Niles' National Register,* vol. LIII, no. 14 (December 2, 1837), pp. 217–218; PC in the Washington, D.C., *Daily National Intelligencer,* December 4, 1837, p. 2; PC in the Washington, D.C., *Globe,* December 5, 1837, p. 3; PC in the Washington, D.C., *Madisonian,* December 9, 1837, p. 2. NOTE: Besides Bausket, the members of the committee for a public dinner at Edgefield whom Calhoun addressed where A[rthur] Wigfall, J[ames] P[arsons] Carroll, M[aximilian] LaBorde, J. Jones, F[rancis] H[ugh] Wardlaw, and J[ohn] W. Wimbish.

Edward W. Johnston's prospectus for the Bedford Female Academy at Liberty, Va., 11/3. Johnston, formerly associated with South Carolina College, proposes to operate the academy on principles of "a less multifarious education, which formed the Virginia lady, some sixty years ago, before Northern improvements came in." His methods "will leave the child the feelings, opinions, the manners and principles proper to Southern birth, and fit to be the basis of an *Education purely Southern.*" Johnston lists as references John C. Calhoun, William C. Preston, Thomas R. Dew, Benjamin W. Leigh, and other prominent South Carolinians and Virginians. [Edward W. Johnston was a brother of Joseph E. Johnston.] PC in the Richmond, Va., *Enquirer,* November 10, 1837, p. 4, and November 17, 1837, p. 4.

[Anna Maria Calhoun,] Fort Hill, to [Patrick Calhoun, West Point, N.Y.,] 11/6. Anna explains that her long silence is attributable to a fever from which she is just beginning to recover. John C. Calhoun is home on a short visit and leaves tomorrow with Maria Simkins for Abbeville where he will meet Francis [W. Pickens], who will take Maria [his sister-in-law] home. Calhoun then goes to visit his brothers, William, James, and Patrick [in Abbeville District], all of whom have been ill recently. Anna congratulates Patrick on his standing in his class at the Military Academy and tells him of Calhoun's pleasure with Patrick's recent conduct report. Professor [Henry J.] Nott and his wife [Caroline Oley Nott] died in a recent steamboat accident. ALU (incomplete) in ScU-SC, John C. Calhoun Papers.

To J[ohn] R. Mathew[e]s, [Clarkesville, Ga.?]

Fort Hill, 26th Nov. 1837

My dear Sir, Your two letters, the one of the 19th Inst[ant], and the other written before your visit to Milledgeville [Ga.], enclosing a letter to Mr. [George W.] Featherstonhaugh, were received a few days since. I sealed and forwarded the letter to Mr. F., as you requested. He is exceedingly anxious to spend the next summer in our vicinity with the view to a thorough examination of the mineral resources of our mountain region. I hope he may not be disappointed in his arrangement.

I am much gratified to learn, that publick sentiment is so sound in this State and Georgia on the great question of the day. I felt in taking the course I did, that I assumed a very heavy responsibility, but I saw as clearly as I do the light of heaven, that any other would be fatal to us, and I did not hesitate. We are in the midest [*sic*] of one of the most important junctures, we ever passed. A false step would have been irretrievable; even the most correct course without union among ourselves may be unavailing. To consolidate the credit and the currency of the country is to consolidate the government itself.

I do hope your information in relation to our friend [James] Hamilton [Jr.] may be correct. I feared from my last conversation with him, that he would go wrong, which I would greatly regret. He has not been in his true position ["for some time" *interlined*]. There is no one, whose cooperation I would value more highly.

I intended to set out on the 28th Inst[ant] for Washington, and to take Columbia [S.C.] in my way. The Board of directors of our great railroad ["will" *interlined*] meet on the 1st Monday in next month at the latter place, but I fear, as anxious as I am to be present, that I cannot leave home for a week or ten days. I had the misfortune to lose my overseer [William P. McDow, who died] in my absence at the extra session, (the best I ever had,) which has so deranged my affairs, as to make it almost indispensable for me to remain at home some time longer to get them right again.

I believe that the French Broad route [for the railroad] may be considered as substantially abandomned [*sic*]. No one has the least idea, that it can go on, unless N[orth] Carolina, Tennessee, & Kentucky should agree to construct the work through their respective States, of which I do not think there is the least probability.

The present inclination is to join Georgia; to purchase out the Hamburgh ["road" *interlined*] and unite with the Athens [Ga.] interest, and ultimately to connect with the State road from the Suck to the Chattaho[o]chee [River]. I confess this appears to me the most rational course. It was my original conception. Should it be adopted, it may delay the improvement of our noble river [the Savannah?], but so fine a stream cannot in this age of improvement & activity long remain neglected. I hope you have succeed [*sic*] in your arrangement to get a charter for its improvement. It will be the first step, out of which much may grow.

Mrs. [Floride Colhoun] Calhoun has just got the bug destroyer, which you were so kind as to send her, and for which ["she" *interlined*] is much obliged to you. It is an invaluable article in its place.

I will give an early attention to our unfortunate mail arrangements. I had supposed ever[y] thing was fixed when I left Washington. Yours truely, J.C. Calhoun.

ALS in DLC, John C. Calhoun Papers.

To A[RMISTEAD] BURT

Fort Hill, 29th Nov[embe]r 1837
My dear Sir, I expected to set out this morning for Columbia, but I find that my private affairs will require me to remain home a few days longer. I hope, however, that I will be able to reach Columbia some day next week. I write to apprise you of the fact, so that you may not be disappointed at my non arrival at the time I expected to be there.

I hope all is going on well. Truely, J.C. Calhoun.

ALS in NcD, John C. Calhoun Papers.

To H[ENRY] BALDWIN, [Associate Justice, U.S. Supreme Court]

Fort Hill, 2d Dec[embe]r 1837
My dear Sir, I am under great obligation to you for the volume on Constitutional Views &[c.] &[c.], which you were so kind as to transmit to me.

I have read it with very great satisfaction. Your exposition of the origin, the nature and character of our system is demonstrabuly[?] clear; so much so as to place them beyond the sphere of controversy. Fortunate would it have been for our country, if they had always prevailed. Under no other view, can the system be preserved. As explained by you, it is one of great beauty and harmony. Regarded in any other light, it becomes the mere vulgar system of the numerical majority, which has been so often tried and condemned. It is, in fact, but one of the forms of despotism.

As far as you have carried your conclusions, there are but very few points, in which I do not fully concur. There are important questions lying beyond, which I could wish you had discussed in the same masterly manner. Having clearly shown, what the system is—that its components parts [*sic*] are States—that the two, the General and State governments were created, and adopted by the same authority; the one by each State sepera[t]ely for itself, and the other conjointly with its confederates, for federal purposes; the two in fact making but one Government, it appears to me, the right of State interposition follows as a necessary consequence, and is indispensible [*sic*] to make the ["practice" *canceled and* "action" *interlined*] and the theory of the system conform. Without it, be the theory what it may, practically it must be a consolidated Gov[ern]ment, and work precisely, as if it was made by the people of the United States in the ag[g]regate, which you have so clearly shown not to be a fact. It seems to me, that this is the great question, on which the true character of the system must practically depend, and on which, I would be happy to exchange ideas when we meet.

For what you have done, you will please accept my thanks—the thanks of one, who has the profoundest attachment to our admirable system, and whose first and highest desire is, to ["transmit to contribute" *canceled and* "aid" *interlined*] in transmit[t]ing our free institutions to the latest generation. With great respect I am & & J.C. Calhoun.

ALS in PHC; variant PC in Jameson, ed., *Correspondence*, pp. 384–385. NOTE: Baldwin's book discussed herein was *A General View of the Origin and Nature of the Constitution and Government of the United States, Deduced from the Political History and Condition of the Colonies and States, from 1774 until 1788, and the Decisions of the Supreme Court; with Opinions in the Cases Decided at January Term 1837, Arising on the Restraints on the Powers of the States* (Philadelphia: John C. Clark, 1837).

To "Capt." J[AMES] ED[WARD] COLHOUN

Fort Hill, 2d Dec[embe]r 1837
My dear Sir, I expected to leave here yesterday, but could not make my arrangement to leave home so soon. My presence here for a few

days longer is indispensible [*sic*], so deranged was my business in consequence of the death [in Sept.] of [my overseer, William P.] McDow and the sickness on the place. I intend to leave home on Wednesday [12/6]; and, tho' too late for the board [meeting], I hope to see [Robert Y.] Hayne and most of the directors. The movements and discrepetancy[?], to which you refer, I think, may be easily explained. It is to cover the retreat. I hold it manifest, that there is no intention of taking the French Broad route, except N[orth] Carolina, Tennessee & Kentucky will carry the ["route" *canceled*] road through their respective limits, of which there is but little prospect. This I think appearent [*sic*] from the Report. I will, however, write you from Columbia.

I will send the ["spring" *interlined*] wheat; but fear that I shall not get at my Red River cotton, in time to send you the seed. It is place[d] quite back in the Gin House, and was intended for the last ginning, and cannot be got at till the other is out of the way. I do not think it material, however; for it has degenerated much, from mixture[?] & want of care in my absence; and I would not advise you to try it. I have not yet got in my corn, or cotton, but hope to finish both next week. I shall make upwards of 4,000 bushels of corn, and about 65,000 pounds of cotton off of 90 acres. Can you not send me a boat, or engage one of the boats, as they pass you from An-[der]sonville, to take down my crop[?] Several loads may be had here ["on the (Seneca) River" *interlined*]. I would wish to send down in March or April. Do let me hear from you.

Do you bring up salt from Augusta? If so, I would be glad to get from you two ["or three" *interlined*] sacks when my waggons [*sic*] go down for the cotton seed at Christmas. If you have it not, I would take it as a particular favour, if you would ["buy" *canceled and "get" interlined*] me ["in Augusta" *interlined*] three sacks and have them brought up by that time. The article is $2 the bushel here.

Your brother [John Ewing Colhoun] leaves for Charleston tomorrow. He is late in going down, and I fear nothing will be done [in regard to the sale of Bonneau's Ferry], unless you can go. I do think you ought to go. It is important; and will not take you more than 8 or 10 days. If you do not, ["you do," *canceled*] you had better give him precisise [*sic*] instructions, as to price & terms, and leave him to sell subject to them.

I saw [Robert?] Anderson. He says the tittle [*sic*; title] of the land, for which the note that your mother [Floride Bonneau Colhoun] indorsed ["was given," *interlined and "is" canceled*] is still in the ["hands" *canceled*] heirs of Mays, whose Executor [Baylies John?] Earle is, and will of course be an offset to it ["for its Value" *interlined*]. I will endeavour to see Earle at Columbia.

Write me at Columbia, and let me know whether I can get the sault [*sic*; salt] through you & what prospect there will be of a boat.

All are well and send their love to you. Affectionately, J.C. Calhoun.

ALS in ScCleA.

To [JAMES EDWARD COLHOUN]

[Fort Hill] 3d Dec[embe]r [1837]

D[ea]r Sir, I send down Daniel for the load of cotton seed. The wagon body is very large, and if you cannot spare of your best kind sufficient to fill it, I would be glad that you would ["get" *interlined*] what may be required from [George] McDuffie, or some of your neighbours. If you have the three sack[s] of salt, which I requested you to get for me from Augusta send it by the wagon.

I send by Daniel the spring wheat and a vial of skinless oats seed, said to be of an excellent quality. Truely, J.C. Calhoun.

ALS in ScCleA. NOTE: The condition of this letter and its lack of a postmark suggest that it was probably hand-delivered by Daniel. A somewhat indecipherable endorsement (by the recipient?) reads: "Dec. 7[?] 1837. See letter of Dec. 2, 1837." This perhaps indicates 12/7 as the date of receipt.

SYMBOLS

◫

The following symbols have been used in this volume as abbreviations for the forms in which papers of John C. Calhoun have been found and for the depositories in which they are preserved. (Full citations to printed sources of documents, some of which are cited by short titles in the text, can be found in the Bibliography.)

Abs   —abstract (a summary)
ADI   —autograph document, initialed
ADS   —autograph document, signed
ADU   —autograph document, unsigned
AEI   —autograph endorsement, initialed
AES   —autograph endorsement, signed
AEU   —autograph endorsement, unsigned
ALI   —autograph letter, initialed
ALS   —autograph letter, signed
ALU   —autograph letter, unsigned
CC   —clerk's copy (usually not for retention by the writer)
CCEx   —clerk's copy of an extract
CSmH   —Henry E. Huntington Library and Art Gallery, San Marino, Calif.
CtY   —Yale University Library, New Haven, Conn.
DLC   —Library of Congress, Washington, D.C.
DNA   —National Archives, Washington, D.C.
DNDAR   —Daughters of the American Revolution Library, Washington, D.C.
DS   —document, signed
DU   —document, unsigned
EI   —endorsement, initialed
En   —enclosure
Ens   —enclosures
ES   —endorsement, signed
EU   —endorsement, unsigned
Ex   —extract
FC   —file copy (usually a letterbook copy retained by the sender)
GAHi   —Atlanta Historical Society
GU   —University of Georgia Library, Athens
LS   —letter, signed
LU   —letter, unsigned
M-   —(followed by a number) published Microcopy of the National Archives
MH   —Harvard University Library, Cambridge, Mass.
MiU-C   —William L. Clements Library, University of Michigan, Ann Arbor
NcD   —Duke University Library, Durham, N.C.

NcU	—University of North Carolina Library, Chapel Hill
NHi	—New-York Historical Society, New York City
NHpR	—Franklin D. Roosevelt Library, Hyde Park, N.Y.
NN	—New York Public Library, New York City
OFH	—Hayes Memorial Library, Fremont, Ohio
PC	—printed copy
PDS	—printed document, signed
PEx	—printed extract
PHC	—Haverford College Library, Haverford, Pa.
PHi	—Historical Society of Pennsylvania, Philadelphia
RG	—Record Group in the National Archives
RPB	—John Hay Library, Brown University, Providence, R.I.
Sc-Ar	—South Carolina Department of Archives and History, Columbia
ScCleA	—Clemson University Library, Clemson, S.C. (John C. Calhoun Papers in this depository unless otherwise stated)
ScSpW	—Wofford College Library, Spartanburg, S.C.
ScU-SC	—South Caroliniana Library, University of South Carolina, Columbia
TxU	—University of Texas Library, Austin
ViU	—University of Virginia Library, Charlottesville

BIBLIOGRAPHY

⫿

This Bibliography is limited to sources of John C. Calhoun documents and to the more important references used in the preparation of this volume.

Alexandria, D.C. and Va., *Gazette*, 1808–.

Anderson, John M., ed., *Calhoun: Basic Documents*. State College, Pa.: Bald Eagle Press, c. 1952.

Augusta, Ga., *Chronicle*, 1785–.

Augusta, Ga., *State Rights' Sentinel*, 1834–1836.

Biographical Directory of the American Congress, 1774–1949 . . . . House Document No. 607, 81st Congress, 2nd Session. [Washington:] U.S. Government Printing Office, 1950.

Boucher, Chauncey S., and Robert P. Brooks, eds., *Correspondence Addressed to John C. Calhoun, 1837–1849*, in the *American Historical Association Annual Report* for 1929 (Washington: U.S. Government Printing Office, 1930).

"Calhoun–Gouverneur Correspondence, 1823–1836," in the *New York Public Library Bulletin*, vol. III, no. 8 (August, 1899), pp. 324–333.

[Calhoun, John C.,] *Speeches of John C. Calhoun. Delivered in the Congress of the United States from 1811 to the Present Time.* New York: Harper & Brothers, c. 1843. [Some copies of this work have the alternate title page: *A Selection from the Speeches, Reports, and Other Publications of John C. Calhoun, Subsequent to His Election as Vice-President, (Including Also His First Speech in Congress in 1811), and Referred to in His "Life."*]

Charleston, S.C., *Courier*, 1803–1852.

Charleston, S.C., *Mercury*, 1822–1868.

Charleston, S.C., *Southern Patriot*, 1814–1848.

[Cleveland, John B., compiler,] *Controversy between John C. Calhoun and Robt. Y. Hayne as to the Proper Route of a Railroad from South Carolina to the West.* [Spartanburg, S.C.: 1913.]

Coit, Margaret L., *John C. Calhoun: American Portrait.* Boston: Houghton Mifflin Company, c. 1950.

Columbia, S.C., *Southern Times and State Gazette*, 1830–1838?.

Columbus, O., *Ohio State Journal*, 1811–1904.

Congressional Globe . . . 1833–1873 . . . . 46 vols. Washington: Blair & Rives and others, 1834–1873.

Cook, Harriet Hefner, *John C. Calhoun—The Man.* Columbia, S.C.: privately printed, c. 1965.

Cralle, Richard K., ed., *The Works of John C. Calhoun.* 6 vols. Columbia, S.C.: printed by A.S. Johnston, 1851, and New York: D. Appleton and Company, 1853–1857.

De Bow's Review. New Orleans: 1846–1880.

Edgefield, S.C., *Advertiser*, 1836–.

Freidel, Frank, *Francis Lieber: Nineteenth-Century Liberal.* Baton Rouge: Louisiana State University Press, c. 1947.

Greenville, S.C., *Mountaineer*, 1829–1901.

Guide to the National Archives of the United States. Washington: General Services Administration, National Archives and Records Service, 1974.

Haynes, George H., *The Senate of the United States, Its History and Practice.* 2 vols. Boston: Houghton Mifflin Company, 1938.

[Hunter, Robert M.T.,] *Life of John C. Calhoun, Presenting a Condensed History of Political Events from 1811 to 1843.* New York: Harper & Brothers, c. 1843.

Jameson, J. Franklin, ed., *Correspondence of John C. Calhoun*, in the *American Historical Association Annual Report* for 1899 (2 vols. Washington: U.S. Government Printing Office, 1900), vol. II.

Jenkins, John S., *The Life of John Caldwell Calhoun.* Auburn, N.Y.: James M. Alden, 1850, 1851. (There are at least four later editions.)

Magoon, E.L., *Living Orators in America.* New York: Baker and Scribner, 1849.

Meriwether, Robert L., W. Edwin Hemphill, and Clyde N. Wilson, eds., *The Papers of John C. Calhoun.* 12 vols. to date. Columbia: University of South Carolina Press, 1959–1979.

New York, N.Y., *Courier and Enquirer*, 1827–1861.

Niles' Weekly Register. Baltimore: 1811–1849.

Norfolk and Portsmouth, Va., *Herald*, 1805–1861.

Pendleton, S.C., *Messenger*, 1807–?.

Peters, Richard, ed., *The Public Statutes at Large of the United States of America, 1789–1845* . . . . 8 vols. Boston: Little, Brown and Company, c. 1848.

Register of Debates in Congress . . . 1824–1837 . . . . 14 vols. Washington: Gales & Seaton, 1825–1837.

Remarks of Mr. Calhoun, in the Senate of the United States, on the Bill Authorizing an Issue of Treasury Notes, on the 19th September, 1837. No place: no date.

Remarks of Mr. Calhoun, of South Carolina, on His Proposition to Cede the Public Lands to the New States Upon the Payment of One-Third of the Gross Amount of the Sales. In Senate of the United States, February 7, 1837. Washington: printed by William W. Moore & Co., 1837.

Remarks of Mr. Calhoun, of South Carolina, on the Reception of Abolition Petitions, Delivered in the Senate of the United States, February 1837. Washington: printed by William W. Moore & Co., 1837.

Remarks of Mr. Calhoun, on the Bill Authorizing an Issue of Treasury Notes. Delivered in the Senate of the United States, September 19, 1837. Washington: Blair and Rives, 1837. (Two editions of this pamphlet with nearly identical title pages but different pagination were published by Blair and Rives.)

Remarks of the Hon. John C. Calhoun, of South Carolina, on the Bill to Regulate the Deposites of Public Money. In Senate, June 1836. Washington: printed by Duff Green, 1836.

Richardson, James D., ed., *A Compilation of the Messages and Papers of the Presidents, 1789–1902.* 10 vols. [Washington:] Bureau of National Literature and Art, 1903; and other editions.

Richmond, Va., *Enquirer*, 1804–1877.

Richmond, Va., *Whig*, 1824–1888.

Shanks, Henry T., ed., *The Papers of Willie Person Mangum.* 5 vols. Raleigh: North Carolina Department of Archives and History, 1950–1956.

Speeches of Mr. Calhoun of S[outh] Carolina, on the Bill for the Admission of Michigan. Delivered in the Senate of the United States, January, 1837. Washington: printed by Duff Green, 1837.

Speech of Mr. Calhoun, of South Carolina, in Senate, January 18, 1836, on the Motion to Refer the Messages of the President of the United States, concerning the Relations of the United States with France, to the Committee on Foreign Relations. [Washington?: 1836.]

Speech of the Hon. J.C. Calhoun, of South Carolina, on the Abolition Petitions. Delivered on Wednesday, March 9, 1836. Washington: printed by Duff Green, [1836?].

Speech of the Hon. J.C. Calhoun, of South Carolina, on the Bill to Prohibit Deputy Post Masters from Receiving and Transmitting through the Mail to any State, Territory, or District, Certain Papers therein Mentioned, the Circulation of Which is Prohibited by the Laws of Said State, Territory, or District. Delivered in the Senate, April 12, 1836. Washington: no publisher, 1836.

Speech of the Hon. John C. Calhoun, on His Amendment to Separate the Government from the Banks. Delivered in the Senate of the United States, October 3, 1837. Washington: printed at the Globe Office, 1837.

Stokes, Anson Phelps, *Memorials of Eminent Yale Men: a Biographical Study of Student Life and University Influence during the Eighteenth and Nineteenth Centuries.* 2 vols. New Haven: Yale University Press, c. 1914.

Swisher, Carl Brent, *Roger B. Taney.* New York: The Macmillan Company, c. 1935.

Thomas, E.S., *Reminiscences of the Last Sixty-Five Years, Commencing with the Battle of Lexington; Also, Sketches of His Own Life and Times.* 2 vols. Hartford: printed by Case, Tiffany and Burnham for the author, 1840.

United States Democratic Review. Washington and New York: 1837–1859.

U.S. Senate, *Journal of the Executive Proceedings of the Senate of the United States, 1789–1852.* 8 vols. Washington: U.S. Government Printing Office, 1887.

U.S. Senate, *Journal of the Senate of the United States.* 24th and 25th Congresses.

U.S. Senate, *Senate Documents.* 24th and 25th Congresses.

Waring, Alice Noble, ed., "Letters of John C. Calhoun to Patrick Noble, 1812–1837," in the *Journal of Southern History*, vol. XVI, no. 1 (February, 1950), pp. 64–74.

Washington, D.C., *Daily National Intelligencer*, 1800–1870.

Washington, D.C., *Madisonian*, 1837–1845.

Washington, D.C., *Reformer* and Baltimore, Md., *Merchant*, 1837.

Washington, D.C., *The Globe*, 1830–1845.

Washington, D.C., *United States' Telegraph*, 1826–1837.

Wiltse, Charles M., *John C. Calhoun.* 3 vols. *Nationalist, 1782–1828; Nullifier, 1829–1839; Sectionalist, 1840–1850.* Indianapolis: The Bobbs-Merrill Company, Inc., c. 1944, 1949, 1951.

INDEX

⫿

Bomford, George: mentioned, 110, 122.

Bonham, James Butler: mentioned, 6.

Bonneau, John Ewing: from, 258, 285, 357, 510, 514, 522, 630; mentioned, 301, 511.

Bonneau's Ferry, S.C.: sale of, 489, 510–511, 630–631, 645–646.

Bowie, James: mentioned, 6.

Boydton, Va., *Virginia Expositor and Southern Advocate*: mentioned, 516.

Branch, John: mentioned, 471.

Branchville, S.C.: mentioned, 290.

Breckinridge, John: introductions of, 123.

Brent, John: claim of legatees of, 174.

Brisbane, Abbott H.: mentioned, 356–357.

Broglie, Achille Charles Léance Victor, Duke de: mentioned, 38.

Brown, Bedford: and reception of abolition petitions, 23, 27, 100, 145–147, 365–366; and tariff, 467–468, 471; mentioned, 350.

Brown, Elias: to, 6.

Brown University: document in library of, 530; mentioned, 530.

Buchanan, James: and volunteer bill, 192, 195–196; debates Calhoun on admission of Michigan, 332–335, 349–350, 352–355; favors incendiary publications bill, 234; in abolition petition controversy, 30, 44, 77, 94–95, 97–98, 103, 106–107, 110, 112, 387–388, 392; mentioned, x, 21, 78, 136, 174, 179, 229, 320, 355, 371, 429, 442, 477, 479, 481, 541, 546, 586, 606; on U.S.-French relations, 33, 38, 47, 79–80.

Bulloch, William Bellinger: statement by, 265.

Burke, Aedanus: mentioned, 97.

Burke, Edmund: invoked by Calhoun, 416, 601.

Burt, Armistead: mentioned, 301–302, 307–308, 505; to, 250, 433, 622, 643.

Burt, Martha Calhoun: mentioned, 250–251, 434, 622.

Butler, Behethaland Foote Moore: illness of, 245.

Butler, Benjamin F.: mentioned, 221.

Caesar, Julius: mentioned, 363.

Caldwell, Pinkney: from, 10; mentioned, 237, 285.

Calhoun, Andrew Pickens: mentioned, 277, 493, 504, 511, 518, 523–524, 531, 536, 588, 627, 630.

Calhoun, Anna Maria: from, 89, 518, 641; mentioned, 13, 70, 177, 201, 245, 250, 296, 311, 358, 385, 434, 444, 492, 498–499, 502, 515, 524, 534, 627; Northern tour of, 260, 278, 280; to, 536, 587.

Calhoun, Ezekiel: mentioned, 621.

Calhoun, Floride Colhoun: mentioned, 13, 258–259, 277, 280, 296–297, 302–303, 358, 514, 536, 588, 636, 643.

Calhoun, James: mentioned, 250, 300, 518, 641.

Calhoun, James Edward: mentioned, 518.

Calhoun, James Montgomery: to, 621.

Calhoun, John Caldwell (grandson of John C. Calhoun): mentioned, 511, 525, 624, 630.

Calhoun, John C., Jr. (son of John C. Calhoun): mentioned, 357.

Calhoun, Margaret Green: mentioned, 259, 277, 511, 630.

Calhoun, Martha Cornelia: mentioned, 358; proposed medical treatment of, 489, 513.

Calhoun, Patrick (brother of John C. Calhoun): mentioned, 250, 628, 635, 641.

Calhoun, Patrick (son of John C. Calhoun): mentioned, 280, 488–489, 492–493, 499, 510–511, 514, 588, 624; to, 518, 524, 641.

Calhoun's Mills, S.C.: mentioned, 29.

Calhoun, William: mentioned, 250, 525, 628, 641.

White, George O.: Calhoun mediates dispute of, 265.

White House: mentioned, 305, 361; society at, 11–12.

White, Hugh L.: and appropriations for Indian removal, 189–191; as Presidential candidate, 257, 301; mentioned, 100, 159, 461.

White, Joseph M.: mentioned, 442.

Whitner, Joseph N.: as trustee of Pendleton Academy, 369; witnesses deeds, 522, 627.

Whitney, Reuben M.: mentioned, 139–140, 204.

Wigfall, Arthur: to, 636.

Wilkins, William: mentioned, 100.

Wilky, ——: mentioned, 10.

Williams, Abner: appointment of opposed, 453–454.

Williams, John R.: mentioned, 332.

Williams, William: from, 495.

Williams, William George: mentioned, 113, 117, 307–308, 356, 433.

Wilmington, N.C.: mentioned, 155, 405.

Wimbish, John W.: to, 636.

Wine: duties on, 470.

Winnsboro, S.C.: mentioned, 291.

Wisconsin Territory: removal of Indians from, 189–192.

Wise, Henry A.: mentioned, 47, 430.

Wofford College Library: document in, 525.

Woodbury, Levi: and deposits, 169, 181–182, 204–207, 320, 421, 450–451; and removal of David Melvill from office, 171–172; and Treasury surplus, 12, 14–17, 80–81, 114–115, 209, 217, 314–315, 323–326, 328, 540–541; from, 369; mentioned, 221, 252, 355, 360, 374, 440, 471.

Woollens: duties on, 457, 460, 471.

Wright, Elizur, Jr.: from, 625.

Wright, Silas: advocates tariff reduction, 451, 454–457, 465–466, 468–471, 473; and admission of Michigan, 126–127, 133, 136; and public deposits, 141–142, 188, 202–209, 216, 218–225, 228, 239–242, 324–325; and reduction of the revenue, 312, 321, 360, 451; and surplus revenue, 79–83, 86, 114–116, 462–465, 477, 479, 486–487, 538, 540–541; as member of Senate Select Committee on the Deposit Bill, 229, 243–244; mentioned, x, 78, 100, 313, 366–368, 381, 441–442, 458, 545, 573, 581, 618; on abolition petitions, 42–44.

Yale College: introductions to, 188, 233; mentioned, 346.

Yale University: documents in libraries of, 188, 233.

Yancey, Benjamin C.: Calhoun mediates dispute of, 265.

Yates, Mrs. ——: mentioned, 588.

York County, Pa.: petition from, 100–101.

York, S.C.: mentioned, 291.

Young, George H.: from, 261; to, 262.